Architectural Guide Iran
From the Safavids to
the Iranian Revolution

How to Use this Book

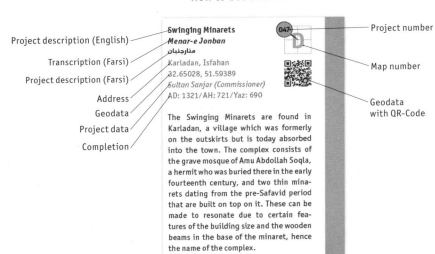

Project description (English) — **Swinging Minarets**

Transcription (Farsi) — *Menar-e Jonban*

منارجنبان

Project description (Farsi) —

Address — Karladan, Isfahan

Geodata — 32.65028, 51.59389

Project data — *Sultan Sanjar (Commissioner)*

Completion — AD: 1321/AH: 721/Yaz: 690

Project number

Map number

Geodata with QR-Code

The Swinging Minarets are found in Karladan, a village which was formerly on the outskirts but is today absorbed into the town. The complex consists of the grave mosque of Amu Abdollah Soqla, a hermit who was buried there in the early fourteenth century, and two thin minarets dating from the pre-Safavid period that are built on top on it. These can be made to resonate due to certain features of the building size and the wooden beams in the base of the minaret, hence the name of the complex.

Architectural Guide Iran
From the Safavids to the Iranian Revolution

Thomas Meyer-Wieser

DOM
publishers

Contents

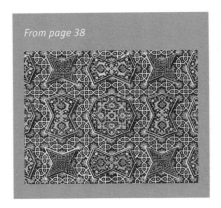

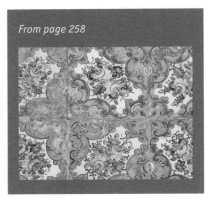

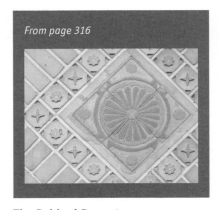

Introduction

View of Tehran at the foot of the Alborz mountains

View of the ruins of Persepolis, seat of the ancient Persian empire, today UNESCO World Heritage Site

From the Safavids to the Iranian Revolution

The rise of the Safavids in the mid-fifteenth century led to a new era of Iranian architecture. They established an economically-robust and politically-stable political system and created a kind of "Iranian national state" in which Twelver Shia was imposed as the state religion, resulting in Iran's particular religious development, which is still practised to this day. These political and social upheavals led to a new architectural expression. The iconographic decor of the Harun Velayat mausoleum in Isfahan demonstrates the Safavid's zeal to promote Twelver Shia as the sole state religion by the highly-developed motifs of flowers, plants and paradise. In 1587, Prince Abbas was chosen as Shah of Persia. Similar to the European sovereigns of mercantilism, Shah Abbas promoted craft, commerce and industry, reformed the lease and taxation system and standardised the coinage. The expansion of infrastructure – roads, bridges, fountains, canals, dams and caravanserais – increased the effectiveness of the internal and external trade. The new Shiite monarchy, merging the glory of the ancient Persian Empire with the ancestry of the Prophet's family, manifested itself in the visionary master plan for the new capital, Isfahan. The axial juxtaposition of religion, politics and economics in the "Maidan-e Naqsh-e Jahan" transformed the new town centre into an icon of imperial power where absolutism and centralism were visually and spatially tangible. The vision of Shah Abbas the Great was so sustainable that later generations developed it further and perfected it. The grandiose building Mader-e Shah testifies to this renaissance, which demonstrates to the whole Islamic world not only the power and fame, but in particular the legitimacy of the Safavids. With the collapse of the Safavid Empire, infighting erupted, in which Karim Khan Zand gained recognition in 1759 and developed Shiraz into a residential town and significant cultural centre. The town was extended along the north-south axis, where rich merchants bought land and established gardens and villas, leading to the golden age of Persian garden culture. The Persian garden highlights the contrast between the arid landscape outside and the cool, shady vegetation inside.

Bagh-e-Eram consists of a walled-in quadrangle, divided into more-or-less equal parts by four water channels. In the centre of the upper third lies a two storey pavilion with southwest orientation, which was reserved for the reception of

View of Tehran with Alborz mountains in the background

View of Isfahan from Kuh-e Sofeh

guests. The private quarters occupied by members of the family are situated in the perimeter wall. Poets loved to draw comparisons between garden and paradise, where one can rest on comfortable cushions, with the fruits of the garden within easy reach.

A chieftain of the Qajar, Aqa Mohammed Khan, had the last ruler of the Zand dynasty assassinated in 1794 and began an internal Persian conquest which, even measured by the standards of the eighteenth century, became known as one of the cruellest in history. After fifteen years of war, having killed almost all competitors for the throne, he chose Tehran, then a small village near the far older Ray, as the Shah's residence and capital. In 1873, Nasreddin Shah was the first Persian monarch to visit Europe. The journey took him from Russia through Germany, England, France, Switzerland and Italy to Austria for the Vienna World Fair, where Persia was represented with its own exhibition pavilion. Subsequently, traditional Tehran acquired a touch of European flair by the building of a theatre reminiscent of the Royal Albert Hall in London, as well as the first clock tower in the style of Big Ben. The first five-storey building in Tehran, Shams ol-Emareh, combined references to pre-Islamic heritage (especially Sassanid) with strict European neoclassical forms going back to Andrea Palladio (who was only known in Iran by narratives and postcards). It culminated in a new imperial style that had never existed previously and has never been repeated.

On 31 October 1925, the last Qajar Shah was removed by the Iranian parliament with only four dissenting votes, and Reza Khan was proclaimed Shah. During his reign began the systematic industrialisation of the country and the promotion of private investment. The road and

railroad network was expanded, which strengthened the Europeanization of society. For the planning of these projects, European architects were predominantly engaged, who designed historic buildings like the telegraph building in Tehran, whose appearance is dominated by typical renaissance elements. In the 1930s, archaeological excavations led to the rediscovery of Persepolis and thus the rediscovery of the ancient national identity. Allusions to the pre-Islamic heritage, in particular the Sassanid, were supplemented with European neoclassical forms. This mixture culminated again in a new imperial style, which reaffirmed the power of the Pahlavi through references to the old monarchy, and at the same time restricted the influence of the clergy by using pre-Islamic symbols. About a dozen of these buildings were erected in Tehran. Tehran's police building and the Bank-e Meli Iran dating from 1933 are exact copies of the Darius Apadana Palace at Persepolis. Gabriel Guévrékian, an Iranian of Armenian descent, who studied in Vienna under Oskar Strnad and cultivated friendships with Joseph Hoffmann and Adolf Loos, lived in Paris, knew Le Corbusier and was co-founder and first secretary of the Congrès Intenationaux d' Architecture Moderne (CIAM). He arrived in Iran in 1933 at the invitation of Shah Reza Pahlavi and was appointed town architect and city planner of Tehran. The modern movement in Iran addressed a different clientele to in Europe, namely the country's elite, and therefore much earlier became a lifestyle propagated through advertisements and articles in contemporary magazines.

Great Britain and the Soviet Union forced Reza Shah Pahlavi to resign. His son and successor, Mohammad Reza Shah, was inaugurated on 17 September 1941 as the second Shah of the Pahlavi dynasty.

Ruins of Apadana Palace in Persepolis

Tehran was transformed into a global city, with explosive growth in area as well as height of buildings, not least thanks to the revenue from the oil industry, nationalised in 1951. With the aid of foreign planners, huge urban projects were developed, like a new city centre in the north and the residential area Shahrak Ekbatan, one of the largest housing complexes in the Middle East. The construction industry boomed, which at the end of the Pahlavi reign led to an investors' architecture that resulted in a crisis of modern architecture in Iran, and simultaneously in Europe and the United States. Young architects sought a way out, and the golden age"of Iranian contemporary architecture began. Arches, vaults, domes and other elements of the traditional architectural vocabulary were newly interpreted. For example, the Centre for Management Studies, probably the most complete and meaningful

experiment in new Iranian architecture, is reminiscent in form and structure of a traditional madrasa, built around a courtyard where architecture and nature stood in contrast to each other.

Starting in September 1978, regular mass demonstrations took place, culminating in the Muharram protests, with over 2,000,000 participants protesting at the Freedom Tower. The angry crowd demanded the removal of the Shah and the return of Ayatollah Khomeini. On 16 January 1979, Mohammed Reza Shah hurriedly left the country. On 1 February, Khomeini arrived in Tehran. Islamic institutions and their influence on the armed forces and administrative institutions were accompanied by executions and imprisonments, overshadowing Iran's domestic events. In September 1980, the Iraqi army crossed the Iranian border. One of the longest, bloodiest wars in

recent history began, halting any further development of the country. The Iranian revolution was a cultural revolution. The universities closed, and the professors and architects of the golden age left the country. Social, cultural, national and religious ideals were reconsidered, and the quest to establish an Islamic identity became the dominant idea. A half-hearted postmodernism prevailed For more than a decade, style elements of the Islamic past were quoted without a mandatory functional context. The shrine of Imam Khomeini and the construction of Negarestan are examples of this time.

The generation of revolutionary architects slowly disappeared, and an independent young generation dictated the scene. In 1995, Bahram Shirdel returned to Tehran after a successful career in the US and Canada. Although none of his ideas have been realised so far, his projects, which oscillate between organic and technological architecture, have a huge influence on both students and the establishment. The first manifestations of a new generation are the ingenious conversion of a swimming pool – which cannot be used in Islamic law – into a furniture gallery, or the construction of the Mellat Park Cineplex, shaped like a living organism. The seven-storey high Sharifi-ha in northern Tehran also shows a new understanding of architecture. It conforms to the traditional Iranian residence, typically consisting of summer and winter quarters, and turns it into three rotating boxes which can be opened or closed depending on the season. It is still not clear whether the administration will trust these pioneers, or whether they will follow the ideas of the Ministry of Housing and its outdated design principles.

The Garden as
Anticipation of the Town

The Garden as Anticipation of the Town
The Key to Persian
Architecture and Garden Design

Pottery with a representation of
a chahar bagh, ca. 2000 BC

Source: Drawing Ernst Herzfeld, Die Vorgeschichtlichen
Toepfereien von Samarra, Berlin 1930

The Importance of Water

The Iranian plateau is located in the
centre of the Old World. It forms the link
between India and Russia, China and
Arabia, the desert and the oceans. With
a surface of more than 1,500,000 km^2,
the plateau forms the eastern part of
the Middle Eastern fold belt. It is clearly
defined on all sides by the Persian
Gulf and Indian Ocean in the south,
the Caspian Sea and the Turan Lowland
in the north, the Mesopotamian plain in
the west and the Indus plain in the east.
The highlands surrounding the mountain
ranges are closely grouped together in
the northeast and northwest and connect
to the central and western Asia range.
The average elevation of the Elburz

Iranian landscape near Natanz

Source: Hattstein, Markus/Delius, Peter (Islam: Kunst and Architektur)

Mountains around the Caspian Sea is between 3,000 and 4,000 m; at its southernmost bend sits the 5,670 m high volcanic crater of the Demawend. The central Iranian mountain ranges divide the interior highlands into different basins.

Water is the key to Persian architecture and garden design, and the origin of this water is crucial. Throughout the Iranian plateau, the amount of rain is less than 40 cm per annum. Heavy rainfalls and a subtropical climate are only prevalent along the Caspian Sea. On the highland itself, the main source of water comes from the snow that falls on the mountain tops during the winter months. In spring, the thaw creates thousands of streams that tumble down through steep ravines. Only a few are perennial, and some grow into substantial rivers winding their way to the sea. However, most rivers flow into the desert, where they are absorbed by the hot sand.

The Four-Part Garden, *Chahar Bagh*

A pottery fragment dating from ca. 2000 BC, excavated by Ernst Emil Herzfeld in the ruins of Samarkand, bears the image of four cross-shaped channels with stylized trees in the intermediate spandrels. This type of floor plan, in which one axis may be longer than the other, became the standard design of the Persian garden which was known as chahar bagh. Around 2250 BC, the Akkadian kings took the title Lord of the Four Quarters, indicating a link between this archetypal

Daryache, or little sea, as a Persian garden element

concept and the kingdom. Thus, the construction of a paradise garden became a symbolic act where the king placed himself in the centre of everything and reenacted the creation in his own way. Water basins lined with trees of life are depicted on some of the vessels, whilst others show a world divided into four quadrants, some with a pool of water in the centre.

The First Gardens

The first gardens mentioned in myths and literature and often verified by excavations were created near the Euphrates and Tigris rivers in Mesopotamia in the northwestern foothills of the Zagros Mountains, in the present-day province of Chuzistan and the Nile valley in Egypt. The earliest gardens were oases which were fenced-in to protect them from animals, sandstorms and robbers. A natural source supplied the water necessary for survival, and the shade of trees provided protection from the harsh heat. The oasis dwellers soon developed irrigation systems which were initially purely functional, proving to archaeologists the transition from a nomadic to a sedentary lifestyle. Lush plant growth symbolized paradise for the dwellers, whilst they connected the rest of nature with evil ghosts and dangers like dying of thirst. Trees, water and soil were considered sacred from the earliest times. With growing agricultural development, farming, fruit gardens and pleasure gardens became increasingly important. The idea of the garden as a paradise spread throughout the ancient world through military conquests and trade relations. The Silk Road, the main trade route between China and the Western world, had traversed Persian territory since the second century BC.

Relief representation of a hillside garden outside of Nineveh, ca. 645 BC

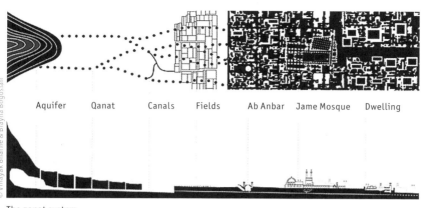

Source: The Qanat transect
© Vinayak Bharne & Blayna Bogosian

Aquifer   Qanat   Canals   Fields   Ab Anbar   Jame Mosque   Dwelling

The qanat system

The Qanat System

The most important water source is a typical Persian invention called qanat or kariz, an invention which can be dated back to the Achaemenid period. Because water evaporates quickly in open irrigation channels on the Iranian plateau in the summer heat, the ancient Persians built a network of underground aqueducts. This was accomplished by digging a shaft at the foot of the mountain which reached down to the water table, sometimes 30 or 40 m deep in porous rock. The groundwater level and the point where the water should reach the surface were arranged in a way that the surface could be reached by a slightly inclined tunnel. From there, a horizontal tunnel was painstakingly dug by hand. Vertical shafts were built at intervals of about 50 m to remove the excavated material and ensure the air supply of the underground workers. The aerial view of a qanat looks like a series of giant mole-hills. Its length varies from a few hundred metres to several kilometres. The longest qanat ever recorded near Yazd measures 70 km. Once the tunnel is completed, it provides a steady amount of clear, cold water throughout the year. A good channel supplies about 1 m^3 per second, which is sufficient for the permanent irrigation of 200 m^2 of arable land. About 50 m ahead of a settlement, the tunnel becomes an open channel. It is first used by the owner or those who buy the largest amount of water; the channel then flows into a deep pool, which is surrounded by pavilions, orchards and gardens, and finally it is used to operate grain mills. In more densely populated areas the water is divided into smaller channels that-line the streets. Behind the village, many small channels reach farmland until every precious drop is absorbed by the earth.

Source: Meyer-Wieser, Thomas

Qanat near Yazd

Passargadae: former garden in the Palace of Cyrus

Source: Meyer-Wieser, Thomas

The *paradeisoi* of the Achaemenids

The writer Xenophon, who in 401 BC joined the Greek auxiliaries in the campaign of Cyrus the Younger against his brother, the Great King, learned much about the Persian way of life and praised the local rulers for not only mastering the art of war, but also promoting farming, irrigation and gardening in their provinces. In his Socratic dialogue about home economics, *Oeconomicus*, the *paradeisoi* are first mentioned as luxuriant pleasure gardens created by the Persian rulers everywhere they stayed during their journeys through the empire: "The great Persian king provides ... in all parts of the country which he inhabits and visits ... gardens, so-called paradeisoi, which are filled with all the good and beautiful things provided by the soil". Xenophon translates the ancient Persian word *paradeiza*, a combination of *pariri*, which corresponds to the English *all around*, and *daeza*, meaning *wall*, with the Greek *paradeisos*. The Greek word was later translated into Latin whereby the term became established as the Garden of Eden in the European world – right through to Milton's *Paradise Lost*. This dialogue, translated into Latin by Cicero, valued by Virgil and frequently read by renaissance humanists, helped to promote the concept of a geometric paradise garden in Europe. Xenophon is said to have established such a garden at his retirement home in Greece, Lucullus eagerly adopted the concept, and Virgil is also said to have been inspired to create a so-called "paradise" around a Roman temple. The *Oeconomicus* reports further that Lysander, the Spartan general, admired the geometric order of the design, the symmetry of the rows of trees and the perfume of the flowers. But he was even more astonished by the fact that Cyrus himself had designed the enclosure in all detail and partly planted some of it with his own hands. Around two thousand years later a miniature of the Babur-Nameh depicts the founder of the Mughal Empire, Babur, at exactly the same activity – an amazing example of continuity through the ages.

Spring of Chusrau

After the fall of the Achaemenid Empire, the Hellenistic and Roman conquerors kept the paradise garden concept alive until the rise of the Sassanid dynasty, when a so-called "Iranian renaissance" in the Middle East took place from the third to the seventh century AD. The concept

Babur supervising the work in Bagh-e Vafa

of paradeiza was expanded by establishing game reserves where royal hunts took place. The palace architecture also became gigantic, as in the ruins of Ctesiphon, Taq-e Kesra. On the marble floor of the throne hall of this palace, the Arab conquerors discovered the legendary carpet, the Spring of Chusrau. Described in detail by Persian historians of the tenth century, the pattern of

this work of art, measuring 26 × 11 m and made of pure silk, was based on the design of the royal gardens. The surface depicted flowerbeds and streams of water crossing in front of individual pavilions, just like in a real garden. The royal craftsmen used gold thread to represent the soil, glittering crystal for the water in the canals and beads for the gravel-covered paths. The fruit

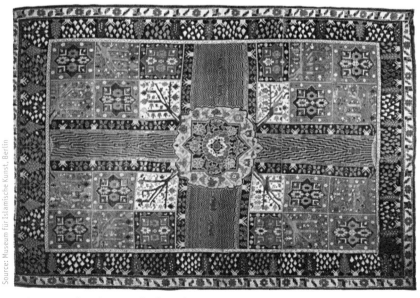

Garden carpet of northwestern Persia, 17th century

Source: Moraqqa'-e Golshan, Golestan Palace, Tehran

Kamal al-Din Bihzad: Sultan Hossein Mirza, miniature of the 16th century

trees in the geometrically-designed fields were worked in silver and gold; flowers and fruits were depicted by precious stones. The palace was almost completely destroyed by the Arabs in 642. Contemporary historians report that the carpet was cut into countless pieces and distributed as booty among the Arab conquerors.

Fin Garden as Image of Paradise
Bagh-e Fin

The image of nature being framed, exalted, refined and assembled into a geometric mandala, where the sovereign could display and enjoy his power as a reflection of the great creation, must have been attractive to the Muslim rulers

Source: Penelope Hobehouse

External wall of Bagh-e Fin in Kashan

as well. The concept of the Akkadian chahar bagh expanded west to Andalusia
and eastward to India. The floor plan of
Bagh-e Fin in Kashan instantly reminds
us of a Persian garden carpet because
all the elements – channels, gardens,
flowers and pavilions – are arranged in
a similar pattern. The Persian garden is
not a place for walks. The prince went
to an open pavilion to meditate, listen
to music, listen to poems or write his
own verses. The Bagh-e Fin deserves our
full attention because it is an admirable
example of the monumental royal gardens and can be seen as the epitome of
the Persian garden culture.

The spatial concept of Bagh-e Fin in
Kashan shows the typical features of
a royal garden palace. This villa subur-
bana consists of a garden surrounded by
high walls and divided into four roughly
equal parts by a coordinated system of
watercourses. Various entrances are created in the perimeter wall. The main
entrance in the north is reached via
a ceremonial road lined with tall trees.
In the centre of the complex lies a two-
storey pavilion, a classic biruni reserved
for the reception of guests, located in
the upper third of the garden and oriented
to the southeast. An entrance to the west
allowed direct horse access to the stables
and the andaruni, the part of the garden
palace reserved as private quarters for
women, children, staff and members of
the family. It is integrated into the enclosure and housed in the complex bordering
the stables. The bathhouse mentioned
earlier consisted of separate rooms and
pools for hot and cold water.

Bagh-e Fin, in its present form, was created during the reign of Shah Abbas I,
but we know that as far back as 1504,
Shah Ismail used it to receive his guests
in a walled garden. The buildings erected
later probably date back to Shah Abbas I.
who used them for stopovers when travelling through the country with his entourage. There is proof that Shah Abbas II
visited the garden in 1659. The turquoise
tiled channels, with their fountains
still functioning thanks to gravity, and
the ancient cypresses date from the seventeenth century. However, the original building at the central intersection

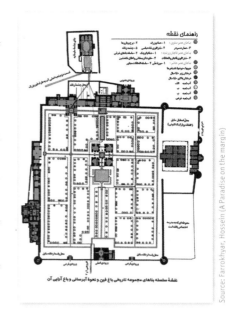

Kashan, Bagh-e Fin, floor plan
● building of the Safavid period
● building of the Zand- and Qajar period
● current building
○ streams, pools, ponds
● trees younger than 150 years
● trees older than 150 years
● underground water supply
○ underground water supply
● underground water supply
○ secondary underground water supply

of the water channels decayed over
the years and was restored by Fath-Ali
Shah between 1799 and 1834, using old
designs. Bagh-e Fin is primarily known
to Persians for a cruel murder that took
place here: The Persian prime minister was murdered in the bathhouse of
the garden in 1852 by order of the young
Nasir-ad-Din Shah.

This fairytale complex is based on
an advanced form of chahar bagh, with
a main channel directing the view from
the monumental entrance through
the main palace as far as the southern end of the garden. Several transverse water channels – small rivulets
that flow into a pool – and raised walkways in the dappled shade of dark, fragrant cypresses contribute to the unique
beauty of this garden. The garden accen-
tuates the contrast between the arid,
inhospitable landscape outside the walls
and the lush foliage inside. Outside,
the water is scarce and precious; inside,

Source: Farrokhyar, Hossein (A Paradise on the margin)

Source: Meyer-Wieser, Thomas

View into the main axis in Bagh-e Fin

it flows in abundance. The arid landscape is replaced by colourful leaves, flowers, tiles and painted plaster. The axis symmetry contrasts with the almost impenetrable greenery. Fragrant orange trees are surrounded by densely planted cypresses along the paths. These dark, tall and mostly gnarled pine trees form a second wall in the garden, again accentuating the geometry of the space, whilst softening its severity by the unique beauty of their shape. A cool, shady space is created along with the lush vegetation, which intensifies the contrast of its heavenly character to the dry, hot climate outside the garden walls.

The water reservoir is placed in the southern half of the garden, a basin full to the brim and covered by a perforated marble slab that allows water, the source of life, to well up. The pool is fed by a large cistern, supplied with mountain water via a qanat. Water basins can be found in all sorts of shapes and sizes. They are usually placed on the main axes of courtyards or gardens, with their longitudinal axis perpendicular to the axis of the larger area. They are always built on slight slopes, taking advantage of gravity, and are often interspersed with small waterfalls below the basins.

The sides and floors of the channels are covered in blue tiles to make the water appear bright and cheery until it flows

into one of the large, tree-lined pools that suggest a dark, unfathomable depth. The Persian garden lacks dramatic fountains but is rather focused on the quiet enjoyment of the precious element of water. The gardens were established on slightly sloping ground, making it possible to build running, gurgling and babbling channels where inclined stones placed at different levels and decorated with a fishbone pattern resulted in the fast, quiet stream becoming a gushing torrent. A soft bubbling and trickling is the most beautiful sound to the Muslim ear because it evokes tranquility – similar perhaps to an Englishman enjoying the crackling of an open fire.

The dark, reflective quality of the surface of the water in big pools was generally much admired. The pools were not cleaned very often. The way the side walls of the basins were formed is also

Source: Farrokhyar, Hossein
(A Paradise on the margin)

Water reservoir with openwork marble slab in Bagh-e Fin

Cistern of Bagh-e Fin

typical of the Persian design, with a retention pond collecting the overflow. When water supply is adequate, these pools overflow constantly, so that even from a short distance the water appears to be infinite.

A pavilion stands in the centre of the garden at the intersection of the north-south and east-west channels. This place cannot be described in words. It radiates a special meditative aura by most effectively orchestrating the elements through light, sound and the alternation of peace and flow. The tabular basins and wells were often intended as mirrors, reflecting the depth of the sky and complementing the surrounding buildings symmetrically. The embanked water embodies the halt of time, giving the courtyard and garden a timeless, otherworldly character and showing the eternal universe in transient elements.

The image of paradise, which forever dominated Persian thinking, is that of an exquisite garden. Poets loved to compare earthly gardens with the Koranic paradise. According to the suras of the Qu'ran, paradise consists of four gardens grouped in two pairs in which symbolic fruits grow – figs and pomegranates, olives and dates. A system of intersecting paths runs along channels which represent the four rivers of life – water, milk, wine and honey. Those who feared

Blue tile-lined channels in Bagh-e Fin

the Lord's presence could rest comfortably on cushions woven with silk and gold, with the fruits of the garden close at hand. There are virgins present who have been touched neither by jinns nor by men and who only have eyes for their beloved. They are like rubies and corals. Should the reward for good deeds be anything but great?

Court life in the gardens is depicted in detail in contemporary miniatures. Descriptions of Timur's receptions are found in the *Zafar nama*, the book of victories of Sharaf al-din Ali Yazdi. Although none of them exactly depict the reception

Reflecting pool in front of the gazebo in Bagh-e Fin

of the Spanish diplomat and author Ruy González de Clavijo on 8 September 1404, many details are the same and the atmosphere is shown very vividly. Clavijo came to Samarkand with the delegation of the Sultan of Egypt, whose gifts for Timur included ostriches and a giraffe. The giraffe must have been exhausted after the 3,000 km march from Cairo! Clavijo reported from his audience with Timur, who was then seventy years old and almost blind: "... just outside the town, we came to a large garden where a pavilion stood. Holding each envoy by the forearm, guards led us into the garden through a big gate, which was covered in gold and blue tiles. We came to a place where a senior court official was sitting on a raised divan, and we all paid our respects. Then we came to other divans where several young princes were sitting, the nephews of His Majesty, to whom we also paid our respects. After passing through another place, we reached Timur, who was sitting under a kind of portal, similar to the entrance of a beautiful palace. He did not sit on the floor but on an elevated sofa in front

Interior view of the gazebo in Bagh-e Fin

Source: Babur-nameh

Bishandas, Miniature of Bagh-e Vafa

Bishandas, Bagh-e Vafa

of a fountain which spouted a water column into the air, with red apples floating in the water. His Royal Highness sat on something that looked like a small mattress, tightly stuffed and covered in silk, leaning on his elbow against round pillows stacked behind him. He wore a plain silk jacket and a tall white hat adorned with a ruby."

One of the most beautiful teahouses in Iran lies on the thoroughfare next to a beautiful Ayvan built by Fath-Ali Shah for his own use. Teahouses have always existed. In a 1972 travel guide, we read

that a tea house is the "Iranian equivalent of a pub or a simple guesthouse in our countries". But these are hardly places for spontaneous social gatherings, nor places for encounters between men and women. It appears that the centuries-old coffee or tea house culture as a place of encounter and exchange, which is found in other Muslim countries, never existed in Iran. This could be because coffee was associated with the unpopular, or even hated Arab invaders. However, chai, a scented tea from the Caspian Sea area, has always been popular.

Source: Reichmann, Caroline

Bagh-e Fin, teahouse in the garden

Bagh-e Fin, Teahouse in the garden

Caravanserai
Karvansara

A caravanserai was a walled hostel on caravan routes. For a small fee, travellers could safely spend the night there with their livestock and merchandise and also stock up on food. Large caravanserais also served as warehouses and trans-shipment centres. The first caravanserai emerged in the late tenth century in Central Asia. Military fortifications increasingly took over economic and religious functions and became fortified hostels. Under the Safavids, the system of caravanserais was expanded and had adequate infrastructure to secure and promote trade. The distance from one caravanserai to the next was about 30 to 40 km, which corresponded to the daily stages of a caravan. The caravanserais lost their function in the twentieth century with the introduction of new means of transport. The layout of a caravanserai usually formed a square or rectangle, sometimes an octagon. It had a large courtyard, surrounded by rooms lined with arcades. Stables and shops were situated on the ground floor. The lodgings and eating areas for travellers were located upstairs. Many caravanserais had workshops, bathrooms, kitchens, tea and coffee shops and medical facilities. Musicians played for entertainment. Some had small mosques or prayer rooms. The caravanserais were run either by private operators or belonged to a charitable trust, or waqf, an institution that served a public cause or a charitable purpose and was funded mostly by the private sector.

Winter and Summer Resort
Yaylaq and Qishlaq

The custom of Persian rulers to take yaylaq and qishlaq, a sort of summer and winter break, gave rise to the creation of a dense network of royal gardens along the routes they travelled. The entire

Exterior view of the Caravanserai En-Rashin

Source: Hochueli, René

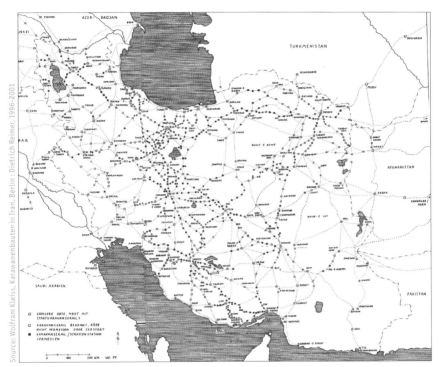

Source: Wolfram Kleiss, Karawanenbauten in Iran, Berlin: Dietrich Reimer, 1996–2001

Wolfram Kleiss, Map of Iran with routes and caravanserai

Source: Charlotte Heer Grau

Courtyard of the Caravanserai En-Rashin

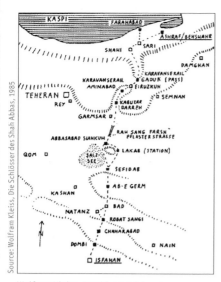

Wolfram Kleiss, Road from Isfahan to
Mazandran, also called Rah-e Sang Farsh

Persian court and its entourage went
hunting from one place to another, right
into the Masanderan province, the preferred hunting ground of Shah Abbas.
The chronicler Iskandar Bayg reports
that the king spent "most of his qishlaq
in this area and its hunting grounds". In
1031, after the Hegira, Mirza Taqi Khan,
the vizier of Tabaristan province, ordered
the widening and paving of the most
important road in Masanderan used by
the king and his entourage. The map from
Isfahan to Farahabad redrawn by Wolfram
Kleiss in his book *Safawidenstraße*
shows the stopovers which, according to
Iskandar Bayg, remained at a distance of
four farsakh (roughly 25 km), and consisted of hostels, catering facilities, gardens and bath houses. Such facilities,
referred to by Kleiss as overnight and
hunting lodges, were used by the king
and his entourage only for short stays
on their journey. In Masanderan, however, they took on the character of veritable royal residences. The most frequently
visited places were Farahabad and Ashraf,
where the king built palaces and gardens
of which only ruins remain today.

Safavid Palaces in Farahabad and Ashraf

In 1611-1612, Shah Abbas I had two summer residences built in the Mazandaran
province, the palace complexes in Ashraf

and in Farahabad, the latter located near
the Caspian Sea. Apart from his capital
Isfahan, these were the Shah's preferred
places. Pietro della Valle, an Italian
explorer, describes life in these Safavid
palaces and gardens and reports on his
first audience with Shah Abbas in the hall
of public audiences at Ashraf on 4 March
1618: "The main entrance to the palace
lies opposite a long and beautiful road.
When we arrived there we disembarked
but did not proceed to the large lawn that
serves as a forecourt. We kept to the right
until we arrived at another palace which
leads to a large garden gate. At the end
of the square, close to the palace, stands
a beautiful big tree where more guards
were stationed. We entered the massive
gate at the end of a straight wide road
lined with hedges and gardens. Beyond
the first door I noticed a small courtyard
which appeared to be a kitchen or pan-
try because I saw many containers and
plates filled with food. From this small
courtyard we proceeded through a second entrance into a covered atrium, followed by another guarded entrance which
led straight into the garden. The garden
was not very large. Exactly in the centre
stood the *divan khane*, a slightly raised
loggia or portico with two steps leading
up to it, completely open at the front and
surrounded on the other sides by walls
with windows. Opposite the entrance
was a door. The main axis with waterways
runs from the entrance of the garden to
the 'divan khan' through this door on
the other side to the end of the garden".
Pietro della Valle describes the arrangement of gardens south of the maidan as
follows: "Beyond the door through which
we entered is a beautiful large lawn which
serves as forecourt of the king's palace
and where people gather when they want
to see the king or speak to him. A partly
man-made hill with soil brought in from
outside rises next to the bathhouse. On
this hill, which can be accessed by steps,
lies a garden planted with orange and
lemon trees, flowers, all kinds of fruits
and fragrant herbs. In the centre of this
garden, which is not very large, stands
an octagonal building, also small but tall
and divided into rooms, all painted and
gilded but very small in size as dictated by

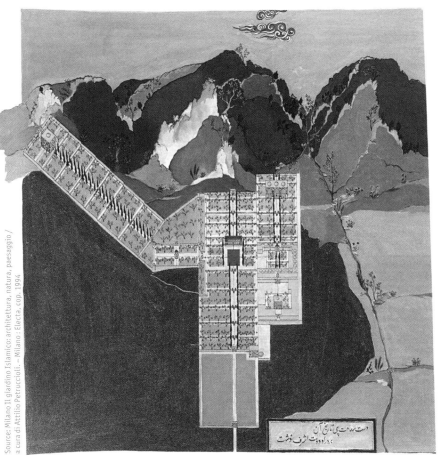

Mahvash Alemi: Reconstruction of the Gardens of Ashraf

custom. This place is only used by women."
The Bagh-e Tappe of Ashraf is depicted
in a miniature illustrating the Khamsa,
a collection of poems by Nizami, one of
the greatest romantic poets of Persian
literature. The subject of young girls taking a bath whilst secretly watched by
their older lord was obviously popular as
it gave the painters the opportunity – in
contrast to Islamic practice – to show
scantily clad women in a relaxed atmosphere. Of the gardens west of the Maidan,
Pietro della Valle writes: "After descend-
ing the stairs we saw the king's house to
the right of the lawn, with a small garden and a gatehouse facing the mountains and the *divan khane*. A fountain
casts its water very high into the air, with
water being run through all the rooms of
the house right up to the roof. This house
is also small, and the rooms are tiny. It has
many balconies on all sides and contains

Tasvir-i Qiyath al-Mudhahhib: Miniature in
the Collection of the Khamsa Poems by Nizami
Source: Aga Khan Development Network (AKDN)

Fata Morgana at Salt Lake
near Rah-e Sang Farsh

Northern section at Resmeh through salt pan
along Rah-e Sang Farsh

a space which has doors and windows on all four sides and two giant mirrors which are like windows and give the illusion of seeing many similar rooms on all sides as well as some other secret rooms, which they call khalvatkhane, meaning *houses of loneliness*." The reconstruction of the royal residence of Ashraf by the Iranian landscape architect Mahvash Alemi shows a similar structural arrangement to the Dawlat Khaneh-ye in Esfahan: close proximity of royal palace to public square, an arrangement of public buildings serving as the vestibule to the palace grounds and consisting of pavilions, gardens and courtyards, forming a perfect frame for court life.

Stone Carpet Path
Rah-e Sang Farsh

Shah Abbas I built a direct road from Isfahan to his castles on the Caspian Sea in Ashraf and Farahabad, the royal road through Dasht-e Kevir, which was enhanced by caravanserais and several hunting lodges. The total distance from Isfahan to the Caspian Sea was approximately 570 km. In the centre of the route lies the massif of Siah Kuh, with the building complexes of Abbasabad and Ain-e Rashidi on its northwestern edge, with Robat Lakab on the eastern slopes in the direction of the next station, Sefid Ab. Today the areas around the Siah Kuh are again rich in wildlife, especially gazelles, and were previously also populated by ibex and wild donkeys. Thus, this area was not only a transit route for caravans, but also a hunting ground for the Safavid and Qajar dynasties. Located on the direct route from Isfahan to Farahabad, the stopover in Sefid Ab or Abbasabad offered a pleasant halfway break, and one is therefore not surprised by the concentration of ruins of castles in both places. Between the stations Abbasabad Siah Kuh and Resmeh near Garmsar, the road crosses a salt pan. The king commissioned the building of the Rah-e Sang Farsh, or Stone Carpet Path, a banked and paved dam of 25 km in length, which runs straight through the salt pan and is still preserved, or at

Caravanserai Maranjab

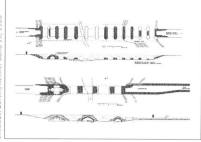

Archäologische Mitteilungen aus Iran / Hrsg. Deutschen Archäologischen Institut, Berlin, Reimer Band 19, 1986

Rah-e Sang Farsh: Southern Bridge (below),
Northern Bridge (top)

Source: Charlotte Heer Grau

Remains of the Southern Bridge
at Rah-e Sang Farsh

least visible, to this day. The stone carpet path has eleven passages of salty runnels with two wider riverbeds below. The rah-e sang farsh is 4.5 m wide, plus two shoulders of about 80 cm each. The path slightly slopes by about 15 cm from the centre to both sides and is made up of large rocks and gabions. One kilometre north of the southern end of the Rah-e Sang Farsh lie the remains of the foundations of a 17 m wide bridge with four passages, which was built on an embankment. The bridge with rounded piers and bridgeheads is 4.5 m wide, which is equivalent to the surface of the rah-e sang farsh. This path was used in 1629 to take Shah Abbas I's body on his last journey from Farahabad to Kashan, where he is buried.

Caravanserai and Castle Maranjab
Karwansara va Qaleh-ye Maranjab

The caravanserai Maranjab is a typical lodging and hunting castle, used by Shah Abbas I and his entourage for short stays on his route from Isfahan to his

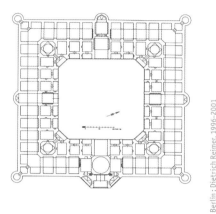

Source: Wolfram Kleiss, Karawanenbauten in Iran, Berlin: Dietrich Reimer, 1996–2001

Caravanserai and Castle Maranjab: floor plan,
section and elevation

Source: Charlotte Heer Grau

Caravanserai Maranjab, inner courtyard

Source: Charlotte Heer Grau

Roofscape of the Caravanserai Maranjab

castles on the Caspian Sea. The caravanserai and the Safavid palace Maranjab lie 61 km northeast of Kashan, 690 m above sea level, on the southern shore of the salt lake Daryaceh-ye Namak. Marendjab is a courtyard caravanserai with four ayvans, two stables, round intermediate and corner towers, a dome above the entrance and a protruding portal. The dimensions are approximately 58 × 57 m without protrusions, and the courtyard measures 30 × 29 m. The caravanserai was built from burnt bricks. The restoration work was interrupted by the Islamic revolution in 1979. The second building, the Marendjab station, is a rectangular courtyard with round corner towers and a cistern in the centre of the yard, adjacent to the Safavid caravanserai and connected to it by a wall. It is probably of Qadjar origin.

Caravanserai Sefid Ab
Karwansaray-e Sefid Ab

The Caravanserai Sefid Ab is close to a Safavid palace, 49 km east of Marendjab on the Safavid royal road and about 985 m above sea level. The Castle Sefid Ab is half a kilometre north of the ruins of the caravanserai on a plain which forms the land barrier between the salt lake and the great salt desert. A rich freshwater source rises between the caravanserai and the camp of the game wardens, and its water was channelled through conduits, traces of which can be seen along the ground to the castle where a walled garden was created on the west side. The remains of several building lines are still visible. The ruins of the castle lie in an area which today is almost barren in autumn and where only a few camel

Source: Reichmann, Caroline

Safavid dome at the main entrance of the Caravanserai Maranjab

View over the ruins of the Caravanserai Sefid Ab

thorn trees thrive. The outer perimeter of the complex measures 86 × 47 m and consists of two courtyards, with the southern courtyard attached to the original building. The entrance to the original complex was by way of an ayvan at the south front. During alterations, most likely shortly after the addition of the southern courtyard, a partition wall was built in the ayvan, shortening its depth. The passage from the ayvan to the courtyard in the far right corner of the ayvan is designed to block the view from the ayvan to the courtyard. Due to this fact alone and even more so by altering the ayvan, the northern courtyard with its corresponding rooms must be considered the harem part of the palace, whilst the southern courtyard was assigned to the male entourage of the travelling or hunting king. The western hall measuring 18.5 × 5.5 m, at a height of 5 m, is the largest hall of the castle. There is a narrow exit on its western side which leads to the garden. The hall is divided by large high niches, with small niches arranged in between. In addition, the interior is enlivened by the transverse arches of the vaults. The vaults are built of burnt bricks, the walls of rubble masonry mixed with burnt bricks. The walls are plastered, with fillet cornices. The spatial

impression is very strongly Safavid, such that for this building, which shows no date, stylistic considerations lead to the conclusion that the origin can be specified as Safavid, regardless of the speculations about the Safavid royal road. Apart from the caravanserai and the Safavid palace, there is an aqueduct that supplies water to the castle from a source close to the caravanserai.

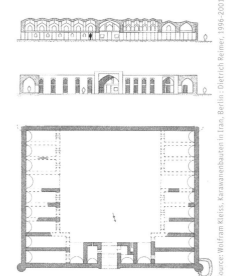

Section, elevation and floor plan of the Caravanserai Sefid Ab

The Safavid Dynasty

1501
The Foundation of the Empire

Iran under the Safavid
صفویان

The origins of the Safavid go back to the chaos of the Mongol invasion, when Islam was spread among farmers, city dwellers and nomads in the vast area between eastern Anatolia, northern Syria, Armenia, Kurdistan and western Iran. This movement was strongly supported by Sufi sheikhs and Islamic brotherhoods and often took on very unorthodox, extreme shiitic forms. These included sectarian groups who followed their leaders in eschatological expectations. These leaders often appeared as Mahdi or even God incarnate, so the group could not be regarded as Muslims in the eyes of most Sunnis. In this troubled, largely unstructured but religiously quite creative environment, Sheikh Safi ad-Din acted as master of a Sufi brotherhood. In 1301 he founded a Sufi order in Ardabil which quickly gained momentum, became a centre of a religious mass movement and created socially revolutionary expectations of salvation. Safi and his direct descendants were strict Sunnis until the mid-fifteenth century, when the order adopted the principles of Twelver Shia, giving greater militancy to his doctrine and creating a uniformed unit called qizilbash, or red hats, named after their red turbans.

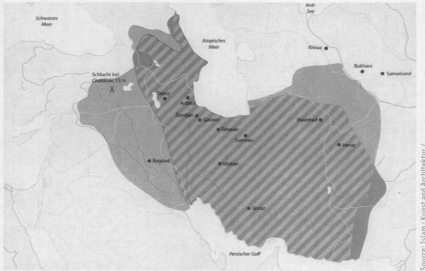

Source: Islam : Kunst and Architektur / Markus Hattstein and Peter Delius, Könemann, 2000

Dominion of the Safavids in the 16th and 17th Centuries

▨ Safavid dominion ca. 1512

— Contested areas between Ottomans and Safavids after 1512

▨ Safavid dominion early 17th century (under Shah Abbas I)

— Contested areas between Ottomans and Safavids during 17th century

Shrine and Grave of Sheikh Safi ad-Din

001

Aramgah-e Sheikh Safi ad-Din

آرامگاه شیخ صفی‌الدین اردبیلی

Ayatollah Taleghani, Ardabil
38.24849, 48.29137
Mirza Shah Hossein Isfahani
AD: 16.–18. Jh. / AH: 950–1200 /
Yaz: 920–1160

Source: Magel, Lutz

The Khaneghah Sheikh Safi ad-Din in Ardabil in northwestern Iran is a unique building complex dating from the sixteenth to the eighteenth century with bazaars, public baths, residential units, religious and public institutions. During the reign of the Safavids the khaneghah was the largest Sufi centre in Iran. The building had great political and national significance as the shrine of the founder of the Safavid dynasty. Ardabil became a pilgrimage site and a centre of Islamic mysticism with outstanding sacral architecture and art. Under the great-grandson of the first Safavid Shah, the building complex became a grave sanctuary. He was also buried there, and subsequent rulers went to the sanctuary every year with their royal household to honour the memory of the ancestors. This necessitated new building additions, whilst the classrooms and the residential dwellings fell into decay. The area of the grave sanctuary is accessed via a spacious courtyard, with the lodgings of the former pilgrims arranged in the walls. A forecourt arranged transversely to the main axis leads further into the main courtyard where the longitudinal walls are decorated by high rectangular niches, elaborately carved lattice and adorned in the upper part with a tile mosaic. The octagonal prayer hall lies to the north. Sixteen wooden pillars once supported the dome, where the rituals of the dervishes took place. The lantern house, which served as a prayer hall, is reached through the eastern longitudinal wall of the main courtyard. This is where the ritual climax of the pilgrimage was celebrated. On the southern

Source: Meyer-Wieser, Thomas

Baq'a Sheikh Safi ad-Din

Chini-khaneh (Porcelain House)

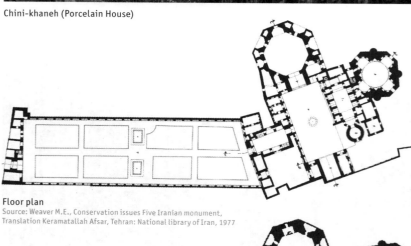

Floor plan
Source: Weaver M.E., Conservation issues Five Iranian monument,
Translation Keramatallah Afsar, Tehran: National library of Iran, 1977

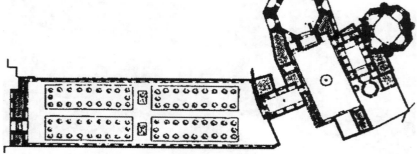

Ardabil plan of complex
Ganjanameh, Cyclopedia of Iranian Islamic Architecture, Shahid Beheshti University (Floor Plan)

Allah-Allah cupola

narrow side there is a domed area separated by an iron grate, where the Shah would sit during the ceremony. At that time the floor was covered by a carpet made specifically for this space, now kept in the Victoria and Albert Museum in London. The lantern house is followed by the grave tower of Sheikh Safi al-Din and the burial chamber of Shah Ismail. Ismail's wooden sarcophagus is a masterpiece of sixteenth-century Persian intarsia: Ivory, lapis lazuli and gold were artfully inlaid in the wood. The Porcelain House is reached via the old, largely ruined residential dwellings. The irregular octagonal floor plan with plaster cladding on the walls and ceiling niches is impressive. This space, once used as a ballroom, is now a museum. The ornamentation and interior design show influences of Ilkhanid and Timurid architecture with the religious message of Sufism. The complex, its architecture and decoration combine spiritual and aesthetic aspects in a harmonious work of art whose authentic image is preserved to this day.

1501–1548
Tabriz – First Safavid Capital

Ismail, who later became the first Safavid Shah, was only twelve years old when he became the head of the qizilbash in 1499. Despite his youth he proved to be a charismatic leader of extraordinary and ambitious character. His understanding of Islam went well beyond accepted Islamic doctrines, but he remained true to the eschatological expectations and messianic promises of its original doctrine: Ismail appeared as the hidden imam and mahdi respectively, and at the same time as the incarnation or "shell" of God and the divine light, which previously was manifest in Ali, the prophets and the imams. His followers revered him as divine, immortal and invulnerable. Charisma must be sustained: Ismail gathered his qizilbash, advanced to the east with about 7,000 men and conquered Tabriz in July 1501, where he appointed himself the Shah of Azerbaijan, proclaiming himself Shah-hanshah, King of Kings of Iran, and minted coins in his name. In Tabriz, he ordered the Friday prayer to be performed on behalf of the twelve Imams, had the first three caliphs cursed and at the same time threatened to put to death everyone who refused this curse – an act often described as the introduction of Shia as the Iranian "state religion". But Iran was still not conquered at that time; the Safaviyya was at best at the edge of the broad Shiite flow, and the concept of a "state religion" in the Islamic context is anything but clear. Until 1512 the qizilbash conquered western and central Iran as well as large parts of Afghanistan, Iraq including Baghdad and the Shia shrine of Najaf, Kerbala and Kaziamain and Khurasan. However, their home country Anatolia remained in Ottoman hands. Involved in the succession struggles, Selim I acted ruthlessly and with great brutality against the qizilbash and inflicted a crushing defeat on Ismail in 1514 in the Battle of Chalderan that damaged his aura of invincibility – but did not prevent the establishment of the Safavid dynasty. Following Chalderan, the Ottomans briefly occupied Tabriz. An important consequence of the occupation was the forced migration of hundreds of skilled metal workers to Istanbul, which spelt the end of the pre-eminence of Tabriz as a cultural centre. After he was defeated by the Ottomans, Shah Ismail retreated at Khoy to lead a life of royal pleasures – hunting, drinking wine, and feasting – until his death in 1524. When Shah Ismail died he left his successors with a difficult legacy. In the course of these struggles the royal residence gradually migrated into the Iranian heartland.

Development of the urban area of Tabriz, from the 8th to the 20th century

In 1501, Shah Ismail I entered Tabriz and proclaimed it the capital of his Safavid state. Thus, under the first Safavids, Tabriz rose from a regional to a national capital for a short time. But the newly established Empire lacked both time and resources to confirm their Safavid domination through monumental buildings in the newly conquered capital. In fact, they used existing structures to perform their new kind of Shiitic legitimacy and therefore, few traces of Safavid urban planning or Safavid monumental buildings can be found in Tabriz. Moreover, Tabriz was temporarily occupied by the Ottomans after the battle of Chaldiran in 1514. Retaken by Iranian forces, the town remained the Safavid capital until 1548, when Shah Tahmasp I transferred it to Qazvin to avoid the growing threat of the Ottoman army. In the summer of 1721, a large earthquake occurred in Tabriz, killing about eighty thousand of its residents. For this reason, one hardly finds any buildings from earlier periods in the city. One important change after the Islamisation of Persia in Iranian cities was the emergence of religious institutes, characterised mainly by the Masjid-e-Jameh, as the major religious and political centre. Main government buildings and the residences of the governor and the market centre were located beside it. The second important change was the substantial improvement in their economic role, which can be seen by the rise of the bazaar as the main centre of economic activities. Increasing interregional trade between the tenth and fifteenth centuries led to the growth of cities. Another characteristic of the spatial structure of Islamic cities was the segregation of residential and commercial areas, attributed to the need to separate private from public spaces in Islamic culture. In the nineteenth century, Tabriz exemplified the physical structure of the traditional Iranian city. Its structure was influenced by urban experience during the Islamic period before it was influenced by the impact of the twentieth century.

Development of the urban area of Tabriz in the 8th century

Development of the urban area of Tabriz in 1830

Development of the urban area of Tabriz in the 11th century

Development of the urban area of Tabriz in 1900

Development of the urban area of Tabriz in the 13th century

Development of the urban area of Tabriz in 1966

City of Tabriz

Source: www.iranmap.com

Location of Tabriz on the Silk Road

The geographical location of Tabriz on the major east-west historical trade routes, the Silk Road and Spice Route, made it the ideal main trading centre in northwestern Iran. This exposed situation frequently made Tabriz the bone of contention of the region. Attacks by Mongols, Russians and Turks shaped the history of the city. The famous Italian explorer Marco Polo, who travelled along the Silk Road and passed Tabriz ca. 1275, described it as "a great city surrounded by beautiful and pleasant gardens. It is perfectly positioned, and the goods brought here come from many regions. Latin merchants, especially Genovese, came here to buy the goods that came from foreign lands."

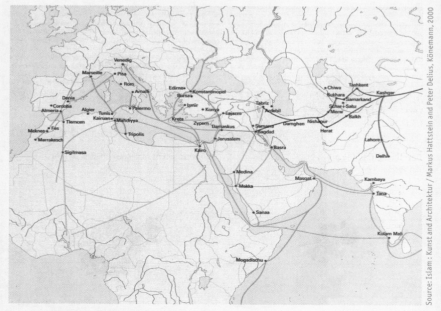

Source: Islam: Kunst and Architektur / Markus Hattstein and Peter Delius, Könemann, 2000

Location of Tabriz on the Silk Road

——— trade routes   ——— gold trading road   ——— silk road

Jameh Mosque
Masjid-e Jameh
مسجد جامع تبریز

002 B

Rasta Kuche St., Tabriz
38.08099, 46.29042
Hossein-Qoli-Khan Donboli et al.
(Commissioners)
AD: 11th cent./AH: 5th cent./
Yaz: 5th cent.

In this historically important place, Shah Ismail ordered the Friday prayer to be performed on behalf of the twelve Imams, had the first three caliphs cursed and introduced Shia as the Iranian state religion in July 1501. But the Masjed-e Jameh of Tabriz is an ensemble of different buildings, created or rebuilt in various periods. The most ancient part of the mosque is its vast roofed area. It has an arch and domes, based on octagonal brick pillars covered with delicate and artistic plasterwork dating from the eleventh century. The mosque was repaired during the rule of the Mongol Ilkhanid dynasty when additional sections were added. Its high altitude minbar and plasterwork, rebuilt recently by experts from the Iranian Cultural Heritage Organisation, are reminders of that era. During the rule of Aq Qoyunlu Yaan a tall, tiled dome was built in the northern corner

Masjid-e Jameh, plan and section

of the mosque – the remains of which can still be seen. The present mosque was constructed after the 1721 earthquake during the early years of the rule of Qajar dynasty. Its height, solid structure and fine architecture make for a compelling sight, and experts admire the skills of its architect. Another part of the congregational mosque is a shabestan called Alchaq-Masjed, which is located in the southeast of the ensemble. During repairs carried out in recent years, the remaining Safavid period vaults were removed and a new prayer room with a large span was built. The shabestan, known as the Hojat-ol-Eslam mosque, is an old building which has been repeatedly restored.

Masjid-e Jameh, Sheikh-e Sadeq Shabesta

Masjid-e Jameh, Hojat-ol-Eslam, Shabesta

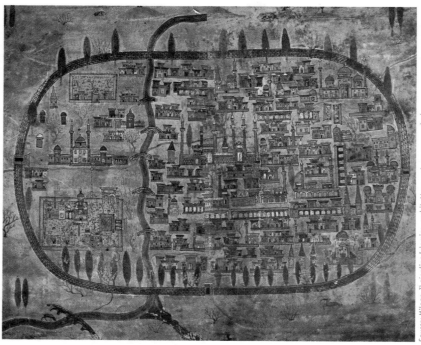

Source: Milano, Il giardino Islamico: architettura, natura, paesaggio / a cura di Attilio Petruccioli. – Milano : Electa, cop. 1994

N.S. Matrakci, Plan of the city of Tabriz, 16th Century

Saint Mary's Church
Kelisa-ye Maryam
کلیسای مریم مقدس

003 B

Rasta Kucha Aghzi Square,Tabriz
38.07899, 46.28819
unknown
AD: 12th cent., 1785/AH: 6th cent., 1199/
Yaz: 6th cent., 1154

Since the Safavid dynasty was of Azerbaijani origin, the aristocracy and culture of this country played an important role in the rise of the empire. Moreover, the contacts of Armenians with Christian merchants were extremely important for the newly established power, and form an important thread to understand Safavid history. Saint Mary's Armenian Church is the largest and oldest Christian church in town and a notable centre for Armenian national and religious ceremonies. It was built in the sixth century, and Marco Polo referred to it in his travel chronicles on his way to China. A board of Armenian peers governs the well-attended church. For many years, Saint Mary's served as the seat of the Azerbaijani Armenian archbishop. It is a handsomely built edifice, with annex buildings sprawled over a large area. The aedicula beside the church, topped with a cupola-like turret, is a formal reference to the Church of the Holy Sepulchre in Jerusalem. It was not simply a copy of the holy site; it was believed that through the combination of image, dedications and devotional acts, the sacred topography of the Holy City could be relocated – re-created, as it were, at a new site. The significance of Saint Mary's lay in the belief that sanctity or spiritual value could be associated with people, places or objects, and that by being captured in matter, the numinous qualities could be transferred from the original location. Such supposed transfers of holiness were common in the Middle Ages and were a routine component of Christian pilgrimages.

Source: Wikimedia Commons

Saint Mary's Church

Sahibabad Garden
Bagh-e Sahib-abad
باغ صاحب اباد

Mahadiye Str., Tabriz (destroyed)
38.084638, 46.294031
Commissioner unknown
AD: 1258/AH: 655/Yaz: 627

According to the anonymous 1674 history *Tarikh-e Alam Ara-ye Safavi*, Ismail was enthroned in Tabriz and played polo in the maidan in front of the garden. The first vast official and ceremonial space, Sahib-abad, was created in 1258, around which the most important public buildings were erected and where army parades took place, but which could also be used as a meeting place. The plan of the city of Tabriz drawn by the Ottoman painter Matrakci during his first Persian campaign is the first graphical document showing the Bagh-e Sahibabad in the sixteenth century. It shows the urban core with bazaars and mosques to the south of the river Mahan, whilst gardens were situated to the north of the river. Among these was the royal garden in which stood the turquoise, octagonal Hasht Bihisht palace built by Uzun Hasan Aq Quyunlu. The garden was accessed through a maidan flanked to the east by the Sahib-abad mosque, malletss for playing polo can be seen in the miniature. The palace and garden were destroyed in 1636 by Ottomans. In the Qajar period, the maidan was turned into a fresh produce bazaar. The centre of government moved from the Sahib-abad, where public buildings were arranged around a vast square north of the Mehran Roud river to its present location south of the river, close to the Aala Gate. Sahib-ul-Amr square was built in the historical area of Sahib-abad.

Citadel of Tabriz
Arg-e Tabriz
ارگ تبریز

Imam Khomeini and Ferdowsi Street, Tabriz
38.07239, 46,28875
Falaki Tabrizi
AD: 1318–1339, 19th/
AH: 718–739/Yaz: 736–715

This strategically-important and-much besieged city has had a citadel, variously rebuilt and resited, at least from early Safavid times. Arg-e Ali Shah is the remnant of an unfinished fourteenth-century mausoleum and a nineteenth-century military castle and barracks in the city centre. The original construction was built between 1318 and 1339, during the Il-khanate, in the southwestern area of the Mongol Empire. The roof of the mausoleum collapsed during construction and the project was stopped. Centuries later, during the Russo-Persian Wars of 1804–1813 and 1826–1828, the compound was reconstructed as a cannon foundry as well as military headquarters and barracks, and a small palace was added to the original plan. During the Russian invasion of Tabriz in 1911, the Arg was used as a command centre. In the Pahlavi era, non-original parts were destroyed, and the southern part of the Arg was turned to an urban park, Bagh-e Mellat. After the Iranian revolution the park was renovated. Everything from the Qajar era was removed and a new mosque was built next to the castle; the superstructure of the new mosque undermines the architecture. Despite the regulations of the Iranian Organisation for Cultural Heritages and the courts, the construction of the new structure continued and will be finalised.

Source: Voyage en Perse, avec Flandin, éd. Gide et Baudry, 1851

Eugène Flandin, Remains of the Citadel of Tabriz

Source: Bachellerie Olivier

Arg-e Tabriz, view from the south

Blue Mosque
Masjid-e Kabud
مسجد کبود

Emam Khomeini Av., Tabriz
38.07359, 46.30108
Jahan Shah ibn Qara-Yussef
Turkmen (Commissioner), Nematollah bin
Mohammad ul-Bavvab (Calligraphist)
AD: 1491/AH: 896/Yaz: 870

This completely roofed mosque, which is unusual in Persian designs, consists of a domed central building with four ayvans, connected to the outside on three sides with side domes and on the fourth side to a small domed structure toward Mecca. The various Kufic and Thulth inscriptions, the exquisite arabesque patterns and the admirable chromatic compositions of these façades, which are truly amazing, were created by Nematollah bin Mohammad ul-Bavvab. He was a well-known calligrapher and writer and the main architect of this building. His inscriptions show that Jahan Shah and the Qara Qoyunlu tribe were Shiites and devoted to the Holy Prophet's family, and that this building was the first decorated mosque in which the names of the Rashidun caliphs were omitted and the words "Ali is the Friend of Allah" and the revered names of Hassan and Husayn adorned its walls and vaults in various ways. According to existing sources, the construction of the Mosque was completed in 1491, but work on its auxiliary buildings took place after this date. The Blue Mosque bears its name because of the previously used cobalt blue tiles, and it was one of the most beautiful buildings of the Timurid period. The decoration can be compared with Timurid works in Herat, Samarqand and Khorasan, and the design can be

Entrance portico of Masjid-e Kabud

compared with Ottoman buildings, especially the great mosques of Orhan and Yeshil in Bursa. Many travellers and historians have described this building in their writings, expressing their admiration for its majesty and beauty. As in other Ottoman Külliyes, the original building included a school, a public bath, a soup kitchen and a library, all of which disappeared during the earthquake in 1721 as well as due to poor maintenance. Only parts of the mosque have survived, and what remains is a testimony to its earlier grandeur and splendour. Reconstruction began in 1973 thanks to the initiative of Tabriz architect Reza Me'maran Benam. The domes of the mosque were recently rebuilt, the main one as a twin-shell, hollow structure. However, the tiling is still incomplete. The mosque is now almost permanently closed, but renovation and eventual reopening seem inevitable.

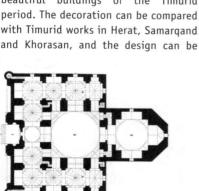

Plan of Blue Mosque

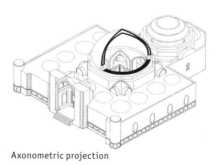

Axonometric projection

Source: Voyage en Perse, avec Flandin, éd. Gide et Baudry, 1851

Saheb ol Amr Mosque by Eugène Flandin, ca. 1851

Shah Tahmasp Mosque
Masjid-e Shah Tahmasp
مسجد صاحب الامر

Shahid Madani, Tabriz
38.08410, 46.29570
Hossein-Qoli-Khan Donboli
(Commissioner)
AD: 1636/AH: 1046/Yaz: 1004

The Mosque of Shah Tahmasp I, son and successor of Shah Ismail, is located on the east side of Sahibabad garden. In the Aq Quyunlu period, a large hospital, a sofreh-khaneh and a khaneqah were built around this square. In 1636, Shah Tahmasp I had a mosque built opposite these buildings. However, the building was destroyed by the Ottoman ruler Murad IV after invading Tabriz in 1638. Once Persian troops had regained control over the city, the mosque was rebuilt under the Safavid Shah Sultan Husayn,

but suffered great damage during the 1721 earthquake that struck the city soon after. Consequently, the entire square, along with the mosque, was reconstructed by Goli Khan Donboli. In order to please the people, the mosque was dubbed Saheb ol Amr, Master of Command, one of the titles of the Mahdi, the last Shia Imam. Legend has it that someone – whether in a dream or in reality – saw the Twelfth Imam in the mehrhab of this mosque. As a result of this anecdote, this site acquired special spiritual value among the people of Tabriz and became a place of pilgrimage. In 1850, Mirza Ali Akbar Khan, the interpreter for the Russian Consulate, had some other parts of the dome rebuilt and added mirrors to the corridor. When a new avenue was being built, the northern section and part of the northwestern corner were unfortunately demolished.

Source: Sargozasht-e Gozargah-e Iranian Islamic Architecture, Shahid Beheshti University

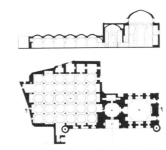

Masjid-e Shah Tahmasp, floor plan and section

General view of the mosque

Bazaar of Tabriz
Bazar-e Tabriz
بازار تبریز

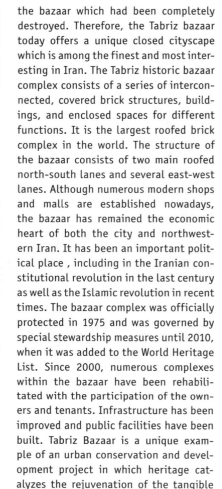

Sadeqyeh Bazaar, Tabriz
38.08245, 46.29315
Amir Ahmad Khan
(Commissioner)
AD: 13th cent., ca. 1780/
AH: 6th cent., ca. 1193/
Yaz: 6th cent., ca. 1149

Tabriz has been a place of cultural exchange since antiquity, and its historic bazaar complex is one of the most important commercial centres on the Silk Road. Tabriz and its bazaar were already prosperous and famous in the thirteenth century when the town became the capital city of the United Ilkhanid Empire, which stretched from Hindu Kush to Egyptian territory, for forty years. Its proximity to the Caucasus and Turkey made it one of the most important commercial cities of Persia until the end of the eighteenth century saw the expansion of Ottoman power and the opening of the Suez Canal in 1869. However, the bazaar is only 230 to 240 years old and has been subjected to repeated historical restorations in order to maintain its commercial role as an urban and architectural focus of the city. After the 1721 earthquake, which caused the death of tens of thousands of people, Amir Ahmad Khan ordered the rebuilding of

the bazaar which had been completely destroyed. Therefore, the Tabriz bazaar today offers a unique closed cityscape which is among the finest and most interesting in Iran. The Tabriz historic bazaar complex consists of a series of interconnected, covered brick structures, buildings, and enclosed spaces for different functions. It is the largest roofed brick complex in the world. The structure of the bazaar consists of two main roofed north-south lanes and several east-west lanes. Although numerous modern shops and malls are established nowadays, the bazaar has remained the economic heart of both the city and northwestern Iran. It has been an important political place , including in the Iranian constitutional revolution in the last century as well as the Islamic revolution in recent times. The bazaar complex was officially protected in 1975 and was governed by special stewardship measures until 2010, when it was added to the World Heritage List. Since 2000, numerous complexes within the bazaar have been rehabilitated with the participation of the owners and tenants. Infrastructure has been improved and public facilities have been built. Tabriz Bazaar is a unique example of an urban conservation and development project in which heritage catalyzes the rejuvenation of the tangible and intangible memories of the historic city of Tabriz.

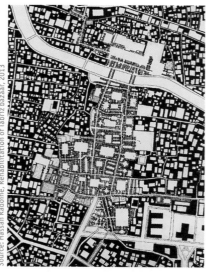

Source: Hassan Radoine, Rehabilitation of Tabriz bazaar, 2013

The urban structure of Tabriz Bazaar

Haji-Mohammad-Qoli Timcheh and Sara
Timcheh-ye va Saray-e Haji-Mohammad-Qoli
تیمچه و سرای حاج مهمد قلی

Rasta Bazar-e Jadid, Tabriz
38.08148, 46.29139
Haji-Mohammad-Qoli (Promoter)
AD: after 1780 1828/AH: after 1243/
Yaz: after 1197

This bazaar ensemble, reconstructed after the 1721 earthquake, combines closed and open spaces including two passageways, a timcheh and a sara. The timcheh is located at the intersection of the passageways, but unusually the entrances are located at the corners so that the axis of the area's entrance

Haji-Mohammad-Qoli Timcheh and Sara,
central space of the timcheh

Timcheh Malek,
central space of the timcheh

forms a 45° angle with the main axis of its base. The designer probably adopted this geometry because of the limitations of the site and in order to create a larger central area, but since he did not want the area's entrance to appear slanted, he used devices in the ceiling's detail and geometry to compensate for this discrepancy. Thus the main arches are rotated in respect of the main axes and are aligned with the arches of the passageways. Consequently, a clear-cut, crystal-like space has been created which can be considered the result of the rotation. The location of the stairways on the sides enhances the standing of the upper floor. In fact, this ease of access to the upper floor is characteristic of the ensemble as it transformed its upper floor chambers from secondary spaces into valuable and easily accessible ones. The vault culminates in a central sun-like geometric pattern, in the centre of which an aperture sheds light on the vault, putting the crystalline refinement of this space in relief.

Malek Timcheh
Timcheh-ye Malek
تیمچه ملک

Rasteh Bazar-e Qadim
38.08148, 46.29139
unknown
AD: after 1828 / AH: after 1243 /
Yaz: after 1197

Malek Timcheh is a handsome Qadjar-period bazaar building, reconstructed after the 1721 earthquake. The timcheh has a simple portico followed by a short two-storey passageway, starting with a circular and continuing with a tripartite arch connected to the starting point of the dome by round elements. The central area of the timcheh is a composite space which appears to have taken shape from the replication of its central cell. With its elongated shape, the timcheh has succeeded in adapting itself to the form of the parcel as well as establishing a three-way link. This unique area can be viewed as a combination of five

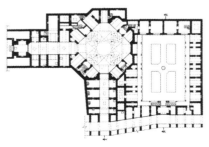

Haji-Mohammad-Qoli Timcheh and Sara,
ground floor plan

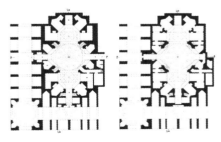

Timcheh Malek,
first- and second-floor plans

Source: Ganjanameh, Cyclopedia of Iranian Islamic Architecture, Shahid Beheshti University

Timcheh Malek, part of the central space of the timcheh

Timcheh Malek, three-dimensional projection

visualised the design of the entire space. The ceiling plays an important role in the design. The dome has no central light aperture. Rather, several lights are located in the vault's sides. This refined spatial layout has been realised with simple materials: bricks with white pointing, plaster rasmis, wooden doors and windows and brick-framed plaster surfaces.

Haji-Sheikh-Kazem Timcheh   011
Timcheh-ye Haji-Sheikh-Kazem
تیمچه هاج شیخ کاظم

Kaffashan Bazaar, Tabriz
38.07990, 46.29312
Haji-Sheikh-Kazem (Commissioner)
AD: ca. 1830 / AH: ca. 1245 / Yaz: ca. 1200

main parts: a square with equally chamfered corners based in the central area, two semi-octagons in the northern and southern areas, and two semi-hexagons based in the eastern and western ones. Rather than surrounding the central area, the chambers are situated around the four peripheral ones. The stairways leading to the upper floors are located at the four corners of the central floor. The area has been given a centre by enlarging its base and increasing the height of the central dome. The design of the floor, the walls and the ceiling is uniform and unbroken and their intimate connection shows that, from the very beginning, the designer

The Haji-Sheikh-Kazem Timcheh, also reconstructed after the 1721 earthquake, consists of a composite area which appears to have penetrated into the surrounding buildings. Since the timcheh communicates with other areas on four sides, the 45° turn in respect to the bazaar structure has allowed communication to be established whilst preventing the timcheh from appearing too large despite its complexity. The refined vaulting consists of a tall dome-shaped vault surrounded by four shorter half-vaults in harmony with the geometry. This layout allows the timcheh excellent connection with the surrounding

Haji-Sheikh-Kazem Timcheh, section

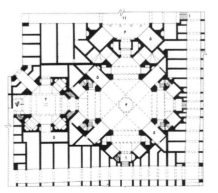

Haji-Sheikh-Kazem Timcheh, ground floor plan

Central ceiling space of the timcheh

areas, particularly the main passage of the bazaar, where the connection has been ensured by small passageways lying lower than the corridor level. A second focal point of the ensemble is a small timcheh west of the main one, which provides space for more chambers and allows the connection between the ensemble and the Gorjiar sara via a passageway.

Amir Ensemble
Majmueh-ye Amir
مجموعه امیر

Amir Bazaar, Tabriz
38.07900, 46.29384
Samad Memar
AD: 1840/AH: 1255/Yaz: 1209

The founder of Amir Karvan sara and timcheh is Mirza Mohammad Khan, the Amir Nezam of Zangneh. The architect of the complex was Samad Memar. The Amir Ensemble comprises a large central sara with two timchehs, one on its northwest and another on its south side. The elaborate design of the bazaar buildings of Tabriz is conspicuous in this ensemble. The sara has a large courtyard which was considered a caravanserai. Surrounded by two-storey façades, the navicular courtyard follows a four-ayvan design. The ayvans' arcs are taller and their frames rise as high as a full storey above the roofline. Thus, the central ayvans on

the four sides of the courtyard reinforce the geometry of the design, giving unity to the two-storied façades and building the numerous and varied constituent elements of the courtyard's inner area. The façades are made of dark bricks with white interstices. The southern timcheh is two-storied, with a non-conventional yet perfectly regular and symmetrical base. This timcheh constitutes a unified area which may be viewed as the aggregate of a central square with equal chamfered corners and four surrounding halfoctagons. The vaults' heights are in harmony with the shape of the base and vary in proportion to it. The interior façade of the timcheh is made of dark brick with white pointing. The fine intersecting curves on the ceiling joining the walls to the vault culminates in a large shamseh covered by the timcheh's topmost circular vault. Stone, brick, wood, clay and plaster were the main materials used throughout the bazaar and in a professional way that shows a high level of control of small details.

Majmueh Amir, three-dimensional projecion

Majmueh Amir, central space in the southern timcheh

Timcheh Malek, part of the timcheh's central space ceiling

Mozaffaryeh Timcheh
Timcheh-ye Mozaffaryeh
تیمچه مظفریه

Sarraj-ha Bazaar, Tabriz
38.08086, 46.29228
Bela-Kazem
AD: 1850/AH: 1267/Yaz: 1305

Timcheh Malek, cross section

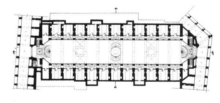

Timcheh Malek, ground floor plan

This timcheh, one of the most beautiful buildings in the bazaar of Tabriz, is devoted to carpet selling. It was built in 1850, during the reign of Qajar monarch Naser al-Din Shah and the regency of Mozzafar-ed-Din-Mizra, after whom it was named. It is said that its construction was commissioned by Haji-Sheikh-Jafar from the architect Bela-Kazem. The timcheh has an elongated shape with an entrance at each end. These two entrances have equal architectural importance. Both of them have unusually-shaped but symmetrical bases, as well as delicate and elaborate ceiling decorations, and are connected to the semi-hexagonal areas of the two ends of the passage. The form of the base does not change and has identical vaults that give it the appearance of a small bazaar. The entire interior façade is made of dark bricks with pointing and, except for a fine ceiling decoration, the building is plain. The brickwork is employed to meet both structural and ornamental needs and, accordingly, there is an architectural coherence between the structure and the wall surfacing.

Timcheh Malek, central space of the timcheh

Source: Ganjnameh, Cyclopedia of Iranian Islamic Architecture, Shahid Beheshti University

Timcheh Malek, part of the timcheh's central space ceiling

Mir-Abol-Hasan Sara
Saray-e Mir-Abol-Hasan
سرای میر ابو الحسن

014 B

Sarrajan Bazaar, Tabriz
38.08148, 46.29139
Mir-Abol-Hasan (Promoter)
AD: ca. 1870 / AH: ca. 1285 / Yaz: ca. 1240

Axonometric projection

Floor plan

This sara, built during the reign of Naser al-Din Shah, is an extensive ensemble comprising a large courtyard, a small bazaar and chambers laid out around it and linked together. The sara has a large entrance corridor whose axis is perpendicular to the bazaar axis, and two chahar-suqs have taken shape at their intersections. Thus, the ensemble constitutes a complete combination of a bazarcheh, a timcheh-like chahar-suq, a passageway, a corridor and its surrounding chambers. The constituent elements, the rhythm of façades and spaces, their crests and depths are complete and studied. The chambers, which are of different sizes, are intermittently repeated around the courtyard. The relatively fixed rhythm is modified and reinforced by the ayvan-like openings at the centre of its side. Thus, they serve as basis for unifying and strengthening the design elements, and give meaning to the refined melody of the chambers. An unusually- but regularly-shaped small pool, surrounded by four rectangular flower beds, decorates the courtyard.

Western side of the sara

Mansions of Tabriz

Most historical houses in Tabriz date back to the Qajar dynasty. Almost all valuable historical monuments of Tabriz were destroyed in an earthquake during the last night of 1854, reducing Tabriz to debris and ruins. However, some of the strong and stable monuments such as Alishah Ark, Tabriz Bazaar, Ostad va Shagerd mosque, Jameh Mosque and Kabud Mosque remained, in spite of the damage they suffered. Following this earthquake, in the beginning of the Qajar dynasty, construction flourished in Tabriz and the people started building a new city full of beautiful and – of course – *strong* houses, on the ruins of the destroyed Tabriz. Today, these mansions can be seen in the central parts of the city. However, during some decades, these places also suffered damages requiring reconstruction and renewal. In recent years, the trend for mending the historical houses of Tabriz has resumed. For instance, Mashrouteh house, Sharbat Oghli House and the houses of Behnam Ganjalizadeh and Sadaghiani and Amirnezam have been converted to cultural spaces after renovation and reconstruction. Even at present, many of these houses are being renewed and renovated. Architecture of these houses is local-Iranian and the wonderful geographical correspondence makes it absolutely appropriate for Tabriz. Since Tabriz is located on an earthquake zone, the structure of Qajar houses in Tabriz were built using a combination of framed and vault constructs: The basement usually had vault construct, while the next floor would have framed construct.

Behnam House, southern view

Source: Muhammad Ali Kaynejad, Mohammad Reza Shirazi; The Traditional Houses of Tabriz, 2011

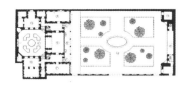

Ground floor plan and section

Behnam House
Khaneh-e Behnam
خانه بهنام

015

Ark-e-Jadid, Tabriz
38.07101, 46.29530
Behnam Family (Commissioner)
AD: ca. 1790 / AH: ca. 1204 / Yaz: ca. 1159

Behnam House was built as a residential home during the latter part of the Zand and early part of the Qajar dynasty. The Behnam family was a dynasty of state bureaucrats since the beginning of Qajar rule. Its members were mainly mostowfis, or tax accountants. During the reign of Naser al-Din Shah, this building was substantially renovated and embellished with ornamental paintings. The house consists of a main building, referred to as the winter building, and a smaller structure called the summer building. Like many traditional houses in Iran, the house has an inner andaruni, the private quarters, and an outer biruni courtyard, the former being the larger of the two. During a 2009 renovation project, some hitherto-unknown miniature frescoes were discovered and restored. The Behnam House was part of a restoration project of three adjoining houses by the Fine Arts, Architecture and Carpet Departments of the University of Art. Traditional methods and materials such as brick, lime, sand and glass were used throughout. This kind of successful – and, equally importantly, inexpensive – rehabilitation of old and discarded buildings has led to many other similar projects in the region, helping to revive local knowledge and training.

Source: Muhammad Ali Kaynejad, Mohammad Reza Shirazi; The Traditional Houses of Tabriz, 2011

Ottomanesque fireplace

Garden elevation

Amir Nezam House
Khaneh-e Amir Nezam
خانه امیرنظام

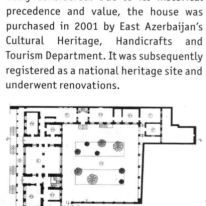

Sheshgalan Avenue, Tabriz
38.08311, 46.30600
*Amir Nezam Garrousi
(Commissioner)*
AD: ca. 1803 / AH: 1341 / Yaz: ca. 1292

In 1803, the crown prince of Fat'h-Ali Shah, Abbas Mirza, resided in Tabriz, which was the country's military command headquarters during wars between Iran and Russia. The house of Amir Nezam was erected during the era of Naser-ed-Din Shah by Ali Khan Amir Nezam Garrousi, who was the king's chief of staff. Ali Khan Amir was among the affluent and renowned dignitaries of his time and held important political and military posts. He was appointed Iran's ambassador to London and also supervised and protected Iranian students studying in European cities. In Naser-ed-Din Shah's memoirs about his third trip to Europe, many references were made to this building. Today only parts of this building remain. Like other historical buildings of Tabriz, the house has two courtyards which have small gardens and large ponds. The porch of the building has sixteen pillars, embellished with plasterworks. Its adorned multi-coloured orosi windows, plaster and mirror works in its halls enhance the beauty of this building. There is a large pond in the basement,

which is one of its most attractive areas. The Stone Hall has an exquisite marble inscription made in memory of the reconstruction of Tabriz after the devastating 1721 earthquake. Because of constant neglect over a long period of time, the building had fallen into such a poor state of repair that demolition was seriously considered. Due to its historical precedence and value, the house was purchased in 2001 by East Azerbaijan's Cultural Heritage, Handicrafts and Tourism Department. It was subsequently registered as a national heritage site and underwent renovations.

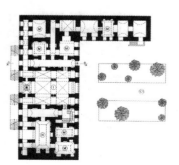

Floor plan

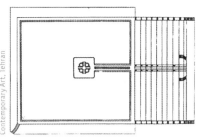

Bagh-e Shah Goli, site plan

Bagh-e Shah Goli, aerial view

Shah Goli Park
Bagh-e Shah Goli
شاه گلی

Ferdows Street, Tabriz
38.02532, 46.36559
Abbas Mirza Qajar (Commissioner)
AD: about 1835 / AH: about 1250 /
Yaz: about 1205

017

Bagh-e Shah Goli dates back at least to the late eighteenth century, but it more likely originates from a much earlier time – some specify the date of origin as far back as the fourteenth century – and was later rebuilt. Bagh-e Shah Goli was firstly used as a water store, fed by the Mehran river and used both for watering the gardens and drinking water. The high terraces date from the nineteenth century. During repairs to the central pool, the governor of Tabriz, Abbas Mirza Qajar, ordered the construction of an octagonal pavilion as a summer house.

The pavilion, once crowned by a dome, stands on a peninsula in the middle of this artificial lake, and on the eastern side of a high man-made mountain, supplied by water sources that flow down the hillside over five cascades. The most beautiful part of the house is a skylight and a passage decorated with colourful glasses and mirrors. Despite the romance of the resulting summer photos Bagh-e Shah Goli offers the visitor a rather disappointing sight when the surrounding trees and orchards are bare and the surrounding suburb of Tabriz appears behind the branches. Until 1937, the mansion and gardens were deserted. The Tabriz Municipality secured it, changing it into a park with minimal restoration measures. Due to the decay of the building, it was destroyed in 1961, and a new structure was erected on the same site in 1970. Today Bagh-e Shah Goli is a popular weekend resort for locals.

View from the man-made mountain

Constitution House, main elevation

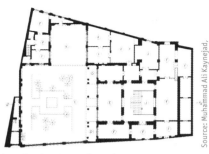

Constitution House, floor plan

Source: Muhammad Ali Kaynejad, Mohammad Reza Shirazi, The Traditional

Constitution House
Khaneh Mashrouteh
خانه مشروطه

Motahhari Ave, Tabriz
38.08056, 46.28833
Haji Vali Me'mar-e Tabrizi
AD: 1868/AH: 1285/Yaz: 1237

The Iranian constitutional revolution originated in Tabriz and culminated during the reign of Mohammad Ali Shah of the Qajar dynasty. The house was constructed in 1868 on order of Haji Mehdi Koozekanani, a merchant in the Tabriz Bazaar. With the constitutional revolution simmering in Tabriz, Haji Mehdi joined it and became one of its major financial supporters. He also used the house as a meeting place of the revolution heads and a place for publication of an underground paper of the pro-constitutional movement. The most famous people among them were Sattar Khan, Bagher Khan, Seqat-ol-Eslam Tabrizi and Haji Mirza Aqa Farshi. Located in the Rasteh Koucheh district near the city's historical bazaar, the two-storey building was constructed in 1868 by Haji Vali Me'mar-e Tabrizi. The main front of the building is located on the north and west sides. On the first floor of this front, the north side has a terrace with side rooms opening to it. The main part of the building located in the northern front has two floors. In the centre of the ground floor is a central space with coloured decorations. The original veranda on the south side consists of eight columns with stone columns. The most beautiful part of the house is a skylight and passage decorated with colourful glass and mirrors. The house gained historic importance once more just after World War II when it was used as Azerbaijan's Democratic Party's meeting centre. In 1975, it was registered by the Cultural Heritage of Iran. Statues of Sattar Khan and Baqer Khan, known as Sardar-e Melli (National Commander) and Salar-e Melli (National Leader) respectively, are found at the entrance of the building as a reminder of the era's passion for fighting.

Haidarzadeh House
Khaneh-e Haidarzadeh
خانه حیدرزاده

Heydarzadeh Alley, Tabriz
38.07297, 46.29545
Haji Habib Lak
AD: ca. 1870/AH: ca. 1285/Yaz: ca. 1240

Haidarzadeh's House is a historical mansion situated in Maghsoudieh, on the south side of the Tabriz Municipality Palace. There is no document showing the date of construction, but studies revealed that the house was designed in about 1870 by Haji Habib Lak. The house was registered in the list of National Remains of the Country in 1999. It covers an area of 900 m² and has two floors. The house has two interior and exterior yards. There is a Howz-Khaneh in the basement, a large room with a small pool and a fountain in the middle, ornamented with colourful bricks and a vault. Other parts of the house are connected by a hall. The building was decorated with wooden orosi-windows, stuccoes, colourful glass, brickwork and paintings. The main room, shah neshin, is one of the most attractive rooms of the house. Haidarzadeh House was restored in 2001 and is currently used as the Tourism Information Centre of East Azerbaijan Province and Tabriz.

Shabestan and Spring-House of Haidarzadeh House

Part of the Haidarzadeh House's Spring-House ceiling

1548–1598
Qazvin – Second Safavid Capital

Tabriz remained the Safavid capital until 1548, when Shah Tahmasp I, the son of Ismail, saw himself incapable of defending Tabriz against the attacks of the Ottoman Sultan Suleiman and had no choice but to transfer the capital to Qazvin to avoid the growing encroachment of the Ottoman army on his capital. In order to stop the advance of the Ottoman, Shah Tahmasb used a specific military method which entailed creating massive destruction around the attacking force and then exhausting it through violent and scattered counter attacks. This method, apart from immense damages to the residents or farmers, resulted in the roads being closed, making trade extremely difficult. Qazvin, one of the most ancient regions,

is situated in the northwest of Iran. It is located on the Silk Road between three economic centres: Hamadan, Rey and Tabriz. Because of its excellent location for trade, and the important role its historical bazaar had gained in the life of the whole city, Qazvin was chosen as capital. Particularly during the reign of Shah Tahmasp I, Qazvin gradually developed and expanded into one of the era's largest commercial trading centres.

Development of the Urban Area of Qazvin from the 8th to the 20th century

When Shah Tahmasp I decided to transfer his capital from Tabriz to Qazvin, he was engaged in a large urban development

Development of the urban area of Qazvin in 644

Development of the urban area of Qazvin in 1350

Source: A. Mohammad Moradi; F. Nassabi; Sepah (Shohada), a historical avenue, as a joint axis in city of Qazvin's Integration theory, 2011

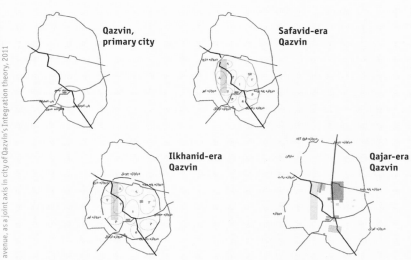

Development of the urban area of Qazvin from the Ilkhani to the Qajar era

program, the largest part of which concerned the gardens for the residence of his court, a garden city. He developed it into the famous baghistan, or garden city, named Saadat, built to the north of the existing town and linked to it via a Khiyaban and two maidans.

After the garden city was completed in 1557, Shah Tahmasp moved from the old palace, known as the dawlat khanwh of Shah Ismail, to the new one. The Safavid palace architecture owes its glory to Tahmasp I. The architecture, gardens and water circulation in the palace area of Qazvin, all of which were described by the court poet and historian Abdi Bayk Navidi, seem to reflect the Shah's preferences in architecture. One such preference was the interior painting of buildings such as Chehel Sotun, and his palace in general.

The most striking decoration in Isfahn's Cheh Sotun hall shows Shah Tahmasp receiving the Mughal Emperor Homayun, who was at the time a refugee at Tahmasp's court. On his return to India, Homayun was able to take two of the finest miniaturists with him, who were then instrumental in creating the great Mughal school of painting in India. Of course, Homayun did not only take painters with him; he also returned with sufficient ideas concerning architecture and garden design to influence the entire course of subsequent architectural development in Mughal India.

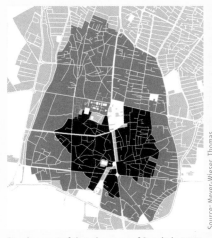

Source: Meyer-Wieser, Thomas

Development of the urban area of Qazvin in 1598   Development of the urban area of Qazvin in 1847

Pascal Coste, Qazvin Sara Hadj Rida, 1840

Pascal Coste, Qazvin Sara Shah, 1840

Source: Eugen Wirth, Die Orientalische Stadt, Mainz, 2000

Bazaar of Qazvin
Bazar-e Qazvin
بازار قزوین

Rasteh Vazir, Qazvin
36.26570, 49.99978
Commissioner unknown
AD: ca. 1500/AH: ca. 900/
Yaz: ca. 870

020

The bazaar of Qazvin is a remnant of the early Safavid period and its architectural features are extremely interesting. Although the nucleus of this bazaar points to the pre-Safavid times, during the reign of said dynasty the bazaar, had witnessed expansion. Each row or alley of the bazaar was allocated to a certain guild, and each segment was comprised of a mosque, bath and arcade. The Qeysaryeh of Qazvin has four entrances: The northern entrance leads to the Sarbaz arcade, whereas the southern, eastern and western entrances lead to the covered arcades of the Vazir Inn and the intersection of the bazaar, respectively. The Sa'd-ol-Saltaneh Bazarcheh is an archaic relic of the Qazvin bazaar, with a beautiful vestibule. The important features of the bazaar are as follows: The two-storey Sarbaz Arcade is located to the north of Qeysaryeh; the arcade has an arched entrance; its false arched ceilings are adorned in reintal fashion, and its yellow and pink tiles display hunting scenes and floral design. The wooden sash doors are

another interesting feature. The covered, two-storey arcade with chambers alongside is located to the south of Qeysaryeh. The Arcade of Haji Sayed Kazem is within the bazaar and opposite the leather merchant alley. This alley is currently reserved for leather products. The Razavi Arcade, which deals in timber, was constructed by Haji Seyed Abol Qasem Razavi Esfahani. His descendants are currently in charge of it. The Dervish Mehdi Arcade is located at the large intersection south of the mint. At present this is an area for dispatching goods. Haji Mohammad Taqi's eponymous arcade was formerly the iron mongers segment of the bazaar; today it is used to dispatch merchandise.

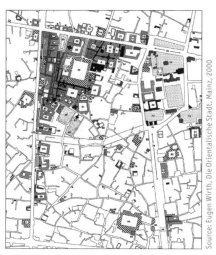

Eugen Wirth, Qazvin Historical Old Town

Source: Eugen Wirth, Die Orientalische Stadt, Mainz, 2000

Source: Voyage en Perse, avec Flandin, ed. Gide de Baudry, 1851

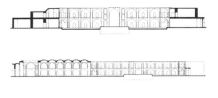

Eugène Flandin, Shah Caravanserai, 1851

Shah Caravanserai
Karwansaray-e Shah
کاروانسرای نبی

Bazaz-ha Rashteh, Qazvin
36.26730, 49.99857
unknown
AD: mid-16th cent./AH: mid-9th
cent./Yaz: mid-9th cent.

021

The Shah caravanserai, today known as Nabi caravanserai, belongs according to Eugen Wirth to the few surviving Safavid buildings in Qazvin and fully conforms to the model of caravanserais built within a bazaar. It consists of a simple courtyard with a corridor laying along its entrance axis and a multitude of chambers surrounding it on two floors. The courtyard's roofline is uniform and its overall appearance is therefore strongly influenced by the nearby Shah Mosque. A structural analysis of this caravanserai shows that the whole complex is constructed from similar cells of different magnitude and complexity. The same spatial and architectural logic makes them linkable among each others. This cell-structure can clearly be seen in the arrangement of the bazaar-like corridor at the entrance: the shopping niches are laterally interconnected and form comb-like passageways. The same kind of niche, arranged around a courtyard, is also used to form the caravanserai.

Source: Ganjanameh, Cyclopedia of Iranian Islamic Architecture, Shahid Beheshti University

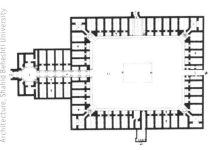

Eugen Wirth, Qazvin Historical Old Town

Western Corridor

Sara entrance on the western side

Haji Reza Caravanserai
Karwansaray-e Haji Reza
کاروانسرای حاج رضا

Saad-os-Saltaneh Bazaar, Qazvin
36.26661, 49.99916
unknown
AD: mid-16th cent./AH: mid-9th
cent./Yaz: mid-9th cent.

Safavid bazaars' caravanserais usually consists of a large yard surrounded by chambers and an entrance. In Haji Reza Caravanserai, the entrance is quite elaborate, assuming the appearance of a timcheh and a caravanserai. Its proximity to

Haji Reza Caravanserai, Section

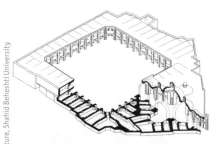

Haji Reza Caravanserai, Axonometric projection

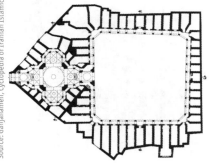

Haji Reza Caravanserai, Second floor plan

the large and plain surface of the yard makes its elaborate refinement more conspicuous. The timcheh has a cross-shaped space and is two stories high. Analytically, this cross-shaped space can be considered a combination of a central part surrounded by four adjoining parts. The central part has a regular octagon in which four sides are smaller than the four others, along with a base and a tall dome pierced with a central aperture. Each of the four lateral parts has a semi-octagon base and a roof made of a vault and a half-vault. The aggregation of these domes and tops has also created a handsome composition in the building's exterior volume, which is visible from within the courtyard. Bricks reign unrivalled inside the timcheh and the diversity of the brick-work patterns further emphasises this supremacy. Tiles are also used here and there on walls, vaults and particularly arch spandrels. Simple ceiling decorations ending at the base of the dome and the lateral vaults connect the ceiling and the walls.

Saad-os-Saltaneh Ensemble
Majmueh-ye Saad os-Saltaneh
مجموعه سعدالسلطنه

Rasteh Vazir, Qazvin
36.26893, 50.00066
Sa'd al-Saltaneh Isfahani
(Commissioner)
AD: 1888–1896/AH: 1305–1313/
Yaz: 1257–1265

The Saad-os-Saltaneh ensemble is a large Qajar-era caravanserai on the site of the former gardens and parks of the Safavid palace district. It is one of Persia's best preserved urban caravanserais. The commissioner was Saad al-Saltaneh Isfahani. The ensemble is one of the largest commercial complexes in Iran and, indeed, a commercial town in the heart of the bazaar. This ensemble may be seen as a museum of various types of arches, vaults, structures and open and closed spaces, all made of simple, basic elements, namely bricks. The main street of Qazvin, today named Imam Khomeini Street, runs north of the structure, and one of the bazaar's passages, which follows a meandering, non-geometric path,

Source: Ganjnameh, Cyclopedia of Iranian Islamic Architecture, Shahid Beheshti University

Saad os-Saltaneh Ensemble, Western side of the northeastern courtyard and axonometric projection

borders it on the west. A bathhouse and the Nabi (Shah) mosque stand opposite the ensemble. The most important part of the plan is the main courtyard, with two courtyards flanking it on the eastern and western sides; on its southern side is a large space at the intersection of two covered bazaar passages connecting various closed spaces. Two large courtyards, where animals were kept and goods were unloaded, are visible on the south side of the ensemble. The caravanserai is built on a square plan with four ayvans facing the courtyard. The interiors are decorated with muqarnas and ceiling decorations. The hujrehs (travellers' rooms) are situated one metre above ground level. A regular octagon behind the southern ayvan has a large dome, with four adjacent semi-domes. The east-west axis of the octagonal space is called Caesar's Hall and is connected to the bazaar.

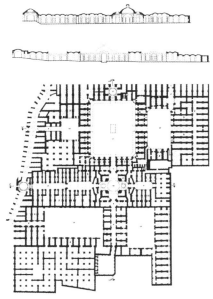

Saad os-Saltaneh Ensemble,
Ground floor plan, section and elevation

Western Chaharsu of the ensemble in the bazaar

Western Bazaar's main passage of the ensemble

Negarossaltaneh Cafe 024
Cafe Negar os-Saltaneh
کافی نت نگار السلطنه
سیستم عامل

Rasteh Vazir, Qazvin
36.26895, 50.00025
Ershad Malakooti
AD: 2010/AH: 1431/Yaz: 1380

Cafe Negar os-Saltaneh is an exquisitely restored coffee shop in the centre of the Saad-os-Saltaneh ensemble. The architect and manager Ershad Malakooti created a tastefully-decorated and carefully-furnished café with an incomparable Iranian atmosphere. The coffee is excellent alongside chocolate cake or local sweets. This popular coffee shop opened in 2010 and became a second home for women, students and intellectuals. Coffee shops are often the only places where Iranians can socialise or use free wifi in a country without bars. However, their popularity has been countered by government raids, regulations and even shutdowns for supposedly "not following Islamic values". It is especially hard to argue that coffee shops symbolize Western immorality when coffee has been a part of Persian and Middle Eastern culture long before the development of the Western world. But despite the continuous efforts against them, the coffee shops return.

Saadat Garden 025
Bagh-e Saadat
باغ سعادت

Helal Ahmar, Qazvin
36.26867, 50.00397
Shah Tahmasp I (Commissioner)
AD: 1548–1598/AH: 954–1007/
Yaz: 917–967

When Shah Tahmasp I died in 1576, the empire ruled by his sons was brought to the brink of disaster. Shah Ismail II and Shah Mohammad, ruling in succession, did not rule long enough to make their marks. Their rule ended when the majority of the emirs sided with the sixteen-year-old Abbas Mirza, who, aided by his tutor, marched to Qazvin in 1587 to public demonstrations in his favour. Once enthroned in the Chehel Sotun palace in the Saadat garden, Shah Abbas ordered his slaves to use their scimitars to behead the emirs who had been compromised in the past, or who posed a threat to his tutor's authority. The twenty-two heads were then exposed on spears in the maidan, marking the first day of his reign. The Saadat garden was the centre of these dramatic events, and the maidan at its door was the best place to display his might to his opponents. The garden complex was accessed through a public promenade, Khiyaban Sepah, that ran from the Great Mosque to the Ali Qapu Gate. From here, a promenade aligned with the gate led north inside the royal garden to the shah's

Aqa Mirak, Miniature of Bagh-e Saadat, 1539 – 1543

pleasure pavilion. The garden incorporated fourteen plots with various square, hexagonal, octagonal, and round shapes as well as a number of talars. The gardens were partially built over in the Qajar period. Today only a small part of the garden, along with Forty Columns Palace and Ali Qapu Gate, survives.

Source: www.iran-daily.com

Ali Qapu
Sardar Ali Qapu
عالی قاپو

Helel-e Ahmar Str., Qazvin
36.26583, 50.00309
Shah Tahmasp I (Commissioner)
AD: mid-16th cent./
AH: mid-9th cent./Yaz: mid-9th cent.

Access to the Royal Palace was controlled by several gates, which were strategically positioned to point out the various functions of the palace. Ali Qapu reminds every Iranian of the famous mansions in Isfahan which were built during the Safavid era. However, this edifice - also from the Safavid era - was built in the city of Qazvin before the capital was relocated to Isfahan. Sardar Ali Qapu is located at the beginning of Sepah Street and is one of seven gates at the entrance to the royal Safavid citadel. It served as a prestigious main entrance to the Safavid government and palace complexes. It consists of a domed room with a high entrance ayvan connected to two open, two-storey wings, in the upper floors of which drums would often be played on special occasions. Whilst the outside of the middle part is structured by pilasters and three superimposed ogival niches, the façades of the side wings are flanked by half-columns and pilasters. The spandrels of the entrance ayvan are adorned by multi-coloured, flower-shaped tile mosaics. The Thuluth inscription on a bright blue background inside the ayvan deserves special attention; it was made by the famous calligrapher Ali Reza Abbasi. Above the inscription, the wall is broken up by a tendril-shaped window, whose soffits are decorated with blue floral tiles. The vault of the semi-dome in the entrance ayvan is decorated with muqarnas. Due to its function as police headquarters for Qazvin, Ali Qapu has never been properly photographed or studied.

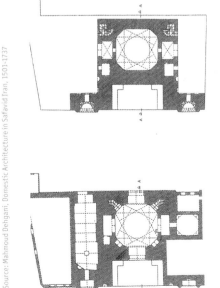

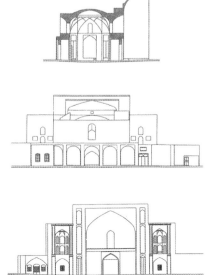

Mahmoud Dehgani, Ali Qapu, Qazvin, ground floor plan, section and elevation

Source: Panoramio

Forty Columns Palace
Kakh-e Chehel Sotun
چهل ستون

Maidan-e Azadi, Qazvin
36.26867, 50.00395
Shah Tahmasp I (Commissioner)
AD: 1510/AH: 915/Yaz: 879

The Chehel Sotun, literally Forty Columns, is a unique remnant from the Safavid palace complex. In the development of Persian palace architecture, the pavilion foreshadows the fully developed style of Safavid pavilions exemplified by the Hasht Behesht at Isfahan. The royal palace in Qazvin consisted of several pavilions in various gardens and courtyards. So the Safavid palace was rather a building ensemble than a single monumental castle. The ensemble consisted of three parts: the Dawlatkhaneh for public audiences, the harem or khalvatkhane for private life and the buyutat-e saltanate for the functioning of the court. Between this complex and the city lay the maidan, the great square which served as the vestibule to the royal palace. The only other surviving part of the palace is a free-standing portal structure, Ali Qapu. Both Shah Ismail II and Shah Abbas I were enthroned there. The palace precinct is located in what must have been the centre of the later Safavid city. The bazaar, the Friday mosque, and the pre-Safavid city lie to the west and south of it, which suggests that the site was originally near the northern perimeter of the city because before the seventeenth century, citadels and royal residences in Iran were generally located adjacent to city walls. The pavilion itself was built in 1510 and is generally attributed to Shah Tahmasp I. The interior was radically altered in the Qajar period, but in the 1970s it was largely restored to its original appearance. The building consists of two floors. On the ground floor a quadrangular central room communicates with the surrounding gardens through four ayvans, one on each side. Each ayvan was originally connected to the central room by three short passages. The four corners between the ayvans contain four rooms, each of a different design. On the exterior there are oblique walls instead of corners, so that the plan is that of an unequal octagon. Around the exterior of the structure, eight massive columns and eight corner piers with engaged columns support a gallery encircling the upper storey, reached via a curved staircase leading from the southeastern corner room. Upstairs, thirty-two slender wooden supports carry the roof of the gallery. The main portion of the upper floor consists of a large cruciform hall, with four corner rooms, each with a small adjacent chamber. Whereas the rooms on the ground floor and the ayvans are vaulted, all the rooms on the upper floor have flat wooden ceilings. Restoration work in the 1970s revealed the remains of

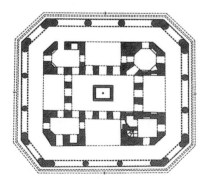

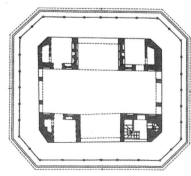

Mahmoud Dehgani, Chehel Sotun Palace, Qazvin, floor plan

Source: Mahmoud Dehgani, Domestic Architecture in Safavid Iran, 1501-1737

wall paintings on both levels. Upstairs, on the south wall of the western arm of the cruciform hall, there is a vivid depiction of a harem girl wearing European dress in the style of the sixteenth and seventeenth centuries. The high quality of the surviving wall paintings suggests a date in the period when Qazvin was the capital. Today, the pavilion houses a museum of calligraphy.

Sepah Avenue
Khiyaban-e Sepah
خیابان سپه

Sepah Avenue, Qazvin
36.26262, 50.00363
Shah Tahmasp I (Commissioner)
AD: 1498−1548/AH: 903−954/
Yaz: 867−917

Sepah Avenue, today Shohada Street, was constructed from 1548 to 1598 in the era of Shah Tahmasp I, and it is officially the first boulevard in Iran registered in the national heritage list. The name of the avenue means *the path of the river*, and one or two big rivers in this axis provided water to Ja'afar Aabad Garden and the City's southern gardens, so it is assumed that the avenue was constructed on the current axis. Sepah Avenue was a promenade, a part of the Safavid master plan, located inside the city's borders, and did not extend outside the town. It is constructed in one of the oldest parts of the city. Sepah Avenue has a pivotal role in this historic context. It appears that it ran from Ali Qapu's entrance to the end of the open space in front of Jameh Mosque. At this time, an entrance gate was built at the end of the avenue. The large

Qazvin, public spaces in Safavid town planning

■ building complex of the palace district
▨ gardens and parks of the palace district
▨ open spaces for public events and ceremonies
= still-recognisable patterns of Safavid town planning
● buildings preserved until reign of Shah Abbas II (1642-1666)

Chahar Bagh Promenade corresponds to the course of today's Khiyaban-e Shohada, but was twice as wide at that time. Not long after that, the avenue was extended to the front of Jameh Mosque. According to Safavid sources, the entrance of Jameh Mosque was strengthened when in 1639, Shah Safi I had this avenue extended to Imamzadeh Hoseyn by about 1 km. Moreover, there is evidence of the existence of large gardens at this site. Ja'afar Abad Garden is the best example of this. To the east of the square in front of the Ali Qapu lay Maidan-e Asp, which was mainly used for polo matches and horse races.

Khiyaban-e Sepah, Qazvin, December 2010

Jameh Atiq Mosque
Mesjid-e Jameh Atiq
مسجد جامع عتیق

Sepah Square, Qazvin
36.26117, 50.00184
unknown
AD: from 807 / AH: from 4th cent. /
Yaz: from 4th cent.

Unlike other mosques, the Jameh Atiq Mosque is approached through two ayvans and a gateway harmoniously designed in 1663, built simultaneously with the construction of the second part of Sepah Avenue. However, it is much older. It is recorded that Harun al-Rashid, on his way to Khorasan in 807, stopped in Qazvin to lay the foundations of a congregational mosque on a Zoroastrian fire temple. Even today, part of the southwestern corner of the mosque is known as Harun's vault. From Seldjuk time the north ayvan of 1153 still exists, surmounted by two minarets, whose shafts are visible from the basement. The impressive southern cupola, whose undivided large squinches are reconciled to the dome, was built in 1106. Its diameter is 15 m and, together with the equally large dome of Nezam-al-Molk in Isfahan's Friday Mosque, it is one of the largest preserved domes of its time. It is worthwhilst to pay attention to the inscription bands at the base of the dome. The upper one is written in Kufi, the lower in Naskhi, both dated 1107. They are some of the most impressive inscriptions of the time, with their typeface interspersed with tendrils and buds. The mosque was set on fire and damaged in 1220 during the Mongol invasion. Later, additions were made, the last one during the late Safavid era. The western and southern ayvan date back to and bear inscriptions of that time. The northern ayvan also likely dates back to the reign of Shah Tahmasp I. Parts of the mosque have been turned into a public library.

Mesjid-e Jameh Atiq, section

Mesjid-e Jameh Atiq, three-dimensional projection

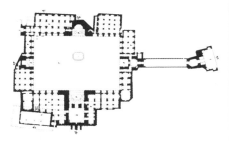

Mesjid-e Jameh Atiq, ground floor plan

Mesjid-e Jameh Atiq, main entrance ceiling

Eugène Flandin, Mosquée royale et terrasses de maisons, Casbin

Shah Mosque
Masjed al-Nabi
مسجد النبى

030

Imam Khomeini Ave., Qazvin
36.26837, 49.99901
Mirza Shirazi
AD: ca. 1524 / AH: ca. 930 / Yaz: ca. 893

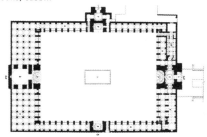

Masjed al-Nabi, ground floor plan

In his travel account, Jean Chardin alludes to the construction of this mosque by Shah Ismail: "Just as he had one storey of it built, he moved on to the other world, and its completion was carried out by his successor, Shah Tahmasp ...". Describing the building he writes: "The mosque is located at the end of a wide alley, Bab-e Homayoon, planted with large old trees, at the entrance of which stands the great royal palace ... ". The names of Mizra Shirazi, the architect in charge of the construction, and the master tileworker Ismail Kashi-paz appear in the inscriptions of the mosque. The row of trees at the centre of the forecourt was planted by Aqa Baha'. Later, Masjed al-Nabi, formerly Shah Mosque, was affected by urban planning during the reign of Shah Tahmasp I, as was the later town planning of Isfahan. The mosque lay on the southeast side of the former maidan. Whilst the great Shah Square in Isfahan still exists, the large Qazvin maidan was increasingly obstructed over the centuries, and circa 1990, the last remaining site had to give way for a commercial building. Fat'h-Ali Shah, the Qajar monarch, extended the mosque between 1805 and 1808, commissioning the architect Ustad Mirza Shirazi, who designed the present building. The Shah Mosque is now one of the largest four-ayvan mosques in Iran.

Masjed al-Nabi, courtyard (northwestern corner)

Saqqa-khaneh and part of the northern side of the courtyard

Imamzade Hossein
Imamzadeh-ye Hossein
امامزاده حسین

031

Salamgah Str., Qazvin
36.25780, 50.00080
*Shah Tahmasp I, Zainab Beygum
(Commissioner)*
AD: mid-16th cent., 1943/
AH: mid-9th cent., 1361/
Yaz: mid-9th cent., 1313

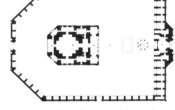

Imamzadeh-ye Hossein, ground floor plan

Imamzadeh-ye Hossein is interesting because it is part of the representative planning along the processional way built by Shah Tahmasp I. It was re-established as a pilgrimage centre in the mid-sixteenth century. The tomb is named after the two-year-old, deceased son of Imam Hossein who passed away whilst travelling to Khorasan in Qazvin in 821 with his father and was buried at this site. Later more members of the Safavid dynasty were buried here. According to existing sources, parts of the complex were built during the reign of Shah Tahmasp I, and Shah Tahmasp's daughter Zainab Beygum extended it in 1630, during the reign of Shah Safi. The original shape of the mausoleum is unclear. The structure was entirely rebuilt in 1895 and its verandas and the inside of its dome were adorned with mirror-works. The mausoleum is reminiscent of a generous complex with its own walled garden, rows of plants, small ayvans, niches, grave stones and precious blue and cream-coloured tile decorations. The façade of the main gate has six slender minarets. The fascinating effect of geometric tile patterns to the right and left of the inner minarets and the tympanum is based on the experience of centuries. Directly behind the gate there is a pavilion-like, octagonal drinking fountain which is one of the finest of its kind in Iran.

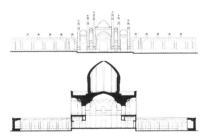

Imamzadeh-ye Hossein, section and elevation

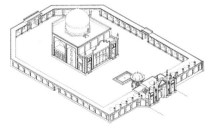

Imamzadeh-ye Hossein, axonometric perspective

Source: www.tishinet.ir

Tomb of the Four Prophets
Peighambarieh
مسجد چهار انبیاء و بقعه پیغمبریه

Peighambarieh Street, Qazvin
36.26860, 50.00272
Mirza Masud Shaykh al-Islam
AD: mid-16th cent./AH: mid-9th cent./
Yaz: mid-9th cent.

The Place of the Prophets is one of Iran's most fascinating Judeo-Christian-Islamic sites. According to tradition, four prophets are buried here, all of whom are believed to have lived sometime between the life of Jesus and the life of Muhammad. One of the four prophets, Khalid e Nabi, espoused the teachings of Jesus but also foresaw the coming of Muhammad, offering an important historic connection between the two faiths. The other three, Shamun, Yuhanna and Yunus, proclaimed Christianity, and may be connected to the tradition of the Three Wise Men, or the Three Holy Kings. According to the Christian tradition, the Three Wise Men came from the east to worship the King of the Jews, bearing gifts of gold, frankincense and myrrh. There is some confusion as to whether they were around before, during or after the life of Christ. The four are considered to be of great historic importance in the tradition of the various eastern churches in Asia. The shrine was built in the sixteenth century. It consists of a pillared veranda with two pairs of wooden columns, stone dado and stucco-decorated walls. From the street the shrine does not appear special. Only when you pass the gate to the courtyard can you see the sparkling interior clad with thousands of mirror shards. Inside, there is a sarcophagus protected by a latticework wrought of silver and gold. The building is topped by a striking blue, onion-shaped dome.

Heidarieh Madrasa
Madrasa-ye Heidarieh
مسجد حیدریه

Mohamadie Str., Qazvin
36.26528, 50.00556
unknown
AD: 1119/AH: 512/Yaz: 488

The Heydarieh Madrasa dates in substantial parts back to the Seljuk period, but played an important part in the master plan of Shah Tahmasp I. The madrasa was almost completely destroyed in the 1119 earthquake. A vizier of Seljuk Malik Shah I had the complex rebuilt. Here the early Islamic concept of the kiosk mosque was applied, as the mosque-madrasa was built on the ruins of a Zoroastrian fire temple. In general, architecture of pre-Islam has been very influential for the construction of mosques in Iran. They acquire their distinctive character by enriching the Arab hypostyle form with two elements deeply rooted in pre-Islamic Iranian architecture: the domed chamber, based on the baldachin of the Zoroastrian fire temple, and the great vault, or ayvan, a more secular element of Sassanid palaces serving as the audience chamber of the Shah. Popularly, the Heydarieh Madrasa is still known as Fire Temple, or Ateschkade. It is hidden behind the raised walls, near the Ali-Qapu Palace. Today only the courtyard, the domed prayer hall and the ayvan still exist from historical times. The remaining parts of the building have a uniform height and contain no further ayvans. A remaining Kufic inscription is worth looking at because it is one of the most splendid discovered in Iran. Furthermore, there is a mehrab made of stucco. Today the Madrasa's mosque is home to an elementary school with a library and auditorium.

Source: iranpedia.ir

Heidarieh Madrasa

Mausoleum of Sayyed Ismail 034
Imamzadeh-ye Sayyed Ismail
امامزاده اسماعیل

Sahid Ansari Str., Qazvin
36.264844, 50.002309
*Haji Mohammad-Ebrahim Shalviri
(Commissioner), et al.*
AD: ca. 1500 / AH: ca.900 /
Yaz: ca. 870

Imamzadeh Sayyed Ismail was built under the Safavids on the side of Maidan -i-Shah. The construction of the mausoleum dates back to the early Safavid period. The shrine is composed of a main space with four interconnected verandas on its sides. The plan of the sanctuary is an octagon, in which four high arcades are linked to the verandas on each of the four major sides. Tthe dome is decorated with tilework on the exterior and ceiling decoration and plasterwork on the interior The tilework of the dome was commisssioned by Haji Mohammad-Ebrahim Shalviri. The main resting place of Imamzadeh lies in the fact that the eastern and western verandas are similar due to their structures. The only difference lies in the fact that the eastern veranda leads to a street whilst the western veranda connects to a newly established hussainiya, or ceremonial hall. The northern and southern verandas have identical and homogeneous plans. The dome was tiled circa 1930. The building' cellar contains the grave of Sayyed Ismail, the son of Imam Jafar Sadegh. His tombstone has been stolen. The courtyard of the northern side was roofed-over in recent times and then removed during repairs carried out in 1987. At the same time, the mausoleum's northern ayvan and façade were repaired and the dome adorned with tile.

Source: Ganjanameh, Cyclopedia of Iranian Islamic Architecture, Shahid Beheshti University

Mausoleum of Sayyed Ismail, Gondbad-khaneh

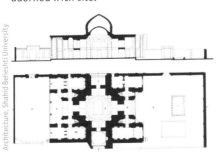

Source: Ganjanameh, Cyclopedia of Iranian Islamic Architecture, Shahid Beheshti University

Mausoleum of Sayyed Ismail, ground floor plan and section

Mausoleum of Hamdollah Mostowfi 035
Aramgah-e Hamd-ol-Allah Mostowfi
آرامگاه حمدالله مستوفی

Kashani St., Mahjur St., Qazvin
36.26426, 50.01067
Commissioner unknown
AD: 13th cent. / AH: 8th cent. /
Yaz: 8th cent.

This enigmatic building is believed to be the mausoleum of Hamd-ol-Allah Mostowfi, an Iranian historian and geographer at the time of Ilchane. His works include the poetic opus *Zafar-Namah*, or *Book of Victory*, narrating the history of Iran from the advent of Islam to his time. He is also the author of a history of the origin of the earth up to 1330, *Tarik-e gozida*, as well as the geographic description of Persia and Mesopotamia, *Nozat al-qolub*. The building dates back to the thirteenth century. The Turkish-style, pointed, blue dome originally had a plain brick exterior that was later covered with simple grey-green tiles. The monument is characterised by a strong emphasis on pure form and a great restraint in decoration, radiating an almost modern aesthetic. A single opening on the west ern side allows entry to the completely hollow interior of the building. Inside,

Source: Kambiz Haji-Qassemi (Ganjanameh)

Mausoleum of Hamdollah Mostowfi

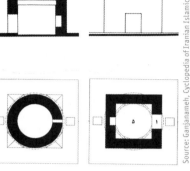
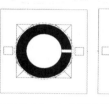

Source: Ganjanameh, Cyclopedia of Iranian Islamic Architecture, Shahid Beheshti University

Aramgah-e Hamd-ol-Allah Mostowfi,
ground floor plan, section and elevation

below the dome, there is a circular decoration with muqarnas containing a brief biography of Hamdollah Mostowfi. Part of the conical dome had collapsed in recent times. It was summarily repaired in 1940 and thoroughly restored in 1949 by the Ministry of Culture. This building was again restored in 1979 by the Iranian National Organisation of Preservation of Historical Monuments.

Sardar Madrasa
Madrasa-ye Sardar
مدرسه سردار

036

Tabriz Avenue, Qazvin
36.26432, 49.99126
Sardar Hossein-Khan, Sardar Hassan-Khan (Commissioner)
AD: 1815 / AH: 1231 / Yaz: 1184

The Sardar Madrasa is located in Tabriz Avenue and is a remnant of the Qajar era, dating back to the year 1815. As the inscription on the portal indicates, the Sardar Madrasa was commissioned by the brothers Sardar Hossein-Khan and Sardar Hassan-Khan, commander in the Qajar army. This cubical shaped structure is two storeys high. The cornices are made of stone, though the structure itself was constructed of brick and adorned with coloured tiles. Epigraphs in the Naskhi script display the poetical verses of the late Mohtasham-e-Kashani.

These inscriptions surround the courtyard of the school. The chambers are located in the eastern and western sectors of the school. The upper floor is similar to the floor below, the only difference being that there are four narrow chambers which form the lateral or side rooms. To the south of the school courtyard is a vast terrace which connects to a mosque, with a ceiling resting on three brick arches. The conical dome is on the central arch. The entrance of the structure is in the centre of the northern front. This leads to a large vestibule which adjoins the sleeping area from the two sides. The entrance of the school is adorned with coloured tile work, in addition to poetical verses in the Naskhi script which were carved on marble in a spectacular manner. The madrasa was active until 1920. Thereafter, the number of students dwindled and it was eventually closed in 1945, the building beginning to fall into ruin. From 1965 onward, it served as a primary school for a short while, and the building were restored from 1975 to 1979. During these operations, the tile work was consolidated, an orosi on the northern side was repaired and the dome was given a steel girdle. Further repairs were carried out in 1990. On the outside, opposite the northern portal, stands an abanbar (water reservoir) disguised with tile mosaic. The façade of the portal is

Madrasa Sardar, view into the courtyard

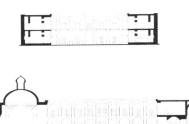

Madrasa Sardar, section and elevation

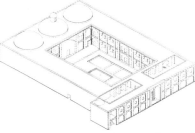

Madrasa Sardar, axonometric perspective

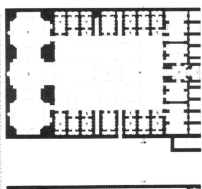

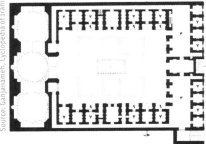

Madrasa Sardar, ground floor plan

completely covered with multi-coloured tiles that depict vines, arabesques, palmettes, bouquets and strewn flowers. This ornamentation continues in the portal niche, which additionally contains a stone relief band. Sardar cistern is situated opposite Sardar School and Mosque, established by two brothers, the warriors of Fat'h-Ali Shah of the Qajar dynasty. This cistern enjoys beautiful tilework and there is also a marble inscription on the portal showing the date of 1859. The plan of the reservoir is in a square shape, each side of which is about 20 m. There is also a great column at the centre of this square, which bears the load of four ribs. In other words, the square design of the cistern on the ceiling is further divided into four smaller squares, and each of these parts has a cupola. There is also a small wind catcher at the heart of every cupola that functions as a ventilator.

643–1598
Pre-Safavid Isfahan

The history of Isfahan can be dated back to the Palaeolithic age. In recent archaeological excavations, artefacts from this as well as the Bronze and Iron ages were discovered. Ancient Isfahan was part of the Elamite empire. Under the name Gabai, the town developed into one of the most important cities of the Medes, which was incorporated into the Achaemenid empire by Cyrus II. The settlement north of the river Zayandeh Rud and close to the river crossing, which later became the Sharestan Bridge, is said to have been one of the royal seats of the King of Kings. In the time of the Parthians, Isfahan became historically known as a provincial capital called Aspadana, later Sepahan, which means Place of the Army, and during Sassanid times developed into a military centre with a strong fortress which was manned by many Zoroastrians, Jews and Christians. Even in those days the area around Isfahan, with its various religious communities, must have had a cosmopolitan character. Correspondingly, the settlement area at the time of the Arab conquest was divided in two major districts: Jay, which is the successor of the Achaemenid city Gabai, with the fortified Qa'leh Tabarak, and the northern

district of Yahudieyeh, the Jewish Quarter in the centre of today's old town of Isfahan. Isfahan was conquered and Islamised by the Arabs in 643. With the beginning of the Islamic era, not only religion but also lifestyle and culture, social structures and even the calendar changed. The development to a wealthy commercial town under the Abbasids and its role as the royal residence of the Buyids dynasty can only be inferred archaeologically from the progressive development of the Friday Mosque and the nearby marketplace. The Seljuks conquered large areas in Iran in the eleventh century. Nizam al-Mulk, one of the most important viziers in Islamic history, ruled the Seljuk Empire successfully between 1072 and 1092. Under his reign, the city of Isfahan became one of the most important urban settlements in the world at that time. Finally, Isfahan fell victim to the Mongol conqueror Timur Lenk in 1387.

Development of Isfahan ca. 643

The history of Isfahan in Islamic times evolved from the merger of the towns Yahudiya and Jay. A city wall with twelve gates enclosed the city centre around the Friday Mosque, and the Ṭabarrak Citadel at the southwestern end of the town was built during this time. With the exception of the elaborate portal of the Jurjir mosque, the Buyid time in Isfahan is only documented through written accounts of medieval travellers and geographers. Nevertheless, traces of the city walls, the connecting roads and the city districts still exist. The centre of Isfahan was located around the Friday Mosque and the old maidan since the Seljuk period. The major transport and supply axes of the town started at the old maidan. Along these, line bazaars were established which still exist today in the north and northwest. When Togrel Beg, the first Seljuk sultan, chose

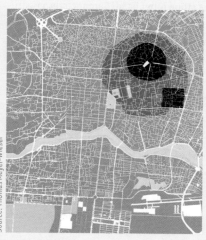

Source: Thomas Meyer-Wieser

Development of Isfahan ca. 643
compared to 1150 (AH)

Isfahan as the centre of his empire in 1051, several important buildings were erected which characterise the political and cultural ambitions of the dynasty. The city walls and gates were renovated and reinforced, and the city centre, the Friday Mosque, a royal residence and administrative building, a madrasa and the bazaar were developed around or close to the former main square, Maidan-e Kohne. Only the Friday Mosque, some minarets and ruins remain of this medieval city, in contrast to the descriptions of Naser-e Kosrow and other medieval correspondents who described Isfahan as the wealthiest and most populous city of its time. The few remaining monuments of the Turkmen and Timurid successor states from the fifteenth century remain largely unexplored, though the famous, carved stucco mehrab in the Friday Mosque is noteworthy. The lack of monumental buildings from the first century of Safavid rule can be explained by the fact that at that time Tabriz, then Qazvin, served as the capital. Under their patronage, two important buildings were erected in the early sixteenth century: the mausoleum of Harun Velayat and the Masjed-e Ali. Their strategic location on the southern edge of the Seljuk town centre shows the determination of the Safavids to demonstrate their imperial claims in the medieval town.

Silk Road
Jaddeh-ye Abrishem

Isfahan is located on the southern route of the Silk Road, a network of caravan routes linking the Mediterranean by land to East Asia via Central Asia. Trade routes in Iran can be traced back to the fourth millennium BC. Around 110 BC, silk became an important trading product. Documents from the first century BC mention silk in Roman markets in the eastern Mediterranean area, particularly in the Phoenician cities Tyre and Sidon, and silk became a coveted luxury product in Rome. Not only merchants, scholars and armies travelled along the Silk Road from east to west or vice versa, but also ideas, religions and entire cultures. The main artery of the Silk Road crossed the Iranian border at presentßday Sarakhs, passing Damaghan to Rey south of Tehran, and from there via Saveh and Hamadan to Ctesiphon and Palmyra, the main centre of the silk trade between Parthia and Rome. The establishment of connecting roads had always been an important concern of Persian rulers. Isfahan, as capital and centre of the empire under the Safavids, played a strategically-important role and became the centre of a trade network spanning several continents. Shah Abbas I's expansion program included not only the restoration of the routes that had existed for millennia, but also the expansion of a densely-interwoven road network between the caravanserais, which grew to 999 in Iran. These caravanserais were generally spaced at intervals of 25 – 30 km. Tabriz could be reached from Isfahan in 24 days, Merev in 12 and the Persian Gulf, via Shiraz, in 22 days.

Source: The Mandala Collaborative- Wallace, McHarg, Roberts and Todd

Old and new connecting roads

Fire Temple
Atashgah
آتشگاه

Atashgah, Isfahan
32.64812, 51.57034
unknown
AD: 6th cent. BC/AH: ca. 1200/
Yaz: ca. 1200

On a lone limestone hill, 8 km west of Isfahan, stands a Zoroastrian Fire Temple with beautiful views of the surrounding gardens and fields. The fire temple was a place of worship which housed the sacred fire. Here priests and the faithful performed rituals and maintained the eternal fire. In Zoroastrianism, fire is considered a purifying force and is identified with the truth. The fire temple looks like a fortress. Archaeological research in 1967 came to the conclusion that in the sixth century BC, the building originally consisted of two thick adobe walls, five storeys high, and later, in

the third century AD, became a place of eternal fire. The temple, measuring 5 m in diameter, is built from mud bricks, with the walls built from different materials such as sand, lime and bamboo. The main room was originally covered with a dome to preserve the sacred fire over the centuries. The first fire altars were built by the Achaemenids. The clearest examples in antiquity can be found in the Sassanid places of worship, where the symbolic fire burned in the centre, or in the comparable Chahar Bagh design of the Sassanid paradise gardens. The Chahar Taq was added to the design vocabulary of Islamic architecture as a traditional concept with far-reaching implications which represented the architectural manifestation of Creation. The cubical volume of the base, which is seen as human being, earth and earthly paradise, is a symbol of the *unmoved mover*. The four pillars symbolize the four elements, the four directions, the four winds, the four seasons as

Aerial view of the Fire Temple near Isfahan

Source: azsafar

Fire Temple on a chalk hill near Isfahan

well as the four colours. The rectangular volume is overlaid by a round dome symbolising the lightness and total mobility of mind, a form with neither beginning nor end. Its only reference point is the centre, spanned by a metaphysical axis connecting the dome to the cube.

Cemetery Throne of Steel
Maghbareh-ye Takht-e Foulad
تخت فولاد

038

Baba Rock-ol-Din, Isfahan
32.62750, 51.68306
unknown
AD: ca. 750/AH: ca. 130/
Yaz: ca. 120

Takht-e Foulad is the historic cemetery of Isfahan and one of the oldest cemeteries in the world. According to ancient sources, Joshua, the son of the prophet Noah, is buried here. In pre-Islamic times, it served as a Jewish cemetery. From the eighth century on, Muslims (including many famous personalities like Baba Rokn ed-Din, who lies in the oldest structure of the cemetery; poet and calligrapher Wale Isfahani; and the famous Safavid mystic and scholar Mir Fendereski) were increasingly buried here in mausoleums. During the Safavid and Qajar dynasties, Takht-e Foulad was the official state cemetery. Later, a number of graves were removed and converted into residential plots. A new cemetery, Bagh-e Rezvan, was opened in Isfahan east of the town in 1984 to relieve the pressure on the old, overcrowded cemetery. Restoration of shrines and mausoleums commenced in 1994. The martyrs' cemetery of the Iran–Iraq war is close by.

Eugène Flandin: Takht-e Foulad, from Voyage en Perse avec Flandin, 1851

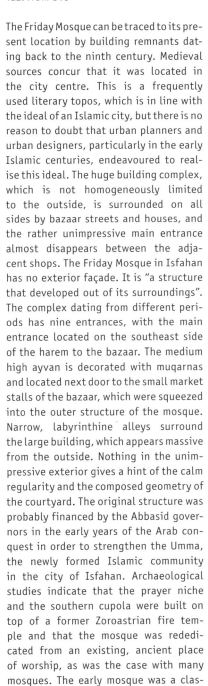

Friday Mosque
Masjed-e Jameh
مسجد جامع

Khiyaban-e Hatef, Isfahan
32.66972, 51.68528
various
AD: from 771/AH: from 154/
Yaz: from 140

The Friday Mosque can be traced to its present location by building remnants dating back to the ninth century. Medieval sources concur that it was located in the city centre. This is a frequently used literary topos, which is in line with the ideal of an Islamic city, but there is no reason to doubt that urban planners and urban designers, particularly in the early Islamic centuries, endeavoured to realise this ideal. The huge building complex, which is not homogeneously limited to the outside, is surrounded on all sides by bazaar streets and houses, and the rather unimpressive main entrance almost disappears between the adjacent shops. The Friday Mosque in Isfahan has no exterior façade. It is "a structure that developed out of its surroundings". The complex dating from different periods has nine entrances, with the main entrance located on the southeast side of the harem to the bazaar. The medium high ayvan is decorated with muqarnas and located next door to the small market stalls of the bazaar, which were squeezed into the outer structure of the mosque. Narrow, labyrinthine alleys surround the large building, which appears massive from the outside. Nothing in the unimpressive exterior gives a hint of the calm regularity and the composed geometry of the courtyard. The original structure was probably financed by the Abbasid governors in the early years of the Arab conquest in order to strengthen the Umma, the newly formed Islamic community in the city of Isfahan. Archaeological studies indicate that the prayer niche and the southern cupola were built on top of a former Zoroastrian fire temple and that the mosque was rededicated from an existing, ancient place of worship, as was the case with many mosques. The early mosque was a classic, Arab hypostyle mosque developed from the house of the prophet during the reign of the sixth Umayyad caliph al-Walid, with columns supporting arches of masonry, interconnected at the height of the impost by tie beams, and a courtyard at right angles to the harem, with a cleaning well in the centre. Between 1072 and 1092 the Grand Vizier Nezam-al-Molk ordered the construction of a dome over the prayer room of the mosque. This square chamber, covered by a semi-dome, is bordered at the corners by massive round columns of impressive dimensions, which is reminiscent of a Chahar Taq of pre-Islamic, Sassanid architecture associated with a Zoroastrian fire temple. The rival and successor of Nezam-al-Molk, Abu'l-Ganayem Taj-al-Molk Parsi, endowed a second dome near the north gate in 1088, which was outside the mosque and was probably intended for royal ceremonies. Whilst the southern dome of Nezam-al-Molk commands respect with its massive and heavy proportions, the northern dome of Taj-al-Molks inspires through lightness and elegance in the way shapes are arranged into complex geometric patterns. The double-leaf dome creates a larger outer profile and allows a measured transition of the interior. The flow of forces of the dome is a sophisticated system of tapered arches, starting from the centre and forming two- or three-dimensional elements. The pattern of wide arches, which are supported by smaller ones, the deeply carved corners alternating with shallow niches and intersecting pentagons are all perfectly integrated into the building, as structural as well as decorative material covering the masonry. In this respect, the north dome represents the highlight of Seljuk architecture in Iran. As revolutionary as adding the two domes was for the mosque, the next Seljuk intervention into its structure led to a total transformation of the original hypostyle mosque to a new, unprecedented mosque style. In about 1120 the courtyard of the mosque was complemented by four arches and four ayvans. In the centre of each side, ayvans emerged: a long, narrow entrance ayvan in the north and three wider and less deeply vaulted halls on the other three sides

Courtyard

of the courtyard. Unlike the rigid juxtaposition of the roofed prayer hall and the open courtyard of the Arab mosque, the four ayvans of the Persian mosque direct the view to the courtyard, thus creating a connection between the interior and the courtyard, resolving the architectural contradiction of the Arab hypostyle mosque. The four-ayvan-court is not characterised by any apparent orientation. Nevertheless, the qibla ayvan is slightly larger and more important in its ornamentation and general composition than the others. In the Friday Mosque in Isfahan it is even flanked by two minarets, an early application of a motif which played a major role in later mosque design. The façade of the courtyard is determined not only by the large ayvan but also a two-storey arcade. The small ayvans sitting on top of each other, which are significantly higher on the ground floor, hide the single-storey structure inside. The importance of Masjed-e Jameh of Isfahan in Persian architecture is confirmed by the fact that many rulers and patrons left their traces in this mosque. During the reign of Öljeitü and in the post-Mongol period, the area behind the western ayvan was converted

Shabestan

Side wall with inscriptions

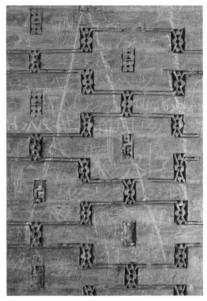

Wall decoration with inscriptions

into a prayer hall. There, the Il-Khanid vizier Mohammad Savi and the calligrapher Badr designed a wonderful mehrab, famous for its complex composition and masterly stuccowork, in 1310. It is decorated with three-dimensional stucco bands in thuluth-writing, which shows the names of the twelve Shiite Imams in twisted leaf tendrils and lotus flowers. The mihrab is located in a remarkable brick vault behind the western ayvan and is equipped with a menbar artfully decorated with intarsia, which is undated but is clearly one of the oldest, most important parts of the mosque. The Muzaffarid

added a small, remarkable Koranic school on the eastern side of the mosque ca. 1350, whilst the Timurid added one of the finest winter prayer halls of Iran and, more importantly, covered the courtyard façades with mosaic tiles. The Safavid-also left traces in the Friday Mosque. They equipped the four-ayvan complex with muqarnas vaults, covered them with tile and crowned the most important, qibla-ayvan with two thin minarets. The fact that the Safavid Shahs Ismail I and Tahmasp used the walls of the mosque to publish royal decrees attests to the social importance of the building.

Library

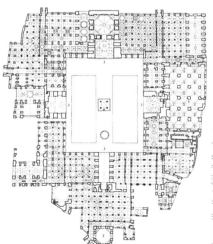

Floor plan

Kohne Square
Maidan-e Kohne
ميدان كهنه

Maidan-e Kohne, Isfahan
32.66745, 51.68456
Ahmad ibn Muhammad al-Chasib,
Ahmad ibn Muhammad al-Farghani
AD: 861/AH: 247/Yaz: 230

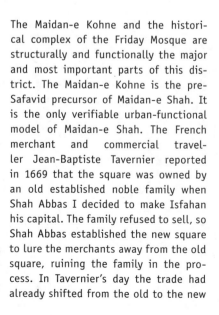

The Maidan-e Kohne and the historical complex of the Friday Mosque are
structurally and functionally the major
and most important parts of this district. The Maidan-e Kohne is the pre-
Safavid precursor of Maidan-e Shah. It
is the only verifiable urban-functional
model of Maidan-e Shah. The French
merchant and commercial traveller Jean-Baptiste Tavernier reported
in 1669 that the square was owned by
an old established noble family when
Shah Abbas I decided to make Isfahan
his capital. The family refused to sell, so
Shah Abbas established the new square
to lure the merchants away from the old
square, ruining the family in the process. In Tavernier's day the trade had
already shifted from the old to the new
square. Part of the surrounding arcades
had collapsed and trade was limited to
foodstuffs. Even if the historic part of
Tavernier's report is probably nothing
more than a nice story, there is no doubt
that Shah Abbas I copied the old maidan
and robbed it of much of its prestige.
In 1864, the mosque Ali Harun Velayat
and the Friday Mosque were situated to
the north and south of the area which
Kaempfer and Jean Chardin described as
the Old Square. Life in the old maidan and
its immediate surroundings was undoubtedly very active. Like rays of light meeting in a focal point, floods of people and
goods came together. The square was
lined with shops, and until the fourteenth century, it presented a colourful
image comparable to the Maidan-e Shah
of the Safavid time. In front of the surrounding buildings, itinerant traders
sold their goods, second-hand dealers
displayed their wares, and street artists
entertained the public. In the Chahar-Su
intersections close to the Old Maidan,
goods from foreign countries were for
sale. There was silk from Kufa, brocade
from Byzantium, high-quality cloth from

Source: Luperto, Claudia

Egypt, precious stones from Bahrain, ivory from India and many other goods. The previously undeveloped area of the old maidan was occupied by a flea market and by itinerant traders in second-hand clothing. The square was largely destroyed in the 1950 s and 1960s by the Haussmannian creation of new roads demanded by the modernisation program of the Pahlavi. It was recently restored by NJP Consulting Engineers after several years of planning. The aim of their design was not only to preserve the historical and cultural identity of the complex, but also to adapt it to the current requirements and to revitalise the surrounding urban context. The project was officially opened in September 2013.

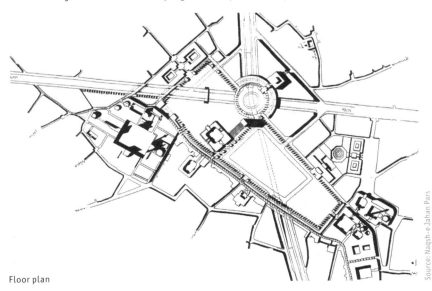

Floor plan

Source: Naqsh-e Jahan Pars

Jurjir Mosque
Masjed-e Jurjir
مسجد جورجیر

041

Khiyaban-e Hakim, Isfahan
32.66378, 51.67465
al-Sahib Kafil-Kufat ibn Abbad
AD: ca. 949/AH: ca. 337/Yaz: ca. 318

The portal of the Jurjir mosque was only rediscovered during restoration work in 1955. It is the only remnant of the Buyid Mosque built by al-Sahib Kafil-kufat Ibn Abbad in 1055. It consists of a deep entrance portal which is surrounded by side walls with several projecting and receding vertical elements, completed by a tripartite semi-dome whose centre part was left open as a bow window. The side portions of the hemispherical, concave, triangular plates are adorned with writings in Kufic ductus script that form keyhole-like niches on the pillars. The geometric relief patterns, which were created with fine brickwork, show the typical technique of the Buyid era, with a repetitive stucco pattern creating a second decorative feature. The attention to the surface relief, in both wall

Portal of Jurjir Mosque

elements as well as decoration, enlivens the façade with an intense play of light and shadow. The portal of the former Jurjir Mosque is today one of the side entrances to the Hakim Mosque, a late work of the seventeenth-century architect Ali-Akbar Isfahani, who integrated the Buyid-era relic into its structure.

Source: Aga Khan Visual Archive

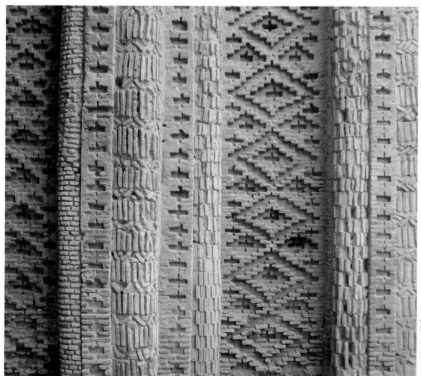

Detail of decoration

Source Hochueli, René

Pol-e Shahrestan, the oldest bridge over the eternal river

Shahrestan Bridge
Pol-e Shahrestan
پل شهرستان

Shahrestan, Isfahan
32.62716, 51.71775
unknown
AD: 1050/AH: 440/Yaz: 420

Pol-e Shahrestan is the oldest bridge over the so-called "eternal river" Zayandeh Rud, and the furthest downstream. It is located near the village of Shahrestan, about 3 km east of the city boundary of Isfahan. This bridge was on the southern route of the Silk Road to Shiraz. It is assumed that the stone pillars and the bow-like breakwaters originate from the early Sassanid. The brick arcatures above were built by the Seljuks in the eleventh century. The edifice clearly goes back to Roman prototypes: The arches are combined with gates in the pier to allow for maximum flow when water levels are high. The Pol-e Shahrestan is considered an architectural masterpiece of its time, but it is hardly used today. The Abbasid Caliph al-Rashid Bellah was murdered here in 1138 by a Shiite; the Shahzadeh Hosein shrine in Shahrestan may be his last resting place.

Pol-e Shahrestan, ca. 10 km from the city centre

Roofscape of bazaar buildings

Bazaar of Isfahan
Bazar-e Isfahan
بازار اصفهان

043

Bazar-e Bozorg, Isfahan
32.66226, 51.67796
unknown
AD: ca. 1000/AH: ca. 390/Yaz: ca. 370

The development of bazaar and city in Isfahan appears to be more closely interwoven than in other Middle Eastern towns; city and bazaar form a homogenous whole. This is not surprising because the bazaar is the economic heart of the traditional Middle Eastern town and therefore the location of almost all its economic activity – from the humblest workshops to the organisation and financing of long-distance trade spanning continents. Today we no longer find bazaar buildings in Isfahan that date back to the pre-Safavid period. Nevertheless, it can be demonstrated that not only the locations of important sections of the bazaar, but also the outline of many bazaar streets have the same origin. For example, the main route of today's bazaar follows the connecting road between the old city centre and the former southern city gate. Therefore the layout of the lines and the aligning of the core area of the Isfahan bazaar can be traced back

Shop in the Spice Bazaar

Source: Luperto, Cludia

Ceiling of Chahar-su

to the Middle Ages, and we can assume an uninterrupted continuity of the line bazaar from the eleventh century to the present day. Apart from the indications already mentioned, its age can also be confirmed by the following observation: The main bazaar road had accumulated masses of building rubble and trash over the centuries which caused it to be raised like a dam by more than 2 m above the level of the adjacent courtyards. During excavations for the sewerage system in this area of the bazaar in 1974, it was discovered that the street rested on top of about 4 m of huge cultural debris, supported by solid sand and clay.

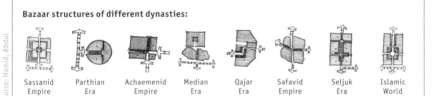

Bazaar structures of different dynasties:

| Sassanid Empire | Parthian Era | Achaemenid Empire | Median Era | Qajar Era | Safavid Empire | Seljuk Era | Islamic World |

Source: Hamid, Abdul

Source: Hochueli, René

Roofscape

Oil Press Seih
Assarkhaneh Shahi
اسار حانه سهی

Khiyaban-e Allameh Majlesi,
Isfahan

32.66869, 51.68310
Seih (Commissioner)
AD: 1120/AH: 515/Yaz: 490

Oil presses of this type once existed in large numbers in the bazaar of Isfahan. However, the Assarkhaneh Seih is the only remaining complete and fully functioning plant. It is set over two floors, one at street level, the second one below ground when seen from the alley, but because of the vast difference in level between the street and the surrounding terrain, the latter opens to a small courtyard. The actual pressing chamber occupies the centre of the building, which is double volume. Two long pressure levers made from tree trunks are installed here. Oil is pressed through these from olives crushed by archaic methods. Octagonal rooms are located in the basement on either side of this room where the olives were prepared for the pressing process by using a round, horizontally placed millstone on the ground, which has an axis in its centre to which a wooden arm is attached with a joint. At one end of the arm, a round grinding millstone is fixed by means of a friction bearing. A camel moving in a circle is harnessed to the longer end of the arm, causing the upper millstone to move and crush the olives. The construction cannot be precisely dated. The fact that buildings of this type were not as easily abandoned as other shops, due to their rather high investment, makes a Safavid origin likely.

Ali Minaret and Mosque
Menar va Masjed-e Ali
مناره علی

Maidan-e Kohne, Isfahan
32.66556, 51.68306
Mizra Kamal od-Din
AD: ca. 1150, 1522/AH: ca. 545, 928/
Yaz: ca. 520, 891

The Ali minaret is the most famous minaret in Isfahan. It is situated on the northwest side of the Ali Mosque. The brick cylinder is divided into three parts complemented by two balconies resembling carnations. The height of the minaret is approximately 48 m, with a diameter of 6 m. The lower part of the minaret is decorated with polygons, crosses, hexagonal and octagonal stars and diamonds. In the central part, jagged diamonds form diagonal intersecting strips on the left and right, narrowing due to the conical shape. The minaret is decorated with two inscriptions in nashki increasing the variety of geometric patterns. The Ali Mosque and minaret were built during the reign of the Seljuk Sultan Sanjar in the mid-twelfth century. The decorative brickwork of the minaret from the Seljuk period was preserved, whilst the mosque was largely rebuilt and redesigned under the Safavid Shah Ismail I. The mosque's design is based on the four-ayvan typology, with prayer halls grouped around an open courtyard. The Qibla wing south of the courtyard houses a vaulted prayer hall with a mehrab and minbar. The street elevation is formed by an arched portal with two flat, large alcoves of equal size and a small panel with a blind arch. A gilded thuluth inscription by the calligrapher Shams od-Din Tabrizi is located

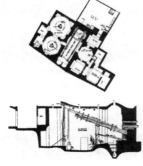

Floor plan and section of oil press

Aerial view of Ali Minaret

in the recess of the portal; it dates back to the reconstruction by the architect Mizra Kamal od-Din during the Safavid period. Even the stellar vault of the portal is decorated with glazed tiles; above the entrance is a plaque from 1522, quoting Musaddiq as the author of the tilework. Blue and turquoise tiles with large floral motifs and a wide band with a white Kufic inscription are used on the exterior of the dome.

Source: Arnold Henry Savage Landor

Swinging Minarets, 1904

Jafar Mausoleum
Maghbareh-ye Jafar
امامزاده جعفر

046

Chaharrah-e Shekar Shekan,
Khiyaban-e Hatef, Isfahan
32.66333, 51.68444
unknown
AD: 1324/AH: 756/Yaz: 693

Two inscriptions on a gravestone and the façade date the building to 1324. The inscription on the grave stone indicates that Jafar eben-e Hassan eben-e Hossein eben-e Mohammad eben-e Ali eben-e Hossein, a direct descendant of the prophet, is buried here. André Godard considered this building one of the few built by Mongols in Isfahan and points out similarities to buildings in Azerbaijan. The mausoleum, originally surrounded by a large courtyard, is partially occupied today by residential buildings; it was recently restored.

Swinging Minarets
Menar-e Jonban
منارجنبان

047

Karladan, Isfahan
32.65028, 51.59389
Sultan Sanjar (Commissioner)
AD: 1321/AH: 721/Yaz: 690

The Swinging Minarets are found in Karladan, a village which was formerly on the outskirts but is today absorbed into the town. The complex consists of the grave mosque of Amu Abdollah Soqla, a hermit who was buried there in the early fourteenth century, and two thin minarets dating from the pre-Safavid period that are built on top on it. These can be made to resonate due to certain features of the building size and the wooden beams in the base of the minaret, hence the name of the complex.

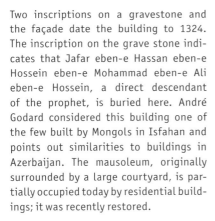
Source: Ganjanameh, Cyclopedia of Iranian Islamic Architecture, Shahid Beheshti University

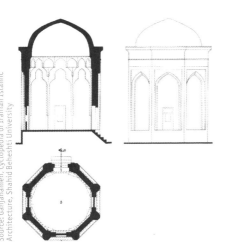

Floor plan, section and north elevation of Jafar Mausoleum

Source: Gasser, Markus (Bild- & Planführer für Studienzwecke)

Menar-e Jomban

Qu'ran School Emamiyeh, Baba Qasim
Madrasa-ye Emamiyeh, Baba Qasim
مدرسه امامیه (بابا قاسم)

Khiyaban-e Hatef, Isfahan
32.66111, 51.68417
Sultan Abu al-Hassan Talut Damghani (Commissioner)
AD: 1355 / AH: 756 / Yaz: 725

The Emamiyeh Madrasa was commissioned in 1355 by Sultan Abd-el-Hassan Talut Damghani in honour of his teacher Baba Qasim Isfahani. It was declared a national monument in 1940. The large courtyard and ayvan are equipped with tile decor similar to the Friday Mosque. The tile decoration of the north portal no longer existed in 1965, and a large crack ran through the north ayvan, resulting in most of the masonry being destroyed. At the same time, the cells of the upper floor were in poor condition and had been confiscated by neighbours. The school was later renovated. Today the north ayvan is again broken and the brickwork is in poor condition. The mihrab of the Emamiyeh Madrasa is now in the Metropolitan Museum of Art in New York. It consists of a mosaic composed of small tiles, forming various geometric and floral patterns and inscriptions. The inscription

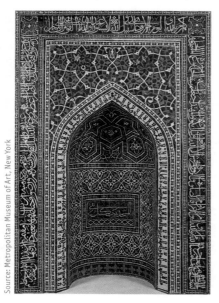

Source: Metropolitan Museum of Art, New York

Prayer Niche Emamiyeh Madrasa, today Metropolitan Museum of Art, New York

Source: Panoramio

Interior of Natural History Museum

in muḥaqqaq, a traditional italic font going from the lower right to the lower left, quotes the Surah IX, *The Repentance*, from the Qu'ran. A second inscription with words of the Prophet in Kufic letters is next to the pointed arch of the niche and a third, cursive inscription, is set in a frame in the centre of the prayer niche. The bottom of the niche just below the central inscription was restored in the mid-1920s, together with a large part of the main inscription.

Natural History Museum
Talar-e Teymuri
موزه تاریخ طبیعی

Khiyaban-e Ostandari, Isfahan
32.65808, 51.67415
unknown
AD: ca. 1450 / AH: ca. 854 / Yaz: ca. 770

The so-called Talar-e Teymuri, a building within the royal gardens, Bag-e Naqsh Jahan, is today the home of the Museum of Natural History in Isfahan. The building is attributed to the Timurid dynasty, although there is no archaeological or written evidence. At the entrance of the museum a group of rather sad, non-threatening dinosaurs made of fiberglass welcomes you, but do not be put off by this: Inside, you will find a treasure trove. The building has large halls and a talar decorated with stucco muqarnas. It is questionable whether the building is suitable for stuffed animals; particularly dinosaurs suffer from the cheap plastic display shelves. The building was altered in 1988 in an unsettling folk architecture.

Maghbareh Darb-e Emam, exterior view

The two Safavid domes of the Mausoleum

Mausoleum Darb-e Imam
Maqbareh Darb-e Imam
مقبره درب امام

Khiyaban-e Hammam-e Vazir,
Khiyaban-e Dardasht, Isfahan
32.66888, 51.67716
Mirza Shah-Hossein Isfahani
AD: 1453 / AH: 857 / Yaz: 822

This remarkable mausoleum, Darb-e Imam, is located just west of the Friday Mosque in a cemetery dating from the tenth century, with shrine structures and courtyard-like designs associated with different construction periods and styles. The mausoleum was built in 1453 for the two descendants of the fourth caliph and son of Muhammad Ali, the key figure of Shia Islam. Two domes were added in the Safavid era, the larger one in 1601 and the smaller one in 1670. The unusual proximity of the cupolas is characteristic for this complex. After crossing the courtyard, the visitor's attention is immediately drawn to the monumental portal, the pischtak, a typical element of Seljuk architecture. This is of particular importance because its intricate mosaic tile pattern is so intense in its blue colours and so fine in its craftsmanship that one is immediately reminded of the Blue Mosque of Tabriz. The two panels above the arches on either side of the main portal are decorated with a repeating hexagonal pattern which shifts at a certain distance, resulting in each element taking the place of an identical element in the original pattern. Ornate geometric ornaments have a long tradition in Islamic culture. However, some ornaments created from the twelfth

Portico of Darb-e-imam shrine with two overlapping girih-patterns

Representation of the overlapping girih-patterns

Source: Peter Lu, Harvard University and Paul Steinhardt, Princeton University

century differ in their complexity from earlier ones: They are based on hundreds of decagons, and the design is so complex and precise that it could not possibly be achieved with ruler and compass. Peter Lu and Paul Steinhardt have shown that these complex mosaics, called girih in Persian, were actually created with a set of only five different tiles. These five tiles decorated with lines are shaped like a decagon, a pentagon, a hexagon, a crystal, a rhombus and one resembling a bow-tie. Islamic artisans were able to create a multitude of patterns with these tiles. Thus a pattern was developed which is today called quasi-crystalline. Such patterns were not known in the Western world until much later: In 1974, the British mathematician Penrose discovered several related, small, non-repeating patterns which always retain a certain order.

Mausoleum Harun-e Velayat, Sanctuary of Aron
Maghbareh-ye Harun-e Velayat
مقبره هارون ولايت

Maidan-e Kohne, Isfahan
32.66583, 51.68278
Mirza Shah-Hossein Isfahani
AD: 1512/AH: 918/Yaz: 881

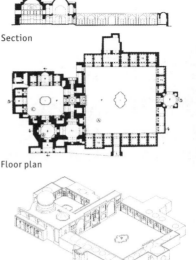

Section

Floor plan

Axonometric projection

Source: Ganjanameh, Cyclopedia of Iranian Islamic Architecture, Shahid Beheshti University

The two main buildings dating from the sixteenth century, the mausoleum of Harun Velayat and the renovation of the Masjed-e Ali, were built under the auspices of the new ruling elite, the Safavids. Durmis Shamlu Khan, the Safavid governor of Isfahan, endowed the building of Harun-Velayat and Kamal-od-Din. Sah-Huseyn commissioned alterations of neighbouring Masjed-e Ali. In both buildings, but especially in the mausoleum of Harun-Velayat, the inscriptions of the façade refer to the parallels between the biblical Aaron and the first Shia Imam, Ali Ibn Abi Taleb. By using the most perfect flower, plant and paradise motifs on mosaic tiles, the iconographic program also conveyed an intense Shiite propaganda that was consistent with the Safavid enthusiasm for promoting Twelver Shia as the sole state religion. The choice of the strategic position on the southern edge of the Seljuk town centre shows the determination of the early Safavid to realise their own imperial ambitions in the medieval town. Imamzadeh Zadeh Harun Velayat closes Maidan Kohne off to the southwest. The complex consists of the mausoleum of Harun Velayat, the son of the seventh Shiite Iman, a small madrasa on the west side and the hosseiniyeh, a large courtyard, in the north. The inscription above the entrance indicates the name of Mirza Shah-Hossein Isfahani, who had been asked to build the mausoleum. In his youth he worked as a builder and architect, became a civil servant and was possibly murdered in 1533. The other buildings were probably based on older constructions, which were expanded in 1512 during the reign of Shah Ismail under the supervision of his vizier Dormesh Khan. The shrine on the north side of the vast courtyard is surrounded by corbel arches. Four of these display swastika motifs formed of glazed and untreated brick. The blue dome of the shrine has a double shell with a diameter of 7.5 m on

Entrance of the Maghbareh-ye Harun-e Velayat

Source: Claudia Luperto

Side entrance of the Mausoleum

Source: Claudia Luperto

Source: Claudia Luperto

Side entrance of the Maghbareh-ye Harun-e Velayat

an octagonal base. The interior is richly decorated with paintings and faïence, giving the pilgrimage centre a strong spiritual atmosphere. According to the travel diary of Jean Chardin, Muslims as well as Jews and Christians worshipped here in the seventeenth century, since a saint, Mualla Nasir, is buried here. The Seljuk era minaret, built entirely of brick, rises abruptly to the right of the entrance portal. It is ca. 48 m high and has a tapered cylindrical shaft with two balconies. The minaret is decorated with a pattern of interlocking stars and fine diamonds and bands in Kufic script. Harun-e Velayat marks the beginning of the Iranian renaissance architecture in Isfahan, which flourished under Shah Abbas I.

Source: Heinz Gaube, Eugen Wirth, Der Bazaar von Isfahan, Wiesbaden, 1978

Interior view of Zulfikar Mosque

Zulfikar Mosque
Masjed-e Zulfiqar
مسجد ذوالفقار

Bazar-e Dar-Bag-Qalandarian, Isfahan
32.66417, 51.67861
Shah Tahmasp I (Commissioner)
AD: 1543/AH: 950/Yaz: 912

The Masjed Zo-l-Feqar is a small mosque in the bazaar of Isfahan built during the time of intense Shiite propaganda to elevate Twelver Shia to the state religion. Zulfikar is the name of the double-furrowed, two-edged sword of Ali Ibn Abi Tali – said to have been given to him by Muhammad in the battle of Badr – which became an important symbol of the Shiites, representing resistance against oppression and inhumanity. The mosque consists of a rectangular prayer hall, covered by five rib vaults over a long, rectangular ground plan between four powerful belts. The hall is accessible from the bazaar Dar-Bag Qalandarian and an adjacent courtyard to the north. The portal facing the bazaar was later altered. According to the inscription, the mosque was built in 1543, during the reign of Shah Tahmasp I. Its courtyard is bordered by three ayvans in the north, east and south; adjacent to its southeastern corner is a hammam.

Origin of the Four-Ayvan Mosque

One of the key elements in the development of eastern Islamic architecture is the large spatial portal, the ayvan (also ivan or aiwan). The term is derived from the Persian ayvan, meaning a type of room. The first major ayvan in history was built in Taq-e Kasra, the palace of the legendary King Khosrow in Ctesiphon not far from Baghdad, where it served as a throne hall. The Abbasid caliphs adopted the ayvan. The first examples can be found in the eighth century in the desert palaces of Syria and Palestine. Later the ayvan was incorporated into the court-like madrasas, whereby each of the four Sunni law schools was arranged around a courtyard, with an ayvan allocated as a lecture hall, thus creating the new typological basis for the four-ayvan mosque which refers to the influence and the enormous spread of the ayvan-madrasa, the layout of which was adapted for the Persian mosque, giving it a completely new look. By making the ayvan part of the four colonnades and occupying their centre, the courtyard of the mosque, which was previously bordered by columns or pilasters in simple undefined colonnades, was enriched by this new element and obtained decisive architectural axes. Despite the new partitioning there is no fundamental spatial hierarchy and none of the four directions is particularly accentuated. Although the qibla ayvan is larger than the others, the difference is hardly noticeable and all four portals occupy an equally strong position. Incorporating the ayvan into the formal language of religious architecture during the twelfth century caused tensions in the inner balance of the building itself. The previous homogeneity of the columned hall was changed by ayvans and divided the open space into four parts. Despite the novelty that the ayvan represents, a basic concept of Islamic architecture is retained. The four sides of the empty courtyard preserved their equality despite the new monumentality. The large ayvan with their apparent spatial depth multiply the line of vision instead of directing it to one point. Similar to the courtyard of the early Arab mosque, the viewer is confronted with a space that is characterised by a variety of both orientations and perspectives. It is an infinite outside with all the characteristics of an interior, because the yard is completely enclosed. The inclusion of the ayvan in the basic scheme of the mosque had far-reaching consequences not only for the layout of the rooms, but also for the relationship between the interior and exterior of the building. The ayvan became an essential part of Persian religious architecture by not only changing the layout but also the construction of buildings.

Friday Mosque in Damghan
Masjed-e Jameh, Masjed-e Tarikhaneh, Damghan
مسجد دامغان

Damghan, Semnan
36.16436, 54.35426
unknown
AD: 789 / AH: 173 / Yaz: 158

The Friday Mosque in Damghan is the oldest mosque in Iran. Built between 750 and 789, the small building shows an innovative solution in the development of the early mosque, despite its modest dimensions and design. The main elevation of the courtyard, the qibla side, undergoes an important change. The arcade of the middle nave, or the mihrab nave, which is considerably wider than the rest of the arcades, is framed by a pistaq rising above the roof-line. Yet the two heavy cylindrical brick pillars supporting the pistaq do not differ from the rest of the structure. The hall looks homogeneous and the barrel vaults of the naves are perpendicular to the outer wall, which seems to extend the depth of the short hall. The small mosque is very solid. Its structure consists of two very different parts: a lower one, with heavy cylindrical columns, and an upper superimposed part with arches and vaults. The superimposition of both parts can be seen in the crude connection of pillar and arcade: some are clearly separated whilst in others both structural elements form a unit. The pointed arches of the arcade of the courtyard are framed by half-columns which reach from the floor up to the roof line, giving the courtyard façade an unfinished look. The Persians, who had no previous experience in the construction of columned halls, suddenly found themselves confronted with a new problem. The differentiation of the various components (columns, arcade, pistaq) and the hierarchical importance of the centre are the timid beginnings of a new development which evolved only a century later. The mosque with pistaq or ayvan did not conform to a pre-defined architectural building type in Iran. It is rather an unintentional reintroduction of traditional elements which were first used as standard design in palaces and later also in mosques. The design of the Friday Mosque in Damghan represents a transition between the simple, early Arabic hypostatic mosque and the four-ayvan mosque. John D. Hoag described the building as follows: "The Tarik-Hana mosque is Arabic in its design but Sassanid in its construction."

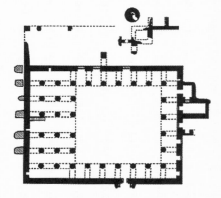

Ground floor plan of Friday Mosque in Damghan
Source: Keppel Archibald C. Creswell,
A Short Account of Early Muslim Architecture, 1989

Friday Mosque in Damghan, 8th or 9th century

Friday Mosque in Nain
Masjed-e Jameh, Nain
مسجد جامع نایین

Nain, Isfahan
32.86194, 53.09056
unknown
AD: 960/AH: 349/Yaz: 329

054 A

Built in 960, the Friday Mosque in Nain on the central Iranian plateau is well preserved. The oldest part is very similar to the Friday Mosque in Damghan. The vaulted naves stand at right angles to the outside wall, and the later additions give the interior a more complex look, particularly in the wider northwest corner of the hall. The orientation in the prayer room varies constantly with the changing direction of the arched naves. Compared to that of Damghan, the mosque shows some important innovations. The mihrab vault is similarly wider than the others. The apex of the pointed arch in the middle of the qibla-pistaq reaches the height of the roofline. The pistaq itself rises above the roofline by a few centimetres in an unspectacular way. The almost-continuous pistaq, which no longer rests on pillars but goes further down to a higher or lower pedestal, is a novel solution. The columns as supporting and freestanding elements disappear from the courtyard façade and are replaced by creative half-columns. This new composition represents an important intermediate step in the development of the ayvan mosque. Although the court façade gives the impression that it consists of ayvans or a series of downwardly extended pistaqs, it still lacks the spaciousness of the genuine ayvan. The Friday Mosque in Nain was built as a Sunni mosque, which was "Shiite-tised", so to speak, over the years. The important symbol of Shiites, Zulfikar, the double-ridged, two-edged sword of the Prophet, is depicted on a pillars from a very early renovation.

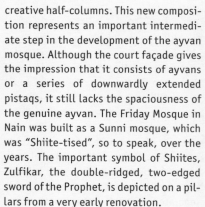

Sections

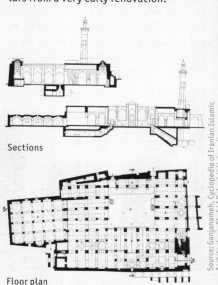

Floor plan

Source: The David Collection, Hans Munk Hansen

Friday Mosque in Zavareh
Masjed-e Jameh, Zavareh
مسجد جامع زواره

Zavareh, Ardestan
33.44889, 52.49361
Abu Taher Hossein ibn Ahmad
AD: 1136 / AH: 531 / Yaz: 505

The four-ayvan mosque was built for the first time in Zavareh, a small town at the edge of the Iranian central desert. Whilst most of the Persian mosques of the early 1100s had one or more ayvan added, the Zavareh Mosque is a so-called

Section

Source: Ganjanameh, Cyclopedia of Iranian Islamic Architecture, Shahid Beheshti University

Floor plan

"monument from one mould". O. Kühnel described the mosque, built in 1136, as follows: "There are four ayvans around an almost-square courtyard, one of which is wider than the others and is closed off at the rear wall, leading to a passage to the adjoining domed room with the mihrab". The large mihrab ayvan opening to the courtyard is connected to an enclosed space, a combination which became standard design in large and small mosques. The position of the mosque in the old town of Zavareh shows its urban character. There are two entrances on the road axis. When the doors of the mosque are open, the northeast side of the building looks like a public colonnade and the courtyard of the mosque like a square. Just as Persia "Iranised Islam", so to speak, a new type of mosque evolved in Iran which differs from the Arab origin. Thus, at a relatively early stage of development, the Islamic prayer hall had taken on a spatial and formal design that was no longer the result of a collection of buildings of different dimensions and spatial properties. The time of the development of a four-ayvan mosque is no accident. It will remain one of the mysteries of history why the first attempt to realise a uniform design principle for the Persian mosque was made in Zavareh, a small, inconspicuous desert town.

Isfahan, Capital of Shah Abbas the Great

When Tahmasp I died in 1576, the empire ruled by his sons was brought to the brink of disaster. Shah Ismail II and Shah Mohammad, ruling in succession, did not rule long enough to leave their marks. Their rule ended when the majority of the emirs sided with the sixteen-year-old Abbas Mirza, who, aided by his tutor, marched to Qazvin in 1587 to public demonstrations in his favour. Once enthroned in the Chehel Sotun palace in the Sa'adatabad garden, Shah Abbas ordered his slaves to use their scimitars to behead the emirs who had been compromised in the past, or who posed a threat to his tutor's authority. The twenty-two heads were then exposed on spears in the maidan. It marked, in the memory of the emirs, the first day of his reign. The Sa'adatabad garden was the centre of these dramatic events, and the maidan at its door was the best place to display his might to his opponents.

After some dynastic turmoil Prince Abbas, the later Shah Abbas the Great, consolidated the empire. He inherited an empire weakened by a war between the Turkmenian Qizilbasch and the Safavid princes and princesses, which lasted for decades. Under his rule the assault of the Uzbeks was stopped in 1595, Bahrain was occupied in 1601, the Ottomans expelled from Azerbaijan, Armenia and Georgia in 1603, and in 1623 even Iraq and Baghdad were recaptured. Due to a skilful economic policy, the country began to enjoy not-inconsiderable wealth, which is reflected in the development of the infrastructure, particularly in the new capital Isfahan, which has an excellent road system from this time. He also limited the influence of the Turkmenian military by building up troops of Christian slaves. In the interior, Abbas consequently and successfully continued his grandfather's politics of centralisation. One main element of his politics was the establishment of a standing

army with cavalry, infantry and artillery, following the Ottoman example, which was recruited from east Iranian farmers, Qizilbash and Caucasians. With this reformed army he led successful wars against Mughals, Uzbeks and Ottomans. Similar to the European rulers of his time, Shah Abbas promoted craftsmanship, trade and industry. This included reforms of the lease and taxation system as well as standardisation of the monetary system. The improvement of the infrastructure, i.e. roads, bridges, fountains, channels, dams and caravanserais, benefitted both domestic and foreign trade and increased the effectiveness of the caravanserais along the routes. These improvements were refinanced by the imposition of route taxes in gold and silver, which mainly affected Europeans. Abbas claimed the monopoly for the lucrative silk trade and generally tried to control the production of luxury goods. The existing caravan routes to Anatolia and Syria were vulnerable due to ongoing wars with the Ottomans, and burdened by extensive transit taxes even in peaceful times. The promotion of maritime trade via the Indian Ocean was therefore an obvious alternative. The big trading companies of England, France and Holland conducted important commercial transactions with the Safavids. The Safavid era gained real importance through the state support of Twelver Shia, which made Iran the only important Shia state in Islamic history after the reign of the Ismaili Fatimids. The implementation of the Shia had obvious political motives as it helped to protect the reign of the Safavid against the predominantly Sunni neighbours. In re-establishing the royal power, the major part of the traditional military aristocracy was replaced by a new Gholam-elite, mostly converted Cherkess, Armenians and Georgians, who pledged their loyalty solely to the Shah. The Safavid empire reached its economic peak during the reign of Shah Abbas I. The Safavids established a permanent and thoroughly-organised political system, which stopped the 250-year-long political division and foreign domination. The Safavid state enforced an increasing standardisation of its population structure, created a kind of Iranian nation state and declared the Shia of Twelve as the principle of the government.

Urban Area of Isfahan ca. 1629

When Shah Abbas I decided to proclaim Isfahan as capital of the Safavid empire, the economic centre of the town was the Maidan-e Kohne. In contrast to previous rulers, who lived in the area of the old town near the maidan and in palaces southeast from there, Shah Abbas I moved his court to the southeastern end of the town. His master plan, which extended far out to areas never before occupied by royal buildings, was without precedent. The new public square, Maidan-e Naqsh-e Jehan, and the Chahar Bagh Promenade were the cornerstones of the Safavid plan. The first building phase concentrated on the royal square, which was levelled and enclosed by a rectangular perimeter wall of one-storey cells between 1590 and 1591. A monumental door on the west side of the square, Ali Qapu, the Sublime Gate, marks the threshold between the public town and the private royal gardens, which Shah Abbas I had developed as his residence. These political and ceremonial buildings were partnered by the Qeysaryeh Bazaar, or royal market, on the north side of the maidan. The second building phase began in 1596 with the building of the Chahar Bagh Promenade on the west side of the royal gardens. This avenue, about 2 km long, connected the palace across the Allahverdi Khan bridge to Bagh-e Hezar Jarib, a royal garden lying outside the town at the foot of the Soffe Mountains. The royal gardens and garden pavilions were developed along this promenade over the next ten years, whilst the villas and residential quarters of the new Safavid elite were built on the south side of the avenue. The Armenian suburb of New Julfa, established in 1603 and 1604 by forcibly-relocated trading families, and the residential district Abbasabad, for traders exiled from Tabriz, are among the most remarkable urban developments from this period in Isfahan. The spatial, architectural, functional and iconographic aspects of the Safavid town are so coherent that they refute the oft-repeated assumption that it was developed in phases.

Shah Abbas' Master Plan

The urban planning represents the vision of a new order that articulates the concept of royalty in Twelver Shia and merges the royal splendour of the ancient Persian kingdom with the legitimacy of the family of the Prophet. The implementation of the visual-spatial aspects of this vision depended not only on the brilliant imagination of Shah Abbas but also on the commitment of the politically-empowered nouveaux riches, the new gholam elite

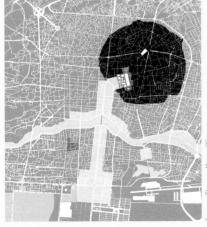

Urban area of Isfahan ca. 1629

Source: Thomas Meyer-Wieser

who closely observed the implementation of the master plan. The design of the maidan, with its axial juxtaposition of religion, politics and economy, transformed the old urban centre into an icon of absolute imperial power. Together with the Chahar Bagh Promenade and the planned neighbourhoods of the elite, Shah Abbas transformed the medieval town into a proper capital. It became one of the most populous and prosperous cities of the seventeenth century, a city where the various elements of the early modern enterprises of absolutism and centralism were optically and spatially demonstrated to great effect.

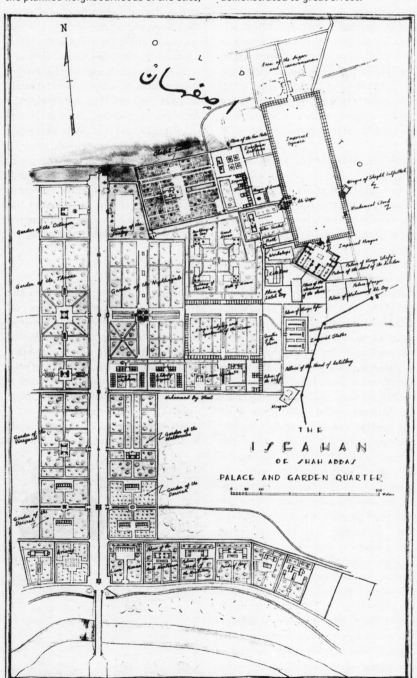

Donald N. Wilber, Reconstructed Plan of the Palace and Gardens in Isfahan

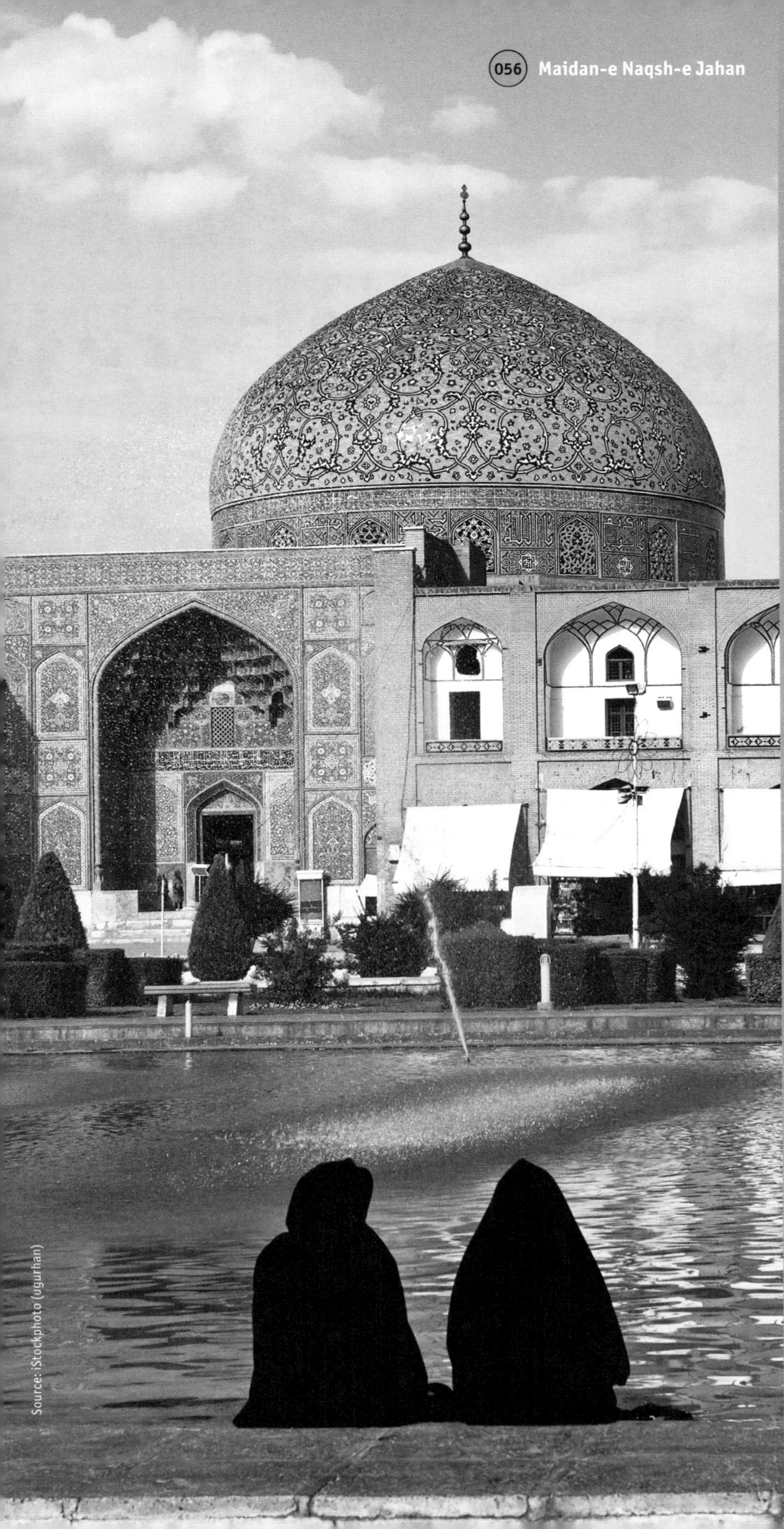

Source: iStockphoto (ugurhan)

Source: Claudia Luperto

Shah Square, Imam Square
Maidan-e Shah,
Maidan-e Naqsh-e Jahan
ميدان نقش جهان

056

Maidan-e Shah, Isfahan
32.65778, 51.67722
Shah Abbas I (Commissioner)
AD: 1595/AH: 1004/Yaz: 964

The nearly 9 ha Maidan-e Naqsh-e Jehan is one of the largest city centres in the world. The existing centre from the Seljuk period was near the Friday Mosque. In the course of planning the residential town between 1590 and 1595, Shah Abbas I ordered the development of this place into the new city centre on open land between the old town centre and the Zayandeh Rud river, about 1 km to the southwest. A radical intervention in the existing building structures was thus prevented. The original name of the square Naqsh-e Jehan, or Image of the World, was later changed to Maidan-e Shah, or King's Square (its present name) after the Islamic revolution. The place forms an elongated rectangle 560 m long and 160 m wide and is almost exactly aligned in a north-south direction. It was also planned as cour d'honneur, marketplace, court, sports field – Shah Abbas I was a passionate polo player – and fairground and is surrounded by major monumental buildings, namely the Royal Palace, Mosque and Bazaar, which are connected by a double-storey

Source: Ernst Hoeltzer Collection

Shah Square ca. 1870 (before Europeanisation)

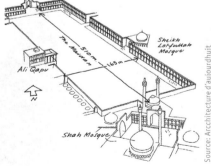

Birds-eye view of the square

Source: Arcchitecture d'aujourdhuit

arcade surrounding the square. Starting in 1602, the Maidan-e Naqsh-e Jehan was expanded by a second row of shops. Although this reduced the open area, it completed the square and doubled the sales area of shops, which were connected by a covered walkway. Religion was one supporting pillar in the emerging Safavid state, trade and commerce the other. Shah Abbas' ambition was to turn Isfahan into not only the most magnificent, but also the richest town in the Middle East. His vision was to be achieved by a well-designed commercial centre, where each guild and each craft had its place and where trade and industry were supported by ensuring safety and providing a generous infrastructure. Before long, significant trade routes between China and Europe were routed via Isfahan. Unlike in other desert towns, the presence of the bright turquoise domes and precious glazed tiles of mosques and madrasas, colourful gardens, elegant palaces and spacious houses conveyed the image of a prosperous city. The sight may have appeared to visitors like a fata morgana, a beautiful mirage, a veritable paradise on earth, after the many deprivations of an exhausting journey by caravan.

Royal Palace
Dowlatkhaneh
دولت خانه

Maidan-e Shah, Isfahan
32.65700, 51.67482
Shah Abbas I (Commissioner)
AD: from 1598/AH: from 1007/
Yaz: from 967

The most complete example of a Persian royal palace is Dawlatkhaneh in Isfahan, of which Engelbert Kaempfer made an interesting drawing published in his book *Planographia Sedis Regiae*. The Dawlatkhaneh in Isfahan encloses a conglomeration of parks and buildings of various designs, which consisted functionally of three parts, namely the Dawlatkhaneh for public audiences, the harem or khalvat khan for private use and the buyutat-e saltanati for the administration necessary for the functioning of the state. Between this complex and the city lies the maidan, the great square which served as the vestibule to the royal palace. From Ali Qapu, the central archway, a passage led along the barracks and the Mosque of the Royal Guard westwards to the proper palace. The talar-e tavileh, or riding hall, was located to the south. Further to the right lay the area with the royal magazines, shops stocking garments for the royal household as well as the royal library and scriptorium, a European watchmaker and jewellers. Few were granted the privilege to enter this area – only noblemen, invited guests, servants and guards. For these few, the secluded interior provided a delightful sight of woods and gardens, ponds and fountains as well as countless blue-tiled channels with running water. Separate buildings in a more remote part housed the many children of the Shah and the older members of the royal family. These buildings are no longer in existence, and contemporary accounts do not shed much light on the secluded life in the harem. The rear area culminated in the royal gardens along the Chahar Bagh Prom which opened to the landscape. The north side contained two formal, walled, rectangular gardens, the Bagh-e Khalvat, the garden of solitude, and the Bagh-e Chihil Sutun, the garden of forty pillars, both equipped with various pavilions and connected by a small vineyard. The perimeter walls of these gardens were lined with interconnecting galleries, enabling the Shah to move undetected from one enclosed space to another. A diagonal passage linked the harem to a pavilion at the top of Chahar Bagh Promenade, a structure with latticed balconies, from where the ladies could watch the formal receptions of ambassadors and courtiers.

The Safavid court ceremony showed many similarities with French absolutism, particularly the emphasis on the availability of the ruler, who showed himself in public at every opportunity. The Safavid Shah manifested his royal power through permanent presence, pomp and availability. His image as a monarch accessible to the public characterised the ceremonies and the design of the palaces of Isfahan. Although Shah Abbas I's successors made alterations to the palace and extended the ritual pomp, they still followed the traditions he had established. Their reign moved away from his informal style, but compared to the Ottoman or Mughal court, the Safavid ceremonies remained relatively informal, dominated by large banquets where the Shahs conversed with their guests.

Ali Qapu Entrance Palace
Ali Qapu
عالى قاپو

Maidan-e Shah, Isfahan
32.65722, 51.67667
Shah Abbas I, Shah Abbas II (Commissioner) et al.
AD: from 1598/AH: from 1007/
Yaz: from 967

Access to the Royal Palace was controlled by several gates, which were strategically positioned to show the various functions of the palace. It was commissioned by Shah Abbas I, who in 1597

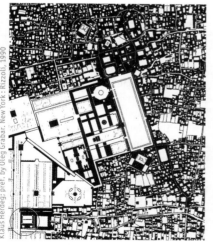

Klaus Herdeg: Reconstruction of Dawlatkhane of Isfahan, 1990

Source: Formal structure in Islamic architecture of Iran and Turkistan-Klaus Herdeg; pref. by Oleg Grabar. New York: Rizzoli, 1990

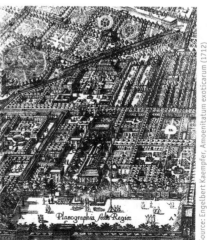

Engelbert Kaempfer: Planographia sedis regiae, Dawlatkhane of Isfahan, 1712

Source: Engelbert Kaempfer, Amoenitatum exoticarum (1712)

Ali Qapu from Maidan-e Shah

Source: Thomas Meyer-Wieser

celebrated the Nowruz festival in this building. The Ali Qapu entrance palace served as the seat of justice, the gateway to the royal residence and to host gala events. It was built together with the Qeysaryeh and the bazaar portal during the first phase of the new town centre. Shortly after Shah Abbas II ascended the throne, he instructed his Grand Vizier, Mirza Mohammad Taqi Saru, to build a talar in front of the existing five-storey tower. This addition radically changed the purpose of the original palace. The transformation of a court of law to a ceremonial reception palace created a new threshold between the public and royalty. Whilst the seat of administration and the king were hidden deep inside the palace in Ottoman Topkapi Sarayi in Istanbul or Mughal Red Fort in Delhi, the ceremonial palace in Isfahan formed the threshold between king and populace. As the Safavid court increasingly tended towards more elaborate festivities and large receptions, an audience hall with a level ayvan and exposure to the maidan offered almost-ideal conditions. Especially impressive is the viewing platform, where an imposing flat roof supported by eighteen cedar pillars was

Ali Qapu, ceiling of the talar

Source: René Hochueli

designed as an open portico. In the centre of the porch lies a marble basin, supplied with water by a machine driven by oxen. This spacious veranda was the ideal place for the king and the court to watch polo matches and other events which were held in the Maidan-e Shah. Royal audiences and receptions for foreign envoys took place here. The fifth and final floor, added about in 1615, consisted of private music rooms. It shows a very special type of embellishment: In front of the wall and ceiling area, a gypsum layer was added, in which the outlines of vessels in various shapes and sizes were carved. This structure, together with the glass and metal bottles embedded therein, apparently resulted in very special acoustics highly appreciated by musicians.

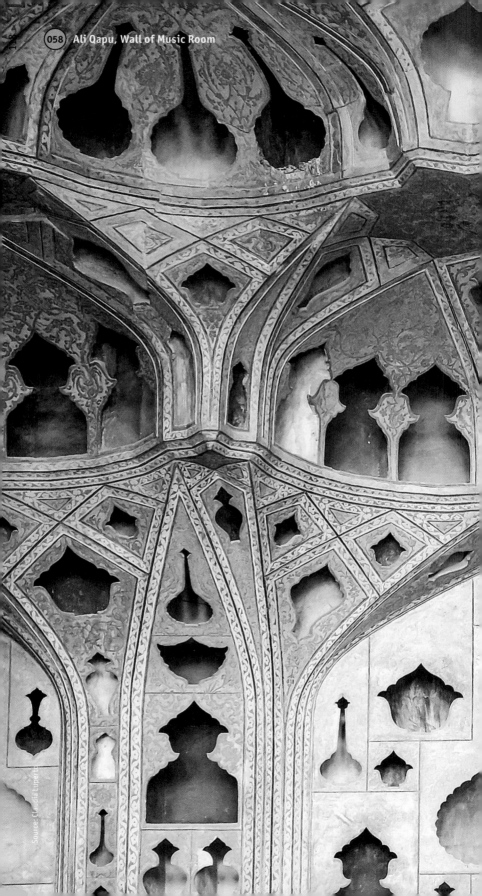

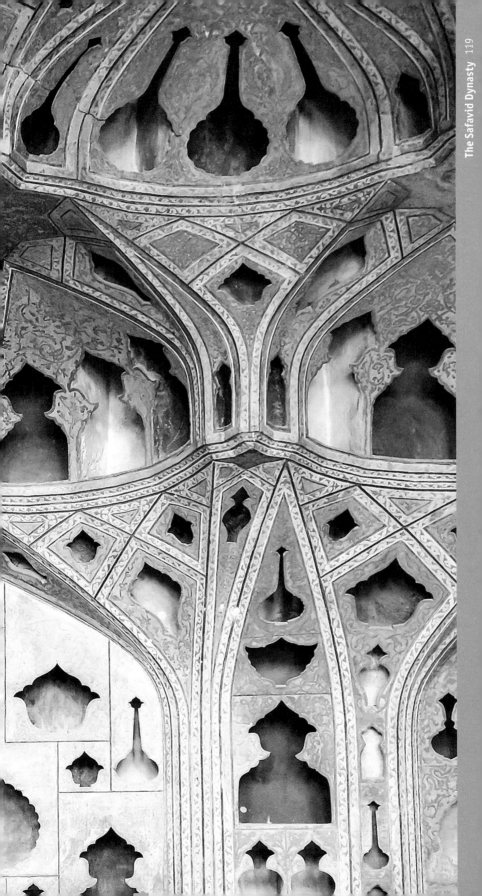

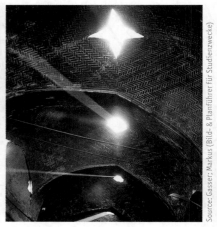

Jørn Utzon, Munk Hansen: Great Bazaar, 1959

Great Bazaar, ceiling

Great Bazaar of Isfahan
Bazar-e Bozorg
بازار بزرگ

Maidan-e Shah, Isfahan
32.66056, 51.67639
Shah Abbas I (Commissioner)
AD: 1598/AH: 1007/Yaz: 967

The decision of Shah Abbas I to build a new central bazaar area on the southern axis, in the part of the town where the court centre of Isfahan developed under him and his successors, was obvious: The court, with its myriad of courtiers, guards and visitors, had such a high demand for goods and services that it required the establishment of a new business and commercial centre nearby. The resulting shift in focus necessitated the construction of a new maidan and a new field-bazaar, the Qeysaryeh, as well as the surrounding streets. The basic pattern of the design of the field-bazaar, adjoining Maidan-e Shah on the north side, consists of a nine-square grid, which, however, was not faithfully executed. The architects designed their buildings about 200 m west of the old bazaar street, linking them to the southern axis. Its layout and that of the surrounding buildings had little influence on the southern bazaar, which continued to follow the slightly winding old route to the southern gate. The construction of the Maidan-e Shah and the adjoining field-bazaar marked the completion of today's old town and bazaar. All future development followed the newly defined field of forces, according to which the significance of the old maidan was substantially reduced. Still, it retained its influence on the further development of Isfahan. It remains today in the most densely populated part of the city. Next to it stands the Great Mosque, which was never a serious rival for the Shah Mosque at Maidan-e Shah.

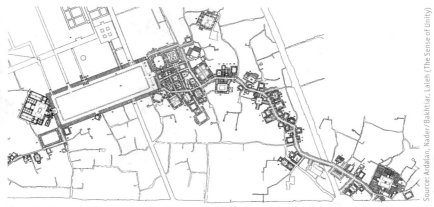

Nader Ardalan and Laleh Bakhtiar, The Bazaar of Isfahan, Twentieth Century

Source: Markus Ritter

Qeysaryeh Bazaar Gate, north side

Qeysaryeh Bazaar Gate
Serder Bazar-e Qeysaryeh
سردر بازار قیصریه

Maidan-e Shah, Isfahan
32.66029, 51.67681
Shah Abbas I (Commissioner)
AD: 1602/AH: 1011/Yaz: 971

Opposite the entrance to the King's Mosque, probably built whilst extending the maidan with a second row of shops and the addition of a floor in 1602, the monumental entrance to the bazaar was constructed at the northern end of the square. The portal with figurative murals and large clock and bell (no longer extant) was not only the entrance from the square to the Qeysaryeh, but in the opposite direction, before the modern road breakthroughs, it was also the only architecturally-composed access to the Maidan, continuing to the palace district. Its role as the main portal to the square and palace area is confirmed by its formal position: Of all the buildings at the Maidan, the atrium of the portal has the greatest depth. In contrast to the other sides, the arcades on the north side of Maidan-e Shah consist of two rows interspaced with the monumental portal with a deep atrium in the longitudinal axis of the square. The portal was flanked by two elongated wooden galleries on the upper floor. They formed an impressive frame for the portal and the atrium as well as a third floor. Travellers in the seventeenth century referred to it as a place of the ruler's musicians, naqqara Khane, or the drum tower, where "... music made by kettle drums, oboe and other instruments could be heard every night at sunset and whenever the Shah entered or left the square". The custom of drumming at sunset, which is much older than the Safavid period, is still practiced in today's Iran and Islamic India. The musicians presumably also attended receptions on the maidan and performed at polo tournaments. Reports by European and Iranian chroniclers show that Shah Abbas I included the bazaar area in royal ceremonies. A walk through the illuminated and decorated bazaar was a fascinating show, similar to the visits to factories and shopping malls during today's state visits, and was always on the agenda at receptions. Shopkeepers and artisans had to be present to exhibit their most precious goods and at the same time pretend to pursue their normal activities. The murals of Agha Reza-e Abbasi, the most famous Persian miniature painter and calligrapher of the Isfahan School, point to specific feats of Shah Abbas I. Behind the gate lie the barrel roofs and domes of the Royal Bazaar, connected to the old line bazaar. "Here", reported Chardin, "the most exquisite goods and products are found, and there is such a multitude of shops that anything available in the world can be found." The entrance to the bazaar is closed at night, but nowadays only for symbolic and not for security reasons.

View into Khiyaban-e Chahar Bagh

Chahar Bagh Boulevard
Khiyaban-e Chahar Bagh
خیابان چهارباغ

Khiyaban-e Chahar Bagh, Isfahan
32.65239, 51.66837
Shah Abbas I (Commissioner)
AD: 1602/AH: 1011/Yaz: 971

West of the palace lies Chahar Bagh Boulevard, which was not planned as a road but as a promenade, as it was then on the outskirts of the town. It started in the northwest corner of the palace, running down to the river in a straight line of about 1.5 km, crossing a magnificent bridge and leading to a great royal garden, Hezar Jerib. Eight rows of plane trees were planted along the 50 m long promenade, with roses and jasmine planted in-between. Most of the trees were planted in the presence of Shah Abbas, who added gold and silver coins as fertiliser. Five water channels ran along the avenue; the centre channel was paved with stones. Differences in the level were accentuated by individually-designed pools. On the orders of Shah Abbas I, high ranking officers and dignitaries had to establish gardens and build villas along the Chahar Bagh as well as on both river banks. This is a clear indication of the change from polycentric tribal feudalism towards a centralised, absolutist state. Jean Chardin wrote in 1668 that it was the most beautiful avenue he had ever seen. French envoys conveyed his description to the court of Louis XIV in Paris, influencing Le Nôtre's design on the spatial axis of the Champs-Élysées in 1670. The Chahar Bagh retained its charm until the end of the nineteenth century, when a nephew of Shah Abbas, who was governor at the time, ordered the felling of most of the ancient trees. Today, the large ceremonial axis and the gardens of the Safavid court have degenerated into an architecturally-undefined but vital shopping street. If someone in a leadership position had applied just a little understanding, the former atmosphere could have been preserved. On both sides of the Chahar Bagh there are still some remarkable late-Qajar and early-Pahlavi buildings constructed shortly before or after World War I.

Presentation of the Chahar Bagh Boulevard by Eugène Flandin

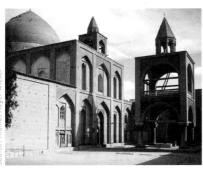

Source: Thomas Meyer-Wieser

Courtyard elevation of Kelisa-ye Vank

Vank Cathedral
Kelisa-ye Vank
کلیسای وانک

Khiyaban-e Kelisa-ye Vank,
Julfa, Isfahan
32.63491, 51.65583
David I. Julayetsi (Commissioner)
AD: 1606, 1664 / AH: 1015, 1075 /
Yaz: 975, 1033

062

The cornerstone of the Armenian-Apostolic Vank Cathedral was laid as far back as 1606, but the church was only built in 1655-1664 under the supervision of Archbishop David. In comparison to other magnificent buildings in Isfahan, the exterior of this almost insignificant-looking, ecclesiastical building reflects the glorious history of the Armenian community in architecture and style. The Vank Cathedral had great influence on the architecture and decor of the Orthodox churches in Iran and Iraq. The construction lasted from 1606 to 1655, as changes to the original plan were constantly made. Finally, the cathedral was completed as a mix of a Christian church and a mosque. The enormous interior is covered by a mosque-like dome with a cross at the top. The bell tower stands free in the yard, with Christian tombs at its base. The altar is raised, which is common in western churches. The plain exterior contrasts sharply with the interior, which is richly decorated with jewels and ornaments. Looking up just after entering, one can admire the Persian floral motifs that decorate the ceiling. Ornate paintings and carvings and precious tiles adorn the walls of the church. The masterful blue and gold frescoes in the dome depict the creation of the world, the expulsion from paradise, scenes from the life of Jesus, Armenian martyrs and the Last Judgment. The churchyard contains a memorial to the Armenian Genocide of 1915 in Turkey. A stone building, decorated with scenes from the Bible on the outside, houses a small museum and a valuable library containing over 700 Armenian manuscripts. These documents gave researchers priceless information on the history and culture of Armenians in Isfahan. Among these manuscripts one can find the foundation edict of Julfa signed by Shah Abbas I as well as sacred relics such as garments, monstrances and chalices, art treasures of the Safavids, Armenians and Europeans, as well as photographs, maps and documents about the Armenian genocide. There is also a printing device and the first book printed in Iran. One highlight of the museum is a pen drawing of Abraham by Rembrandt.

Source: Flandin, Eugène (Voyage en Perse)

Vank Cathedral presented by Eugène Flandin

Bridge of Thirty-Three Arches (063)
Si-o-Seh Pol
سی و سه پل

Maidan-e Enghelab, Isfahan
32.64444, 51.66750
*Allahverdi Khan Undiladze
(Commissioner)*
AD: 1607/AH: 1016/Yaz: 976

Brick building with thirty three arches

In 1596, when Shah Abbas I commissioned the Chahar Bagh, the construction of a bridge was planned, to connect the northern and southern sections of the promenade. Between 1602 and 1607, Chancellor Allahverdi Khan Undiladze made it a reality. The bridge is considered a masterpiece of Safavid engineering. The two-storey viaduct is designed like a brick building on stone pillars, about 300 m long and 13.5 m wide. As its name suggests, the bridge consists of thirty-three arches. The middle track was designed for pack animals and was bordered on both sides by covered passageways. Wide stairs lead to the pedestrian promenades, which run along the entire bridge on the upper floor. On the sidewalk, massive pillars form small pavilions used by picnickers enjoying the shade, the sound of water and the fresh wind of the river valley. At the southern end, there is a significantly larger arch, housing a famous tearoom. Frescoes adorned the interior walls until the nineteenth century, when they were removed because they were perceived as obscene.

The edifice even fascinated seasoned travellers like Lord George Curzon of Kedleston, from the United Kingdom, who wrote: "It is hard to believe that one has to travel all the way to Persia to see possibly the most noble bridge in the world." Lord Herbert Kitchener, a British Army officer, had its dimensions taken during his transit from Sudan to India. Due to over-exploitation of ground- and surface water, as well as declining rainfall, the Zayandeh Rud has run dry for much of the year for over a decade, since the year 2000. The Bridge of Thirty-Three Arches served as a model for the Khajou Bridge, built some fifty years later.

The Bridge of Thirty-Three Arches, a masterpiece of the Safavid era

Source: Claudius Duttwyler

Source: Claudia Luperto

Source: skyscrapercity, Churches and Cathedrals Of The World

Kelisa-ye Maryam, fresco in the pendentives

St. Mary's Church
Kelisa-ye Maryam va Hakup
کلیسای مریم و هاکوپ

Maidan-e Julfa, Julfa, Isfahan
32.63591, 51.65820
Khaje Avdik (Commissioner)
AD: 1607, 1613 / AH: 1015, 1021 /
Yaz: 976, 982

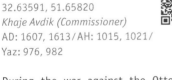

During the war against the Ottomans in 1603 and 1605, Shah Abbas I ordered the deportation of the Armenian population of Julfa, relocating them to Isfahan and granting them freedom to practice their culture and religion. In memory of their hometown, the Armenian Quarter in Isfahan was called "New Julfa". The Armenian cultural and religious community of Isfahan is not only tolerated, but also respected and supported by the Muslim population and the government. St. Jacob's Church, built in 1607 on the site of the future St. Mary's Church, is the city's oldest church. The increase of the Armenian population led to a shortage of space, so in 1613 Chadsche Avdik, an important silk merchant, decided to build at his own expense St. Mary's Church, where he was buried after his death. The magnificent interior combines frescoes, stucco reliefs and tiles with oil paintings imported from Venice.

Source: Persian Tourism Guide (2015)

Roof of St. Mary's Church

Source: Architectural Review, Mai 1976

Shah Crossroads
Chahar-su Shah
چهار سو شاه

065

Bazar-e Mokhless, Isfahan
32.66106, 51.67759
Shah Abbas I (Commissioner)
AD: 1613, 1803 / AH: 1022, 1218 /
Yaz: 982, 1172

The Chahar-su Shah also dates from the Safavid time and was rebuilt in 1803. There is another large dome three blocks north, behind which the bazaar alley curves by 45° to the east. It is clear that from here an alley as an extension of the southern bazaar of Mokhless originally continued, which supports the thesis that the old bazaar road proceeded west from Samsirgaratan Bazaar.

Zovelian House,
Polsheer House
Khaneh-ye Zovelian,
Khaneh-ye Polsheer
خانه زولیان، خانه پلشیر

066

Tabrizi-ha, Julfa, Isfahan
32.63056, 51.64694
Wesir as-Salih Talai (Commissioner),
Reza Ghanei
AD: ca. 1615, 2001 / AH: ca. 1020, 1422 /
Yaz: ca. 980, 1371

Chahar-su Shah

The Polsheer House is a remarkable place. It combines Persian, Armenian and European identities and was the headquarters of an Armenian merchant family, later serving as British consulate and now housing Polsheer, a contemporary Iranian architectural office. The house dates back to the seventeenth century. It was built by Armenian merchants, the Aghanourian family, who were also agents of the British government, so the building also served as a British consulate. This is testified by the Victoriana, copper engravings of portraits, buildings and steamships which were affixed on the plaster in the interior. The architectural heritage of the building differs from western tradition in some important aspects. There are no movement axes in the building. Instead, the circulation happens around the central courtyard – upstairs via a hallway, downstairs directly across the courtyard. Ecological aspects are of prime importance. The rooms facing south are used in winter, when the sun's heat is welcome. The rooms that open to the east and west side, which enjoy the cool breeze and escape the unrelenting heat of the morning sun, are known as shah neshin, seat of the king. The architect Reza Ghanei bought the building in 1987, shortly after the end of the Iran–Iraq war, initially as a centre for cultural exchange with the University of Cologne until political problems put an end to this plan. It then became his architectural office. A rectangular pool is located in the courtyard. Like the rest of the building, it is based on modern Iranian design. Asymmetrically-arranged, traditional peacock-blue tiles line the basin. The planting of the courtyard, with flowers arranged in patterns reflecting carpets – like in many Persian gardens – bridges the gap to the cubistic gardens of Guévrékian. The long

Source: Caroline Reichmann

Inner courtyard of Zovelian House

and complex history of the building is also the history of Iran. It is colourful, complex, influenced by a variety of cultural sources and yet very Iranian – a wonderful building. Resisting the tendency toward complete globalisation, Ghanei promotes a construction that is conscious of history and local traditions. In 2002, Ghanei received the UNESCO Asia-Pacific Heritage Award for his meticulous restoration, which took three years.

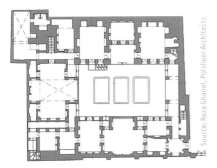

Source: Reza Ghanei, Polsheer Architects

Ground floor plan after Ghanei's restoration of Zovelian House

Source: Caroline Reichmann

Ayvan from the Qajar period in Polsheer offices, Zovelian House

Thousand Hectare Garden
Bagh-e Hezar Jarib
باغ هزار جریب

067

Khiyaban-e Chahar Bagh-e Bala,
Isfahan
32.62222, 51.66444
Shah Abbas I (Commissioner)
AD: ca. 1616/AH: ca. 1025/Yaz: ca. 985

Gardens like Bagh-e Hezar Jarib, easily accessible from the town, served as a retreat from the urban bustle. Rather than retreating to the summer palaces in Mazenderan, as was the custom of Shah Abbas the Great, the later Safavid spent the hot summer months in the garden palaces south of the city. Founded in 1616, Bagh-e Hezar Jarib no longer exists; it has been absorbed into today's city. Only a 12 m long piece of the enclosure remains. Engelbert Kaempfer describes this garden as a hortus suburbanus situated on a rise at the end of Cahar Bagh. It was a very large garden divided into two areas. It apparently contained several entrance loggias, balakhane, a central Imarat, a harem and even a maidan for polo tournaments and archery. The garden was watered by canals that drew their water from Zayandeh Rud, and consisted of beds with fragrant herbs, fruit trees and flowers. According to Kaempfer, the most beautiful feature in this garden was its main channel, shah juy, adorned by pools and cascades. It was framed on both sides by plane trees and could be seen from the talar. It was a highly articulated axis that rivalled the most successful creations found in European baroque gardens. The Italian explorer Pietro della Valle was also impressed by the beauty of the major axis of the royal gardens, stating "The garden was full of trees and rich

Source: Drawing by Mahvash Alemi

Mahvash Alemi: Reconstruction of Bagh-e Hezar Jarib according to Traktat Irshad al- Zira'ah

in fruits, but nothing can rival the beauty of the main path that starts at the house and leads to the end of the garden. This path, like all the others I later saw in the royal gardens, was covered with flag stones and lined with rows of cypresses; in the centre, a water channel formed graceful fish ponds as well as some attractive cascades, where the stone was treated in different ways so that the water was leaping and gurgling over it in several places where the path slopes downwards".

Saint Georg's Church
Kelisa-ye Gevork
کلیسای گئورگ

068

Khiyaban-e Hakim Nezami,
Julfa, Isfahan
32.63788, 51.65434
unknown
AD: ca. 1616/AH: ca. 1025/Yaz: ca. 985

This is the second oldest church in the Julfa district. The interior design of the church is kept very simple. The church is famous for the thirteen stone

Elevation of Saint Georg's Church

Source: Wikimedia Commons

Interior: Adoration of the Magi

Masjed-e Sheikh Lotfollah

blocks which were removed from the Etschmiadsin Cathedral, the Armenian Apostolic Centre of Armenia, and brought here. The stones make Saint Georg's church one of the holiest places in Julfa, maintained by the Armenian community with great devotion. The entrance is decorated with a ceramic tile artwork depicting the adoration of the Magi and dating from the reign of Sultan Husein.

Sheikh Lotfollah Mosque 069
Masjed-e Sheikh Lotfollah
مسجد شیخ لطف الله
Maidan-e Shah, Isfahan
32.65722, 51.67889
Mohammad Reza ibn Ustad Hosein Banna Isfahani
AD: 1619/AH: 1028/Yaz: 988

To the east of the square, opposite the Sublime Gate and the Royal Palace precinct, lies the colourful blue entrance gate of the Sheikh Lotfollah Mosque. It was designed in 1602 by the architect Muhammad Reza ibn Ustad Hosein Banna

Masjed-e Sheikh Lotfollah, corridor

Isfahani and – according to the inscriptions of the calligrapher Ali-Reza Abbasi – completed in 1618 – 1619. In 1622, Shah Abbas I dedicated it to his late father-in-law, Sheikh Lotfollah, a spiritual scholar native of Lebanon, whose name it bears to this day. The building is unique in several respects. Its inscription identifies it as Masjed, but the complex has only one single domed room, with no minarets or courtyard with ablution facilities common in mosques. In literature, the building is usually referred to as a private prayer house of the royal family, which is unknown in Iranian architecture. It was designed as an integral part of the transformation of Isfahan to the new imperial capital: Shah Abbas and his architects and consultants used the symbolic value of the location – outside the palace and only accessible by means of a theatrical entry through the public Maidan – to demonstrate the piety of the court. The main room covering an area of 19 × 19 m contains a prayer niche, or mihrab, which is oriented to the direction of prayer, the qibla, in such a way that the construction is ca. 45° offset to the square. This is achieved through a complicated covered passage leading from the entrance façade to the north side of the prayer hall. The façade, which was restored in the 1930s under the direction of André Godard, consists of a marble base covered in tiles with tightly intertwined floral and plant motifs. These were made in the haft rangi technique that was

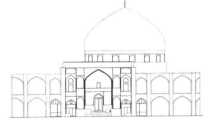

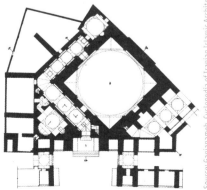

Source: Claudia Luperto
Source: Andrew Schneider

Above: Ornate front

Left: view into the inner dome

developed due to Shah Abbas' impatience to complete his buildings, and replaced the expensive, time-consuming mosaic art of the early Safavid and Timurid periods. Depending on the movement of light, the colours of the dome tiles change from pink to beige to caramel. Blue colour dominates in the interior, but it is striking that many elements are worked in a reddish ochre, a colour that is usually reserved for women. The mosque was also connected to the Sublime Gate situated opposite by an underground passage under the Maidan-e Shah to protect the female members of the royal family from prying eyes.

This passage was rediscovered during the construction of a large water basin in the 1950s. In his travelogue *The Road to Oxiana*, the British travel writer Robert Byron delighted: "I have never encountered splendour of this kind before. Other interiors came to mind as I stood there, to compare it with Versailles, or the porcelain room at Schönbrunn, or the Doge's Palace or St. Peter's. All are rich; but none so rich. Their richness is three-dimensional. It is attended by all the effort of shadow: In the Mosque of Sheikh Lutfulla it is a richness of light and surface, of pattern and colour only. The architectural form is unimportant. It is not smothered as in rococo; it is simply the instrument of a spectacle, as earth is the instrument

of a garden. And then I suddenly thought of that unfortunate species, modern interior decorators, who imagine they can make a restaurant, or a cinema or a plutocrat's drawing-room look rich if given money enough for gold leaf and looking glass. They little know what amateurs they are. Nor, alas, do their clients."

Source: Ganjanameh, Cyclopedia of Iranian Islamic Architecture, Shahid Beheshti University

Floor plan and eastern elevation

Source: Jaroslava Hašková (Mapio.net)

Courtyard elevation of Kelisa-ye Beit ol-Lehem

Source: Nuran Zorlu

Pendentives of Kelisa-ye Beit ol-Lehem

Bethlehem Church
Kelisa-ye Beyt ol-Lahm
کلیسای بیت لحم

Khiyaban-e Nazar, Julfa, Isfahan
32.63639, 51.65778
*Khajeh Petros Vali Janian
(Commissioner)*
AD: 1628/AH: 1038/Yaz: 997

Another impressive church in Julfa is the Bethlehem Church, which is located on the site the Armenians believe to be the true birthplace of Jesus Christ. The church was founded in 1628 by the Armenian Khajeh Vali Petros Janian whose portrait is found on an inner wall of the church. It has the largest dome of all churches in Isfahan. The influence of Islamic architecture is strong, integrating many Islamic elements such as onion domes, arches and even minarets as spires. The frescoes created by Armenian artists are much more delicate than those in the Vank Cathedral, combining Persian and Armenian ornaments similar to the Safavid buildings in their patterns, colours and designs. The backgrounds are often finished in black or gold and depict scenes from the bible which are depicted much more realistically than the almost-comic ones in the Vank Cathedral.

Royal Bath
Hammam-e Shah
حمام شاه

Bazar-e Mokhless, Isfahan
32.66056, 51.67722
Shah Abbas I (Commissioner)
AD: 1629/AH: 1039/Yaz: 998

The Hammam-e Shah belongs to an early building complex of the Bazaar north of Maidan-e Sah. Jean Chardin wrote that Shah Abbas I commissioned this bath for his personal use but occasionally

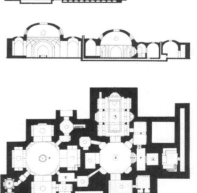

Source: Ganjanameh, Cyclopedia of Iranian Islamic Architecture, Shahid Beheshti University

Hammam-e Shah: floor plan and section

Garmkhaneh of Hammam-e Shah

Morteza Bekhradi at his home, 2014

allowed it to be opened to the public. The bathhouse was still in use until recently. The building is already mentioned in a waqf document from 1605. The Hammam-e Shah is accessible from the main entrance of Mokhless Bazaar and from a passage to the side entrance of the Karbasforusha Bazaar. The painstaking faïence work lends a special appearance to the building within the bazaar. Like most Iranian baths, the building consists of two main areas: sar bineh, the dressing room, and garmkhaneh, the warm bath hall. A fairly large area next to the bath hall is occupied by a swimming pool, chal-e hose. The sar-bineh is a large, octagonal hall, in the centre of which sits an octagonal pool. Large elevated platforms with flat vaults define the space on four sides and also define separate areas. The central area of the sar-bineh is lit by a large skylight, and each platform has its own skylight. The design of the swimming hall is octagonal and surrounded by alcoves. The north side of the garmkhaneh adjoins an area which is called kiseh-kesh-khane and is fed by a large water basin. The chal-e hose, whose large pool was used in summer for swimming, is located on the opposite side.

Bekhradi House
Khaneh-ye Bekhradi
خانه بخردی

Kujeh-e Sonbolestan, Isfahan
32.66669, 51.67481
Morteza Bekhradi
(Commissioner) et al.
AD: ca. 1650/AH: 1060/Yaz: 1020

Bekhradi House was built during the Safavid dynasty. It lies in Sonbolestan, a pre-Islamic village which was absorbed into the city structure. The house lies west of the remains of the Jamaidan palace which dates from the Seljuk period. The Bekhradi house is registered in the list of national historic buildings. It is the first and only Safavid house that has operated as a traditional boutique hotel since 2005. Mr. Bekhradi, the current owner, adhered to the original architectural design in the restoration, which lasted from 1999 to 2005, whilst the interior was completely renovated. The hotel offers a total of five suites, ranging in size from one to three rooms, all including bathrooms. The talar has been repurposed as a dining room, and a traditional tearoom has been installed in the basement. The hotel can accommodate up to nineteen guests.

Aerial view of the complex

Shah Mosque
Masjed-e Shah
مسجد شاه

Maidan-e Shah, Isfahan
32.65444, 51.67750
Ali Akbar Isfahani,
Mohib Ali Beikollah
AD: 1630/AH: 1040/Yaz: 999

073

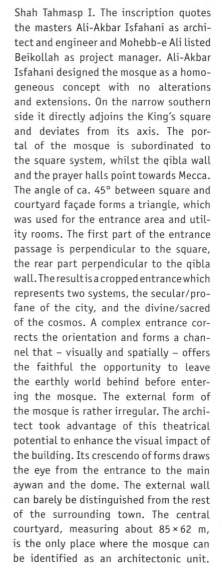

The Masjed-e Shah on the southern side of the Maidan-e Naqsh-e Jehan represents the crowning glory of the building works carried out under the patronage of Shah Abbas I. The Shah Mosque emphasises the importance of the monumental square as a new urban centre. The early Safavid reign was characterised by the debate over the legitimacy of the Friday prayer during the absence of the Mahdi. Heated theological discussions exposed the contrast between the Safavid Shiites and the Sunnis, especially the Ottomans, who were accused of apostasy and illegitimacy. It was only after the judgment by the religious authority, presided over by Shaikh Lotfollah and Shaikh Baha-e that the political-religious dilemma was resolved, paving the way for the construction of the mosque. The monumental edifice on this important urban site reaffirms the legitimacy and authority of the Safavid as well as the interconnection of politics and business on the one hand and Twelver Shia as the state religion on the other. According to the inscription at the entrance ayvan, Shah Abbas I commissioned the building of this mosque and dedicated it to his grandfather Shah Tahmasp I. The inscription quotes the masters Ali-Akbar Isfahani as architect and engineer and Mohebb-e Ali listed Beikollah as project manager. Ali-Akbar Isfahani designed the mosque as a homogeneous concept with no alterations and extensions. On the narrow southern side it directly adjoins the King's square and deviates from its axis. The portal of the mosque is subordinated to the square system, whilst the qibla wall and the prayer halls point towards Mecca. The angle of ca. 45° between square and courtyard façade forms a triangle, which was used for the entrance area and utility rooms. The first part of the entrance passage is perpendicular to the square, the rear part perpendicular to the qibla wall. The result is a cropped entrance which represents two systems, the secular/profane of the city, and the divine/sacred of the cosmos. A complex entrance corrects the orientation and forms a channel that – visually and spatially – offers the faithful the opportunity to leave the earthly world behind before entering the mosque. The external form of the mosque is rather irregular. The architect took advantage of this theatrical potential to enhance the visual impact of the building. Its crescendo of forms draws the eye from the entrance to the main aywan and the dome. The external wall can barely be distinguished from the rest of the surrounding town. The central courtyard, measuring about 85 × 62 m, is the only place where the mosque can be identified as an architectonic unit.

Source: Caroline Reichmann

Passage to the courtyard

Source: Caroline Reichmann

Wall cladding

The rich faïence ornamentation indicates that in this courtyard one is in the heart of the building from which everything else is arranged in the proper order. It is simultaneously external and internal, whilst the ceiling is heaven itself. Indeed, the design of the courtyard façade appears to have been the architect's primary concern. The interior walls of the ayvan and the courtyard façades are clad in glazed tiles. Every visible surface of this amazing structure is covered, internally and externally, with square, multi-coloured, mostly dark-blue tiles on a solid marble slab. If the aim of Islamic architectural ornament is the dissolution of solid mass, it is completely achieved here. The main dome is constructed of two shells: the outer shell is 14 m higher than the inner, elevated on a high drum with a sixteen-sided transition zone. Calligrapher Ali Reza was responsible for the craftsmanship. In order to save time, a new combustion technology for glazed tiles, haft rangi, was employed for the first time, replacing the use of inlaid mosaic. This technique made it possible to bake up to seven colours on one tile simultaneously, without the colours running into each other. The Shah Mosque is a masterpiece of the Islamic renaissance. The almost thousand-year-old Iranian-Islamic mosque architecture "created a tradition which has influenced all subsequent Iranian architecture and found its crowning glory in the mosque of Shah Abbas with its play between outer portal, inner ayvans and vaulted prayer rooms".

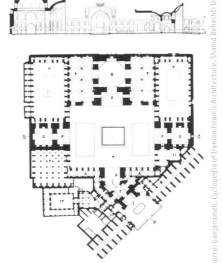

Floor plan and section

Source: Ganjanameh, Cyclopedia of Iranian Islamic Architecture, Shahid Beheshti University

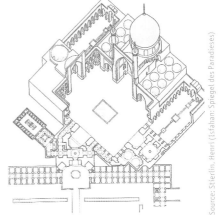

Axonometric projection

Source: Stierlin, Henri (Isfahan: Spiegel des Paradieses)

Middle Eastern Palace Architecture

Royal Palaces and Gardens

The striking lightness of Middle Eastern palaces compared to their European counterparts can be explained from their archetype – the tent – on which many are based. In his travelogue from the fourteenth century, Ibn Battuta described the travelling court of a Tartar Sultan and Abu al-Fazl, the biographer of the Mughal ruler Akbar, informs us in detail about the system and arrangement of such royal tent cities. It is believed that this portable royal architecture not only influenced many pavilions but sometimes also parts of the city design, which may have absorbed the structure of the camp

Junayd: Divan Khwaju Kirmani: Prince Humay in front of the palace of Princess Humayun, 1396

in strongly geometric form. Ruy González de Clavijo and his contemporary Ali Yazdi reported on feasts and receptions that took place in these palaces as well as outdoors, in meadows and open parks with no permanent structures.

One of the greatest festivals was the celebration of the wedding of Ulugh Begh, the grandson of Timur. About 20,000 tents were erected haphazardly for the royal party in the space of three to four days. Butchers and cooks offered their wares, bakers kept their ovens warm and wooden cabins were erected as bathhouses, each with its own boiler for hot water. On the day of the wedding, people dressed in their finery, taxes and debts were paid and everyone flocked to the camp where the "air smelled better than nutmeg and the water was sweeter than sugar, so that one thought it was part of the gardens of paradise". In the centre of the complex was the royal camp, cordoned off by a 300 m long wall made of silk. This wall was "as tall as a rider on his horse", secured between posts, crowned by a pinnacle of coloured fabric, with only a single doorway.

The tent of the ruler was situated inside this wall. Clavijo's description makes it possible to reconstruct this pavilion. "It had the shape of four squares. It measured three lengths of a lance in height, such as used by soldiers on horses, and the sides were about 30 m from corner to corner. The ceiling of the pavilion was round so that it formed a dome supported by twelve posts, each as broad as a man's chest. The posts were painted in blue, gold and other colours. Four of the twelve posts were erected in the corners, with two more in-between. The exterior walls of the pavilion were made of silk fabric woven into white, black and yellow ribbons. At each corner a rod was attached, crowned by an apple with a crescent. The bars were very high and formed the framework of a tower made of silk, creating a kind of pinnacle. There was a hallway from the bottom to the tower to maintain the whole edifice. It was a wonderful sight which is difficult to describe". Clavijo was fascinated by the light and colourful tents and the festivals, of which he described at least a dozen.

Something of these ephemeral, temporary residences is inherent to most Middle Eastern palaces, even where they crystallised into an aesthetically highly ornate architectural language. It is no coincidence that the tales of *A Thousand and One Nights* are interspersed with images of magically-built, easily-moved palaces that can rise and disappear in the blink of an eye. The palaces were mostly composed

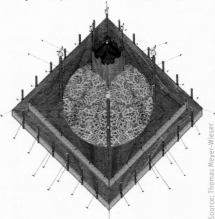

Source: Thomas Meyer-Wieser

Reconstruction of Timur Lenk's tent

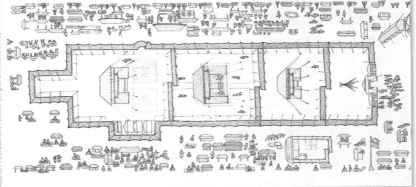

Source: Petruccioli, Attilio (Il giardino Islamico)

Attilo Petruccioli: Reconstruction of an Imperial Camp

Timur Lenk in his garden in Samarkand

Source: Hattstein, Markus / Delius, Peter (Islam: Kunst and Architektur)

of several royal, domestic, economic and administrative complexes which were often only loosely connected by intermediate courtyards or gardens. Within such composite structures, linear spatial sequences, perspective alignments and elaborate stairways were deliberately avoided. The connecting lines were interrupted, offset orbroken to prevent unwanted interference and to maintain the independence of each part.

This, of course, did not spell the absence of symmetry and axial order, but only played a role in the individual spatial components and were expressed by gardens, pools or opposing gates whose balanced arrangement gave each courtyard a self-contained character. The complexity of the palace was not immediately obvious to a stranger; it was a safety precaution, but also a means to surprise visitors. Eyewitness accounts

Topkapi Sarail in Istanbul

Source: Petruccioli, Attilio (Il giardino Islamico)

Arched roof in Hasht Behesht Palace

and Middle Eastern storytellers portray hidden wonders and treasures of palaces. They describe intricate passageways, leading through covered interior passages, arcades and open garden courtyards, allowing ever-changing views of water features, rare plants, wild animals, birds and golden trees with rare fruits, until the throne hall is reached, where the sultan sits under a canopy amid precious rugs and silk cushions.

The legendary kings who created this splendour were Alexander the Great, the Sassanid king Cuhusrau and, above all the biblical King Solomon who (according to the Qu'ran) had a host of jinns at his beck and call who instantly granted him every wish for precious halls and paintings. It was he who conjured up the mirrored crystal floor which the Queen of Sheba mistook for a water surface, according to Piero della Francesca.

Piero della Francesca: Meeting between Solomon and the Queen of Sheba 1454 – 1459

1629–1722
The late Safavid in Isfahan

Shah Abbas the Great ordered the execution or blinding of several of his sons and grandsons without giving them a political education or preparing them for rulership. The Safavid rulers raised their princes in an atmosphere of terror, intrigues and rumours as prisoners of the harem, causing most of them to develop into naïve eccentrics or severely mentally-disturbed people, which ultimately contributed to the decline of the Safavid empire. The central government lost its influence under these successors. Only Shah Abbas II reformed and consolidated the empire. Under his aegis, close trade contacts with the European maritime powers of England and Holland were established. Towards the end of the seventeenth century, under the rule of Sultan Husayn, a sharp economic decline took place. His reign saw the downfall of the Safavid dynasty, which had ruled Persia since the beginning of the sixteenth century. He had a reputation for being easy-going and had little interest in political affairs. He was nicknamed Yakhshidir, "Very well!", the response he was said to give when asked to decide on matters of state. Sultan Husayn's rule was relatively tranquil until he faced a major

revolt in Afghanistan, in the easternmost part of his realm. In 1709, Afghan Sunnis of the Ghilzai tribe rebelled and successfully broke away from Safavid rule. In 1716, Safavid expeditions to bring them back under control ended in failure. In the meantime, Sultan Husayn was confronted by other rebellions resulting from revival of Shia Islam. In 1722, the Afghan ruler Shah Mahmud Hotak and his army swept westward, aiming at the shah's capital Isfahan. Rather than biding his time within the city and resisting a siege in which the small Afghan army was unlikely to succeed, Sultan Husayn marched out to meet Mahmud's force at Golnabad. Here the royal army was thoroughly routed and fled back to Isfahan in disarray. Mahmud's siege of Isfahan lasted from March to October 1722. Lacking artillery, the Afghans were forced to resort to a long blockade in the hope of starving the Persians into submission. The siege of Isfahan in 1722 by Afghan invaders, the massacre, the looting and destruction mark the end of Isfahan as the capital with a tragedy as terrible as its rise had been spectacular. This, as well as the growth of European trade especially from the Dutch, degraded Isfahan's significance The subsequent history of architecture and urban planning of Isfahan pales beside the Safavid period.

Urban area of Isfahan ca. 1722

The master plan of Shah Abbas I was so sustainable that subsequent urban development adhered to these planning principles and anchored new urban functions in Safavid town planning. The palace area and the large garden district from the sixteenth century developed into a true dwelling place for the blessed, and Shah Safi I, Shah Abbas II and Shah Suleiman expanded this with ceremonial palaces. The new residential areas southwest of the city were connected with the suburban palaces on the Zayande Rud over the Khaju Bridge, and by the eponymous Chahar Bagh-e Khaju Avenue. Smaller mosques and madrasas are scattered throughout the city, of which many were endowed by ladies of the royal court or by senior officials, such as the Grand Vizier Saru Taqi or the court physician Hakim Mohammad Dawood. The bazaars were embellished with additional caravanserais or with domed buildings and other public facilities at intersections. The last

Safavid Shah, Soltan Huseyn, commissioned the construction of a complex of madrasa, caravanserai and bazaar of considerable urban and architectural interest. His extreme religiousness and his refusal to limit the power of the clergy went hand in hand with his visual and literal retreat into the bosom of the harem. The baroque splendour of the Madrasa Mader-e Shah is a testament to the amazing development of the city during its hundred years as the Safavid capital.

Development of the urban area of Isfahan ca. 1722

Source: Thomas Meyer-Wieser

Beq'a Baba Rokn od-Din, elevation

Source: Caroline Reichmann

Mausoleum Baba Rokn od-Din (074)
Beq'a Baba Rokn od-Din
بابا رکن الدین شیرازی
Takht-e Foulad, Isfahan
32.62444, 51.68111
Shah Abbas I (Commissioner)
AD: 1629/AH: 1039/Yaz: 998

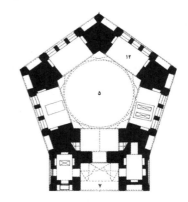

The inscription on the tombstone of Baba Rokn–al–Din dates back to 1367, but according to the inscriptions on the building the construction was commissioned by Shah Abbas I and completed under Shah Safi. Jean Chardin noted in his travelogue that the mausoleum was covered with faïence inside and out. Several celebrities, including Allaverdi-Khan were buried next to Baba Rokn–al–Din. The mausoleum is located in the cemetery Takht-e Foulad, and the tombstone of Baba Rokn–al–Din is the oldest there. Today the exterior façade is covered with turquoise-coloured ceramic tiles, and the area between the arches is decorated with faïence. The pentagonal plan bears a resemblance to the Villa Farnese in Caprarola or the Castel del Monte.

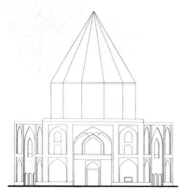

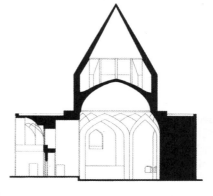

Plan, section and north façade of the Mausoleum

Source: Ganjnameh, Cyclopedia of Iranian Islamic Architecture, Shahid Beheshti University

Caravanserai Koohpayeh
Karvansaray-e Koohpayeh
کاروانسرای کوهپایه

Rah-e Isfahan-Nain,
ca. 75 km from Isfahan
32.71328, 52.43578
Shah Abbas I (Commissioner)
AD: from 1630/AH: from 1040/
Yaz: from 999

According to the village elders there was an inscription on the building attributing the construction to Shah Abbas I and dating back to 1630. The caravanserai was temporarily used as a police station and is still largely intact. The building ranks among the largest caravanserais in the country. As in other caravanserais the courtyard is enriched by ayvanaches with rooms situated below. Four ayvans are grouped around the central courtyard, three of which have sehdaris at the back. These rooms were reserved for wealthy travellers. The stables are located behind the common rooms. They are interspersed in the middle by the rooms behind the ayvan and thus divided into four sections, which are accessible from the corners of the courtyard. Spacious lodgings for camel drivers are located near the entrance. The caravanserai is entered from the southeast. The high entrance portal is flanked on two floors by ayvanaches and protrudes from the front façade, thereby generously accentuating the entrance. The alternating larger and smaller arcades, flanking towers, pinnacle and brick decorations contribute to the importance of the building and transform it into grandiose architecture. Two octagonal rooms, accessible only from the outside, flank the portico and distinguish the construction from other caravanserais. Above these rooms there are further rooms which are oriented only towards the outside and lend a soft, non-desert element to the building. A large vestibule on two floors creates the impression of a timcheh.

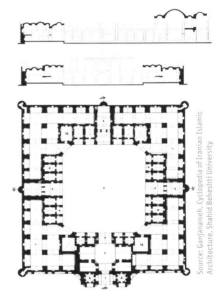

Source: Ganjanameh, Cyclopedia of Iranian Islamic Architecture, Shahid Beheshti University

Plan and section

Source: Ganjanameh, Cyclopedia of Iranian Islamic Architecture, Shahid Beheshti University

View into the courtyard of Koohpayeh Caravanserai

Above: Pascal Coste, Interior of the Palace Sar Pushideh
Left: Engelbert Kaempfer, Engraving of a reception in the Talar-e Tavile

Riding School
Talar-e Tavile
تالار طویله

Maidan-e Shah, Isfahan
32.65650, 51.67547
Shah Safi I (Commissioner)
AD: from 1630/AH: from 1040/
Yaz: from 999

During the reign of Shah Safi, the successor of Shah Abbas the Great, two new palaces were constructed, the Talar-e Tavile in the Dawlat Khan and the Khan Ayne on the southern bank of the Zayande Rud. Neither is extant. The architectural arrangement of Talar-e Tavile is unusual: Instead of a square design, the plan is based on the longitudinal axis, and the traditional relationship between solid and void is abandoned in favour of complete emptiness. Porticoes were not new, but the special feature of this hall opens a new chapter in Persian architectural development. In contrast to the horizontality of the porticoes in Achaemenid palaces or contemporary talars, Talar-e Tavile consisted of a series of columned spaces completely open on three sides and representing a new architectural type. European descriptions tell us that the Talar-e Tavile was specifically used for large feasts, sometimes with more than 500 guests. Building and rebuilding was the rule of the time. In the early nineteenth century, a pavilion, Sar Pushideh, was built at the behest of Said al-Daula Mirzac. Unfortunately, this structure did not outlast the century. The drawing shows how the walls of a typical gazebo were essentially turned inside out, probably so that the shelter could be used in cooler temperatures.

Pascale Coste, Perspective of Mirror Pavilion, 1840

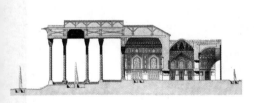

Section

Elevation

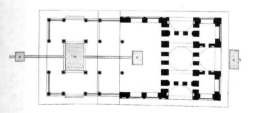

Pascal Coste, Plan of Mirror Pavilion

Garden of Happiness
Bagh-e Saadat Abad
باغ سعادت آباد

Zayandeh Rud, Isfahan
32.63667, 51.68333
Shah Safi I (Commissioner)
AD: from 1630/AH: from 1040/
Yaz: from 999

On the south bank of the river, at the eastern end of the new city, a royal garden extended to the Pol-e kahju Bridge. The area was called Saadat Abad, "place of bliss" and was described by several contemporary poets. The most important buildings there were Haft Dasht (Seven Wonders), Ayne Khan (Hall of Mirrors) and Namakdan (Salt Cellar). The engraving by Pascal Coste shows the Hall of Mirrors as he saw it in the mid-nineteenth century, with the Pol-e kahju Bridge in the background. The building was destroyed at the end of the nineteenth century. With its talar, a type of porch in front of other rooms, it looked very similar to the Chehel Sotun. Ayne Khan illustrates the fundamental importance of the garden as

Source: Voyage en Perse, avec Flandin, ed. Gide et Baudry, 1851

an intrinsic part of court life. The palace, composed of semi-open elements such as ayvan and talar, perpetuates the continuity of the garden space, even if that space is then surrounded by walls. The dominant transparency as well as the spatial and visual connection to the exterior, which was achieved in Talar-e Tavile and Ayne Khan, marks a turning point in Iranian palace architecture. Of similar size was Farahabad, a palace town built in the early eighteenth century by Shah Soltan Huseyn. This was the main residence of the last Safavid king, and the Afghans orchestrated the siege of Isfahan from Farahabad in 1722.

Engelbert Kaempfer, Reception at Bagh-e Saadat Abad

Source: London, British Library, ms. Sloane 5232

Courtyard of Masjed-e Saru Taqi

Saru Taqi Mosque
Masjed-e Saru Taqi
مسجد ساروتقی

078 D

Bazarche Masjed-e Saru Taqi,
Isfahan
32.65314, 51.68000
Grand Vizier Saru Taqi (Commissioner)
AD: 1643/AH: 1053/Yaz: 1012

The builder of the mosque, Saru Taqi, was Grand Vizier under Shah Safi I and Abbas II. He had caught the eye of Shah Abbas the Great, who in 1612 appointed him governor of Mazandaran province. In 1617, Gilan was also put under his administration. In 1634, he was promoted to Grand Vizier. He was considered incorruptible

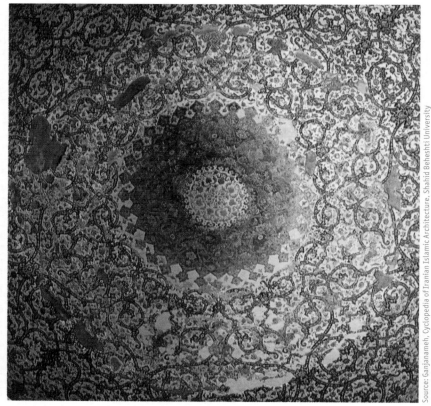

Dome in the Square Prayer Hall

Source: Ganjanameh, Cyclopedia of Iranian Islamic Architecture, Shahid Beheshti University

Courtyard of Madrasa-ye Jadde-ye Kuchak

and intolerant of misappropriation and embezzlement. The main purpose of his policy was to strengthen the position of the Shah against the emirs. Conspirators from the royal court murdered him and his family in 1645. A wooden door from the bazaar street opens to the mosque through an ayvan enclosed at the top with stalacites. The entrance leads to a vestibule, then a two-nave hall and another room. The archaic yard is octagonal, with ayvans to the northwest and southwest. A high ayvan leads from its southeast side into a square prayer hall covered by a dome. In the centre of all four sides, plastered, lime-washed ayvans recede, painted to emphasise the structure of the building. The courtyard and the hall on the north side are more recent. Mohammad Hosain Khan had strongly promoted construction activity in the area, and in view of the fact that the shape and decoration of the courtyard are reminiscent of other complexes from the first half of the nineteenth century, the restoration of the yard can be dated back to his governorship.

Small Madrasa of the Grandmother
Madrasa-ye Jadde-ye Kuchak
مدرسه جده کوچک

Bazar-e Qannad-ha, Isfahan
32.66611, 51.68111
Delarm Khanom (Commissioner)
AD: 1646 / AH: 1056 / Yaz: 1015

An inscription on the gate dates the construction of Madrasa Jadde-ye Kuchak to the year 1646. According to written sources, the construction was commissioned by Delarm Khanom, the grandmother of Shah Abbas II, and completed by Valid Aqa. The word jadd means both ancestor and grandmother; written sources confirm that the younger grandmother of Shah Abbas simultaneously commissioned the building of the Madrasa Jadde-ye bozorg. Kuchak (lesser) and bozorg (greater) refer to the size of the construction and also to the rivalry between the two women. The school is still in use, but the recently-installed steel doors and windows diminish its architectural quality.

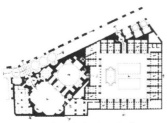

Floor plan of Masjed-e Saru Taqi

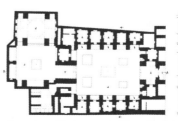

Source: Ganjanameh, Cyclopedia of Iranian Islamic Architecture, Shahid Beheshti University

Floor plan of Madrasa-ye Jadde-ye Kuchak

Source: Ganjanameh, Cyclopedia of Iranian Islamic Architecture, Shahid Beheshti University

View into the Saray-e Saru Taqi

Saru Taqi Commercial Building (080)
Saray-e Saru Taqi
سرای سارۆ تقی

Khiyaban-e Baru-Ashraf, Isfahan
32.66222, 51.67972
Grand Vizier Saru Taqi
(Commissioner)
AD: 1646/AH: 1056/Yaz: 1015

The Saray-e Saru Taqi lies in an area of the bazaar that is no longer prosperous, but the quality of the building is testimony to the high standard of the Safavid period. The northern entrance is located in the Saray, whilst the southern portal forms a half-dome in the bazaar, which is executed in excellent muqarnas brickwork. The small mosque of the complex is also situated here. A tulut inscription by the calligrapher Muhammad-Reza Emami gives 1646 as the building date. The founder was the Grand Vizier Saru Taqi, a reformist civil servant and head of government who was killed in a conspiracy. The atmosphere of the building, the perfection as a whole and the details, shapes and proportions of the Safavid period make this complex one of the most significant bazaar buildings in Iran. Unfortunately, large parts of the building are now destroyed and conservation measures need to be taken urgently. The large complex consists of several sarays, a vestibule and a passage which forms the backbone of the design

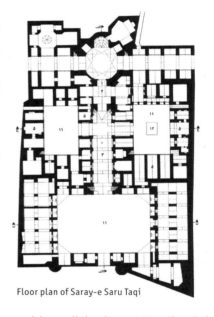

Source: Ganjanameh, Cyclopedia of Iranian Islamic Architecture, Shahid Beheshti University

Floor plan of Saray-e Saru Taqi

and draws all the elements together. As is usual, the vestibule is at the entrance and shows the mastery of the Safavid architects in connecting rectangular shapes. The passage begins with a semi-octagonal, elegantly-domed space in whose corners two staircases are cleverly placed. The saray consists of a simple courtyard surrounded by two-storey arcades with identical size rooms. Varying the width of the central openings in the north and south introduces diversity into this rhythm. The openings are formed by small ayvans which are interconnected upstairs, forming a loggia-like access.

Large pool in front of the main entrance of Forty Columns Palace

Forty Columns Palace
Kakh-e Chehel Sotun
کاخ چهلستون

081 D

Khiyaban-e Ostandari, Isfahan
32.65722, 51.67194
Wesir as-Salih Talai (Commissioner)
AD: 1647, 1706 / AH: 1057, 1118 /
Yaz: 1016, 1076

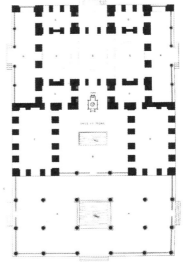

Pascal Coste: floor plan, 1840

Forty Columns Palace, situated in the royal garden opposite the private chambers (the Chehel Sotun), is a well-preserved building and a highlight of every visit to Isfahan. It is the largest building of the palace district. With the adjacent gardens extending to the Maidan-e Shah in line with the axis of the maidan, the core of the building was possibly part of the overall urban planning of Shah Abbas I. However the palace itself was built during the reign of his successor, Abbas II, and was restored in 1706 after a fire. It is located behind an elongated water surface, 110 × 20 m, and consists of three distinct parts which lie transversely to the actual rotation axis. A stately talar in the front area is followed by banquet and reception halls. Kakh-e Chehel Sotun marks the conclusion of the architectural implementation of the experiments which began with Talar-e Tavile. It created the formal framework for the practice of celebration as an imperial ritual, a peculiarity of the Safavid court. The French traveller

Jean Chardin excellently described these opulent rituals taking place in Chehel Sotun, where a large number of guests conversed and discussed politics with the Shah. This type of feasting and entertaining, where the Shah personally acted as host, was the Safavid response to the demand that the Shah as a representative of the Imams was accessible to everyone. This was in sharp contrast to the reserved manner of Ottoman and Mughal sultans, who were prohibited public displays of such profane activities as eating or drinking, particularly in company. A detailed drawing by Eugène

Ceiling at Forty Columns Palace

Flandin allows insight into the palace. The layout of the pavilion reflects Persian ingenuity, where the open outer space and the enclosed interior space were interconnected in such a way that it was difficult to say where one begins and the other ends. The front of the pavilion is dominated by a large porch with twenty overlong wooden pillars reflected in a long water basin. There is consensus that the name of the palace, Forty Pillars, refers to these, but this interpretation may be incorrect as the word for forty in Persian also translates to "very many". Already in the seventeenth century some authors, reporting on palaces and gardens of Safavid rulers,

realised that the buildings were based on designs used by the Achaemenids. Indeed, when the Perso-Armenian Petrus Bedik described the palace of Cyrus in Persepolis as theatrum quadraginta columnarum, he identified it as the archetype of the Chehel Sotun. This is frequently pointed out in writings by European travellers. In the nineteenth century Charles Texier wrote: "Present-day customs of the Persian court can be found in just about all traditions which were practiced at the court of Carius and which are revealed to us when we examine the monuments of this period carefully. To my mind, Chehel Sotun, the favourite residence of Shah Abbas II, mirrors the great throne room of Persepolis." A fusion of inside and outside is enhanced by the generous use of glass which virtually removes the wall area. The ceiling of the portico is brightened by coloured wood mosaic into which small mirrors in different shapes are inserted, and the muqarnas vaulted entrance-ayvan is covered with small pieces of glass which refract the light. Other surfaces were enhanced with large continuous mirrors of Venetian glass, gifts of the Doge. In the centre of the terrace, four massive stone lions spout water into a marble basin and the royal throne was obviously placed in the ayvan behind. The wall

Soffit of Forty Columns Palace

Shah Abbas receiving the Uzbek Khan

behind the throne is covered in mirrors, lending this area an airy, intangible character. Four entrances lead from the talar to the reception room, which takes up the entire width of the pavilion. Six large oil paintings hang on the upper half of the walls, helping the viewer to visualize the turbulent and pleasurable court life of the seventeenth century. One of these paintings shows Shah Abbas at a reception of the Khan of the Uzbeks. Both sit on cushions and Shah Abbas, with cloth turban and moustache, holds his cup out to be refilled. In the background, servants bear golden platters, and in the foreground, girls with castanets and tambourines are dancing. Other paintings show historical events like a battle against the Ottoman

Outside of the palace

Porch with wooden columns

Eugène Flandin: Palais de Tchehel-Sutoun, Ispahan, 1840

Sultan. The adjoining rooms are decorated with delicate patterns surrounded by flowers and birds, scenes designed in the style of miniature paintings. The second coronation of Suleiman I, originally Shah Safi II, took place in this palace in 1668 and was attended by Jean Chardin. In Chardin's day, sumptuous banquets were frequently held in the main hall, lasting three or four hours. On these occasions the Shah sat on a throne covered with expensive fabrics and richly embroidered with pearls, gold and silver. In September 1970, an international architectural congress on the "interaction of tradition and technology" took

Source: Voyage en Perse, avec Flandin, ed. Gide et Baudry, 1851

place in the Forty Columns Palace and was attended by Louis Kahn, Buckminster Fuller, George Candilis and Paul Rudolph. Queen Farah Diba Pahlavi, a former student of architecture and an enthusiastic patron of architecture and the arts, presided. In the 1970s, her role acquired a strong political dimension when she was appointed royal regent and was given the title Shahbanou, literally "woman king", a title bestowed on female monarchs by the Sassanids. The concept of Shah and Shahbanou as royal couple should be seen as a gesture of gender equality and created a modern, pseudo-historical image of the Pahlavis.

Courtyard of Madrasa-ye Jadde-ye Bozorg

Big Madrasa of the Grand-mother
Madrasa-ye Jadde-ye Bozorg
مدرسه جده بزرگ

082

Bazar-e Qannad-ha, Isfahan
32.66556, 51.68083
Younger grandmother of Shah Abbas II.
AD: 1648/AH: 1058/Yaz: 1017

The Madrasa Jadde-ye Bozorg is located in the bazaar. The courtyard is classical, with four ayvans, and the decoration in glazed pottery is remarkable. An inscription on the gate dates the building to the year 1648. Sources say that the younger grandmother of Shah Abbas II ordered its construction at the same time as the elderly grandmother, Delarm Kanom, built her madrasa. The construction dates back to the late Safavid period, restored in the early 2000s. Today the loggias of the façades are closed with wooden doors.

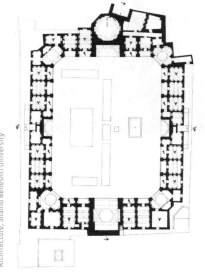

Floor plan of Madrasa-ye Jadde-ye Bozorg

Khaju Bridge
Pol-e Khaju
پل خواجو

083

Maidan-e Khaju, Isfahan
32.63667, 51.68333
Shah Abbas II (Commissioner)
AD: ca. 1605/AH: ca. 1060/ Yaz: ca. 1020

The Pol-e Khaju bridge was built in 1650 by order of Shah Abbas II on the foundations of an earlier bridge from the fifteenth century, which linked Isfahan to the old road to Shiraz. It is 132 m long and 12 m wide and connects Chahar Bagh Khaju with suburbs to the south of the river. It rests on a broad foundation, which has tip-shaped spouts facing the flood side to break the flow of the water and guide it through the lower arched passages. In order to achieve this effect even at high water levels, the buttresses also have pointed lobes. The floodgates attached to the arches can be closed if necessary to dam the water. This was used to irrigate gardens on higher ground when the water level of the river was too low. As is the case with other Safavid bridges, the Pol-e Khaju is not only a means of crossing the river, but also a recreation area. The bridge is constructed on two levels: On the lower level there are open niches with shaded seating; the upper level consists of a passage enclosed by walls and lined with an arcade. Its centre contains an octagonal pavilion with

viewing platforms, which shows a particularly interesting application of the ayvan: The arcades lining the central driveway open in two half-octagonal ayvans towards the river. The art of creating open spaces that overlook canals and gardens serves to enhance the sight of Zayandeh Rud, itself unusual and spectacular. The causeway is designed as a place of delight and is a veritable "water architecture" that could be admired from the talar of the pavilion in Bagh-e Saadat Abad. The centre aisle served caravans and long distance trade, whilst the slightly-elevated outer arches were reserved for pedestrians. The bridge has been described by many travellers, including in 1684 the German physician and explorer, Engelbert Kaempfer, and in 1892 the Marquess Curzon of Kedleston, who called it "the most handsome bridge in the world". Persian and European chroniclers describe the festivities in the central pavilion and along the bridge which served as a stage for fireworks, boat races and the like. (Shortly after its completion, Shah Abbas II ordered the bridge to be decorated with lights and flowers for the Nouruz festival.) The interior surfaces of the pavilion and the walls of the central passage were covered in tiles (now sadly lost) with a distinctive striped pattern. Sir William Ousley's observation of so-called "erotic" images suggests that at least part of the wall paintings were of a figural nature, similar to those seen on the walls of the palace of Chehel Sotun, which appeared risqué to Ousley's Victorian eyes. Jean Chardin quotes an inscription on the wall decoration: "The world is truly a bridge; pass over it. Weigh and measure all that you meet with on your passage. Evil surrounds the good everywhere and penetrates it."

Pascal Coste: view of Khaju-Bridge

Source: René Hochueli

Hakim Mosque
Masjed-e Hakim
مسجد حكيم

Khiyaban-e Hakim, Isfahan
32.66306, 51.67444
Muhammad Ali ibn Ustad
Alibeyk-e banna Isfahani
AD: 1663/AH: 1074/Yaz: 1073

The Hakim Mosque close to the bazaar was built between 1656 and 1663 during the reign of Shah Abbas II. Doctor Hakim Mohammad Dawud, a converted Jew and court physician of Shah Safi and Shah Abbas II, moved to India, where he prospered under the Great Mughals and endowed the mosque in his name. The Hakim Mosque replaced the Buyid Jurjir mosque of which only the gate remained. Hakim Mosque, with its four hectares, is the largest four-ayvan Mosque in Isfahan after the Friday Mosque. In contrast to the other Safavid mosques, large areas, particularly in the ayvan and the dome over the mehrab, are alternately decorated with glazed and unglazed tiles. The architect,

Mohammad Ali Isfahani, was the son of the master-builder Ali Beg, whose name is mentioned in the foundation inscription of the king's mosque. By commissioning artists and architects connected to royal projects, Hakim Dawud competed with native Gholams and the elite of the Safavid court. Masjed-e Hakim shows that a mosque is not a consecrated place like a church or an antique temple but first and foremost a public building serving a variety of functions. It is meeting place for the daily prayer, a Qu'ran school, a community centre with similar functions as in the West, sanitary facilities

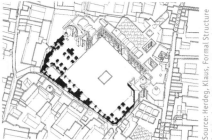

Source: Herdeg, Klaus, Formal Structure in Islamic Architecture of Iran and

Klaus Herdeg: Axonometric projection of Hakim Mosque

View of the two-storey Madrasa-ye Molla-Abdollah

and shelter for travellers. It is the first sign of the community one encounters in the residential street and therefore a vessel of the community. The Hakim Mosque does not have one imposing entrance but rather five different ones, and is therefore often used as a shortcut; it is a public, monumental space like the Roman Forum. The internal organisation of the maidan, the courtyard of al-Hakim, a typical residential house or a living space always follows the same pattern. A longitudinal axis dominates the space; one or more transverse axes define the rooms behind. The relationship between space and courtyard is similar to those in the examples mentioned, a logical sequence from the niche in the wall to the room, from the room to the inner courtyard and from the entrance of the mosque to the maidan.

Qu'ran School Molla-Abdollah (085)
Madrasa-ye Molla-Abdollah
مدرسه ملاعبدالله

Chahar-su Shah, Isfahan
32.66017, 51.67819
Shah Abbas I (Commissioner)
AD: 1677 / AH: 1088 / Yaz: 1046

The main entrance to the Madrasa-ye Molla-Abdollah is from Chahar-su-Shah, and there is a side entrance from Zalman Street. In his *Journal*, Jean Chardin in 1711 called this mosque the largest and most beautiful mosque of Isfahan. An inscription on the south ayvan dates the madrasa to the year 1677. It

was endowed by Shah Abbas I, and its name refers to a famous scholar, Molla-'Abdollah Shusstari, who was its first rector. A water channel, Madi-e Fadyan, branches off from Zayandeh Rud and flows through the central courtyard, giving it a special atmosphere. The yard is enclosed by double-storey buildings, now once more used by theological students as classrooms. In the 1930s, the original use was abandoned and the building was used for commercial purposes. From the main gate a long, slightly-offset passage leads into the yard. At its northeast side is the mosque which is part of the madrasa, a rectangular basilica covered by nine cloister vaults on four pillars. The courtyard is bordered by four cells on two floors, arranged in pairs around the middle ayvan. The basic structure of the building does not differ from a saray of the same age. Instead of geometric decorations of the frontal fields encountered in some sarays, plant decorations are found here.

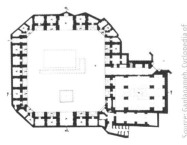

Floor plan of
Madrasa-ye Molla-Abdollah

Source: René Claudius Duttwyler

Source: Claudia Luperto

Exterior view of Hasht Behesht

View into the garden

Eight Paradises
Hasht Behesht
هشت بهشت

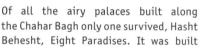

Khiyaban-e Bagh-e Goldaste, Isfahan

32.65336, 51.67010

Shah Suleiman (Commissioner)

AD: 1669/AH: 1080/Yaz: 1038

Of all the airy palaces built along the Chahar Bagh only one survived, Hasht Behesht, Eight Paradises. It was built near the former Bagh-e Bolbol, Garden of the Nightingale, shortly after the accession of Shah Suleiman, and was one of the most richly-decorated buildings in town. It was not built in the public area of Dawlat-Khan, but south of the harem. Its location as well as its architectural design both point to private use. Descriptions of leisurely outings of the ladies of the court took place here, which concurs with the architectural and decorative features. As the name suggests, the building

Dome with masterly muqarnas vault

Source: Caroline Reichmann

Source: Claudia Luperto

Interior of the palace

was constructed on an octagonal base with cut corners, accentuated by massive, two-storey columns perforated by niches with pointed arches. All four sides are equipped with spacious verandas supported by a pair of tall, thin wooden columns. The conventional floor plan has an unusual corner configuration, as illustrated by Pascal Coste. Especially charming is the view from the central interior space; the supporting structure relates to the dome as usual, but the lantern and the portals are wide open to the outside, and the cladding is kept as bright as possible. At the centre of the octagonal pavilion there is a hall with a muqarnas vault which is one of the masterpieces of Islamic art. Although it apparently turns the court into an interior, its real intention is to visualise the circling

Pascal Coste, view of Hasht Behesht, 1840

Source: Monuments modernes de la Perse mesurés, dessinés et décrits, éd. Morel, 1867

celestial sphere. The skylight inserted into the dome drum lights up all facets of the highly complex stalactite structure, as if it were the inside of a crystal splitting the light into finest particles, thereby capturing the immediate quality of the light beam, transforming and showing it in countless shades of light and dark. On the upper level, the construction has galleries and rooms, each of which has its own shape and decor. Some are equipped with water basins and fountains, which are fed through a system of lead water pipes set into the wall; others are completely lined with mirrors. Four ayvans opening to the garden make the connection between garden and palace. The central basin, with its numerous fountains, was fed from a channel leading around the building, which Engelbert Kaempfer described in 1685 as follows: "The pavilion is located in the middle of a quadragonal courtyard paved with stones. A channel flows around it and marble benches are placed here at regular intervals. Two avenues, aligned from north to south and lined with plane trees lead to the pavilion, whilst water flows in

Eugène Flandin: Hasht Behesht with central water basin, 1840

Source: Voyage en Perse, avec Flandin, éd. Gide et Baudry, 1851

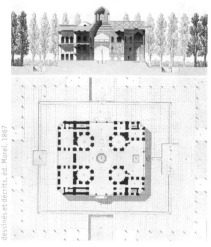

Source: Monuments modernes de la Perse mesurés, dessinés et décrits, éd. Morel, 1867

Pascal Coste, floor plan and section, 1840

Qu'ran School Kasse Garan
Madrasa-ye Kaseh Garan
مدرسه کاسه گران

Maidan-e Qiyam, Isfahan
32.66806, 51.68500
Muhammad Momen ibn Ali Beik,
Muhammad Ibrahim ibn Ismail Banna
AD: 1697 / AH: 1109 / Yaz: 1066

The Madrasa Kasse Garan was commissioned in 1697 by Mir-Mohammad-Mehdi Hakim-ol-Molk Ardestani, who worked in India as a doctor and was amply rewarded with jewels for healing the Great Mughal Aurangzeb's daughter. He donated said jewels for the construction of this madrasa. On the gate, Muhammad Momen, the son of Ali Beik, is named as architect, and on the southern ayvan Muhammad Ibrahim ibn Ismail Banna. The construction dates back to the Safavid period and, based on the data available, can be placed in the reign of Shah Suleiman. The Madrasa Kasse Garan is part of the transformation of the Maidan-e Kohne carried out by NJP Consulting Engineers. The saray in the bazaar, which was largely destroyed in the 1950s and 1960s by the modernisation program of the Pahlavi, as well as the madrasa, will be restored in the course of the new square design and clearly separated at the back by the surrounding traditional context. Such detachments are today still observed in many places in the country. Whilst in the 1920s the continuity of neighbourhoods was interrupted by newly created streets, today the individual historical monument is taken out of its context and left to stand alone to fully display its architectural effect as a historic monument.

transverse channels to a pool populated by swans and ducks". The building itself, along with the garden, looks like a late echo of the Timurid period, with its preference for holding court outdoors. For the French writer Jean Chardin, Hasht Behesht was an "ornamental masterpiece of colourful extravagance and indulgence in decorative abundance, a mirror of the superficial love of luxury of the court and symbol of the decadence of the ruling monarch". The garden of Hasht Behesht has, in recent years, been transformed into a lovely public park.

Source: Monuments modernes de la Perse mesurés, dessinés et décrits, éd. Morel, 1867

Pascal Coste, Interior perspective of the palace, 1840

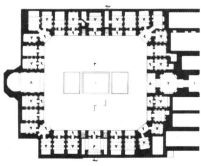

Floor plan of Madrasa-ye Kaseh Garan
Source: Ganjanameh, Cyclopedia of Iranian Islamic Architecture, Shahid Beheshti University

Source: The Architectural Review, May 1976

View into the courtyard

Mosaver al-Molk House
Khaneh-ye Mosafer al-Molk
خانه مسافر الملک

088 D

Khiyaban-e Malek, Isfahan
32.65369, 51.68654
Mosafer al-Molk (Commissioner)
AD: ca. 1650/AH: ca. 1060/Yaz: ca. 1020

The Khaneh-ye Mosaver al-Molk is one of the best preserved and very typical seventeenth-century houses in Iran. The original entrance is at the end of an elongated passage and is accessed via a traditional octagonal entrance which leads to three other houses. Between the entrances are pedestals used by the guards to sit and chat. The rectangular reception room where the host welcomed his guests is located at the end of the typical bent access, thus visually protecting the private areas. The spatial arrangement of the court follows the classical scheme: The public areas in the north are built over the basement and lend prominence to the house's main area, which is enhanced by the height of the rooms. Two staircases lead to the upper floor, which traditionally served as guestrooms or for the ladies of the house to take part in festivities without being seen. The side wings on one side contain the living quarters for the family of the parents and on the other side the quarters for the married daughters or sons. They consist of a central space flanked by a bedroom and a cloakroom. In the hot season, the family used the summer apartments on the south side of the court. These are grouped around the badgir, a massive, octagonal wind tower that rises from the ground floor through to the roof, divided into vertically-arranged ventilation ducts that open in all four directions and can be closed individually for control. Like all traditional houses, the Mosaver-al-Molk house is built of sun-dried mud bricks made from the soil of the property. This also explains why the houses are, without exception, below street level. The brickwork was built on a stone foundation. The floors in the building are made of brick, while the interior walls are plastered. The exterior walls, the brick domed roof and the wood ceiling were sealed with a waterproof mixture of clay and straw.

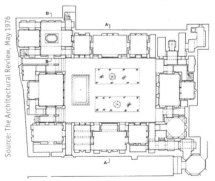

Source: The Architectural Review, May 1976

Floor plan

Source: Claudia Luperto

Entrance façade to Madrasa-ye Nimavard

Qu'ran School Nimavard
Madrasa-ye Nimavard
مدرسه نیماورد

Bazar-e Nimavard, Isfahan
32.66547, 51.67919

Zeinab Beigum (Commissioner)
AD: 1706 / AH: 1117 / Yaz: 1075

The madrasa Nimavard is located on the east side of Nimavard Bazaar near the intersection. The inconspicuous exterior hides – apart from the Medese Mader-e Shah at Chahar Bagh which is not readily accessible for visitors – one of the finest theological schools in Iran. Inside there is a beautiful Persian garden, which was planted as a traditional four-ayvan complex. A rectangular water basin lies in its centre, bordered by four sunken flower beds planted with trees, a Chahar Bagh symbolizing the Garden of Eden. The almost-square courtyard is bordered on all sides by high ayvans and four, two-storey cells arranged in pairs. Three cells can be accessed from the receding corners. The building bears no inscription to suggest its date of origin. Above the gate, a religious inscription from the 1930s is attached. About this time, a thorough restoration seems to have taken place. When Jean Chardin described Nimavard in 1677, the madrasa evidently did not yet exist as he did not mention it in his book. The historian Ansari names the founder as Zeinab Beigum, wife of Muhammad Mahdi Ardestani who was the builder of the Madrasa Kasse Garan, and 1705 as the year of construction.

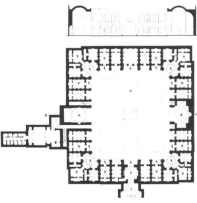
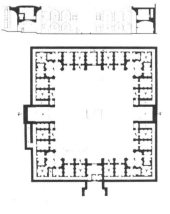

Source: Source: Ganjanameh, Cyclopedia of Iranian Islamic Architecture, Shahid Beheshti University

Floor plans and section

089 Madrasa-ye Nimavard

Source: Markus Gasser (Bild- & Planführer für Studienzwecke)

Aerial view of the complex

Caravanserai and Qu'ran School Mother of Shah and Bazaar Honar

090

Karvansara va Madrasa-ye Mader-e Shah va Bazar-e Honar

کاروانسرا و مدرسه مادر شاه و بازار هنر

Khiyaban-e Chahar Bagh, Isfahan

32.65170, 51.66990

Shah Sultan Husayn (Commissioner)

AD: 1706 / AH: 1118 / Yaz: 1075

The Mader-e Shah complex is one of the most extraordinary examples of Safavid architecture in Isfahan. The power and glory of the Safavids, but especially their legitimacy as rulers of Persia had to be clearly demonstrated to the Islamic world. The architect succeeded in producing an organic whole, which offered the traveller many amenities. Apart from the lodgings and the necessary housekeeping facilities there were ayvans where one could sit and chat late into the night or listen to musicians and storytellers by the dim light of oil lamps. There was also a shady garden with its canal and a huge, vaulted bazaar with eighty shops located on both sides of the longitudinal axis where one could buy the necessary provisions for the voyage. The mosque of the madrasa also offered pilgrims an opportunity for reflection. The Caravanserai and Qu'ran School Mother of Shah and Bazaar Honar is a religious foundation, or waqf, which donated property, buildings and so on for a charitable purpose. If successful long-distance traders or governmental, military or religious leaders made huge profits – legally or illegally – they

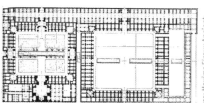

Maxime Siroux, ensemble of the foundation Mader-e Shah

Source: Maxime Siroux Ancient roads and monuments of Ispahán,

Pascal Coste: School of Mother of Shah, minaret and details

preferred to invest their money in urban real estate which they then turned over to religious foundations. This ensured that they were safe from expropriation and largely beyond the reach of the sovereigns. The income of the foundations had to be only partially used for religious purposes; a part could be retained by the donor, and the rights from a waqf were inheritable. Even with political upheavals, a change of dynasties or valid conviction of the founder, the foundation remained protected by religion. Thus pious foundations were in past centuries the safest way to secure property titles,

to finance income and retirement and to safely pass it all on to one's descendants. It goes without saying that there were repeated infringements of the law, and income was diverted for personal gain. The rulers endowed such complexes – in or out of the town – mostly in their lifetime – and supported them with generous donations. This income was used not only for the maintenance of the building but also the payment of the staff, students and imams who could live there and pray for their salvation. The necessary revenue was generated by renting out bazaars, business premises and caravanserai.

View of the cupola of Madrasa-ye Mader-e Shah

Pascal Coste, Courtyard of the Caravanserai, 1840

Caravanserai Mother of Shah (091)
Karvansaray-e Mader-e Shah
کاروانسرا مادر شاه

Khiyaban-e Amadegah, Isfahan
32.65138, 51.67056
Shah Sultan Husayn
(Commissioner)
AD: 1706/AH: 1118/Yaz: 1075

This caravanserai, built about 300 years ago, was called Mehmansara Abbasi or Karvansaray-e Mader-e Shah. *Mehmansara* can be translated as "guesthouse" or "hotel", *karvansaray* or caravanserai as "hostel". But a caravanserai was not only a hostel; it was also a warehouse and trading centre. The Caravanserai Mother of Shah was built under Sultan Husayn in the seventeenth century and dedicated to his mother. Even then the buildings enclosed a large, square garden, through which a water channel ran which offered visitors a refreshing and peaceful atmosphere. The structure of the caravanserai is solid and functional: On ground floor were shops leading to the yard; accommodation for the travelling merchants was upstairs. Wholesalers, who belonged to the upper classes of society, rented space in urban caravanserai, and local traders

Source: Abbasi Hotel

Courtyard of Abbasi Hotel

Source: Coste, Pascal (Monuments modernes de la Perse)

as well as domestic and foreign agents were able to view and purchase the goods here. The court of the caravanserai was a very lively trading centre. After the fall of the Safavid dynasty, the caravanserai was badly damaged and used by the cavalry. In 1957 the government decided to convert the caravanserai into an international hotel, which was designed by French architect Maxime Siroux, who had previously studied caravan buildings in Iran. The basic structure of the complex was maintained. The renovation had two aims, namely the preservation of the original court façades and the transformation of hodshrehs, the former living quarters of the caravanserai, into a first class and unique luxury hotel with modern rooms. In 1971, the hotel complex was enlarged by Ali Bakhtiar & Associates by creating a beautiful addition, built in a typical contemporary Iranian brick style and divided into an old and a new part. The rooms in the historic part were partially decorated with gold and turquoise walls in Safavid and Qajar style, which have a high, somewhat abstruse quality. The movie *Ten Little Indians*, starring Oliver Reed and Elke Sommer, was filmed in the complex in 1974.

Source: Abbasi Hotel

Lobby of Abbasi Hotel

Entrance to the classroom

Qu'ran School Mother of Shah ⓿92
Madrasa-ye Mader-e Shah
مدرسه مادر شاه

Khiyaban-e Chahar Bagh, Isfahan
32.65168, 51.66900
Shah Sultan Husayn
(Commissioner)
AD: 1706 / AH: 1118 / Yaz: 1075

Ironically, Shah Sultan Husayn spent the last night before his beheading in the Madrasa-ye Mader-e Shah as prisoner of the Afghans. In comparison to the classic Safavid buildings of Shah Abbas, this magnificent building shows profound stylistic innovations which are not immediately apparent upon entering. For example, the ayvans of the madrasa are much more complex than those of the Shah Mosque. The sober simplicity of the Shah Mosque arises from rectangular or sometimes triangular floor plans, which always result in very clear and balanced façades, with wide surfaces enlivened by large ceramic fillings. The Qu'ran School Mother of Shah is quite different. On each side of the ayvan there is a sort of apsis with smaller niches within, resulting in an almost baroque spatial look. Where the Shah Mosque forms smooth, rectangular, calm surfaces, the Madrasa has chamfered corners and recesses, which in turn form small ayvans within large ones and divide each space infinitely, whereby its ceilings split further into stalactites,

pendentives and facets. There is a strict logic in this multiple zoning – nothing is arbitrary, and everywhere you see the tendency to bring all the principles of the Safavid era to their ultimate conclusion. The ornamentation, too, emphasises this in the linear dryness of the dark bands, following the lines of force. But this is only a visual structuralism; in fact, the curving technology has developed so far that the pendentives and facets have almost no relief and therefore serve no load-bearing function. Even the stalactites no longer have a structural purpose: They are added to the smooth vaults by using wooden scaffolding clad with gypsum. Furthermore, the supporting structure of the dome no longer shows the typical profile of the Persian keel arch with four centre points arranged in a semicircle; rather, it has a blunt profile that is flattened to a third of its height. The southern dome shows an interweaving of black, yellow and white arabesques on a turquoise background. The previous emphasis on floral patterns is reduced in favour of a simpler contrast between masonry and yellow mosaic panels. The theological college surrounds an idyllic courtyard where the Farshadi channel was reinterpreted as a central pond, lined with tall cypresses and pine trees. Even today, the restored buildings radiate the power of a peaceful oasis in the centre of Isfahan.

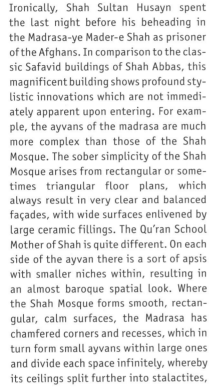

Source: René Hochueli

Ayvan of the madrasa

Source: Flandin, Eugène (Voyage en Perse)

Garden

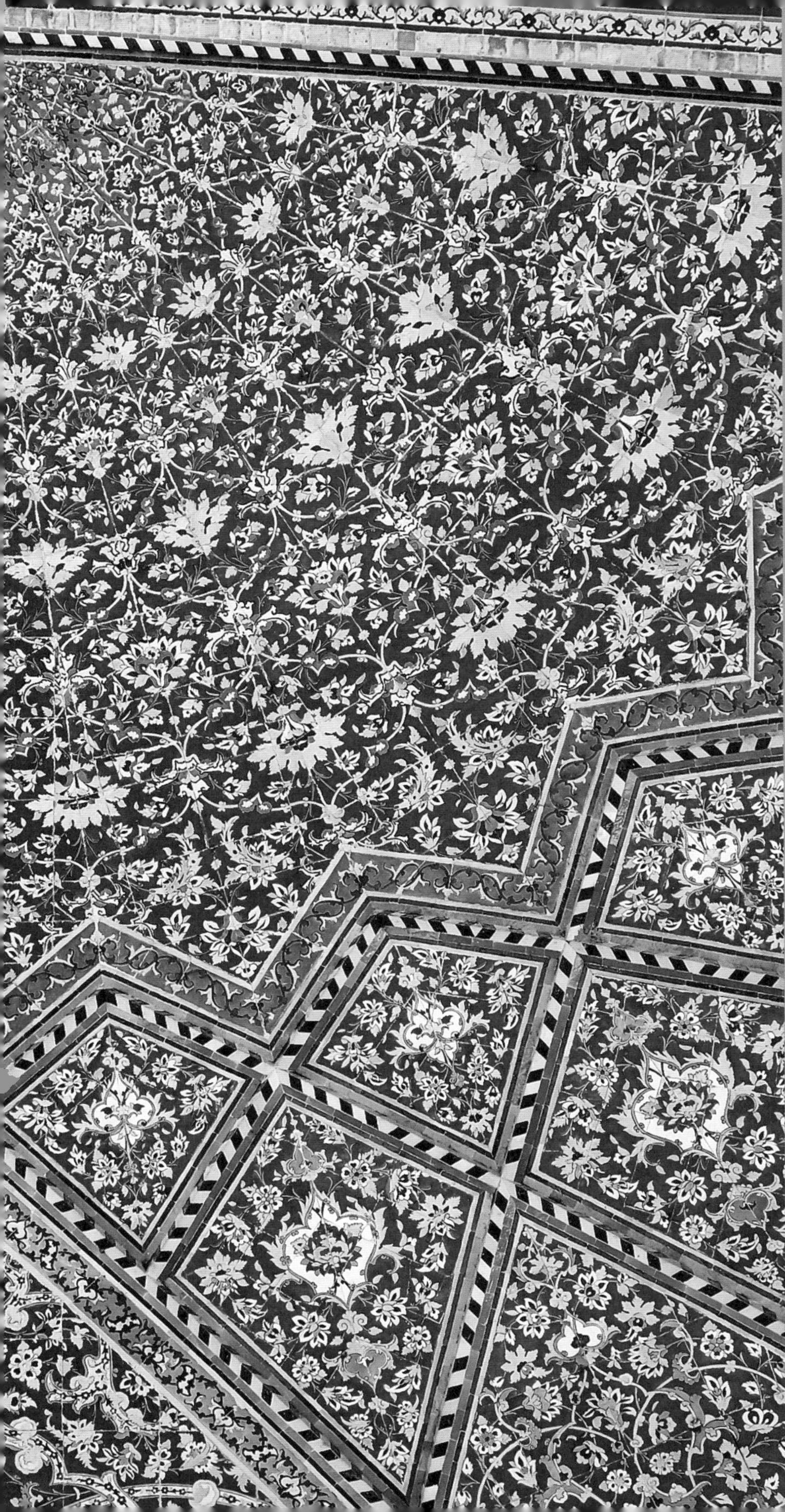

The bazaar as original Islamic heritage, here Bazar-e Honar

Honar Bazaar
Bazar-e Honar
بازار هنر

Khiyaban-e Chahar Bagh, Isfahan
32.65230, 51.66960
Shah Sultan Husayn
(Commissioner)
AD: 1706 / AH: 1118 / Yaz: 1075

Trade played a dominant role in the Islamic town, along with religion and welfare. With the expansion of the Islamic empire, trade relations experienced a similar expansion. Markets and warehouses in towns like Isfahan were stocked with precious goods, and many European companies maintained permanent representation until the end of the eighteenth or sometimes into the nineteenth century. Business centres of this type neither existed in the ancient Middle East, nor in classical antiquity or medieval Europe. Thus, the bazaar (*suq* in Arabic) is perhaps the only fundamentally distinctive feature of the Middle Eastern town that is *not* rooted in the ancient Middle East, and which therefore must be seen as an independent Islamic cultural heritage. The transformation of the bazaar into an enclosed, consistently functional system is one of the great achievements of the Islamic Middle Ages. The Bazar-e Honar is elongated, illuminated only by regular beams of sunlight, like an interior passage with built-in cabinets on both sides. The individual store opened and closed like a closet from the alleyway, usually offering only enough space for the owner and his wares. The bazaar is one of the few remaining business centres consisting of the previously-common typology of double-storey units for artisans, with shops on the ground floor and workshops upstairs. They inspired the designs of the French *passage* in Paris or the Italian *galleria* in Milan or Naples.

Tohid House
Tohid Khaneh
توحیدخانه

Khiyaban-e Ostendari, Isfahan
32.65722, 51.67583
unknown
AD: 17. / 18 Jh. / AH: 1411 /
Yaz: 1359

The recently-renovated Tohid Khaneh, situated just behind the Ali Qapu, today serves as a school of arts and crafts of Isfahan. It is a good example of a khanqah, a place of meditation for Sufi monks. The term is often incorrectly translated as monastery. A sixteen-angular pavilion stands in the middle of a large courtyard, which is surrounded on four sides by hojrehs often encountered in traditional madrasas. The pavilion has large arches on the four main sides. These ayvan-like elements are the same height as the surrounding walls. The one situated opposite the qibla wall is adorned with rich, finely-crafted faïence. The central space is vaulted with a semi-dome which rests on a short tympanum.

Source: Aga Khan Award for Architecture

Tohid-Khaneh, formerly a place of meditation for Sufi monks

Garm-khane of the bathhouse

Secondary room of the hammam

Source: Markus Gasser (Bild- & Planführer für Studienzwecke)

Bath Ali Qoli Aqa
Hammam-e Ali Qoli Aqa
حمام على قلى آقا

Khiyaban-e Masjed Seyyed, Isfahan
32.66778, 51.66750
Ali Qoli Aqa (Commissioner)
AD: 1710/AH: 1122/Yaz: 1079

The hammam was created in 1710 by Ali Qoli-Aqa, a eunuch who served in the harem of Safavid Shah Suleiman and Shah Sultan Husayn. It was part of a larger complex that consisted of a mosque, a bazaar, a saray and a chaharsu. The bath was used until 2000 but is no longer in use today. The complex consists of a large and a small bath-house, was alternately used by men and women and has two main areas, a cold sar bineh and a warm garm-khane, which are placed as close to each other as possible. It is also noteworthy how a regular floor plan was placed on an irregular plot, contributing to the perfection of the design. The sarbineh is designed as an octagon, surrounded by regular platforms. The pillars and the difference in height of the ceiling between central and side rooms define the passageway and the rest area.

On one side it opens to the vestibule, on the other to main-dar, which connects it with the garm-khane and leads to other service rooms including a coffee shop. Another area, the chal-e hose, is used for swimming in summer. Skylights accentuate the geometry of the ceiling and provide a chiaroscuro effect that enhances the relief and lights the bathroom.

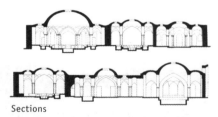

Sections

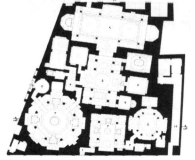

Floor plan

Source: Qassemi, Kambiz Haji (Ganjnameh)

Source: Qassemi, Kambiz Haji (Ganjnameh)

View into the courtyard of the caravanserai

Caravanserai Scheich Ali Khan 096
Karvansaray-e Sheikh Ali Khan
کاروانسرای شیخ علی خان

ca. 35 km northwest from Isfahan
32.93294, 51.51317
Ustad Taher ibn Reza Isfahani
AD: 1729 / AH: 1142 / Yaz: 1098

The inscription at the entrance indicates that the caravanserai was commissioned by minister Sheikh Ali Khan Zanganeh in 1729 and built by architect Ustad Taher, son of Reza Isfahani. The caravanserai covers an area of 80 × 80 m around a yard measuring 35 × 50 m. In the centre of the courtyard elevations are four ayvans flanked by ayvanaches, which are connected to the rooms behind. The stables extend beyond this space. They are accessible via the corners of the courtyard. On the south side of the caravanserai, two independent units were built around two smaller courtyards which probably served as private accommodation. The entrance of the building is in the centre of the south side, and its high portico with two-storey flanking arcades protrudes from the front façade. The arcades widen the façades in both directions, and by reducing their depth at the side end, the architect combines them with the massive circular wall, creating a perfectly-designed façade. The vestibule is skilfully vaulted and lit over two floors. On the courtyard side, it appears as an ayvan, facing an ayvan of equal height on the opposite side, which houses the two-storey shah-neshin. The arrangement of the high building elements on the entrance axis, on the one hand, and the symmetrical arrangement on the east-west axis, on the other, increase the architectural importance of this building in turn.

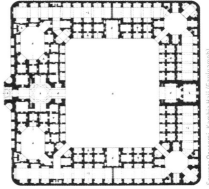

Floor plan

Source: Qassemi, Kambiz Haji (Ganjnameh)

1722–1779
From Capital of the Empire to Provincial Town

The early Safavid rulers, as heads of the Sufi order and with their religious charisma, could still limit the power of the Shiite clergy. But when weaker characters took over, the clergy gained more and more influence over state affairs which soon had an effect on the religious minorities: Jews and Zoroastrians faced humiliations, while Christians fared little better because Armenian merchants were needed to conduct business with Europeans. The decline of economic prosperity in the late seventeenth century was due to a number of factors: The shifting of trade routes mainly damaged the Iranian silk trade; the incompetent Shahs who had grown up in harems were manipulated by courtiers; the rise of local nobility at the expense of the central government resulted in reduced tax revenues and led to an even more ruthless exploitation of the taxpayer. With the collapse of the Safavid

Source: Thomas Meyer-Wieser

Urban area of Isfahan up to 1779

kingdom after the conquest of Isfahan by the Afghans, the Afsharid General Nadir Khan unified Persia and expelled the Afghan Ghilzai. He formally fought for the Safavid Shah Tahmasp II, who was politically powerless. In 1730, Nadir Khan gained control over the whole of Persia, but with Shah Abbas III, a Safavid was again appointed as Shah of Persia. He only ascended the throne himself in 1736 as Nadir Shah and founded the Afsharid Dynasty. The government of Nadir Shah was marked by constant campaigns. For instance, after the submission of Ghilzai in Afghanistan, he started a campaign against the Great Mughals of India. With the conquest of Delhi in 1739 at the Battle of Karnal, the "peacock throne" came to Persia. Other campaigns led him to Bukhara and Khiva. In 1747 he expelled the Ottomans, who had taken occupation after the overthrow of the Safavids, from Azerbaijan and the Caucasus. Despite his great military successes, Nader Shah could not stop the economic decline of the empire, and because of the high taxes required for the maintenance of the army, the economy suffered further. He had also neglected the administrative and financial consolidation of his rule, resulting in the rapid decline of the dynasty. Nader became increasingly cruel as a result of his illness and his desire to extort more and more tax money to pay for his military campaigns. New revolts broke out and Nader crushed them ruthlessly, building towers from his victims' skulls in imitation of his hero Timur. Nader Shah was assassinated in 1747. He was surprised in his sleep by Salah Bey, captain of the guards, and stabbed with a sword. After his death, heavy infighting erupted in Persia again. In 1796, the Afsharid Dynasty was overthrown by the Qajar. In the meantime, the Zand princes asserted themselves in large parts of Persia.

Urban area of Isfahan up to 1779

During the reign of the Afghan Ghalzai, who were annihilating each other in civil wars, and the subsequent turmoil under Karim Khan Zand and Nadir Shah, urban development stagnated. Zel os-Soltan, the eldest son of Naser al-Din Shah, was governor of Isfahan from 1872 to 1907. Intending to stir up fear and terror among the people, he ordered the indiscriminate destruction of important Safavid palaces because they were reminders of the splendour of the glorious past. One of these was Chehel Sotun Palace, which was, however, rescued by Malek ol-Tojar, a well-known businessman. There is no record of the many buildings he reduced to rubble, but they included Ayne Khan, the Hall of Mirrors, Sar Pushideh and Khyaban-e Cahar Bagh (the latter of which managed to retain its charm to the end of the nineteenth century, when Zel os–Soltan ordered most of the old trees to be cut down).

Today, the large ceremonial road and the gardens of the Safavid court have degenerated into an architecturally-undefined but lively shopping street. The palace zone, the large garden area from the sixteenth century, developed into an undefined business district of the Qajar period.

Source: Claudia Luperto

Renovation of a Safavid dome

Zariy Baf House
Khaneh-ye Zariy Baf
خانه زری باف

Khiyaban-e Chahar Bagh-e Paeen/
Kujeh-ye Rashtiha, Isfahan
32.66306, 51.67056
Zariy Baf (Commissioner)
AD: ca. 1670/AH: ca. 1180/Yaz: ca. 1130

The name means House of the Gold Brocade Weavers, and the two courtyards were possibly part of a larger complex originally belonging to this weaver guild. The octagonal entrance hall led to two different entrances, part of other courtyards and gardens. The smaller yard is a perfect miniature of a house that may have been inhabited by the guild guard. On the north side of the larger courtyard is an unusual building that was probably used for storage of the precious material, and also as an exhibition space. Behind the first rooms are hidden areas, based on a cross-shaped ground plan and dominated by a central chimney that lit and ventilated the five rooms.

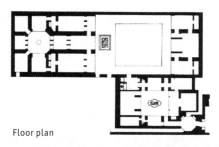

Floor plan

Pool in the courtyard of Khaneh-ye Zariy Baf

Rooftop view of Saray-e Golshan

Golshan Complex
Saray-e Golshan
سرای گلشن

Bazar-e Golshan, Isfahan
32.66325, 51.67814
*Haggi Aqa Muhammad Zamani
(Commissioner)*
AD: 1779/AH: 1193/Yaz: 1148

The Saray-e Golshan is part of the town's largest commercial complex. It lies on the east side of the Bazaar Golshan and is connected to it by two dehlizes (shopping arcades). Just before the passage opens into the courtyard, stairs lead north and south from it to the upstairs rooms and the roof, which offers a magnificent view over the bazaar street. The saray courtyard is accessed from the passages. The ship-shaped courtyard is surrounded by low, single-storey shop buildings with keeled arches which, despite their different dimensions, are harmonious and emphasise the spaciousness of the court. The courtyard has large flower beds and a round pool. The lush vegetation creates a green oasis in the middle of the town. The ground-floor plan gives the impression that the architects first designed a courtyard away from the remaining sarays, around which they then developed the single-storey building as an independent, adjustable

Source: Claudia Luperto

building mass filling the gaps between the existing buildings. From the four corners of the courtyard, passages connect the saray with the surrounding rooms. The location of the entrances at the corners of the courtyard and the water basins in front of it are characteristic and resulted in the main activities taking place here. A passage in the northeast leads to a small, ship-shaped saray, which is surrounded by single-storey buildings whose decorative woodwork recalls better times. The southeastern corridor leads to the small mosque of the complex. The single-storey space is very carefully executed in brick, ceramic and stucco work and has a completely different spatial quality than the rest of the saray. The mosque has a roofed octagonal courtyard from which various niches split off. The northeastern niche leads through a door to a covered prayer hall (a later addition). The saray was commissioned by Haggi Aqa Mohammad Zamani, who occasionally served as deputy of the governor of Isfahan at the time of Karim-Khan Zand. In 1782, the building became part of the waqf of the Najaf sanctuary. A religious inscription on a bronze ring above the south gate bears the date 1212/1797. To the west of Saray-e Golshan lies the small, attractive hall from the early twentieth century, Timcheh

Poshti, which is directly accessible from the bazaar, between the two dehlizes of Saray Golshan. It is a scaled-down copy of Malek Timcheh, with three domes, but unlike the latter, it has a nearly square-shaped, two storey northern annex that was once used for offices. The upper floor is accessed via a projecting wooden gallery. Today, the structure is in poor condition. Since the wall is set against Saray Golshan, the date of origin must be after 1780, but probably, like Malek Timcheh, it was only built ca. 1900.

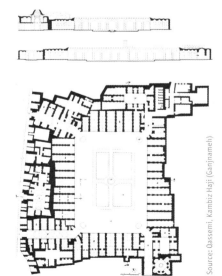

Floor plan and sections

Source: Qassemi, Kambiz Haji (Ganjnameh)

Source: Caroline Reichmann

View into the courtyard of Arastoie House

Arastoie House
Khaneh-ye Arastoie
خانه ارسطویی

099

Khiyaban-e Hasht-Behesht,
Isfahan
32.65250, 51.68361
unknown
AD: ca. 1650/AH: ca. 1070/Yaz: ca. 1130

The Arastoie house is a residence dating from the Qajar period, comprising 400 m². Since its renovation it has been owned by the cultural heritage preservation of Isfahan and is used as classrooms by the Calligraphers' Association. The Arastoie house was built as a typical residence of the middle class. The alcove on the west side, the most beautiful room in the house, has decorative stucco elements and murals. The courtyard façade is made of mud plaster reinforced with straw. Lines from poems by Kamal-od-Din Mohtasham Kashani are inscribed on the outdoor room. The house was not only used as a residence but also as assembly hall, Rosh Khaneh, hosting meetings to commemorate Imam Hussein and his companions in Karbala.

Sadr Khaju Madrasa
Madrasa-ye Sadr-e Khaju
مدرسه صدرخواجو

100

Khiyaban-e Chahar Bagh-e Khaju,
Isfahan
32.64608, 51.68203
Haji Mohammad Hossein Khan Sadr Isfahani (Commissioner)
AD: 1802/AH: 1217/Yaz: 1178

The really remarkable Madrasa Sadr-e Khaju was commissioned by Haji-Mohammad Hosein Khan Sadr Isfahani, governor of Isfahan and Minister under Qajar Fath-Ali Shah, who also built the Boulevard Chahar Bagh-e Sadr. The school was built between 1838 and 1842 when the avenue was inaugurated, and was used until 1919 when it was converted to a mental hospital. The cells and yard as well as the laundry and bath of the school were renovated in 1957 and again used by the students. In 2014, the madrasa once again began renovations, which are still in progress.

Source: Qassemi, Kambiz Haji (Ganjnameh)

Courtyard of Madrasa-ye Sadr-e Khaju

Source: Qassemi, Kambiz Haji (Ganjnameh)

Courtyard of Saray-e Haji Mohammad Sadeq

Haji Mohammad Sadeq Saray (101)
Saray-e Haji Mohammad Sadeq
سرای حاج محمد صادق

Bazar-e Mokhless, Isfahan
32.66194, 51.67833
Mohammad Sadeq (Commissioner)
AD: ca. 1830/AH: ca. 1246/Yaz: ca. 1200

The saray located on the east side of Bazaar Mokhless has two floors, with the upper floor accessible via a mahtabi. Although the building dates back to the Safavid period, later modifications conceal the Safavid elegance. For example, the chamfer of the almost-square courtyard in its north- and southeast corners was replaced by a colonnade. The original design was based on a symmetrical octagonal courtyard which looked terraced due to the recessed upper floor. In addition to the courtyard being

enlarged, this offset allowed easy access to the upstairs rooms with a minimum of stairs. The façade consists of a combination of two differently-sized ogee arches. The lintel of the narrower openings is decorated with inscriptions on brick, which reduce the height of the arches. These different spans with varying heights create a very pleasing visual rhythm, which is perhaps the most important architectural contribution of this saray. The attractive courtyard design goes back to the original construction. The long, river-like water pool flanked by flower beds is the main element of the landscape design. Although the similarity of the four courtyard façades and the octagonal floor plan should preclude the dominance of one of the axes, the pool and the flower beds make the east-west axis appear longer and more pronounced.

Source: Qassemi, Kambiz Haji (Ganjnameh)

Floor plan of Madrasa-ye Sadr-e Khaju

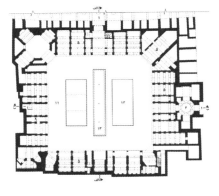

Floor plan of Saray-e Haji Mohammad Sadeq

Source: Qassemi, Kambiz Haji (Ganjnameh)

Entrance façade of the caravanserai

Mother of Shah Caravanserai (102)
Karvansaray-e Mader-e
Shah Mourchekhourt

کاروانسرای مادرشاه مورچه خورت

Rah-e Isfahan-Delijan, Mourche,
ca. 35 km from Isfahan
33.01317, 51.49925
Haji Seyyed Mohammad Bagher Shafti
(Commissioner)
AD: 1835 / AH: 1251 / Yaz: 1204

The French architect Maxime Siroux
writes that ambassadors and diplomats rested in this caravanserai on their
way to Isfahan and changed their robes
for the grand entrance at court before
they continued on, accompanied by

their entourage. He dates the building
in the reign of either Shah Abbas II or
Shah Suleiman. It is one of the biggest
caravanserais in Iran. A large rectangular
courtyard lies in the centre of the site.
Four central ayvans with flanking ayvanaches form a regular, homogeneous
courtyard façade, with all walls having the exact same dimensions. There is
a storage and/or living space behind every
ayvan. The stables of the caravanserai are
executed in two different ways: either as
a square supported by columns in the corners of the building, which is accessible
via the chamfered corners of the courtyard; or as elongated stables located
behind the living quarters on the northwest and southeast side, accessed via
the outermost arcades. Maxime Siroux
assumes that the large stables in the corners were probably used to accommodate
the elephants that were often used in ceremonial royal receptions. The entrance of
the caravanserai is at the southwest side.
A high portico with flanking arcades protrudes from the façade. The brick decoration of the pinnacle crest, together
with the watch towers at the corners of
the building, form an impressive façade.
The vestibule is composed of a double-
storey, octagonal space, with the common
areas for the caravanserai guards next
to it. On the opposite side of the courtyard lies the northwestern ayvan with

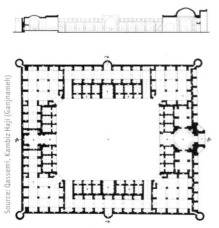

Source: Qassemi, Kambiz Haji (Ganjnameh)

Floor plan and section

Source: Qassemi, Kambiz Haji (Ganjnameh)

Courtyard of Masjed-e Seyyed

a cruciform entrance hall behind it. The bath and the water cistern are located outside the caravanserai. The caravanserai continued to be used during the Qajar period; it was then abandoned, and was thereafter used as barracks until recently. Since 2013, Mahestan Nagshe Jahan has planned to rebuild the caravanserai as a regional tourism centre. The master plan has apparently been approved, the first infrastructure facilities are already in place, and the caravanserai is in danger of Disneyfication.

Seyyed Mosque
Masjed-e Seyyed
مسجد سید

Khiyaban-e Masjed-e Seyyed, Isfahan
32.66472, 51.66389
Haji Seyyed Mohammad Bagher Shafti (Commissioner)
AD: 1839/AH: 1255/Yaz: 1208

103 D

The Masjed-e Seyyed is one of the four Friday Mosques in Isfahan. It was endowed by Haji Seyyed Mohammad-Baqer Shafti Rashti Bid-Abadi. After his death, his son Seyyed-e Sani, and later his grandson Mohammad-Baqer Sani, continued his work. According to the inscriptions, the construction appears to have taken 130 years. The floor plan is based on the principle of the four-ayvan-mosque

and is in line with other Friday mosques. Instead of minarets there is a clock tower on the south side. On the west side is a shabestan, which takes up the entire length of the court. Under the main dome is a large-scale arabesque reminiscent of the Madrasa-ye Mader-e Shah, illustrating the big difference between the original paradigm and the Qadjar time, the decline of the golden age. On the northeast side there is a small blue dome belonging to the shrine of the aforementioned clergyman. It has an amazing entrance to a small Bazaar. The shrine contains interesting elements, such as pendentive domes, mirror work and iron railings.

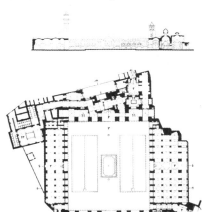

Source: Qassemi, Kambiz Haji (Ganjnameh)

Floor plan and section

Courtyard of Saray-e Haji Karim

Haji Karim Saray
Saray-e Haji Karim

سرای حاج کریم

Dar-e Bagh-e Qalandaran, Isfahan
32.66444, 51.67889
Haji Karim (Commissioner)
AD: ca. 1870 / AH: ca. 1290 / Yaz: ca. 1240

104

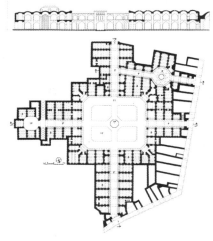

Floor plan and section

The Saray-e Haji-Karim is located on the east side of Isfahan Bazaar and shows all the characteristics of Qajar architecture. The small, double-storey, navicular courtyard forms a pleasing protected space with a pool surrounded by four flower beds covering most of the area. Large old plane trees create a lush green atmosphere. The ingenious surroundings of the courtyard are enhanced by the recess of the upper floor. The protruding parts in the symmetry axes, which house large rooms with four windows, contribute further to this refinement. Originally all the windows were made of wood and showed similarities to residential architecture. The dark, recessed openings under these protrusions are in strong contrast and enhance the four quadrants of the courtyard. The simple construction of brickwork and wooden windows emphasises this contrast. The relation of the saray to its surroundings is also direct and clear: Four rectangular corridors in the centre of the courtyard façades link it to the neighbourhood. The northern, southern and western passages lead directly to the bazaar, whilst the eastern corridor comes to a dead end with a small saray and modest timcheh. Thus the right-angled, geometrical arrangement, with its two distinct main perpendicular axes, could be incorporated into the non-geometric, free-flowing system of bazaar streets, with two perfect access points. Halfway through the southern connection, another passage with a pretty double-storey timcheh in its centre branches off. The timcheh and the dehlize have two floors and are equipped with shops on both sides. Upon entering the court, the height is reduced to one level, allowing for rooms over the entrances. Like the Saray Mokhless, the complex was built in the second half of the nineteenth century. In view of the older techniques used, it can be assumed to be pre-1870.

Gondbad-Khaneh (Domed Hall) of Masjed-e Rahim Khan

Rahim Khan Mosque
Masjed-e Rahim Khan
مسجد رحیم خان

Khiyaban-e Ayatollah Taleghani,
Isfahan
32.65917, 51.66278
Aqa Juni, Ali Ashgar
AD: 1878 / AH: 1295 / Yaz: 1248

105

Floor plan

At the east end of Taleqani Street, you can see the high dome of Rahimkhan Mosque. It was commissioned during the Qajar period by Mir Sayyed Hassan Mojahed-e Isfahani, whose work was continued by Muhammad Rahim Khan Beiglarbeigui and his brothers. The architect of the mosque was Aqa Juni, and the shabestan was executed by Ali-Asghar. Other artists involved were the calligrapher Hassan Khan, the ceramicist Aqa Jan and the painter Ali. The mosque has three gates, and the north side is completed by the noteworthy shabestan. Two large platforms are located in the yard, similar to the Friday Mosque. A three-dimensional wooden framework was inserted under the great dome. The inscriptions confirm that construction took place between 1878 and 1886. An inscription on a stone pillar states that Rahim Khan endowed the mosque. Under Reza Pahlavi, it was used as barracks for five years, then as a poorhouse for three years before it was restored to its original purpose some forty years ago.

Entrance decoration of Rahim Khan Mosque

Courtyard of Saray-e Mokhless

Mokhless Saray
Saray-e Mokhless
سرای مخلص

106 **D**

Bazar-e Mokhless, Isfahan
32.62889, 51.68472
Haggi Mir Mohammad Tabatabay
(Commissioner)
AD: ca. 1880 / AH: ca. 1297 / Yaz: ca. 1250

The building is located near the northeast end of Maidan-e Sah, at the busy Bazaar Mokhless. It is one of the largest sarays of the city and ca. 1880 was considered to be the noblest in Isfahan. It was commissioned by the merchant Haggi Mir Mohammad Tabatabay in place of a previous Safavid building. The construction consists of a rectangular, central courtyard where rooms were laid out on two levels. The rooms upstairs are recessed except for the façades of the main axis, and enlarge the yard, whilst in the middle of each side u-shaped projecting structures rise which appear like small copies of the Qeysaryeh gate, reminding one of the courts of four-ayvan mosques. Each of the projections forms an entrance that connects the courtyard with the Bazaar. The configuration of the western corridor, which forms the main entrance of the saray, is more elaborate and divided into three parts which only differ by the middle vault having a circular skylight and being more richly decorated.

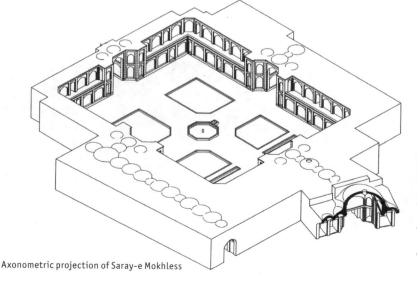

Axonometric projection of Saray-e Mokhless

The middle part is thus distinguished only by decoration and different lighting, and the centre of the access is emphasised. The landscaping echoes the rhythm of the façade. An octagonal water pool surrounded by four flowerbeds is located at the intersection of the two axes and creates a balance between the emptiness of the court and the mass of the adjacent volume. The architects very deliberately juxtaposed the closed, semi-dark room of the bazaar and the light composition of the court; the bazaar is like a river flowing with the mass of people, whilst the saray next to it forms a quiet pond. The design places great emphasis on this stillness next to the hustle and bustle, and all elements concentrate on this.

a groined vault over a long-rectangular floor plan with a lantern in the apex. The structural condition indicates that the timcheh Atiq-e Forusha definitely originated after Saray-e Golshan, i.e. in the early nineteenth century.

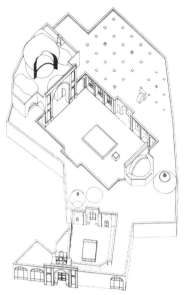

Source: Qasseni, Kambiz Haji (Ganjnameh)

Atiq Forusha Timcheh
Timcheh-ye Atiq-e Forusha
تیمچه عتیقه فروشها

107

Bazar-e Golshan, Isfahan
32.66250, 51.67750
unknown
AD: ca. 1900 / AH: ca. 1315 / Yaz: ca. 1270

The Timcheh-ye Atiq-e Forusha is located on the west side of the Bazaar Golshan between the portals of Madrasa-ye Sadr in the south and Saray-e Fahr in the north. By way of a harmonious portal placed between the passes of the bazaar and beyond a 5 m-deep gatehouse, you arrive in an octagonal, vaulted building, surrounded on two floors by sales stalls. Its floor level is about half a metre below the bazaar street, a testimony to the centuries of use which had raised the main alley with debris and building rubble to above the level of the adjacent courtyards. The stores in the axes of the structure are wider than those in the corners. All are covered by groined vaults between walings. The central space is spanned by

Axonometric projection of
Rokn ol-Molk Mosque and School

Rokn ol-Molk Mosque and School
Masjed va Madrasa-ye Rokn ol-Molk
مسجد رکن‌الملک

108

Khiyaban-e Feyz, Isfahan
32.66347, 51.67750
Mirza Suleiman Khan Shirazi (Commissioner)
AD: 1902 / AH: 1320 / Yaz: 1272

The Rokn-ol-Molk mosque was built in the Qajar era close to the Takht-e Foulad. It was built by Mirza Suleiman Khan Shirazi, who was a prominent figure in Isfahan, and known as Rokn-ol-Molk, the Column of the Kingdom. The entrance portal of the mosque is decorated with Rokn-ol-Molk's verses written in white lettering on azure brick background. Next to the rooms on both sides of the entrance lies his grave, with his poems engraved on tiles. The mosque is an example of the innovative and interesting Qajar era architecture. The monument was listed in 1996 as an Iranian national heritage site.

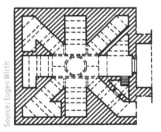

Source: Eugen Wirth

Floor plan of Timcheh-ye Atiq-e Forusha

Source: Claudia Luperto

Interior of Timcheh-ye Malek

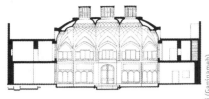

Source: Qassemi, Kambiz Haji (Ganjnameh)

Section of Timcheh-ye Malek

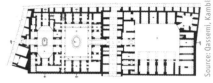

Ground floor plan of Majmueh-ye Malek

Malek Ensemble
Majmueh-ye Malek
مجموعة ملك

109 D

Bazar-e Mokhless, Isfahan
32.66222, 51.67694
unknown
AD: 1904/AH: 1322/Yaz: 1274

The Malek complex is located on the west side of the main bazaar. The inscription at the entrance indicates that it was built in 1904 under the Qajar ruler Mozaffer od-Din Shah. The structure combines three areas: a timcheh, a saray and a craft centre, or bahar-band. These elements are arranged along the east-west axis, which also forms the symmetry axis of the buildings and lies transverse to the main axis of the bazaar. A bazaarcheh between the saray and the craft centre breaks the connection, but its ingenious design still shows the unity of the three parts. The first and most important part is the timcheh, which was eponymous for the entire ensemble. At the entrance, an atrium is followed by a short, differently shaped passage that makes the visitor aware that he is entering a new space, which abruptly confronts him with a new world. The navicular structure of the timcheh, the transverse water basin in the centre, the design and execution of the walls and the lighting invite contemplation; few visitors pass through this room without lingering. The saray consists of a small rectangular courtyard, which appears open due to the double-storey colonnade and offers better light and a larger façade development – a trick which amplifies its volumetry. By cutting back the colonnade of the upper floor in the middle of each side to an octagonal opening, the architect achieved an entirely new expression. A passage on the west side of the courtyard leads to the craft centre, which consists of a rectangular courtyard with a pond in the centre surrounded by a single-storey room. Apart from the elaborate entrance area, the design of the bahar-band is not worth mentioning.

Talar Saray
Saray-e Talar
سرای تالار

110 D

Bazar-e Dartalar, Isfahan
32.66556, 51.67944
unknown
AD: 1917/AH: 1335/Yaz: 1286

The commercial building Talar is located in the northwest of the bazaar on an irregular but rectangular plot. The central

Source: Qassemi, Kambiz Haji (Ganjnameh)

Courtyard of Saray-e Malek

Source: Qassemi, Kambiz Haji (Ganjnameh)

Courtyard of Saray-e Talar

Source: Qassemi, Kambiz Haji (Ganjnameh)

Greenery in the courtyard of Madrasa-ye Sadr

Sadr Madrasa
Madrasa-ye Sadr
مدرسه صدر

Bazar-e Samaversaz-ha, Isfahan
32.66222, 51.67694
*Haji Mohammad Hossein Khan
Sadr Isfahani (Commissioner)*
AD: 1917 / AH: 1335 / Yaz: 1286

opening on each side of the courtyard forms a single-storey, ayvan-like opening, with the exception of the southern one, which forms the main entrance to the saray and is thus the most important place in the courtyard. The entrance to the saray is today barely visible from the bazaar, but it seems that it used to have a double-height portico that led directly into the saray. Upon entering the bazaar, the height of the passage is reduced to one level. Although the building dates back to the Qajar period, the influence of the mature Isfahan architecture, which lived on in the buildings of the town even after the Safavid dynasty, can be retraced in the proportions, the half-arches, windows and doors. The inner walls of the shops are plastered, which makes them appear hollow. The floor plan of the courtyard has been greatly changed and is now cluttered and chaotic.

The madrasa was commissioned by Haji Hossein-Khan Sadr Isfahani, Prime Minister under the Qajar ruler Fath-Ali Shah. The construction and the façade were unfinished when he died. The inscription above the entrance names Ali as architect of the building, Ghaffar as ceramic artists and Abolqassem Kashisaz as a manufacturer of faïence facing in the madrasa library. The madrasa library was endowed by Sayyed Mohammad-Reza Khorassami and completed in 1945. The madrasa was recently restored and extended with a steel structure for the winter prayer hall on the north side. The courtyard is designed as a Chahar Bagh and artistically planted with irregularly-placed pines and cypresses.

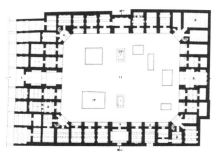

Floor plan of Saray-e Talar

Source: Qassemi, Kambiz Haji (Ganjnameh)

Floor plan and section of Madrasa-ye Sadr

Shah Nematollah Vali Shrine in Mahan

Space and Surface in Persian Architecture

The following article is in many parts similar to the chapter of the same title in
the book *Ispahan: image du paradis* by Henri Stierlin, which is partly quoted verbatim
for better comprehension of architectural conditions in Persia.

The Isfahan Oasis

The oasis Isfahan is located 1,400 m above sea level and is dominated by the Zagros Mountains. Desert rocks form the background to turquoise domes and high minarets and break up the maze of brick domes and roofs. The vegetation, which greatly surprises the newly-arrived traveller, was certainly lusher in seventeenth-century Isfahan than it is today, due to urbanisation and traffic.

The mountain ranges form a natural boundary of the fertile oasis. The silhouette of the mountains, which accompany vast deserts on the way to Isfahan, seems infinite. But then one is suddenly confronted with a large, open valley where the royal city lies. The beholder is surprised by the immense contrast between the world of sand and rock and this enormous oasis, this fertile, green valley, interspersed with domes and houses revealing the size of the town, whilst the foliage of the big plane trees shields the buildings like a lattice.

In 1840, a hundred years after the devastating fall of the Safavid dynasty, the French architect Pascal Coste he surveyed and recorded the most important monuments of Isfahan and wrote in his excellent work *Monuments modern de la Perse mesures, dessinés et décrits*, published in Paris in 1867: "If a traveller approaches Isfahan from any direction, he immediately notices that he is facing a vast, beautiful city. If he arrives in summer, the gardens outside and inside the town cover everything with their green foliage and hide the rather low buildings from the view. Only the minarets of numerous mosques scattered throughout the whole town stretch their elegant steeples into the air, conveying an immediate notion of the size of the town to the visitor."

In his travelogue *Vers Ispahan*, which appeared in 1904, Pierre Loti makes the same observation and mentions: "At dawn we finally depart for Isfahan! For an hour the path leads us through a drab desert area with bumpy, brown loamy ground, which seems perfect to increase the surprise once the city of gleaming blue domes amid the oasis comes into view, promising freshness. It is like a curtain opening up on a stage, because suddenly two arid mountains part in front of us and a Garden of Eden reveals itself slowly to our eyes. In the foreground, meadows welcome us with big white flowers that dazzle the eye like snow in stark contrast to the dusty monotony of the desert. Next a veritable forest of poplars, willows, oaks and plane trees appears, until we discover the many blue domes and the countless blue minarets of Isfahan! This is a grove and a town at the same time."

Thus Loti describes his impression of a typical Middle Eastern oasis town. To "settle" means something completely different in the Middle East, and does not meet our Western ideas; to "claim land" in Europe means to clear ground by clearing, to "irrigate" means to make it suitable for agricultural use, to "cultivate" means to make it suitable for building. In the Middle East, "planting" means to create an oasis, a habitable place in the desert, usually located near a spring or in a wadi, where shade could be provided. The Middle Eastern town and its homes are always first found in an oasis, a densely planted area.

Isfahan, building mass dyed black

Source: Thomas Meyer-Wieser

Space and Surface in Persian Towns

If we compare the plan of a typical Persian town with the plan of a typical European one, the following difference becomes obvious: In the European town the houses are positioned as individual buildings or in rows, an object or a figure on a more-or-less untouched ground. The area narrows to alleys and spreads to streets and squares; however, it always remains a natural, self-evident surface where the buildings are placed and where every house presents itself as an individual element because of its more-or-less imposing façade. The Persian town, on the other hand, develops on three different levels: The most important one is formed by the flat roofs covering most of the area, the second underlying level consists of paths and squares and creates holes in the urban fabric, and finally the third level is formed by buildings which break through the continuous building mass. Thus the Persian urban fabric is diametrically opposed to the occidental one, because its order is always determined by courtyards and

squares, by space and not by volume as in Europe. The Middle Eastern and European town form two completely different models which appear like two readings of a figure-ground diagram illustrating the changing of the figure-ground phenomenon: One is close to black, the other almost white; one forms an accumulation of voids in a largely unstructured mass, the other a collection of masses in a largely pristine emptiness. In both cases each surface supports a completely different category of shape – space in the one, volume in the other.

Continuous Spatial Structure

The continuous spatial structure determines urbanism and architecture in Persia. One spatial unit flows into the next one without any interruption or the need to leave the atmosphere created by space and surface. One moves rather in an artfully-arranged sequence of transitions where each building is part of a harmonious whole. In this totality there is never an isolated building which looks lost, but everything fits into the urban fabric

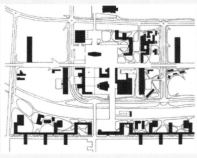

St. Dié, 1945, building mass dyed black

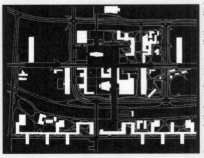

Source: Colin Rowe/Fred Koetter (Collage City)

St. Dié, 1945, exterior space dyed black

Source: Claudia Luperto

Roofscape of Kashan

which is crossed by several major arteries, roads and bazaars and at the same time finds its focus in the courtyards and squares. A break between the individual elements is avoided by fusing the key elements of the construction plan into a homogeneous whole. Arches, vaults or a series of domes cover the streets and the alleys, which wind like underground tunnels through a neighbourhood. Each quarter forms an entity in itself similar to a row of houses in Europe except that in the Persian concept, each element fits completely into the whole structure and is not distinctive as an individual.

Inside and Outside

In the Middle Eastern town, one always moves within a certain space, that is *within* an often-covered street, *within* a courtyard of a house, *within* a madrasa,

Source: Claudia Luperto

Busy bazaar street in Kashan

a caravanserai, a mosque and also *within* a town square, which is restricted by a contiguous environment. The Safavid architecture therefore is not understood as a compilation of individual separate buildings but as a clearly defined space, where the built-up area is subject to a rhythmic order. The homogeneity of this surface is expressed firstly in the continuous sequence of roofs, which immediately stands out when one looks down on the whole town. These flat or vaulted brick roofs covering the houses and bazaars form a kind of reference plane, an artificial "floor" located on the second floor, and is reminiscent of a desert covered by dunes. Two different features break up this area stretching right over the town, namely the shafts of the interior courtyards and the openings for the squares on the one hand and in contrast to this, the elevations formed by the domes and minarets of public buildings, the mosques and the madrasas. These two types of breaks, the holes and bumps, are the only elements that provide variations to the horizontal uniformity of the roofs. It is the rhythm in the space, the vibration in shape and volume in Isfahan that lends the town its charm. Isfahan welcomes the visitor like a great adventure and enchants him by an eternal play between light and shadow, through a constant movement like breathing in and out, as if hurrying back and forth, as if constricting its volumes before literally exploding.

Courtyard versus Terrace

The same observation can be made of a house if we compare a built-up volume like a residential building erected in the mid- twentieth century in Tehran, and a hollow body, a courtyard house from the mid-nineteenth century, both of almost the same dimensions and both with an almost identical use. As the comparison involves two interpretations of the same spatial program, it could also serve to turn the thesis "form follows function" on its head. But if we

Above: Roofscape of Timcheh-ye Bakhshi in Kashan

Left: Interior of Timcheh-ye Bakhshi

Courtyard of Khaneh-ye Borujerdiha

compare these two buildings formally, we realise that Villa Shahab Khosrovany stands as an object-like building block in a largely untreated outdoor space, whilst the courtyard building Khaneh-ye Borujerdiha is a hollow mould punched out of an unstructured mass. In the case of the villa, everything is based on a single, central idea, on a single universal, organising principle, a display of total design, of the triumph of the common, of the predominance of an overwhelming idea and the denial of the exception – whilst on

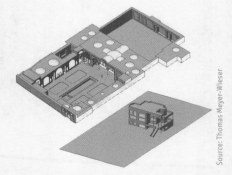

Source: Thomas Meyer-Wieser

Courtyard house versus veranda house: Khaneh-ye Borujerdiha versus Villa Shahab Khosrovani

the contrary Khaneh-ye Borujerdiha is trying to avoid any reference to a dominant idea, is seemingly haphazard and negligent and proposes the opposite of any totality. The first is a radiating object that can be transported from place to place, the second a specifically created hollow mould for a particular site. The Khaneh-ye Borujerdiha can be interpreted as a Villa Shahab Khosrovany whose outside is turned inside, like a casting box for the building block of Villa Shahab Khosrovany. The Khaneh-ye Borujerdiha refers to the immediate environment, which is hardly the case for the villa Shahab Khosrovany. Through the explicit spatial relationship to its surroundings, the courtyard house absorbs the idea of the town, whilst Gabriel Guévrékian's building, created from its inner need, considers the site rather as a symbolic structure. The first tells us of of historical necessity, the other of historical continuity; one glorifies the common, whilst the other focuses attention on the particular.

Side façade of the courtyard of Khaneh-ye Borujerdiha

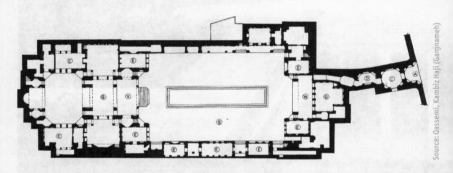

Floor plan of Khaneh-ye Borujerdiha

Courtyard of Khaneh-ye Borujerdiha

Entrance to reception area of Khaneh-ye Borujerdiha

Source: Claudia Luperto

Biruni of Khaneh-ye Borujerdiha

Spatial Planning

The Borudjerdi and Tabatabaei Houses are probably the most famous houses in Kashan. Depending on their purpose and importance, the rooms of these houses not only differ in size but also in height; they follow a spatial plan in the interior where size and arrangement of the rooms is dictated by function and interconnects them partially on different levels. "Free thinking in space" is the guiding principle in the arrangement of these houses, "the

planning of rooms at different levels and not bound to a single floor, and the composition of interrelated spaces into a harmonious, indivisible whole and an economic structure." This was an important idea which entered into European architecture only ca. 1910 via Adolf Loos, a Viennese architect. Essential for the complex design of the building's interior is the passage through the house as a flow of impressions, and therefore the conscious percipience of the fourth dimension, namely time.

Source: Claudia Luperto

View into the biruni of Khaneh-ye Borujerdiha

Detail of biruni of Khaneh-ye Borujerdiha

The Zand Dynasty

1759–1779
Shiraz, Residential Town of Karim Khan Zand

In the succession struggles after Nader Shah's assassination, almost all provincial governors declared independence, established their own states, and the entire empire of Nader Shah fell into anarchy. Finally, the Kurd Karim Khan, one of Nader Shah's generals, gained control of the central and southern parts of Iran, declared Shiraz as his capital and became ruler of Iran. By 1760, Karim Khan had defeated all his rivals and controlled all of Iran except Khorasan. Many territories that were once captured by the Ottomans in the late Safavid era were retaken, and Iran was once again a coherent and prosperous country. In order to add legitimacy to his claim, Karim Khan placed the infant Shah Ismail III, the grandson of the last Safavid Shah on the throne. Ismail was a figurehead king and the real power was vested in Karim Khan. He chose to call himself Vakil ol Ro'aya, Advocate of the People. The Zand era was a time of relative peace and economic growth for the country. Through an equitable tax policy, the development of irrigation systems and the promotion of the trade with India, Shiraz became an important cultural centre. In foreign policy, Karim Khan attempted to revive Safavid-era

trade by allowing the British to establish a trading post in the port of Bushehr. This strengthened the hand of the British East India Company in Iran and increased their influence in the country. However, Karim Khan's heirs failed to secure his gains. When Agha Mohammad Khan, the founder of the Qajar dynasty, came to power, he besieged Shiraz for six months in the winter of 1777. Thousands died of hunger and cold. When Shiraz finally fell to the Qajar in 1794, they took their revenge on Shiraz by destroying the city's fortifications and extinguishingthe Zand dynasty. 20,000 men were blinded and the women and children were enslaved.

Development of the Urban Area of Shiraz up to 1779

The Zand era was an era of relative peace and economic growth for the country. Karim Khan Zand made Shiraz his capital and ordered the construction of several architectural projects there. A brisk construction activity started: He built the Vakil bazaar, which, with its brick vaults, is among the finest in Persia, and the Vakil mosque, with floral-patterned tiles dating back to Qadjar times. The size and internal differentiation of the new bazaar is a good example of the town's economic recovery. The regent also had the city walls dating from the Atabak dynasty strengthened, creating public spaces in front of each gate and shading them with plane trees. During his reign the city expanded along the north-south axis. The main road, today Karim Khan Zand Avenue, was already built under the Safavids in the seventeenth century and was modelled on the Khyaban-e Chahar Bagh in Isfahan. Its mostly single-storey and densely-built residential

Source: Thomas Meyer-Wieser

Development of urban area of Shiraz up to 1779

Gateway to the oasis Shiraz with the Musalla Gardens

areas were limited mainly to the east and west sides of the town, where he commissioned the building of Arg-e Karim Khan, his fortress-like residence around a green courtyard with shady trees and ponds. He also tended to older gardens like Bagh-e jahan nama and renovated the impressive garden Bagh-e nazer with its octagonal pavilion. This is where he received foreign ambassadors. After Iranian painting reached its height at the end of the seventeenth century, a special school of painting was established during the Zand era in the seventeenth and eighteenth centuries. The art of this era is remarkable and, despite the short life of the dynasty, a distinct Zand art emerged. Many Qajar artistic traits were copied from the Zand examples. To this day, Karim Khan Zand has a reputation as one of the most just and able rulers in Iranian history. A wealth of anecdotes portray him as a compassionate ruler, genuinely concerned with the welfare of his subjects, as in *L'assedio di Sciraz*, a melodrama composed by Nicolò Gabrielli. After the Islamic revolution, the Zand was the only dynasty whose names on public places and monuments were not removed by the new republican government.

Qu'ran Gate
Darvazeh Qoran
دروازه قرآن

Bulvar-e Ayatollah Rabbani,
Shiraz
29.63562, 52.56185
Adud al-Daula (Commissioner)
AD: 10th cent., ca. 1950/AH: ca. 340,
ca. 1370/Yaz: ca. 320, ca. 1320

The Qu'ran Gate originates from the tenth century and was constructed under the rule of Adud al-Daula. The gate is situated at the city exit towards Isfahan at the foothills of Mount Baba Kuhi. When travellers arriving in Shiraz from the north reached the highest point of the pass, they rejoiced for centuries at the view down to the city and cried "Allahu Akbar"; therefore this bottleneck is called Tange-ye Allahu Akbar. During the Zand dynasty the gate was damaged by several earthquakes. During the restoration under Karim Khan Zand, a small room was added over

the passageway, where two handwritten copies of the Qu'ran, transcribed by Sultan Ibrahim Bin Shahrukh Gurekani were kept, so that anyone who left the town through this gate passed under the Holy Qu'ran. The custom of starting a journey by passing under the Qu'ran was said to bless the traveller and grant him a safe return. The two Qu'rans were removed in 1937 and transferred to the Pars Museum, where they are still exhibited. Hosein Igar, a merchant, restored the arches of the gate in 1949. In the course of the remodelling of the road in 1950, this gate was dismantled, moved and faithfully restored, so that the road now leads around the Qu'ran Gate and probably no longer guarantees the traveller a safe return. Today it is part of the city park developed by Iranian architect Mehrdad Iravanian, and it is a popular destination for Shirazi, where they relax during their leisure time, smoking water pipes in the chai-khaneh at the foot of Baba Kuhi or enjoying picnics with their families.

Garden of the Throne
Bagh-e Takht
باغ تخت

Karimkhaneh Castle Bus Stop,
Shiraz
29.63658, 52.54478
Atabek Qerakhe (Commissioner)
AD: ca. 1300/AH: ca. 700/Yaz: ca. 670

In his book *Persian Gardens and Pavilions*, Donald Newton Wilbur writes: "Clearly visible from the presumed site of the Bagh-i-Naw is the crumbling complex known today as the Bagh-e Takht, or Garden of the Throne. Some hundreds of metres to the west, it abuts a rocky hillside and owes its existence to the presence of a spring which gushes from the rock. An early history of Shiraz indicates that a local ruler of the eleventh century, Atabek Qaracheh, was responsible for constructing a garden at this spot." Around 1300 the governor Atabek Qerakhe built a residence in the northwest of Shiraz, at the foot of the mountain Baba kuhi, which he called Bagh-e Takht, Garden of the Throne. The imposing and generous height of the palace gave the ruler a view over the city and the plain and symbolised his claim to power. The seven terraces are preserved in their basic form to this day. They are unique in the country. Irrigation was provided via a spring. To keep the living and reception rooms cool in summer, the water first passed through these rooms, then through the garden and into a pool. The garden is connected to the lower level by seven terraces, each having a height of about 3 m. A water channel, which was designed as a series of cascades, formed the longitudinal axis which flowed into a rectangular pond, called daryacheh, or little sea, with a fountain and equipped with

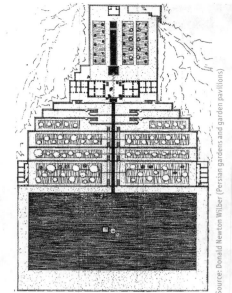

Floor plan

Source: Donald Newton Wilber (Persian gardens and garden pavilions)

boats. Although Shiraz is surrounded by mountains, this so-called "hanging garden" was the only one which took advantage of the topography, giving it special status. The numerous gardens were similar in topographic respects. For instance, they were usually planted on steep slopes in suburban terrain, had steep terraces with the palace standing on the level, and included a vast flat area at the foot of the slope, as well as an orchard with a large pool. Takht-e Qajar in Tehran was based on the same design. The palace enclosed a fixed andaruni, or private courtyard; public life took place at the foot of the hill. Guests were received in a large talar, which enclosed the slope towards the lake, and in the ayvan of the pavilion in the centre of the orchard. The topography and the diversity of its buildings transformed the Bagh-e Takht into a very impressive complex.

View of Bagh-e Takht

Source: Pascal Coste (Monuments modernes de la Perse)

Courtyard of the New Mosque ca. 1950

New Mosque
Masjed-e No
مسجد نو

Maidan-e Ahmadi, Shiraz
29.61083, 52.54167
*Mozafer ad-Din Abu Shoja Saad
ibn-e Zangi (Commissioner)*
AD: ca. 1190 / AH: ca. 585 / Yaz: ca. 560

Sources tell us that the mosque was commissioned by Mozafer ad-Din Abu-Shoja Saad ibn-e Zangi. It was reportedly his home, but when his daughter fell ill, he vowed to remodel it as a mosque after her recovery. It is also reported that a room adjoining the qibla-wall of the mosque was the living room of the Persian poet and mystic Saadi. The mosque was renovated many times, so that nothing of its original structure is retained today.

Friday Mosque Atiq
Masjed-e Jameh-ye Atiq
مسجد جامع عتیق

Maidan-e Ahmadi, Shiraz
29.60778, 52.54472
Amr ibn al-Layth (Commissioner)
AD: ca. 1250 / AH: ca. 547 / Yaz: ca. 620

The most interesting and oldest building in the historic centre of Shiraz is the Friday Mosque, also known as Mesjed-e Jameh-ye Atiq. First built in 875 during the reign of Saffarid ruler Amr ibn al-Layth, it was rebuilt, restored, and extended a number of times thereafter. Most of the present day structure – a four-ayvan courtyard mosque – dates from the seventeenth century. Damaged by numerous earthquakes, it was restored extensively after 1935. The centre of

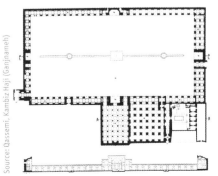

Floor plan and section of Masjed-e No

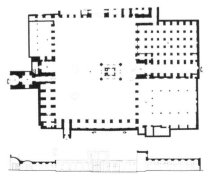

Floor plan and section of Masjed-e Jameh-ye Atiq

Masjed-e Jameh-ye Atiq

Source: Qassemi; Kambiz Haji (Ganjnameh)

its courtyard is occupied by the Khuda Khane, House of God. Commissioned by Injuids ruler Mahmud Shah in 1351 for the storage of Qu'rans, this small kiosk is also known as Bayt al-Mashaf, the House of Books. Both the mosque and Khuda Khane are aligned with qibla slightly east of south. The kiosk known as Khuda Khane consists of a rectangular core, with a loggia of three arched bays on each side, with solid circular towers projecting at the outer corners. The ensemble is raised on a marble platform. Only the towers, the platform and ruined inner walls remained of the original structure in the early twentieth century. It was rebuilt between 1937 and 1954 by the Archaeological Service of Iran under the supervision of André Godard, based on the original design.

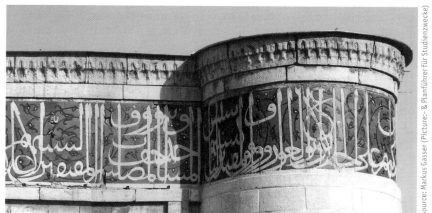

Frieze at the Khuda Khane of Masjed-e Jameh-ye Atiq

Source: Markus Gasser (Picture- & Planführer für Studienzwecke)

Front view of the Shah-e Cheragh Shrine

Seyyed Mir Ahmad Shrine
"King of Light"
Imamzadeh-ye Mir Ahmad
"Shah-e Cheragh«
(شاه چراغ) امامزیده سید میر احمد
Maidan-e Ahmadi, Shiraz
29.60917, 52.54389
Tash Khatun (Commissioner)
AD: ca. 1300/AH: ca. 700/Yaz: ca. 670

The most notable religious site in Shiraz is the shrine of Syed Amir Ahmad. Apart from the shrines of Imam Reza in Mashhad and of Fatima Masuma in Qom, the third most important pilgrimage destinaton in Iran is the shrine of Shah-e Cheragh in Shiraz. Amir Ahmad and his brother Mir Muhammad, who were both brothers of Imam Reza, took refuge in Shiraz following the Abbasid persecution of the Shiite sect. The brothers' tombs, originally only simple mausoleums, became celebrated pilgrimage destinations in the fourteenth century when the pious and art-loving Queen Tashi Khatun established a mosque and theological school near the tombs. Known locally as Shah Chirag, or King of Light, the exquisite tomb of Amir Ahmad is a place of truly stunning beauty. The construction date of the mausoleum is not clearly identified. It was restored in the Safavid period, when new parts were added to it. In the Qajar period, the dome was once again restored and the interior of the gondbad-khaneh was adorned with mirror works on the orders of Qavam-ol-Molk. Behind the portal building, adorned predominantly with tiled ornaments in blue tones, lies the vast courtyard followed by the lobby supported by columns on the right side of the main building. The blue-tiled large dome, rebuilt in 1958 in the typical Shiraz bud form, rises above it. At the centre of the shrine stands the sarcophagus protected by a silver Zarih lattice from 1827. The interiors are furnished with magnificent mirror mosaics. The enormous dome above the shrine is inlaid with hundreds of thousands of pieces of finely crafted tiles and the interior walls are likewise covered with myriad pieces of dazzling cut glass intermixed with multi-coloured tiles. To this day, the faithful make pilgrimages to this site to ask for blessings in the grave mosque which is decorated with magnificent tiles and beautiful mirror artworks. Women seek a partner, help with a birth or a cure for a variety of ailments; men wish for success. Or they come to die there. The dead are carried around the shrine in coffins before burial. Pilgrims touch the silver latticework of the shrine or kiss it. It is never quiet under the dome. Mosque guards in long robes, with high hats wrapped from green cloth, maintain order. The mausoleum Shah-e Cheragh consists of a large high domed room, surrounded by four large, open niches forming a cross-shaped floor plan. The tomb is not located in the centre of the dome as usual, but in the western niche. The main façade is flanked by two minarets, which were recently complemented by a veranda. At the same time the courtyard was extended on all sides and connected to the courtyard of Imamzadeh Mir-Mohammad.

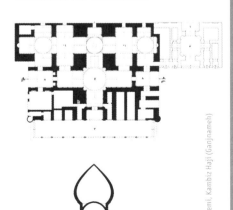

Floor plan and section

Exterior view of Imamzadeh-ye Ali ibn-e Hamzeh

Ali ibn Hamzeh Shrine
Imamzadeh-ye Ali ibn-e Hamzeh
امامزیده علی بن حمزه

117

Khiyaban-e Hafez, Shiraz
29.62222, 52.55278
Azodal Daula Dailamite
(Commissioner)
AD: ca. 1300/AH: ca. 700/Yaz: ca. 670

The Imamzadeh Ali ibn Hamza is listed here because it is much more easily accessible than the shrines Seyyed Mir-Ahmad or Imamzadeh Mir-Mohammad. Today's building structure of Imamzadeh arose after the earthquake of 1814. It was commissioned by Azodal Daula Dailamite, but was rebuilt several times over the centuries. Originally the shrine stood on a large historic cemetery, which was levelled in 1926 and redesignated as an art school and public park. Imamzadeh is the Persian term for the descendant of an imam, by which are meant the descendants of one of the Twelve Imams. The term is not only used for a person but also for the shrine or mausoleum where he is buried. The Islamic concept of life after death goes back to Jewish and thus indirectly to Persian and ancient Middle Eastern sources. The world then was the place of the last judgment, of reward and punishment.

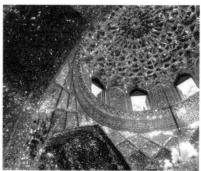

Vaulted ceiling of the shrine

Source: Charlotte Heer Grau

Front view of Madrasa-ye Khan

Khan School
Madrasa-ye Khan
مدرسه خان

Khiyaban-e Lotfali Khan-e Zand, Shiraz
29.61111, 52.54667
Allahverdi Khan (Commissioner)
AD: 1615 / AH: 1024 / Yaz: 984

The Madrasa-ye Khan lies southeast of the Vakil Bazaar at the edge of the historic centre of Shiraz. Originally it was surrounded by gardens, and the cells were oriented both to the courtyard and to the gardens. The construction of the Madrasa-ye Khan was started in the late sixteenth century by the then-governor of Shiraz, Allahverdi Khan, and was completed in 1615 under his son Imam Qoli Khan. The fortified exterior harbours one of the most beautiful madrasas in Iran. Inside there is a wonderful garden, consisting of six laterally-lowered beds planted with trees. The centre is dominated by an octagonal basin; two long, river-like pools in the main axis form the backbone of the design. The courtyard is bordered on each side by a high ayvan lined with cells on two floors. The east and west façades have a different rhythm, arising from the alternation of openings of different widths, showing the high standard of Safavid architecture. The sober simplicity of the eastern ayvan shows the Safavid architects' mastery of creating an archaic space experience where nothing seems arbitrary. During the unrest caused by the takeover of Karim Khan Zand, the madrasa was badly damaged and later restored on his orders. Despite the fact that the walls and tiles lining the madrasa were partially destroyed during the Iran–Iraq war, the atmosphere of the building, both perfect as a whole as well as in the details, shapes and proportions, make it one of the major madrasas of Iran. It is still used as a religious school but allows visitors who show patience and good manners.

Source: René Hochueli

View into the ayvan of Madrasa-ye Khan

Vakil Bazaar
Bazar-e Vakil
بازار وكيل

Bazar-e Vakil, Shiraz
29.61498, 52.54680
Karim Khan Zand (Commissioner)
AD: 1773/AH: 1187/Yaz: 1143

Ceiling of Bazar-e Vakil

The 1.5 km long Vakil bazaar is considered the finest example of a cross-bazaar with several large, simultaneously built khans. It consists of two rectangular, crossing line-bazaars. In the centre, a few metres away from Saray Mushir-ul-Mulk, the bazaar axis splits toward the Masjed-e No and Jame atiq, the main mosque. The bazaar axes are still relatively well-preserved. The new roads created across the traditional texture in the 1930s were an inevitable intervention, which was necessary due to the pressure to modernise the city to keep up with the enormous demographic development. The old town was spared massive changes and a degradation of traditional structures. The modern streets are consistent with the existing roads. The whole bazaar complex was divided into parcels of about 400 m, and the roads were widened. Although some architecturally and historically interesting buildings were destroyed or partially removed, the traditional city structure remained largely intact. Another remarkable fact is that these renovations made it possible to access individual bazaar areas by modern means of transport. This is certainly one of the main reasons why the bazaar substance of this town is relatively well-preserved.

Vakil Mosque
Masjed-e Vakil
مسجد وكيل

Bazar-e Vakil, Shiraz
29.61417, 52.54517
Karim Khan Zand (Commissioner)
AD: 1773/AH: 1187/Yaz: 1143

The Vakil mosque was built between 1751 and 1773 on behalf of Karim Khan Zand, but was restored several times in the nineteenth century during the Qajar period. It is one of the largest mosques from the eighteenth and nineteenth centuries. Its decoration and tile work were probably incomplete at the time, as is attested to by the names of the Qajar monarchs Fath-Ali Shah and Naser al-Din Shah, as well as others mentioned

Roofscape of Bazar-e Vakil

Source: René Hochueli

Source: Claudius Duttwyler

Source: René Hochueli

Tiling over the Mihrhab of Masjed-e Vakil

in different inscriptions concerning its completion and restoration. Presumably the mosque originally had no cladding. The ayvans and courtyard were decorated with typical Shirazi haft rangi tiles, a characteristic feature of the art and crafts of Shiraz. The tile work in this building is one of the best examples of the art of Iranian tile workers and painters in the latter half of the eighteenth century. Every available surface that could be moulded into something else with hammer and chisel seems to have been worked on, and the overall effect is awe-inspiring. The entrance gate of the Vakil Mosque is very artistically decorated and flanked on two sides by the passages to the left and right. Vakil Mosque has only two ayvans instead of the usual four,

Source: René Hochueli

Shabestan in the Masjed-e Vakil

situated on the northern and southern side of a large open court. The simplicity of the arcades and colonnades places the mosque's age near that of the early Islamic buildings. Its decor in terms of colour is more restrained than that of the Safavid period. It is striking that the plants are not stylised, but are reproduced realistically and stand out against a plain, light background. The courtyard leads to the main room. The shabestan located behind the southern ayvan is an excellent example of a hypostyle mosque. It is supported by forty-eight monolithic spiral columns crowned with corbels of acanthus leaves. The tile decoration here focuses on the qibla wall with mihrhab niche, which is vaulted with muqarnas. The fourteen-stepped mimbar is hewn from one block of marble. It is said that Karim Khan Zand once joked that this block cost him as much as its weight in gold. It was used as a venue for Friday prayers until a few years ago. Much renovation work has been done in recent times to maintain this ancient mosque. Improvements have been made to the tilework, lighting systems, plaster works, courtyard flooring and all other aspects of the mosque necessary to keep it in good condition. Vakil Mosque is one of the most important artistic and historical buildings remaining from the Zand period and was registered as a national heritage building ca. 1960.

Source: Qassemi, Kambiz Haji (Ganjnameh)

Sarbineh in Hamman-e Vakil

Vakil Bath
Hammam-e Vakil
حمام وكيل

Khiyaban-e Taleqani, Shiraz
29.61467, 52.54503
Karim Khan Zand (Commissioner)
AD: 1773/AH: 1187/Yaz:1143

The Hammam Vakil was commissioned by Karim Khan Zand probably ca. 1751. The bath is adjacent to the Vakil Mosque and the cistern. Apart from the usual areas such as sar bineh and garm-Khaneh it contains several service sectors. The octagonal sar bineh, which also has an octagonal pond, is the largest area of the complex. Four sunken foot-baths with stairs in front are situated on the side platforms, accentuating the secondary spatial axis. The ceilings are decorated with frescoes from the Qajar period , which usually depict mythological themes like the sacrifice of Isma'el by Abraham, the ascension of Mohammad, Joseph and his brothers and Shirhin and Farhad. The garm-khane is designed as a rectangular area, which is divided by four columns. Two alcove-like spaces are vaulted and equipped with a square basin. The heating with its storerooms is located behind the khazinehs, which served as private washrooms.

Garden of view, Pars Museum
Bagh-e Nazar
باغ نظر

Bulvar-e Karim Khan Zand, Shiraz
29.61601, 52.54500
Karim Khan Zand (Commissioner)
AD: 1774/AH: 1188/Yaz: 1144

The garden was one of the most important impressive sites which Karim Khan Zand built directly southeast of his residence. It served for recreation and the reception of royal guests and foreign ambassadors. The octagonal koshk is characteristic of the garden, a pavilion with the typical roof construction which became known

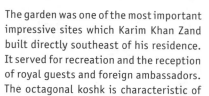

Source: Qassemi, Kambiz Haji (Ganjnameh)

Floor plan and section of Hammam-e Vakil

Source: Nirupars Netzwerk für alles Persische

Pavilion of Bagh-e Nazar

as "European hat", as well as the pool and fountain. The four principal directions of the pavilion are about 4 m wide, whilst the remaining sides measure 2.5 m. In the centre of the wider sides, large windows afford a view of the garden and pool surrounding the pavilion. The exterior façade was created from yellow brick. The interior, reached by three steps, is decorated with tiles in typical flower and bird paintings. In the centre of the pavilion stands an octagonal marble basin. The domed ceiling and the arc-like façade design with numerous niches and murals make the interior appear larger and more impressive. The garden lost its importance with the decline of the Zand dynasty. The Qadjar successor, Agha Mohammad Khan, had valuable building components relocated to his palace in Tehran, and the garden was neglected for years. Later the Qajar Shah had the corpse of Karim Khan Zand, who was buried in the eastern alcove of the pavilion, removed as an act of revenge; it was returned in the Pahlavi period. Between 1797 and 1834, Hosinali Mirza Farmanfarma ruled the Fars province. He had the garden restored as a reception and pleasure palace and added prestigious new buildings to the southwest and southeast. The walls and ceilings of the pavilion's interior were covered with

Source: Zolfaqari, Amir Huseyn

Interior of the reception room

mirror mosaics depicting floral patterns. Because of the light reflecting in the mirrors, they were called "mirror and sun buildings". In 1931, the urban expansion began with the development of the public road network. This took up large parts of the northern and eastern sides of the garden, today covered by roads, administration buildings and a public library. Since 1935, the entire complex served as a state museum, an initiative of the then-Culture Minister Ali Asqar Hakmat. Restoration of the pavilion started in 1971, and it was reopened in 1981.

Source: Charlotte Heer Grau

Courtyard with water basin

Citadel Karim Khan Zand
Arg-e Karim Khan Zand
ارگ کریم خان زند

Maidan-e Shohada, Shiraz
29.61764, 52.54478
Karim Khan Zand (Commissioner)
AD: 1774/AH: 1188/Yaz: 1144

In 1759, Karim Khan Zand chose Shiraz as his capital and had his residence built west of the historical centre, on the site of the former Safavid fortress. This enabled him to use the existing water supply. From outside the architecture of the building resembles a citadel because of its high walls and four towers. However, it is a purely residential building with a palatial central complex, which is located on the northwest side. All the secondary rooms, stables, arsenal, guard-room, parade grounds as well as the garden were placed outside the walls. The rooms within the enclosure were lavishly fitted out for the ruler's family and for official receptions and formed a carefully-designed holistic artwork. Above the entrance on the south side there is a coloured-glazed ceramic image depicting the mythical struggle between Rostam and an evil spirit. The reception and living rooms are located on the northwest side and open to the large, leafy courtyard. The rooms are about 1 m above ground level and are reached by

a portico located in the middle. From here you have a marvellous view across a small basin to the large pond in the axis of the garden. The central reception rooms on the northwest side consist of a hall with wooden columns of about 8 m high which are partially decorated with floral pictures. After the defeat of Karim Khan Zand and his successors, the original stone columns were moved to Tehran and replaced by the present wooden columns. Wind vents are arranged on the roof of the portico, ensuring pleasant air circulation in the rooms. Whilst the exterior

Source: René Hochueli

Detail of the façade

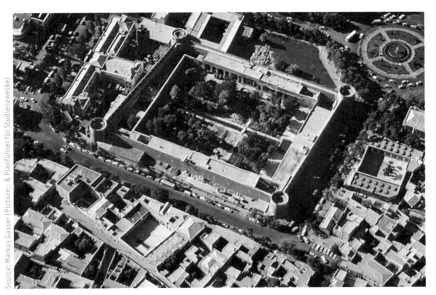

Source: Markus Gasser (Picture- & Planführer für Studienzwecke)

Aerial view of the complex

façades of the reception and living rooms are sparsely decorated, the interior walls and ceilings were elaborately adorned with stucco work and coloured murals. The castle-like, historically rather unusual character of the house is explained by the fact that the owner was a soldier and therefore may have had many personal enemies. In 1779, only five years after completion of the residence, Karim Khan Zand and his descendants were murdered by a political adversary. Between 1928 and 1935, the arsenal, the parade ground and parts on the southeast side of the bazaar were levelled to make way for a new road, and on the west and east side of the complex new administrative and service buildings were erected by Mohsen Fouroughi and Vartan Hovanessian. From 1935, the Arg-e Karim Khan Zand was used by the city administration and later as a prison until 1967. In 1972 it was given protection status as a national building deserving of protection. As part of a new urban concept, the thoroughfare on the south side was moved underground, creating one of the first traffic calming "pedestrian zones" in Iran.

Source: René Hochueli

Bottom view of the talar

Source: René Hochueli

Mosaic over the main entrance

Source: Behrooz Barsin (TU Berlin)

Aerial view of the garden

Garden of the Image of the World
Bagh-e Jahan Nama
باغ جهان نما

Khiyaban-e Hafez, Shiraz
29.62892, 52.55858
Karim Khan Zand (Commissioner)
AD: 1774/AH: 1188/Yaz: 1144

The existence of this garden can be traced back to the fourteenth century. It enjoyed the heyday of its development between 1766 and 1774, when Karim Khan Zand had the garden redesigned, adding an impressive pavilion, a guest house and outbuildings. Between 1797 and 1834, the site served as a government guest house and at times as residence of the British consul. From 1979 until 2002, the building was used as a radio and television studio. Today it is used as

a public park. The centre of the square garden is a 10 m high, octagonal pavilion. The outer walls have different widths: four sides measure about 10 m, the remaining sides 4 m. The wider sides have large windows allowing a beautiful view over the garden. The pavilion is located approximately 1 m above garden level. In its centre lies an octagonal marble basin with a fountain. The upper parts of the interior façade are decorated with murals, a Shirazi design of flower and bird motifs. Apart from the pavilion there are two more buildings on the southeast and southwest side of the garden which originally served as guesthouses. These are presently under reconstruction. Originally the single-storey building on the northwest side was a secondary building used by staff, and it is currently used as office for security personnel.

Source: Behrooz Barsin (TU Berlin)

Mural with classic flower and bird decoration

Mausoleum of Seven Graves
Takiyeh-ye Haft Tanan
هفت تن

Bulvar-e Haft Tanan, Shiraz
29.62889, 52.56222
Sufi-Orden (Commissioner)
AD: 1774/AH: 1188/Yaz: 1144

It is assumed that a member of the Zand family ordered the building of this suburban villa. Set in a beautiful garden with cypresses, pine trees and citrus

Aqa Sadeq, mural with classic floral and bird motifs in the portico

trees, the terrace of the main building is decorated with murals. Seven highly respected Sufi dervishes lived and meditated here and are buried in the garden. Karim Khan Zand had the building walled and refurbished with decoratively designed rooms as a place of worship, which was used as a place of pilgrimage until the Islamic Revolution of 1979, when the Sufi fell from favour. Since then, Haft Tanan has been used as a museum for stone tablets and text fragments. Between 2007 and 2009 the archetypal building was repaired by the Office for Cultural Heritage. The area, measuring 85 by 30 m, lies at the foot of Mount Baba Kuhi. On the northeast side is a portico, flanked on both sides by double-storey rooms. The building is about 1.5 m above garden level and is accessible via five steps. The walls of the portico

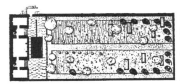

Floor plan

are decorated with wall paintings depicting flowers and birds as well as a portrait of the Safavid king Shah Abbas I and Sufi motifs like Abraham sacrificing Ishmael, and Moses with a flock of sheep. The murals were created by Aqa Sadeq, a well-known Shirazi artist of the eighteenth century, and restored between 1957 and 1958. On the southwest side of the mausoleum are common rooms used as sanitary and utility rooms. Today they are used for administration and as workshops for small restoration work.

View over the tombs of the seven Sufis

Takiyeh-ye Haft Tanan, courtyard

1787–1925
Shiraz, New Beginning under the Qajar

The brief period of cultural rise of Shiraz was followed by a more than hundred year period of decline when no major urban changes took place. The Qajar king Agha Mohammad Khan chose Tehran as his capital in 1796. This shift to north moved the Fars province and its capital Shiraz to the periphery. The city wall and corresponding moats, replaced in the Zand dynasty, were gradually demolished in the second half of the nineteenth century, earlier than in most other Iranian cities, where this measure was only implemented after 1920. This was due to structural damage caused by earthquakes. The motives were not so much to obtain building materials or land but rather the new rulers' intention to exclude Shiraz from being used for military purposes by political opponents. The consequences of the loss of capital status were exacerbated by strong earthquakes. As a result, the population shrank by about half by 1867, down to approximately 25,000 residents.

The earthquakes also destroyed the irrigation system, which severely affected agriculture and horticulture. In 1897, *Meyers Lexikon* still stated: "The streets of the city, which is frequently exposed to earthquakes, are dirty, narrow and uneven, buildings and city walls dilapidated, the famous gardens overgrown, the castles in the neighbourhood neglected".

Development of the Urban Area of Shiraz up to 1779

The remaining palaces of the Zand dynasty on the north-south axis were used for the provincial administration. The Zand Avenue – the former city gate, Bagh-e Shah – now served as east-west axis which was developed as the connection between the old town and the new districts on the west side, with rows of trees and grass strips in the centre. Along the avenue, still within the old town, rich landowners and merchants bought land and built villas surrounded by large gardens. Of particular note are three families who dominated individual city districts. The Qavam Al Molk family, which was among the politically most influential families of this dynasty, renovated its urban residence, which had a beautiful courtyard to the east of the old town, in 1870. In 1882, the businessman Mirza Abul Hasen Khan Moshir Almolk built a country house in the southwest, outside Bagh-e Jennat. Yet Shiraz had not recovered from the heavy setbacks at the end of the Qajar dynasty; the town had only about 30,000 residents in 1913.

Source: Thomas Meyer-Wieser

Development of urban area of Shiraz up to 1779

Source: Thomas Meyer-Wieser

Garden of Eden
Bagh-e Eram
باغ ارم

Bulvar-e Eram, Shiraz
29.63570, 52.52575
Haji Mohammad Hasan Memar
AD: 1091, 1338, 1813/AH: 484, 739, 1228/
Yaz: 460, 707, 1183

The Bagh-e Eram, today the most famous garden of Shiraz, is located north of the city. Its name derives from a legendary garden on the Arab peninsula mentioned in the Qu'ran as "the one decorated with columns". The origin of the garden dates back to the Seljuq dynasty. In 1091, Atabek Qerajeh built his residence here. Towards the end of the Mongolian Ilkhanid dynasty, the governor chose Bagh-e Eram as his residence. The poet Hafez sang about its beauty and Timur Lenk was inspired by it. At the beginning of the second half of the nineteenth century, the merchant and landowner Mirza Hasen Khan Nasir Almolk acquired the garden and constructed a new reception hall. He commissioned the architect and builder Haji Mohammad Hasan Memar to design the building and the garden. The property was owned by the Nasir Almolk family until the 1930s. When the last descendant, Mohammad Naser Khan, was unable to pay his taxes, the governor had the property confiscated and made it his headquarters. The living quarters are designed in such a way that they divide the garden into a formal front part and a smaller rear part for family use. The pediments of the palace façade show coloured tiles images, for example, a mythical royal couple with Rostam, Naser al-Din Shah on a white horse, Farhad and Shirin, Joseph and Zuleika and different animal species. The long garden axis, focus of all the elements, creates the balance between the checkerboard-like fields. The slightly recessed beds on both sides of the paths are planted according to ancient Persian tradition, with fruit trees, which blossom in spring. The three-storey high, formal reception building also forms the central point here. The wing facing the garden is framed by a richly-decorated open portico with a magnificent façade clad in colourful tiles with geometric and floral patterns. The rooms in the basement are intended for hot summer days; the walls and floors are covered with coloured tiles. A canal flows through a pool in the middle of the room before it empties into the large pool in front of the house. Lateral stairs lead from here to the piano nobile, from where the view through the main axis is extended to the south and picturesquely opens to the barren hills that form the border of the oasis. The garden has been part of the University of Shiraz since 1980 and is now used as a botanical garden and recreational area. Unfortunately, the palace is no longer accessible.

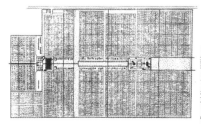

Ground floor plan
according to Donald Newton Wilber

Source: Donald Newton Wilber
(Persian gardens and garden pavilions)

View through the central axis of the garden

Orange Garden of Qavam
Bagh-e Narenjestan-e Qavam
باغ نارنجستان قوام

Khyiaban-e Lotfali Khan Zand,
Shiraz
29.60784, 52.55257
*Mohammad Reza Khan Qavam
al-Molk (Commissioner)*
AD: 1836, 1846 / AH: 1252, 1262 /
Yaz: 1206, 1216

Elegance and opulence are typical of the taste of the Persian upper class. Bagh-e Narenjestan-e Qavam, together with the adjacent Zinat ol Molk House, forms the Qavam complex built by Ali Mohammad Khan in 1880. He was mayor of Shiraz and coordinator of the powerful Khamseh nomadic tribes. The Narendjestan Garden with its buildings served as administrative headquarters. Simple matters were dealt with in the offices at the entrance. The way to the reception rooms led through the garden, planted with palms and orange trees along water basins, to the talar, the pillared porch of the main building which is surmounted by several pediments. These display the royal symbols, such as the lion and the sun. The residence is called Narendjestan because orange trees were planted along the way between the offices and the reception room. The pavilion's mirrored entrance hall opens onto rooms with painted walls and ceilings. The ceilings in the upstairs rooms are particularly interesting, with beams painted with European-style motifs, including Alpine churches and buxom German ladies. His son, Mohammad Reza Khan Qavam ol-Molk, renovated the estate

View from the talar

Soffit in the main building

Source: René Hochueli

Plinth detail

in 1884 and created the courtyard garden in its current form. It continued to be used as a residence until 1966, when the then-successor, Abrahim Qavam, bequeathed the entire complex to the University of Shiraz. In the ensuing years, it was renovated under the patronage of Shahbanu Farah Diba Pahlavi. Between 1969 and 1979, the complex was put at the disposal of the Asia Institute, run by American archaeologist and historian Arthur Upham Pope and his wife Phyllis Ackermann, who published several volumes on Iranian art and architecture. The complex has been managed by the University of Art and Architecture since 1999 and is used as a museum. As expected, the town house also follows the well-known design. The main building houses the biruni, whilst the entrance and offices are located along the road.

A south-facing pavilion in the centre, set about 1.5 m above garden level, opens onto a typical Qajar talar decorated with mirror mosaics and stained-glass windows. The wooden sliding windows on the garden façade are striking. The interiors are decorated with elegant Qajar mirror mosaics, tile decor, frescos and inlays. Ceilings and exteriors are also decorated with mirror mosaics and plaster ornaments with floral patterns. The wood-panelled ceilings bear traditional flower and bird motifs created by Lotfali Khan Soratger. The familiar courtyard design is focused on water pools and central paths lined with roses. The courtyard façade of the entrance buildings is decorated with colourful ceramics depicting three servants in typical Zand attire, framed by motifs with floral, landscape and hunting scenes merging into each other.

Source: René Hochueli

Joist system in the talar

Reception building of Bagh-e Delgosha ca. 1930

Heart-Refreshing Garden
Bagh-e Delgosha
باغ دلگشا

Bulvar-e Bostan/
Bulvar-e Delgosha, Shiraz
29.61939, 52.57472
Mirza Ali Akbar Qavam al-Molk Shirazi
(Commissioner)
AD: 1839/AH: 1255/Yaz: 1209

128

Bagh-e Delgosha is one of the oldest gardens of Shiraz. Its construction is attributed to the Sassanid but it was used continuously in different periods of time and became one of the most famous gardens in Shiraz in the Safavid era. It underwent restoration work during the Zand as well as the Qajar eras. The garden was first mentioned ca. 1370 when

Shiraz peacefully fell into the hands of the Timurid. It is believed that Timur Lenk used it as seat of government. In 1839 a merchant, Qavam Almolk Mirza Ali Akbar Shirshzi, acquired the garden. He built the present reception building and surrounded the estate with mud walls. The members of the family used the garden as their main residence until 1969, when it was acquired by the city council. In the centre of the garden is the three-storey reception building. The main axis of the garden extends from its entrance gate as far as the basin in front of the mid- garden building. On either side of this axis are two citrus orchards. Two walkways are on the eastern and western sides of the main building, and a third walkway is located north, with pine and cedar trees planted alongside it. Other trees found at Bagh-e Delgosha Tare are several old sour orange trees as well as palms, walnut trees and a few other species. A big, beautiful basin stands in front of the twin-columned portico south of the building. The mid-garden pavilion comprises a large hall with four alcoves constructed in the architectural style of the Sassanid palace of Bishapur, still preserved in its original condition. This building is on three floors, with its frontage covered by Muarraq tiling. Part of the pavilion was destroyed in a fire two

Reception building of Bagh-e Delgosha

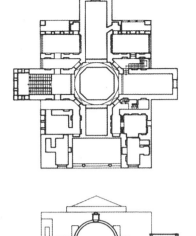
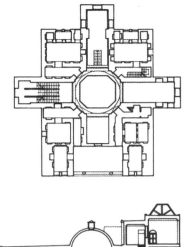

Source: Bagh-e Irani (Iranian New Art)

Floor plan and section of the reception building

decades ago but was reconstructed during the past decade. Its entrance is on the narrow southwestern side. Four steps lead to the audience hall, which is about 1 m above garden level and allows a view over the open porch into the countryside. In the centre of the hall sits an octagonal basin of hewn limestone with a fountain. The ceiling and interior walls are decoratively stuccoed with floral patterns, whilst the exterior façades are covered in colourful ceramic tiles in geometric patterns. The calligraphic inscriptions, framed by floral arabesques, are also

impressive. The private residential building, reserved for women, children and family members, lies outside the present walls on the northeast side. It was separated from the garden in 1959 by the construction of a road and is currently closed to the public. Bagh-e Delgosha satisfactorily represents the elements and systems of Persian Gardens with its antiquity, design, geometrical garden space, exploitation of qanats, vegetation system as well as the selection of plants suitable for the climate. However, urbanisation has somewhat harmed it.

Source: Charlotte Heer Grau

Basin in the garden axis

Interior of the Qajar talar

Garden of Paradise
Bagh-e Jannat
باغ جنت

Samavarsaz-ha, Shiraz
29.61339, 52.47383
Mirza Abul Hasan Khan
(Commissioner)
AD: 1839 / AH: 1255 / Yaz: 1209

In 1839 the merchant Mirza Abul Hasen Khan commissioned the building of a villa southwest of the town. The property was about 54 ha and known under the name Bagh-e Jannat. From the mid-1920s, most trees were felled, and the military has used the site since 1979. New buildings were erected in the southwest and northwest areas which served as hospital, administration and function venue. In 2004, the city of Shiraz bought the southwest and northwest parts of the garden, which were redesigned and opened to the public in 2008. The park is surrounded by densely populated neighbourhoods with a predominantly low-income population as well as industrial areas. It is bound on all sides by busy roads. The gate house from 1839 no longer exists.

View into the courtyard of Bagh-e Jannat

Source: René Hochueli

Source: Hossein Majidi

Two-storey reception building with water basin in front

Rose Garden, Afif Abad Garden
Bagh-e Golshan, Bagh-e Afif Abad
باغ عفیف آباد

Samavarsaz-ha, Shiraz
29.62305, 52.49817
Mirza Ali Mohammad Khan Qavam al-Molk (Commissioner)
AD: 1575, 1863 / AH: 983, 1300 / Yaz: 944, 1233

The garden is first mentioned in 1575 when it was used by Governor Jaqob Khan Zolqader for receptions and as a residence. In 1863 the nobleman Mirza Ali Mohammad Khan Qavam ol-Molk bought the garden, enclosed it by a wall and built a single-storey apartment building, andaruni, with a double-storey reception building, biruni, situated in the upper third of the garden oriented to the southeast. It combines various decorative elements such as portico, stucco and tile work with designs from pre-Islamic and Islamic periods. The entrance to the building is located on the northeast side and is flanked by two, 5 m high pillars. On the southeast side is a typical portico, called shah nashhin, or royal seat. From here, one looks over the pools and the garden, with its wide lawns and tall cypresses. The walls of the reception building bear plasterwork, murals and tiles with floral motifs. The floor in the entrance hall shows flower and bird motifs and western European landscapes. The offices, service rooms and bath house are located next to the entrance on the east side of the garden. The walls in the bath house are clad with colourful tiles embedded in miniature-like landscape pictures, showing battle and hunting scenes from *Shahname*, the *Book of Kings* by Ferdosi. The reception building divides the longitudinal axis. The northwest half has an open, 55 m long canal with paths on both sides, whilst the southeast side has a limestone pool measuring 28 × 15 m. Originally there was an elongated open channel near the basin, which extended to the edge of the garden. The new Governor Naser Aldols Abrahim Khan resided here from 1902. Towards the end of the Qajar dynasty, his wife Afife inherited the garden, which was then named after her. The garden was owned by the Pahlavi family from 1941 to 1969, and a few rooms upstairs (including the bedroom of Shahbanu Diba, with its original decor) are preserved as they were used by the last Shahs. Between 1969 and 1991, Bagh-e Afif Abad was used by the military, which built the symmetrical areas and buildings on the southwest side and installed a museum of ancient weapons in the basement of the reception area.

Source: René Hochueli

Zinat ol-Molk House

Zinat ol-Molk House
Khaneh-ye Zinat ol-Molk
خان زینت الملک

Khyiaban-e Lotfali Khan Zand,
Shiraz
29.60785, 52.55207
Mirza Ebrahim Khan
AD: 1879, 1886/AH: 1296, 1303/
Yaz: 1248, 1255

Khaneh-ye Zinat ol-Molk is a beautiful edifice on the west side of Bagh-e Narenjestan-e Qavam. This house was originally the Qavam ol-Molk family's stunning andaruni, or private residence. There is an alley between Narenjestan (the biruni, or working place of Qavam) and the private residential building. The complex was built between 1879 and 1886 and is named after its last owner, the daughter of the builder Qavam. Its construction is attributed to Mirza Ebrahim Khan, the great-grandson of the elder Qavam and grandfather of the present Qavam ol-Molk. An underground passage under Sang Dakhakhiha alley, which is today closed to the public, connects these two buildings. The rectangular courtyard has a number of trees and two water basins, one in front of

the edifice and the other on the east side of the courtyard. There are a number of buildings around the yard that served different purposes during the year. The main hall of the building lies on the west side of the courtyard. This double-storey building is decorated with paintings and mirrors. It has fretwork doors and windows in the Qajar style. Twenty rooms are embellished with paintings, stucco decoration and mirrors; intricate mosaic floors were designed to resemble ornate Persian rugs. The detention house and stable no longer exist. Today, most of the finely-decorated rooms show exhibits of the Fars History Museum, whilst others serve as exhibition space for young Shirazi artists. The downstairs museum houses an archaeological collection put together by Arthur Upham Pope, an American historian and scholar who taught at the Asia Institute in Shiraz between 1969 and 1979. Pope spent fifty years of his life working here, and dedicated numerous antique artifacts to it. The museum's collections of his photographs and slides is also preserved here. The complex is a significant representation of Iranian architecture during the Qajar period.

View into the courtyard of Moshir Complex

Moshir Complex, Golshan
Majmueh-ye Moshir, Golshan
مجموعه مشیر (گلشن)

Bazar-e Ordu, Shiraz
29.61339, 52.54619
*Mirza Abul-Hasan Khan Moshir
al-Molk (Commissioner)*
AD: 1871/AH: 1288/Yaz: 1241

According to an inscription at the entrance, the Moshir or Golshan complex was commissioned in 1871 by the governor of Fars province, Mizra-Ab-ol-Hassan Khan Moshir-ol-Molk. It is one of the most sophisticated buildings in the bazaar of Shiraz and relatively well-preserved. A two-storey courtyard unit upstairs, which is slightly recessed and accessed via a front corridor, incorporates a ship-shaped courtyard. The centre part of the north façade protrudes and emphasises the overlying dome, which is designed as a timcheh. The corners of the courtyard are designed quite differently, depending on the requirements. The façade design is extremely skilful. Various types of ogee arches, circular arches and half-arches span the openings. The courtyard design is also carefully thought-through – a large

rectangular pool is flanked by four flower-beds on the north and south sides. Since the courtyard is lower than the shops, it offers a special view over the canopy formed by the tall trees and the beds in the yard. The inner courtyard façades consist mainly of brick, used to vault and decorate the rooms and passages. This sophisticated system peaks in the octagonal entrance vestibule which is covered by a cap-like squat vault. The combination of wood and brick creates a warm, friendly atmosphere. The vestibule is connected to a finely-worked portico, which in turn contributes to the sophistication of the saray (which, with its narrow, double-storey façade, is similar to the entrance of a mosque).

Ground floor plan

Excursion into prehistory

Excursion into prehistory
Achaemenid Empire

The Achaemenid Empire was the first Persian Empire. Its first expansion occurred in 550 BC under Cyrus II, following the defeat of the Medes. The expansion continued under his successors, up to the largest expansion, which reached its peak ca. 500 BC. The Achaemenids occur in Western history primarily as opponents of the Greeks. Benchmarks are the battles of Marathon and Salamis. From this perspective, the prominent role of the kingdom with regard to the history of the Near East and the development of ancient Greece was largely ignored. The idea of ancient Persians as murderous and cruel barbarians still dominates European thinking. This strong negative and distorted image was influenced by the Greeks, with even the first Greek historian Herodotus often describing bestial details, thereby creating a picture of horror of the Persians. In contrast, it is hardly known that the empire founded by Cyrus II can be considered as one of the first welfare states of the Near East. Apart from inscriptions on monuments, there are hundreds of administrative and inventory texts in Elamite and Aramaic that describe the organisation of the community and everyday life. They show a very different image of the Persian Empire. For example, men and women received the same compensation for the same work (in the form of produce),

Persian Empire at 500 BC

reflecting the very pronounced multilingualism in Achaemenid times. The ancient Persian Empire is therefore an interesting historic example of multicultural communities. Darius had manuals of the sciences, medicine, law, astronomy and geography compiled from all satraps and thus started the lengthy process of combining Asiatic peoples and cultures from India to Iran, Babylonia and Anatolia to Egypt into one single unit. At the end of this process, after more than a millennium, the Great Caliphate emerged; but not only the Arabs, but also the Persians, had already created this civilization.

Persian Empire, 500 BC

Herodotus recounts the romantic story of the insurrection of the Persian king Cyrus against the Medes king Astyages, saying that after his victory Cyrus concluded a friendship treaty with the Medes which was based on equality. At the palace steps of Persepolis you see the representatives of the countries in animated conversation, alternately a Mede and a Persian, and also in the deployment of the twenty-three Satrap delegations you find alternately twelve Persian and eleven Median satraps. Only with the combined forces of two Iranian clans was it possible to conquer the enormous Achaemenid Empire.

Source: iStockphoto (mtcurado)

Ruins of Persepolis near Shiraz

women were granted a sort of paid maternity leave after giving birth, pregnant women were given special rations, and the disabled or people unable to work due to accidents were supported by a type of minimum wage. In addition, there was freedom of religion and freedom of lifestyle or freedom to use other languages, as long as the existing laws were observed. These official records are amazingly written in several languages,

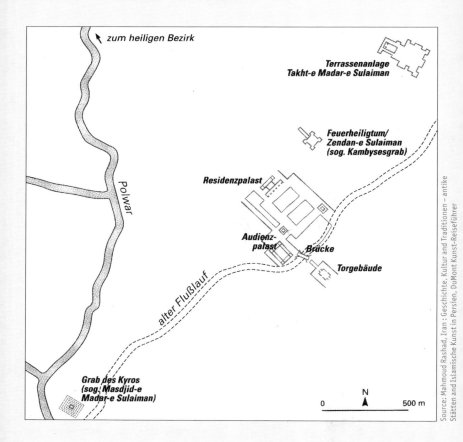

Source: Mahmoud Rashad, Iran: Geschichte, Kultur and Traditionen – antike Stätten and Islamische Kunst in Persien, DuMont Kunst-Reiseführer

Labels on map: zum heiligen Bezirk · Terrassenanlage Takht-e Madar-e Sulaiman · Feuerheiligtum/ Zendan-e Sulaiman (sog. Kambysesgrab) · Polwar · Residenzpalast · Audienz-palast · Brücke · Torgebäude · alter Flußlauf · Grab des Kyros (sog. Masdjid-e Madar-e Sulaiman) · N · 0 – 500 m

Pasargadae, Pasargad
AD: 559 – 525 BC

Pasargadae, the first capital of the Achaemenids, was founded by Cyrus the Great in the sixth century BC. The city extended over about 300 ha. It consisted of a palace and two open-air pavilions, set in an irrigated garden. The raised site of the palace emphasised the rank of the king when he sat before his courtiers in the shade of the portico in front of the palace, looking at the decorative water channels. At that time, the city had a sophisticated irrigation system, consisting of a barrage and a channel leading to Pasargadea. Precise historical indications for a paradise garden in the Achaemenid era can be found in the vast plane of Marv-Dasht east of Zagros Mountains. Among the ruins of its foundations, bright-white, channelled columns rise up to the sky against the backdrop of brown hills. The first Achaemenid garden allowing a reconstruction was the palace garden of Cyrus the Great in Passargadae.

David Stronach's excavations show well-preserved fragments of a geometrically-designed system of open sandstone water channels, interspersed with periodically-repeated square pools surrounding a large garden area. The capital that Cyrus created consisted of a palace and two open-air pavilions, which opened up to the landscape on two or four sides, offering a view into the countryside from protected, slightly elevated colonnades. If we use the later references to ancient gardens by Persian poets, the love of gardens must have originated from a contemplative attitude and a poetic approach to nature. Between the channels, in the square areas below the main paths, Cyrus probably planted different fruit trees in neat rows. Watercourses formed the Passargadae central garden's main and lateral axes. This geometric, rectangular array of channels that divided the site required an artful stone construction for irrigation and ensured a steady flow of water – but the channels and pools were also always decorative.

Palace of Cyrus the Great
Kakh-e Kurosh-e Bozorg
کاخ کوروش بزرگ

Pasargad, Shiraz
30.20272, 53.17794
Cyrus the Great (Commissioner)
AD: 525 BC

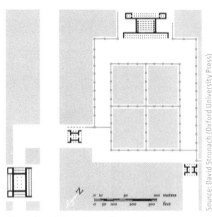

Floor plan of the Palace of Cyrus the Great

Excavations by David Stronach revealed that the central garden of Pasargadae was probably the private garden of the king and formed part of a much larger royal park. He reconstructed a Chahar Bagh measuring 145 × 112 m which was flanked by pavilions providing shade during the heat of the day. Its boundaries were defined by smaller water channels leading from the palace's cross wall in the north to a small pavilion in the south. Stronach assumed that Cyrus' throne was placed in the axis of one of the gardens. Between the channels, in the square areas below the main paths, Cyrus may have planted different fruit trees in neat rows, like pomegranates, which had been cultivated for centuries, as well as sour cherry and almond trees. Also, there were vines and indigenous roses with cloves and colourful bulbous plants such as tulips, irises and poppies planted underneath. Common white bark poplars were probably planted there as protection from the wind, irrigated by jubs. Avenues of indigenous cypresses and Middle Eastern plane trees offered shade.

Irrigation channel in the garden of Cyrus the Great

Excavated fragments of the Palace of Cyrus the Great

Tomb of Cyrus the Great, aerial view

Tomb of Cyrus the Great
Aramgah-e Kurosh-e Bozorg
آرامگاه کوروش بزرگ
Pasargad, Shiraz
30.19389, 53.16728
Cyrus the Great (Commissioner)
AD: 525 BC

The tomb of Cyrus is generally identified with a small stone monument southwest of the palaces of Pasargadae. According to Greek sources, the tomb of Cyrus II was located in the royal park at Pasargadae. "How beautiful the trees are", Lysander wrote after visiting Cyrus in his royal paradise garden at Sardes in today's Anatolia, "planted at an equal distance, how straight in rows, how nicely rectangular they stand". In addition, Xenophon reports that the tomb of Cyrus at Pasargadea was surrounded by water and a garden with symmetrically arranged trees. The tomb of Cyrus the Great stood in a lush garden with trees and flowers. A cenotaph in the form of a small stone house is placed on a base of six stone steps. Its shape is related to Lycian tombs in southern Asia Minor. When, after his return from India, Alexander the Great found the mausoleum broken into and

Tomb of Cyrus the Great

Persepolis, aerial view

looted, he ordered it to be restored and had an epitaph attached which Strabo quoted in his work *Geography*: "O man, whoever thou art, from wheresoever thou cometh, for I know you shall come, I am Cyrus, who founded the Persian Empire. Grudge me not, therefore, this little earth that covers my body." The tomb is simple in form, constructed of large, carefully dressed ashlar blocks set with precision and secured by dovetail clamps. The high grave chamber elevated from the ground is a sign of a Zoroastrian mausoleum as it prevents the contact of the deceased body with the ground.

Persepolis
Takht-e Jamshid
تخت جمشید

Pasargad, Shiraz
29.93500, 52.89028
Xerxes I (Commissioner)
AD: 518 BC

About 50 km northeast of Shiraz, located at the foot of Kuh-e Rahmat, you will find the most impressive historical site in Iran, called Parseh in old Persian, worldwide known under the Greek name Persepolis, the Persian City. At the height of his power, ca. 518 BC, Darius the Great

Charles Chipiez, Bird's-Eye View of Persepolis, 1884

Flight of stairs to the residential palace of Darius l

founded the residence of the Achaemenid kings. He summoned architects, artists, artisans and materials from all parts of the empire. Therefore Urartian, Assyrian, Egyptian, Babylonian, Greek, and Median influences are recognisable in architecture and decoration, but the Achaemenids never just copied foreign cultural ideas but always created something new, so that one can really speak of Persian-Achaemenid art. Under Darius, the Persepolis terrace was initially established, and the construction of the Apadana and the palace of Darius commenced. Darius' son and successor, Xerxes, completed these buildings,

adding the Gate of All Nations as well as his own palace. The Hall of a Hundred Columns was only completed under his son Artaxerxes. Persepolis, the largest and best preserved palace complex of antiquity, is an impressive example of this unique advanced civilization. According to one theory, the monumental structure was erected to celebrate the New Year, Noruz. Since time immemorial, the reawakening of nature in spring inspired Persian art and poetry, and still today the blossoming of the desert is an occasion for celebration. The wise governance of the Achaemenids and the balanced rule of Shahanshah, or King

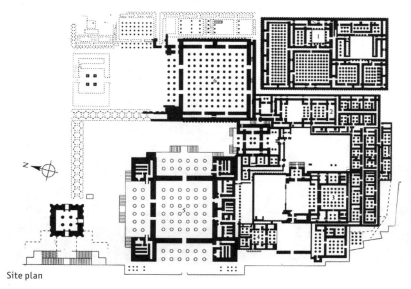

Site plan

of Kings, who allowed the vanquished nations to rule relatively freely as independent satrapies in his name, resulted in a fruitful fusion of all cultures conquered by the Achaemenids. The architectural perfection achieved in Persepolis surpassed everything the Achaemenids produced during their 229-year reign. New in Persepolis is the compact building mass of the entire complex consisting of various individual buildings, which are all arranged on one uniform rectangular coordinate system, connected by open spaces and gateways. The master plan of the terraces in its design and in the selected building materials shows two distinctly separate areas, suggesting completely different functions. In the eastern part of the terrace, directly facing the slopes of Kuh-e Rahmat, stand the buildings like Hundred Columns Hall and the Treasure House, constructed from transient building materials like mud-brick; they are probably part of the private domain of the king. The more important buildings on the west side of the terrace, Apadana, Darius Palace, Xerxes Palace and Tripylon, show a pure stone architecture, suggesting the official audience character of these palaces, which is additionally confirmed by the visible inscriptions that were only discovered on stone buildings. Darius I never completed the palace complex he planned. During his lifetime, most likely only his own palace, the treasury and as well as parts of the Apadana and the Tripylons were completed. The great builder of Persepolis was probably Xerxes I, who executed his father Darius' plans splendidly, except for Hundred Columns

Source: René Hochueli

Persepolis, Cyclopean masonry

Hall, which (except for the propylon) was completed by his son Artaxerxes. It henceforth required only minor modifications or additions, which had no influence on the vision of Darius I. Persepolis had been the symbol of the Achaemenid Empire for nearly 200 years when, in 330 BC, Alexander the Great set fire to the palace, avenging the destruction of the Acropolis in Athens by Xerxes I and bringing about the destruction of the Achaemenid empire. Dutch artist Cornelis de Bruijn, who visited Persepolis in 1704/1705, was the first to make a serious contribution to the exploration of the ruins and identified them as capital of the ancient Persian Empire. His drawings were published in 1711 in *Reizen over Moskovie, door Persie en Indie*. They were the best available accounts right up to the twentieth century.

Source: Cornelis de Bruijn, *Reizen over Moskovie, door Persie en Indie* (1711)

Cornelis de Bruijn, View of Persepolis, 1711

Apadana
Apadana
آپادانا

Persepolis, Shiraz
29.93500, 52.88944
*Darius I the Great, Xerxes I
(Commissioners)*
AD: 518 BC

Cornelis de Bruijn, Darius' Palace, 1711

Source: Cornelis de Bruijn

The Apadana was the largest building on the terrace at Persepolis. It served as an audience hall, and was commissioned by Darius the Great in the first half of the fifth century BC and completed by Xerxes I. It was presumably the main hall of the kings. The pillars were 20 m high and had complex capitals in the form of bulls, lions and raptors. This was the place where the king was offered tribute. The hall is accessed by two monumental staircases in the north and east, decorated with reliefs representing the delegates of the twenty three nations of the Persian Empire. The delegates of the vassal states, Elamite, Parthian, Egyptians and Babylonians who came to Persepolis all had to climb these (stairs) to pay homage to their king. Led by Persians and Medes, some carrying flowers as the artist's indication of the approaching spring, they stride towards the pillars that supported the roof of the huge audience hall. Regularly-recurring images of lotus leaves and flowers as well as cypresses, pine and palm trees testify to the Persians' love of nature and their masterful skill in the art of bas-relief. The term "Apadana" is etymologically ambiguous. The Old Persian word a-pad-an means "unprotected" and refers to the fact that the veranda-like structure is open on one of its four sides and thus exposed to the elements. The term ayvan later used in Islamic architecture derives from it, and refers to both buildings with columns, like the palace of Chehel Sotun, as well as barrel vaults, like the classic four-ayvan mosque. The Apadana was excavated by the German archaeologist Ernst Herzfeld and his assistants Friedrich Krefter and Erich Schmidt between 1931 and 1939. Annemarie Schwarzenbach, who participated in the excavations in 1933, recorded this in her travel diary *Winter in the Middle East*.

Darius' Palace
Kakh-e Techer
کاخ تچر

Persepolis, Shiraz
29.93417, 52.88944
Darius I the Great (Commissioner)
AD: 518 BC

Darius I the Great commissioned the so-called Winter Palace. However, it was completed by his son and successor Xerxes I only in 486 BC after his death. Several inscriptions attest: "Darius the great king, king of kings, king of countries, son of Hystaspes, built this palace". The ruins just south of the Apadana are relatively well-preserved compared to the other buildings, which suggests that the palace was spared in the destruction of Persepolis by Alexander the Great. The reliefs of the palace for the first time depict motifs which became very important in later Achaemenid art, like the king accompanied by a servant with a parasol, or a fight with the lion. The lintels of the Winter Palace are in the Egyptian

Source: Wikimedia Commons

Charles Chipiez, Reconstruction of the Apadana of Persepolis, 1884 style, an interesting innovation that occurs again more than seven centuries later in the Palace of Ardashir in Firuzabad. Near the western entrance was a garden where a small irrigation canal is still visible today, and one can assume that the king sat here and enjoyed the view over the plain.

Restored north façade of the Harem of Xerxes

Xerxes' Palace
Kakh-e Hedish
کاخ هدیش
Persepolis, Shiraz
29.93389, 52.89000
Darius I the Great (Commissioner)
AD: 518 BC

Xerxes' Harem
Haram-e Khashayar Shah
خشایار شاه حرم
Persepolis, Shiraz
29.93389, 52.89111
Ernst Emil Herzfeld
AD: 518 BC

The palace of Xerxes was twice the size as that of Darius. It was called Hedish, or Habitation. A terrace connected it to Darius'. The main room had thirty-six columns and was surrounded by six smaller rooms. To the north stood a portico overlooking Apadana. Xerxes' Palace is badly damaged, as seen in the relief of the Great King. The damage on the right side of the stele is partly caused by natural decay, but a hole was also drilled in the face near the ear in order to blow up the stone with a piece of cork soaked in vinegar, which expands in the heat – a common practice in ancient quarries. The staircase connecting the terraces is among the best-preserved parts of the complex. Ahura Mazda is depicted in the middle of the staircase, flanked by two sphinxes.

Damaged relief of the Great King on a stele from Xerxes' Palace

Xerxes' Harem, the residence of the ladies of the court, was laid out in an L-shape. The main wing was oriented north-south, the extension on the southern part of the main wing was to the west. The core of the main building consisted of a large central portico with a talar, a porch that opened onto a courtyard. The hall had four doors; the jambs are decorated with reliefs depicting Xerxes entering the hall followed by two servants – one with a fly whisk, the other with a parasol. Six apartments arranged in two rows were located south of the portico. Each apartment consisted of a large columned space and one or sometimes two smaller rooms. The west wing contained sixteen similarly designed apartments. Two staircases linked it to Xerxes' palace. The main wing of the harem was excavated and faithfully reconstructed by Herzfeld in 1932. A large part of the building served as living quarters and work rooms for the expedition staff, where the cleaning, labelling, and restoring of objects was undertaken. Finally, the front of the Harem was restored and turned into a museum, displaying some of the objects found at Persepolis. Herzfeld took the opportunity of transforming the harem into a dig house with a modern roof to transpose his perception of Achaemenid architecture as realistically as possible into three dimensions, resulting in one of the most interesting museums in Iran which allows us to understand the spatial quality of the ruins on-site. The museum was reopened in 2002 after the Islamic revolution.

Rustam Relief
Naqsh-e Rostam
نقش رستم

Rah-e Marvdasht-Eqlid,
Marvdasht
29.98861, 52.87444
Various (Commissioner)
AD: ca. 520 BC

Naqsh-e Rostam, a vertical cliff on the southern foothills of Huseyn Kuh, lies about 6 km northwest of Persepolis. The place is exceptionally rich in Achaemenid and Sassanid monuments which are built or carved out of the rock. The Persian name "Pictures of Rostam" refers to the Sassanid reliefs, and the Persians believed that they represented scenes from the life of their legendary hero Rostam. Naqsh-e Rostam consists of four tombs of Persian Achaemenid kings, some partially well-preserved reliefs of the Sassanid dynasty and the enigmatic Cube of Zoroaster.

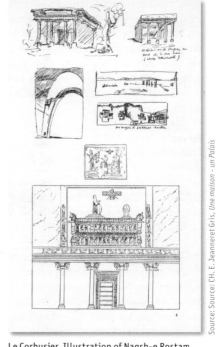

Source: Source: CH. E. Jeanneret Gris, *Une maison - un Palais*

Le Corbusier, Illustration of Naqsh-e Rostam

Achaemenid Tombs in Naqsh-e Rostam
نقش رستم

Rah-e Marvdasht-Eqlid,
Marvdasht
29.98889, 52.87472
Darius I the Great (Commissioner)et al.
AD: ca. 225 BC

The first grave and at the same time the first Persian relief in Naqsh-e Rostam is of Darius the Great. It was created during his reign, probably at the same time as the buildings in Persepolis. The rock grave served as a model for future royal tombs. The façade is cross-shaped and has a total height of almost 23 m. The middle part shows a portico, which is almost entirely modelled on Darius' Palace in Persepolis. The grave façade is 18.5 m tall, almost identical to Darius' Palace. Furthermore, the column spacing is 3.15 m, exactly the same spacing as in the Persepolis palace. In

Overview drawing of Naqsh-e Rostam

Source: Rashad, Mahmoud

Source: René Hochueli

Rock tombs in Naqsh-e Rostam

the middle of the façade is the entrance to the king's burial chamber. It consists of a passage running parallel to the façade, from which three chambers depart at right angles. One chamber is located directly opposite the front door, the other two to the left. The interior of the chamber, unlike the overall construction of the grave, is asymmetrical. Over the millennia, the sarcophagi were repeatedly ravaged by grave robbers who left their traces. Almost all have been completely forced open; four of them are preserved in fragments. It is assumed that apart from the king, his wives and parents were buried here as well. The top and bottom of the grave has a width of 10.9 m. The lower level is plain, whilst the upper level is richly decorated with reliefs and pictures. The king stands on a two-part pedestal, with two lion heads at its ends. The platform is supported by two superimposed rows of fourteen representatives of the empire; another two are right next to the pedestal on the bottom row. King Darius, who is depicted almost twice the size of the deputies, stands on a square, three-step pedestal. In his left hand he holds the traditional bow, the Persian

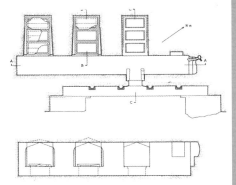

Grave of Darius I the Great

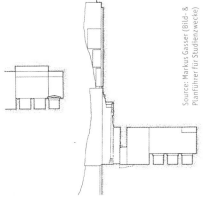

Source: Markus Gasser (Bild- & Planführer für Studienzwecke)

Presumably grave of Xerxes the Great

national weapon, his right hand is raised in worship towards the sacred symbol of Faravahar, the central gesture of this regal scene. To the right is an altar with a fire burning, symbolising purity and the earthly sign of God, an indication of the faith of the great kings, who were probably Zoroastrians. The rock grave of Darius the Great was the only one that could be identified beyond any doubt because it bears two inscriptions by the king. The second one, northeast of Darius' grave is possibly the grave of his son Xerxes the Great, the southwestern one is assumed to be that of Artaxerxes I, and the fourth that of Darius II, the great-grandson of Darius the Great. The rock tombs are all of the same type, with no other examples existing in the Middle East, Egypt or Greece. In his book *Une Maison – un Palais*, published in 1928, Le Corbusier reproduced the primitive huts of Mesopotamian peasants (which portend the splendour of tBabylon and Niniveh, as well as Persepolis and the graves and rock reliefs of Naqsh-e Rostam) as an expression of his view of architecture, which he believes develops from the private house to the public building and, ultimately, to the town.

Rock Relief in Naqsh-e Rostam
نقش رستم

Rah-e Marvdasht-Eqlid,Marvdasht
29.98917, 52.87500
Ardashir I (Commissioner)
AD: ca. 225 BC

The earliest relief from the Sassanid dynasty depicts the founder of the new Persian Empire, Ardashir the Great. It shows King Ardashir accepting the ring of power from Ahura Mazda. Both ride towards each other, Ardashir from the left and Ahura Mazda from the right. Unlike seen on previous reliefs, Ahura Mazda is at eye level with Ardashir and has the appearance of a man. Below the two horsemen are two defeated adversaries, the Parthian king Artabanus IV under Ardashir and the devil Ahriman under Ahura Mazda. The scene symbolises the victory of good over evil. Perhaps the most famous relief in Naqsh-e Rostam is the one of Shapur I, Ardashir's son and heir. It shows the triumph of King Shapur I over the Roman emperor Marcus Julius Philippus and Publius Licinius Valerian, the latter having been captured by Shapur after a crushing defeat in Edessa,

Rock relief with presentation of Shapur I

Source: René Hochueli

Entrance to the Cube of Zoroaster

Cube of Zoroaster

something unique in the history of Rome. Philippus Arabs is kneeling before Shapur, Valerian stands before him; his arms are held by Shapur to symbolize the capture. Shapur himself is sitting on his royal horse, followed by the high Zoroastrian priests Kartir. The next relief is immediately adjacent, mounted on an Elamite relief dating back to ca. 1000 BC. It depicts King Bahram II holding a huge sword in his hand. On the right side, three powerful statesmen are depicted paying their respects to the king.

Cube of Zoroaster
Kaba-ye Zartosht
كعبة زرتشت

143 **A**

Rah-e Marvdasht-Eqlid, Marvdasht
29.98833, 52.87389
unknown
AD: ca. 520 BC

Opposite the graves is a nearly 13 m high building, whose exact purpose is not entirely clear. The Ka'ba-ye Zartosht is a fifth-century BC Achaemenid tower. The name probably dates back to the fourteenth century, when many pre-Islamic sites were identified with figures and events of the Qur'an or the Shanahme. The Kaba was illustrated in the works of seventeenth century Western travellers who visited Naqš-e Rostam, such as Chardin, De Bruin and Kaempfer. They entered its single chamber, which was easily accessible since the structure lay half buried in rubble. The Kaba is a square tower built of white limestone blocks, laid without mortar but joined by iron cramps. It measures 7.25 m a side, with a height of 12.50 m. Taken together with the three-step plinth and the slightly pyramidal roof, the building has a total height of 14 m. Each face of the building is decorated with slightly-recessed false windows of black limestone, which have no other purpose than to break the monotony of the structure. A frieze of similar, alternatively protruding and receding rectangular stones forms the upper cornice. The structure has one square inner chamber, access to which is through a doorway with a decorated lintel in the upper half of the tower. The chamber was once accessible by a flight of stairs, of which only the lower half has survived. The door was of solid stone that was originally firmly closed but has since disappeared. The Kaba has been variously interpreted as a fire temple, archive, or mausoleum. However, the theory that a sacred fire burned inside the building fails due to a lack of a chimney or any form of ventilation. Another theory is that it was a library for sacred scriptures, where prayers and ceremonies were held. Most scholars consider it an Achaemenid royal tomb. Weissbach and Demandt observed that it resembled the description of Cyrus's tomb by Lucius Flavius Arrianus and Strabo more closely than the monument in Pasargadae attributed to this king. The massive foundation would make sense for the mausoleum of a Zoroastrian ruler, since it would prevent the seepage of cadaveric poison into the soil.

Excursion into prehistory
Sassanid Empire

The Sassanid Empire originated in the third century and was the second Persian Empire. It stretched over the territories of present-day Iran, Iraq and Afghanistan. The king of the Persians, Ardashir Babakan from the house of Sassan, again succeeded in uniting the Iranian tribes, and in 226 AD founded the New Persian Empire of the Sassanid. He is seen as the creator and organiser of the empire, which destabilised the Roman Empire from the start. Aware of the Achaemenid tradition, he not only created a centrally organised state, but also declared Zoroastrianism as the state religion. He sent the following message to the Roman emperor: "Romans, what you occupy in Asia is my heritage". When Severus killed the messengers, the war against Rome began, which ended with the biggest defeat in Roman history. In the first war, the Roman Emperor Gordian fell. After further heavy defeats, the Roman Emperor Valerian himself sought out the Shah. The undertaking ended in a disaster for the Romans; Valerian and over 70,000 Roman legionaries were taken captive. The Romans also had to commit to high reparations. The young Sassanid Empire gained the highest reputation in the world at that time. During this tim,e Roman prisoners constructed numerous bridges and dams; the most famous being the still-extant Caesar's Bridge.

Firuzabad
فیروزآباد
AD: 224

The plain of Firuzabad has been inhabited since prehistoric times, as valuable copper was mined there. It is surrounded by high mountains, with very few approach roads, all of which are easily defensible. Because of this quality of safety, Firuzabad was chosen by Ardashir Babakan as a refuge and command center during the revolt against the Parthians. Over an area of 12 km, the complex in Firuzabad includes the archaeological sites of the town Ardashir Khureh, the castle Qal'ah Dokhtar and the palace Kakh-e Ardashir Babakan, as well as rock reliefs from the time of the founding of the Sassanid empire, including petroglyphs commissioned by Ardashir to commemmorate his victories.

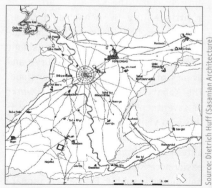

Plain of Firuzabad

Source: Dietrich Huff (Sasanian Architecture)

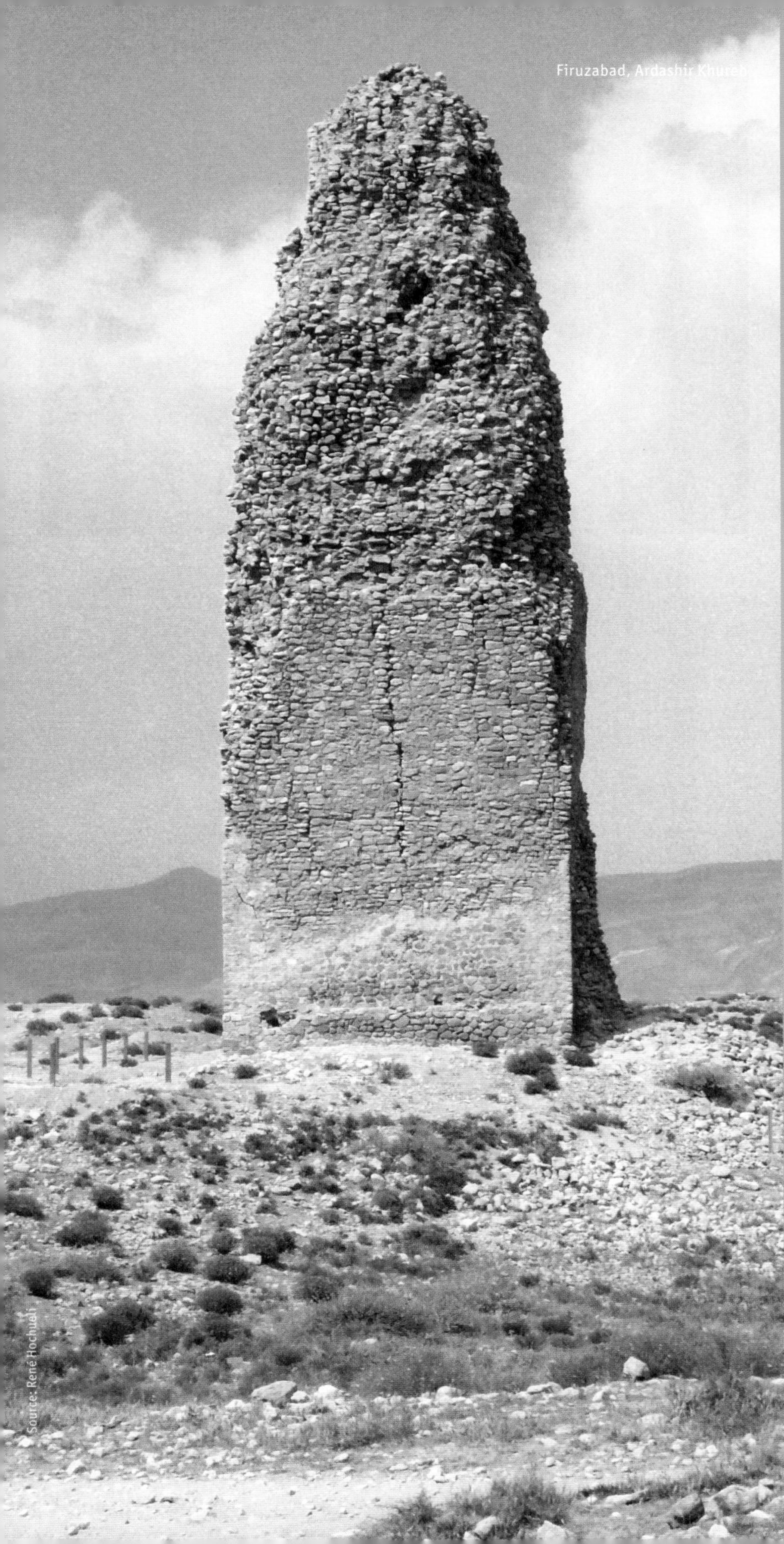

Firuzabad, Ardashir Khureh

Source: Georg Gerster (L'Iran vu du ciel)

Aerial view of Gur at Firuzabad

Ardashir Khureh
Shahr-e Gor
اردشیرخوره
Firuzabad
28.85278, 52.53250
Ardashir I (Commissioner)
AD: 224

The city of Gur, also called Ardashir Khureh, is located near Firuzabad, about 110 km south of Shiraz on a fertile plain surrounded by precipitous mountains. A perennial river, Tang-ab, flows through it in a north-south direction. Almost all historical sources ascribe its foundation to the first Sassanid king Ardashir, who is said to have founded it on the occasion of his victory over the Parthian king Artabanus. Originally created as a perfect circle with a diameter of 2 km, the town is surrounded by two circular clay walls and a 35 m wide moat. The interior is divided into twenty sectors by twenty radial and several concentric roads. The city centre boasts a tower-like edifice, Terbal, a 9 m wide and 30 m high pillar of rubble masonry, which was the core of a stairwell. Ernst Herzfeld interpreted it as part of a palace or government building, which probably symbolized the divine and centralist monarchy propagated by Ardashir. However, this did not preclude

Source: René Hochueli

Ardashir Khureh

(BAB HORMIZD)

DEH SHAHR
(DORFRUINEN)

IMAMZADEH
SHAH HAIDAR

TAKHT-I
NISHIN

ZISTERNE

(BAB BAHRAM)

IMAMZADEH
DJA'FAR

(BAB MIHR)

IMAMZADEH
BUZURG

MINAR

FAHRWEG

WALL

GRABEN

WALL

(BAB ARDASHIR)

Ground floor plan

Source: Markus Gasser (Bild- & Planführer für Studienzwecke)

a practical use; the tower enabled visual contact with the fortifications above the gorge of Tang-ab, and in addition to the military function, it served to survey the city, whose four main axes of the city gates led through the tower. These gates are still visible as gaps in the remains of the wall. Moreover, you find traces of radial channels, paths, walls and field boundaries up to 10 km from the central tower. The circular structure was inspired by the pattern of the round military camp from Assyrian times; government buildings and the residences of the aristocracy gathered around the palace in concentric, hierarchical circles.

Source: Voyage en Perse, avec Flandin, éd. Gide et Baudry (1851)

Eugène Flandin, Ancient Monument in Firouzabad

Maiden Castle
Qaleh-ye Dokhtar
قلعه دختر

Firuzabad
28.92056, 52.53000
Ardashir I (Commissioner)
AD: ca. 220

4 km northeast of Ardashir Khureh's ruins lies Qaleh-ye Dokhtar, a castle on a steep rock at a bend in the river Tang-ab. It appears to have been Ardashir's first fortress, which he probably later gave up for structural reasons in favour of his second palace. The name of the site refers to the Zoroastrian water deity, Anahita, who was called The Maiden. The ideal location of the castle was chosen for strategic reasons: The plateau is inaccessible from three directions, and the fourth, which opens onto the river, was protected by an extensive defence system of walls and towers. The first shield wall was an outer bailey to the river side, whilst the second enclosed the core of the complex, together with the casemates. The main gate to the fortification was at the south end of the defence wall. In the two outer baileys extending towards the river, water wells were found, which connected directly to the river via a tunnel. Moreover, the position of the fortress allowed control of the road and thus control of the northern access to the plain of Firuzabad. In Sassanid times, the road ran below Qaleh-ye Dokhtar, and, unlike today, led across the river after the bend, where remains of pillars of a bridge still

View of Qaleh-ye Dokhtar from Tang-ab

Source: Thomas Meyer-Wieser

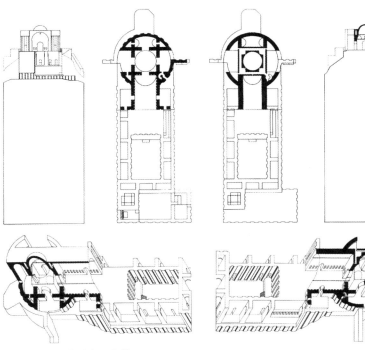

Reconstruction of Qaleh-ye Dokhtar

Source: Franz Oswald (Lehrgerüst)

exist. The entrance to the castle was through a high gate in a rectangular tower and across a ramp which was accessible on horseback, leading to a courtyard with blind niches. The stairs continued to the next level which was completed by a large 14 × 23 m wide ayvan in front of a domed rotunda, supported on all sides by very thick walls, presumably to ensure stability. The dome and the rooms on top floor were accessible via a spiral staircase on the south side. The main rooms are arranged in a round donjon, which protrudes from the fortified walls like an architectural symbol. The ayvan (also called ivan or aiwan), a building type adopted by the Parthians, appears even more spacious and airy. This barrel-vaulted hall is open on one side and offers a cool space open to a landscaped courtyard with a central water basin. The ayvan cannot clearly be defined as an exterior or an interior space, but is both, which idea developed into one of the most characteristic features of Persian and Central Asian architecture. During his visit in 1923, Ernst Herzfeld noted that "from the outside, hall and cupola form a huge round tower, a donjon, a veritable Castle of the Grail

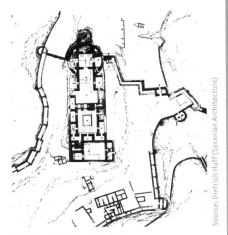

Qaleh-ye Dokhtar, site plan

Source: Dietrich Huff (Sasanian Architecture)

in the most fantastic surroundings, a counterpart to the great Throne Hall of Khosrow in Ctesiphon!" Qaleh-ye Dokhtar is remarkable in several respects. For the first time in the history of architecture, the ayvan appears as an independent space, not just the ante-chamber of a domed hall. The use of squinches as a solution to the transition from square to circle is applied here for the first time and is a characteristic of Sassanid construction, which was later developed further in Islamic architecture.

Ayvan of Kakh-e Ardashir-e Babakan

Stucco cladding in the Palace of Ardashir

Palace of Ardashir
Kakh-e Ardashir-e Babakan
کاخ اردشیر بابکان
Firuzabad
28.89800, 52.53922
Ardashir I (Commissioner)
AD: 224

About 5 km northwest of the capital Ardashir Khureh, Ardashir I built his magnificent palace Kakh Ardashir Babakan in 224 AD. The palace was built next to a pond which is fed by a natural source

associated with Anahita, the Zoroastrian deity of water and growth. The view from a particularly magnificent, now partially-collapsed ayvan, is over a garden courtyard with its picturesque pond. Today, all that remains of the garden are the 12.6 m wide vaults and the façade of a huge talar. Both palaces, the Qal'ah Dokhtar and Kakh Ardashir Babakan have the same design but in very different arrangements: 12 m wide ayvans and square domes (rectangular barrel vaults around a courtyard) as royal reception halls, small rooms upstairs as private living quarters. From the architectural configuration, however, it appears that the palace in the plain was more a place of conviviality where guests were able to socialise with the imperial ruler. The structurally less-ambitious and more-solid construction clearly proves that the palace was planned later; the lack of fortifications and the monumental layout show that it

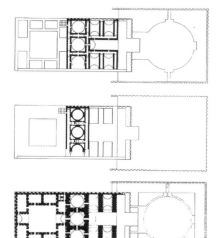

Reconstruction of Kakh-e Ardashir-e Babakan

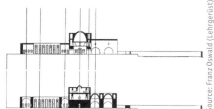

Source: René Hochueli

Squinch in the Palace of Ardashir

Sassanid Rock Relief
Naqsh Barjasteh Sasani
نقش برجسته ساسانی

Firuzabad
28.89811, 52.54689
Ardashir I (Commissioner)
AD: 225

In the Tang-ab gorge, below Qal'ah Dokhtar, there are two rock reliefs and the ruins of a Sassanid bridge from the fifth century. The first rock relief depicts Ardashir's coronation. The second, the oldest and also the largest Sassanid rock relief, is located halfway between Qaleh-ye Dokhtar and the palace of Ardashir. It depicts Ardashir's victory over Artabanus who subsequently took the official title Shahanshah, King of Kings. The river exits the plain through another narrow gorge in the south. Alexander the Great had a dam built on this site, which flooded the plain and the surrounding villages. The lake still exited at the beginning of the third century, when Ardashir I regained the town through the construction of water channels and a tunnel. This is probably the background to the ancient and medieval reports of Ardashir giving orders to cut through mountains.

was built after the consolidation, when Ardashir's hegemony was established and military considerations were no longer an issue. The walls of the rectangular, 104 m × 55 m building consist largely of hewn, relatively small stones joined with mortar and then plastered. The Parthians and Sassanids also worked with stucco, a mass of lime, gypsum and sand which they used to reinforce adobe walls. This malleable mass also allowed the creation of ornaments that gave their palaces a distinctive touch. These ornaments can be seen as a precursor to floral and geometric decor developed by the Umayyads in Syria and Spain, and later the Abbasids throughout the Middle East. In the centre of the palace are three square halls whose domes are not completely closed, but which all have a fairly large opening that illuminates the space below. Again, a squinch was used to place the domes over the square spaces. Robert Byron, British travel writer and nephew of Lord Byron, visited the palace in February 1934 and described it in his book *The Road to Oxiana* as a prototype in the evolution of the squinch. In Byron's opinion, lauded monumental buildings such as St. Peter's Basilica and even the Taj Mahal would likely never have existed without this Sassanid precursor.

Source: René Hochueli

Rock relief with coronation of Ardashir

The Qajar Dynasty

1779–1865
From Village to Capital of Iran

When Nader Shah died in 1747, the Afsharid rule fell apart. The turmoil and civil wars ended only when a Turkmen tribal leader named Aqa Muhammad Khan, who had been castrated in childhood by the Afsharid Adel Shah, ordered the assassination of the last Persian ruler of the Zand dynasty in 1794, starting an intra-Persian conquest which, measured even by the standards of the eighteenth century, was one of the cruellest recorded in history. It is said that in Kerman alone he ordered the eyes of 20,000 residents to be torn out because they thwarted his army and refused to surrender the town without resistance. After fifteen years of war, Aga Mohammed Khan had killed off almost all his competitors for the Persian throne, made Tehran – which was just a small village near the much older and more famous Ray – his capital, brought the entire country under his control and united it. The Qajar, known as Qizilbash during the rise of the Safavid, served under them in the sixteenth and seventeenth centuries as ambassadors and administrators. In 1796, Aga Mohammed Khan proclaimed himself Shah of Persia. At a time when the French Revolution ushered in the end of absolute monarchy in Europe, a despotic ruler came to power in Persia, thus establishing an absolutist dynasty, which was replaced only in 1924. Aga Mohammed Khan and his successors led Persia into political insignificance within a century. In two wars against the Russian Empire, Persia lost vast areas in the north of Iran and became economically and politically dependent on Russia. The war against the Afghans led to the loss of Persian-dominated Afghanistan and resulted in economic and political dependence on Britain. Persia's total overestimation of its own resources and the waging of preventable wars without adequate strategies led to further warfare, resulting in the partial loss of state sovereignty and economic and political dependence on Russia and Britain.

Development of Tehran ca. 1856

Qajar Aga Mohammed Khan chose Tehran as the Shah's residence and capital in 1789. A small settlement of orchards and underground dwellings, close to the more famous city Ray, had already been expanded to a city by the Safavid with a citadel, bazaar and ramparts. From this period only the gateway Bagh-e Meli remains, but not in its original form. In the early seventeenth century, ca. 3,000 houses existed inside the town walls which encompassed five districts with four gateways on 4 km². Practical advantages were offered by its position in the centre of the west-east axis of the Persian Empire: a mild climate, good soils and water as well as protection from attacks offered by the Alborz Mountains.

Source: Thomas Meyer-Wieser

Development of Tehran ca. 1856

Bazaar of Tehran

Bazaar of Tehran
Bazar-e Bozorg
بازار تهران

Bazar-e Bozorg, Tehran
35.67417, 51.42447
unknown
AD: from 1500/AH: from 900/
Yaz: from 870

Hajeb al-Doleh

According to its foundation dates, the Bazaar of Tehran is one of the most recent in Middle East. The town plan of Major August Krziz from 1857 gives us an idea how the floor plan of the Tehran Bazaar might have looked in the mid-nineteenth century. An approximately 2 km long road connects the two gates, Semiran in the north and Shah Abdol Azim in the south. Important for the development and evolution of Tehran Bazaar was the building of the Arg, the fortified royal residence, in the late eighteenth century. Residential areas and bazaar infrastructure expanded rapidly around the Arg. In the nineteenth century, Fat'h-Ali Shah built several mosques in the Bazaar district, including the Masjed-e Shah. Only then did Tehran take on the appearance of a capital city. With the town's increasing importance, the Bazaar became an important trading centre for long-distance trade as well as for the local market. The Bazaar today consists of a total of 10 km of roads and tens of thousands of small shops. The bazaar's transverse axes alone are several hundred metres long. In addition, several minor bazaar axes (raste) open onto the main axes. The length of some of these minor axes is larger than many major axes in smaller, traditional Iranian towns. Today Tehran, with its large urban area and thirteen million inhabitants, handles by far the largest trading volume in the country. Tehran Bazaar even enjoys countrywide importance in certain areas, and has greatly expanded in the last hundred years. This continuity and unbroken vitality of the bazaar were achieved by a significant change in the goods offered and also an increasing social distinction of its customers. Lower- and middle-class people in particular still prefer to shop in the bazaar for products other than their daily needs, supporting the undiminished vitality of the bazaar. If one compares today's bazaar to last century's, one realises that the holistic picture has been preserved. Previously-open areas in the central bazaar districts are now occupied by department stores, and old alleyways leading to the residential areas were converted to malls in the late nineteenth century. The former bazaar road leading to the city gate Shemiran is now crossed by modern streets.

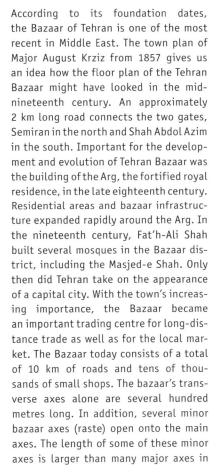

Timcheh-ye Mahdieh

Sabz-e Maidan

Golestan Palace
Kakh-e Golestan
كاخ گلستان

Maidan-e Panzdah-e Khordad,
Kakh-e Golestan, Tehran
35.67975, 51.42122
Shah Abbas I, Karim Khan Zand,
Fat'h-Ali Shah (Commissioner)
AD: from 1750/AH: from 1170/
Yaz: from 1130

The Golestan Palace complex is located in the heart of old Tehran. The palace today consists of two interconnected gardens: a smaller in the west, Bagh-e Takht-e Marmar, which is aligned to the north-south axis, and a larger one in the east, Bagh-e Golestan, with a more-or-less square floor plan. The palace was not only a place for affairs of the state but also served as the residence of the Qajar kings. Tehran's first fortifications were built in the 1550s under Safavid Shah Tahmasp I. These enclosed the royal citadel, which consisted of a small palace and an audience hall. To the north of the buildings, Shah Abbas the Great planted a Chahar Bagh and a plane tree garden. The earliest surviving building structures date back to the Zand dynasty. In 1760, Karim Khan Zand commissioned the architect Ustad Gholam Reza Tabrizi to renovate the Safavid city wall and to erect new buildings, an audience chamber as Divan Khaneh, today Imarat-e Takht-e Marmar and the Khalvat-e Karim Khan. After his death in 1779, Aqa Mohammad Khan Qajar came to power, moved the capital to Tehran in 1785 and chose Golestan as his residence and administrative centre. He enlarged Divan-e Dar-ol Imareh and built Imarat-e Khoruji, which remained unfinished after he was assassinated in 1797. His successor, Fat'h-Ali Shah, was the first Shah to initiate major urban development in Tehran. Maidan-e Shah and Maidan-e Toop Khaneh were created at the entrance of the old royal castle. Most changes in the Golestan Palace were made during the reign of Naser al-Din Shah. Since there was no more space within the old fort, royal palaces, embassies and residences for foreigners were constructed outside the city walls. During the approximately fifty years of Naser al-Din Shah's reign,

Golestan Palace was converted to his winter residence and centre of government. His Prime Minister, Amir Kabir, bought land on the east side of the garden and had the palace complex enlarged. The most important building created there was the Kakh Shams ol-Emareh at the southeast corner of the garden. In 1867, this five-storey building, flanked by two towers, was built on the north side just before the completion of the andaruni, the private quarters of the palace. Between 1868 and 1873, Takiyeh Dowlat, a theatre for religious ceremonies, was constructed. It is the largest building in Golestan Palace. In 1873, Naser al-Din Shah initiated the construction of a number of buildings with a continuous two-storey high façade on the northwest site of the Golestan garden. This necessitated the demolition of significant parts of Khalvat-e Karim Khani and the Golestan Palace, which were replaced by pools, lawns, flowers and trees. The last building commissioned by Naser al-Din Shah, Kakh-e Abyaz, is completely European and neoclassical, without a trace of Islamic forms or ornaments. Although both Reza Shah Pahlavi and his son Mohammad Reza Shah were crowned in Golestan Palace, they moved the seat of government to Saadabad in northern Tehran, and under the Pahlavis, Golestan Palace was only used to host important foreign guests. During their rule, about three quarters of the Golestan complex was demolished to make way for modern office buildings in the city centre. The gate of the palace was removed in 1929 to ensure that the Iraqi king could arrive by car for his reception. Water basins were filled in under the pretext of eliminating the mosquito plague, and the andaruni, no longer considered fashionable, was demolished to accommodate the Ministry of Finance. Under Shah Reza Pahlavi II, the palace retained its ceremonial importance, but other major parts were altered or destroyed. In 1946 the dilapidated Tekiei Dowlat on the south side of the complex was demolished to build the bazaar branch of Bank Melli. In 1959, during the visit of Queen Elizabeth of England, the Narenjestan mansion was replaced by a guesthouse for foreign state guests. In the early 1960s,

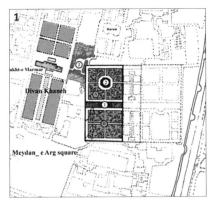

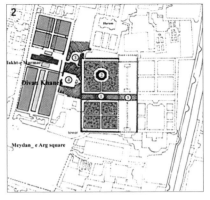

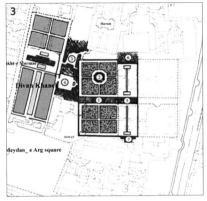

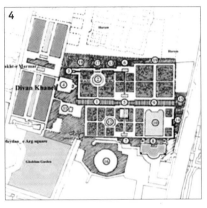

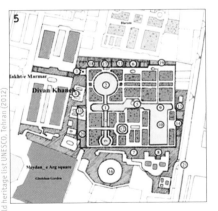

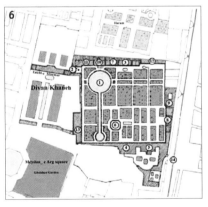

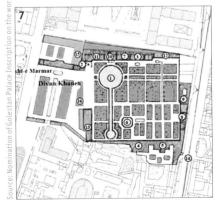

1 Golestan Palace in the Karim Khaneh-ye Zand era, 1759–1779
2 Golestan Palace in the Aqa Mohammad Khan era, 1786–1797
3 Golestan Palace in the Fat'h- Ali Shah era, 1797–1834
4 Golestan Palace in the Naseri III era, 1869–1878
5 Golestan Palace in the Naseri V era, 1883–1895
6 Golestan Palace in the Pahlavi I era, 1925–1941
7 Golestan Palace in the Pahlavi II era, 1941–1979

Detail of the palace decoration with lion and sun

in preparation for the 2,500th anniversary of the Iranian monarchy, substantial restoration work was carried out on Talar-e Salam and Howz Khane. At the same time, a large hall was built for this ceremony, and a faïence-clad courtyard façade plus a number of Qajar buildings were demolished to make way for it. Due to the severe financial situation of the country after the Islamic revolution and the outbreak of the Iran–Iraq war, no funds were available for the preservation of the monument. Restoration and repair work was intensified from 1996, so that the complex today has a fresh look and is frequently visited by Iranians. Golestan Palace was declared a UNESCO World Heritage site in 2013.

Marble Throne Building
Imarat-e Takht-e Marmar
تخت مرمر

Maidan-e Panzdah-e Khordad, Kakh-e Golestan, Tehran
35.68028, 51.41917
Karim Khan Zand (Commissioner)
AD: 1759 / AH: 1173 / Yaz: 1129

Imarat-e Takht-e Marmar is arguably the most important building of the Golestan Palace due to its historical, political and social importance. The foundation was laid in 1759 by Karim Khan Zand. During the Qajar period, under Fat'h-Ali Shah, the building was expanded to serve as residence and administrative

Imarat-e Takht-e Marmar, exterior view

Imarat-e Takht-e Marmar, Marble Throne

Source: Eugène Flandin (Voyage en Perse)

Eugène Flandin and Pascal Coste, exterior view of the Marble Throne Building

centre of the country where ceremonies like A'id and Norouz were celebrated and foreign ambassador were received. Takht-e Marmar consists of a long rectangular area with three parts: the shahneshin, or seat of the Shah, and two symmetrical wings, each about 1.5 m above the courtyard level and open to the garden, allowing an unobstructed view of the King on his throne. From the main entrance an 80 m long water basin leads to the throne room. The two-storey building is opened up by a magnificent talar, supported by two twisted marble columns with muqarnas capitals. These 8 m high columns were allegedly brought by Aga Mohammad Khan from Arg-e Karim Khan Zand in Shiraz in 1771, as was the carved yellow marble base decorated with flowers, parrots and eagles. The walls and ceiling of the talar are decorated with mirror mosaics, stained glass, marble works and oil paintings depicting Fat'h-Ali Shah,

foreign ambassadors and war scenes. The Imarat-e Takht-e Marmar also accommodated the marble throne commissioned by Fat'h-Ali Shah in 1806 to replace the precious Peacock Throne, Takht-e Tavous. He called it Takht-e Suleiman, after the throne on which Solomon was supposedly was taken up to heaven by genies and fairies, which was depicted almost literally by the court painter Mirza Baba Shirazi, who also designed the throne. Takht-e-Marmar is bordered by the distinctive Ministry of Finance building, built between 1948 and 1950 at the north side of the complex. Sadly, the thereto perfectly-preserved living spaces and gardens of the palace were destroyed during construction.

Imarat-e Takht-e Marmar, floor plan

Source: Claudia Luperto

Above: Imarat-e Takht-e Marmar, main ayvan   Next page: Imarat-e Takht-e Marmar, façade detail

Karim Khan's Alcove

Source: Firouzeh Mirrazavi (Iran Review)

Karim Khan's Alcove
Khalvat-e Karim Khani
خلوت کریمخانی

Maidan-e Panzdah-e Khordad,
Kakh-e Golestan, Tehran
35.68028, 51.41917
Karim Khan Zand (Commissioner)
AD: 1759/AH: 1173/Yaz: 1129

East of the Marble Palace lies a small terrace vaulted with arches, Khalvat-e Karim Khani. As the name suggests it dates from the time of Karim Khane-e Zand, and Khalvat means isolated place. Naser al-Din Shah is said to have often visited this terrace when he was looking for peace and quiet. His valuable marble grave has now been placed there and is well worth a visit. The terrace, raised by 1.5 m, has four entrances: one from the south, three from the east, each surmounted with arches, with the centre arch being wider and higher. The basic structure of Khalvat-e Karim Khani is similar to Ayvan-e Takht-e Marmar as it also forms a terrace with a small marble throne. The former is much smaller and less rich, but exquisitely decorated with multi-coloured tiles. The highlight is the inner vault covering the ceiling, based on spiral, geometric elements. Some depict animal scenes, for example a lion killing a deer above the portrait of the Sultan, probably an allegory of the Sultan's victory over his enemies. In the centre of the vault is an octagonal pool through which water from a qanat flows to a lower basin that was originally surrounded by a Chahar Bagh.

Qasr Prison
Zendan-e Qasr
زندان قصر

Marv Dasht, Tehran
35.72361, 51.44833
Nikolai Markov,
Arash Mozafari (Renovation)
AD: 1790, 2012/AH: 1205, 1433/
Yaz: 1160, 1382

Qasr Prison in Tehran was one of the earliest political prisons. It was previously a garden with a large palace established by Fat'h Ali Shah. In 1924 it was converted to a prison by the Russian architect Nikolai Markov under Reza Shah Pahlavi. It had 192 cells for 700 prisoners, including one hundred single cells where some of the most famous politicians and activists like Ayatollah Mahmoud Taleghani, a member of the Constitutional Council after the Islamic Revolution, and Mohammad-Ali Rajayi, second President

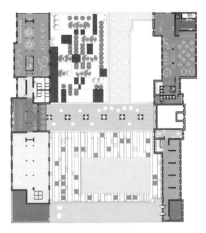

Arash Mozafari, ground floor plan of
Qasr Prison

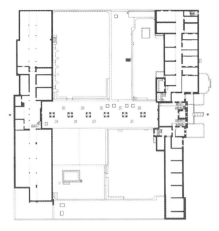

Arash Mozafari, second floor plan of
Qasr Prison

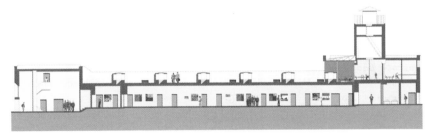

Arash Mozafari, section of Qasr Prison

of the Islamic Republic, were detained.
The prison was closed in 2008 and converted into a museum. The women's
prison, the station towers and the mosque
were preserved and restored by the Iranian
Cultural Heritage and Preservation
Department. The complex is currently used
by the More Pooya Software Company and
by artists, graphic artists and photogra-
phers. The garden has been restored.

Source: Qasr Prison Garden Museum, Tehran

Prison after conversion to a museum, with an adjoining garden

Antoin Sevruguin, Imrat-i Badgir, ca.1880

Wind Tower Building
Imarat-e Badgir
عمارت بادگیر

153 G

Maidan-e Panzdah-e Khordad,
Kakh-e Golestan, Tehran
35.67903, 51.42169
Fat'h-Ali Shah (Commissioner)
AD: 1813 / AH: 1228 / Yaz: 1183

Among the most beautiful buildings of the Golestan complex is the Imarat-e Badgir, built by Fat'h-Ali Shah in 1813. Remarkable for its tile-decorated badgirs, the current Imarat-e Badgir is the result of Naser ed-Din Shah's major renovation and reconstruction work carried out in 1853. This building consists of a main hall and its adjoining rooms with four Badgirs at the corners. The Badgirs are tiled in blue, yellow, and black. The Imarat-e Badgir also has a Howz Khaneh in the basement, which worked with the four Badgirs to circulate and cool air by passing it over pools of water. The Howz Khaneh is now used as the Golestan Palace's photo gallery, which exhibits images from the Qajar period, particularly from enthusiastic amateur photographer Naser al-Din Shah. The hallmark of the building, the badgir, or wind catcher, is a traditional Persian architectural element used for centuries in Iran for the ventilation of buildings. It is a solidly-built tower, reaching

from the lowest level of a building right up to above the roof. If the temperatures in the building are higher than outside, the chimney effect causes cold air to flow through the Badgir. If the wind blows, the flow reverses. The pressure on the upwind side pushes cold air through the Badgir into the rooms below. If the air flows over a water surface, an additional cooling effect occurs. Apart from the air exchange, the air flow in the Badgir also allows circulation of air within the building. When the kings spent the summer in Tehran and did not

Veranda

Source: UNESCO, World Heritage Convention (2012)

Wind catcher decorated with tiles

leave for the countryside, they would use this building and the Howz Khaneh. The façade of Imarat-e Badgir is decorated mainly with tile work, fresco, and a combination of mirror work, stucco work and stone engravings. Small terraces on the side of the main terrace serve as the entrance to the rooms and are all decorated with painted arabesques. Other remarkable features of Imarat-e Badgir are its symmetry and inclusion of spaces such as the alcove, the vestibule, the passages and chambers. If a line were drawn in the centre of the plan, the building

would be divided into two similar, equal parts. The entrances to the building are also symmetrically connected to the interior by fourteen steps through the courtyard. Beyond the terrace, there is the square-shaped hashti that takes you to the chambers, central hall, terrace, and the enclosure to the south of the edifice. The walls here are decorated with Western-style paintings of nude women, bowls of fruit, flower vases and scenery. This hall is home to one of the most unique sets of decoration. Among the significant decorative elements here are two wooden-plaster spiral columns with Zand-era patterns. Decorated from the bottom to the top with floral paintings, they are of decorative rather than structural function. There is also a splendid orosi with arabesque mirror works. In this hall, one of the most elaborate royal edifices in Iran, one can see all types of architecture-related art: lattice work, stone reliefs, stone painting, oil paint on fresco, mirror work, mirror painting, tilework, and wood embossing.

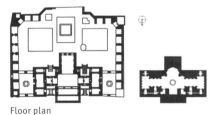

Floor plan

Source: UNESCO, World Heritage Convention (2012)

Interior decoration

Source: Claudia Luperto

Brick pillar in the courtyard

Masjed-e Shah

Shah Mosque,
Imam Khomeini Mosque
Masjed-e Shah,
Masjed-e Imam Khomeini

مسجد امام خمینی

Bazar-e Bozorg, Tehran
35.67628, 51.42203
Fat'h-Ali Shah (Commissioner)
AD: 1834/AH: 1250/Yaz: 1204

The Shah Mosque, today named after Imam Khomeini, is located on the northern edge of the Great Bazaar. It was completed in 1834 at the time of Fat'h Ali Shah. The two minarets were added later, in the time of Naser al-Din Shah. The main entrance with a hall-like gateway is finished off with a niche with magnificent stalactite. Visitors enter into the courtyard through four narrow passages. The square courtyard with a pool has a side length of about 60 m. It opens towards the main prayer hall covered by a blue dome. The prayer hall is covered by more than forty small domes. The characteristic elements of this mosque are the arcades covered in yellow glazed tiles, which add a particularly beautiful glow to the light in the mosque. The Imam Khomeini Mosque is a working mosque and one of the largest and most frequently visited in Tehran. Several busy bazaar roads lead through the courtyard. Although the building dates back to the early eighteenth century, it should mainly be visited to observe Islam in action.

Spring of Ali
Cheshmeh-Ali

چشمه علي

Shahr-e Rey,
ca. 15 km south of Tehran
35.61028, 51.44972
Fat'h-Ali Shah (Commissioner)
AD: 1834/AH: 1250/Yaz: 1204

In an attempt to celebrate royalty, many visual depictions of the Shah and his court were produced. Rock reliefs, often adjacent to Sassanid sites in Ray, Fars, and Kermanshah, reflected the Qajar Shah's desire to be seen by his own people and by future generations as the heir to the ancient Persian Empire. The Sassanid rulers usually mounted rock reliefs on

Niche in the Shah Mosque

Source: Eugène Flandin (Voyage en Perse)

Eugène Flandin: Cheshmeh Ali

a steep rock face above a pool, depicting their triumphs and religious beliefs. In 1834, Fat'h-Ali Shah chose exactly the same site in Ray to show himself in the Achaemenid and Sassanid style. He had a rock relief mounted in the rock wall above the Cheshmeh Ali. In the centre of the relief image, Fat'h-Ali Shah sits surrounded by his sons and inner circle. The central part of the relief is framed by two slender columns with three-part capitals. Whilst on the left side of the image only four figures are shown, the right side of the column depicts a complete scene. The main character is again Fat'h-Ali Shah. He holds a falcon in his fist; a servant stands behind him, holding a parasol or canopy over him. The relief is finished at the top with a series of elongated inscriptions. According to travelogues from that time, there used to be a Sassanid horsemen relief on this site which Fat'h-Ali Shah had replaced with his own image. The main events of Fat'h-Ali Shah's reign were the disastrous wars with Russia, increasing contacts with Western powers, establishment of relations with the British government, inconclusive French attempts under Napoleon at securing the support of the Shah against the British, and the realisation by some Persians that, compared to Europe, the country was lagging behind and required a thorough overhaul of its institutions and a critical re-examination of its cultural attitudes.

Source: Wikimedia Commons

Rock relief with Fat'h-Ali Shah as central figure

Exterior view of Khaneh-ye Qavam od-Dowleh

Qavam od-Dowleh House
Khaneh-ye Qavam od-Dowleh
خانه قوام الدوله

Khiyaban-e Mirza Mahmud Vazir,
Tehran
35.69149, 51.41461
*Mirza Mohammad Khan Qavam
od-Dowleh (Commissioner)*
AD: 1834/AH: 1250/Yaz: 1204

Ahmad Qavam was one of the most influential Iranian politicians. He headed several ministries and was prime minister several times. He was a leading figure in the political transformation of Iran from an absolutist to a constitutional monarchy. The villa Qavam od-Dowleh is located in the Sarcheshmeh district of Tehran. The house was built in 1834 for Mizra Mohammad Khan Qavam od-Dowleh. It is a three-storey building, surrounded on the north and south sides by two large courtyards and large halls, adorned with European and Iranian stucco. The quality of the stucco work and the harmony of decorative elements lend the building a unique character. The building is decorated with mirrored stalactites in beautiful geometric patterns, frescoes by Loft Ali Khan Suratgar, stucco wall and ceiling coverings, coloured orosi windows and decorative brickwork. Worthy of note is a set of portraits of women from the nineteenth century, kept in the mansion and framed by mirrors; they are among the world's oldest colour photographs.

Shah-Abdul-Azim Shrine
Astaneh Hazrat Abdul Azim
استانه حضرت عبد العظیم

Shahr-e Rey,
ca. 15 km south of Tehran
35.58572, 51.43539
*Mirza Mohammad Khan Qavam
od-Dowleh (Commissioner)*
AD: 1834/AH: 1250/Yaz: 1204

The Shah-Abdol-Azim shrine in Ray is a place of pilgrimage near the grave of a descendant of Hasan ibn Ali, the son of the fourth ecumenical caliph. Abdul Adhim al-Hasani died in the ninth century. The sanctuary consists of a main gate with access to various courtyards and a mosque. Expansions were undertaken during the Buyid dynasty, and major repairs were carried out by the Safavids. The dome was gilded in 1835 in the Qajar era on the instruction of Naser al-Din Shah. Several important personalities are buried there, among them Naser al-Din Shah who was murdered on this site. In 1888, the first Iranian railway line, from Tehran to Abd-al-Azim in Ray, was launched here. Initially planned as a horse-drawn railway, it was operated as a narrow-gauge railway. Today the Tehran Metro connects Ray with the city.

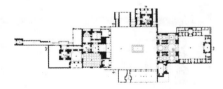

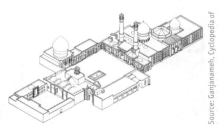
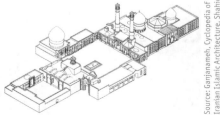

Floor plan of Qavam od-Dowleh House

Axonometric projection and floor plan of the Shrine

View into the Place of Royal Artillery

Place of Royal Artillery
Maidan-e Toop-Khaneh-ye Mobarakeh

میدان امام خمینی

Maidan-e Imam Khomeini, Tehran

35.68575, 51.42147

Amir Kabir (Commissioner)

AD: 1851/AH: 1267/Yaz: 1221

In days gone by, the Silk Road caravans traversed the Place of Royal Artillery, now called Imam Khomeini Square; today there are traffic jams. The square originally lay in front of the northern entrance to the royal palace and was connected to the citadel through a gate in the city wall, Darwaze Dowlat. Under Mirza Taghi Khan Amir Kabir, first chancellor of Naser al-Din Shah Qajar, the Place of Royal Artillery was moved from the south side to the north side of the citadel and a new arsenal, or ghur khaneh, was built at the southwest corner of the square. Until the end of the Qajar period, cannons were

mounted on the square, giving off salutes at official occasions such as the start of the Iranian New Year. In 1904 Top-khaneh square was further developed by adding two square-shaped floors measuring 220 m × 110 m north of the citadel. The ground floor was a storage space for cannons and ammunition, and the upper floor served as lodgings for gunners. Maidan-e Toop-Khaneh, unlike other squares of that time, did not have the uniform elements of the past; instead, modern elements were created in the square. In the four sides of Toop-Khaneh Square, offices like the Shahi bank, Nazmyyeh, the police station, Ghorkhaneh Gate, the post office, the telegraph office, gates and entrances were located. "The four sides of the square had an organised and constant façade composed of half-arcs on two floors and an exterior passage that surrounded the whole square." The square was the urban communication centre, a ceremonial venue and the centre of social and cultural life.

Maidan-e Imam Khomeini

Source: Wikimedia Commons

Entrance gate

Polytechnic School
Dar al-Fonun
دارالفنون

159 G

Khiyaban-e Naser-e Khosrow, Tehran
35.68379, 51.42186
Amir Kabir (Commissioner), Nikolai Markov
AD: 1851/AH: 1267/Yaz: 1221

The first three years of Naser al-Din Shah's reign saw a number of basic reforms introduced by his capable reformist and hard-driving chief minister Amir Kabir. He attempted to organise the military and equip it with modern weapons; he tried to balance the budget and replenish the empty coffers of the treasury by cutting down on unnecessary expenditure; he sent students abroad to study Western techniques and sciences; he engaged foreign advisors and founded the first polytechnic school in the capital. The "House of Arts", as it was called, was the first institute of technology and was the first secular university in Iran.

It was established by Amir Kabir, the foreign minister under Naser al-Din Shah. One of his main concerns of was to modernise the Iranian economy and find connectivity to industrial development in Europe, for which he needed engineers with university degrees. Moreover, Amir Kabir wanted to build an army that was powerful enough to protect the country from foreign invaders. The institute was planned by the Iranian-educated Mirza Reza Mohandes, and built by the architect Muhammad Taqi Khan Memar-Bashi, under the supervision of the Qajar prince Bahram Mirza. Facilities included an assembly hall, a theatre, a library, a cafeteria and a printing shop. Towards the end of the nineteenth century, sixteen Iranian and twenty-six European professors taught medicine, natural sciences, engineering, geology, military sciences and humanities. Dar al-Fonun's printing shop published outstanding scientific papers in the Persian language and opened Iran's first photo studio. Teachers from the West introduced their ideas about politics and society to Iran. It is therefore no surprise that students and graduates of Dar al-Fonun played an important role in the Constitutional Revolution of Iran in 1905, which led to the abolition of the absolute monarchy and the introduction of a constitutional monarchy with a constitution and a parliament. The building was destroyed in

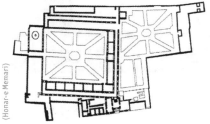

Source: Amir Bani Mas'ud (Honar-e Memari)

Ground floor plan

Antoin Sevruguin: Kakh-e Saltanat Abad, view with the large water basin, about 1933

1925 by Mirza Yahya Khan Qaragozlu, then-Minister of Education, and rebuilt based on the design of the Russian architect Nikolai Markov, who planned the expansion around a large courtyard surrounded by fifty classrooms, a theatre, a print shop, a library, a large dining room and various workrooms and laboratories. The east portal, decorated with two columns and tiles in the traditional star pattern, stands at Naser-e Chusrau Avenue. With the establishment of the University of Tehran in 1935, the Dar al-Fonun lost importance as a university and was converted to a high school.

Saltanat Abad Palace
Kakh-e Saltanat Abad
کاخ سلطنت آباد

Rostam Abad, Tehran
35.76053, 51.45644
Naser al-Din Shah (Promoter)
AD: 1859 / AH: 1276 / Yaz: 1229

The construction of the Saltanat Abad complex, ordered by Naser al-Din Shah in the village of Rostam Abad, commenced in 1859 and was completed in 1887. Situated in northeast Tehran, it consists of a castle with various, usually freestanding individual buildings like a Hawz-Khana, a covered area with a pool, the bedrooms, Khab-gah, living rooms, Haram-Khana, and Abdar-Khana, and the kitchen which is famous for its exquisite tile work. In the spacious pool in front of the palace a vessel was anchored, where proud owners could put out to sea. The main building has two floors; the walls and ceilings are decorated with excellent Qajar plasterwork. The metal roof is adorned with a golden globe, the symbol of royal power. The architecture and stucco decorations are an important contribution of Qajar style architecture. Next door is another building with a five-storey tower. In the basement of this palace is a remarkable Hawz-Khana with a magnificent hall, decorated with seven coloured tiles that realistically depict various episodes from Naser al-Din Shah's time. The tower of the palace, known as the Borj-e Homaiuni, is also decorated with frescoes, gypsum stalactites and stucco. The top floor has a platform to enjoy the view. The façade of the tower is covered with seven-coloured tiles depicting Naser al-Din Shah's army.

Antoin Sevruguin: Kakh-e Saltanat Abad, view from inside the garden, 1880–1930

1778
The Earthquake of Kashan

A 6.1-magnitude earthquake occurred in Iran in December 1778 on the western side of the desert. The earthquake was strongly felt in Ray, Qom and Isfahan cities. The event claimed about 8,000 lives in the city of Kashan and destroyed almost all the houses there, mainly buildings and palaces in the city. Heavy damage occured in large areas in the north and south of Kashan. The water supply became contaminated in the epicentral region, causing an outbreak of cholera. Daily aftershocks of the earthquake continued for a month. The earthquake destroyed the towers and ramparts of Jalali palace, but by the order of Karim Khan the palace was repaired by the governor of Kashan, Abdolrazzagh Khan. The city started a reconstruction program, and numerous large houses from the eighteenth and nineteenth centuries were rebuilt, incorporating the finest examples of Qajar aesthetics. The rebuilding of Kashan after the earthquake resulted in a great agglomeration of Qajar dwelling architecture, and numerous unique architectural samples of that period are preserved to the present day. Ustad Ali Maryam, an Iranian architect of the nineteenth century, became famous for his reconstruction work after the earthquake of 1778. Three of his buildings in particular achieved great prominence: the Tabatabai mansion, the Borudjerdi-ha mansion and the Timcheh Amin-o-Dowleh. He developed the typical nineteenth-century architectural style of Kashan, using traditional elements like stucco.

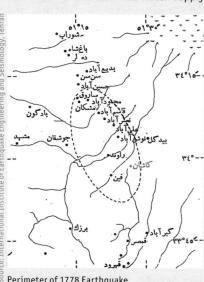

Perimeter of 1778 Earthquake

Hammam-e Khan, view of the roof

Khan Bath
Hammam-e Khan
همام خان

Feyz Sq. Bozorg Basar, Kashan
33,98504, 51,44965
*Abd-or-Razzaq-Khan
(Commissioner)*
AD: 1774 / AH: 1298 / Yaz: 1187

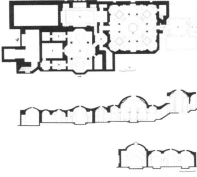

Hammam-e Khan, floor plan and section
Source: Ganjanameh, Cyclopedia of Iranian Islamic
Architecture, Shahid Beheshti University

The bathhouse, located below ground to keep warm in winter and cool in summer, was one of the few bazaar-era buildings to survive the earthquake of 1778 undamaged. It is still owned by the same family. Hammam-e Khan was commissioned in 1774 by Abd-or-Razzaq Khan, governor of Kashan during the reign of Karim Khan Zand. The bathhouse has three sections: a sar bineh, a garmkhaneh and a chal-e hose. The first is a large vaulted locker room with wooden or stone benches along the walls, covered with mats and carpets, with a fountain in the centre. Ceilings and walls are decorated with scenes from *Shahnama*, Ferdowsi's *Book of Kings*. The steam room, or garm-khaneh, is generally rectangular. The floor is steam-heated and made of marble or tiles. Traditionally, for a full-body wash there was a large water-filled basin, or kazina, over a stove stoked with manure and leaves. A dallak, or attendant, would pour water onto a hot tile to generate steam. First, the customer had a massage, then his hair and beard were dyed with henna. After that, he was treated with a pumice stone to smoothen the soles of his feet and his palms, and then his nails were cut. The third area, the chal-e hose, contained a swimming bath used by several people at the same time. Generally there were two baths, one with hot water and the other with cold. According to Jean Chardin, "the water was covered with a thick layer of fat or lather. ... and it was only changed once or twice a year as religion dictates that water is not impure. Public baths therefore often carry diseases".

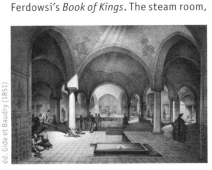

Eugène Flandin: Interior of Khan Bath in Kashan, 1840

View into the small yards flanking the octagonal reception hall

Tabatabai Mansion
Khane-ye Tabatabai
خانه طباطباییها

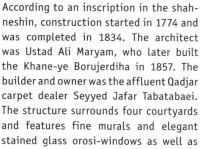

Alvi St. / Qaleh Jalali Str., Kashan
33.97480, 51.43912
Ustad Ali Maryam
AD: 1774 / AH: 1298 / Yaz: 1187

According to an inscription in the shah-neshin, construction started in 1774 and was completed in 1834. The architect was Ustad Ali Maryam, who later built the Khane-ye Borujerdiha in 1857. The builder and owner was the affluent Qadjar carpet dealer Seyyed Jafar Tabatabaei. The structure surrounds four courtyards and features fine murals and elegant stained glass orosi-windows as well as a variety of classic traditional elements of the lifestyle of the time. The outer part, which is accessible to visitors, is called biruni, and the private, residential part, which is not open to the public, andaruni. A columned ayvan, slightly recessed from the edge and facing a rectangular pool, sits in the centre of the southern front on the courtyard. The southern front constitutes the most important spatial structure of the mansion. It is taller then the other parts and is crowned by a semi-circular arc that forms the highest point of the building's skyline. The richly-decorated columns and the beautiful details of the coloured-stucco carvings of the walls and ceiling of the ayvan further empha-sise its importance. Behind the ayvan

View into the small yards flanking the octagonal reception hall

Source: Tishineh, Iran

Cupola in the reception hall

lies a reception hall with a shah-neshin linked to a small yard at each end. Thus, the windows of the hall overlook open space on three sides. Surrounded by two-storey buildings, the small yards flanking the octagonal reception hall have an octagonal pool in the centre. The main entrance of the mansion is situated at the southeastern corner and combines several consecutive spaces linking the entrance arch to the courtyard. The large, impressive cellar located under the openc recessed space of the northern front, has a central part surrounded by a number of areas. Generally speaking, the subterranean area ranks among the important summer spaces of the edifice. The second, smaller and obviously

Axonometrical projection
Source: Ganjanameh, Cyclopedia of Iranian Islamic Architecture, Shahid Beheshti University

more private part of the mansion consists of two small courtyards on the northern and southern fronts. The mansion has two distinct sections representing independent yet connected houses. The larger section has a rectangular courtyard with small areas at the corners.

Source: Penelope Hobhouse, Jerry Harpur

Arabesques on the walls and pilasters of the courtyard

Bazaar Kashan
Basaar-e Kashan
بازار كاشان

Masjed-e Soltani, Kashan
33.98267, 51.44659
unknown
AD: 1778/AH: 1191/Yaz: 1147

Eugen Wirth: Bazaar Kashan

Source: Eugen Wirth, Die Orientalische Stadt, Mainz (2000)

Bazaar Kashan, one of the major bazaars of the Seljuk and Zand periods, was completely destroyed by the earthquake in 1778. Although it was adequately restored and partly rehabilitated by Ustad Ali Maryam in the Qajar period, particulary under Fath-Ali Shah and Naser al-Din Shah, important and valuable parts of it were lost when new roads were builit during the reign of Pahlavi I. Nevertheless, this structure still ranks among the country's most splendid bazaar complexes where complete examples of such buildings are found. In its structure and function as well as its architectural design, Bazaar Kashan shows three main bazaar types, namely line, area and central bazaar. Once a city such as Kashan engaged in long distance trade, the structure of the bazaar became much more complex. Added to the traditional bazaar alleys, which were the location for craft and retail, khane or saras sprung up as offices, warehouses and long-distance trading companies. These completely introverted buildings were connected by a network of parallel, axial or irregular bazaar alleys. The formation followed certain processes which resulted in the characteristic shape and structure of this bazaar. Topographic or local circumstances, or simply the intersection of two major bazaar axes, emphasise or highlight a centre or an intersection and lead to the development of an area bazaar. Such interactions of profane, commercial and religious institutions demonstrate the fascinating interrelationships within the bazaar and contribute to its distinctive quality.

Bazaar of Kashan

Source: Wikimedia Commons

Pascal Coste: Bazar Haji Seid Hussein Kashan, 1840

Source: Monuments modernes de la Perse mesurés, dessinés et décrits, éd. Morel (1867)

Courtyard, southwest side

Aqa-Bozorg Mosque
Mesjed-e Aqa Bozorg
مسجد آقا بزرگ

Kamal-ol-Molq Sq., Kashan
33.97822, 51.44533
Haji Sha'ban-Ali Posht-Mashadi
AD: 1842/AH: 1260/Yaz: 1211

The Aqa-Bozorg Mosque in Kashan is one of the most beautiful mosques in Iran. It is famous for its precise, symmetric architecture and attractive appearance. The mosque was commissioned by Haji Mohammad-Taqi newly-e Khanban so that Haji Molla-Mehdi Naraqi II, known as Aqa-Bozorg, could teach his students there. It was finished in 1842 by the master architect Mimar Ustad Haji Sa'ban-Ali, assisted by his student Ustad Ali Maryam, who later on became one of the most famous architects of his time. The subterranean winter prayer hall was built several years before the madrasa and mosque of Haji Ali Sha'ban-Posht-Mashhadi. Agha Bozorg is famous for its symmetric design. The mosque consists of four porches, two ornate minarets and a brilliant brick dome. Writings about this building inform the reader that its orientation in relation to the qibla distinguishes it from other similar edifices in that its courtyard's main axis is not aligned with the qibla, and its prayer niche is located at its southwest corner. Two large ayvans are richly decorated with red, blue and yellow tilework against the brick backdrop, as well as calligraphy bands by calligraphers like Hossein, Assadollah and Mohammad-Hassan. The ayvan in front of the mehrab has two minarets with a brick dome. The gondbad-khaneh was originally open to all sides. It was later extended in the west by Mohammad-Ali, the son of Aqa-Bozorg, who also completed the mosque by adding a large winter prayer hall. The wooden front door is adorned with as many jewels as there are verses in the Qu'ran. The imposing dome is built on an octagonal podium and consists of double layers. The lower level of the dome carries the weight of the ceiling and sits on strong pilasters, whilst the outer cladding appears to enlarge the dome. Various verses from the Qu'ran are inscribed on and around the dome, which creates harmony with the rest of the structure. The massive courtyard is one of the most notable features of the mosque. It is flanked by a number of chambers and arcades and has another smaller court sitting at a lower level than the outer one. This sunken garden, or gowdal baqche, has a small pond with a fountain and is surrounded by another series of chambers and arcades which are used in the summer months for protection from the heat. Although the magnificent mosque of Agha Bozorg is decorated with coloured tiles and mosaics, its appearance is ascetic in nature. The cobbled veranda and brick walls of the mosque make it look simple yet elegant. This building has been restored several times without changing its substance.

Source: en.sepehrgasht.com

Outside finish of the openings

Borudjerdi-ha Mansion
Khane-ye Borujerdiha
خانه بروجردیها
Alvi St., Qal'e-Jalai St., Kashan
33.97452, 51.44087
Ustad Ali Maryam
AD: 1855/AH: 1271/Yaz: 1224

165 A

Khane-ye Borujerdiha is one of the most famous mansions in Kashan. It was commissioned in 1855 by Haji Hasan Saiyed Natanzi, a rich carpet dealer of Kashan, who imported the carpets from Borudjerd in Lorestan Province. The house consists of a biruni, the part of the building reserved for guests, and an andaruni, the domain of the wives, children, servants and members of the household. When the mansion was built, Khane-ye Tabatabai was used as the blueprint in view of the Borudjerdi family's intention to marry into the Tabatabayi family. However, the Tabatabayi family only agreed to the marriage on condition that the bride's house would be as beautiful as the mansion constructed by Ustad Ali Maryam for their family. The wedding finally took place after a construction period of more than eighteen years! The mansion has an elongated courtyard, at opposite ends of which stand its two important special structures. The façades of these two fronts are taller than that of the two other. The first ensemble, forming the southwestern front of the courtyard, is the more important part of the edifice and includes a large majestic reception hall of hasht-o-nom-hasht shape surrounded

Source: Claudia Luperto

Western courtyard façade

Façade of summer area

Walls of the Shahneshin

on two levels by various rooms and other spaces. In front of the reception hall, an area connects the hall to the ayvan overlooking the courtyard. Two large covered spaces flank this area, ensuring communication between the lateral rooms of the ensemble. Most of the rooms in this part of the building are lavishly decorated. The interior design was done by court artist Sani ol-Molk, better known as Kamal-ol-Molk, who adorned the reception hall with murals of Qajar Shahs. The main rooms are situated at both ends of the long courtyard. The more representative parts are located along the southwest façade where the elongated octagonal reception room is surrounded by a number of rooms on two floors. An intermediate portion connects

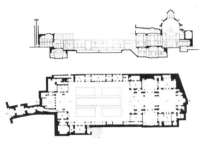
Floor plans and sections
Source: Ganjanameh, Cyclopedia of Iranian Islamic Architecture, Shahid Beheshti University

it to the ayvan facing the yard. Most of the main rooms are painted, especially the reception talar, which is crowned by a dome decorated with a yazdi bandi pattern interspersed with light openings, so that the space shines like a pearl. The outside finish of these openings gives the house a special expression that is depicted on many Iranian postcards. The high courtyard façade, situated in front of the impressive roof volume, gives the ayvan its full glory. The arrangement of these elements, flanked by two badgirs, reminds the visitor of the importance of this house. The elongated pool flanked by flowerbeds reinforces this impression. The second courtyard contains another comparatively-modest structure. The walls are covered with stucco birds and flowers. The central courtyard, accessed from the side, has a pond flanked by trees and flowerbeds. This area served as a retreat for the family.

Entrance corridor to Borudjerdi-ha Mansion

Source: eurasia.travel

Imamzadeh Habib Ibn Musa

Imamzadeh Habib Ibn Musa 166 A
Imamzadeh-ye Habib Ibn Musa
امامزاده حبیب بن موسی
Emam Khomeini St., Kashan
33.98679, 51.45767
Mohammad-Sadeq Esfahani
(Promoter)
AD: 1859 / AH: 1238 / Yaz: 1228

The Safavid family obviously had a soft spot for Kashan, as Shah Abbas I requested that he should be buried there in preference to Ardabil, Qom or Mashhad. His body lies inside the thirteenth-century Imamzadeh named after Habib Ibn Musa, who is believed to have been a descendant of the seventh Imam Musa ibn Qasem. The tomb of Shah Abbas the Great is now part of a large mosque complex that was rebuilt in Qajar times. His black marble cenotaph stands to the right of the entrance of the crypt. In fact, no-one really knows where Shah Abbas is buried. Three coffins were prepared after his death, possibly to ensure that his bones would not be disturbed by enemies after his death, or perhaps to signal that he ruled over the whole of Iran. One coffin was taken to Ardabil, one to Mashhad, and one to Kashan, but it is not known which coffin held the body of Abbas. Iskander Beg does not mention this tale at all; he recounts how Shah Abbas' funeral cortège left Mazanderan, leaving his aunt, a daughter of Shah Tahmasp and other women of the royal household in charge of the royal treasuries and workshops. Devoted Sufis shouldered the bier. Later in Kashan: "The people came out to meet the funeral procession and showed their great grief. The throng around the bier was so great that the emirs and other nobles could hardly make their way through the crowd. The bier was taken to the Imamzadeh Habib Ibn Musa, situated behind the burial ground outside the city". There, the body lay in state, with incense, long candles, and "every kind of meat and sweetmeat", as well as a roster ensuring that the Qu'ran was recited continuously throughout the ceremony.

Floor plan and section

Amin-od-Dowleh Timcheh
Timcheh-ye Amin od-Dowleh
تیمچه امینالدوله

Khayyat-ha Basar, Miyanchal
Basar, Kashan
33.98423, 51.44880
Farrok-Khan Amin-od-Dowleh (Promoter)
AD: 1868 / AH: 1284 / Yaz: 1237

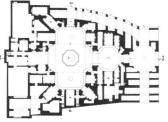

One of the most important buildings in Kashan bazaar, which constitutes a complete example of a timcheh, is Amin-od-Dowleh Timcheh, built in 1868 during the reign of Nasr-od-Din Shah. The timcheh was also designed by Ustad Ali Maryam, who reportedly made a scale model of the building when he designed it. The Timcheh-ye Amin od-Dowleh was commissioned by Farrokh-Khan Amin-od-Dowleh, an influential statesman of the Qajarid court, who was "trusted by the state". It is located at Khayyat-ha Basar, where Persian carpets are still sold and traded. The timcheh has a vestibule and a central area around which rooms are laid out on two floors. The central area of the timcheh has a regular base but a composite form which can be considered a combination of a navicular shape and two half octagons joined to its extremities. This layout can also be seen in the ceiling. All three parts are covered by circular vaults, with the central one being larger and higher. Each vault features a rare yazdi-bandi ceiling decoration with cross lines creating triangular and diamond shapes. The surface is subdivided into a triangulated grid in which each of the facets is kept at approximately the same scale. The nave of the timcheh gives an optical effect of a diamond in cruciform shape and an acoustical effect of diffusion. The subtle lighting of the area enhances the elegance of these chiselled vaults. Light apertures are located in the apex and on the sides of the vaults. The main aperture of the centre vault is large and dodecagonal, and those of the lateral vaults are octagonal. Unlike these central apertures, the lateral ones are directional and have herringbone-shaped curves, and all seem to be pointed towards the central apertures. The ceiling gently joins the surrounding walls, and its finely patterned surface is gradually replaced by their relatively coarse patterns, showing a combination of refinement and solidity.

Source: Ganjanameh, Cyclopedia of Iranian Islamic Architecture, Shahid Beheshti University

Floor plan

Vestibule and its connection to the central space

Southern and eastern sides of the central space

Central space ceiling decoration

Source: Thomas Meyer-Wieser

New Saray
Saray-e No
سرای نو

Qayseriyeh Bazaar, Kashan
33.98584, 51.45111
unknown
AD: 1778/AH: 1191/Yaz: 1147

At the front of the great bazaar of Kashan stands a building whose design is unique in several aspects and must be considered an innovation of the Qajar period. The first unusual feature in this design is its regular decagonal base, which affects its exterior. As far as we know, the use of this form is unprecedented except in the Jalali Fortress, also located in Kashan. Another odd feature is the tiered three-storey area encircling the courtyard. Care was taken in the span arrangements, façade and decoration to prevent any point in the yard from being too prominent. The design remains non-directional, as the form of

its base dictates. The main entrance leads directly to the first floor through a downward stairway and a simple passageway. Therefore, the yard is directly visible from the bazaar through its entrance, and the light attracts the passerby's attention to the existence of the saray.

Bakhshi Timcheh and Saray
Timcheh va Saray-e Bakhshi
تیمچه و سرای بخشی

Khayyat-ha Basar Kashan
33.98475, 51.44918
*Haji-Hossein Bakhshi
(Commissioner)*
AD: 1909/AH: 1326/Yaz: 1278

The remarkable Bakhshi Timcheh and saray complex date from the Qajar period and were commissioned by Haji Hossein Bakhshi. The design consists of a number of open and closed spaces; a timcheh, a saray and a vestibule which connects them on the inside but also to the bazaar. Additional rooms are arranged around it, forming a precise geometric order along the bazaar. The central, main space of the timcheh has an elongated shape that widens in the middle. The expansion and vaulting emphasise the importance of the space. The middle of the vault is surmounted by smaller, dodecagonal skylights; the flanking domes are smaller and also have octagonal skylights. The rooms of the timcheh are higher than the ground and are connected and accessed by stairs leading to anterooms. The Bakhshi Timcheh and Saray form an extremely interesting roofscape which is worth

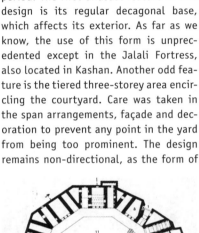

Floor plan

General view of the saray

Source: René Hochuli

Bakhshi Timcheh, outside view

View into Bakhshi Timcheh

seeing. The saray has two floors and its ship-shaped courtyard is located one floor lower than the timcheh. The upper floor is recessed, enabling the viewer from the courtyard to see a two-storey structure with ayvan-like recesses on the shorter sides. The major axis is also accentuated, the geometry of the court is amplified and the rhythm of the façade varies. The Timcheh is connected on the south side by a short, single-storey passage that serves as the entrance vestibule of the saray and the timcheh. A short passage connects this timcheh like a vestibule to the saray. The saray has two floors, and its yard lies one storey below the timcheh's floor. In the past, this yard was probably accessed via a stairway which connected it to the vestibule's cellar, but today it is entered through a long, narrow stairway added later to the saray. The second floor of the saray is recessed in the shape of a half octagon at its junction

Axonometric projection
Source: Ganjanameh, Cyclopedia of Iranian Islamic Architecture, Shahid Beheshti University

with the passage to the timcheh and its opposite side. Thus, a viewer standing in the yard is faced with a two-storey area, with ayvan-like recesses at the centre of its smaller sides. In this way the main axis of the design is suddenly accentuated, the geometry of the yard is reinforced and the façade's rhythm is diversified. The yard is paved with bricks and today has only one, neglected flower bed. Based on its position lower than the timcheh, it appears that it used to be a sunken garden, with its treetops visible from within the timcheh's vestibule and passage.

Source: eurasia.travel

Bakhshi Timcheh, outside view

1865–1924
First Influence of European Architecture

The first modern architectural developments in Iran took place during the Qajar period, following the reforms of Abbas Mirza, Amir Kabir and other intellectuals who promoted the rule of law, public education and welfare. With the objective of achieving economic and national independence, they laid the foundation of a new Persian architecture. Increasing communication between Iran and Europe led to a growing awareness of European art and architecture, which was obviously the intention of the government. In the eighteenth and early nineteenth century, an interesting comparison began between local Iranian and European architectural parameters, and at the end of the nineteenth century, influences and changes from all over the world came into play. This change began in the 1850s with the architecture of pre-modernism in Iran; Iranian architectural historians speak of first western influences in Iranian architecture. The pre-modern architecture originally manifested itself in representative public buildings but not private dwellings. Encouraged by his chief minister, Mirza Hassan Khan Sepahsalar, the Shah made a trip to Europe followed by two further visits where he was accompanied by a number of his courtiers. These visits resulted in a certain appreciation of Western manners and methods, and some purchases were made, including a printing press. The basic problems of the country, however, remained unresolved, and the opposition to the status quo increased.

Development of Tehran ca. 1873

Tehran's first fortification wall was demolished in 1857 to allow an extension, based on plans influenced by European architecture. The new wall encompassed a territory five times its previous size, and featured a moat and twelve gates. The vast Place of Royal Artillery with surrounding buildings, was created. Wide arterial roads instead of labyrinthine narrow streets and a ring-road along the former city wall were important developments for the economic life of the town. Nasr-al-Din Shah was the first Persian monarch to visit Europe in 1873; further visits took place in 1878 and 1889. The Shah was reportedly amazed by the technology he witnessed. Subsequently, the traditional city of Tehran was given a touch of European flair by the erection of a theatre resembling the Royal Albert Hall in London, as well as the first clock tower in the style of Big Ben. But the city really only opened to the West in the twentieth century, under the succeeding Pahlavi dynasty. The Qajar period marks the transition from traditional to modern architecture in Iran. References to pre-Islamic Iranian heritage, especially the Sassanid, were complemented with severe European neoclassical forms. This mixture culminated in a new imperial style.

Source: Thomas Meyer-Wieser

Development of Tehran ca.1873

Source: Wikimedia Commons

Sun Building Palace
Kakh-e Shams ol-Emareh
کاخ شمسالعماره

170 **G**

Maidan-e Panzdah-e Khordad,
Kakh-e Golestan, Tehran
35.67933, 51.42228
Moayer ol-Mamalek, Ali Mohammad Kashi
AD: 1861/AH: 1278/Yaz: 1231

Shams ol-Emareh is probably the most impressive building of the Golestan Palace. The building is located in the east of the complex and is accessible from the palace and the Nasser Khosro Road. It covers an area of 664 m², spread over five floors, in which each room is assigned a specific function – a very European model. The ground floor is designed as a hybrid structure that splits into two towers from the first floor, with the third and fourth floor and the viewing platform erected on top of these. A clock, a gift from Queen Victoria to Naser al-Din Shah, was installed between the two towers, and its bells could be heard throughout the city. Whilst most buildings in Iran are

Source: Claudia Luperto

Basement entrance

Faïence plinth detail

introverted and enclosed, this construction is entirely extroverted and, being a high-rise building it allows a wonderful view over the city and the countryside. Naser al-Din Shah brought the idea of building a skyscraper back from his trip to Europe, and pictures of European buildings supported his plan. He commissioned Moayer ol Mamalek and Master Ali Mohammad Kashi with the design. Construction commenced in 1865, and the building was completed two years later. The first five-storey building in Tehran, Shams ol-Emareh, is also one of the first Iranian buildings where Western influences can be observed, especially in the design of the façades which boast twin columns, pillars, arches, round windows and elongated balconies. These influences go back to Andrea Palladio, whose buildings, however, were only known through verbal accounts and postcards. At that time, architects did not have the opportunity to travel abroad and study the buildings on site. Shams ol-Emareh is also the first building in Tehran

View of Kakh-e Shams ol-Emareh

using modern materials such as cast-iron pillars and cast-iron balustrades, and the upstairs rooms are equipped with wall heaters. The combination of traditional Iranian architecture and classical European styles resulted in a unique architecture that did not exist previously and was never repeated. On the one hand, the building is strongly reminiscent of the Safavid Ali Qapu Palace in Isfahan, but at the same time it also consciously incorporates the formal language of European architecture.

Shams ol-Emareh, mirror wall lining

Mosque and madrasa with central water basin

Sepahsalar Mosque and School
Masjed va Madrasa-ye Sepahsalar
مسجد سپهسالار

Khiyaban-e Mostafa Khomeini, Tehran
35.68889, 51.43333
Haj Hossein Lurzadeh
AD: 1861 / AH: 1278 / Yaz: 1231

171

Although Qajar architecture is often referred to as not being innovative, the details seen on the Sepahsalar mosque – such as the use of faïence or mirror mosaic in the Indian tradition – show an advance in the ornamentation, which testifies to the splendour achieved with this fantastic technique. Sepahsalar Mosque is also known as Motahari Mosque, named after Martyr Morteza Motahari who was a leader in the 1979 revolution. It is a classic courtyard-mosque with a central ayvan on each side. It was built in the Qajar era by order of the incumbent chancellor during the rule of Naser al-Din Shah. Mirza Hassan Khan Sepahsalar was the Grand Vizier and

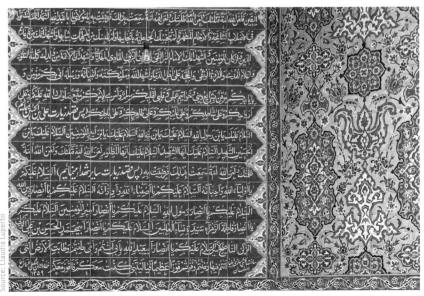

Use of Indian-style faïence

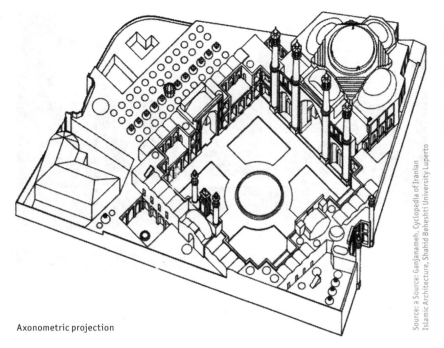

Axonometric projection

also the Minister for Foreign Affairs and Commander-in-Chief during the Shah's reign. The mosque has eight minarets and sixty rooms, including a main prayer hall with forty-four columns and a large domed hall, followed by four ellipsoidal semi-domes. The entrance is on the west side. It is no longer created as a traditional, high rectangular portal, but set back and covered with a shallow muqarnas vault, so that the two flanking minarets dominate the silhouette. The entrance leads into a vaulted entrance hall from which several passages lead to the courtyard of the mosque. This is surrounded by double-storey, continuous arcades, which open to the cells occupied by students. The spacious courtyard is shaded by stately trees and dominated by a round pool in the middle. The four ayvans have classic shapes, deep arched niches decorated with stalactites. The most important and dominant feature of the courtyard is the south ayvan, which is very high and deep and leads to a spacious, vaulted maqsureh. The façade of the ayvan has four minarets constructed in the same style and with the same proportions as those at the entrance of the mosque. Parallel to the courtyard is the shabestan, which is accessed through a door in the east ayvan as well as a passage on the north side. The most spectacular feature of the mosque is the extravagant colourful tile decoration. Geometric motifs and calligraphic characters mix with compositions based on a naturalistic treatment of flowers and fruits which shows similarities to contemporary European and Chinese examples. The floral tiles and brick decoration of the minarets are dominated by ochre, pink and a small amount of blue. In contrast, the colours used in the dome are white, turquoise and bright shades of blue, whilst the ochre content is negligible.

Section

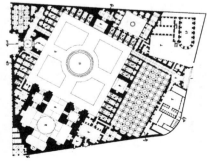

Floor plan

Antoin Sevruguin: Embassy of the United Kingdom ca. 1933

Embassy of the United Kingdom
Sefarat-e Britania
سفارت بریتانیا

198 Khiyaban-e Ferdowsi, Tehran
35.69611, 51.41833
James Wilde
AD: 1869/AH: 1286/Yaz: 1239

Naser al-Din Shah reigned for nearly fifty years. During his reign, contacts with the West intensified, and the intervention of the Russian and British governments in Persian affairs continued. The British Embassy, originally built on the northern outskirts of Tehran, is today part of the city. The U-shaped main building is surrounded by its garden. There is an open pavilion in the centre whose shape is inspired by the chattris of Indian Mughal architecture. The embassy was designed by the British architect James Wilde in 1860. The completion of the building took nearly 16 years, since the dome, together with some of the large glass windows, were imported from the United Kingdom, causing unforeseen problems. In 1872 the concession for the import, export, purchase, and sale of tobacco was given to a British company. This was met with opposition from the populace and the ulema. The Shah was pressured into cancelling the concession, and the country suffered the financial consequences of the cancellation. This movement is often regarded as a prelude to the Constitutional Revolution as well as the first instance in the modern period when the ulema managed to successfully rally the urban populace to take a stand against the government.

Asli Castle
Kakh-e Asli
کاخ اصلی

Kakh-e Golestan, Tehran
35.67883, 51.42064
Naser al-Din Shah
(Commissioner)
AD: 1873 / AH: 1290 / Yaz: 1243

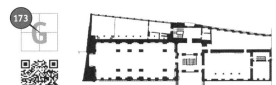

Floor plans
Source: Nomination of Golestan Palace for Inscription of the World Heritage List 2012

After his visits to Europe between 1873 and 1882, Naser al-Din Shah was greatly influenced by Russian neoclassicism of the late nineteenth century. In 1873 he initiated the erection of a series of neo-classical buildings with a homogeneous double-storey façade on the north side of the Golestan garden. This led to the demolition of significant parts of Khalvat-e Karim Khani. The new complex consists of the Talar-e Ayineh which is reminiscent of St. Petersburg and includes a museum building, and other smaller halls which are lined with mirror mosaics like many other ayvans and halls of the Golestan Palace. The museum hall was the first building in Iran purposely built as a museum. Apart from objets d'art and weapons, Naser al-Din Shah displayed the gifts he brought back from his travels or received from foreign envoys. During the reign of Naser al-Din Shah, the Royal Jewels were also exhibited in this hall. After the famous Peacock Throne, the Takht-e-Tavoos, was transferred to the National Jewel Museum

of the Central Bank, the king used the hall for important receptions. The hall has exquisite mirror work. The ceiling and walls are covered with plasterwork, the floors with mosaics. In the middle of the complex, Talar-e A'ineh overlooks the Golestan garden from the second floor. Although not very large, the Mirror Hall is the most famous hall in the palace. Kamal-ol-Molk, the best known painter of the Qajar period, created a famous painting of Talar-e A'ineh, now exhibited in the adjacent Talar-e Salam. The oil painting shows the interior of the hall, its mirror work and chandeliers before the renovation in 1907. The square mirrors on the ceiling vividly reflect the walls, objects and carpets.

Source: Golestan Palast

Kamal-ol-Molk, Oil painting of Talar-e Aineh, 1882

Exterior view

Kamal-ol-Molk, View of the interior, 1892

Royal Theatre (demolished)
Takiyeh-ye Dowlat
تکیه دولت

Kakh-e Golestan, Tehran
35.67883, 51.42064
Ali Mehrin
AD: 1873/AH: 1290/Yaz: 1243

174

The Tekiyeh Dowlat, commissioned by Naser al-Din Shah Qajar in 1868, was the Royal Theatre of Tehran and the most famous place in Iran, where ta'zieh performances, the Shiite passion plays in honour of Husain, took place. The architecture is reminiscent of the Royal Albert Hall in London which Naser al-Din Shah visited on his European tour together with the Princess of Wales and her sister, Tsesarevna, the daughter of Alexander III of Russia. The theatre was large enough to accommodate 20,000 visitors, and in the opinion of many western visitors it surpassed the largest opera houses in

Europe in luxury and splendour. Samuel G. Benjamin said during his first visit that it was comparable to the Arena of Verona. The building was designed by the architect Ali Mehrin and built as a round, 60 m wide and 24 m-tall brick building, painted white on the outside and clad with tiled walls and pillars on the inside. The building had three entrances, one for men, one for women and one from the citadel for use by the Shah and the royal family. The ceiling, originally planned as a wooden structure, was spanned with steel ribs covered with a tent roof on the advice of French engineers. The courtyard was surrounded by twenty arches three-storeys high with a width of 7.5 m, which contained the boxes of the ministers and governors as well as a large veranda for the Shah. The hall was illuminated by more than five thousand candles on stands and wall mounts. An electric chandelier was later installed in the centre of the ceiling. The Takiyeh Dowlat was used until the end of the Qajar period; the funerals of Naser al-Din Shah and Mozaffar od-Din Shah took place here. It was used for the last time on 6 December 1925 at the constitutional meeting when Ahmad Shah was deposed and Reza Khan Pahlavi appointed as temporary head of government. After that, the Takiyeh was abandoned and fell into disrepair. It was demolished in 1947 and Muhammad Reza Shah built the bazaar branch of Bank Melli in its place.

The Shah and the Royal Family at the State Concert at the Royal Albert Hall, 1889

Cossack Garrison
Imarat-e Qazaqkhaneh
عمارت قزاقخانه

Khiyaban-e Kushk-e Mesri,
Tehran
35.68922, 51.41683
Karim Taherzadeh, Behzad Tabrizi
AD: 1879 / AH: 1296 / Yaz: 1249

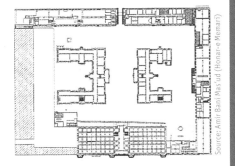

The Cossack garrison was built under Naser al-Din Shah as a garrison of the Persian Cossack brigade outside the city and was one of the earliest and largest military zones of Tehran. The Cossack brigade was established in 1879 and was a military unit commanded exclusively by Russian officers. The brigade served as bodyguards of the Shah and also protected Russian envoys. Its formation was part of the modernisation process of the Persian armed forces, implemented with the help of foreign military experts. On his second journey to Europe in 1878 Naser al-Din Shah visited St. Petersburg. He was accompanied by Cossacks from the Russian border and was so impressed by their smart uniforms, precise commands and modern armament that he wanted to establish a similar force in Persia. The tsarist government in St. Petersburg of course immediately saw an opportunity to increase its

Floor plan and exterior view

influence in Persia and promptly agreed to assist. After the October Revolution in 1917 and the collapse of the Russian monarchy, the Russian officers were replaced by Persians. Reza Khan's hour had come; he overthrew the government on 21 February 1921, was appointed as the new prime minister and founded the Pahlavi dynasty. In 2010 the Tehran College of Design bought and remodelled the Emarat Qazak Khaneh.

Front of the Imarat-e Qazaqkhaneh, today the Art School of Tehran

East elevation of the White House

White House
Kakh-e Abyaz
کاخ ابیض

Khiyaban-e Kushk-e Mesri,
Tehran
35.68040, 51.42134
Naser al-Din Shah
AD: 1883/AH: 1300/Yaz: 1253

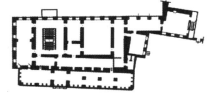

The Ottoman Sultan Abdul Hamid II sent many precious gifts to Naser al-Din Shah, and it was reported that there were enough to fill an entire castle. After his trips to Europe, where he visited the major museums, the Qajar ruler decided to set up an exhibition hall worthy of these gifts in the Golestan Palace, and a new building was constructed next to the Talar-e Adsch. It is believed that Naser al-Din Shah himself designed this building, which had to

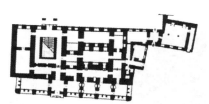

Floor plans

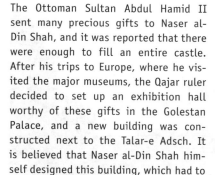

West elevation

be large enough to accommodate Abdul Hamid's carpet. The palace was completed in 1883, and has since accommodated one of the most interesting, sometimes slightly bizarre ethnological collections in Iran. Showcases display wax figures with costumes of different ethnic groups in lifelike surroundings. There are also household items, tools, musical instruments, water pipes and traditional jewellery. The façade of the building is created in the Russian neoclassical style of the eighteenth century. The coronation of Mohammad Reza Shah Pahlavi occurred here on 17 September 1941.

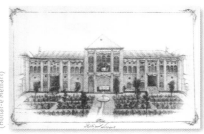

Engraving by Abootorab Ghaffari, 1883

Saheb Qaranieh Palace
Kakh-e Saheb Qaranieh
کاخ صاحبقرانیه

Niavaran, Tajrish, Tehran
35.81281, 51.47144
Haj Ali Khan Hajeb od-Dowlah
AD: 1889/AH: 1307/Yaz: 1259

Kamal-ol-Molk, Oil painting of Hauzkhaneh in the Niavaran Palace, 1889

Saheb Qaranieh palace is the oldest building of the Niavaran palace complex. Its origins can be dated back to the reign of Fat'h-Ali Shah; however, most of the buildings existing today were built in the time of Naser al-Din Shah. Even the name of the palace, Lord of the Centuries, is derived from a title awarded to Naser al-Din Shah. The site originally consisted of more than forty buildings attributed to the architect Haji Ali Khan Hajeb-od-Dowlah. There was a big reception building (biruni) containing the imperial mirror hall and surrounded by a vast garden with several pools, and several smaller residential buildings for the king's wives (andarunis). But when Mozaffer-ed-Din Shah and Ahmad Shah came to power, the andaruni lost importance and was made smaller. The summer palace is particularly interesting because it shows the architectonical development of the Golestan Palace, especially the progressive influence of European and particularly Russian architecture. Its white porticos give a colonial atmosphere and have the quality of a stage design. The main building consists of two storeys, with the top floor displaying excellent mirror mosaics and stucco in the Mirror Hall. On the ground floor there is the famous room, Hauzkhaneh, with a water basin painted by Kamal-ol-Molk. One of his most famous paintings is on display at the Golestan Museum. The sprawling

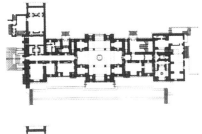

Floor plans and elevation

building – with offices, reception rooms for ambassadors and foreign envoys, tea room, lounge with bar, dining room, private rooms and even a fully-equipped dental practice – was repeatedly used by famous Iranian film makers as a backdrop for historical films and television series.

Source: Iranian Historical Photographs Gallery

View from Midan-e Toop-Khaneh-ye Mabarakeh, ca. 1938

Shahi Bank
Bank-e Shahi
بانک شاهی

Immam Khomeini Square,
Tehran
35.68616, 51.42306
Haj Ali Khan Hajeb od-Dowlah
AD: 1890/AH: 1307/Yaz: 1259

178 **G**

Bank Shahi, floor plan

Shahi Bank was the first bank of Iran, founded in 1890 in the eastern wing of Toop-Khaneh Square next to the gate of Cheragh Gaz Street. In terms of architecture, the historical construction was a unified one, and decorative elements of Iranian architecture (segmented bowls in the half-dome of the entry portal, mosaics and stucco) are among its significant features. Ghorkhane or Takhshaee was a large building housing the production of artillery, ammunition, fireworks and war materials. Ghorkhaneh was located in the western part of Toop-Khaneh Square, and its gate opened to the square. In the Qajar era, some of the arcs of Ghorkhaneh's gate were destroyed to make space for the Nazmyyeh building. A building with thirteen entrances, as high as the previous building on the square, with a gabled roof and a columned façade, was erected on this site.

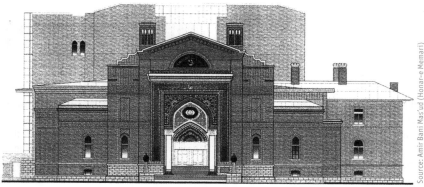

Source: Amir Bani Mas'ud (Honar-e Memari)

West elevation

Source: Wikimedia Commons, Mino Saberi

Nasr Theatre, façade of the oldest surviving theatre in Tehran

copies of Western themes and techniques. Despite Pahlavi censorship, Iranian drama flourished in the mid-twentieth century, with ground-breaking new forms merging Western innovations and Iranian tradition. After a brief period of great artistic freedom, the revolution of 1979 imposed political control of the theatre, but it remained an important art form that remains at a high artistic level and tackles topical subjects.

Nasr Theatre
Teatr-e Nasr
تئاتر نصر

Khiyaban-e Lalehzar, Tehran
35.68972, 51.42222
unknown
AD: ca. 1900 / AH: ca. 1320 / Yaz: ca. 1270

The former home of the Nasr Theatre, the oldest theatre in Tehran, still exists. It is located on Lalehzar Street, which was one of the most prestigious streets in 1900 and runs from the former central Toop-Khaneh, now Khomeini Square, to the north. Iran is the only Islamic country with its own, centuries-old tradition of drama. This has its roots in the Shiite religious practice of performing rituals to commemorate the violent death of the third Shiite Imam and martyr Hossein. A unique genre of scenic performances with songs and processions was developed, which is still of great importance to the local culture. European – and thus, secular – theatre has also existed in Iran since the mid-nineteenth century. It experienced a big boom in the 1960s, but the performances were by no means

Source: Ali Martin (Tehran: Past & Present)

Khaneh-ye Alam os-Saltaneh, Motive from the Shahnameh

Alam os-Saltaneh House
Khaneh-ye Alam os-Saltaneh
خانه اعلم السلطنه

Khiyaban-e Hafez, Tehran
35.70969, 51.39764
unknown
AD: ca. 1900 / AH: ca. 1320 / Yaz: ca. 1270

The building was constructed in 1900 during the reign of Mozaffar ad-Din Shah. Later, the property came into the possession of Kazem Bannat Nezam, a merchant of Qazvin, who was known as A'lam os-Saltaneh. The architect combined Iranian and Western design. The north-south and east façades acknowledge the symmetry, whilst the west façade is treated completely asymmetrically and bears no relation to the others. The window frames and sills of the mansion are decorated with brick patterns. In addition, the gable elements in particular are decorated with faïence depicting motifs from Shahnameh. The building now houses the Ministry of Jihad-e Keshaverze.

Source: Ali Martin (Tehran: Past & Present)

Entrance façade of Khaneh-ye Alam os-Saltaneh

Ferdowsi Villa and Garten
Imarat-e Bagh-e Ferdows
باغ فردوس

Khiyaban-e Valiasr, Tuzi,
Tehran
35.802185, 51.422478
Moayyer ol-Molek (Commissioner)
AD: ca. 1900/AH: ca. 1320/Yaz: ca. 1270

This Garden of Paradise is located in Tajrish, a neighbourhood in northern Tehran. The complex was originally commissioned as a summer residence by Haji Mirza Aqasi, a Sufi believer and the Prime Minister of Muhammad Shah. Subsequently, the building underwent several changes of ownership until it was purchased by Mohammad-Vali Khan, Sepahsalar-e Tonekaboni. He was the leader of the revolutionaries who demanded the liberation of the State of from the royalist forces. He was appointed defence minister in the first constitutional government, which ended in 1909 with the dethronement of Mohammad-Ali Shah Qajar. He then became prime minister. The impressive gate of the garden dates from this period. In the reign of Naser al-Din Shah, the palaces were renovated and renamed Bagh-e Ferdows. Naser al-Din Shah's son-in-law asked architects from Isfahan and Yazd to build a new mansion, which he called Rashk-e Behesht, Envy of Paradise. The main building consists of two superimposed halls with a gabled steel roof. The lower one has an elaborate stucco ceiling, and the doors and windows are made of wood and coloured glass. Since 2000, this attractive, formerly Qajar summer residence has been home to the Iranian Film Museum, which provides an insight into the long and successful history of Iranian filmmaking, showing film clips of Iranian filmmakers such as Abbas Kiarostami, Mohsen Mahmalbaf, Jafar Panahi and Majid Majid. The museum shop also sells hard-to-find DVDs of Iranian movies. A highlight of the museum is the plaster decoration of the cinema ceiling.

Exterior view of the Villa in the Ferdows-Garden with the representative double staircase

Source: Hamid Reza Norouzi Talab (Tehran: Past & Present)

Imar-e Kafe Pars at Khiyaban-e Lalehzar

Qazali Cinema Complex at Khiyaban-e Lalehzar

Lalehzar Street
Khiyaban-e Lalehzar
خیابان لاله زار

Khiyaban-e Lalehzar, Tehran
35.68983, 51.42267
Naser al-Din Shah
(Commissioner)
AD: ca. 1900/AH: ca. 1320/Yaz: ca. 1270

In the nineteenth century Lalehzar was a meadow on the outskirts of the capital and was given its name because of the many wild tulips growing here. It was a popular meeting and recreation place for the upper class. After his first trip to Europe, where he was enthusiastically received – especially in Paris, where he was escorted by elephants during his reception in the Champs-Elysees – Naser al-Din Shah decreed that an avenue similar to the one in Paris would be built in the middle of the park. Trees were cut down and channels dug, and Khiyaban Lalehzar was created. In later years, Fat'h Ali Shah's grandchildren built the Grand Hotel there, the first modern Iranian hotel, and at the end of the century the first carriages in Iran drew up in front of it. Electrification started here, and the first streetcar drove through Khiyaban Lalehzar, where luxury shops, cinemas and theatres had ben established The area became known for its cabarets, cafés, restaurants and nightlife. The first Iranian silent film and the first Iranian sound movie premiered in Lalehzar. Eventually the theatres and cinemas closed one after the other, and the street lost its glamour. Today, the avenue is just a city street with small shops and street vendors in the busy, crowded, old downtown area. In the place where the first magnificent modern hotels of the Qajar princes were built, an elderly man now sits and sells wire, screws and electrical parts. But there are still traces of the old glory, ornamental tiles, plaster and masonry of faded lustre.

View into Lalehzar Street

Commercial building on the street

Source: Kamyar Adl

Ahmad Shahi Pavilion
Kushk-e Ahmad Shahi
کوشک احمد شاهی

Niavaran, Shemiranat, Tehran
35.81186, 51.47231
Ahmad Shahi (Commissioner)
AD: ca. 1900 / AH: ca. 1320 / Yaz: ca. 1270

183 F

The Ahmad Shahi Pavilion is located near the main building of the Niaveran garden. It served the last Qajar ruler, Ahmad Shah, as a summer residence. Ahmad Shah ascended the throne at the age of twelve. The country at that time experienced a rather-chaotic mix of newly won freedoms and a traditional system of government, with unstable cabinets following one another, all unable to govern effectively. World War I saw the incursion of Russian, British, and Ottoman troops into Persia, adding to the disorder and economic problems of the country. The Shah was inexperienced, lacked a strong personality, and was too fond of spending time in Europe. Political factions borne out of unwonted freedom were engaging in disruptive conflicts in Parliament and in the press; corruption was rampant. The intervention of British and Russian agents in Persian affairs was reaching new heights. In 1907 the two great powers had come to an agreement to divide the country into zones of influence, with the Russians receiving a free hand in the north and the Caspian provinces, whilst the British were to enjoy the same privileges in the south, that is, Fars province, Khuzestan, the Persian Gulf and the Sea of Oman, with central Persia left to the Persians. In 1915, a new agreement between the two powers no longer acknowledged even the central neutral zone. In 1917, however, Russia underwent a Bolshevik revolution and soon renounced its tsarist imperial policies and its privileges in Iran. The British, on the other hand, further consolidated their grip over the Middle East and India. In 1919, by making gifts of money to the prime minister and several other ministers, the British made an agreement with the Persian government which practically placed

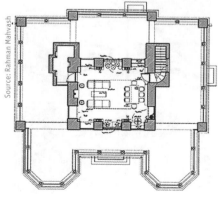

Source: Rahman Mahvash

Upper floor plan

Persia under the governorship of Great Britain. This gave rise to loud, nationalistic protests in the country and was also rejected by the League of Nations. The country was now thoroughly disenchanted with the results of the hard won freedom, the incompetence of the successive cabinets, the inefficacy of the Shahs, and the corruption of the bureaucracy. A strong and stable government became the people's desideratum. The architecture and design are from the late Qajar period. The exterior façades of the pavilion are kept in brick throughout. A tiled entrance leads into the central hall leading to more rooms.

The staircase is located on the northeast side. The central hall on the upper floor, used as a music room, is surrounded on all sides by a portico. From the early 1950s, the pavilion was used as a venue for family celebrations of the Pahlavis. In the early 1960s, Mohammad Reza Pahlavi decided to expand Niaveran and had the pavilion redesigned as his office by the same French designers who decorated the Oval Office in the US White House. Starting in 2010, the Ahmad Shahi pavilion was restored to its original, pre-Pahlavi design by the architect Rahman Mahvash. The official reopening was scheduled for 2015.

Terrace of the pavilion

Source: Amir Bani Mas'ud (Honar-e Memari)

Exterior view of the Parliament Building

House of Parliament
Imarat-e Baharestan
عمارت بهارستان

Khiyaban-e Lalehzar, Tehran
35.69014, 51.43360
Naser al-Din Shah
(Commissioner)
AD: 1906/AH: 1324/Yaz: 1276

On 5 August 1906, Mozaffar ad-Din Shah issued a decree to establish a Parliament. Between 1905 and 1907, the Persian Constitutional Revolution took place, which led to the establishment of a parliament. A movement to create transparency in government practices and to place its operations on the basis of law rather than the whims of the Shah and his agents, it gradually developed as a result of encounters with the West and the increasing awareness of the so-called backwardness of the country. The Imarat Beharestan not only played an important role in the development of constitutional government, but also embodied the spirit of the national architecture of the last Qajar years, which tried to unify tradition and modern Western (especially Russian) architecture. Jafar Khan, professor at Dar ol-Funun, was the architect of the first building in the west of today's complex, which he designed as a "brick baroque" building. After a fire in 1891, the French architect and sculptor, Fabius Boital, is said to have rebuilt the south façade in the neoclassic style of the French parliament; three years later, Karim Taherzadeh Behzad added the colonnaded façade and the entrance of the north façade in the Apadana style of Persepolis. The first Parliament elected by quotas from different districts and layers of society, including Qajar princes, met on 7 October 1906. Soon two factions emerged: one, the radical Socialist-Populist party, and the other the Moderate Party. As the nerve centre of politics, the large square, named after a residence building on its west side that was converted to the first Iranian parliament, witnessed many receptions, demonstrations, clashes and battles. The significance of the place, however, has changed. After the revolution, the parliament building was abandoned and is now used as a library and museum.

Source: Freer Gallery of Art- Arthur M. Sackler Gallery

Antoin Sevruguin: Baharistan Square, 1930–1940

View from the garden

Entrance portal

Negarestan Garden
Bagh-e Negarestan
باغ نگارستان

Shari Atmadar, Tehran
35.69450, 51.43289
Kamal-ol-Molk (Commissioner)
AD: ca. 1910, 2013 /
AH: ca. 1330, 1434 / Yaz: ca. 1280, 1383

185

The Negarestan Garden is close to Baharestan Square in downtown Tehran. In 1910, the painter Mohammad Ghaffari, better known as Kamal-ol-Molk, started a famous art school here that influenced Iranian painting over almost seven decades. The garden, a historical monument of Qajar period, was converted to a museum for Kamal-ol-Molk and his students in 2013. Kamal-ol-Molk was born in 1847 in Kashan and was undoubtedly one of the most important Iranian artists of his time. He developed an interest in calligraphy and painting from a young age. After primary school he moved to Tehran and studied painting at Dar-ol-Fonoun for three years. During a visit to the school, Naser al-Din Shah became aware of his talent and invited him to become a court painter, where he was awarded the title Kamal-ol-Molk – Perfection of the Country. During his years spent at the court, Kamal-ol-Molk created some of his most important works, which reflect the unique atmosphere and culture of the Qajar dynasty and represent one of the highlights of visual arts in modern Iran. After Naser al-Din Shah's death, he immigrated to Europe at the age of 47, where he remained for about four years. In 1898 he returned to Iran, but soon left again due to the increasing pressure of Mozaffar ed-Din Shah. After spending two years in Iraq, he returned to Iran and established the Sanaye Mostazrafeh Art School, better known as Kamal-ol-Molk Art School, whose aim was to promote new talent. Kamal-ol-Molk was not limited to painting but also taught other crafts such as weaving, mosaic design and woodwork at the school. When he refused to cooperate with Reza Khan Pahlavi, he was forced to resign and was exiled to Nischapur, where he devoted himself to agriculture. Kamal-ol-Molk died in 1940 and was buried near the grave of Sheikh Attar.

View along the central axis

Hans Holein: floor plan and isometric drawing for the conversion of Glass and Ceramics Museum

Ahmad Qavam House, Glass and Ceramic Museum
Khaneh-ye Ahmad Qavam os-Saltaneh, Muzeh-ye Abgineh va Sofalineh
موره آبگینه و سفالینه

Khiyaban-e 30 Tir, Tehran
35.69342, 51.41508
Hans Hollein (Modification)
AD: 1919, 1978/AH: 1338, 1398/
Yaz: 1289, 1347

Staircase in today's Glass and Ceramics Museum

This unique complex was built by Ahmad Qavam os-Soltaneh, a well-known statesman of the late Qajar and early Pahlavi era, as a residential and business building in the 1920s. The buildings were erected in a 7,000 m² garden now located in the centre of Tehran. The complex consisted of two almost identical buildings – the biruni, the outer, and the andaruni, the inner area. Today the biruni houses the Iranian Glass and Ceramics Museum. The building consists of brick work in Seljuk style, glazed panels depicting legends from Shahnameh, stucco, faïence, mirror work and inlays – all of the highest quality. The mansion is two stories high and shows a blend of classic Rococo, Art Nouveau and Persian style. The building is rectangular in shape, with an entrance portico and a balcony above. The rooms are arranged on two floors in a circle around the stairwell. Until 1951, the property was the residence of Ahmad Qavam os-Soltaneh. After he left Iran, the Egyptian government bought the complex and established their embassy there. In 1976, the Farah Pahlavi Foundation bought the house, had it restored by Hans Hollein in 1977–1978 and converted into a museum. Hollein simultaneously worked on the museological concept. The galleries were reinforced by columns to cope with increased traffic from the public. The ornate interior walls could largely be retained, display cases with built-in lights were designed by Hans Hollein are placed in the centre of the rooms. A number of structural changes were inevitable, and the existing rooms were adapted accordingly. Most fireplaces were left in place, although they are no longer used for heating purposes. Unfortunately, Hollein could not oversee the exterior space design or extension. The Muzeh-ye-Abgineh-va-Sofalineh contains one of the most complete collections of Holein's works.

Ettehadieh Residence
Aqamat-e Ettehadieh
اقامت اتحادیه

Khiyaban-e Ettehadieh, Tehran
35.69086, 51.42178
Mirza Ebrahim Khan Amin os-Soltan (Commissioner)
AD: ca. 1920/AH: ca. 1318/Yaz: ca. 1270

One of the few relics of Lalezar Street is the Mirza Ebrahim Khan Amin os-Soltan estate, which served as coffeehouse for Naser al-Din Shah. Only a part of the garden still exists, which fortunately was registered as a national heritage site. The building, which stands at the end of

Pavilion of Ettehadieh Residenz

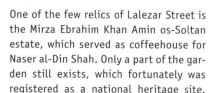

the cul-de-sac Ettehadiyeh, was used as the film location for a highly successful Iranian TV series in 1976, directed by Nasser Taqvai and based on a book by Iraj Pezeshkzad. The story takes place at the time of Iran's occupation by the Allies during World War II. Most of the story is filmed in the narrator's home, a huge, early twentieth century-style Iranian mansion where three wealthy families live under the tyranny of a paranoid patriarchal uncle. The first-person narrator is a high school student in love with his cousin Layli, who is his "Dear Uncle's" daughter. The story revolves around the narrator's efforts to stall Layli's pre-arranged marriage to her cousin Puri, whilst the narrator's father and Dear Uncle plot mischief against each other to settle past family feuds.

Ferdowsi International Grand Hotel
Hotel-e Bozorg-e Ferdowsi
هتل بین المللی بزرگ فردوسی

Khiyaban-e Ferdowsi, Tehran
35.68983, 51.42267
unknown
AD: ca. 1920/AH: ca. 1339/Yaz: ca. 1290

Old black and white photographs in the lobby of the hotel speak of a "glorious past". The "Ferdowsi", situated at what was then the northern edge of the New Town, was once one of the first hotels in Tehran and, before the revolution, also one of the better establishments. It was opened in the 1920s. The façade and the interior were renovated at some stage, which brought about pleasing changes whilst still retaining a touch of Persian heritage. The six-storey hotel has 220 rooms, suites, royal suites and a restaurant that offers excellent traditional and modern Iranian cuisine.

Grand Hotel Qazvin
Hotel-e Bozorg-e Qazvin
گراند هتل قزوین

Peighambarieh Street, Qazvin
36.26704, 50.00234
Ustad Ali July
AD: 1922/AH: 1340/Yaz: 1291

At the end of the Qajar dynasty and the beginning of the Pahlavi era, under governorship of Sadossaltane, Grand Hotel Qazvin was constructed in central Qazvin, west of Chehel Sotun Palace, by a well-known architect of Qazvin, Ustad Ali July. This building is one of the oldest remaining hotels in whole country. According to travelers who have personally resided in the hotel, all the furniture and appliances of the hotel are in the European style and the interior decoration is fully luxurious. The main entrance is in the west wing with wooden covers on each side. It reaches the hall in the middle storey. There are pillared halls with ribbed vaults on each side. All the hotel's main rooms are in the first floor. There are 17 rooms with views over the street and to the yard on the east and west wings. In addition, there are several rooms on three different floors that are smaller and linked to the service space and grand cinema as well. According to the history, Grand Hotel Qazvin has been a place of political incidents such as Reza Khan's planning of a coup d'état. It is the oldest guest house in Iran.

Ferdowsi International Grand Hotel

Grand Hotel Qazvin

Source: Caroline Reichmann

Gate to the National Garden
Sardar-e Bagh-e Melli
سردر باغ ملی

Khiyaban-e Imam Khomeini,
Tehran
35.68600, 51.41697
Jafar Khan Kashani
AD: 1921/AH: 1340/Yaz: 1291

190 G

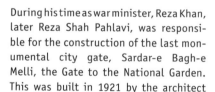

During his time as war minister, Reza Khan, later Reza Shah Pahlavi, was responsible for the construction of the last monumental city gate, Sardar-e Bagh-e Melli, the Gate to the National Garden. This was built in 1921 by the architect Jafar Khan Kashani, when it was still a parade ground. Although the portrayal of machine guns, heavy artillery and Cossack uniforms give the faïence on the door a contemporary look, the theme of soldiers guarding a checkpoint is very old, and is reminiscent of the Apadana staircase in Persepolis. Today, Bagh-e Melli is a government complex where the police headquarters, the Ministry of Foreign Affairs, the National Museum, the Malek Museum and the Museum of Posts and Telecommunications are located. This gateway was the symbol of Tehran before the Shahyad monument was built.

Source: Claudia Luperto

Tilework with military motifs on Sadar-e Bagh-e-Melli

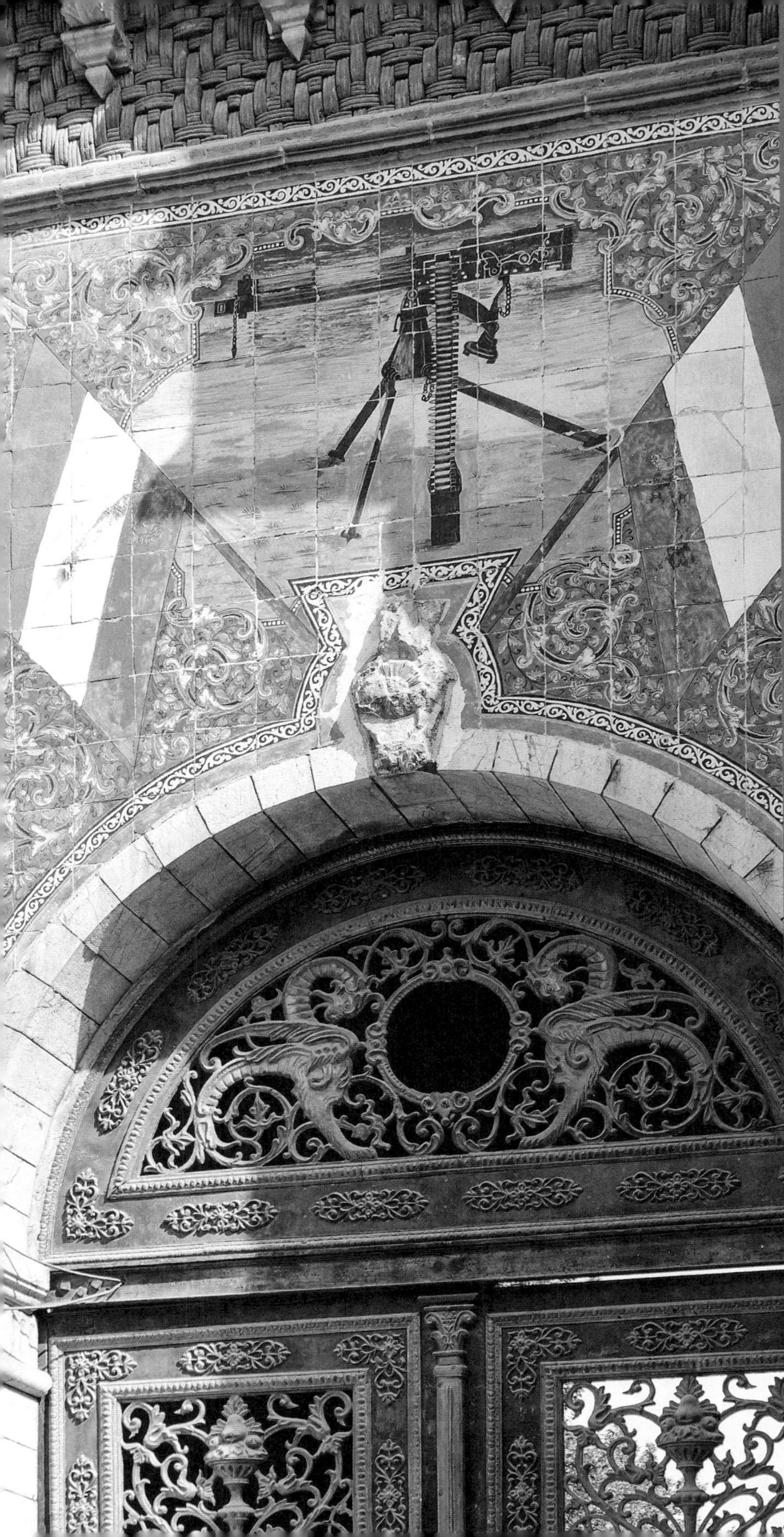

The Pahlavi Dynasty

1924–1933
Discovery of the National Identity

On 31 October 1925, Ahmad Shah Mirza, the last Qajar ruler, was deposed by the Iranian Parliament with only four dissenting votes. Reza Khan, commander of the Cossack Brigade unit stationed in Qazvin, and later defence minister, was appointed Shah on 12 December 1925 by parliament, thus founding the Pahlavi dynasty. When he ascended to the throne, a new economic and cultural era began in Persia. After his government came to power, the systematic promotion of industry and private investment started. This meant that from 1929, many landowners and feudal lords invested their capital in the import of capital goods for industrial plants, which was an important step for urban development. The road and railroad networks were established, which occurred simultaneously with an increased Europeanization of society. Reza Shah often travelled to Turkey and was heavily influenced by Kemal Atatürk, whom he used as a guide for the country's attempts at modernisation, which resulted in imitation and rivalry. All policy objectives, education, business and culture were viewed through a Western lens. This required new infrastructure, with museums, ministries, and railway stations. The question was, who could design these modern buildings, and what should they look like? The government and the architects agreed that local architects could not cope with this task, and instead agreed to ask European architects for their expertise and to become involved in the renovation of the country. Reza Khan envisioned the future of Persia as a modern state, with a modern economy and industry, capable of eventually being ranked alongside European societies. He set out with great determination

Source: Thomas Meyer-Wieser

Development of Tehran ca. 1920

to reform the military, administrative, educational, and judicial systems of the country as well as its social structure.

Development of Tehran ca. 1920

During the reign of Reza Shah Pahlavi, the city structure changed considerably and Tehran finally became the capital of the country. In 1925, Tehran's old town was razed and started growing rapidly. The community law enacted in 1930 made it possible to realise the master plan for urban revitalisation. The construction of large avenues was pursued and swaths were cut through the old city fabric, followed by the demolition of the city walls. For the first time Iran had a government functioning along Western lines. In 1933 the first state budget was adopted, which led to the immediate construction of various ministries: Foreign Office, Ministry of War, Treasury, courthouse and public services such as a post office, railway station and Archaeological Museum. The new dominant architecture broke with tradition. It is characterised by a monumental European style, particularly German, national style with neo-Achaemenid influences and Qajar elements mainly seen on residential buildings. In the 1930s, archaeological excavations led to a rediscovery of Persepolis and thus to a rediscovery of Iran's own national identity. This gave architects the opportunity to develop a new design vocabulary. References to Persepolis were very welcome in Reza Shah's power strategy as this enabled him both to confirm his power by referring to the ancient monarchy and to limit clerical influence by using pre-Islamic symobls. This style is strongly influenced by the neoclassic European architecture of the late nineteenth century and was mainly applied to government buildings, schools, universities and banks. About a dozen of these buildings were erected in Tehran, recognisable by their application of symmetry and geometric forms. The combination of these approaches – the European and the Iranian – led to a special neoclassical style which found its own national expression in Iran.

Source: Amir Bani Mas'ud (Honar-e Memari)

Exterior view of former Post and Telegraphs Building

Post and Telegraphs Building (demolished)
191 G

Sakhteman-e Post

ساختمان پست

Maidan-e Imam Khomeini, Tehran

35.68492, 51.42178

Louis Maurice Adolphe Linant de Bellefonds

AD: ca. 1925/AH: ca. 1344/Yaz: ca. 1295

In the 1920s, mainly European architects were invited to design important representative buildings which were realised in a short time. These architects recommended the imitation of European Historicism, an artistic style that draws its inspiration from a combination of different styles or the use of new elements, creating completely different aesthetics. By copying the European style selected, the government hoped to achieve European quality. A dozen public buildings in this style were planned between 1921 and 1933. Around 1920, German architects built the Post and Telegraphs Building in Tehran, using the design principles of the Renaissance. The dominance of typical Renaissance elements such as loggias, domes and triangular pediments can be observed in the entire building. Sakhteman Post represents an edifice whose architects neither used the locally available materials nor local elements. It is a non-Iranian building; it could stand in any other capital. The European Historicism did not win recognition in Iran. On the one hand, the rediscovery of Persepolis in 1933 led to the government losing interest in this style, and on the other hand the style was accepted neither by the local architects nor the population. To this day, such buildings are seen as examples of a failed attempt at the blind adoption of foreign solutions taken from a different context. This period also saw the development of factories, office buildings and universities, and the increasing use of new building materials such as steel, concrete, copper and glass. New construction techniques led to a mixture of European and Iranian styles and trends. In fact, the Persians were the first nation who established an efficient communication system. "Neither snow, nor rain, nor heat, nor gloom of night stays these couriers from the swift completion of their appointed rounds." This famous quote by Herodotus about the messengers of the Achaemenids points to the importance of the ancient communication system. The whole country was crossed by an extensive network of roads and connected by galloping messengers; 111 relay stations between Susa and Sardis facilitated the work of the couriers, who covered an astounding distance of 2,683 km in one week.

Alborz High School

Alborz High School
Dabiristan-e Alborz
دبیرستان البرز
Khiyaban-e Enghelab/
Khiyaban-e Hafez, Tehran
35.70277, 51.41128
Nikolai Markov
AD: 1925/AH: 1344/Yaz: 1295

The Alborz High School, formerly the American School, one of the architectonical gems of Tehran, is still hidden behind road buildings north of Enghelab Street and only accessible through an alley. The Alborz High School was established as a primary school in 1873 by a group of American missionaries. It is one of the first modern schools in the Middle East. Its position in the Iranian intellectual elite is equal to Eton College or Phillips Exeter Academy. In the early 1900s, the College was transformed into a high school and in 1925 received a permanent home, built by Nikolai Markov in neo-Qajar style. During World War II, the school was no longer under American management and was reformed under the auspices of Reza Shah. The Alborz High School enjoyed its most successful period up to 1979 and after the Iranian revolution. Nikolai Markov, an architect of the avant-garde at that time, studied architecture and Persian literature in St. Petersburg. After the Russian revolution, he decided to stay in Iran. His designs, particularly of educational centres, are influenced by the traditional Iranian Islamic and pre-Islamic architecture. The Alborz High School is his first work; many others followed: schools, public buildings, factories, urban residences, mosques and churches. Markov was a leading figure of Iranian architecture between 1920 and 1940.

Elevation of Alborz High School

Elevation of Kafeh Naderi

Interior of the coffee shop today

Café Naderi
Kafeh Naderi
کافه نادری

520 Khiyaban-e Jomhuri-ye
Eslami, Tehran
35.69444, 51.41639
Khachik Madikian
AD: 1927 / AH: 1346 / Yaz: 1297

Café Naderi is the place where modern Iranian literature began to flourish. Its name is automatically connected with the poet Sadegh Hedayat who, like his colleagues Bozorg-e Alavi, Mojtaba Minovi, Ahmad Shamloo, Nader Ebrahimi' and Lili Goestan, sat talking here all night long. It was founded by an Armenian immigrant, Khachik Madikian, in 1927 and named after the then-Naderi Avenue. Khachik Madikian began his career as a confectioner and was the first to offer European food to Iranians. The Naderi was the second hotel built in Tehran after the Grand Hotel at Lalehzar Street. The construction in western, German style was started simultaneously with the construction of

the buildings for the Iranian railway and a number of banks. Nothing has changed in the café; chairs, cups and even the cutlery are still the same. The decor is also unchanged, and the tablecloths seem to have the same colour as 50 or 60 years ago. Time seems to have stood still in the café's garden. It is easy to imagine how comfortably one could sit here under trees in the heat of a summer evening.

Shah Reza Hospital
Bimaristan Shah Reza
بیمارستان شاه رضا

Navid, Tehran
35.71117, 51.41878
Karim Taherzadeh Behzad
AD: ca. 1928 / um AH: 1347 /
Yaz: ca. 1298

Shah Reza Hospital was a new building type defined on the basis of modern medical requirements. It was designed by Karim Taherzadeh Behzad, who is considered one of the pioneers in the development of Iranian architecture in the

Elevation of Shah Reza Hospital

Orientation panel of the palace

Side view of the Green House

twentieth century. He was exiled for political reasons and continued his education at the Academy of Fine Arts in Istanbul, and later at the Academy of Arts in Berlin. On his return in 1926 he was the first Iranian architect who had been trained abroad. The first building erected by Behzad in Iran is the Ferdowsi Mausoleum in Tus, Khorasan. The architecture of Shah Reza Hospital combines historical approaches and Persian identity. The creative implementation of local and non-local elements led to the development of a new architectural language.

Saadabad Palace Complex
Kakh-e Saadabad
کاخ سعدآباد

Khiyaban-e Ayatollah Maleki, Tehran
35.81667, 51.42417
Reza Shah Pahlavi (Commissioner)
AD: ca. 1930/AH: ca. 1350/Yaz: ca. 1300

Saadabad Complex is a walled building complex with eighteen palaces in the Shemiran area in northern Tehran. The site originally served as a Qajar summer residence. In the 1920s, Reza Shah Pahlavi expanded the compound several times and used it for official and residential purposes. His son Mohammad Reza Pahlavi continued this tradition from the 1970s. After the Islamic revolution, the palace was converted to a museum. Of the eight entrances to the complex, two of them were reserved for the royal family, namely the Nezamieh Gate, the former entrance of Mohammad Reza Shah's family and the remarkable Darband Gate in the purist style of the 1930s. Today, the official residence of the President of Iran is adjacent to this complex.

Green House
Kakh-e Sabz
کاخ سبز

Khiyaban-e Ayatollah Maleki, Tehran
35.81786, 51.42225
Reza Shah Pahlavi (Commissioner)
AD: ca. 1930/AH: ca. 1350/Yaz: ca. 1300

This palace was constructed by Reza Khan to the northwest of Darband on the hillock of Saadabad. Built in 1927, the Green Palace is the oldest building of the complex. It has a mirrored pavilion, an entertainment area, a dining room, bedroom and an office. The façade of this palace is decorated with green stones. Its name is attributed to the green marble cladding. A great Middle Eastern rear terrace stands in contrast to the simple entrance. The southern windows allow a fantastic view over Tehran. A multi-faceted mirror hall is adorned with a finely knotted carpet measuring about 70 m² which was made in Mashhad and is one of the masterpieces created by reputable Iranian carpet weavers. The entire interior of the palace is executed in traditional Iranian handicraft, but most of the decorative items were imported from Europe in 1974 – 1975. The well-preserved living area has an informal atmosphere.

Façade detail of the Green House

Entrance to the White House

boots, the remains of a larger-than-life statue of Reza Shah. White marble from Yazd covers the floor. The ballroom has a 145 m², finely-knotted Mashad carpet. Murals with mythological scenes from the *Shahname* decorate the dome of the banquet hall. Chandeliers, antiques and paintings impress with their magnificence. Many gifts to the royal family from all over the world are displayed in the palace's wings. Two garden pavilions are decorated with contemporary Persian miniatures and calligraphy created by the Iranian artist Hossein Behsad and the Armenian Klara Abkar.

White House
Kakh-e Sefid
کاخ سفید

Khiyaban-e Ayatollah Maleki, Tehran
35.81708, 51.42350
Boris Gchbryhay, G. Paladin, Sheykhan Karim, Hasan Raza
AD: ca. 1930 / AH: ca. 1350 / Yaz: ca. 1300

The White House, the largest building of the complex, was the ceremonial and reception palace of Reza Shah and his son. In 1982 it was converted in 1982 into Muze-ye Mellat, a folk museum. The façade of the palace is modern and plain. A wide staircase leads to the first floor. In front of the façade on the left stands a pair of large bronze equestrian

Black House
Muzeh-ye Honarha-ye Ziba
موزه هنرهای زیبا

Khiyaban-e Ayatollah Maleki, Tehran
35.81472, 51.42389
Reza Shah Pahlavi (Commissioner)
AD: ca. 1930 / AH: ca. 1350 / Yaz: ca. 1300

The Black House took its name from its black marble base. Today it is a museum exhibiting paintings of Iranian and foreign artists collected by Farah Diba. Court paintings from the Safavid and Qajar time are on display. Art from the seventeenth to the twentieth century is covered, and the last floor contains Persian paintings from the Safavid to the Pahlavi era, including some works of Kamal-ol-Molk.

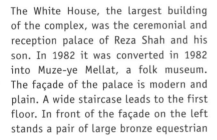

Lounge of the White House

Faramaz Pilaram, painting in the Museum of Fine Arts, *Untitled*, Oil on Canvas, 1982

Spiral stair of the White House

Carriage House
Kalskhaneh Qajari
کالسکه خانه قاجاری

Khiyaban-e Ayatollah Maleki,
Tehran
35.81886, 51.42100
unknown
AD: ca. 1930/AH: ca. 1350/Yaz: ca. 1300

The museum in the northwestern part of the Saadabad complex was the carriage house of the complex in the Qajar period. The Iranian brothers Omidvar, to whom the museum is dedicated, documented their ten year trip around the world, which they started in 1954, with pictures and films. Aborigines, Maori, Pygmies, Eskimos and Indians of the Amazon basin were extensively studied and documented. Abdullah and Issa Omidvar came from a wealthy Tehrani merchant family. When the brothers grew up in the 1930s, it was a time of sweeping political reforms in Persia. Shah Reza Pahlavi enforced secularisation and a radical adaptation of the society to western standards along the lines of Turkish President Kemal Atatürk. Everyone, including the members of the Omidvar household, was prohibited to wear a chador, turban or caftan, but only European clothes. Their parents embraced European culture and travelled extensively with their youngsters, even abroad, and sometimes in their own car,

which was not common even in the best circles. In 1935, when the country's name changed to Iran, Issa and Abdullah were not yet ten years old but, in contrast to most of their friends, had bicycles with which they explored their surroundings. Their adventurous mother passed on her wanderlust to her sons at an early age. Issa and Abdullah started globetrotting in the early 1950s. They prepared for their first major expedition for three years. After their father ordered two motorcycles from England, they started to travel eastward in 1954. The first stops were Afghanistan, Pakistan and India, followed by Thailand, Malaysia and Indonesia. In Jakarta they put their motorbikes on a plane to Australia. From there they flew to the Philippines, Hong Kong and Japan, before going to the Arctic, where they spent five months with the Inuits. Next they crossed the American continent and even crossed the Antarctic. They only returned home seven years later. Indian wooden figures, Asian cookware, Native American weapons, shrunken heads from the Amazon – souvenirs of this and other trips around the world are on display at the Omidvar Museum, which opened in September 2003 in Tehran. The brothers' second big journey, which began just three months later and lasted until 1967, is also documented in this treasure house. It took them through Europe,

Photo of the ten-year trip around the world of the Brothers Omidvar

Source: Nirupars, Netzwerk für alles Persische

the Middle East and across Africa. In addition to the objects collected, ranging from elephant tusks and primitive tools, Middle Eastern daggers and masks to hunting trophies and Pygmy teeth, are press cuttings and pictures. They prove that Issa and Abdullah did not merely travel as adventurers, but rather had a wider scope. "We did not see ourselves as anthropologists," said Issa, now eighty years old and still living in Tehran, where he runs a small textile trimming shop and regularly visits his museum in Saadabad, "but we had asked ourselves a few questions, and we looked for answers in the most remote corners of this planet: How do people live? What distinguishes the individual nations and tribes? How does one come into contact with them?" Their enquiring minds resulted in tens of thousands of photographs, dozens of film rolls, masses of tapes, several mostly-untranslated books and countless articles, written not only for *National Geographic*, but also for the likes of the German weekly entertainment magayine *Bunte*, which published a series of their travelogues in the 1960s, for which they apparently received the incredible sum of 11,000 marks. Abdullah still hankers after his old passions, travel and filmmaking. Decades ago, love made him move to Chile, where he published a tourism magazine and helped establish one of the largest cinema centres in Latin America. The most beautiful relics of the Omidvar wanderlust are kept in a glass box in front of the museum: one of the brothers' motorcycles and the khaki coloured Citroën 2CV used in their second expedition. This robust and fuel-efficient van had been given to them in 1964 by the manufacturer.

Hassan Abad Square
Maidan-e Hassan Abad
میدان حسن آباد

Maidan-e Hassan Abad, Tehran
35.68617, 51.41014
Mirza Alikhan Mohendes,
Ghelidj Baghelian; Amir-Massoud
Anoushfar (Modification)
AD: ca. 1930, 2003 / AH: ca. 1350,
1424 / Yaz: ca. 1300, 1373

In 1870, when the city began to expand, Hassan Abad Square lay in an open field. In the time of Reza Shah Pahlavi, four symmetrical, curved buildings were constructed at the corners in neo-Palladian style, resulting in an attractive, round piazza. Hassan Abad is a traditional, commercial neighbourhood that lay outside the walls of Tehran at the northwest corner. It evolved in the Qajar period and was named after the Prime Minister Mirza Hassan al Mostofi Mamalek. The district has a homonymous square,

Motorcycle and Duck, with which the Omidvar brothers went on their expedition

Upper floor of one of the buildings on the square

Source: Ali Martin (Tehran: Past & Present)

Source: Elnaz Sarbar

which was developed in neo-classical style by the Armenian architect Ghelidj Baghelian and his civil engineer Leon Tadossian in the 1930s. The four corners of the square were originally occupied by identical buildings erected by Mirza Alikhani Mohendes. The southeastern segment was demolished in 1963 to make way for a bank. The present restoration of the square aims to repair the existing structure appropriately. The program plans to rehabilitate the square with traffic-calming measures and also create access to the underground station.

Façade of the original square design

Source: Amir Bani Mas'ud (Honar-e Memari)

The Drama of Persepolis

We owe much of what is known about Persepolis to the passionate archaeologist Ernst Herzfeld, who started systematic excavations on the site. In 1931 Herzfeld and his assistant Friedrich Krefter began to excavate the Persian metropolis Persepolis – the largest palace complex of antiquity. In a ruined fortress wall they found 30,000 clay tablets, the palace archive of the fallen ancient city. It was one of the largest archaeological inscription finds which included receipts, employment contracts and delivery notes. It made Ernst Herzfeld famous worldwide, because these tablets made it possible to reconstruct the former empire and its daily business and to carry out a complete reassessment. Previously the image of Persepolis was mainly drawn by the Greek conquerors who had defamed the Persians as tyrants and brutal despots. For example, the ancient Greek historian Herodotus spoke of palace intrigues, harem murders, cruel despotism and decadence at the Persian court. However, the excavation was soon shattered by the troubles of the time. The Nazis came to power in Germany, and the archaeologist Herzfeld was not Aryan enough for their liking. In 1934, Herzfeld was removed from the excavations in Persepolis. He was on his way to London for a research visit when a former colleague, now a Nazi elevated to the rank of SS-Obersturmbannführer, denounced him. Alexander Langsdorff wrote that Herzfeld was a "typical international Jew" who abused his diplomatic passport. In 1935 Herzfeld was relieved of his professorship, forced to retire and deported from Germany. He moved to Princeton where he taught at the University with other German emigrants and Nobel Prize winners such as Albert Einstein.

Source: Freer Gallery of Art· Arthur M. Sackler Gallery

Ernst Herzfeld, Archaeologist and Iranologist at Persepolis ca. 1934

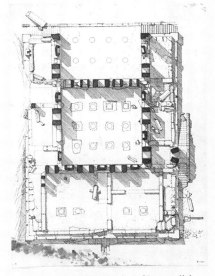

Ernst Herzfeld, isometric plan of Persepolis' Tachara Palace, 1905

Source: Bahman Jalali

Police station at Enghelab Street, 1979

Shah Reza Street, Islamic Revolution Street
Khiyaban-e Shah Reza, Khiyaban-e Enghelab Islami
خیابان انقلاب اسلامی

201 G

Khiyaban-e Enghelab, Tehran
35.70188, 51.43335
Reza Shah Pahlavi (Commissioner)
AD: ca. 1932/AH: ca. 1351/Yaz: ca. 1302

Khiyaban-e Enghelab Islami, or the Islamic Revolution Street, today runs where Qajar ramparts limited Tehran to the north until 1932. In the 1920s, Shah Reza Pahlavi started to open his country to the West and to expand the city into a metropolis, whereby the existing substance was not handled with any great care. The building work along the Shah Reza Avenue took place in the 1930s in a relatively short time and therefore shows a fairly homogenous design of pre- and early modernism with mostly four- to five-storey buildings. Brick and plaster was mainly used for the façades. Such a coherent ensemble is rarely seen in Tehran. Unfortunately, in the on-going modernisation, historically-valuable buildings were often demolished and replaced by mediocre architecture. Despite its importance to the city, Enghelab Street suffers from heavy traffic and a lack of amenities, except perhaps for Student Park.

House of Professor Adl
Khaneh-ye Professor Adl
خانه پرفسور عدل

202 G

Khiyaban-e Sokhanvar 4–6, Tehran
35.68856, 51.40350
Nikolai Markov
AD: ca. 1932/AH: ca. 1351/Yaz: ca. 1302

Shortly after the Iranian revolution, between 1903 and 1905, Professor Mostafa Adl drafted the Iranian Civil Code which was enacted by Parliament

Source: Iran Historical Photographs Gallery

Khiyaban-e Shah Reza, 1963

Source: Ali Martin (Tehran: Past & Present)

Khaneh-ye Professor Adl

and is still in use today. The mansion that belonged to Professor Adl is located at the intersection of Sokhanvar Street and Vali Asr Street, opposite the Marble Palace. It is a single-storey building with a basement and annex, probably designed by the Russian architect Nikolai Markov. It was completed in 1932. The stately residence is decorated with outstanding stucco work. In the second decade of Nikolai Markov's activity, he tended to horseshoe arches sitting on two pillars and elegant reveals or cornices reminiscent of traditional eclectic style, suggesting a symmetrical neoclassical historicism. Markov was one of the first to introduce Orientalism in Tehran's residential architecture. The villa he designed in the "oriental style" was much talked-about and important for the future development of Iranian residential architecture. The building picks up a general Islamic repertoire, inspired by neo-Orientalist North African especially Mauritanian forms and relates to the 1842 publication *Sections and Details of the Alhambra* by Owen Jones. Although Jones turned in the preface to *Grammar of Ornament* against the thoughtless copying of ornaments, his epochal work was a popular model for the "Arts and Craft movement" in England and therefore influenced the renewal of arts and crafts in all of Europe and the Middle East.

Sara Rushan
Saray-e Rushan
سرای روشن

Khiyaban-e Naser Khosrow, Tehran
35.68094, 51.42278
unknown
AD: ca. 1932 / AH: ca. 1351 / Yaz: ca. 1302

The style of pre-modern eclecticism as it appears in Shams ol-Emareh was used until the 1930s. A prominent example is the Rushan shopping arcade. This building complex is a synthesis of different elements from Qajar architecture, European Baroque or Rococo and ancient Persian symbols. The European elements (the triangular gable with putti, the impost capital and the two pinnacle-like towers with Corinthian columns) were mounted in the centre of the two-story building. The architect also placed Iranian ogee-arched windows in combination with turquoise and yellow floral mosaics. Other Iranian, pre-Islamic symbols like Ahura-Mazda are found under the pediment. Such compilations clearly show that eclecticism was not the appropriate solution for the needs of the time. The architect was unable to set rules for new style combinations, nor to move from a merely bizarre merging of different elements towards a symbiosis. Thus the eclecticism was largely ignored.

Elevation of Saray-e Rushan

1934–1941
Arrival of Modernism in Iranian Architecture

The long history of Russian and British interventions in Persian affairs fostered widespread resentment against the two great powers. As a result, Germany, which did not have a history of dealing with Persia and stood against Russia and Britain in World War II, was accorded a measure of sympathy. Its ideology of Aryan supremacy added to the people's admiration without their realising the nature of Nazism. From mid-1930s, young architects who studied in Europe brought these ideas to Iran and tried both to reshape the public and private sectors of Iranian architecture. Certainly one of the most important architects was Gabriel Guévrékian. In 1933, he accepted an invitation from the Iranian government to take part in its national modernization projects. Immediately after his arrival in Tehran, he was he was nominated by Reza Shah to be chief architect of Tehran municipality. In 1934, Reza Shah made a formal diplomatic request that the country should be referred to as Iran rather than Persia, the traditional name, with its cultural connotations. That same year, the Anglo-Persian Oil Company and the University of Tehran were founded. On 7 January 1936, the chador for women was banned. With the outbreak of World War II, Iran declared its neutrality. After Hitler's attack on the Soviet Union, the Allies planned a supply line through Iran, which could not be accepted due to the declared neutrality.

Development of Tehran ca. 1941

The three styles (eclecticism, historicism and the national neoclassicism) were replaced in the mid-1930s by modernism. In this architecture, there was no influence of Persian traditional architecture. It was built without local adaptations. The railway station of Tehran, the courthouse, the university buildings for medicine and law and the campus of Tehran University exemplify the architecture from the second Pahlavi era. Guévrékian, Vartan Hovanesian and Mohsen Foroughi were the protagonists of this movement. Guévrékian, an Iranian of Armenian descent, studied under Oskar Strnad in Vienna and cultivated friendships with Joseph Hoffmann and Adolf Loos. He lived in Paris, was a friend of Le Corbusier and co-founder and first secretary of the "Congrès internationaux d'Architecture moderne" (CIAM), founded in 1928 as a think tank to explore new aspects of urban planning and architecture. It is thanks to Guévrékian and his colleagues that fellow Iranians experienced the impact of modern European architecture first-hand. The variety and the geographical scope of their projects reflect the centralisation policies of Reza Shah. To eliminate local autonomy, he had everything planned, even the most remote towns. The broader Western concept of "modernity" is difficult to apply to twentieth-century Iran.

Source: Thomas Meyer-Wieser

Development of Tehran ca. 1941

Source: CIAM

Group photo with Gabriel Guévrékian at the First CIAM-Congress in La Sarratz, 1928 (third from left)

Source: hamgardi.com

Front elevation of the Police Building

Police Building
Kakh-e Shahrbani
کاخ شهربانی
Melal-e-Mottahed, Tehran
35.68750, 51.41750
Mirza Alikhan Mohendes
AD: 1933 / AH: 1353 / Yaz: 1303

One of the most prominent examples in the development of an Iranian national style is the Mirza Alikhan Mehendes police building of 1933, an exact imitation of Darius' Apadana Palace at Persepolis. All details, such as capitals, roof friezes or reliefs, were studied on site and rebuilt as a detailed imitation of the palace. The combination of European and Iranian designs led to a special neo-classical style which combined modernity and tradition and found its own national expression in Iran. The floor plan is modelled on Hans Pölzig's IG Farben Building which was still considered very modern in the 1950s. The arrangement of the wings and of the main building allowed all offices to have adequate natural light and ventilation. The front of the building looks impressively massive; inside it shows a clear lightness. The entrance is located in the central axis of the building. It is preceded by a temple-like portico which elevates it in a dignified way – a relatively common feature in administrative buildings of the time.

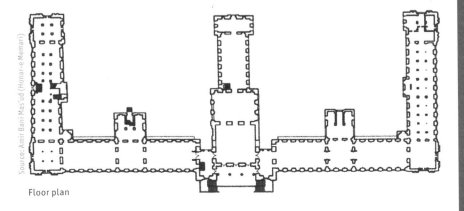

Source: Amir Bani Mas'ud (Honar-e Memari)

Floor plan

Entrance to the headquarters of Bank-e Melli Iran

Central Bank of Iran
Bank-e Melli Iran
بانک ملی ایران
Khiyaban-e Ferdowsi, Tehran
35.69217, 51.41967
Hans Heinrich
AD: 1933/AH: 1353/Yaz: 1303

Bank-e Melli Iran was established in 1927 as the first National Bank of Iran by resolution of the Iranian parliament. The bank began its operations in September 1928 and in the ensuing years opened branches in major Iranian cities. The head office of the bank, built in 1933 in Ferdowsi Street in Tehran, is another example of the Iranian national style of that time. The responsible architect, Hans Heinrich, based the massive building structurally on contemporary German architecture. Achaemenid motifs such as capitals, pilasters, window frames, roof mouldings and the two lions at the entrance dominate the façade. The four columns crowned with bull heads at the entrance portal are elements adopted true to detail from the Apadana Palace in Persepolis. The window embrasures also show similarities with the entrance gate of Darius' Palace. Even the roof frieze with lotus flowers was adopted from the Achaemenid palaces and used as architectonical decor.

Officers Club
Bashgah-e Afsaran
افسران باشگاه
Khiyaban-e Sur Esrafil/
Khyiaban-e Davar, Tehran
35.68986, 51.41503
Gabriel Guévrékian
AD: 1933/AH: 1353/Yaz: 1303

One of the first architects to return to Iran in that time was Gabriel Guévrékian. An Iranian of Armenian descent, he studied in Vienna under Oskar Strnad and cultivated friendships with Joseph Hoffmann and Adolf Loos. Later he lived in Paris, was friends with Le Corbusier, founding member and first secretary of the Congrès Internationaux d'Architecture Modern (CIAM) which was founded in 1928 in La Sarraz, Switzerland, by architects and critics as a think tank for new aspects of urban planning and architecture. This is important, because it caused modernity to be taught first-hand in Iran. In 1933, Guévrékian returned to Iran at the invitation of the Iranian Government and remained in Tehran for four years. Shah Reza Pahlavi appointed him as City Architect and Town Planner of Tehran. His tenure covered major new buildings for houses, residences and several government buildings. The Officers Club in Tehran, which he designed with Vartan

Garden façade of Villa-ye Malek Aslani in Tehran and Khaneh-ye Kuzeh Kenany in Tabriz

Hovanessian, was the first building realised by Guévrékin in Tehran. It is still strongly influenced by national neoclassicism of the early Pahlavi time.

Villa Malek Aslani
Villa-ye Malek Aslani
ویلا ملک اصلانی

Shemiran, Tehran
Site and state unknown
Gabriel Guévrékian
AD: 1934 / AH: 1354 / Yaz: 1304

Avant-garde projects re-interpreting the Iranian house are rarely found in the Iran of the 1930s. An innovative project of this time is Gabriel Guévrékian's villa for the Malek Aslani family, where modern design meets local architecture. The symmetrical division of the façade with a centre talar and the two sides, biruni, the reception room which is reserved for guests, and andaruni, the part of the house occupied by the wife, children, staff and members of the family, are elements implemented

Floor plans and elevation of Villa-ye Malek Aslani, 1935
Source: Elisabeth Vitou/Dominique Deshoulières/ HubertJeanneau (Gabriel Guévrékian)

in a more modern architectural language. Much like in a traditional house, both the ladies' and the gentlemen's living rooms had a connection to the main room, which was larger and penetrated deeper into the building. The Qadjar architects set an ayvan in front of these rooms, and by using vertical sliding glass doors opened the rooms to the terrace, which led into the garden via a central staircase. The pool in the garden was also part of this concept. The architect managed to connect the Qadjar spirit with modern European living ideas, resulting in a house which was not alien to the Iranians and, as Bruno Taut said, is of "value to the whole world".

Entrance to the Officers Club

Source: Thomas Meyer-Wieser

Street side of the Ministry of Foreign Affairs

Source: Old Tehran

Street view of General Post Office

Ministry of Foreign Affairs

Vezarat-e Omur-e Kharejeh
وزارت امور خارجه

Khiyaban-e Kushk-e-Mesri,
Tehran
35.68825, 51.41603
Gabriel Guévrékian
AD: 1934/AH: 1353/Yaz: 1304

Gabriel Guévrékian designed the building for the Ministry of Foreign Affairs to resemble two symmetrical buildings connected by an third, elongated, central part. The respective entrances to the two side pavilions, whose volumes were highly structured, form a succession of avant-corpss. The construction differs significantly from the original design. It lacks a clear, underlying stylistic feature or intuition. Rather, it is a creative combination of formal elegance, precious materials, intensity of colours and thematic sensuality which was typical of art deco. It is characterised by the stylised and flat display of floral and organic motives. The lack of shade and naturalness promotes the modern and often striking impression of the architecture of this era.

The industrial production and the carefree, eclectic mix of style elements of different origins are important prerequisites.

General Post Office

Sakhteman Edari-ye Post
ساختمان اداری پست

Khiyaban-e Imam Khomeini,
Tehran
35.68611, 51.41778
Nikolai Markov
AD: 1934/AH: 1354/Yaz: 1304

The extension of the main post office was officially opened in 1934. It was built under the direction of the Russian architect Nikolai Markov. The architecture of the building is a combination of Islamic, Achaemenid and Safavid elements. The brick façade with its stairs and stone pillars emanates a beauty that belongs to the unique style of the Reza Shah Pahlavi era. In 1990, the extension was turned into the Posts and Telecommunication Museum. The museum consists of three floors. The east and west wings are symmetrically arranged around a courtyard, reminiscent of a caravanserai.

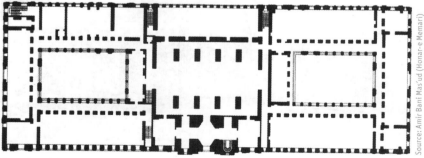

Source: Amir Bani Mas'ud (Honar-e Memari)

Floor plan of General Post Office

Façade detail of
General Post Office

Mausoleum in honor of the Persian poet Ferdowsi

Tomb of Ferdowsi
Aramgah-e Ferdowsi
آرامگاه فردوسی

210

Tus, Razavi Khorasan
36.48594, 59.51733
*Karim Taherzadeh Behzad,
Houshang Seyhoun (renovation)*
AD: 1934/AH: 1354/Yaz: 1304

An important example is the design of the Tomb of Ferdowsi, the poet and author of the tenth-century national epic, the *Shahnameh*, to celebrate Ferdowsi's millenium in 1934. The building functions as a boost to national pride based on the *Shahnameh*'s representation of ancient Iran, with its distinctive pre-Islamic design and Zoroastrian ornamentation. The Tomb of Ferdowsi was originally designed by the Iranian architect Haji Hossein Lurzadeh, who, among others, created the Masjed-e Sepahsalar, the Ramsar Hotel and part of the interior of the Marble Palace. The present building dates back to Karim Taherzadeh Behzad, who replaced the dome created

Interior of Tomb of Ferdowsi in the 1930s

by Lurzadeh, using mainly elements of Achaemenid architecture. The design of Ferdowsi's tomb looks very similar to the grave of Cyrus the Great at Pasargadae. The deliberate reference to Achaemenid architecture was politically motivated. Referring to the ancient monarchy, Reza Shah Pahlavi confirmed his power, and through the use of pre-Islamic symbols restricted the influence of the clergy. Thirty years after its construction, the monument was renovated under the direction of Hushang Seyhoun. A prolific and innovative architect with diverse interests in architecture, painting, craftwork and sculpture, Seyhoun designed many memorable public spaces and monuments, including the commemorative mausoleums of Avicenna in Hamadan, Nader Shah in Mashad, Ferdowsi in Tus, Omar Khayyam and Kamal-ol-Molk in Nishapur. Seyhoun is renowned for his integration of Persian traditional elements in his clearly modern architectural designs. His work often involves inventive new forms and styles based on combinations of diverse cultural sources. At the beginning of World War II, the government primarily produced symbols for the growing national identity; images of a glorious past, like newly-built or renovated mausoleums of national heroes, poets and scholars. A so-called "scientific" process was staged where tombs of relevant historical figures were seized, the remains exhumed and autopsied. Thereafter, they were reconstructed

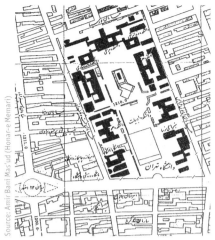

Site plan of Tehran University

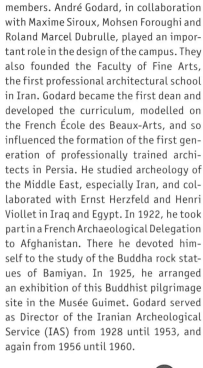

based on skull and bone measurements and presented to the Iranians as Aryans from the supposedly glorious past and as a model of a modern nation, by producing life-size sculptures, colour portraits, photographs, stamps, postcards, coins and utensils. An important event in this marketing exercise was the re-internment of historical figures in the original tomb in a modern grave during an official royal ceremony.

University of Tehran
Daneshgah-e Tehran
دانشگاه تهران

University Campus, Tehran
35.70433, 51.39500
Mohsen Foroughi, Maxime Siroux, Roland Marcel Dubrulle, André Godard et al.
AD: from 1934 / AH: from 1353 / Yaz: from 1304

The main campus of Tehran University is located in the city centre. It is a good example of modernism of the early Pahlavi time. Tehran University was opened in the winter of 1934. It was founded seven centuries ago, as a houza, or religious school, where not just religious studies but also mathematics, astronomy, medicine, literature, biology, physics and chemistry were taught. In modern times it developed into an academic institution similar to western establishments. The scientific staff consists today of 1,650 full-time faculty members and several hundred part-time adjunct and affiliate members. André Godard, in collaboration with Maxime Siroux, Mohsen Foroughi and Roland Marcel Dubrulle, played an important role in the design of the campus. They also founded the Faculty of Fine Arts, the first professional architectural school in Iran. Godard became the first dean and developed the curriculum, modelled on the French École des Beaux-Arts, and so influenced the formation of the first generation of professionally trained architects in Persia. He studied archeology of the Middle East, especially Iran, and collaborated with Ernst Herzfeld and Henri Viollet in Iraq and Egypt. In 1922, he took part in a French Archaeological Delegation to Afghanistan. There he devoted himself to the study of the Buddha rock statues of Bamiyan. In 1925, he arranged an exhibition of this Buddhist pilgrimage site in the Musée Guimet. Godard served as Director of the Iranian Archeological Service (IAS) from 1928 until 1953, and again from 1956 until 1960.

Medical Faculty
Daneshkadeh-ye Pezeshki
ساختمان دانشکده ی پزشکی

University Campus, Tehran
35.70578, 51.39422
Maxime Siroux, Mohsen Foroughi
AD: 1934 / AH: 1353 / Yaz: 1304

The main building of Tehran University is based strongly on the Palais de Chaillot built for the world exposition of 1937. The monumental design at the apex of the campus, realised by Maxime Siroux and his former assistant, Mohsen Foroughi, structures the axis to the main entrance. Their aim was to emphasise the centre of the building with a towering entrance

Entrance ayvan of the neo-classical main building of Tehran University

gate and consciously create the effect of two stone arms appearing to embrace all those who are interested in art, science and technology. Siroux was one of the most prolific foreign architects in Iran for three decades. He arrived in Iran in the early 1930s as an archaeologist and soon became involved in the reconstruction program. Siroux was chief architect of some important ministries such as education, industry and mining, agriculture, home affairs and finance. This allowed him to work in various fields including the restoration of traditional tombs and mosques as well as new buildings for hospitals, schools, universities and stadiums. As Siroux was directly involved in a number of rehabilitation projects, he interpreted local architecture in his buildings, using traditional features such as domes, wind-catchers and ayvans with great sensitivity for regional, climatic and cultural needs. Siroux collaborated with the Iranian architect Mohsen Foroughi, particularly on the university buildings and the buildings for the ministry of finance. The range of Siroux's work, in its stylistic and volumetric diversity, is breath-taking. The most important buildings realised by him are the medical faculty of Tehran University, the extensions to the Muzeh-ye Iran-e bastan and villas for ministers and officials. Being intimately familiar with the principles of Persian architecture, he was able to interpret the traditional elements in an innovative way. As a professor at Tehran University, Siroux also wrote scientific papers on pre-Islamic and Islamic buildings and an excellent study on caravanserais and small buildings along the caravan route. Markov, Godard and Siroux remained active and influential until the late 1950s. As partners in Reza Shah's modernization program, they played a key role in the creation of the education system, professionalized the profession and left their Iranian heirs a legacy of written and executed work that showed possibilities for a new architecture.

University Club
Bashgah-e Daneshgah
باشگاه دانشگاه

University Campus, Tehran
35.70200, 51.39467
Roland Marcel Dubrulle
AD: 1934/AH: 1353/Yaz: 1304

After completing his studies, Roland Marcel Dubrulle moved to Iran in 1935, where he worked until 1942. His buildings reflect the style of the late 1920s and early 1930s in France. Roland Marcel Dubrulle is a representative of functionalist architecture pre-World War II. This movement saw the highest architectural task in the creation of social benefits,

Street view of University Club

Source: Oruj Travel

Tabriz, Municipality Palace, elevation

therefore the floor plan as *plan sociale* moved into the centre of attention and had to consider needs such as air, light and sun. Unlike in pure functionalism, Roland Marcel Dubrulle's designs are visual architecture which relate to the image of his time. New media like film and photography play an important role. The integration of the graphic gave his work its strength. He contradicts the credo of *function × economy*, with an act of sensory experience that offers more than just function.

Municipality Palace
Kakh Saat
کاخ شهرداری

Saat Square, Tabriz
38.07361, 46.29555
German engineers,
Avedis Ohanjanian, Arfa'ul Mulk
AD: 1938 / AH: 1357 / Yaz: 1318

Tabriz Municipal Palace, also known as Saat Tower, is the city hall and main office of the municipal government of Tabriz. It was built between 1934 and 1938 under the supervision of German engineers, in collaboration with Armenian architect Avedis Ohanjanian and based on German Wilhelminism, an essentially neo-Baroque, extraordinarily prestige-oriented style calculated to give expression to the German state's claim to imperial

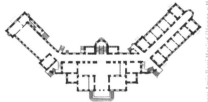

Source: Amir Bani Mas'ud (Honar-e Memari)

Tabriz, Municipality Palace, plan

power. After World War II, the building was used by the Azerbaijan Democrat Party as a Government Office. When Iranian troops regained control of Tabriz in 1947, the building was again used as the Tabriz municipal central offices, a function that continues to the present day. During the 1990s, in an attempt to instal an elevator, one of the patios of the Saat was damaged. The dome at the top of Saat tower was reconstructed on 2008 with new khaki-coloured fibreglass instead of the original silver colour. Since 2007, a part of the building has been converted to a municipal museum or city museum of Tabriz. It was opened in 2007 to coincide with the hundredth anniversary of the establishment of the municipality in Tabriz. The museum has different halls for vintage cars and antique cameras, a hall dedicated to the Iran–Iraq war, a publishing hall, a carpet hall, a contemporary art hall, a calligraphy hall, the hall of wisdom, and more.

Hafez Mausoleum

Tomb of Hafez
Aramgah-e Hafez, Hafeziya
آرامگاه حافظ

Khiyaban-e Hafez, Shiraz
29.62540, 52.55832
André Godard
AD: 1935/AH: 1354/Yaz: 1305

In 1435, the governor Shams Aldin Mohammad Yaqmai commissioned the building of a monument with a dome and water basin for the famous poet Hafez of Shiraz in the cemetery. The monument was rebuilt by Shah Abbas the Great, and repaired in the reign of Nader Shah. In 1767, Karim Khan Zand had a marble

Gravestone of Hafez

tombstone placed there, inscribed with one of his poems: "Bring wine and the lute to me when you come to my grave / then, delighted to see thee / I shall rise dancingly from the grave." In 1935, Colonel Ali Riyazi, Head of the Cultural Authority, ordered the redevelopment of the site and appointed the French architect André Godard. Preserving the covered Zand-dynasty portico, Godard divided the site in such a way that a garden with Hafez' tomb in the centre was established on the north side, bound by four yellow brick buildings. These serve as souvenir shops and workshops as well as one of the most beautiful tea houses, situated on a water basin framed on two sides by beds with citrus trees and cypresses. The tombstone of Hafez is slightly raised in an open pavilion with a diameter of about 6 m. The copper-clad dome is supported by eight marble columns and is similar to the hat of a dervish. The green patina of the roof harmonises with the design of the inside, which is lovingly clad in tiles with geometric and floral images and calligraphic inscriptions. In front of the pavilion are two elongated

Source: Behdari, Yousef / Bavani, Pardis khabaz (CAOI)

Mausoleum of the poet Hafez in Shiraz

pools, which are design elements providing visual and acoustic stimuli and cooling. The Hafeziya has been a popular resort sanctuary for Shirazi for many years. They drink tea, rest in the shade of pine trees and recite the poet's poems. Like visitors over many centuries, present-day visitors still query fate by randomly opening a copy of Hafez' collected works and interpreting it. A copy lies on the tomb for just this purpose. Goethe was sixty-five years old when he discovered the Persian poet. He read his *Divan*, only recently translated into German, and felt an intimate spiritual bond with the fourteenth-century Persian poet which crossed geographical, religious and cultural boundaries. This inspired him to write his last great collection of poems, the *West-Eastern Divan*.

Source: Eugène Flandin (Voyage en Perse)

Eugène Flandin: Gravesite of the oet Hafez

344

Villa Dr. Siassi
Villa-ye Doktor Siassi
ویلا دکتر سیاسی
Shemiran, Tehran
Site and state unknown
Gabriel Guévrékian
AD: 1935/AH: 1354/Yaz: 1305

The Villa of Ali-Akbar Siassi, a remarkable Iranian intellectual, psychologist and foreign minister, was designed by Gabriel Guévrékian in the 1930s. The building is rectangular but breaks the overall symmetry of the south façade with an extension, opening generously to the garden. Guévrékian organised the floor plan on five levels, giving an overview of the whole house upon entering, which was unimaginable in the traditional Iranian architecture in those times. The interior of the villa follows the model of a *Raumplan*, developed by Adolf Loos in 1910 which made the size and height of rooms dependent on their function and arranged them in multi-level, partially interlocking boxes, which from the outside approached a cubical shape. The two-storey ground floor is extended by a large canopy, supported by four rectangular columns, and forms a terrace upstairs. The stern rhythm of the façade is softened by the materials and the design of the ground floor terrace. The garden uses the traditional Persian vocabulary – a central water axis – complemented with European elements. The villa is a functional and simple building, which corresponds in many respects to Loos' Moller House.

Girls School of Performing Arts
Honarestan-e Dokhtaraneh
هنرستان دختارانه
Khiyaban-e Sarhang Sakhaie, Tehran
35.69028, 51.41250
Vartan Hovanesian
AD: 1935/AH: 1354/Yaz: 1305

In 1935, Vartan Hovanesian also returned to Iran, where he won the competition for the Girls School of Performing Arts. After working as a designer in a carpet factory in Tabriz and serving an apprenticeship in Tehran, he studied architecture and urban design at the Ecole d'Architecture Spéciale in Paris and worked on the reconstruction after World War l in the office of Henri Sauvage. He then established his own office in Paris. The influence of Henri Sauvage shaped his architectural style, showing an affinity for the modern movement and the Bauhaus. However, Hovanesian adapted the modern forms to cultural and climatic conditions. In the Girls School of Performing Arts, he commits himself to the international style and incorporates western functionalism like a simple façade with horizontal windows, showing that the walls are non-supporting in the façade design. The building is a three-storey building with a plinth and an accentuated centre avant-corps. The horizontal window bands and the horizontal concrete strips are highlighted by vertical structural elements which are higher than the other parts of the building. The complete structure is formed by the interpenetration of different levels, which are expressed in protruding and recessed elements. Vartan Hovanesian was also editor of the Iranian architectural periodical *Me'mari-ye Nowvin* in which the modern ideas were disseminated.

Source: Vitou, Elisabeth/Deshoulières, Dominique/Jeanneau, Hubert (Gabriel Guévrékian)

Floor plan and elevation of Villa Dr. Siassi, 1935

Bina House
Khaneh Bina
آشپزخانه مدرن

Shemiran, Tehran
Site unknown
Mohsen Foroughi
AD: 1935 / AH: 1354 / Yaz: 1305

Designed in 1935, Bina House was built by the Iranian architect Mohsen Foroughi and exhibits the founding tenets of the rationalist movement: practicality, a purification of decorative features, roofs, terraces, light and hygiene. A heliotropic house overlooking the city, the villa celebrats a new lifestyle that favoured body and nature. Bina House was built for a major politician and modernity lover. It seems as if a new generation of western-oriented elite emerged, which also aimed at a fundamental renewal of existing social and political structures. The house is a reflection of European ideas and demonstrates simple cubes and curved balconies parallel to contemporary work by French modernists. Its opening to the outside is significant: the street façade became an expression of Western presence. Although the building is oriented to the street, the eye can not catch the complex at a glance. So it is

necessary to go around it in order to get an overall idea. The plan does not focus on the interior rooms: rather the building expands and spreads out on all sides. Mental boundaries between inside and outside are cut through. The unusual building was developed in a time still dominated by traditional ideas. The topsheet tried to be free from the burden of the old and adorn itself with the new. The modernists were interested in a new architecture of international connotations, to confirm their own position on the issue of renewal. Although the examples of private residential building from this period are few, they are crucial, since they played a leading role for development in the coming decades.

Khaneh Bina, published in *Architect* Magazine, No. 6, June 1937

Street view of Girls School of Performing Arts

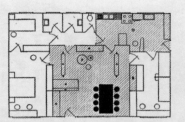

The Modern Kitchen
Ashpaz Khaneh modern
آشپزخانه مدرن

Vartan Hovanesian
AD: 1935/AH: 1354/Yaz: 1305

After World War I, the modern movement to cope with the dramatic housing shortage and the currency crisis emerged in Europe. But Iran was neither affected by World War I nor was it an industrial nation. Against this background, the new building aimed at a different clientele, namely the elite of the country. The modern movement became a lifestyle in Iran much earlier than in Europe and was promoted via advertisements and articles in contemporary magazines. The upper classes sought a design along the European model, especially for houses. Thus, the Frankfurt kitchen, developed by Margarete Schütte-Lihotzky for standardized housing developments, found its way to Iran, where it was to satisfy the needs of a very different society from the West.

Memari-ye Nowvin Nr. 4:
The Modern Kitchen

Residential Buildings at Shah Reza Street (today Enghelab Street)

Residential Buildings at Shah Reza Street
Khaneh-haye Khiyaban-e Shah Reza
خانه های خیابان شاه رضا

219 G

Khiyaban-e Enghelab, Tehran
35.70167, 51.41083
Vartan Hovanesian
AD: 1935/AH: 1354/Yaz: 1305

Of the architects who mainly built residential properties in Tehran, Vartan Hovanesian was perhaps the most prolific and influential. His apartment buildings show both aesthetic and functional characteristics which were well received in the market. The use of round shapes, curved windows, circular balconies or triangular projections refer to art nouveau, which Vartan Hovanesian came across during his collaboration with Henri Sauvage. His residential buildings show a new concept for Tehran: mixed purpose structures, three to five-storey high corner buildings with separate entrances to public and private areas. The units were adapted to the prevailing social conditions, with roof gardens and roof yards replacing the traditional courtyard. His designs and his creative use of concrete had an enormous influence on the development and acceptance

Vartan Hovanesian, Shah Reza residential buildings (today Khiyaban Enghelab Islami)

Veresk Bridge on the railway line between Tehran and Sari

of modern architecture in Iran. From the flying floors of his Darband Palace, which attracted international attention, to his distinctive use of clear horizontal and vertical lines, he created an unmistakable architectural vocabulary.

Veresk Bridge
Pol-e Veresk
پل ورسک

Veresk, Mazandaran, Iran
35.90339, 52.99028
Walter Inger, Ladislaus von Rabcewicz (Engineer)
AD: 1936 / AH: 1355 / Yaz: 1306

As part of the trans-Iranian railway construction, the construction of a large number of special structures such as tunnels and bridges was required to enable travel through the wild and jagged parts of the country. The most impressive building along the route is still the Veresk Bridge. It is an engineering masterpiece of the company Kampsax. The bridge was started in 1934 by Germans, under the direction of Austrian engineer Walter Stockinger and the German Ladislaus von Rabcevisc, and opened in 1936. The structural engineer

and designer was the Swiss national Hans Otto Nater. Reza Shah himself attended the opening ceremony, which took place near his hometown. The bridge is 110 m above ground and has a wingspan of 66 m; when it was completed it was the highest bridge in the world. It was built of stone, sand and cement with very simple tools such as hand drills and dynamite. Below the bridge stands a monument commemorating the workers who lost their lives during construction as well as the chief engineer, Walter Stockinger, who wanted to be buried here. The bridge is located between a number of loop tunnels so that it appears several times. Winston Churchill called it Victory Bridge during World War II, because Reza Shah refused to blow up the tunnels and bridges ordered by the German army to ensure vital war supplies for the Soviets. The political significance extends far beyond the military one. With the establishment of this supply route, the United States became the determining political factor in Iran. They took over the role of the British, who up to this time had decisively influenced Iranian politics. In 1977, the Veresk Bridge was added to the list of national monuments.

Axonometric projection of Villa Heim by Gabriel Guévrékian in Paris,1927

Source: Vitou, Elisabeth/Deshoulières, Dominique/Jeanneau, Hubert (Gabriel Guévrékian)

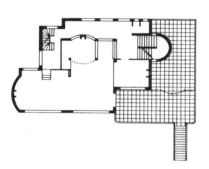

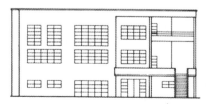

Floor plan and elevation of Villa Shahab Khosrovani, 1936

Source: Vitou, Elisabeth/Deshoulières, Dominique/Jeanneau, Hubert (Gabriel Guévrékian)

Villa Shahab Khosrovani
Villa-ye Shahab Khosrovani
ویلا شهاب خسروانی

Shemiran, Tehran
Site and state unknown
Gabriel Guévrékian
AD: 1936/AH: 1355/Yaz: 1306

The Villa Shahab Khosrovany, built by Gabriel Guévrékian in 1936 in Tehran, generally follows the five points for a new architecture, which Le Corbusier had formulated in the 1930s to support the basic principles of mouvement moderne. He used pilotis, freestanding pillars, which make the building to appear as a floating box. The flat roof became an accessible toit jardin which was cultivated and replaced the ground lost by building. Reinforced concrete was used so the house no longer needed load bearing walls. Posts carry the ceiling, and drywall partitions divide the floor plan as plan libre. The façade libre, independent from the supporting system, is designed according to the view from inside. And because the façade no longer has a support function, it can accommodate fenêtre en longeure, or elongated windows, which allow the brightness and transparency so important for mouvement moderne. This was hard to imagine in Iran at that time. Guévrékian built a house that opened completely to the outside in Tehran, where the houses traditionally are oriented inward, and tried to realise liberated living even in an open floor plan by separating the rooms from each other not by walls but by differences in elevation. The similarity to the Villa Heim built by Gabriel Guévrékian a few years previously in Paris, or the Villa Stein in Garches by Le Corbusier in 1926, is obvious and shows how prevalent the evolving modernity in Iran was compared to Europe.

Faculty building of Law and Political Science of Tehran University

Faculty of Law and Political Science
Daneshkadeh-ye Hoghoogh va Olum-e Siasi
دانشکده حقوق و علوم سیاسی

222 G

University Campus, Tehran
35.70289, 51.39419
Mohsen Foroughi
AD: 1937 / AH: 1356 / Yaz: 1307

In addition to the Faculty of Medicine, the university's main building, the Faculty of Law and Political Science, and the Faculty of Literature and Humanities mirrored opposite is another central point of the university. The design by Mohsen Forugie, a student of André Godard and Maxim Siroux, convinces through its pure forms, the harmonious integration into the gently sloping terrain and the - for its time – revolutionary choice of building materials – concrete without plaster and paint. The building was officially opened in 1937, just before the outbreak of World War II. The structure is a reflection of European ideas, and with its simple cubes shows parallels to the current works by French modernists. Mohsen Foroughi, son of a famous statesman and writer, graduated from the École des Beaux-Arts in Paris. He returned to Persia in 1937 and taught at the various faculties of Tehran University. Together with André Godard and Maxime Siroux, he was instrumental in the design of Tehran University's master plan and the related buildings, including the Faculties of Law and Political Science. Although he took a radically modern approach to building design, Foroughi had an excellent knowledge of traditional architectural principles, such as the use of ayvans or faïence panels. His influence as an architect was considerable, but his greatest contribution can be seen in the development of architectural training. He was involved in the founding of the first school of architecture, was a founding member of the Persian Architect Society and published the first Persian architecture magazine. Mohsen Foroughi was also active in politics. In 1956 he was a member of the city parliament of Tehran, from 1966 to 1978 a member of the Senate and for about three months, just before the fall of the Shah, he was Minister of Education and Culture. After the revolution in 1979, he was imprisoned; his magnificent art collection was confiscated and transferred to the Archaeological Museum of Tehran. He was released from prison in 1982 and died ten months later.

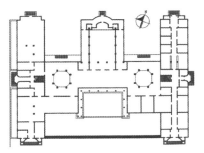

Floor plan of the Faculty of Law and Political Science, Tehran

Symmetrical structure of Tehran Railway Station

Source: Goruma, Berlin

Railway Station Tehran
Istgah-e Rah Ahan-e Tehran
ایستگاه راه اهن تهران

Maidan-e Rah Ahan, Tehran
35.65806, 51.39778
Karim Taherzadeh Behzad
(design), Philipp Holzmann
AD: 1937/AH: 1356/Yaz: 1307

The Trans-Iranian Railway was built between 1927 and 1938 by order of Reza Shah Pahlavi. The railway connects the capital, Tehran, to the Persian Gulf in the south and the Caspian Sea in the north. The Trans-Iranian Railway was opened in 1939 and during World War II was important as a means of transport of the allied forces. The two-storey, doubly symmetrical station building in the style of a reduced neoclassicism was designed by Karim Taherzadeh Behzad (brother of the famous Iranian miniaturist Hussein

Behzad) and the Ukrainian engineer Veladislav Veladislavic Garaditski, and built by the German company Philipp Holzmann AG. The main entrance is in the centre of the northern façade, and other entrances lead to the side wings. The façade is articulated with colossal, unchamfered half-columns taking up the entire building height. The architecture of the railway station is strongly influenced by historic approaches to contemporary fascist German and Italian architecture. No specific Nazi style is used, but Behzad simplified its neoclassical design language to the extreme, reducing details and enlarging them to monumental proportions. He plays with an eclectic selection of traditional elements and motifs, which he applied more simply and less decoratively than in the Shah Reza Hospital, completed almost ten years earlier.

Source: Philipp Holzmann AG

Staircase and interior of the Railway Station Tehran

Source: Claudia Luperto

Richly decorated entrance to Malek National Library and Museum

Malek National Library and Museum
Ketabkhaneh va Muzeh-ye Melli-ye Malek
کتابخانه و موزه ملي ملك

224 **G**

Melal-e Mottahed, Bagh-e Melli, Khiyaban-e Imam Khomeini, Tehran
35.68694, 51.41636
Nikolai Markov
AD: 1937 / AH: 1356 / Yaz: 1307

The first National Library in Iran was the library of the Dar ol-Fonun, founded in 1851. In 1899, the Library of the Nation was opened. The official opening of the National Library on Melal-e Mottahed Street was in 1937. It combined several collections of older libraries, including rare and valuable manuscripts. The manor house of Haji Hossein Aqa Malek, closely interconnected with the structures of the bazaar, forms an important part of the ensemble. The house is a quiet oasis in the bustle of the bazaar, as if it had retained the serenity of its owner through all the years. Haji Hossein Aqa Malek inherited the mansion, which was built in the Qajar style, and had it converted into a library and a museum by Nikolai Markov in 1937. The house bears the stamp of both periods, the Qajar and Pahlavi, in the brick masonry, plaster, wood and iron work. It was included in the list of the historic sites in 1997.

View to the domed Marble Palace

Main elevation of Marble Palace

Marble Palace
Kakh-e Marmar
کاخ مرمر

Khiyaban-e Valiasr,
Khiyaban-e Imam Khomeini,
Felestin, Tehran
35.68906, 51.40203
Joseph Leon, Fathallah Firdaws
AD: 1938 / AH: 1357 / Yaz: 1308

225 G

The Marble Palace is located in a garden at the intersection of Vali Asr Street and the Imam Khomeini Avenue. It was built between 1935 and 1938 at the behest of Reza Shah Pahlavi by the French engineer Joseph Leon and the Iranian architect Fathallah Firdaws. The architecture of the palace is a blend of East and West. At the palace entrance stand two statues modelled on Achaemenid soldiers, created by the Iranian artist Jafar Khan. They reflect this eclectic architecture. The Marble Palace is crowned by a large dome, which is a replica of the Sheikh Lotfollah dome in Isfahan. Until the 1960s, the palace was the main city residence of the Pahlavi and is therefore strongly identified with the person Reza Shah Muhammad, since all three of his marriages as well as his forty-eighth birthday party were celebrated here. He also recuperated in this palace after the assassination attempt of 10 April 1965. Thereafter, the palace was no longer occupied. From 1977 to 1981, it was used as a museum. Today, it serves as a meeting place of the Supreme Court and the State Council.

Detail of the interior dome in Marble Palace

Street façade of Kampsax company branch

Kampsax Company
Sherkat-e Kampsax
شرکت کامپساکس

Maidan-e Ferdowsi, Tehran
35.70197, 51.41722
Alexander Belyn
AD: 1938/AH: 1357/Yaz: 1308

In 1933, the planning of the trans-Iranian railway was awarded to a Danish-Swedish consortium headed by the Kampsax company, who contracted the Russian architect Alexander Belyn in 1938 to build a branch office in Tehran. The expressionist architecture, in contrast to the new objectivity, used round and jagged shapes emphasizing the special plasticity of construction and the quality of craftsmanship. The liveliness of the façades is achieved by the selective setting of brick patterns. This expression was meant to convey the dynamic of the time, but also the violence and tensions inherent to the interwar period.

Rear façade of the company building

Main elevation of Hotel Ramsar with grandiose entrance stairs

Hotel Ramsar
Hotel-e Ramsar
هتل رامسر

Khiyaban-e Hotel, Ramsar
36.90306, 50.65833
Haj Hossein Lurzadeh et al.
AD: 1938/AH: 1357/Yaz: 1308

Ramsar is the only place on the Caspian Sea where the impression of a riviera could be created. Therefore, it was a preferred destination in the Pahlavi time. An approximately 2 km long palm-lined avenue between mountain and sea forms a boulevard flanked by the two most important structures, the Ramsar Hotel and the casino attached to it. Gheribian, an Iranian architect educated in Germany, is named as the author of the palatial hotel. Other sources attribute the building to Haji Hossein Lurzadeh, who created Masjed-e Sepahsalar, the Ferdosi Mausoleum and part of the interior design of the Marmar Palace. The design combines elegance of shape, precious materials, intensity of colour and sensuality, leaning heavily on European art deco of the period between the wars. Building commenced in 1938 and the hotel opened in 1943. It is one of the few hotels in Iran included in the list of registered National Monuments. In 1971, the Ramsar Convention for the protection of wetlands was held here, resulting in one of the oldest international agreements for nature conservation. The current government plans to convert it into a museum.

Source: Institute for Iranian Contemporary Historical Studies (IICHS)

Hotel Park ca. 1973

Source: Behdari, Yousef/Bavani, Pardis Khabaz (CAOI)

Panahi House, garden side

Panahi House
Khaneh-ye Panahi
خانه پناهی

Khiyaban-e Taleghani, Tehran
35.70708, 51.42431
Roland Marcel Dubrulle
AD: 1939/AH: 1358/Yaz: 1309

The architectural arrangement of Panahi house is exceptional: A carefully designed "holistic artwork" is created within its walls. An open, northwest-oriented pavilion, about 1 m above the garden level, opens to the courtyard on a typical, 6'-high talar, which was landscaped and contained an elongated pool. This hall, open on two sides and spanned by a high ceiling, offers a cool lounge which is both an external and an internal space and appears large and airy. It offers a beautiful view over the water to the asymmetrical main axis of the garden. The front of the pavilion is dominated by an overlong column reflected in the water basin. The courtyard design shows other known characteristics where water basin, pathways, roses and evergreen shrubs play the leading role. The Panahi House, which consists of semi-open elements, continues the flow of the outer space, even if it is directed to a walled garden. By dominating transparency and spatial and visual connection to the outdoors, Roland Marcel Dubrulle succeeds in re-interpreting the Iranian palace architecture.

Amjadiyeh Stadium/
Shirudi Sports Complex
Majmueh warzash-e Amjadiyeh
مجموعه ورزشی امجدیه

Mofatteh St, Tehran
35.71028, 51.42750
Roland Marcel Dubrulle
AD: 1939/AH: 1358/Yaz: 1309

The Amjadiyeh Stadium, today known as Shahid Shiroudi Stadium, is one of the oldest sports stadiums in Iran and, prior to the construction of the Azadi Stadium, was the largest football stadium in Iran. It was built in 1939 and when it was opened it was located in north Tehran, whilst it is now in the centre of the town. The stadium hosted many sporting and cultural events, as well as political meetings. Ever since the Iranian national football team was formed, they played their home matches in Amjadieh Stadium before Azadi stadium was built. It has also hosted the Asian Cup finals in 1968 and the Asian Club Championship in 1970. During the coronation of Mohammad Reza Shah and the Shahbanou of Iran in 1967, many events took place here, including the coronation parade. It has four swimming pools (one of which is Olympic size), a soccer field, rock climbing wall, gym, volleyball, basketball, table tennis, shooting and fencing facilities and was to be the departure site for Operation Eagle, the aborted mission to rescue the American hostages held in Tehran during the Iran Hostage Crisis. The open air bath built in 1939 by Roland Marcel Dubrulle is an early example of modern recreational architecture, where the possibilities of construction were maxed out with reinforced concrete. Enhanced reference to landscapes and a sensitive handling of materials are evident in the pool and diving platform. This trend to staged lightness and playfulness was criticised as being "oversophisticated". The highly acclaimed architecture is still visible, but there is an air of negligence. The changing rooms are closed, the diving platform in front of it is a sad crumbling memorial. The outdoor pools are empty – bathing amusement is not a priority in today's Islamic Republic. The stadium was renamed after Shahid Ali Akbar Shiroudi, a helicopter pilot killed in the Iran–Iraq war.

Amjadiyeh Stadium in the 1960s

Source: Iranian Historical Photograph Gallery

Source: Wikimedia Commons

Street façade of National Museum

National Museum of Iran
Muzeh-ye Iran-e Bastan
موزه ملي ايران

230 G

Khiyaban-e 30 Tir, Khiyaban-e
Imam Khomeini, Tehran
35.68689, 51.41461
*André Godard in collaboration with
Maxime Siroux*
AD: 1939/AH: 1358/Yaz: 1309

The competition announced in 1936 for
the National Archaeological Museum
of Iran with adjacent National Library
brought about one of the most convincing examples of a recourse to the past.
André Godard, in collaboration with
Maxime Siroux, won the competition.
They designed the first archaeological
museum in the country, and André Godard
was appointed as the first director of
the museum by Reza Shah. The building
has two floors with an attic, a dominant
central zone and a monumental entrance
arch which extends over the entire height

Source: Claudia Luperto

Detail of entrance ayvan

of the façade. The Muzeh-e Iran-e Bastan
is characterised by an intimate knowledge of Iranian architecture. The architects conceived it as a modern building
with a traditional façade, referring to
the pre-Islamic architecture of Sassanid
time favoured by the Pahlavi government. The large semi-circular arch at
the entrance replicates the famous arch
Taq-e Kisra, in Ctesiphon, and the elaborate stonework of the building sub-
tly refers to the Persian tradition of
brick construction. One of the pillars
to the right in the entrance hall bears

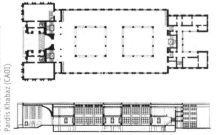

Source: Behdari, Yousef/Bavani,
Pardis Khabaz (CAOI)

Floor plan and section

Source: Caroline Reichmann

Access to the Archaeological Institute

Source: Caroline Reichmann

Entrance detail

a hand-drawn, original plan of the ground floor. The National Museum and National Library showcase what should be preserved as historic cultural heritage. They are the memory framing the burgeoning nation, grounding it and making it legible. André Godard established the gardens of the museum and the National Library together with his compatriot, Maxime Siroux. Asked whether Reza Shah had opened the building personally, the life partner and wife of the architect, Yedda Godard said, "Oh, no, he walked around the building, checked what it could possibly represent, but never entered it". And she added that "he had this strange way ... he was always in fear of ridicule". This style dominated the public buildings in Tehran until the mid 1940s – not least through the personal support of Reza Shah. The museum was expanded by a modernistic white-travertine national art museum in 1972. The second structure, built on the grounds of the old archaeological museum, went through quite a few, hasty changes of the interior, and was still being remodelled when the 1979 revolution swept the country.

Architecte
Arshetekt
ارشتکت

Mohsen Foroughi (Publisher)
AD: 1948/AH: 1367/Yaz: 1326

As an architect, Moshen Foroughi's influence was considerable, and yet his greatest contribution may have been in the development of architecture as a profession. He was instrumental in the creation of the first school of architecture, the Society of Persian Professional Architects, and the founding of *Architecte*, Persia's first professional journal dedicated to architecture. The journal was owned by the architect Iraj Moshiri. Six volumes of *Architecte* magazine were published from 1946 to 1948.

Verso of *Architecte* No. 6, 1948

University of Fine Arts
Daneshkadeh-ye Honarha-ye Ziba
دانشکده هنرهای زیبا

University Campus, Tehran
35.70194, 51.39722
André Godard
AD: 1939/AH: 1358/Yaz: 1309

The university designed by André Godard represents without doubt the milestone of modernity in Iran. It merges the two souls of Godard which is bonded to rationalism and geometry on the one hand, and to expressionism on the other. Rationalism is reflected in the structure of the construction, the formal severity of the design, the clear internal division and the constructive use of materials. The expressionism is revealed in the entrance portico, the elongated windows and in the fact that each part has its special character. The College of Fine Arts is one of the largest colleges of Tehran University. It is considered the father of several academic fields of art in Iran and the Middle East. The college opened in November 1939 under the name honarkadeh, or art school. The first director was André Godard. He established the curriculum and recruited teachers, including Mohsen Foroughi, Hasan Khan Siddiqui and other graduates of the École des Beaux-Arts, as well as the French architects Roland Marcel Dubrulle and Maxime Siroux, Nikolai Markov and the Swiss architect Alexandre Moser. Honarkadeh was modelled on the École des Beaux-Arts

Bank-e Melli

University of Fine Arts as a milestone of early modern architecture in Iran

in Paris. The main focus was on the fields of architecture, painting and sculpture. Teaching and practical work was taught in studios run by a master. The three architecture studios were run by Roland Dubrulle, Maxime Siroux and Mohsen Foroughi, whose focus on traditional Persian forms "distinguished them from the generations that followed".

Bank Melli, Tabriz Branch
Bank-e Melli
بانک ملی

Shohada Sq.,Tabriz
38.07845, 46.29649
Mohsen Foroughi
AD: 1940/AH: 1359/Yaz: 1309

232

At the end of the first Pahlavi era, with the presence of German advisors in various fields and transfer of ancient-oriented approaches to Iran along with dominance-seeking European fascist dictators, some developments took place in architecture as well. The active and extensive presence of foreign, mostly German companies, who were generally engaged in the construction of state buildings (such as police headquarters in various Iranian cities) led to formation of a type of architectural nationalism in building elevations on the basis of western modern architectural models, whilst retaining some limited ornamentation relating to pre-Islamic periods. So Mohsen Foroughi used ancient Iranian architectural symbols and traditional materials like tile, which he used because of its beauty, insulation and easy cleaning potential. Among the other characteristics of this nationalist movement in architecture the use of traditional materials on a foundation of modern architectural features is notable.

Contradiction between nationalist and modern architectural features

1941–1963
Global City Tehran

The allied forces demanded the right of passage through Persia in order to transport food and ammunition to the Soviet Union. They also demanded the expulsion of Germans from Persia, some of whom were engaged in anti-allied activities. Reza Shah, proud of his position and insisting on the neutrality of the country, refused. The British and Soviet armies attacked from the south and the north, respectively; the Persian army could not muster any effective resistance, and Reza Shah had to abdicate his throne, leaving it to his eldest son, the 22-year-old Mohammad Reza, who was sworn in on 16 September 1941 as the second Pahlavi Shah after reaching an agreement with the invading powers. On the first day of his reign, British and Soviet troops marched in Tehran and took over control of the Iranian government. Iran was divided into three zones by the Soviets and the British. The northern zone fell under the administration of the Soviets; the southern zone containing the oil fields was governed by the British. A narrow strip in the middle of the country remained under Iranian administration. The next step was to establish a supply route via the Persian Corridor, across the Caspian Sea and further on to the Soviet Union through which weapons from the Persian Gulf could be supplied to the Red Army on the Eastern Front. The end of World War II did not bring the expected peace for Iran. As agreed, British and US troops began to withdraw their troops, but the Soviet Union refused, triggering the first international crisis after the war, the Iran crisis, which marked the beginning of the Cold War. The economy of Iran was completely destroyed after World War II. Only with US economic aid could the economy be kickstarted again. In 1978, shortly before he was overthrown, the Shah published a book entitled *Towards the Great Civilisation*. In it, he describes his dream of Iran's development; Iran was one of the few countries which succeeded in freeing itself from the state of underdevelopment. Iran had the money, the natural resources, the leadership and the workers to become a modern industrial state. In order to achieve this, Iranians had to adapt to the social norms of a modern industrial society, i.e. order

Source: Th. Meyer-Wieser

Development of Tehran ca. 1963

and discipline, rules and regulations, attentiveness and devotion, and they had to accept new standards and procedures. According to this long-term plan, Iran would achieve the economic status of Europe of 1978 in 1990, and by 2000 it would be economically and socially on par with the European countries.

Development of Tehran ca. 1963

Under Mohammed Reza Shah, Tehran turned into a global city with explosive growth in area as well as height, not least thanks to the revenue from oil which was nationalised in 1951, and at the expense of infrastructure for agriculture and industry. Huge urban projects were developed with the help of foreign planners, for example, a new city centre in the north, and the settlement "Shahrak Ekbatan, one of the largest residential developments in the Middle East, to the west of the city. Here, the international style of American–European modernity was applied, which suggests that the new architecture was international without any consideration being given to local conditions like climate, geography and culture. In 1968, the first master plan for Tehran, covering 25 years, was adopted by Parliament. The primary objective of this plan was to control the growth and structure of urban redevelopment.

Source: Amir Bani Mas'ud (Honar-e Memari)

Advertisement ca. 1945/1315:
New and Old (Please Note the Way of Reading)

Neoclassical façade of Tehran Courthouse

Courthouse of Tehran
Kakh-e Dadgostari
کاخ دادگستری
Khiyaban-e Khayam, Tehran
35.68150, 51.41872
Gabriel Guévrékian
AD: 1946/AH: 1365/Yaz: 1316

233 **G**

The courthouse of Tehran was designed between 1938 and 1946 by Gabriel Guévrékian in the neoclassical style and follows the trend of the late period of the first Pahlavi government. During World War II, the work was stopped for several years so that the building, constructed by the Czech company Skoda, was opened only in 1946. The presence of foreign companies, especially German,

led to a new kind of architectural nationalism aligned to western, fascist models. Of all the public buildings in Tehran realised by Gabriel Guévrékian, the courthouse matches these ideas best. The aerial view shows a symmetrical design which assimilates the traditional typology of European justice palaces. The building has three floors and two ground floors designed as a duplex. The large, rectangular hall – *la salle des pas perdus* – is flanked by two square courtyards. A second hall, arranged at right angles, is also surrounded by courtyards. These walled gardens surrounding the palace and onto which the entrance rooms open on both sides, are novel and beautiful. They lend the courthouse a less-severe atmosphere.

Marble relief in the Courthouse of Tehran by Abdolhassan Sadighi, 1944

Anushiruwan-e Dadgar (Justice Statue) by Gholamreza Rahimzadeh Arjang, 1944

Lalezahr Street façade

The walls on the ground floor are covered with black marble, giving the famous, life-size, white marble statue of the angel of justice by Abdolhassan Sadighi an incredible force. The architecture is influenced by both modern European neoclassical style and architectural characteristics of ancient Iran. It is divided into three parts, with the centre strongly emphasised. Achaemenid-like reliefs on the building façade recall archaeological discoveries in Persepolis and Susa and refer to the history of this land. The use of symmetry and increased volumes, windows on a larger scale than usual and more columns than needed lead to a rhythmic power and greatness embodying the government's ideological ideals and values. At first glance, the majesty and height of the building, with tall windows and numerous columns and bas-reliefs, is entirely consistent. In the main view there are four huge columns and four narrow columns on both sides as well as the lion and sun emblem (now replaced by the Islamic Republic's emblem). On both sides of the entrance there are two carvings by Abdolhassan Sadighi showing the judges in sitting and standing positions, with pens and books in their hands, wearing long Greek robes and scarves. At the top of the entrance sits a Faravahar icon, the symbol of good speech, good thoughts and good deeds. Gabriel Guévrékian's architecture helped to gain recognition for the ancient architectural features of Achaemenid architecture.

Laleh Hotel
Hotel Laleh
هتل لاله

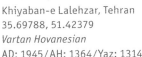

Khiyaban-e Lalehzar, Tehran
35.69788, 51.42379
Vartan Hovanesian
AD: 1945 / AH: 1364 / Yaz: 1314

Vartan Hovanessian set of for Paris in his youth. His architectural formation made him acquainted with artistic advancement in Europe and the architectural trends fashionable at the time in Paris such as classic, modern, art nouveau and art deco. This insight led to a profound knowledge of the principles and details of European architecture of the time. Through an intelligent selection of elements and motives, mainly non-vernacular, Hovanesian displayed his ability to represent this style. So Laleh Hotel is influenced by a group of buildings in Paris known as neo-Hausmannian buildings. The free selection of motives and elements of the past and present and the use of these elements in a combination of different styles, noticeable in the Laleh Hotel building and his personal property in Lalezahr-e No Street, was later called art deco. In the design for Laleh Hotel, Vartan Hovanessian demonstrates his great passion for this style by applying sublime decorations and details of art deco, called Vartan style in Iran, after the architect who so strongly influenced an entire generation of architects in the 1940s and 1950s.

View from Ekbatan Street

Jeep Headquarters
Sakhteman-e Jeep
ساختمان جیپ

Ekbatan Street, Tehran
35.68798, 51.42517
Vartan Hovanesian
AD: 1946/AH: 1365/Yaz: 1316

Vartan Hovanessian's most-published building is the Jeep Headquarters at Ekbatan Street. Due to the shape of the parcel, the building volume forms a parallelogram and plays with a combination of half-cylindrical volumes, cubes and prism with sharp angles. The combination of plane and curved surfaces, modular openings and various divisions forming the basic structure of the body creates different, very animated views. Unlike the neighbouring buildings, the roof is divided into many surfaces giving the impression of large tiles. The frame from first to third floor in the middle of the southern façade, with six decorative columns, emphasises the vertical proportions and creates balance. The building demonstrates Vartan's skill in including elements, decorations and features of art deco. This building can be considered the peak of Vartan Hovanesian's professional life and featured what was later known as "Vartan Style", especially found in Tehran's Twelfth District.

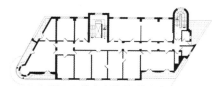

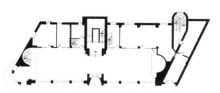

Floor plans and views

Façade of Melli Bank bazaar branch

Melli Bank Bazaar Branch
Bank-e Melli Shobeh Bazar
بانک ملی ایران -شعبه بازار

236

Khiyaban-e Khordad, Tehran
35.67792, 51.42022
Mohsen Foroughi
AD: 1947/AH: 1366/Yaz: 1377

Apart from a number of individual buildings, the main construction activity of the post-war years was carried out by the private sector. Because of the weak economy and the reconstruction, only modest architecture and urban planning projects could be embarked upon. Nevertheless Mohsen Foroughi designed many public buildings and offices for the national bank. Perhaps the best embodiment of Foroughis' style is the bazaar branch of Melli Bank in Tehran. It represents his modern rational approach to public buildings, in contrast to the pre-Islamic imagery of Bank Melli's main building by Hans Heinrich, built about eight years earlier. Although the building in its execution – reinforced concrete, cement mortar – is fundamentally modern, the interior design or the emphasis of the main entrance with a faïence-clad ayvan refers to the principles of traditional Persian architecture. At a time where the citation of pre-Islamic elements was omnipresent, Mohsen

Foroughi used an abstract incorporation of Iranian elements. In the bazaar branch of Bank Melli, the terrace and the entrance area show historic elements such as colonnades or massive square pillars, abstracted from the Achaemenid architecture. The modern office building was built in place of the Tekiei Dowlat, on the south side of Golestan complex.

Interior of Mohsen Foroughi's bank building

Graffiti at Shahid Nematollahi Subway Station

Source: Jamie Han Atta (Kenare/AFP)

Graffiti at the former US Embassy

US Embassy
(Former US Embassy)
Sefarat-e Amrika-ye Sabeq
سفارت سابق آمریکا

Khiyaban-e Taleqani, Tehran
35.70708, 51.42431
Ides van der Gracht
AD: 1948 / AH: 1367 / Yaz: 1318

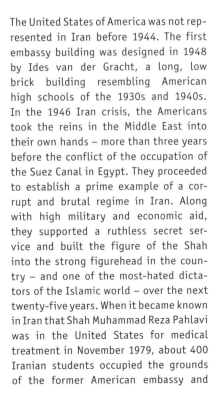

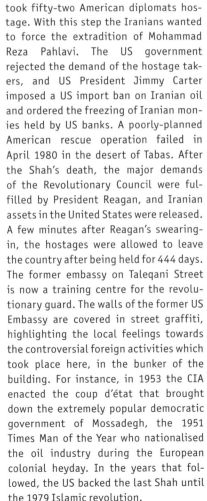

The United States of America was not represented in Iran before 1944. The first embassy building was designed in 1948 by Ides van der Gracht, a long, low brick building resembling American high schools of the 1930s and 1940s. In the 1946 Iran crisis, the Americans took the reins in the Middle East into their own hands – more than three years before the conflict of the occupation of the Suez Canal in Egypt. They proceeded to establish a prime example of a corrupt and brutal regime in Iran. Along with high military and economic aid, they supported a ruthless secret service and built the figure of the Shah into the strong figurehead in the country – and one of the most-hated dictators of the Islamic world – over the next twenty-five years. When it became known in Iran that Shah Muhammad Reza Pahlavi was in the United States for medical treatment in November 1979, about 400 Iranian students occupied the grounds of the former American embassy and

took fifty-two American diplomats hostage. With this step the Iranians wanted to force the extradition of Mohammad Reza Pahlavi. The US government rejected the demand of the hostage takers, and US President Jimmy Carter imposed a US import ban on Iranian oil and ordered the freezing of Iranian monies held by US banks. A poorly-planned American rescue operation failed in April 1980 in the desert of Tabas. After the Shah's death, the major demands of the Revolutionary Council were fulfilled by President Reagan, and Iranian assets in the United States were released. A few minutes after Reagan's swearing-in, the hostages were allowed to leave the country after being held for 444 days. The former embassy on Taleqani Street is now a training centre for the revolutionary guard. The walls of the former US Embassy are covered in street graffiti, highlighting the local feelings towards the controversial foreign activities which took place here, in the bunker of the building. For instance, in 1953 the CIA enacted the coup d'état that brought down the extremely popular democratic government of Mossadegh, the 1951 Times Man of the Year who nationalised the oil industry during the European colonial heyday. In the years that followed, the US backed the last Shah until the 1979 Islamic revolution.

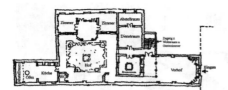

Saremi House as an example of a typical house in Tehran

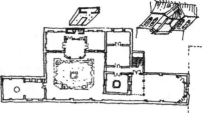

Saremi House, first changes ca. 1950

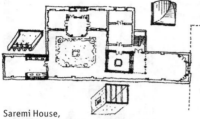

Saremi House, further changes at the end of the 1950s

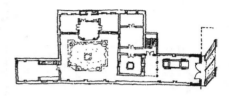

Saremi House, changes at the beginning of the 1960s

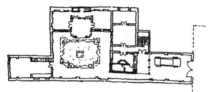

Saremi House, further changes at the end of the 1960s

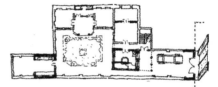

Saremi House, changes at the beginning of the 1970s

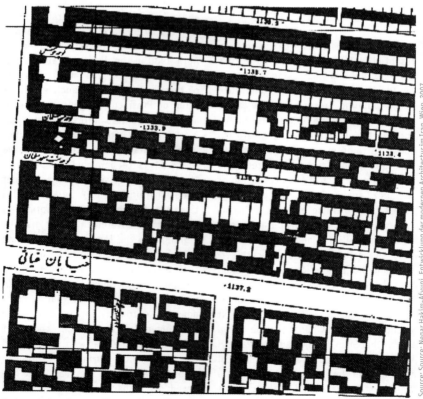

Cadastral plan of terraced houses in working-class district in southeastern Tehran

Source: Source: Negar Hakim-Afyuni, Entwicklung der modernen Architectur im Iran, Wien, 2007

Row houses
Khaneh-ye Shahri
خانه شهری

Shahrak-e-Vali-e-Asr, Tehran
35.64922, 51.34095
anonymous
AD: 1940–1970/AH: 1360–1390/
Yaz: 1310–1340

In an article in the architecture magazine *Memar* in 2006, A. Saremi describes
the transformation of his parents' house,
how modernity changed lifestyle and
housing: "when I came to the university
in the 1940s, we lived in a traditional
inward directed house. During the 1940s,
the first changes began. At this time,
most of the houses didn't had running
water and the homeowner had to install
a water tank on the roof. Now the new
toilet facilities could be integrated into
the house. In the early 1950s the fuel oil
furnaces replaced the coal or wood stoves
in the living rooms and kitchens increasingly. Some years later, the indoor water
tank serving both as laundry and cold
storage room was replaced by an electric fridge. But in the early 1960s,
the floor plan experienced the biggest
change by the newly purchased automo-
bile. The small, old wooden entrance door
was replaced by a large iron door. End of
the 1960s, the room with the water basin
was converted into a bath. And finally,
the new household appliances made
the servant's room superfluous."

Row houses
Khaneh-ye Shahri
خانه شهری

Nord-Tehran, Gish, Tehran
35.70778, 51.38472
Erich Kalantry
AD: ca. 1950/AH: ca. 1370/Yaz: ca. 1320

Row houses, rapidly developed after World
War ll, replaced the traditional, inward
directed courtyard house. In the big cities, the all-round enclosure of the courtyard was abandoned and replaced by
a roadside development with central
courtyard, often of similar or identical
design, situated side by side and joined
by common walls. These terrace houses
were built in two sizes, a simple version
for people with low incomes and a more
sophisticated type for the newly-created
middle class. Thus, the original Middle
Eastern type of living could be maintained as a central courtyard was used as
protected private space. Based on British
terraced home designs, the Iranian variations are similar to their British counterparts and were adapted to suit the climate. Earlier versions were more open,
designed for better circulation of air, and
featured inner courtyards, with a front or
rear garden, or both. A typical Iranian terraced house is usually one or two storeys
high. The manner in which the buildings
were designed varies depending on their
location in an urban area. Such designs
became less common after the 1960s.

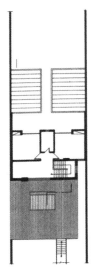
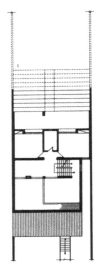

Erich Kalantry, floor plan

Source: Amir Bani Mas'ud (Honar-e Memari)

Entrance courtyard of the Ministry of Finance

Source: Amir Bani Mas'ud (Honar-e Memari)

Model photo of Ministry of Finance

Ministry of Finance
Vezarat-e Omur-e Eqtesadi va Varati

وزارت امور اقتصادی و دارایی

Pamenar, Tehran

35.68170, 51.42082

Roland Marcel Dubrulle, Mohsen Foroughi

AD: 1950/AH: 1370/Yaz: 1325

240 G

The Ministry of Finance was built between 1948 and 1950 by Roland Marcel Dubrulle in collaboration with Mohsen Foroughi on the north side of Golestan Palace. The relatively intact, private living quarters and gardens of the palace were demolished to make room for it. The building's original design in the modernist "new objectivity" style consisted of a five-storey representative entrance building and four comb-shaped office wings. They were equipped with movable partitions; fixed points like stairwells, elevators and utility rooms were placed at the inside corners and at the end of the offices. The four head façades at Naser Khosrow Street create a distinguishing impression of a modern public administration. On its completion, the complex was the largest office building in Iran. Here again, the IG Farben Building in Frankfurt by Hans Pölzig served as a model for this gigantic office block. The building's square wings retain a modern, sparse elegance despite its mammoth size. The Ministry of Finance is considered as an excellent example of functionalism in Iran.

Source: René Hochueti

End buildings of the Ministry of Finance

Seat at the roadside

Pahlavi Street, Valiasr Street
Khiyaban-e Pahlavi, Valiasr
خیابان ولیعصر

Khiyaban-e Valiasr, Tehran
35.73286, 51.41089
Mohammad Reza Shah
(Commissioner)
AD: ca. 1950/AH: ca. 1370/Yaz: ca. 1320

The Khiyaban-e Pahlavi, today Vali Asr Street, covers 19 km, leading from Tehran Station in the south to Maidan Tajrish in the north of the city. The tree-lined street divides the metropolis into western and eastern parts. It is considered one of Tehran's main thoroughfares and commercial centres. The street was built on Reza Shah Pahlavi's orders and called

Pahlavi Street; it originally led partially through undeveloped fields. After the 1979 Islamic revolution the street's name was changed to Vali Asr, a reference to the twelfth Shiite Imam. Vali Asr means Prince of Time, referring to Muhammad al-Mahdi, the hidden Imam. The street reflects the city's development, in 1870 it became Tehran's main axis. At the beginning of the last century rich bazaar merchants built their homes here. At that time, the street was still limited by the city walls. With Reza Shah's Haussmannian urban planning policies, the street became the centre of the imperial district and formed a second city centre. Tehran families now left the south and settled in the new district. The area also had better-quality drinking water that was channelled via a jub from the Alborz mountains to the city. A further extension took place in 1950, under Mohammad Reza Shah. In the 1970s, the villages Vanak and Shemiran were incorporated into the city. With the establishment of trendy restaurants like the Chattanooga or a skating rink and discotheques, the westernisation of Iran to which the Shah aspired was most noticeable in these neighbourhoods.

View into Valiasr Street

Tomb of Saadi
Aramgah-e Saadi, Saadiya
آرامگاه سعدی

Bulvar-e Bustan, Shiraz
29.62222, 52.58250
Mohsen Foroughi
AD: 1952/AH: 1372/Yaz: 1322

The tomb of Saadi, another outstanding Persian poet and mystic, enjoys almost the same popularity as Hafez' – unlike him he left his home town frequently for long journeys. Today, Saadiya lies in a densely built-up and haphazardly-extended residential area at the entrance to a narrow valley with a subterranean spring. As a sign of national identity revival, Shah Muhammad Reza Pahlavi had the new mausoleum designed in 1952 by Mohsen Foroughi, student and assistant of André Godard, builder of nearby Hafeziya. The construction combines contemporary modern European architecture with components from pre-Islamic and Islamic styles. The open entrance area to the tomb is roofed and framed by eight columns clad with red travertine panels in front of a turquoise-tiled façade. The interior, which contains Saadi's grave, is designed as an octagon, with the dome lined with beige marble slabs. The grave chamber is connected to the northeast with a 20 m long and 5 m wide open gallery where the grave of another poet, Shoride Shirazi is situated. Immediately in front of the mausoleum, water flows in an underground channel about 10 m deep, the kariz Saadi. To gain access to this water, a subterranean,

30 m² octagonal room was built in excellent brickwork, which can be reached from the ground floor via steps. Around 90 m from this room, the water flows aboveground. Residents were allowed to collect water here until 1951. In 2005, following the enlargement of the garden area, a structure was built to experience the flowing water here as well.

Memorial and Tomb to Avicenna
Aramgah-e Ibn Sina
آرامگاه ابن سینا

Maidan-e Bu Ali, Hamadan
34.79156, 48.51325
Houshang Seyhoun
AD: 1954/AH: 1374/Yaz: 1324

Ibn Sina was a Persian polymath, who is regarded in the West as one of the most significant Persian thinkers and writers, notably as physician and metaphysician. The Avicenna mausoleum, commissioned at the occasion of the thousandth anniversary of his birth in 1953, was constructed by Houshang Seyhoun and includes a library of his works and a small museum in honour of the famous philosopher. He designed the mausoleum at the age of twenty-eight and described his work as follows: "The mausoleum is not only a grave; it is part of Avicenna's construct of ideas. I tried to express his character through architectural elements regarding geometry and numbers as well as image and sign symbolism". By focusing on pure geometric volumes he reaches a metaphorical expression which

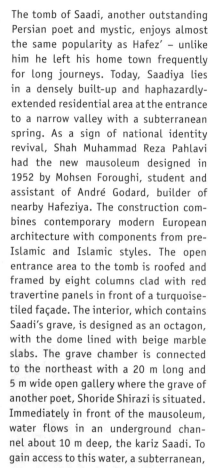

View to the Mausoleum of the Persian poet Saadi through a garden

Hall of the Tomb of Saadi

Source: Behdari, Yousef / Bavani, Pardis Khabaz (CAOI)

Old picture of Avicenna Mausoleum

Source: Wikimedia Commons

Memorial of Kamal-ol-Molk in Neyshabur

consciously resembles Gonbad-e Qabus, a structure considered by the British travel writer and architectural critic, Robert Byron, among the "most spectacular buildings in the world". By designing and building the tombs of famous scientific and literary figures, Houshang Seyhoun between 1950 and 1965 produced a language which combines modern and classical Iranian architecture, and made a first step beyond the mainstream of international architecture.

Tomb of Kamal-ol-Molk
Aramgah-e Kamal-ol-Molk
آرامگاه کمال الملک

Neyshabur
36.16750, 58.80694
Houshang Seyhoun
AD: 1955 / AH: 1375 / Yaz: 1325

Kamal-ol-Molk's tomb was formerly located in the garden cemetery of Sheikh Attar's tomb, near the wall of the garden. In 1954, owing to the enlargement of the garden, the tomb was located within the garden. After World War II, Houshang Seyhoun won several competitions, including for the memorial of Kamal-ol-Molk in Neyshabur. The work began in 1956 and the grave foundation, shell construction and tile cladding, the installation of the grave stone and the torso stone of Kamal-ol-Molk with the construction of the two pools in the courtyard of the shrine, continued until 1959. Houshang Seyhoun meticulously created this tomb based on one of the most famous paintings of Kamal-ol-Molk, *Spring Hall at Golestan Palace*. The innovative design of the arches creating the image is

achieved through a complex geometry and implemented through concrete shell structures. This structure is octagonal in shape, with a tile-clad, onion-shaped dome. Two concave ayvanches at the north side were built in reinforced concrete and innovatively decorated with geometric mosaic tiles in six blue and white shades. The decorative, very artistic mosaic used on curved surfaces narrows toward the symmetry line to ever smaller patterns. The tombstone is made of a black headstone, on which verses in Thulth script are carved. Kamal-ol-Molk's bust installed in the mausoleum was made by one of his disciples, Abu Hassan Sadiqi. Kamal-ol-Molk is considered a pioneer of modern Iranian art. He studied at Dar-ol Fonun School and was appointed as court painter at Naser al-Din Shah's court at the age of eighteen. In 1898, Kamal-ol-Molk went to Europe, where he spent four years. After returning to Iran, he founded an art school, which played a significant role in the development of contemporary art in Iran. Houshang Seyhoun is one of the outstanding personalities of Pahlavi architecture. He studied at Tehran University under the French architect Maxime Siroux for three years and also studied at the École des Beaux-Arts in Paris. Seyhoun represents a new kind of young Iranian architect who returned with high hopes from abroad and risked a step past the international style to find a common language between modern European and traditional Iranian architecture. In 1962, Houshang Seyhoun was appointed dean of the Faculty of Fine Arts at Tehran University. The tomb was registered by the national heritage authority in 2013.

Terminal 1 of Mehrabad International Airport, 1938

Tehran Mehrabad Airport
Forudgah-e Mehrabad
فرودگاه بین المللی مهرآباد

Meraj, Tehran
35.68917, 51.31342
Mohsen Foroughi, William Pereira,
Abdol Aziz Farmanfarmaian
AD: 1955/AH: 1375/Yaz: 1325

Mehrabad International Airport was established in 1938 as an airfield for the Iranian Aviation Club, and in 1949, after World War II, it received recognition as an international airport. In 1955, after construction of the first paved runway, Terminal 1 was built for domestic and international flights by Mohsen Foroughi and his Swedish consultant, William Pereira. The construction attracted attention as Iran was suddenly exposed to completely different standards, functions and technology. Mehrabad International Airport is located about 5 km west of the former city centre. The airport was outside the town when it opened. Through the expansion of the urban area Mehrabad is now in the centre. Imam Khomeini International Airport replaced this airport in 2008, but it is still used for domestic flights as well as pilgrim flights to Mecca. Mehrabad today is the regional hub for Iran Air and Iran Airtours. Extensions were planned by the Iranian architect Abdol Aziz Farmanfarmaian between 1972 and 1974.

Radio City Cinema
Radio Sity Sinema
سینما رادیو سیتی

Khiyaban-e Pahlavi, Tehran
35.69000, 51.42222
Heydar Ghiai
AD: 1958/AH: 1378/Yaz: 1328

Tehran's most luxurious cinema was opened in 1958. It was designed by the Iranian architect Heydar Ghiai, who built many cinemas across the country. Heydar Ghiai received his doctorate at the École des Beaux-Arts in Paris and

Cinema façade with neon lighting, 1958

Courtyard of the architecture office

Courtyard of the architecture office

opened his architecture firm in 1953. (It is now run by his sons.) Stylistically, his work was quite modern, tied to the international style and notable for the use of new technologies and materials such as aluminum. The Radio City Cinema was known for its huge curved façade, lit at night in bright neon colours. In 1973, it was bombed but still operated until the Iranian revolution in 1979. Later, the neon signs were removed and the building turned into a pharmacy. Today it is unused and dilapidated.

Architecture Office
Daftar Kar Meamar
دفتر کار معمار

unknown
Houshang Seyhoun
AD: 1958/AH: 1378/Yaz: 1328

Study trips through the reconstructed Europe gave Houshang Seyhoun a deep understanding of the design principles of modern architecture which went beyond the formal. He developed an architectural vocabulary that combined traditional elements with modern design principles, technology and lifestyle, for which the American architect Frank Lloyd Wright was his model. The design of his own architecture office and garden, which he built in 1958, clearly shows how he implemented his ideas. Building and grounds have a very special relationship in Houshang Seyhoun's architecture. The grounds should enhance the building, and the building derives its form partially from the nature of the site. It grows out of the landscape as naturally as any plant; its relationship to the site is so unique

that it would be out of place elsewhere. Materials are used in a way that enhances their innate character and optimises their individual colour, texture, and strength. Rooms are never simple rectangles but are broken up vertically and horizontally in alcoves, L-shapes, lowered ceilings, and decks, so that space can flow freely from one interior area to the next. An area can never be fully comprehended when viewed from one point but must be slowly experienced as one moves through the space. Ornament is developed as an integral part of the material, not applied. Examples are patterns cast in concrete or carved in stone, leaded glass panels, and tile or glass mosaics. For instance, Seyhoun combined a thin curtain wall façade with traditional Iranian brickwork. He designed his studio and patio adding vistas and niches, like those found in traditional Iranian buildings, thus developing an Iranian modernity which was more than a poor imitation of American and European trends.

Street elevation of the architecture office

Senate Building at Imam-Khomeini-Street, 1962

Senate Building
*Sakhteman-e Majles-e
Sena-ye Sabeq*
مجلس سنای سابق

248 G

Khiyaban-e Imam Khomeini,
Tehran
35.68801, 51.39964
*Mohsen Foroughi, Heydar Ghiai,
Rahmat Safai*
AD: 1959/AH: 1379/Yaz: 1329

The Senate Building, Majles-e Sena in Tehran, was the first government mandate executed by Heydar Ghiai together with Mohsen Foroughi. Yves Ghiai, the son of Heydar, says that this cooperation was mainly achieved due to Mohsen Foroughi's good relations to government. They became famous for this job, and it remains their best-known work and a testament to the inspiring era of modern thinking in Iranian art and architecture. The Senate of Iran was the upper house legislative chamber in Iran from 1949 to 1979. A bicameral legislature had been established in the 1906 Persian constitutional revolution but the senate was not actually formed until after the Iran constituent assembly in 1949, as an expression of Shah Mohammad Reza Pahlavi's desire for more political power. The senate building has an imposing, detached, rasterized marble façade, flanked by two 25 m high bronze pillars by André Bloc in the shape of enlarged chains. The calculation for the dome, one of the most technically-challenging projects in the entire endeavour, was made by the engineer Rahmat Safai. The senate was formally opened by Shah Mohammad Reza Pahlavi in 1960 and, according to the Iranian

100-Rial banknote with Senate Building

Dome of the Senate Building

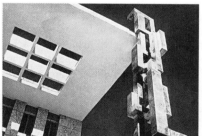

Bronze pillars in form of enlarged chains

View from Ferdowsi Avenue

constitution in force until 1979, was
the second chamber of the Iranian parliament. After the Islamic revolution of
1979, Iran abolished the Senate. Since
the dissolution the building has been
used by the Guardian Council. The building graced the 8-Rial postage stamp
in the Pahlavi period. In the Islamic
Republic of Iran, the building has been
depicted on the reverse side of the 100-
Rial note since 1985.

Maskan Bank
Bank Maskan
بانک مسکن

Khiyaban-e Ferdowsi, Tehran
35.68926, 51.41979
Mohsen Foroughi
AD: ca. 1960/AH: ca. 1380/
Yaz: ca. 1330

Interior view of bank

At the end of his long and produc-
tive career stretching over forty years,
Mohsen Foroughi returned to compact,
geometrically simple forms, but enriched
with subtle symbolism. He takes up
the design language of Oscar Niemeyer
and so invents an architecture oscillat-
ing between lightness and serene monumentality. The bank consists of two volumes: a symbolic rotunda, which serves
as counter area, and a simple rectangular office block with strip windows
where the offices are located, connected to the hall by a covered walkway.
Mohsen Foroughi, the most distinguished

architect of this period, considered himself both an engineer and an architect.
He designed the rotunda as a two-storey concrete structure with elaborate
details and created an amazingly weight-
less effect. The curved space flows harmoniously. Under the ribbed dome, different building structures are integrated
as spectacular as they are obsessively
detailed. This is less a functional building with a striking shape, than rather
an expression of the attempt to inte-
grate a variety of aspects and functions
into a single, logical body, designed to
bear the masses by applying a precise and
effective geometry.

Garden elevation of the villa

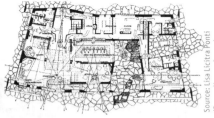

Ground floor

Villa Nemazee
Villa-ye Nemazee
ویلای نمازی

Dezashib, Tehran
(inaccessible)
35.80939, 51.44778
Gio Ponti
AD: 1960/AH: 1380/Yaz: 1330

In the Villa Nemazee in Tehran as well as in two other villas in Caracas, Gio Ponti achieved his desire to build a dream house for customers who dreamed of having one. The client, Nemazee, and the architect developed a friendship, which allowed Gio Ponti to come in contact with Iranian art and culture. On the ground floor of the villa there are wide reception rooms opening to the garden. The centre forms the large dining room which first flows into the playroom and then opens to the outside in a range of perspectives. The steps of the stairs are covered with white marble slabs, whilst the front face is covered with different-coloured marble. The bedrooms and a smaller dining room for private dining are located upstairs. The external panelling is made of ceramic plates cut in a diamond shape. The windows allow a view from one room to the next. The Villa Nemazee is full of compositional surprises. For example, large and heavy walls are juxtaposed against narrow, fine mirror walls. This play of contrasts also extends to the upper floor where along with the terrace, the gabled roof is lined with ceramic tiles, creating a surprising effects. As with previous projects, Ponti engaged his friend, the sculptor Fausto Melotti, for whose sculptures he created a series of niches and irregular openings in the patio.

Four Hundred Units
Chaharsad Dastgah
چهارصد دستگاه

Narmak, Tehran
35.68906, 51.45817
unknown
AD: 1960/AH: 1380/Yaz: 1330

Chaharsad Dastgah, or Four Hundred Units, is probably the first of very few social housing projects in Iran. In the 1960s, 400 houses were built on narrow plots, arranged in characteristic small blocks, each with a neighbourhood square. These were mainly intended for social groups that could not afford

Courtyard of the villa

Interior of Villa Nemazee

Source: Panoramio (Milad Ahsani)

View of the residential area with Burj-e Milad

to buy into the free housing market. The growing economic disparity between the capital city and the rest of the country caused a steady migration into cities and an ever-increasing migration to Tehran. In the years between 1956 and 1976, the population of Tehran tripled, increasing from 1.5 million to 4.5 million, resulting in a massively altered cityscape, especially the poor peri-urban areas in the south.

Source: Panoramio (Reza Ahmadian)

City square in Chaharsad Dastgah

© google maps

Aerial view of the social housing district

Main gate to Tehran University

Source: Caroline Reichmann

Main Gate to Tehran University
Sardar-e Daneshkadeh-ye Tehran
سردر دانشگاه تهران

252 G

Khiyaban-e Enghelab, Tehran
35.70144, 51.39614
Kurush Ferzami
AD: 1961/AH: 1380/Yaz: 1330

500 Iranian Rials

Source: Banknote Currencystore Collection

The main gate of the campus of Tehran university was designed in the 1960s by a graduate of the College of Fine Arts, Kurush Ferzami. Its special design at Enghelab Street is regarded as the symbol of the university and education in Iran. The entrance is edged by a concrete sculpture where several ayvan-like elements form what look like protective hands. Another interpretation sees a pair of wings leading to success and prosperity through science and knowledge. The trellised gate was added later.

Ministry of Petroleum
Vezarat-e Naft
وزارت نفت

253 G

Khiyaban-e Taleqani/
Khiyaban-e Hafez, Tehran
35.70692, 51.41150
*Abdol Aziz Farmanfarmaian,
Yahya Ettehadieh*
AD: 1961/AH: 1381/Yaz: 1331

The Ministry of Petroleum was built by Abdol Aziz Farmanfarmaian and Yahya Etehadieh in 1961. Farmanfarmaian, a

Aerial view of the main gate to University

Main gate under construction

Source: Contemporary Architecture of Iran

descendant of Persian nobility and a member of the Qajar dynasty, is an important contemporary character in Iranian architecture. He studied at the École des Beaux-Arts in Paris. In the 1950s, he held a chair at Tehran university. The headquarters of the National Iranian Oil Company was constructed in 1965 in the international style. The nationalization of the oil production and processing facilities of the Anglo-Iranian Oil Company under Prime Minister Mohammad Mossadegh is a significant event in post-war Iranian history. It took place on 15 March 1951. During this time the monarchy consolidated its economic and political power. It was a time of national revival, which is reflected in the so-called "oriental" design entrance façade. Abdol Aziz Farmanfarmaian and Yahya Etehadieh focused particularly on the exterior of the building. The Vezarat-e Naft attracted the attention of the public, which was suddenly confronted with a completely different urban scale. The thirteen-storey office building above a large basement completely remains in the minimalist and functionalist tradition of European-American modernism, the international style, which Philip Johnson and Henry-Russell Hitchcock showcased in New York in 1932. According to Hitchcock

View from Taleqani Street

and Johnson, modern buildings should look simple, and outer walls should be large, smooth surfaces with regular texture. The international style, modelled over the years on a prismatic tower with glassed curtain wall and filigree construction profiles, was the dominant trend of modernity in the first two decades after World War II. According to many critics, its representatives removed themselves from the functional and humanistic principles of modernity, or were from the outset only engaged with aesthetics. Their architecture exhibits many functional faults which could be mitigated only with mechanical-engineering systems. The international style was also criticised for the repeatability of the shape and monotony of the façades and the aggressive placement of the buildings in the urban space.

Aerial view of the Iranian Ministry of Petroleum ca. 1965

Street elevation of Cinema Rivoli

Cinema Rivoli, Sahra Cinema
Sinema Rivoli
سینما ریوولی

254 | G

Khiyaban-e Taleqani,
Khiyaban-e Shariati, Tehran
35.70758, 51.43469
Yousef Shariatzadeh, Mohsen Mirheydar
AD: 1962/AH: 1382/Yaz: 1332

Cinema Rivoli is characterised by simple geometrical shapes, which in contrast to conventional architectural styles was not a purely aesthetic or artistic choice, but a more functional one. Through accentuated renunciation of luxury elements for the benefit of objectivity and functional aesthetics, Yousef Shariatzadeh and Mohsen Mirheyda wanted to express the social upheaval resulting in the democratisation of society in their architecture. The architecture of Tehran is characterised by a variety of exciting and excellent cinemas, which were principally new urban planning elements primarily designed to cater to the peculiarities of everyday life. They reflect a new concept of public life of the working class. After the revolution of 1979, the Iranian regime closed all cinemas in Tehran and repurposed the buildings.

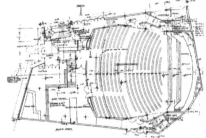

Ground floor plan

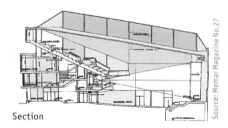

Section

Interior of Cinema Rivoli

Source: Caroline Reichmann

Street elevation of Enghelab Branch

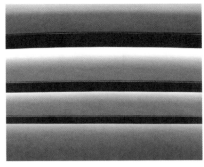

Slab view from below

Melli Bank, Enghelab Branch
Bank-e Melli Shabah-e Enghelab
بانک ملی ایران ءشعبه انقلاب

Khiyaban-e Enghelab, Tehran
35.70081, 51.39964
Jørn Utzon
AD: 1962 / AH: 1382 / Yaz: 1332

In 1958, Jørn Utzon was asked to design a branch of the Melli Bank, Iran's National Bank, in the university district of Tehran. Utzon visited the site only once, together with his collaborator Munk Hansen. During their visit, they did not discuss the project in detail but delved into Iranian architecture, in particular that of the city of Isfahan. The urban fabric of traditional Islamic cities – repeating units, pierced by innumerable leafy courtyards – had a decisive influence on subsequent projects and the development of its additive architecture. The Melli Bank is located on the major Enghelab Street on a large, 26 m wide site. The space design was straightforward: The brief stipulated a large main hall with offices leading from it. An underground parking level was added later. The client wanted the building to be distinct from its neighbours. Utzon put it on a raised platform, recessed and surrounded on both sides by boldly projecting walls, thick enough to accommodate supply lines. One side wall was doubled in size to accommodate an office, private meeting rooms and service rooms. Two additional levels containing administrative offices straddled the outer walls over the entrance. The raised platform provided a dramatic sequence of spaces in the entrance area; visitors pass through a low, dark area, covered with

V-shaped beams, and then enter the open counter hall which expands dramatically up and down, allowing a view over the whole interior. The idea may not be new but Utzon realised it with unusual force. Isfahan's bazaar inspired him to light the counter area from above. Utzon wanted something subdued and diffuse to convey coolness. After having studied the lighting system in Aalto's Baghdad art gallery, he designed a distinctive roof with beams folded from different high plates: The cross-section reminded Utzon of the flowing Farsi writing of the bank's name, an idea which he used in the publication of the project in the architectural magazine *Zodiac*.

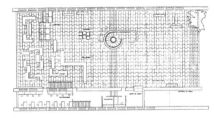

Ground floor plan

Section

Source: Tehran Projects

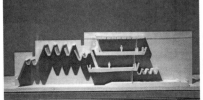

Jørn Utzon, Bank Melli, Enghelab Branch, Section

Source: Wikimedia Commons

Royal Tehran Hilton with Alborz mountains, 1962

Tower of Royal Tehran Hilton, 1962

Royal Tehran Hilton, Hotel Esteghlal
Hotel-e Esteghlal
هتل استقلال

Sohrabi, Tehran
35.79060, 51.41300
Heydar Ghiai, Abdol Aziz Farmanfarmaian
AD: 1962/AH: 1382/Yaz: 1332

The Parsian Esteghlal International Hotel opened in 1962 as the Royal Tehran Hilton. The hotel was designed by local Iranian architect Heydar Ghiai. The British architect Raglan Squire, who designed Hilton hotels in Tunis, Bahrain, Nicosia and Jakarta, is mentioned as design consultant. The hotel originally consisted of a single tower containing 259 rooms. A second tower, with an additional 291 rooms, was added by Abdol Aziz Farmanfarmaian in 1972. The hotel's famous guests during its heyday included Ethiopian Emperor Haile Selassie, King Hussein of Jordan, and astronauts Neil Armstrong, Buzz Aldrin and Michael Collins. After World War II, the Royal Tehran Hilton was the third international hotel in this category in Middle East – after the Babylon in Baghdad and the King David in Jerusalem. After the war, the hotel was a Little America in the truest sense of the word. For American businessmen and tourists it offered – with the added bonus of English-speaking staff – a restaurant serving cheeseburgers and milkshakes, intercontinental phone calls and, most importantly, air-conditioned modernity – a respite from the alien world outside. For the local population the same attributes had a utopian aura: The Hilton was a dream of luxury and delight, a space representing clearly and permanently the new and powerful presence of the United States. It was a luxurious symbiosis between western comfort and the Hollywood version of ancient Persia, which soon proved to be an illusion and therefore had to give way to other trends. The hotel was renamed to Esteghlal Hotel, meaning Independence, following the Islamic revolution in 1979 when all foreign hotel management contracts were cancelled. It is today part of the state-run Parsian International Hotels Company. A third tower is currently under construction.

Tabriz Railway Station
Istgah-e Rah Aha-en Tabriz
ایستگاه راه‌آهن تبریز

Maidan-e Rah Ahan, Tabriz
38.07189, 46.22867
Fernand Pouillon,
Additional buildings by Heydar Ghiai
AD: 1964/AH: 1343/Yaz: 1295

Tabriz was occupied by Russians several times in the first half of the twentieth century and also during both world wars. A railway line to the border at Jolfa, built by the expansionist Russians, was of little importance until recently, but it has increased in significance since the 1990s as a result of Iran's friendlier relations with its northern neighbours. The railway started from Jolfa, a city on the border of

Iran and the modern Azerbaijan republic. In 1967, the Tabriz-Tehran axis came into operation. Tabriz railway station was built during the second Pahlavi era by the French architect Fernand Pouillon. In his autobiography *Mémoires d'un architecte* he reports that he was responsible for the design of several ministerial buildings in Iran, among them the railway stations of Meshed and Tabriz, which is inspired by his Marignane airport design near Marseille. Tabriz railway station is the first station scheduled to be renovated and upgraded as cultural heritage. The Committee agreed to maintain Tabriz station and parts of the exterior architecture of the administrative section. The new addition of the station was designed by a pioneer of the architecture of modern Iran, Heydar Ghiai.

at their best in an unforgettable ambience. The screen, approximately 600 m² (15 m high and 40 m wide), was larger than than in conventional cinemas. The theatre also offered space for a far bigger audience. The floor undulated slightly, raising the front wheels of the cars to ensure a good view of the screen. In addition to classic films, cult films and blockbusters, culinary delights from the 1950s were served: cheeseburgers, hot dogs and milkshakes. Everything recalled the period of rock'n'roll: Girls on roller-skates and popcorn boys served the patrons right at the cars. With the advent of television and, later, home videos, the number of visitors declined in the 1970s. In addition, rising land prices on the outskirts of the city and environmental requirements made it difficult to run the drive-in profitably.

Drive-in Cinema (destroyed) 258
Ranandegi dar Sinema
رانندگی در سینما

Vanak, Tehran
35.76297, 51.40233
Yves Ghiai-Chamlou
AD: 1965 / AH: 1385 / Yaz: 1335

Tehran's Drive-in Cinema catapulted visitors back to the past – to a world where one could still marvel at movies on a big screen in a drive-in cinema. Movie fans, car lovers and nostalgics could enjoy these events of cinematic entertainment

Drive-in Cinema, 1965

Source: Wikimedia Commons

Source: mapio.net

View from Station Square

Aerial view of Moravarid Palace, ca. 2010

Moravarid Palace
Kakh-e Morvarid
کاخ مروارید

Mehrshahr, Karaj
35.78778, 50.88667
Frank Lloyd Wright Associated
Architects: William Wesley Peters with
Nezam Ameri, Kamal Kamooneh,
Hormozdyar Khosravi
AD: 1966/AH: 1386/Yaz: 1336

The Morvarid Palace is a private residence commissioned by Princess Shams Pahlavi, the elder sister of Mohammad Reza Pahlavi, for herself and her husband, Mehrdad Pahlbod, the former art and culture minister, to be built in Mehrshahr near Karaj. The stately home was designed by William Wesley Peters of Frank Lloyd Wright Associated Architects, who had already designed Fallingwater

and the Guggenheim Museum. Thomas Casey was chief engineer, Johny Hill and Cornelia Bryerly were responsible for interior and furniture design, and the landscaping was done by Francis Nemtin. The Morvarid Palace was built on a plot of 170 ha of rolling hills next to a small artificial lake. The building consists of two concrete domes and a ziggurat connected via a ramp, ending in the bedroom of Princess Shams. The other rooms – living room, dining room, lobby and pool – are designed under the two domes as an open-plan living space which is accessible via ramps and stairs. The variety of interior design, exquisite materials, decorations, sculptures and paintings create a holistic work of art, which was tailored to the taste of a Middle Eastern princess. A circular spiral theme is found throughout the palace. Doors,

Entrance of the palace

Entrance stairs

Source: Nezam Amery (Kamooneh Khosrovi Consulting Groop)

Canopy of the palace

Source: Behdari, Yousef / Bavani, Pardis Khabaz (CA01)

Perspex dome inside the palace

furniture, lamps, walls, ceilings and luminaires are decorated like this. Clear, translucent, opaque plexiglass ensures adequate, interesting natural light. In 2002 it received recognition as an architectural monument and was added to the list of cultural heritage buildings. Currently it is used as a recreational centre of the Basiji. Parts of the building are accessible to the public and allow visitors a glimpse into the wonderful world of James Bond from the 1970s. All valuables, including furniture, lamps, carpets, curtains and porcelain are original. If only Frank Lloyd Wright could see how his great architecture is falling into ruin. After nearly thirty years of constant neglect, damage to the plexiglass dome will cause its imminent collapse. Simple covers of the dome and the spiral summarise the current tentative efforts of the state to preserve this architectural jewel. Should the Iranian government decide to preserve the Pahlavi era buildings rather than ignoring them, the restoration of this masterpiece could certainly be a first step.

Villa Behbahani
Villa-ye Behbahani
ویلا بهبهانی

Shemiran, Tehran
David Oshana
AD: 1966 / AH: 1386 / Yaz: 1336

Villa Behbahani, designed by David Oshana in Shemiran in 1966, leans heavily on the design of the Lovell Beach House, the most famous building designed by Rudolph Schindler in Los Angeles. Oshana could realise his architectural ideas for the first time in the Villa Behbahani. The house has large glass surfaces and, like in Schindler's construction, interior and exterior spaces flow smoothly into each other. Oshana combined light metal constructions with structural elements to create a bright, light- and air-permeable ensemble. In addition he specialised in placing his structures in carefully arranged gardens and landscapes. He was mainly inspired by the contrast between geometric shapes and nature, and distanced himself strongly from what he considered dogmatic functionalism.

Source: Behdari, Yousef / Bavani, Pardis Khabaz (CA01)

Garden elevation of Villa Behbahani

Villa Behbahani, detail of façade

Tehran Comprehensive Plan
Tarh-e Jame-ye Tehran (TCP)
طرح جامع تهران

Tehran
35.70000, 51.41667
Victor Gruen,
Abdol Aziz Farmanfarmaian
AD: 1966/AH: 1386/Yaz: 1336

In 1966, the Iranian government instructed the Iranian architect Abdolaziz Farmanfarmaian to develop a master plan for the city of Tehran in collaboration with the American company Gruen Associates. Gruen Associates was one of the hundreds of private companies that worked in Iran between the mid-1960s and the Islamic revolution. The firm represented the generation of American architects who planned so-called garden cities worldwide, initiated by Ebenezer Howard, using shopping malls as the heart of this kind of city. These towns were evergreen, with low density, designed for private transport and with a pinch of American entrepreneurship. The supposedly organic hierarchy of family, neighbourhood, community and city is placed as a kind of flowing park between highways. The ten satellite cities of Tehran rotate around the metro core, and each consists of four municipalities arranged around a community centre, with five districts. In the 1950s and 1960s, Victor Gruen planned several major United States cities like Dallas, Fort Worth in Texas or Valencia in California, and the campus Louvain-la-Neuve in

Belgium. The order of Shah Reza Pahlavi, supported by the necessary petrodollars and the ideological superstructure of the White Revolution, gave Gruen the chance to plan a complete metropolis. Gruen's plan can be described as the ideal image of a metropolis superimposed over the city of Tehran, thus forming something between a central and a linear town. The whole city, old and new, was to be traversed by a network of green valleys in which the immense network of highways and public transportation was embedded. An impressive feature of the new Tehran is the immense landscape park Pardisan, designed by the famous American ecologist Ian McHarg. There are few examples of megacities which are characterised only by one single idealistic vision and, like Tehran, were developed at universities, planned in offices and implemented to such an extent. This large-scale design was one of the first postmodern city designs which American designers were famous for in the 1980s. But only one element of the plan was realised: the more than 200 m high television tower.

Tehran Comprehensive Plan

Source: Ghaffari Associates

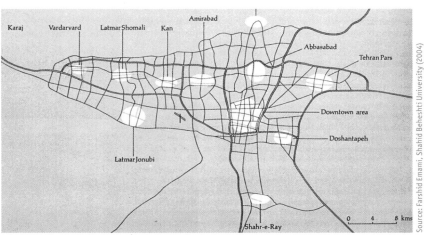

TCP-suggested neighbourhoods

Source: Farshid Emami, Shahid Beheshti University (2004)

Niaveran Palace in the northeastern corner of the complex

Niaveran Palace
Kakh-e Niavaran
کاخ نیاوران
Kashanak, Tehran
35.81167, 51.47306
Mohsen Foroughi
AD: 1967 / AH: 1387 / Yaz: 1337

The extension of Niaveran Palace designed by Mohsen Foroughi in 1958 is located in the northeast corner of the park ,which is partially accessible by the public. The construction of the 2.5-storey building began in 1958 and was completed in 1967. Originally, it was intended as a governmental guest house, but then became the summer residence of the Shah. Mohammad Reza Pahlavi and his family lived here until the Islamic revolution of 1979. The massive flat roof served as a heliport, from which the Shah was flown to the airport when he left the country on 16 January 1979. The very angular palace designed with modern materials and the decorative interior elements are meant to reflect the long history of the country. The bedrooms and the rooms for the children and domestic staff are located on the top floor. Offices, conference rooms and rooms for the service staff are accommodated on the mezzanine floor. The rooms are furnished with valuable pictures and wallpaper, and a number of state gifts are kept here. The ground floor rooms are arranged around a large hall, including a private cinema, dining room, guest rooms, waiting rooms and lateral hall extensions, like the blue saloon used by Reza Pahlavi for state receptions. Jimmy Carter and Mohammad Reza Shah toasted the New Year of 1977 in Kakh-e Niavaran. Carter confirmed after brief talks with the Shah that he fully agreed with the royal view on human rights. He added: "Iran, because of the great leadership of the Shah, is an island of stability in one of the more troubled areas of the world."

Lobby in the palace

Upstairs hall of the palace

Latyan Dam at River Jajrood

Latyan Dam
Sadd-e Latyan
سد لتیان

263

Sadd-e Tanzimi, 30 km east of Tehran
35.79003, 51.67847
Tehran Province Water & Wastewater Co. (Commissioner)
AD: 1967 / AH: 1387 / Yaz: 1337

The Latyan Dam is part of the third development plan, which covered the period from 1962 to 1967 and was aligned with the priorities of education, agriculture and industry. At the same time the dam is a symbol of Iran's independence. After the traumatic experiences of the Abadan crisis, no strangers – especially Brits or Russians – should ever again decide the fate of Iran. The economic planning of Iran was fundamentally reformed by introducing a centrally-managed planning office, which designed, executed and evaluated long-term economic plans. Mohammad Reza Pahlavi considered economic planning as a means to break the deadlock of the Iranian economy, and he succeeded in the years that followed.

Latyan Dam as a symbol of the independence of Iran

Source: Claudia Luperto

Saman Residential Complex within the urban context

Saman Residential Complex 264 G
Mojtame-ye Maskuni-e Saman
مجتمع مسكوني سامان
Bulvar-e Keshavarz, Tehran
35.71003, 51.39883
Abdol Aziz Farmanfarmaian
AD: 1967 / AH: 1368 / Yaz: 1336

The Saman residential complex was built by the company Abdol Aziz Farmanfarmaian in 1967. Architectural firms like Farmanfarmaian at that time had ca. 400 employees. The Saman complex is the first residential high-rise building in Iran. The two almost-identical towers quote Mies van der Rohe's Lake Shore Drive Apartments almost verbatim. Like these, they stand on a nearly-square property located directly on a busy road. They are aligned in parallel and stand at right angles, opening to a small plaza. The 170 residential units, spread over twenty-two floors, result in a building height of approximately 70 m. Around the access core with staircases and elevators in the centre of the building is a square column grid. The apartments were originally accessed by a hallway. They are glazed throughout on the façade side. The buildings are designed as metal structures with bright, flush façades, flat roofs and functionalist floor plans. The outside of both of the buildings is clad in travertine tiles.

1963–1978
The "Golden Age" of Iranian Modernity

In January 1963 the Shah launched his White Revolution, which called for the handing over of farmlands to the peasants, establishing farm cooperatives and banks, granting women the vote, nationalising the forests and mobilising young men and women into the Education Corps, Health Corps, and Agricultural Corps. Dividing the farmlands among the peasants naturally did not please the landlords, and the clergy objected particularly to voting rights given to women, and they did not favour the impingement on property rights either. Changes in global politics and the world oil market allowed Iran in the early 1970s to fully exploit the Organisation of Petroleum Exporting Countries (OPEC)'s collective strength against the weakening position of the western oil companies. The Shah played an important role in leading OPEC to a policy of "price rise, price and production control" between 1970 and 1975, posing as the champion of the oil producers and of the Third World against domination and exploitation by the West. As a result, Persia's oil revenue jumped from USD 1.1 billion in 1970 to 21 billion in 1977. The newly-found riches promoted consumerism and stimulated a variety of industrial, entrepreneurial, and import ventures that tended to clog the ports and the economy as well. The gap between the rich and the poor widened, and this gave further strength to the Islamic protest movement. Between 1963 and 1973, domestic and international tourism also became an important source of income. The construction of educational and health facilities, as well as sports and leisure facilities, was accelerated, and new settlements were planned. In the 1960s, several development plans

Source: Thomas Meyer-Wieser

Development of Tehran ca. 1974

were formulated with similar goals: By using highly developed technologies, a recovery of economic growth and a more equitable distribution of income should be achieved through the increase of the national income, the creation of new jobs and the expansion of social services. The targeted growth in agriculture would supply the population with food and industry with raw materials and so reduce dependence on foreign imports. The fourth development plan called for streamlining of the state bureaucracy. Many sustainable investments in the country's infrastructure were made, such as schools, roads, telecommunications networks, airports, television broadcasting facilities, hotels and tourist resorts.

Development of Tehran ca. 1974

The construction sector further evolved by the guiding principles of "modernism", which at the end of the Pahlavi era led to a disastrous combination of investor architecture in the western style and caused – as in Europe and the US – the crisis of modern architecture in the 1960s in Iran. Young Iranian architects looked for a way out of the dictates of modernity by referring to the theory of Robert Venturi and Denise Scott Brown and pointing to the "complexity and contradiction" of their own architecture as a possible way out. They wished to develop a common language between the modern European and traditional Iranian architecture and strengthen the cultural identity. The so-called Golden Age of Iranian modernity began. Arches, vaults, domes and other elements of the traditional architectural vocabulary were reinterpreted and applied. The Centre for Management Studies is one of the most complete and sensible attempts to develop a new national architecture in the 1970s. The individual tendencies which emerged especially at the end of the second reign of the Pahlavi in the work of Nader Ardalan or Kamran Diba, could not gain a foothold due to the political situation, making it impossible to establish an independent, modern Iranian architecture.

1967
Iranian Pavilion Montreal

Paviliun Iran dar Namayeshgah-e Beyn ol-Melali Montrial

Even vehement supporters of the international style like Abdol Aziz Farmanfarmaian questioned modernity. When designing the Iranian pavilion for the 1967 World Exhibition in Montreal Farmanfarmaian asked himself, "... What can an architect from Iran build next to all the big names? I realised that I could not impress with technology, and so I had the idea to design a building that had to be Iranian. A building made entirely of tiles, only blue, which divulges its origin at first glance and shows that it does not come from India or from China, but from Iran". In line with the theory of post-modernism, he proceeded to design a "decorated shelter", a construction which was functionalist-modern inside and decorated with blue tiles on the outside indicating an association to Safavid mosaics. He thus created a building which at first glance conveyed that it came from Iran. The Iranian pavilion was located on the Île Sainte-Hélène, directly opposite the metro. On two floors, Iran presented its physical characteristics, ranging from high mountains to undulating plains and deserts; from fair-haired aryans to black people; its cultural heritage and archaeological treasures; its mineral and agricultural resources and the industrial development including oil production, and its world-famous carpets, arts and crafts.

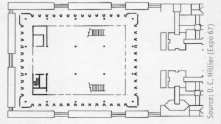

Floor plan

Source: D. C. Hillier (Expo 67)

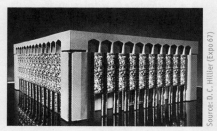

Model of the Iranian Pavilion

Source: D. C. Hillier (Expo 67)

Iranian Pavilion at the World Exposition in Montreal with Safavid-inspired mosaics

Source: Bill Dutfield (Expo 67)

1960–1968
Maison d'Iran à Paris

Sakhteman Khuabegan
Danshejuian Paris

Maison d'Iran was the last of the thirty-eight buildings erected on the site of the Cité Internationale Universitaire de Paris. The project was headed by Farah Diba in the early 1960s. Mohsen Foroughi and Heydar Ghiai were entrusted with the design of the student residence. The project was implemented in cooperation with the French sculptor and artist André Bloc and the architect Claude Parent. The modernist building is the flagship in the career of Claude Parent, who was a child of Le Corbusier and an active member of the "space group" founded by André Bloc in the early 1950s, where artists like Yves Klein and Jean Tinguely were active in the integration of art and architecture. The architecture of the construction borrows much from Russian constructivism, De Stijl movement and Bauhaus theories. Maison d'Iran consists of a main building with the student units and the apartment for the manager, housed in a nearly 38 m high metal structure and a low one-storey building for common areas. The supporting structure was welded together by means of rods made of edged, painted black metal. The architectural expression is determined by the suspension of the four, two-storey blocks in this primary structure and the external fire escape. The house became the seat of opposition against the Shah and was abandoned by the government of the time. It now houses the Fondation Avicenne. In 2008, the building was listed in the inventory of buildings deserving protection.

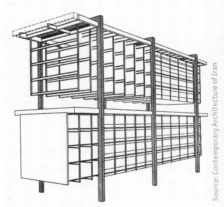

Isometric projection

Elevation of Maison d'Iran, 1967–1969

Maison d'Iran under Construction, 1967–1969

Rudaki Hall, Vahdat Hall
Talar-e Rudaki, Talar-e Vahdat
تالار وحدت

Khiyaban-e Enghelab, Tehran
35.69967, 51.41106
Eugene Aftandilian
AD: 1967 / AH: 1387 / Yaz: 1337

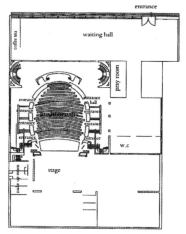

Ground floor plan of Rudaki Halle

Source: Contemporary Architecture of Iran

In the southern part of Enghelab Street, hidden behind other buildings, lies the Talar-e Rudaki (renamed Talar-e Vahdat), which planners intend to expose by breakthroughs at Enghelab Street and allowing accessibility from there. Named after a ninth-century poet, Rudaki Hall is the only opera house in the city centre of Tehran where the dynasty symbolically positioned western modernity in the heart of the growing capital – spatially, visually and architecturally. The hall was built at the initiative of Shahbanu Farah Diba Pahlavi and officially opened on 25 October 1967. The Persian American architect Eugene Aftandilian designed the structure modelled on the Vienna State Opera. In contrast, the ornaments are intentionally based on the formal language of Persepolis, the representative architecture of the Persian empire. Rudaki Hall was the home of the Tehran symphony orchestra and the Iranian national ballet (of which Les Ballets Persans, founded in Stockholm in 2002, considers itself the successor). In addition to orchestra concerts, numerous performances were held with the participation of international musicians and conductors like Henryk Szeryng and Herbert von Karajan. In collaboration with Iranian artists, Maurice Béjart created an original Persian choreography performed in the Vahdat Hall at the 2,500-year celebration of the Persian Empire. The Talar-e Rudaki consists of an opera house with a seven-story administration building attached to it which has rehearsal rooms, a restaurant and a small hall for chamber concerts. On the ground floor is the entrance hall, with ticket counters, buffet and entrances to the 580-seat auditorium. There are three rows of balconies with boxes lined with grey carpets and red satin walls. The stage is divided into four parts. The front part can be lowered by 3 m for opera and ballet performances. The two side panels can be moved up to a height of 6 m. The rear part of the stage is designed as a revolving stage. No opera and ballet performances have taken place here since the 1979 Islamic revolution; instead, performances of original Iranian plays, puppet shows, music and dance (men only) and non-western performances are staged. The pieces shown are quite critical of the regime. Tehran has a very keen, demanding theatre-going public and, judging from the many posters around the theatre and on the doors of many surrounding cafes – from Café Teatr to Café-Pizza Sepidgaah, Rebar cafe to Café Tamandouni – there is a large variety of shows on offer.

Façade on Enghelab Street

Source: Dick Heuff (mapio)

Auditorium in Rudaki Hall

Source: bezanimbiroon.ir

Source: Behdari, Yousef/Bavani, Pardis Khabaz (CAOI)

View into Shafagh Park

Shafagh Park
Park va Farhangsaray-e Shafagh
پارک و فرهنگسرای شفق
Yousef Abad, Tehran
35.72944, 51.40833
Kamran Diba
AD: 1969/AH: 1389/Yaz: 1339

266 F

Ground floor plan

Source: Behdari, Yousef/Bavani, Pardis Khabaz (CAOI)

Shafagh Park, originally known as "Yousef-Abad" Garden, was endowed by Dr. Rezazade Shefeq. This neighbourhood park, planned by Kamran Diba between 1966 and 1969, is home to a community centre with two small libraries, a workshop for children, a community hall and office space. The facilities were partially housed in existing buildings, partially in new structures. Unlike the traditional Iranian garden, the architect decided on an organic layout. This allowed maximum use of the relatively small garden space by creating walkways meandering around artificial hills and densely planted areas. The result was a single, terraced plaza connecting the two opposite ends of the park. An elevated zigzag path leads through the centre and gives an unobstructed view of the lower area which was converted into a children's playground. Kamran Diba is one of the most internationally renowned Iranian architects and urban planners and one of the leading lights of the Golden Age of Iranian modernism. He studied architecture and sociology at Howard University. In 1969, after starting in private practice, he founded DAZ Consulting Architects and Engineers, which he quit in 1980. From 1976 to 1978, Diba was director of the Tehran Museum of Contemporary Art. In his buildings Kamran Diba combines classical Islamic architectural elements with modern spacial concepts. Diba received the Aga Khan Award for architecture for his project "Shustar New Town", exhibited at the Venice Biennale in 1986. He is the cousin of Farah Diba, the former Empress of Iran.

Elevation

Source: Amir Bani Mas'ud (Honar-e Memari)

Source: Behdari, Yousef / Bavani, Pardis Khabaz (CAOI)

Multipurpose building by Hossein Amanat

Multipurpose Building at Alborz High School
دبیرستان البرز

267 G

Khiyaban-e Enghelab/
Khiyaban-e Hafez, Tehran
35.70283, 51.41228
Hossein Amanat
AD: 1970/AH: 1390/Yaz: 1340

Hossein Amanat was ahead of his time. The building next to the Alborz High School is a true hybrid, which by its nature is multi-functional and responds to the requirements of the urban structure. By using contrasting sizes, Amanat combines architecture with everyday urban life and masters the span from microcosm of the individual to the macrocosm of the city. Amanat's construction is more than a multifunctional building, but rather a new type of structure which evolves from an existing concept. The aim is to create a relational design

Source: Behdari, Yousef / Bavani, Pardis Khabaz (CAOI)

Garden façade of Ghasemi House

that analyses technical requirements, social and economic needs and results in an aesthetically convincing building.

Ghasemi House
Khaneh-ye Ghasemi
خانه قاسمی

268 F

Eslamshahr, Tehran
35.61389, 51.49278
David Oshana
AD: 1970/AH: 1390/Yaz: 1340

The Ghasemi house designed by David Oshana in 1970 shows a strong tendency to an architecture characterised by volumetric-sculptural, construction-oriented and coarse shapes. This is an architecture that claims "the aesthetics of truthfulness", with an almost fundamentalist return to the materials of modernity and their sudden appearance in sensual béton brut. This ethic refers to the everyday role of the home environment in the occupant's life, everyday life instead of high culture. And, since the constructions must be readable, beams and timber remain visible, and even lines and installations are always external, not concealed. Materials had to be used raw and unprocessed, so they were subsequently neither clad nor beautified, neither plastered nor painted. Buildings were allowed to be planned only for their exact purpose, never as a memorial to their builders.

Source: Behdari, Yousef/Bavani, Pardis Khabaz (CAOI)

Perspective drawing of Hotel Tehran, 1970

Hotel Tehran (Project)
Hotel Tehran
هتل تهران

Khiyaban-e Dr. Fatemi, Tehran
35.71528, 51.39378
Kenzo Tange
AD: 1970/AH: 1390/Yaz: 1340

Kenzo Tange designed the thirty-storey hotel as a triangular tower at the southeast corner of Laleh Park in 1970. The project presents itself as a pure, strictly geometric glass prism. The shape and the reflective façade are meant to soften the impact of the massive corner structure and harmoniously connect to the park and the surrounding area. The glass-encased,

7.5 m high lobby offers an unobstructed view of the park, the sky and the mountains, whilst the banquet and conference facilities are below ground level. A Japanese garden with waterfall connects the hotel landscape with Laleh Park, thus creating a hotel oasis.

InterContinental Hotel, Laleh International Hotel
Hotel Beyn al-Melali-ye Laleh
هتل بین المللی لاله

Khiyaban-e Dr. Fatemi/
Khiyaban-e Hejab, Tehran
35.71528, 51.39378
Neal Prince
AD: 1971/AH: 1391/Yaz: 1341

InterContinental Hotels opened in 1946 its first hotels for crews and passengers of the Pan American World Airways in countries where no five-star hotels existed. The number of hotels increased with the development of the airline's route in South America and the Caribbean, then reached Europe, Middle East and Asia. Neal Prince, an architect, art historian and collector, dedicated himself to the development of these international hotels and restaurants, which he established as pioneers of branding. The Tehran InterContinental Hotel, which was designed by Neal Prince in 1971, demonstrates how the strategic objectives of management, the knowledge and culture of employees and the company image can be successfully reconciled.

Source: Rhyton Travel, Tehran

Laleh International Hotel at southeastern corner of Laleh Park

Freedom Tower, landmark of modern Tehran

Shahyad Tower, Freedom Tower

271

Borj-e Azadi, Shahyad Aryamehr

برج شه‌ه‌دای آریامهر، برج چرخ آزادی

Maidan-e Azadi, Tehran

35.69975, 51.33808

Hossein Amanat

AD: 1971/AH: 1391/Yaz: 1341

In 1968, the most famous Iranian architects participated in a competition. Surprisingly, twenty-four-year-old architect Hossein Amanat was the winner. He had recently graduated from the University of Tehran when he learned about the competition, and he abandoned plans to continue his studies in the United States, instead forming a small architecture studio in his bedroom to work on a design for the monument. His project for the symbol of the modern state, which was built to mark the 2,500-year celebration of the Persian Empire, consisted of two elements: the commemoration of Shahs, Shahyad-Aryamehr, and a huge open space. The monument is shaped by giant columns forming four arches and standing on a square with

a fountain designed like a Persian carpet. The tower was constructed of reinforced, poured concrete, clad in glistening white marble. Because of the complexity of the arches and curves of the tower structure, the shape of nearly every piece of the stone cladding was unique. Amanat describes the design as the culmination of everything he had learned in his studies and in his travels around Iran, citing many historical precedents as influences. The main archway of the tower combines the parabolic arch of the pre-Islamic ruins at Ctesiphon with the pointed arches of the Islamic period, encapsulating millennia of Persian history. To reconcile the two arch shapes, Amanat took inspiration from the beautifully-detailed squinches found in historic Persian architecture. Even the windows at the top of the tower are influenced by similar features in historic tower structures. The area between the two bulkheads, consisting of rows of indented diamonds, is very reminiscent of Seyhoun's design for the Tomb of Kamal-ol-molk. Only a few years after its completion, the tower became the focal point for demonstrations against the Shah's

regime. Following the 1979 revolution, some expected the tower to be destroyed. As demolition of the tower was considered an impossible undertaking, it was renamed Burj-e Azadi, Freedom Tower. The monument is interesting as it represents modern Iran before and after the revolution. Shahyad Aryamehr managed to represent more than just being the monument to Shahs. It embodies all the contradictory characters of the modern, urban middle class emerging in the Pahlavi time, identified as modern, white and solid and yet playful, deeply traditional and open to other cultures. Hossein Amanat succeeded in reflecting the 7,000 years old history of Iran in this building. The result is a timeless building that serves any political direction as the symbol of freedom. It is one of the most-visited buildings in Tehran. The observation deck, accessed via an elevator, allows a panoramic view of the city. The complex is only partly accessible. The park has been redesigned and reduced in size, and the mausoleum of Reza Shah, built in 1959 by Mohsen Foroughi, was destroyed in the first days of the 1979 Islamic revolution. As for Amanat, as a member of the Baha'i faith and of Jewish descent, he faced persecution in the newly formed Islamic Republic. Allegations against him included accusations that the use of nine windows on each of the main façades of the tower was a Baha'i symbol, prohibited by the new regime. Amanat was forced to flee Iran and settled in Canada, where he continues to practise architecture.

Soffit inside the Freedom Tower at the height of 33 m

Floor plan of the pedestrian underpass

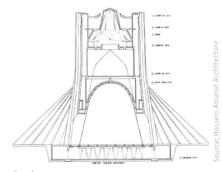

Section

Pedestrian underpass

271 Shahyad Tower, Freedom Tower

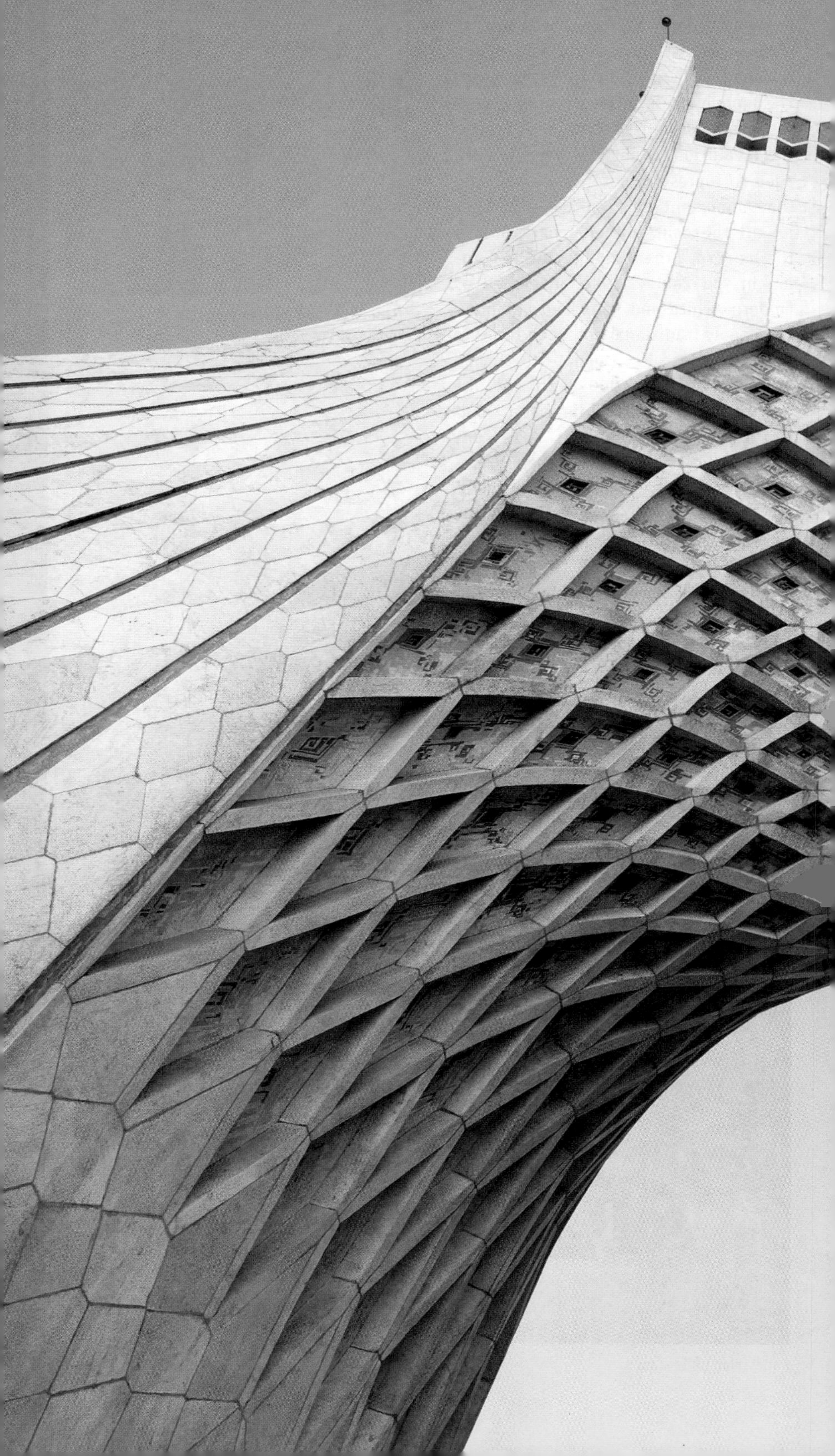

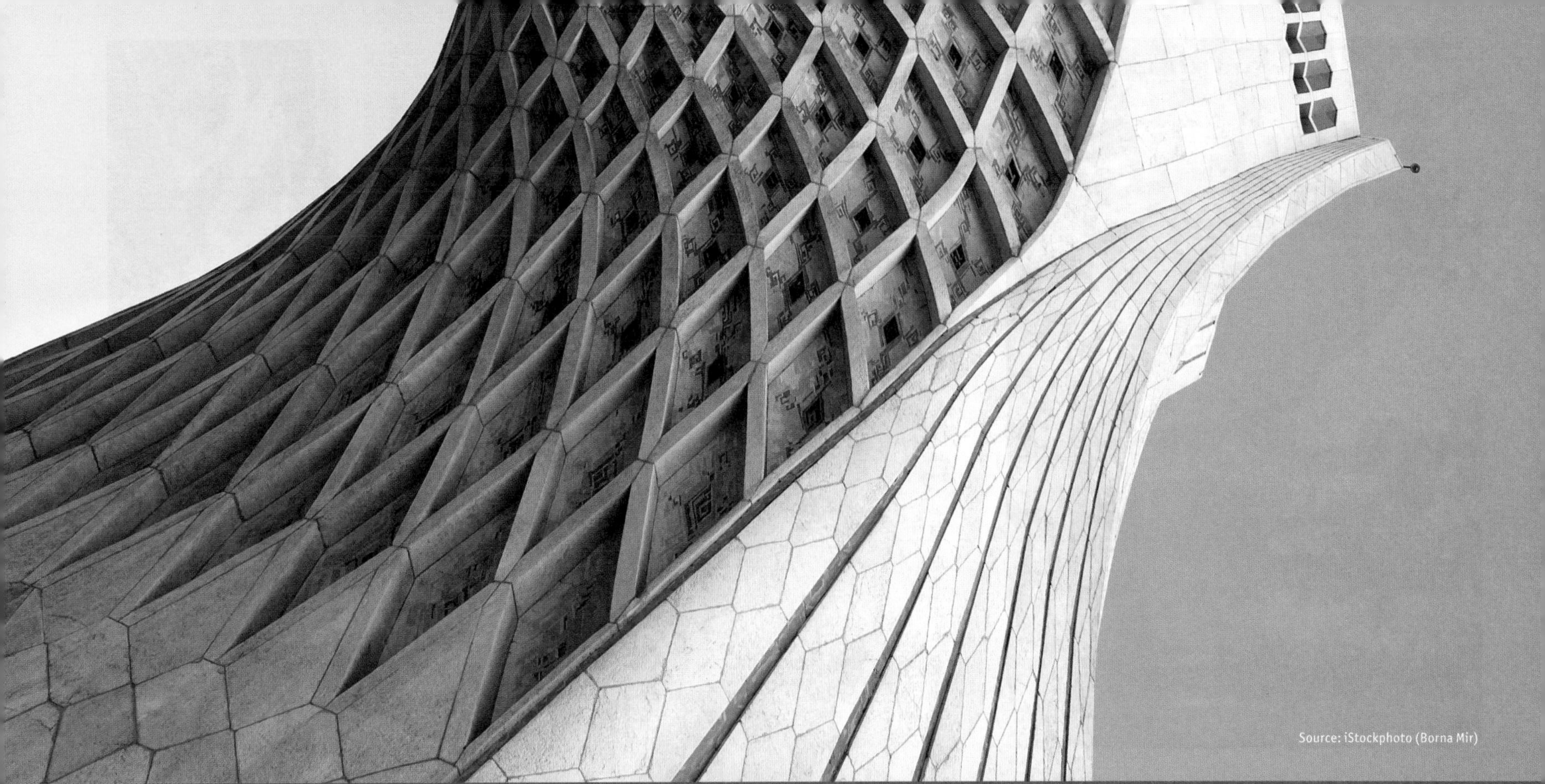

Source: iStockphoto (Borna Mir)

Exterior view of ICMS

Iran Centre for Management Studies (ICMS)
Daneshgah-e Emam Sadegh
دانشگاه امام صادق

Shahrak-e-Gharb, Tehran
35.76767, 51.38231
Mandala Collaborative
AD: 1972 / AH: 1392 / Yaz: 1342

The Centre for Management Studies was conceived by Mandala Collaborative, an architectural firm founded in Tehran by Nader Ardalan in 1972. The design is based on universal principles and specific Iranian references to building and nature. It was heavily influenced by the research Nader Ardalan and Laleh Bakhtiar conducted for their book *The Sense of Unity*, where the authors show Persian architecture as a synthesis of Persian thought and its design. They relate to the basic principle of Sufism, which understands reality as an image of a transcendental

source, finding its symbolic expression in human action, especially in its implementation as a work of art. The Centre for Management Studies is probably one of the best and most meaningful attempts to develop a modern Iranian national architecture. The general plan of the site is both formally and structurally evocative of a traditional madrasa. A Persian "open and secret" garden is defined by a courtyard and forms a rectangular, introverted, specific space, deliberately connecting architecture and domesticated nature. The library occupies the centre of the garden and its symbolic position at the intersection of both axes reminds the students that books contain more knowledge. The disposition of the remaining buildings, lecture halls, administration, service and living area, all arranged around the garden, is symbolic and functional at the same time. The administration and auditoriums are

Interior view of ICMS

Aerial view of ICMS

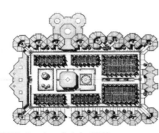

ICMS site plan sketch, 1972

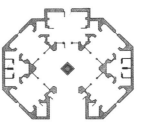

ICMS ground floor plan of the residential unit, 1972

attached to the short sides of the court-yard, the apartments and the dining room to the long sides. The residential units, each accommodating eight students, and four domed rooms with a common room are grouped around an open court-yard opening onto the garden. The build-ing complex, which is made of brick and concrete, harmoniously combines tradi-tional and modern construction meth-ods, thereby providing a stimulating new way to think about humanity and its rela-tionship to the environment.

Abbasabad
Abbas Abad
عباس آباد

Bozorgrah-e Modares, Tehran
35.75064, 51.42994
Louis Kahn
AD: 1974 / AH: 1394 / Yaz: 1344

At the end of 1973, Louis Kahn and Kenzo Tange were contacted regarding the plan-ning of Tehran's new government and administrative centre in the hilly area of Abbasabad. They were commissioned to develop a joint proposal. It is the last project Louis Kahn worked before his death. Kahn collaborated with Nader Ardalan as architect and local coordi-nator. The complex was to be placed on the fringed area south of the hills as one of the ten urban centres proposed in Tehran's Comprehensive Plan. The hilly terrain was left intact and the residential buildings were located along the high-way. The business centre is flanked on one side by sports facilities, the munici-pal administration building and the cul-tural and religious institutions such as university, art gallery, museum of science and mosque. The government offices are located on the other side of the avenue. Here Kahn created a "space of encounter with city and nature in line with the way of life". Residential quarters were planned on the surrounding hills. A rectangular urban square, lined by colonnades and a triangular surface with square blocks in checkerboard pattern, were the main ele-ments of the first proposal.

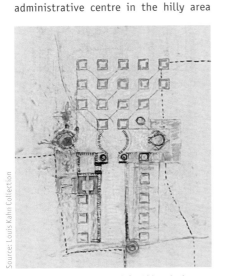

Louis Kahn, Site plan sketch for Abbasabad, Project 1974

Louis Kahn, Clay model for Abbasabad, Project 1974

Source: Thomas Meyer-Wieser

Façade detail of the theatre

Shahr Theatre
Teatr-e Shahr
تئاتر شهر

Khiyaban-e Valiasr/
Khiyaban-e Enghelab, Tehran
35.70008, 51.40562
Ali Sardar Afkhami
AD: 1973/AH: 1393/Yaz: 1343

This beautiful theatre is located in the centre of Tehran. Shahr Theatre was commissioned by Shahbanu Farah Diba in 1967. Ali Serdar Afkhami, an architect of the new Iranian school and student of Houshang Seyhoun, created a building that integrates Greek, Roman and traditional Persian elements such as the pillars of Persepolis, as well as modern elements. The plan and elevation of the theatre are inspired by the circle shaped Tugrul tower in Rey and its construction, an interesting combination of tile and bricks. Another important feature of the city theatre is the circular design. It is designed like a rotunda, modelled on the classic Greek and Roman theatres as well as on Iranian circular tent theatres like Takiyeh Dowlat. The main auditorium accommodates approximately 600 seats, the smaller hall 120. City Theatre is the only theatre in Iran which is not fenced. Thus, indoor spaces are open to areas near Vali Asr Street or Daneshjoo Park, both of which are also part of the building and play a role

in the theatre's audiences. The theatre was officially opened in the presence of Shah Mohammad Reza Pahlavi and Shahbanu Farah Diba on 27 January 1973. Performances at the Shahr Theatre were initially organised by the Office of the Shiraz Arts Festival, and later by the National Iranian Television (NITV). It is home to the only professional theatre company in Iran. The building is endangered; due to the construction of the Vali Asr Mosque on the south side of the theatre and the subway in the north, cracks have developed in the structure.

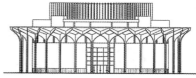

North elevation

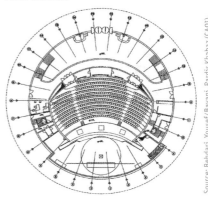

Source: Behdari, Yousef/Bavani, Pardis Khabaz (CAOI)

Ground floor plan

Source: Wikimedia Commons

In the stands of Azadi Stadium

Aryamehr Stadium, Azadi Stadium
Varzeshgah-e Aryamehr, Varzeshgah-e Azadi
ورزشگاه آزادی

275 F

Bulvar-e Azadi Stadium, Tehran
35.72444, 51.27555
Abdol Aziz Farmanfarmaian
AD: 1973/AH: 1393/Yaz: 1343

In 1973, Aryamehr Stadium was built by Abdol Aziz Farmanfarmaian and Associates as a football stadium with athletics track. It lies in west Tehran and was built for the 1974 Asian Games. Originally it was named Aryamehr Stadium, Light of the Aryans, in honour of Mohammad Reza Pahlavi; after the 1979 Islamic revolution it was renamed to Azadi (Freedom) Stadium. Since its opening it has been used for the games of the Iranian top teams FC Esteghlal and Persepolis. It is also the home stadium of the Iran national football team. The revolution of 1979 led to unprecedented investment in sports infrastructure for schools, universities, educational institutions and clubs, intending to uplift the country to international sport standards. The stadium, which can hold approximately 100,000 spectators, is the fourth largest stadium in the world and part of the Azadi sports complex. The stadium is also known for its amazing atmosphere at sold-out games. In the years 2002 and 2003, the stadium was extensively renovated. Among other improvements, the lawn was replaced, lawn heating was installed and new scoreboards were erected. If the Iranian bid for the 2019 AFC Asian Cup is successful, the final will take place here.

Seyhoun Summer Cottage
Khaneh-ye shaleh Seyhoun
خانه شاله سیحون

276 F

Kolokan, Oshan, near Tehran
35.81103, 51.50027
Houshang Seyhoun
AD: 1974/AH: 1394/Yaz: 1344

What makes Seyhoun's Summer Cottage different from all his domestic building designs is his organic approach and drawing on nature. The building is designed and built in harmony with the mountain. Much of this harmony shows itself in the living space. Some of the walls of the space are combined with the mountain rocks, emphasizing the feeling of nature and organic spaces for the observer. Certain similarities with the work of organic architecture, and especially the work of Frank Lloyd Wright, can be seen in this home design and its setting in nature. This harmony between human habitation and natural world can be achieved through design approaches so sympathetic and well integrated with a site so that buildings, furnishings, and surroundings become part of a unified, interrelated composition. Organic

Seyhoun Summer Cottage, in harmony with nature

architecture is also translated into the all inclusive nature of Houshang Seyhoun's design process. Materials, motifs and basic order principles continue to repeat themselves throughout the building as a whole. Organic architecture is essentially also the literal design of every element of the building from the windows to the floors, to the individual chairs intended to fill the space. Everything relates to one another, reflecting the symbiotic ordering systems of nature. Seyhoun noted that the design and construction details of the project were conceived on site as the work progressed.

Post and Telecommunications Office
Sakhteman-e Post va Telegraf va Telefon
ساختمان پست و تلگراف و تلفن

Maidan-e Imam Khomeini, Tehran
35.68500, 51.42167
Abdol Aziz Farmanfarmaian
AD: 1974 / AH: 1394 / Yaz: 1344

The post and telecommunications office was designed in the early 1970s by the Iranian architect Abdol Aziz Farmanfarmaian. It is characterised by a plastic-volumetric, design-oriented and coarse form in the "brutalist style – an architectural style that replaced international postwar modernism with a fundamentalist return to the materials of modernity and its

aesthetics of truthfulness. This architecture refers to the everyday role of architecture in people's lives, the everyday instead of high culture. Some angry architects took exception to the glass fronts. In the era of steel-wrought grid façades, they called for a new Stone Age. The post and telecommunications office forms a purely geometric body achieved by means of visible building materials, especially béton brut with its bumps and marks of the formwork. It evolved from the transformation of the heroic modernity of the 1960s and 1970s, to a new international tendency which strove for urbanity by density and moved away from the functional city with its separation of functions according to CIAM. In fact, the subsequent crisis of the late modernity is not insignificantly connected to the aesthetics of brutalism.

Street view of Post and Telecommunications Office

Model Detail of Shahrestan Pahlavi, 1975

Model of Shahrestan Pahlavi, 1975

Shahestan Pahlavi
Shahestan-e Pahlavi
شهستان پهلوی
Amir Abad, Tehran
35.75064, 51.42994
Llewelyn-Davies International
AD: 1975/AH: 1395/Yaz: 1345

In the mid-1970s, gigantic urban projects were developed with the help of foreign planners, such as Shahestan Pahlavi, Tehran's new town centre in the north on Abbas Abad Hill which, however, was not realised due to the 1979 Islamic revolution. In the words of Jacquelin Robertson, "Then my client lost his throne". The only remains of this mega-project are the Jahan-e Koodak two-storey Haghani highway which was designed as a transport axe, and the more than

200 m high television tower. The project was awarded to Llewelyn-Davies International, the British planners of Milton Keynes, in 1975 after a competitive international bidding process. Shahestan Pahlavi signaled the beginning of a new planning doctrine, namely the shift from the modernist, rational planning to the new urban design, which put more emphasis on the collective memory and traditional urban forms. The result is a project that is determined by the spatial outline around a central axis with a monumental space and lateral transport and green zones. The intent of the designers was that "it leaves options for future architects to implement their own ideas". Within a central axis with waterfalls and one of the largest squares in the world – larger than the Maidan-e

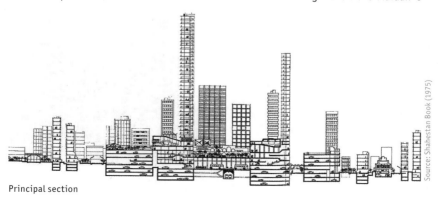

Principal section

Source: Shahestan Book (1975)

Concept of stair-garden in the main axis, 1975

Shah in Isfahan – a cultural district with museums, institutions for performing arts, libraries and subway connection, government offices were mixed with commercial buildings to ensure continuous day and night activity. Detailed sketches for road design and their greening make it clear that Shahestan Pahlavi was to be not only a "microcosm of the mega-city", but also a symbol of modern Tehran, of the emerging urban middle class and its powerful ruler, who would lead his country towards civilization. The whole city was connected with the name of the Shah: The Shahanshah-e highway runs through Shahestan Pahlavi, consisting of Shahanshah Boulevard and the Shahbanu Park. The Shah needed places to be reconciled with the middle class. Shahyad Aryamehr was the aesthetic presentation of Iran's history, Shahestan Pahlavi the symbol of the future, as were the dams and factories which were built all over the country by the Shah.

Source: Shahestan Book (1975)

Concept of Shahanshah Boulevard, 1975

Main entrance, ca. 1976

Courtyard, ca. 1977

Damavand College
Daneshkadeh-ye Damavand
کالج دماوند

Niavaran, Rah-e Lashgark, Tehran
35.80083, 51.50250
*Frank Lloyd Wright Associated
Architects: William Wesley Peters with
Nezam Ameri, Kamal Kamooneh,
Hormozdyar Khosravi*
AD: 1975/AH: 1395/Yaz: 1345

The Damavand College was a liberal arts college for women with an intercultural curriculum, respecting both Persian and western civilization. It was first used during the academic year 1975 – 1976 and was part of the White Revolution, a reform program comprising of six points to modernise and improve the social situation in Iran. The Pahlavi government asked the architect William Wesley Peters of Frank Lloyd Wright Associated Architects to design Damavand College on an 18 ha plot made available by the National Oil Company. The campus consists of a two-storey, U-shaped brick school building. Asymmetric, bastion-like structures form the main entrance and emphasise

the building corners. The central rotunda on the hill accommodates the school library and a cafeteria. The interiors are arranged around open atriums exposed to natural light, or "malls" as Frank Lloyd Wright called them. Wright had originally designed a golden roof. After his death, Olgivanna Wright decided on a bright blue colour "that would age well". The choice of colour along with the earth-coloured brick walls was controversial at first and the building was nicknamed "Big Pink". The only large gold element still existing is the top of the rotunda. The elongated main façade has small, non-structural arches on the outside, whilst the courtyard façade is structured horizontally. The Damavand College is very similar to the main building of the Marine County Civic Centre, north of San Francisco, also designed by Frank Lloyd Wright's son-in-law, William Wesley Peters. The construction is very American, but convinces through its time typical materialization referring to local context. The administration of Payame Noor University has occupied the building since 1988. It is currently difficult to visit the building.

Frances M. Grey in front of the college, ca. 1976

Aerial view of Damavand College, ca. 1976

Tochal Hotel, Dizin Ski Resort 280
Hotel Tochal Pist-e Eski-e Dizin
هتل توچال، پیست اسکی دیزین

Jadde-ye Telecabin, Tehran
35.81889, 51.40678
Marcel Breuer
AD: 1975/AH: 1395/Yaz: 1345

In 1975, after his successful design of the Flaine skiing area in the French Alps, Marcel Breuer was commissioned to make a concept study for a luxury hotel plan with a ski resort on the Valenjak plateau in the Alborz mountains. The position with a breathtaking view of Tehran resulted in a long, low building with an adjoining swimming pool and tennis courts, which, seen from the town, was largely hidden by the brow of the plateau.

Access was to be via a chairlift situated in the parking area at the foot of the mountain, taking visitors to a ski pavilion at the top of the mountain with an intermediate stop at the hotel. Breuer submitted a model, perspectives, schematic floor plans and sections. The project shows a massive base over a swimming pool, a series of protruding and recessed blocks with deeply-inserted balconies and a penthouse. The construction with exotic, so-called "oriental" curves frames a plaza for shops and similar amenities. The project in Breuer's late muscular style is inspired by the Whitney Museum of American Art and refers to similar European projects from the late 1920s, particularly Mies van der Rohe's building for the Weißenhofsiedlung in Stuttgart.

Marcel Breuer, perspective drawing

Model and perspective drawing of Tochal Hotel

Source: Archaeology of Iranian Modernism

Source: Claudia Luperto

Darband chair lift

Source: Claudia Luperto

Darband access road

Source: shahrak-ekbatan.ir

View of Ekbatan District

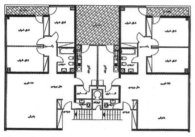

Floor plan of a flat apartment

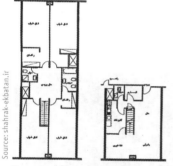

Source: shahrak-ekbatan.ir

Floor plan of a duplex apartment

Ekbatan District
Shahrak-e Ekbatan
شهرک اکباتان

281

Khiyaban-e Nafisi, Tehran
35.70753, 51.30851
Jordan Gruzen
AD: 1975 / AH: 1395 / Yaz: 1345

The original urban design concept of Gruen Associates' and Abdol Aziz Farmanfarmaian's master plan is more-or-less duplicated in Shahrak-e Ekbatan. The satellite city near Mehrabad Airport in west Tehran, with 15,500 residential units, is one of the largest housing estates in the Middle East. It was designed by Rahman Golzar and American architect Jordan Gruzen. Phase 1 of the town was successfully completed before the 1979 revolution by the American company Starrett. At the start, Ekbatan was the largest property development by a privately-held company in

Shahrak-e Ekbatan, aerial view

Source: Satyar Emami (Fars News Agency)

western Asia. The construction group was majority-owned by Rahman Golzar and his family. Following the 1979 revolution, the new government nationalized the group and all its subsidiaries and affiliates and placed its ownership with the ministry of housing, where it remains to this day. The housing development, with schools, kindergartens, shops, restaurants, mosques and health facilities, is a town in itself. The complex comprises thirty-three blocks, with buildings differing in height between five and fifteen floors. Looking at it from the sides, there are five floors on the first level, nine on the second and twelve on the third. The houses stand on short concrete stilts and their façades are articulated by window bands and balustrades. The site is composed of a double row of U-shaped apartment buildings, arranged on a central spine with a shopping centre, forming a wonderful combination of shopping centre and bazaar, selling anything from electronics to perfume and hundreds of handmade cheap tin cups. In the first and third building complex are spacious one-to four-room apartments with an area of between 50 and 240 m². In phase 2, blocks are designed like huge twelve-storey boxes put together at an angle. The second building complex consists mostly of duplex apartments, with hall and kitchen on the first and rooms on the second floor. The interiors are usually a mixture of Stardust and Louis XV. There are green fields between the blocks, gardens and swimming pools, which can no longer be used for swimming since the 1979 revolution. The landscape is designed in a way that combines nature and modern living. Ekbatan is also famous for its graffiti artworks and is the place of origin of artists such as A1one and Oham. On the last

Wednesday evening of the Iranian year, before Nowruz, the Chaharshanbeh-Sure festival is extensively celebrated here. Despite its immense scale, the modern, brutalist architecture of Shahrak-e Ekbatan forms the perfect backdrop to understand the West-Eastern hybrid for which the Pahlavi empire strove.

Habitat Tehran
Tehran Maskan
تهران مسکن

Elahiyeh, Tehran
35.78864, 51.42883
Moshe Safdie
AD: 1976 / AH: 1396 / Yaz: 1346

Due to his success at the World Exhibition in Montreal, the Canadian-Israeli architect Moshe Safdie, was invited by Shahbanou Farah Diba Pahlavi to design a so-called Habitat, with high density living for middle to upper income families and members of the court, to be built in a prestigious location. Safdie combined prefabricated building modules with traditional elements of Iranian architecture, particularly in the design of the atria and the light exposure of the apartments from sunrise to sunset. He planned more than 180 one- to three-bedroom apartments grouped into one building on a steep hill in Elahiyeh. The building offers excellent panoramic views over the city. Each apartment was directly accessible from green, public passages which extended over four levels and were occasionally broken up by public spaces and gardens. The occupants had access to a private rooftop garden, which could be converted into a winter garden, so that the space could be used all year round. The project was stopped in 1978 when it was still in the planning stages.

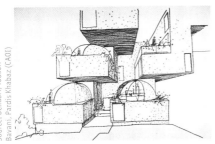

Moshe Safdie, façade of the Habitat in Tehran

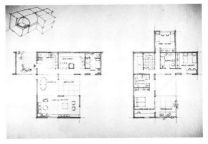

Moshe Safdie, Apartment Type C

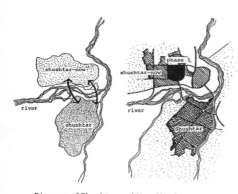

View of New Shushtar with the Old Town in the background

Source: The Aga Khan Award for Architecture (1977)

Diagram of Shushtar and New Shushtar

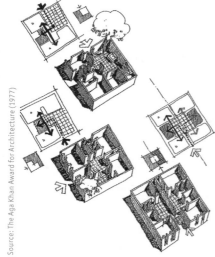

Source: The Aga Khan Award for Architecture (1977)

Concept and typology of Residential Buildings

New Shushtar
Shushtar No
شوشتر نو

Shushtar, Khuzestan
32.06083, 48.84472
*D.A.Z Architects, Planners, and
Engineers, Kamran Diba*
AD: 1976/AH: 1396/Yaz: 1346

283 A

Kamran Diba, together with D.A.Z. Architects and Planners, was commissioned by the Karoun Agro-Industries Corporation and the Iran Housing Corporation to create a new housing estate for 25,000 to 30,000 higher-level employees and industrial workers at the sugar factory in Shushtar. The topography and character of the historic city had a decisive influence on the planning process. The streets and outdoor spaces with their narrow alleys and courtyards respect the climatic conditions, retaining the coolness of night during the hot humid days, and with their dense fabric are reminiscent of a traditional Iranian town. It was very important to Diba to establish the needs of the residents: "I assumed that European planning could be hardly applied for workers' dwellings in Iran. The Iranian working class family cannot use a dwelling that is divided into living and bedrooms. If you know the way

Source: Adle Kamran

Building ensemble of New Shushtar

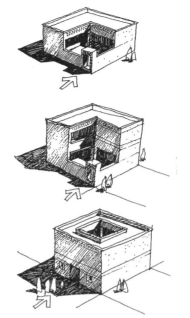

Source: The Aga Khan Award for Architecture (1977)

Concept of growth of the apartment

of the workers' life, you know that they live differently. They don't use any 'hard' furniture such as tables or beds, they use 'soft' furniture. At mealtimes their table-cloth is spread on the ground. The meal is eaten on the ground and afterwards the cloth is re-packed and stowed. They have mattresses to sleep on which are stowed away in daytime. It is clear that such occupants cope better with large multifunctional spaces". The western idea of the house as a unit of living, din-ing and sleeping areas was abandoned in Shushtar. The planners focused on the traditional Middle Eastern concept of living space as a flexible unit and pro-vided a large, re-usable, divisible and multifunctional space". They planned two- and three-room apartments which could be expanded to four-, five- or six-room apartments, depending on the liv-ing standard. Each unit is composed of two areas, the andaruni, the private sphere of the family and the biruni, the guest area, which are connected by the courtyard. Kamran Diba developed not only the plan but also the details along traditional lines. He used long, large walls, which cast shadows and cool the streets during the summer days, similar to the bazaar alleys. The individual apartments are only open to the outside through small,

unobtrusive windows. Detailing refers deliberately to domestic buildings, so that it is familiar to the inhabitants and still gives the impression that they live in a new home where they feel comfort-able. Due to their function as passages, the roads were designed as blind alleys to provide privacy and identity. Cars were parked at strategic points as far away as possible from the common areas. A continuous pedestrian axis forms an important road. All alleyways lead to it and neighbourhoods are designed to encourage movement along this spine, which consists of various courses, gar-dens, schools and bazaars. The contrast between the narrow, treeless neighbour-hood streets and the main axis is obvi-ous. It is also practical. The maintenance of trees and plants along residential streets would have been too expensive for Shushtar. Although the New Town was originally planned for a single com-pany, the housing estate was able to inte-grate different income groups. In order to avoid the character of a "company town", the houses were also offered on the open market and the image of social housing was avoided via the growth concept of individual apartments. Shushtar No sus-tainably shaped the Iranian architecture and urban development debate.

Exterior of the museum

Interior of Carpet Museum

Carpet Museum of Iran
Muzeh-ye Farsh-e Iran
موزه فرش ایران

Khiyaban-e Dr. Fatemi, Tehran
35.71417, 51.39089
Abdol Aziz Farmanfarmaian
AD: 1978/AH: 1398/Yaz: 1348

This architectonically rather uninspiring museum was opened in 1978. The conception, the collection and the design of the museum goes back to Shahbanu Farah Diba, who studied architecture in Paris. Abdol Aziz Farmanfarmaian was charged with the realisation of the construction. The perforated structure around the museum's exterior is designed to resemble a carpet loom and to cast shade on the exterior walls, reducing the impact of the hot summer sun on the interior temperature. Dr. Friedrich Spühler, former director of the Museum of Islamic Art in Berlin and consultant to the Farah Diba Foundation in Tehran, collaborated in the construction of the Carpet Museum. The exhibition space consists of two large halls at ground and upper floor level for handmade carpets and woven kilims. There are over 200 outstanding carpets in the museum, masterpieces of the main centres such as Kashan, Kerman, Isfahan, Tabriz, Khorasan and Kurdistan. One of the oldest and most important is the Sangeshku rug from the Safavid era. On display are the two main types of carpet, nomad and city carpets. Nomad rugs are made of medium to coarse cotton or wool and tend to have a geometric pattern with little detail. Since they are often knotted under rather primitive conditions they are not perfectly symmetrical and often show colour variations that give them a wonderful depth. The city rugs are made in urban workshops throughout Iran from fine wool or silk. They contain up to 160 knots per cm^2 and generally follow regional templates so that their origin can be traced. Even excellent carpets have intentional faults, because only God is perfect. The library affiliated to the museum contains precious books on Persian carpets. A tea shop at the corner of the museum recalls ancient and traditional Iranian tea houses.

Carpet Museum within Laleh-Park

Tomb of Arthur Upham Pope and Phyllis Ackerman

Tomb of Arthur Upham Pope and Phyllis Ackerman

285

Aramga-e Arthur Pope et Phyllis Ackerman

آرامگاه آرتور پوپ و فیلیس اکرمن

Moshtagh St., Isfahan

32.63818, 51.68476

Mohsen Foroughi

AD: 1977 / AH: 1392 / Yaz: 1342

Arthur Upham Pope and his wife Phyllis Ackerman devoted most of their professional lives to the research and publication of Iranian art, architecture, and archeology. Soon after their death, the Society for National Heritage, under the auspices of the Ministry of Culture and Art of Iran, built a joint mausoleum for them. A mirror to their philosophy, the tomb structure was the Society for National Heritage's last major project erected before the fall of the Pahlavi royal dynasty in the 1979 revolution. Mohsen Foroughi worked with Pope on the design. The sketches were approved by Pope in June 1969 and the funeral was held in September of the same year. Formally intended as a revival of the twelfth-century style that he liked, the structure's typology seems to imitate the mausoleum of Ismail the Samanid in

Bukhara. The building's façade is covered in intricately-decorated brick work that features circular patterns reminiscent of the sun. The syncretic style of the shrine is reflective of the ninth and tenth centuries – a time when the region still had large populations of Zoroastrians who had begun to convert to Islam. The two American art historians, who influenced the discourse on Iranian architecture during their lives, became a physical part of the Iranian landscape after their death. Along with medieval historic figures like poets Ferdowsi, Hafez, and Sa'adi, the two American scholars were thus naturalised into the Iranian land as part of its eternal heritage.

Mausoleum of Ismail the Samanid, Bukhara, Uzbekistan, 914-943

Source: Claudia Luperto

Source: Caroline Reichmann

Cultural Centre within Niaveran Garden

Auditorium of the cultural centre

Niaveran Cultural Centre
Farhangsaray-e Niavaran
فرهنگسرای نیاوران

Maidan-e Niavaran, Tehran
35.80814, 51.46922
Kamran Diba
AD: 1978/AH: 1398/Yaz: 1348

From the peaks of the Alborz Mountain, innumerable small rivers flow, irrigating the land and providing the basis for the livelihood of the residents at the foot of the mountain. Many wealthy townsmen established their gardens and summer homes here, irrigated via qanats. The garden of Niarevan served as a sanatorium. Like many of the old walled Persian gardens, the garden was threatened by the the encrouching town and rising land prices. Abandoned and neglected, it was acquired by Shahbanu Farah Diba who wished it to be maintained and used. She had it redesigned by Kamran Diba as a cultural centre and a public park. Kamran Diba retained the existing central axis of the garden, with its water channels and cascades, and clad the open parts of qanats with blue tiles to enhance the symbolic and visual impact of the water supply with

a contemporary design. The qanat supplies water for several mirror pools which run through a tunnel of old plane trees and lead to the cultural centre. The vast space included the secretariat of Farah Diba, who was then the president of twenty four charities and educational institutions, as well as a cultural centre. After revising the program, Kamran Diba suggested accommodating a section of the complex, consisting of the auditorium, gallery, staff restaurant and library, in a separate building open to the public, whilst the royal secretariat would be accommodated in a separate building. By dividing the complex, the concentration of large structural dimensions could be avoided, which meant that fewer trees had to be felled, since the buildings could be erected on the site of the ruined buildings. The cultural centre is located right next to the central axis of the park; two other wings, consisting of stores and a restaurant, enclose a slightly lowered square on three sides, connected to the main axis by a bridge and an open gate. The three elements, water, gate and bridge, form a kind of boundary and convey a sense of interior and exterior, of arrival and departure.

Source: Claudia Luperto

Water channels and cascades in the central axis of Niavaran Garden

Source: Kamran Diba

Axonometric projection of the garden

View from Milad Tower to Shahrak-e Gharb

Shahrak-e Gharb in front of Alborz mountains

West Town, West-Jerusalem
Shahrak-e Gharb,
Shahrak-e Qods

شهرک غرب

Shahrak-e Gharb, Tehran
35.75000, 51.36667
Jordan Gruzen Architects et al.
AD: 1978/AH: 1398/Yaz: 1348

The complex was planned in 1978 by Jordan Gruzen Architects but built by an American company, Starrett. Construction of the Golestan Shopping Centre began a few years after the Iran–Iraq war. The tallest tower of Iran, Milad Tower is located just outside the district. The imposing high rise buildings of Shahrak-e Gharb, the West City, also known Shahrak-e Qods, or Jerusalem, are located in a neighbourhood based on the model of upscale American suburbs with multi-family houses and villas. Around the 1980s, there was only one central shopping centre there, named bazarce, or mini-bazaar. Due to the proximity to shopping centres such as the Golestan, which was opened a few years after the end of the Iran–Iraq war, or the Iranzamin, the Milad-Noor and others, the neighbourhood is now a good address for wealthy bourgeois, diplomats and expats. It is one of the largest districts of Tehran and has easy access to expressways like Chamran Expressway, Hemmat Expressway, Niayesh Expressway, Sheikh Fazl-allah Nouri Expressway, and Yadegar-e-Emam Expressway. Because of the eastward current of the air in Tehran and its constant purification by the adjacent mountains, the air in this town is less polluted than other northern parts of the city.

Secretariat of Farah Diba
Sakteman-e Daftar-e Farah Diba
ساختمان دفتری فرح دیبا

Maidan-e Niavaran, Tehran
35.80992, 51.46997
Kamran Diba
AD: 1978/AH: 1398/Yaz: 1348

The secretariat of Shahbanu Farah Diba, located in the Niaveran Garden, was also built by Kamran Diba between 1970 and 1978. By setting it on different levels and constructing inconspicuous retaining walls, the desired privacy could be ensured. The entrance of the secretariat consists of a spacious central hall illuminated through the roof with indirect sunlight. The floor plan consists of two interlocking, L-shaped structures enclosing the central hall and designed as a split level. The offices have transparent divisions, and open on all sides to the garden. The sense of openness is intensified by levels staggered by half a floor and connected by landings. This allows views through the floors and an open office space that avoids the formal atmosphere of a royal court. The stairs, emphasizing the L-shaped split-levels, are visually connected with the garden by marble slots. Mirrored office doors create a mysterious transparency and irritate by reflecting light and images from the garden.

Secretariat building within Niaveran Garden

View of the spacious complex

Tehran Museum of Contemporary Art
Muzeh-ye Honarha-ye Moaser
موزه هنرهای معاصر تهران

Khiyaban-e Dr. Fatemi, Tehran
35.71128, 51.39053
Kamran Diba, Nader Ardalan,
Anthony John Major
AD: 1979 / AH: 1399 / Yaz: 1349

289 G

Courtyard of the museum

In the 1960s and 1970s, there was grow-ing interest in contemporary stage and visual arts by the Iranian middle classes. Thus the Tehran Museum of Contemporary Art was established on the east side of Laleh Park. It is the most important museum of contemporary art in Iran and also housed the largest collection of contemporary art outside Europe and the United States until the Islamic rev-olution. Western and Iranian critics thought it was irrelevant to collect or exhibit modern or contemporary art in Iran. But how relevant did it seem to them that Europeans, at great cost and effort, assembled so much Eastern art in their museums? The museum was designed in the mid-1970s at the initiative of Shahbanu Farah Diba by Kamran Diba, together with Nader Ardalan and Anthony John Major, and formally opened in 1979. The architecture of the large building is characterised by an ingenious plan which combines traditional elements of Iranian desert regions, such as wind towers, with modern architectural ele-ments. The organisation of the physical concept consists of two major elements. Firstly, there is the entrance hall which accommodates all support facilities such

Ground floor plan

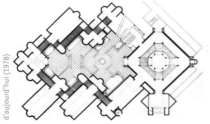

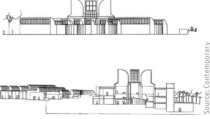

Section and elevation

as bookshop, snackbar, library, offices, lecture hall, cinematheque and storage. Secondly, there is an open courtyard surrounded by a chain of interconnected and articulated galleries. Divided into large and small exhibition spaces, each accommodate large paintings, a single painting, and small paintings and drawings, respectively. In contrast to the modest outer scale, a spacious entrance hall connects the street level with the exhibition space. The galleries are organised along a circular walkway around the inner outdoor sculpture court. As the galleries along the large circulation ramp move downward, the roof of the last gallery meets the entrance level. The snack-bar and outdoor seating area placed on top of it become part of the courtyard, allowing a view of the greenery of Laleh Park. After completing a tour of the building, visitors discover the rare opportunity to experience the galleries from floor to rooftop. The architect creates a rhythm in this promenade through the alternation of static and dynamic spaces, whereby the latter serve as connecting rooms. The contrast between these rooms is enhanced by the lighting: the galleries are illuminated by skylights whereas the passage spaces have side windows directed to the sculpture garden. The last gallery finally ends at the entrance level and opens the roof of the galleries for outdoor use, so that a visitor, after completion of the circular tour, has wandered through the building from bottom to top and experienced the playful quality of the undulating roof landscape as it exists in a traditional desert town. The building is surrounded by a walled sculpture garden, which is placed in a landscaped garden and displays works by famous modern artists such as Henry Moore, Alberto Giacometti and Parviz Tanavoli.

Site plan of Pardisan Park

Pardisan Park
Park-e Jangali-ye Shahrak-e Gharb
پارک جنگلی شهرک غرب

290

Bozorgrah-e Yadegar-e Imam, Tehran
35.74983, 51.34400
Nader Ardalan,
Wallace McHarg Roberts & Todd
AD: 1979 / AH: 1399 / Yaz: 1349

Shahestan Pahlavi's superficiality and grandeur is also evident in other projects of the 1970s. Another grandiose project is the ecology park, Pardisan, to the west of Abbasabad. "Only One Earth" was the motto of the UN World Conference on the Human Environment of the United Nations in 1972 in Stockholm. It was the first UN conference on the environment in general, and also the first time that government officials from industrial and developing countries came together to discuss the effects of increasing environmental degradation and to find common solutions. The right of countries to exploit their own resources within their own territories was confronted by the obligation to ensure that no damage is caused to other countries by these activities. In direct response to the conference, Iran's Department of Environment planned an immense landscape park as an impressive feature of the new Tehran. The park was designed by American ecologist Wallace McHarg, Iranian architect Nader Ardalan and American landscape architecture firm Roberts & Todd – a multifunctional environmental park, a paradise in the desert at the foot of Alborz mountains. The park covers an area of about 300 ha and primarily serves environmental research and educational purposes, with the aim to raise the visitors' awareness of the environment in an entertaining way. The park contains a museum of biodiversity, a museum of wild animals, a theatre, several playgrounds and some other facilities. Pardisan reflects the American gigantism of the planning by Gruen Associates. The idea to create a city of world history around an artificial recreational landscape is similar to Walt Disney's plans for the Epcot theme park in the Disneyworld resort.

12–16 October 1971
2500 – Year Celebration of the Persian Empire

Jashnha-ye 2500 Saleh-ye
Shahanshah-ye Iran
جشنهای ۲۵۰۰ ساله شاهنشاهی ایران

The idea to showcase Iran's brilliant past to the world was not new. The specific occasion presented itself with the celebration of the 2,500th anniversary of the Persian Empire, founded by Cyrus the Great in the sixth century. Domestically, the signs were favourable. The White Revolution reaped its first fruits, the land reform expanded, women's liberation progressed, higher living standards and industrialisation changed the country dramatically, and internationally the state appeared as a western ally, which had an important safety function in the Middle East. It was perfect for Reza Shah Pahlavi's imperial dreams of making Iran the fifth most powerful nation in the world within one generation. Maison Janson from Paris, who specialised in interior decoration for festive occasions and had even rearranged US President John F. Kennedy's Oval Office, suggested erecting a tent city for this celebration in the middle of the Iranian desert, inspired by the royal camp built by François I in 1520 to impress Henry VIII of England. A few months later the model favoured by the Shah and Shahbanou was presented. The contract was signed and the production of the royal tent commenced. Originally, only thirty heads of state were invited, but when the invitations were sent out, sixty-four accepted with their entourages, and everybody was to be accommodated in blue-yellow tents which were actually small apartment houses, made of plastic, consisting of a living room, two bedrooms, two bathrooms and a dressing room. The invitations included monarchs, crown princes, presidents, sheikhs and sultans, selected prime ministers, ambassadors, businessmen and celebrities of the jet set. Finally, more than sixty-nine heads of state and their representatives arrived at the fairytale town. In a patchwork of colours, swirls of salutes, bows and curtseys, the familiar faces stepped off their shiny planes into the Persian light on red carpets. Day and night, escorted motorcades drove from the airport to the imaginary birthplace of this Persian empire, where guests found a camp growing like a star from the Royal Pavilion and accommodating the five continents. The official start of the celebrations was set for 12 October 1971 in Pasargadae, at the grave of Cyrus the Great. The short speech by Mohammad Reza Shah was broadcast live on television and ended with the words: "O Cyrus, Great King, King of Kings, Achaemenian King, King of the land of Iran. I, the Shahanshah of Iran, offer thee salutations from myself and from my nation. Rest in peace, for we are awake, and we will always stay awake." At the spectacular banquet, a meal for one hundred people was flown in from Maxim's of Paris and 5,000 bottles of champagne were popped by international luminaries like the Duke of Edinburgh, Princess Anne, King Haile Selassie of Ethiopia and the former Romanian dictator Nicolae Ceausescu. The next day another event of superlatives followed, namely one of the largest parades ever taking place in the 2,500 year history of the country. It had been conceived by General Fathollah Minbaschian and Minister Mehrdad Pahlbod. After sunset a thirty-minute light show began against the backdrop of the Persepolis ruins. Fireworks concluded the festivities. "This was not the party of the year, this was the feast of twenty-five centuries," said Orson Wells, who was invited to document the celebration in the film *Flames of Persia*. "All Persia participates in the parade", Wells said in a deep voice in the background, and 4,000 actors mimed the story of the country.

This was followed by the blares of hundreds of drummers and trumpeters to reawaken Cyrus and to encourage Darius to stride down the stairs. With the help of his Iranian producer, the film allowed Wells to realise his last and most ambitious film projects, namely *F for Fake* and *The Other Side of the Wind*. During the celebrations, the western press reported enthusiastically about the great event. But after a few days, the tide turned. It began with Khomeini's critical remarks. He described the party as anti-Islamic and declared the participants in the celebration to be enemies of Islam. The criminal system of the Shah had robbed the people of Iran in order to finance his decadent debauchery. *Time* magazine estimated the cost of the celebrations at USD 100,000,000. The French press already talked about USD 200,000,000. In the end, the costs were apparently close to USD 300,000,000. Abd ol-Reza Ansari, who was responsible for the technical organisation of the celebrations, summarised the events in an interview as follows: "In the 1950s, Iran was considered an underdeveloped country. In the 1960s, it was promoted to a developing nation and by the 1970s, it was seen by many guests of the state who came to Persepolis as a country with a rich history which was on the way to becoming a fully-developed industrial nation." For the Shah, Persepolis was an opportunity to show the world that Iran had gained political importance. Many sustainable investments in the infrastructure of the country (road construction, telecommunication networks, schools, airports, television stations, hotels and tourist facilities) were done prior to the festivities. The tent city was completely intact until 1978 and was occasionally used for receptions. Plans to turn it into a luxury hotel did not materialise. During the Islamic revolution the apartments were plundered, in 1982 the former tent city became a military camp, and during the Iran–Iraq war the tents became dormitories for soldiers. Today only the skeletons of the tent coverings are still standing, and the once exquisitely-landscaped gardens are overgrown with weeds.

Parade 03 for 2500 years Celebration of Monarchy

The Persepolis Celebrations, 1971

Tent City in the Iranian Desert

The Islamic Republic of Iran

1978–2000
The Architecture of the Iranian Revolution

Only a few Iranians benefitted from the oil wealth and the economic boom of the country. Furthermore the Shah had prevented any democratic participation and expression of free speech, so even western-minded Iranians turned against him. His failure is the failure of an autocrat who sought to improve the material well-being of people but denied them the democratic rights of the modern world. Religious opposition remained the only possible form of resistance in Iran. The fall of the Shah was inevitable. On 16 January 1979, Mohammed Reza Shah had to leave the country in great haste. When his departure was announced, a tremendous folk festival broke out in Iran. The monuments of the Shah and his father were torn from their pedestals. The rapid collapse of the powerful monarchic regime gave the impression that with a revolution, everything could be changed in a very short time. The fight for a spring of freedom, however, would not last long because the Islamists were organising themselves much faster and more efficiently. They had their institutions, their intellectuals and not least their revolutionary leader, who had

already prepared, theoretically and theologically, the establishment of an Islamic state. The Islamic Republic redefines both the relationship between state and religion and foreign policy relations between Iran and the West. The criticism against the Shah's regime of westernization led to drastic measures in the young republic, such as the expropriation of persons and companies close to old regime. The cultural revolution against universities, which were considered "hotbeds of the disease of westernization", was also a result of this situation. Many professionals fell victim to the broad-based purge of 1980. All universities in the country were initially closed indefinitely. The consequence was the emigration of the elite into exile. As part of this exodus between 1979 and 1980, tens of thousands of Iranians from all sectors of business, science and technology left the country. The institutionalization of the Islamists and the spread of their influence on the armed forces and administrative institutions was accompanied by executions and arrests, a massacre that made even Mohammed Reza Shah, despite his crimes, appear to any independent observer to be an enlightened world citizen. On 22 September 1980, the Iraqi army crossed the Iranian border. Some of the longest and bloodiest static warfare in modern history began. It was not a war between two small poor countries in a strategically-insignificant world region. In the Persian Gulf, two potential regional hegemonic powers that had become emerging nations with the help of oil revenues and state-imposed

Source: Thomas Meyer-Wieser

Development of Tehran ca. 2006

modernisation measures, were at war. The Persian Gulf itself represented a zone of rivalry between the superpowers US and USSR, who repeatedly gave peace researchers occasion to conjure up scenarios of the outbreak of World War III. The beginning of 1981 was not only marked by the Iran–Iraq war, but also a number of internal power struggles and conflicts. It was not until the 1990s that reconstruction became important again.

Development of Tehran ca. 2006

The 1979 Iranian revolution was a cultural revolution. The universities were closed, and the professors and architects of the Golden Age left the country. A generation of architects grew up who could no longer rely on the models of the Golden Age. The political and social upheavals of 1979 led to a break between the architecture before and after the Islamic revolution. Social, cultural, national and religious ideals were reconsidered and the notion to create an Islamic identity became the dominant idea. In addition, the Iranian revolution with its "back to the roots" philosophy produced, parallel to the architectural postmodern trend of the early 1980s, an architecture of memory, which did not see tradition as something that had to be overcome, but regarded it as a collection of possibilities to be used. The return to historical models and roots thus became the leading idea. For longer than a decade, style elements of the past had been used in Iranian architecture without necessarily fulfilling a functional purpose. During

Ayatollah Khomeini

Source: Claudia Luperto

the 1980s and 1990s, the rejuvenation of Islamic culture took centre stage. The use of materials such as masonry and tiles as well as ornamental elements was part of an effort to give buildings an Islamic expression. The shrine of Imam Khomeini, the construction of the Hajj organisation and the Sharif university mosque in Tehran are examples of this time. The war with Iraq took eight long years, and the task of rebuilding the country as fast as possible left no time for fundamentally new ideas, especially not in architecture. Later, when the real estate business gained a foothold again and it was important to find a style for the new bourgeoisie, a few new architectural trends developed. Most widespread were a style called rumi, with a slightly coarse neoclassical approach, and sonnati, a style that drew on regional traditions.

Source: Kamyar Adl

Tejerat Bank Building

Tejerat Bank
Bank Tejerat
بانك تجارت

Khiyaban-e Nejatollah, Tehran
35.70697, 51.41511
Ramin Farshchian
AD: 1979/AH: 1399/Yaz: 1348

The building is characterised by large, light glass surfaces. The construction began before the revolution and was completed in 1979. After the revolution, the government nationalized the domestic private banks and insurance companies, and the banking system was changed to favour the new interest-free Islamic banking regulations. The prohibition of interest is of particular importance. In the broader sense, one should not earn money with money. Instead of granting the buyer a credit, the bank buys the goods directly from the vendor and sells them at a higher price to the buyer, who pays for his purchase in instalments. A typical example is the sale of fish. When fisherman and buyer agree to sell a future catch at a pre-agreed price, the buyer pays for the working time. Risk and reward are shared, although the amount is not fixed. Interest is not paid. The bank however has the option to make a gift. Since it is up to the bank to make a gift, it may be that the money paid in is strictly kept for no reward, but this never happens in practice. The bank may never make a firm commitment on such gifts, as this would be similar to an interest payment. Credit cards do not meet Islamic economic principles, because they mislead people into borrowing at exorbitant prices. Still, credit cards are accepted if some conditions are observed. Cash advance is prohibited, as this corresponds to a credit. Interest payments, whether on credit or not, and late payment of credit card accounts, are prohibited. The credit card holder may use the card only for permitted purchases, for instance a piece of furniture, but not to purchase alcohol.

Varzidekar House
Khaneh-ye Varzidekar
خانه ورزیدکار

unknown
David Oshana
AD: ca. 1980/AH: ca. 1400/Yaz: ca. 1350

The construction began before the revolution and was completed in the 1980s. In designing of Varzidekar house, David Oshana questioned modernity. He developed a mix between classic Iranian architecture and an emerging modernity, which he applied in a syntax going back to Richard Neutra. Iranian architecture elements are translated and compiled into a compact composition of a beautifully regionalist building, perceived at first glance as Iranian. David Oshana took up the flat, stylized, bifurcated leaf tendril, which is so typical of Iranian art, to fill the fields of parapets in an even, vibrating movement. He developed a building that is intentionally traditional and represents the legacy of the golden age of Iranian modernity.

Garden façade of Varzidekar House

Façade detail of Varzidekar House

Source: Behdari, Yousef/ Bavani, Pardis Khabaz (CAOI)

Courtyard of the Institute with reflecting pool

Interior corridor of Management Institute

Management Institute
Moasese-ye Modirat
موسسه مدیریت

Amir Abad, Tehran
35.72331, 51.38178
Hossein Amanat
AD: 1980/AH: 1400/Yaz: 1350

The growth of Iran's industry and international trade in the 1970s prompted Tehran University to establish a faculty of Business Management. Hossein Amanat's building consists of four distinct functional blocks which feature the student union, undergraduate studies, postgraduate studies, a library, auditoriums and small classrooms. The major hub of activity is a central hayat, a quadrangle courtyard inspired by examples of traditional colleges throughout the Middle East. The undergraduate classes, administrative offices and student union surround this hayat, which has a reflective pool at the centre. The two smaller square hayats, accessed diagonally from the corners of the main hayat, house the library and postgraduate department. The layout of the building and the hayats follow the rhythm, geometry, and order of Perso-Islamic architecture. Portals hyphenate the walls, with the main entry portal to the east and another to the south, which provides a transparent connection to an open space for possible future expansion. Addressing ecological concerns, the building faces south and the walls were shaped to shade the windows and protect them from direct sunlight. Natural lighting has been enhanced through skylights, which allow light to enter and keep out the heat.

Buff-coloured brick and reinforced concrete, all local materials, were used to withstand seismic forces and provide the necessary thermal insulation.

Ibrahim Mosque
Masjed-e Ibrahim
مسجد ابراهیم

International Permanent Fairground, Tehran
35.79000, 51.40194
unknown
AD: ca. 1980/AH: ca. 1400/Yaz: ca. 1349

The Ibrahim mosque was built shortly after the 1979 Islamic revolution and named after Abraham. It stands directly next to the fairgrounds and provides a place of worship for visitors. The cube-shaped prayer hall is based on early Islamic forms, whilst the minaret, which is designed as Ziggurat, refers rather to pre-Islamic elements.

Street view of Ibrahim Mosque

Mausoleum of Poets in Sorkhab district of Tabriz

Mausoleum of Poets
Maqhbarat o-Shoara
مقبرةالشعراء

Shahriyar St., Tabriz
38.08364, 46.30356
Gholam Reza Farzanmehr
AD: 1982/AH: 1403/Yaz: 1351

According to experts, Maqhbarat o-shoara' is more than a cemetery and can be considered a literary complex. The building is dedicated to poets, mystics and famous people and is located in the Surkhab district of Tabriz. Some 400 poets, mystics and luminaries from Iran and the region were laid to rest here. The mausoleum was first mentioned by the medieval historian Hamdollah Mostowfi in his Nozhat ol-Gholub. Since the 1970s, there have been attempts to renovate the graveyard area, like the construction of a new symbolic building on the site which was started by Tahmaseb Dolatshahi whilst he was Secretary of Arts and Cultures of East Azerbaijan.

The mausoleum is located in the centre of the complex at a height of 30 m. Gholamreza Farzanmehr, the designer of Maqhbarat o-shoara', said the design was selected from a 1970 competition. Construction operations started in 1972 and were completed in 1982. The design was based on both traditional and modern architecture. Farzanmehr called Maqhbarat-o-shoara' a spiritual and literary resort for intellectuals and educated people. Meanwhile, Tabriz Mayor Sadeq Najafi has said that beautification plans are currently underway.

Self-Service at the Medical School Yazd
Selfservice Olum Pezeshki-e Yazd
ساختمان سلف سرویس علوم پزشکی یزد

Daneshgah, Yazd
31.83417, 54.35583
Mohammad Reza Ghanei
AD: 1984/AH: 1404/Yaz: 1353

The significance of postmodernism in the early days after the revolution shows in the early work of Mohamad Reza Ganehi. He studied architecture in France and founded the architecture firm Polsheer, a firm which tries to implement contemporary Iranian architecture without being influenced by the currents of western architecture. His early buildings show what the new state understood as the

Mausoleum of Poets, aerial view

Source: Contemporary Architecture of Iran

Front and rear view of the Holy Cross Chapel by Rostom Voskanian

rejuvenation of Islamic culture. The project for the university self-service cafeteria for the medical school of Yazd shows great similarity with Safavid monumental buildings. The columns and the cantilevered roof of the refectory refer to the Forty Columns Palace in Isfahan, which the architect externally absorbed but – following Venturi's theory – furnished with a very modern interior core.

Holy Cross Chapel
Salib Moqaddas Japel
عبادتگاه صلیب مقدس

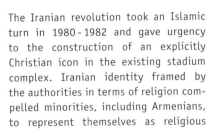

Madoor, Vanak, Tehran
35.76681, 51.40164
Rostom Voskanian
AD: 1987/AH: 1407/Yaz: 1356

The Iranian revolution took an Islamic turn in 1980-1982 and gave urgency to the construction of an explicitly Christian icon in the existing stadium complex. Iranian identity framed by the authorities in terms of religion compelled minorities, including Armenians, to represent themselves as religious minorities. The Holy Cross Chapel was built in the southeast corner of Ararat Stadium complex in 1987. It shows the need – shortly after the Iranian revolution – to manifest religious tolerance and Iranian identity by displaying Christian symbols. Voskanian's scheme was a masterpiece of modern Armenian architecture, a reinterpretation in poured concrete of the best examples of medieval Armenian churches, transformed into an interwoven system of supports, openings and suspensions. Whilst remaining true to the symmetrical and central floor plan of domed architecture of medieval Armenian churches, for instance that of Saint Hripsimeh in Ejmiatsin, Voskanian carves out a novel form that boldly incarnates the elevation and section of traditional churches into an allegorical representation of the Christian cross: simultaneously ancient and avant-garde. An architecture of sculpture or a sculpted architecture, the chapel stands as the most powerful symbol of the endurance of Armenian identity as both ancient and contemporary.

Source: Polsheer Architects Planers Engeneers

Mensa at Medical School in Yazd, reminiscent of the Forty Columns Palace in Isfahan

Street view of Al-Ghadir Mosque

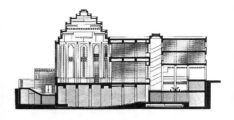

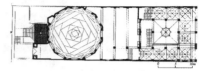

Floor plan and section of Al-Ghadir Mosque

Al-Ghadir Mosque
Masjed-e Al-Ghadir
مسجد الغدیر

Bulvar-e Mirdamad, Tehran
35.75481, 51.48908
Jahanguir Mazlum
AD: 1987 / AH: 1407 / Yaz: 1346

Although it is a small building with dimensions of 15 × 25 m, Al-Ghadir mosque is architectonically important. It was built by the architect Jahanguir Mazlum between 1977 and 1987 and includes a prayer hall, a library and offices for charities. The height and form of the prayer hall forms a scaled-down connection to the public buildings on Mirdamad Boulevard, whilst the meeting room connects to the two- to four-storey high residential units behind the mosque. In addition, the materials are chosen so that the building stands out from the urban environment. The inside of the mosque is

a good example of the post-revolutionary tension between continuity and transformation. The alignment of the interior to the qibla meant that the visitor perceives the mosque as an independent space. The building employs neither the four-ayvan arrangement nor dome and minaret. Instead, Malzum crowned a dodecagonal prayer hall with a series of stacked and rotated squares which grow successively smaller with each level, creating the impression of a prismatic facetted dome, whereby light seeps downward through each triangular opening. Although the ceiling mosaic and decorative stone borders with their glazed blue tiles and Arabic script are traditionally found in Iranian buildings, they have a distinctly modern appearance when juxtaposed with yellow brickwork. The rising squares form an attractive perspective, especially when they are seen from the outside,

Interior of Al-Ghadir Mosque

Imam Khomeini Residential District
Shahrak-e Emam Khomeini
شهرک امام خمینی

Bulvar-e Al-Ghadir, Tehran
35.65672, 51.31175
unknown
AD: 1989 / AH: 1409 / Yaz: 1358

In the decades after the revolution, social housing complexes were built for underprivileged population groups, such as in Shahrak-e-Emam Khomeyni. Two issues shaped the face of the city: On the one hand, Khomeini's promise that all Tehranians had the right to own

View of Imam Khomeini Residential District

Sharif University Mosque

a house, whereupon the city limits of the master plan were ignored and small houses mushroomed on the outskirts. On the other hand, a government decree after the Iran–Iraq war directed in 1989 that each administrative department should be economically self-supporting. Gholamhossein Karbastschi, incumbent mayor of Tehran since 1989, decided to create a new source of revenue by selling the right to a much higher land utilization than was allowed in the Master Plan to builders (i.e. 120 per cent of the land area on two floors for residential areas) without providing the necessary infrastructure. In 1989 the budget of Tehran municipality grew from about USD 24 million to USD 340 million. Only in 1997 did a law allow the administration to sell additional densities, now even up to a maximum of 360 per cent, which increased the problem of extreme densification in the entire north and west of the city. In 2000, the additional density was limited to 300 per cent and made dependent on the width of the street.

Sharif University Mosque
Masjed-e Daneshgah-e Sanati-ye Sharif
دانشگاه صنعتی شریف

Khiyaban-e Azadi, Tehran
35.70353, 51.35208
Hossein Amanat, Mohammad Tehrani
AD: 1989/AH: 1409/Yaz: 1358

The Sharif University of Technology, formerly Technical Aryamehr university, is the most prestigious technical-scientific university in Iran. The university was founded in 1965 on the initiative of Shah Mohammad Reza Pahlavi, modelled on the Massachusetts Institute of Technology and renamed after the 1979 Islamic revolution. In 1975, Hossein Amanat was commissioned to design the university campus, including the architectonically-remarkable Avicenna mausoleum, with its sleek, ingenious central tower. The complex consists of general classrooms, amphitheatres, a library and several faculty buildings. The design aims to create fluid spaces, accommodate the required areas in the most economical way and facilitate its completion in the shortest period of time. The buildings are grouped in a way that creates enclosed courtyards defined by colonnades and arcades. These are integrated into the buildings, similar to traditional Persian schools. An economical construction system using traditional and practical local building techniques was adopted, where loadbearing brick walls are used with concrete earthquake bracings, and prestressed exposed concrete T-beams form the floor slabs. Patterns and frescos were created using the skills of local bricklayers. Students of Sharif university volunteered as unofficial auxiliary police, Basij, which formed a division of the Iranian Revolutionary Guard. Tens of thousands of Basij, some of them very young, perished in the Iran–Iraq war as suicide bombers. The mosque at Sharif university was built in 1989 by Mohammed Tehrani as a monument to these young people, and with its ornamental decoration is an example of early Islamic post-revolutionary architecture.

Mausoleum of Imam Khomeini, with the largest dome in Iran

Mausoleum of Imam Khomeini
Aramgah-e Emam Khomeini
آرامگاه سید روح الله خمینی
Behesht-e Zahra, Tehran
35.54939, 51.36603
Mohammad Tehrani
AD: from 1989/AH: from 1409/
Yaz: from 1358

301

Mausoleum of Imam Khomeini under construction

The Mausoleum of Imam Khomeini contains the grave of Shiite Ayatollah Ruhollah Khomeini, who died in 1989, and that of Ahmad Khomeini, his second son. Some ten million people attended Khomeini's funeral at the time. The shrine is visible from afar – especially at night, it attracts attention by its coloured lighting. It is located about 10 km south of Tehran, near the martyrs' cemetery Behesht-e Zahra. In 1989, architect

Mohammed Tehrani initiated the planning; the project is still under construction. After completion, the complex will extend over more than 20 km, with a tourist centre, a university and a shopping arcade. In the centre, the largest dome in Iran rises to 68 m, under which Khomeini's sarcophagus lies, protected by a zarih, a canopy-covered metal case. The dome rests on a transition zone,

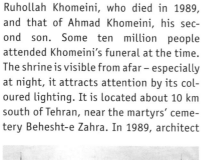

Parviz Moayyed Ahd: Imam Khomeini Mosalla, façade

Imam Khomeini Mosalla with the giant minarets under construction

which has two layers of skylights and stained glass windows decorated with images of tulips, the symbol of Iranian martyrdom. It is supported by eight large marble columns circling the sarcophagus. The shrine is conceived as a large square to be able to accommodate a maximum number of visitors. Because of its size as well as the qibla wall and a maqsura, the mausoleum resembles a mosque. The floor and walls, covered with exquisite carpets, are made of polished white marble. The Khomeini Mausoleum overcomes the architectural past, detached from place and time, in a way that will probably not find a permanent place in Iranian contemporary architecture.

the Eiffel Tower, China the Great Wall and Egypt the Pyramids – and Iran will soon have the great Mosalla showing God's and the Islamic revolution's unity and glory. But much has changed since Khomeini ordered its construction. Zeal has waned, especially among young people for whom the revolution is a distant memory. They see their future more in the largest high-tech location than in the largest mosque. The Iranians are proud. They love big things, whether mosques or airports. Ultimately, the mosque will find a place in the Guinness Book of Records, along with the largest sandwich in the world. The aim is not to enjoy it – it is all about the mention in the book.

Imam Khomeini Mosalla
Mosalla-ye Imam Khomeini
مصلای امام خمینی تهران

Shams Abad, Tehran
35.73486, 51.42564
Parviz Moayyed Ahd
AD: 1990 / AH: 1410 / Yaz: 1359

In the early 1980s, the southern part of Abbasabad was transformed into a Mosalla, a large place for weekly Friday prayer outside the mosque. The similarity to pre-revolutionary Shahestan Pahlavi and the Islamic republic planning is obvious; the square of Shahestan Pahlavi was to be the biggest in Asia, and the Mosalla's minarets the highest in the Islamic world. The gigantic complex for religious events can accommodate 600,000 to 800,000 believers. The central part is already in use. Is there a better symbol of an Islamic republic than the largest mosque in the world? Two minarets are already completed and give a taste of what is to come. The US has the Statue of Liberty, France

Central Municipal Library of Isfahan
Ketabkhaneh-ye Isfahan
کتابخانه مرکزی اصفهان

Khiyaban-e Hasht Behesht, Isfahan
32.65389, 51.67250
Mohammad Reza Ghanei
AD: 1993 / AH: 1413 / Yaz: 1362

The Central Municipal Library of Isfahan was designed as a cube-shaped, five-storey building by Polsheer's Reza Ghaneei, near Maidan-e Naqsh-e Jehan and directly opposite the royal gardens of Hasht Behesht. The design is based on the spatial concept of a palace. It creates a transparent interior, which is separated from the surrounding area by a veil-like grid-wall. The building develops over five floors, three of which are located below ground, respecting the height of Isfahan's historic buildings. The library contains more than 120,000 books and is also the first media centre in Iran.

Three-dimensional animation of the giant Imam Khomeini Mosalla

Façade of the Central Municipal Library of Isfahan

Source: Seyed Hadi Mirmiran (NJP consulting Engineers)

Model photo of the Academies of Islamic Republic of Iran

Academies of Islamic Republic of Iran (Project)
Farhangestan-e Jomhuri-e Eslami-e Iran

فرهنگستانهای جمهوری اسلامی ایران

Abbas Abad, Tehran
35.75375, 51.43364
Seyed Hadi Mirmiran
AD: 1994/AH: 1414/Yaz: 1363

Although the planned city centre of Tehran, Shahestan Pahlavi, was not realised, the location still remained significant after the 1979 revolution. The biggest architectural projects of the Islamic republic emerged here. An important impulse to Tehran's post-revolutionary architectural development was the 1994 competition for the academies of the Islamic Republic of Iran, which took place on the site that had already been earmarked as a cultural and administrative centre during the Shah's regime. Only local architecture offices were allowed to participate. The reference to an Iranian-Islamic identity, which had to be described by the participants, was weighted with 60 per cent. Out of the eighteen participants in the competition, the proposal of Naghsh-e-Jahan Pars by Hadi Mirmiran won first prize. His building design consisted of two main parts, the academies and the complex of conference buildings in addition to a complementary section. The elements of the project are the entrance space, the platform, central courtyard, the dome over the conference complex, the wall of the academies building and a part of the natural topography that deliberately protrudes from the platform. The combination of natural and man-made elements adds to the spatial appeal of the complex. However, because of the references to ancient Islamic architecture, the project was considered by the initiators as too proud and pro-Islamic, which is why it was rejected in favour of a meaningless project with the usual eclectic ingredients. Paradoxically the problem of Mirmiran's design was its remarkable beauty, which had become rare and therefore suspect during the revolution. The design of Mirmiran distinguishes itself from all other contributions by simplicity and clarity; it is the first successful example of architecture relating to history, which was precisely what had been sought since the revolution. Mirmiran studied at the faculty of Fine Arts at Tehran University. From 1968 to 1988, he was Chief Architect of the National Iranian Steel Company, and later Chief Architect in the town planning service of Isfahan. In 1988, he founded N.J.P. Consulting Engineers in Isfahan, which he headed until 2006. The highlight of his career was the construction of the Iranian consulate in Frankfurt, which was completed in 2002.

Source: Naqs-e-Jehan Pars

Rafsanjan Sport Complex with architectural reference to traditional ice houses

Rafsanjan Sport Complex
Majmueh-ye Varzeshi-ye Rafsanjan
مجموعه ورزشی رفسنجان

305 A

Rafsanjan
30.38622, 55.92614
Seyed Hadi Mirmiran
AD: 1994 / AH: 1414 / Yaz: 1363

The sports complex in Rafsanjan realised by Hadi Mirmiran in 1994 shows the same geometric clarity as the design of the academies of the Islamic Republic of Iran. The project leans on traditional forms implemented in a contemporary language that is clearly regional. The architectural concept of the building originated from the typology of traditional ice houses, some of which still exist in this region. In a similar manner to these, Rafsanjan Sport Complex combines an opaque volume (a cone-shaped dome) with transparent elements (a closed wall and a diagonal glazed roof that divides indoor and outdoor pools). The covered and open-air pools are aligned to define a vast surface of water, which is then divided by the transparent diagonal roof. The significant point is that the spatial purity and wholeness of the internal space has been left undisturbed despite the diversity of the complementary areas such as dry and wet sauna, massage rooms, gym, dressing rooms, showers, services, storage, machinery room and

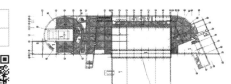

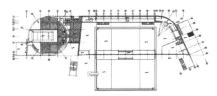

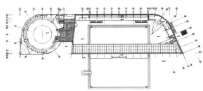

Floor plans of the Sport Complex

Sections

Source: www.archnet.org

water purification plant in the basement, buffet, shop, audience seats, coach room, offices on the ground floor, and a restaurant on the mezzanine level overlooking the pool. The external simplicity of the building is also manifest in the internal space with its diverse divisions.

Curtain wall façade of Navab Safavi House

Living room of Navab Safavi House

Navab Safavi House
Khaneh-ye Navab Safavi
خانه نواب صفوی

306

Khiyaban-e Navab Safavi, Isfahan
32.66611, 51.64861
Mohammad Reza Ghanei
AD: 1994/AH: 1414/Yaz: 1363

The Navab Safavi House, built in 1994, is
a search for the modern Iranian typology.
A plain, dilapidated structure was renovated and expanded to create a family
home. The building is organised linearly
to fit the long and narrow site. A central
axis, which takes the form of a bridge,
links its three layered components.
The core of the house – the old building – contains the kitchen, guestrooms
and a study, with bedrooms above. To
the south is the public area, with a dining hall set over a pool. To the north is
a private area with the children's bedrooms. The entire garden-front consists
of a glazed curtain wall, opening wide
to the outdoor space that was the architect's re-interpretation of the "talar".
The front is deliberately not designed as
a large window, but divided into vertical
segments, subdivided into smaller areas
by curved transverse elements. The pool
in front of it extends beneath this façade
and reflects it. Reza Ghanehi describes
his work: "We wanted the house to appear
strange, yet familiar. If it was not strange
and new, it would not be good architecture, and if it did not look familiar, it
would hardly be what we are looking for."
The house was awarded the *Memar* magazine architectural prize in 2002.

Bar Association
Kanun-e Vokala-ye Dadgostari-ye Markaz
کانون وکلای دادگستری مرکزی

307

Zagros, Tehran
35.73889, 51.41381
Naqsh, e, Jahan-Pars, Seyed Hadi Mirmiran
AD: 1995/AH: 1415/Yaz: 1364

The Tehran Bar Association consists of four floors aboveground and
two floors below. The site is a rectangle located north of Argentine Square.
The building was designed in 1995 by
Seyed Hadi Mirmiran to accommodate
the different administrative, educational
and professional activities of the members of the bar association. The external façade represents a modern abstrac-
tion of the word "justice" in the shape of

Street view of Bar Association

two giant hanging weights with a large pointer between them. At the same time, this façade manifests the floating quality of the interior spaces. In fact the offices, organised in the four floors above the ground, are placed in two floating vertical volumes enclosed in a transparent, luminous space. The sense of floating and complete dominance over the space defines the atmosphere. The slit becomes wider as it proceeds upward. The sense of floating climaxes in the upper floors, as one passes the peripheral corridors which are detached from the sidewalls. In addition to achieving the dramatic quality of offices floating in space, the architect succeeded in providing the spaces with daylight, eliminating the undesirable light coming from the west. Thus it can be said that the use of transparent surfaces in internal and external façades is not merely a formal gesture but expresses the way the building functions. The artistic use of brass and copper in the finish of the two hanging façades, which emphasises the transparency and the void of the internal ambient space through contrast, also improves the effect of the glazed surfaces on urban landscape. The brass and copper finishes are also drawn inward and used as ornaments for the interior hall. The black granite on the ground floor not only reflects the play of light and colour, but the projection of the central axis of the space can also be seen on its hard surface.

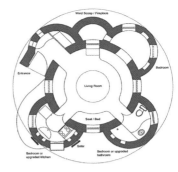

Floor plan of the Emergency Shelters

View of the Emergency Shelters

Interior of a superadobe

Source: Aga Khan Award for Architecture, Cal-Earth

Emergency Shelters (demolished)
Panahgah-haye Ezterari
پناهگاه های اضطراری

Baninajar
31.43603, 49.04131
Nader Khalili
AD: 1995/AH: 1415/Yaz: 1364

308 A

In 2004, a group of fourteen modest buildings in Baninajar was awarded the Aga Khan Award for "improving the understanding and appreciation of Islamic culture". The award referred not only to the architecture but also to the new way of creating temporary dwellings. Nader Khalili constructed these buildings almost ten years earlier as shelters for Iraqi refugees from the first Gulf War. They were constructed from specifically tailored sand bags bound together with wire. All materials had to be purchased and delivered to the disaster area. Superadobe, on the other hand, requires only a small roll of bags and wire, and thanks to the heat-retaining qualities of sand, the shelters remain cool in summer and warm in winter. By applying a layer of plaster, the structure can be permanently sealed and easily retrofitted with plumbing and electricity. Khalili's design would have fit well into Bernard Rudolphsky's *Architecture without Architect*; it costs almost nothing, four unskilled workers can build it in one day and the know-how can be easily passed on.

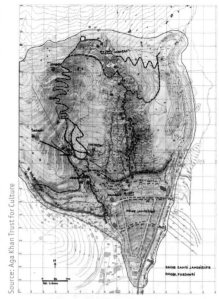

Site plan of the Park Complex

the city. Along these paths, areas for resting, refreshment and entertainment were created within the natural topography, including four cultural houses built to represent the distinctive style of Iran's Azeri, Kurd, Turkmen and Zagros ethnic groups. The paths ultimately lead to a sculpture garden to the east and hiking trails in the upper valleys. The project, completed in 1997, enjoys great popularity and has had a direct and positive impact on the city, alleviating pressure for the development on the slopes of the Alborz mountains and creating an environment where people, nature and culture thrive. An imaginative reinterpretation of the traditional Persian paradise garden adjusted to modern needs, Ferdowsi Park heeds the importance of environmental design within the overall process of urban development.

Ferdowsi Park
Bagh-e Ferdows
باغ فردوس

309

Khiyaban-e Omidvar, Tehran
35.82492, 51.46544
Baft-e Shahr Consulting Engineers
AD: 1996/AH: 1431/Yaz: 1365

The fast population growth in Tehran since the 1950s created a huge shortage for building space, resulting in the destruction of many public and private gardens that once graced the city. As part of a wider range of measures to limit urban sprawl, Tehran municipality supported efforts to protect the natural environment around the Alborz mountains which form the city's northern perimeter. In 1992, the municipality commissioned the park's architects, Bafte-Shahr Consulting Architects and Urban Planners, to prepare a wider study for the outlying areas north of Tehran. The first part of the study to be implemented was a 30 ha park, Ferdowsi Garden, set in series of south-facing gullies scattered with loose rocks and boulders. To assess the site's potential, the design team camped there for a month, and their design was largely based on the natural topography. The initial development was a series of stone paved paths and steps that rise up the hill, providing views over

Provincial Administration
Building
Sakhteman-e Edari-ye Ostan
Farmandar
ساختمان اداری استان

310

Bozorgrah-e Imam Ali, Tehran
35.77917, 51.49111
Farrokh Malek
AD: 1996/AH: 1416/Yaz: 1365

Farrokh Malek from the architectural office Gueno won first prize in a competition for an administrative building in Tehran, where he tried to apply the theory of postmodernism in Iran. He rather obviously uses formal features of Shams ol-Emareh and places them as staffage, or window dressing, on the exterior façade of a rationally-organised office building. Considering that the building's historical model, that of Moayer–ol Mamalek and Ali Mohammad Kashi, was one of the first Iranian buildings where Western influences were cited specifically in the design of the façades, the irony of this postmodernism is clear. But this clear, fundamental misunderstanding of historical reference also shows plainly that a reinterpretation of formal elements from the historical repertoire, which were of formative force in a different social context, can hardly stand for a sustainable historical consciousness.

View of the Navab Safavi Expressway to the north

Qom University Guest House
Mehman Khaneh-ye Daneshgah-e Qom
مهمان خانه دانشگاه قم

Bulvar-e Alghadir, Qom
34.59725, 50.83072
Parviz Foroozi
AD: 1996/AH: 1416/Yaz: 1365

The single-storey residence for the university chairman and visiting scholars is an example of an architectural trend which uses styles and materials such as masonry and tiles, as well as ornamental elements, to give to the building an Islamic look. Even the floor plan is constructed as a geometrical figure, referring to Safavid and Qajar ornamental patterns and worked with incredibly complex geometrical lines whilst still remaining formal. The value of the guesthouse lies in the autonomy of the form. The formalistic consideration of architecture emphasises qualities such as composition, colour, lines and texture. Substantive aspects and relationships are not discussed.

Navab Expressway
Bozorgrah-e Shahid Navab Safavi
بزرگراه شهید نواب صفوی

Bozorgrah-e Navab Safavi, Tehran
35.66861, 51.38167
Gholamhossein Karbaschi (Commissioner)
AD: 1997/AH: 1417/Yaz: 1366

Gholamhossein Karbaschi was mayor of Tehran from 1988 to 1998. Karbaschi supported the modernization effort of the country. He was known for demolishing houses and office buildings without permission, removing revolutionary graffiti from walls, planting thousands of trees and creating large new parks. He also restricted private traffic in central Tehran. Karbaschi was arrested, convicted and imprisoned on charges of corruption, which was regarded as a politically-motivated attack of the government by his supporters. One of his most ambitious projects was the Navab Expressway. He had hoped that the 6 km long highway, with many new buildings on either side, could be started in 1991 and would be finished in 1995. In total, 745,000 m² of living space and 160,000 m² of office and commercial space were created on both sides of the highway. The project was to be self-sustaining and the cost covered by the sale of residential, office and commercial space. A project of this dimension had never before been seen in Iran. A number of architectural companies and urban planners were involved as consulting partners, but the result remained far below expectations on both levels, architectural as well as commercial. Nevertheless the staggered façades form an exciting skyline, in many ways reminiscent of the competition design submitted by Rem Koolhaas for the Parliament of The Hague in 1986.

Administration building versus Shams ol-Emareh

Geometric construction of Qom University Guest House

Skyscraper with copper dome

Armita Office Tower
Borj-e Armita
برج آرمیتا

Khiyaban-e Bokharest, Tehran
35.73261, 51.41656
Behrouz Ahmadi,
Sharestan Architects
AD: 1997 / AH: 1417 / Yaz: 1366

The Armita office tower is a twenty one-storey building on Bokharest Street that culminates in a copper dome. The floor plan is built around a square star, shamseh, an old Iranian motif, which has two mutually-shifted squares normally appearing on the first page of a manuscript, with the title and the name of the author in the centre. Behrouz Ahmadi also refers to the Chrysler building in New York, which was built in the 1930s in the art deco style. A number of skyscrapers in the US and around the world emerged over time, based on the planning and design of the Chrysler building, especially the top of the building. The application of these motifs on the Armita office tower clearly shows that Iranian postmodernism often leads to superficial, purely formal geometric references. It primarily focuses on the façade and hardly develops anything new.

Sadri House
Khaneh-ye Sadri
خانه صدری

Isfahan
Mohammad Reza Ghanei,
Ali Sheikh ol-Islam
AD: 1997 / AH: 1417 / Yaz: 1366

The two architects Mohammad Reza Ghaneei and Ali Sheikh-ol-Islam decided to build two adjacent houses organised around a narrow inner alley which corresponds to the classical housing access of Isfahan and gives access to public and private sectors of the house. The plan is structured as a free floor plan, where the rooms are interconnected at different levels so that they flow into each other but are still separate. Thus, the house appears larger than it actually is. From the side stairs, a connection room leads across the alley to the private sector where the bedrooms are situated, as in Qajar homes. The houses' architecture is not limited to function, construction, material or forms but concentrates on innovations in the interior. In addition to the large façade windows, reminiscent to a talar, daylight penetrates into the house through small, round, hammam-like skylights. However, these are not understood as formal features but as an evolution of a living tradition. In 1994, Sadri House was awarded first prize by the prestigious Iranian architectural magazine *Memar*.

Sadri House with large window

Source: Hamid Reza Norouzi Talab (Tehran: Past & Present)

Complex of Atisaz high-rise buildings at night

Atisaz High Rise District
Mojtame-ye Maskuni-ye Atisaz
مجتمع مسکونی آتی ساز

Bozorgrah-e Chamran, Tehran
35.78500, 51.39028
Atisaz Co.
AD: 1997 / AH: 1417 / Yaz: 1366

A consequence of rapid urbanisation in Iran is an extreme reshaping of the towns, both internally and externally. Parts of the historic cities fell victim to modernisation programs to create roads and housing, whilst rampant growth, whether formal or informal, caused the expansion of the city area. The high-rise complex is located in Evin Atisaz Valley, in north Tehran on the Bozorgrah-e Charman. It is one of the most luxurious residential projects in Iran and was built in 1997 in three stages. In the first two phase,s nine buildings were created and a further five in the third phase. The planning began in the late 1970s but had to be stopped due to the Iran–Iraq war. It was revived only after the war. In 1987, the first 690 units were handed over. After the war, another 830 units were completed and by autumn 2004 the project was completed with 770 additional units. The high-rise complex is equipped with a modern shopping mall, separate swimming pools and saunas for males and females, gardens, fountains, children's playgrounds, waste disposal and schools ranging from kindergartens to high schools.

Source: Tehran24

Atisaz Complex at Bozorgrah-e Charman

Source: www.flicker.com

High-Rise complex with 14 buildings

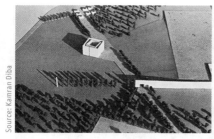

Source: Kamran Diba

Prayer room as sculpture

Prayer Room
Namaz Khaneh
نماز خانه

Fatemi, Tehran
35.71375, 51.39014
Kamran Diba
AD: 1998/AH: 1400/Yaz: 1367

The Namaz Khaneh in Laleh Park is a very simple little prayer room open to the sky, added by Kamran Diba as part of the entrance design to the Carpet museum. The outer shell of this beautiful space, not much larger than nine square metres, is oriented to the street grid, whilst the interior walls are aligned to the direction to Mecca. This fundamental decision creates a space between the noisy environment and the contemplative interior. The two walls are visually connected by vertical slots referring to the two systems, the secular/profane of the town and the divine/sacred

of the cosmos, thus creating an abstract, sculptural object. The architectural contrast between public exterior and private interior space is the most important contribution of Iran monumental architecture to world architecture.

Negarestan Cultural Centre
Markaz-e Farhangi-ye Negarestan
مرکز فرهنگی نگارستان

Khiyaban-e Imam Khomeini, Tehran
35.68750, 51.40172
Manouchehr Iranpour (BIR), Behrouz Ahmadi (AIR)
AD: 1978, 1998/AH: 1398, 1419/ Yaz: 1348,1368

The design of the project began in 1974, but its construction was halted during the 1979 Islamic revolution. The project was resumed under the name of the Qu'ran Museum in 1994. The site is located at the southeast end of Marmar palace. As a sign of respect to the political and historical site, the building is arranged belowground. In the design of inner spaces, important functions are placed in hierarchial order: the central hall and temporary exhibition areas are placed in the upper level, a 400-seat amphitheatre in the middle and the lowest level was devoted to a permanent exhibition of

Source: Amir Hossein Momeni

Prayer Room within Laleh Park

Source: Contemporary Architecture of Iran

Model photo of the Cultural Centre

View of the Cultural Centre Negarestan

historic documents. In addition to these spaces, a large library on the south side of the Central Hall is constructed in three levels. Geometric forms of Iranian historical architecture influence the entire design character. The exposed structure is combined with this pattern at the roof, especially in the amphitheatre and the library. Natural lighting is another feature in the design of interior parts. Sky lights in the roof help to light the inner spaces such as the central hall, the library, the galleries and parts of office spaces during daytime. Durability, minimum maintenance and admirable appearance of the interior surfaces were the main factors in choosing appropriate materials. Brick, concrete and white cement were harmoniously combined.

Dar ol-Shafa Bazaar Bridge
Pol-e Dar ol-Shafa Bazar
دارالشفا بازار پل

318 A

Bazar, Qom
34.64442, 50.88017
Hossein Sheikh Zeineddin
AD: 1999/AH: 1419/Yaz: 1368

The Darolshefa Bazaar Bridge is one of three pedestrian bridges on the north bank of Qom River connecting the residential area with the historical and religious centre on the opposite side. The bridge was developed by Bavand Architects' Hossein Sheikh Zeineddin between 1998 and 1999. It consists of a wide walkway lined by stores which adopt the scale of the historic bazaar. Like the old bridges of Isfahan, the bridge is divided into three spans. Whilst the rhythm remains true to the traditional structure, the dimensions are adjusted to the modern reinforced-concrete structure. The Darolshefa Bazaar

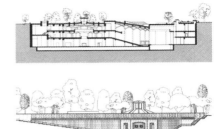

Section and elevation of the Cultural Centre

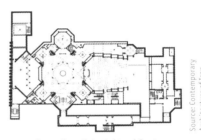

Source: Contemporary Architecture of Iran

Upper floor plan of the Cultural Centre

Bridge shows that the post-revolutionary government in Iran placed great importance to the historically conscious variant of postmodernism and what they understood to be contemporary Iranian architecture by using construction elements or ornaments from building history and incorporating them into new constructions built of brick and decorated with mosaics.

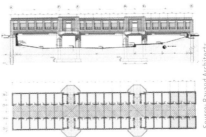

Source: Bavand Architects

Floor plan and section of the bridge

محمدشهر
(ماهدشت)
Mohammad Shahr
(Mahdasht)

گلشهر
Golshahr

اتمسفر
Atmosfer

وردآورد
Vardavard

چیتگر
Chitgar

تهران (صادقیه) اکباتان (ارم‌سبز)
Ekbatan (Eram-e Sabz)   Tehran (Sadeghiyeh)

طرشت
Tarasht

کرج
Karaj

گرم دره
Garmdarreh

ایران‌خودرو
Iran Khodro

ورزشگاه‌آزادی
Varzeshgah-e Azadi

شهرک اکباتان
Shahrak-e Ekbatan

بیمه
Bimeh

دانشگاه شریف
Daneshgah-e Sharif

آزادی
Azadi

استاد معین
Ostad Moein

ترمینال۱ و۲ فرودگاه مهرآباد
Mehrabad Airport Terminal 1&2

میدان آزادی
Meydan-e Azadi

دکترحبیب‌اله
Doctor Habib-o-llah

ترمینال۴ و۶ فرودگاه مهرآباد
Mehrabad Airport Terminal 4&6

شهیدنواب صفوی
Shahid Nawab-e Safavi

شریعتی
Shahrak-e

آباد
Abdi

ت آباد
Ne'mat Abad

آزادگان
Azadegan

Tehran Metro
Metro-e Tehran
مترو‌ی تهران

Tehran
*Tehran Urban & Suburban Railway
Company (Operator)*
AD: 1999/AH: 1419/Yaz: 1368

The original plan of the Tehran subway, the first metro in Iran, was started before the Iranian revolution in the 1970s.

The international tender for the construction was won by the French company SOFRETU, along with the state transport company RATP Paris. Preliminary studies started in the same year, but due to the Iranian revolution and the Iran–Iraq war the project was put on hold in 1982. Work resumed in mid-1985. The north-south connection was treated as a priority, followed by the east-west axis. The metro is very clean, modern and

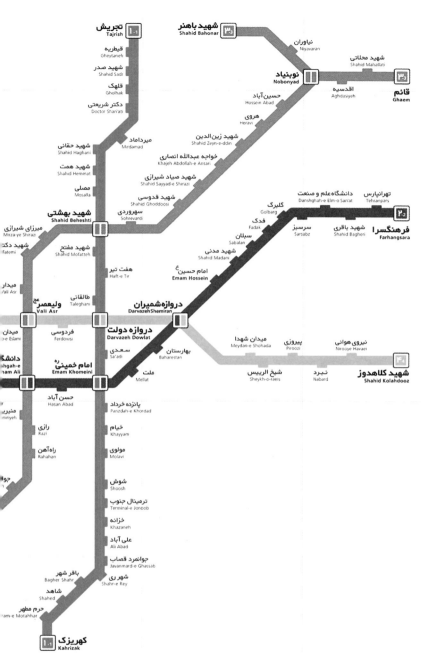

تجريش
Tajrish

شهيد باهنر
Shahid Bahonar

نياوران
Niyavaran

شهيد محلاتى
Shahid Mahallati

نوبنياد
Nobonyad

اقدسيه
Aghdasiyeh

قائم
Ghaem

قيطريه
Gheytarieh

شهيد صدر
Shahid Sadr

حسين آباد
Hossein Abad

قلهك
Gholhak

هروى
Heravi

دكتر شريعتى
Doctor Shari'ati

شهيد زين الدين
Shahid Zeyn-e-ddin

ميرداماد
Mirdamad

شهيد حقانى
Shahid Haghani

خواجه عبدالله انصارى
Khajeh Abdollah-e Ansari

شهيد همت
Shahid Hemmat

شهيد صياد شيرازى
Shahid Sayyad-e Shirazi

دانشگاه علم و صنعت
Danshghah-e Elm-o San'at

تهرانپارس
Tehranpars

مصلى
Mosalla

كلبرك
Golbarg

شهيد قدوسى
Shahid Ghoddoosi

فدك
Fadak

فرهنگسرا
Farhangsara

شهيد بهشتى
Shahid Beheshti

سهروردى
Sohrevardi

سبلان
Sabalan

سرسبز
Sarsabz

شهيد باقرى
Shahid Bagheri

ميرزاى شيرازى
Mirza-ye Shirazi

شهيد مدنى
Shahid Madani

شهيد دك
Fatemi

شهيد مفتح
Shahid Mofatteh

هفت تير
Haft-e Tir

ميدان
Vali Asr

طالقانى
Taleghani

امام حسين ع
Emam Hossein

دروازه شميران
Darvazeh Shemiran

وليعصر
Vali Asr

فردوسى
Ferdowsi

دروازه دولت
Darvazeh Dowlat

ميدان
e Eslami

بهارستان
Baharestan

ميدان شهدا
Meydan-e Shohada

پيروزى
Piroozi

نيروى هوائى
Nirooye Havaei

سعدى
Sa'adi

دانشگ
shgah-e
nam Ali

امام خمينى
Emam Khomeini

ملت
Mellat

شيخ الرييس
Sheykh-o-raees

نبرد
Nabard

شهيد كلاهدوز
Shahid Kolahdooz

حسن آباد
Hasan Abad

پانزده خرداد
Panzdah-e Khordad

نيريه

رازى
Razi

خيام
Khayyam

راه آهن
Rahahan

مولوى
Molavi

شوش
Shoosh

ترمينال جنوب
Terminal-e Jonoob

خزانه
Khazaneh

علىآباد
Ali Abad

جوانمرد قصاب
Javanmard-e Ghassab

باقر شهر
Bagher Shahr

شهر رى
Shahr-e Rey

شاهد
Shahed

حرم مطهر
ram-e Motahhar

كهريزك
Kahrizak

well-organised. About 2.5 million passengers are transported daily in five metro lines. They cover the important areas of the city and run every few minutes. The 5 line is a suburban track with double-decker trains. It runs to the 1.5 million-resident satellite town Karaj, 40 km west of Tehran. Trains are often full to capacity. The first and last one and a half cars are reserved exclusively for women, the middle part is mixed. Many stations are artistically designed, with mosaics and wall reliefs. On the surface too, the subway was an occasion to redesign squares, as at the Hasan Abad station. Orientation in the underground is generally easy: Entrances are easily recognised, the platforms have illuminated panels announcing the route and location of the next train, and on the train itself, the current position is shown by a flashing LED.

Source: Tehran Urban & Suburban Railway Operation Co.

Since 2000
Today's Architect Generation

The guard of the so-called "revolution architects" slowly disappears, and an independent young generation dictates the scene, their mouthpiece being the independent architectural magazine *Memar*. In 1995, Bahram Shirdel returned to Tehran after a successful career in the US and Canada and winning international competitions and awards, and opened his office here. Although none of his projects have been realised yet, he has a huge influence on both students and the establishment with his architectural abstractions – which hold their own next to the works of Peter Eisenman and Zaha Hadid. Geometric concepts and the form-finding process are crucial. This generation of architects, unlike the generation after the revolution, does not want to divorce itself from the international architectural discourse and seeks its own architectural identity, which is not necessarily Iranian-Islamic. The new generation of architects decided to break with the rhetorical and historicist state architecture. Young people started with small

buildings, like houses, condominiums and offices for private clients. Then, seeing the results, even public administrators appreciated the skills of the "disobedient" youth and started to award them commissions for some important public projects. Despite the country's bureaucratic, economic and technological difficulties, these achievements are comparable to those published in international architecture journals. Today's 30- and 40-year-old protagonists are important because more than sixty per cent of the population is younger than 35. They acknowlege that Iranian architecture played an important role in the world's architectural and cultural heritage until 1979 but lost its importance over the last years. It is still not clear whether the administration will trust them or whether they will follow the wishes of the ministry of housing and the outdated structures of municipalities.

Development of Tehran ca. 2006

In 2001, it was decided to develop a new comprehensive master plan in cooperation with the city administration, city council, ministry of interior, ministry of housing and urban development, and the Iranian high council for architecture and urban development. The official name is the "plan to control development and change in the city of Tehran". Work started in September 2004; the district plans will be part of the master plan.

Source: Thomas Meyer-Wieser

Development of Tehran ca. 2006

The document defines the principle of "mutual responsibility of the city administration and the citizens" based on architecture and urban planning. The most important objective is listed as committing to a ceiling of settlement areas. In 2006, Tehran had 7.5 million inhabitants in a surface area of 707 km², which corresponds to a density of 106 inhabitants per hectare. In 2021, this density will rise by an estimated 9 million inhabitants, to 128 inhabitants per hectare. In the outer region of the city, growth opportunities only exist in the west. Therefore, development should primarily take place in urban areas, fallow land and military areas which represent more than 12 per cent of the metropolitan area. The metro and a bus network will be expanded rapidly to achieve a reduction of motorized private transport. Architecturally-valuable structures such as the bazaar, Bagh-e Meli, Arg, Toop-Khane and Hassan Abad, Bahares Baharestan and major roads like Lalehzar, Naserkhosro, Ferdowsi and Saadi will be protected and restored.

Source: Seyed Hadi Mirmiran (Naqsh, e, Jahan-Pars)

Interior view of Frankfurt General Consulate of the Islamic Republic of Iran

2004/2005
Embassy of the Islamic Republic of Iran in Germany

**Frankfurt General Consulate of
the Islamic Republic of Iran**
*Sar Konsulgari-ye Jomhuri-ye Eslami-ye
Iran dar Frankfurt/Main*
Raimundstraße 90, Frankfurt/Main
(permanently closed)
Seyed Hadi Mirmiran
AD: 2005/AH: 1425/Yaz: 1374

The elongated building on Raimundstraße was designed by the Iranian architect Seyed Hadi Mirmiran. When designing the building, he ensured that the building was characterised by architectural elements of Iranian architecture, coupled with transparency and lightness. For example, the building has an oversized, obliquely-placed glass wall which seems to float over the interior like a tent roof at the back, facing the garden. A shallow pool sits close to the glass façade

of the great hall. Spotlights in the sheet of water which throw light against suspended mirrors, making the light shine from under the water. Red Iranian marble was used on walls and ceilings, named Soraya marble after the former Empress. The Frankfurt General Consulate of the Islamic Republic of Iran was the culmination of Mirmiran's career.

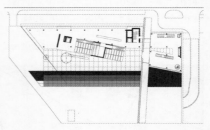

Floor plan

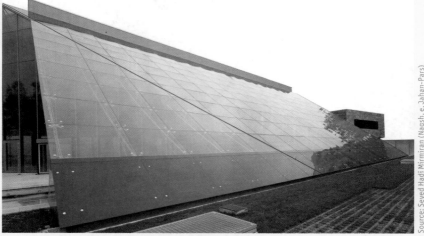

Rear view of Frankfurt General Consulate of the Islamic Republic of Iran

Source: Seyed Hadi Mirmiran (Naqsh, e, Jahan-Pars)

Embassy of Islamic Republic of Iran Berlin
Sefarat-e Jomhuri-ye Eslami-ye Iran dar Berlin

Podbielskiallee 65–67, Berlin
Darab Diba, Jahanguir Safaverdi
AD: 2004/AH: 1424/Yaz: 1373

One of the last new embassies opened its doors in Berlin in February 2005, the Embassy and Consulate of the Islamic Republic of Iran. The building in Podbielskiallee in Dahlem was designed by the Iranian architects Darab Diba and Jahanguir Safaverdi. It is a semi-open building based on an interior courtyard design. The building is set in a residential district with strict building regulations and assumes a rather low profile in order not to disturb the peace of this very chic neighbourhood. The determining factor for the project was the idea to build a bridge between the two cultures and countries. The embassy building extends along its longitudinal axis almost over the whole property. It is divided by incisions and front buildings and develops along a corridor that acts as a central axis and backbone. The length of the building is divided into three unequal parts. The first part is the entrance area, accessed through a convex curved façade. This is followed by the administration area with its corresponding offices. The representative third section, with direct access to the so-called "Persian Garden", completes the space and also the axis of the building. It is a building trying to fulfil many wishes. The police suspect will have to survive many storms, so the protective screen was left permanently in place.

Source: Wikimedia Commons

Embassy Building of the Islamic Republic of Iran in Berlin

Former swimming pool after conversion to a gallery

Ave Gallery
Ave Galeri Mobleman
گالری مبلمان او

Khiyaban-e Vank, Tehran
35.75944, 51.40750
Catherine Spiridonoff,
Reza Daneshmir
AD: 2000/AH: 1420/Yaz: 1369

Reza Daneshmir: Sketches for Ave Gallery

One of the first commissions of Reza Daneshmir and Catherine Spiridonoff was the conversion of a swimming pool to an art gallery at minimum cost. The pool was located in the garden of a painter and designer and could no longer be used to comply with Islamic laws and principles. The main problem was the span of coverage and the connecting staircase. The architects experimented with different options like covers used for industrial buildings, prefabricated stairs or precast elements. Aspects such as cost of construction, the time frame and the spatial quality were also taken into consideration. Looking at the 10 m span and the resulting beam height of about 1 m, and in order to avoid the considerable thickness of the cover plate, the architects decided to halve the roof lengthwise. This made it possible to define the entrance and to clarify the relationship between interior and exterior space. It also provided an opportunity reduce costs. A lightweight roof, supported on a sloped truss, was installed to cover the pool. The depth of the pool is completely utilised, and a series of internal stairs suspended from the same truss lead to the floor of the gallery.

Interior view

External view

Source: Wikimedia Commons

Façade facing the town

Imam Khomeini International Airport

Forudgah-e Beyn ol-Melali-ye Emam Khomeini

فرودگاه بین المللی امام خمینی

Bozorgrah-e Tehran-Qom,
Bozorgrah-e Tehran-Saveh,
35 km southwest of Tehran
35.41611, 51.15222
TAMS-AFFA
AD: 2004 / AH: 1424 / Yaz: 1373

Iranian air traffic slowly began to recover in 1988, after the Iran–Iraq war. This prompted the government to revisit plans for a new airport, 35 km southwest of Tehran. The airport is on the highway from Tehran to Qom. It can be reached from Tehran in forty five minutes to an hour and a half. A subway station is planned and currently being built. The Imam Khomeini International Airport is the largest international airport in Iran and serves as a hub for Iran Air and Mahan Air. The airport consists of two buildings, differing in terms of architecture and function. A light, curved metal roof on tall concrete columns forms the façade to the town. The side to the runway consists of a horizontal metal roof. The passenger flows are completely separated: the arrivals hall is on the ground floor, whilst departures are from a mezzanine level. The original design is based on the concept of the Dallas–Fort Worth airport. It was planned by the architect collective TAMS AFFA, Abdol Aziz Farmanfarmaian and Associates. After the 1979 revolution, the government decided to continue to build the airport with local know-how and support from the French architecture and engineering department of Aéroports de Paris, today ADPI. The opening was originally planned for 1 February 2004, the anniversary of the Islamic revolution. After delays in the completion, the opening took place on 8 May 2004. The airport is modern, bright and well-equipped. It is open around the clock as many flights arrive or depart at night. Travellers should take note that men and women are, in part, processed separately, particularly at security checkpoints.

Source: Wikimedia Commons

Arrival hall

Terrace-like New National Library

New National Library
Ketabkhaneh-ye Melli-ye Iran
کتابخانه ملی ایران

Abbasabad, Tehran
35.75167, 51.43389
Mohsen Mirheydar,
Yousef Shariatzadeh
AD: 2004/AH: 1424/Yaz: 1373

Covered passage

The new building of the national library of Iran is located at Abbassabad in north Tehran. The national library was previously scattered over several buildings in various parts of the city. In 1994, the commission for public buildings of the ministry of housing and urban development announced a national competition to select the best design for the new building of the national library. Pirraz Consulting won the competition and designed an inviting atmosphere. A single, solid, compact and at the same time horizontally-stretched structure provides flexibility and allows for smooth workflow. The building is technically outstanding. Using up-to-the-minute technologies of library management, and considering local and global standards, a contemporary Iranian architecture was created to coordinate the complex work and high standards of construction and detailing. The building has been honoured with various awards, including the Design Award for Environmental Engineering and Architecture in 1997 and the Concrete Prize in 2003, and it was nominated for the Agha Khan Award for Architecture in 2007.

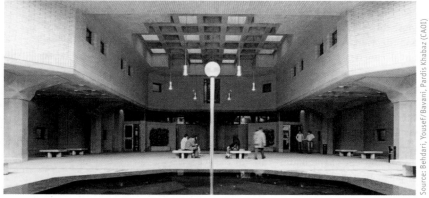

Entrance area

Street façade of the residential building

Interior view

Villa In Darvishabad
Darvish Mahal-e Eqamat
درویش محل اقامت

Nour, Mazandaran
36.57361, 52.01389
Pouya Khazaeli Parsa
AD: 2004/AH: 1424/Yaz: 1373

Top view of the roof

The villa in Dervish by Pouya Khazaeli Parsa – a white cube on pilotis – directs our attention to its synthesis of structure, skin and inventive sequence of spaces, attracting visitors to explore the house in a worthwhilst architectural promenade from the bowels to the spectacular roof terrace with a view of the beach. The villa is cosmopolitan and picks up the heritage of the ideal villa architecture in a language that is in many aspects reminiscent of modernist utopian experiments. The residence wraps around itself in a three-dimensional winding path over a square ornamental pond, which not only cools the air and reflects the sky but also forms the symbolic centre of the house as a geometric axial shape. The language of Parsa's first house – the unadorned structure, the white, black and reddish colour palette, the flat roof terraces – all reminds one of the purist work of Le Corbusier, discovered by the master on his *voyage d'Orient*, and also the projects of early modern architects like Melnikov, Terragni and Guévrékian. In 2004, Khazaeli Parsa, a young Iranian architect, rebuilt an existing ruin of a house at the Iranian coast of the Caspian Sea with a modest budget and dedicated design intent in close coordination with his clients. References to Islamic architecture

were carefully avoided. Khazaeli Parsa rather chose a spatial variation, drawing his inspiration from Le Corbusier's *Le poème de l'angle droit*. The design idea stems from the simple desire to enjoy the view of the Caspian Sea. The house is located in Daryacheh, where the view of the sea is usually obscured. Using a ramp-like way up to the rooms, the house winds ever higher, culminating in a rooftop garden and offering a panoramic view of the nearby sea. The resulting courtyard reinterprets a traditional residential element of Middle Eastern dwelling culture as well as the use of the roof as summer living room and bedroom. The synthesis of Iranian lifestyle with the architectural concept of modernity appears to be successful here. Khazaeli Parsa obtained his master's degree in architecture in 2000 at Tehran's Azad university. He worked in several renowned international agencies, including Shigeru Ban Architects, Shirdel and Partners and Hadi Mirmiran NJP Architects. Today, Khazaeli Parsa is a leading Iranian architect and has received awards in numerous competitions and art biennials.

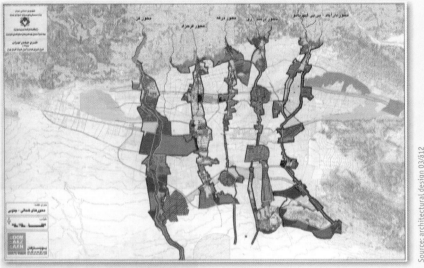

Comprehensive plan of Tehran with incorporated river valleys

Source: architectural design 03/ã12

Comprehensive Plan of Tehran
Tarh-e Jame-ye Shahr-e Tehran
طرح جامع شهر تهران

Tehran
City Planning Office, Tehran
AD: 2006/AH: 1426/Yaz: 1375

The comprehensive plan for Tehran was based on extensive research studies and analyses of the social, economic, political, and physical base of the city of Tehran. A 25-year planning horizon was chosen as the framework for devising alternative development strategies to guide urban growth and the rehabilitation of aging areas of the city. The plan proposed that growth and development be fostered at three levels of self-supporting urban units, each served by an activity centre with a scale of services ranging from small neighbourhoods (5,000 people), to community centres (20,000 to 30,000 people), all the way up to urban regions (300,000 to 500,000 population clusters). Each level of community structure would be integrated closely with its support services including the educational system, residential, commercial and governmental developments. The second most innovative aspect of the plan was its recognition of the need for an integrated mass rapid transportation system, at the same time seeking to minimize the use of private cars. A third series of detailed recommendations in the plan called for rejuvenation of older, existing areas of the city. The plan recommended small, local renewal efforts, using a programmed strategy dedicated to minimizing disruption to the established social and communal fabric of each neighborhood. After a number of areas were physically enhanced, the resident families would all be able to return together, enabling them to retain their long-standing relationships – factors so important to long-term community viability.

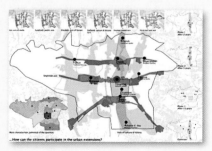

Options of public participation

Zoning plan of Tehran

Source: www.tmicto.tehran.ir

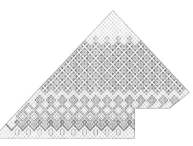

Source: Behdari, Yousef/ Bavani, Pardis Khabaz (CAOI)

Façade drawing of the House of Parliament by Behrouz Ahmadi

Source: Contemporary Architecture of Iran

Pyramid-shaped roof of the Islamic Consultative Assembly, in the evening

House of Parliament façade
Imarat-e Majlis-e Shuray-e Islami
مجلس شورای اسلامی

Maidan-e Baharestan, Tehran
35.69174, 51.43444
Behrouz Ahmadi
AD: 2006/AH: 1426/Yaz: 1375

After the 1979 Islamic revolution, the parliament was renamed Majlis-e Shuray-e Islami, Islamic Consultative Assembly, under the new constitution, replacing the old name Majlis-e Shuray-e Melli, National Consultative Assembly. The change was manifested by a new construction on Baharestan Square in central Tehran. The pyramidal roof was designed by Behrouz Ahmadi, who graduated from Tehran University in 1966. His contribution to the competition was awarded first prize for the design of the façade, which follows almost exactly the client's specifications and refers to style elements of the past. This gave the building a new look, appropriate to the Islamic constitution, so that the Emarat-e Majlis-e Shuray-e Islami can be seen as a strong statement of the new rulers towards the sonnati style, referring to the Islamic regional tradition. The first parliamentary session was held there on 16 November 2004. However, the Majlis-e Shuray-e Islami, as constitutional body of the Islamic Republic of Iran, no longer has a high position within the state structure-like parliament previously occupied together with the senate after the 1906 Constitutional revolution. In the Islamic republic, the opinion of the spiritual revolutionary leader in all matters is crucial and the Majlis-e Shuray-e Islami must ensure that the ideas of the revolutionary leader are implemented.

Source: Meisam Attarzadeh (Sharestan Consultants)

View from Baharestan Street

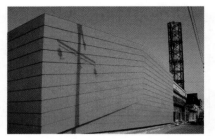

View of main entrance

Wrapping of the existing structure

Shali Shop
Markaz-e Kharid Shali
مرکز خرید شالی

Amol
36.46972, 52.35083
Arsh Design Studio
AD: 2006/AH: 1426/Yaz: 1375

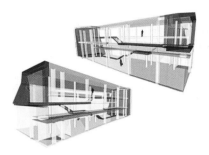

Rendering of the building structure

In this project of converting an old workshop to a shopping centre, the design concept is about wrapping. The bright material wraps around the old building without negating its basic formal and structural characteristics. The façade is like an elegant night gown, showing off the exotic curvature of the body hidden behind it. A sexy tailored dress, not too tight so it leaves something to the imagination of the observer. One feels the burning urge to tear the whole thing apart just to find out what is beneath this flashy cover. The wrap is torn at points to let the openings and cuts take shape. Yet the design is not just about introducing a colourful, eye-catching project, which differs in its architectural form to attract prospective customers. From the designers' point of view, it is a design statement, which hopefully will set the guidelines for renovation and conversion of the aging commercial fabric in the adjacent properties. This is about introducing a new design culture for the forthcoming

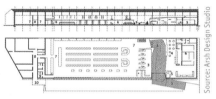

Floor plan and section

revitalization projects of the region, which can be implemented as a prototype for any commercial strip along the arterial roads or through marginal small cities in the area north of Iran. One aspect of the project that is worth pointing out is the fact that the construction teams involved in the site work were not professional, well-trained technicians, and as a result communicating the design concepts and construction details to the working teams was an ongoing challenge for the design team.

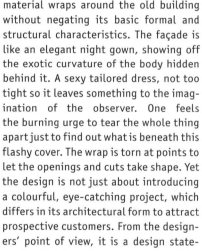

Evening shop

Outer shell

Source: Arsh Design Studio

Source: www.fma-co.com

Curved building mass of cineplex

Mellat Park Cineplex
Pardis-e Sinamai-ye
Park-e Mellat
پردیس سینمایی ملت

325

Bozorgrah-e Nianesh, Tehran
35.77639, 51.40750
Fluid Motion Architects
AD: 2008/AH: 1428/Yaz: 1377

In 2004 Fluid Motion Architects were commissioned to build a cinema complex in one of the most important public parks in northern Tehran. The park is open twenty-four hours a day and is a popular urban meeting place. The long sides of the building are fully glazed, creating the feeling of being outside as well as inside. In addition, the building is designed as a bridge under which one can walk through and it thus becomes part of the park. The long and indeterminate shape of the site makes it possible to instal two movie theatres on the ground floor and two more in the basement. The spatial organisation of the project is defined in a way that an idea of space is created in accordance with the physical program and the structure of the project and also allows interaction with the exquisite natural environment. Hence, by connecting the rotating slopes of the two movie theatres along one another, an extensive covered plaza (ayvan) was created, which is the main benefit of this project for the city and provides a large covered plaza for a variety of other cultural and social events. The connection and curves of the building shape allow the development of smooth and curving ramps along the building façades, so that the paths of the park continue seamlessly as sidewalks in the building. Ultimately, one can say that the shape of the building and its elements are developed like a living organism. Fluid Motion Architects was founded by Reza Daneshmir and Catherine Spiridonoff in Tehran in 2004. Reza Daneshmir taught at several universities and has published several articles in architectural magazines. In 2008, Mellat Park Cineplex was awarded first prize by architectural magazine *Memar*.

Source: www.fma-co.com

System of paths inside the Building

Bridge-like building structure

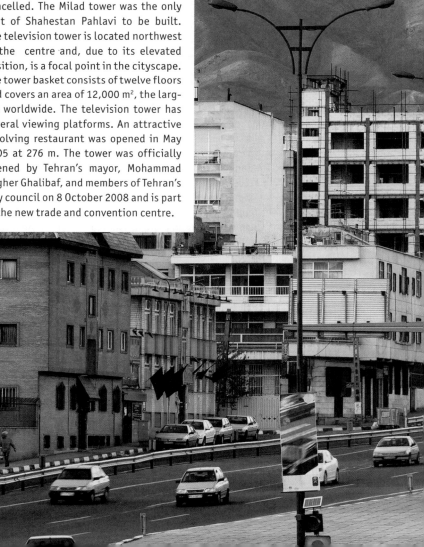

Milad Tower
Borj-e Milad
برج میلاد

Shahrak-e Gharb, Tehran
35.74528, 51.37667
Mohammad Reza Hafezi
AD: 2008/AH: 1428/Yaz: 1377

Milad Tower, the new landmark of Tehran, was designed by Mohammad Reza Hafezi and completed by Boland Payeh Co. in the fall of 2008. At 435 m, it is the tallest tower in the country and the sixth-highest television tower worldwide. The Milad tower was first proposed as part of the Shahestan Pahlavi project in Tehran's Abbasabad district. The project was designed by the American urban planner Jaquelin Robertson. With the advent of the Iranian revolution, the project was cancelled. The Milad tower was the only part of Shahestan Pahlavi to be built. The television tower is located northwest of the centre and, due to its elevated position, is a focal point in the cityscape. The tower basket consists of twelve floors and covers an area of 12,000 m², the largest worldwide. The television tower has several viewing platforms. An attractive revolving restaurant was opened in May 2005 at 276 m. The tower was officially opened by Tehran's mayor, Mohammad Bagher Ghalibaf, and members of Tehran's city council on 8 October 2008 and is part of the new trade and convention centre.

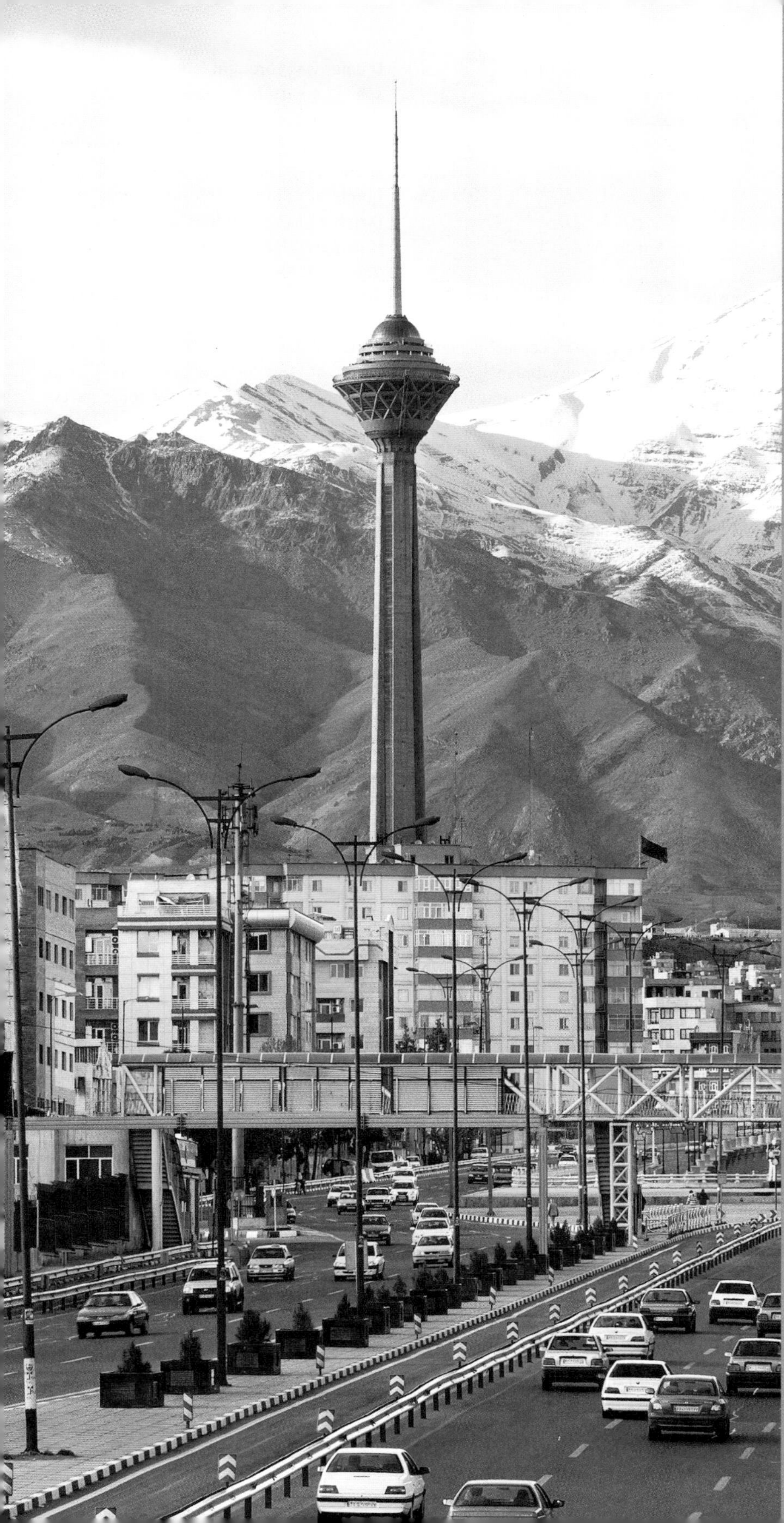

Shahkaram Office Building
Sakhteman Edari-ye
Tejari-ye Shahkaram

ساختمان اداری شاه کرمی

Karaj
35.81689, 50.96647
Hooman Balazadeh
AD: 2008/AH: 1428/Yaz: 1377

The concept of the building goes back to the traditional Iranian orosi window, which consists of small colourful pieces of glass which filter the intense light penetrating inside and create a colourful play of light and shadow on the interior walls. As the building is narrow in comparison to its height, the whole complex is divided into several modules to gain a balanced proportion. These serve various purposes such as entrance, office and commercial units. Light is a significant variable in the façade design. By using transparent and semi-transparent textures, different qualities of light were created with various reflections and angles at night and day. The night light was also modified through using an artificial lighting system that magnifies the dynamic urban views. By the use of this modulation system and the façade design, an Iranian

theme was brought into the interior space, creating the effect of shadows and turquoise reflections of the components installed on the façade. This effect is felt even when the semi-transparent blinds are closed. The north and south façades of the building are made of two transparent layers. The outer layer not only brings a colourful effect of shadow and light inside, but also creates a thermal and light shield for the sharp sunlight on the southern façade. The inner layer of the façade transforms into a semi-transparent layer in some parts, that is textured by double-glazed windows with sand blast modular patterns on the inside. Overall, the main aim of this material combination was to reduce the temperature created by the sun. This climatic need is also modified by the use of sun energy type glass windows. Natural light in the interior is absorbed from the main façade windows, and a series of linear transparent and semi-transparent partitions of glass bricks are installed in line with the transparent façade windows. This strategy not only creates a unity between the interior and exterior but also transfers the natural light into the deeper interior spaces.

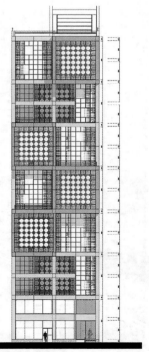

Elevation

Office building in the urban context

Source: Parham Taghiof (www.archdaily.com)

Street view

Source: Parham Taghiof (Nextoffice)

Structure made of two stacked boxes

Villa for a Friend
Khaneh-ye Baraye-yek dust
خانه ای برای یک دوست

Lavasan, near Tehran
35.81833, 51.62278
Nextoffice
AD: 2008/AH: 1428/Yaz: 1377

The steeply sloping terrain provides a stunning vista over the reservoir of Latian Dam which gave the initial idea of framing this delightful landscape by two simple match boxes. Thus, the Villa for a friend is divided into two boxes placed over one another in order to generate different views and to use as much sunlight as possible. Since the yard-like terrace of the upper box is intended to be used for parties and family events, the bedrooms and the connected service areas were located in the lower box to achieve the desired privacy and comfort, whilst the living room, kitchen and a spacious yard were placed in the upper box, which was used by the residents as open areas. The main access is the stairway starting from the lowest level, ending at the building's main entrance in the public area, with an additional shortcut to the private zone available. Slotted wood panels on the balcony side, reminiscent of the work of the Italian painter Lucio Fontana, protect the house from wind and snow during the severe Tehrani winters and simultaneously allow an artificial view of nature.

Iranian Artists' Forum
Khaneh-ye Honarmandan
خانه هنرمندان

329 G

Park-e Honar, Mousavi St, Tehran
35.71031, 51.41946
Bijan Shafei, Parinaz Mirzaei,
Keyvan Khatir
AD: 2008/AH: 1428/Yaz:1377

Honarmandan Park was established during the Qajar period, owned by Kamran Mirza, son of Nasser al-Din Shah. It rose to prominence due to the modernist design of the Austrian gardener Jseph Fischer and was therefore at the time called Fischer Abad. With the onset of World War II, the allies occupied the garden and built some military barracks. After the withdrawal of the allied military forces, the area remained in possession of the Iranian military. After the 1979 Islamic revolution, the area was semi-abandoned. Later it generally went into decay and became a hang-out for drug addicts. In 1999, Tehran municipality decided to rebuild the site and transform it into a cultural centre. Based on the needs of the artists in different fields, the building was reconstructed and lecture rooms, exhibition rooms and different galleries were installed, and the complex opened as the Iranian Artists Forum in February 2000 in the presence of President Mohammad Khatami. Due to unprecedented enthusiasm, the management announced the need for new galleries in 2009 and engaged the services of the previous designers, Bijan Shafei, Parinaz Mirzaei, Keyvan Khatir. Honarmandan Park, or Artists Park, is full of surprises, whether it be the public art displays, the vegetarian cafe, or the former US embassy around the corner. It is a popular tourist attraction.

Chizari Apartment
Apartaman Maskuni-ye Chizari
آپارتمان مسکونی چیذری

330 F

Mahallat, Tehran
35.79970, 51.50848
Bonsar Co., Mohammad Majidi
AD: 2008/AH: 1428/Yaz:1377

Tehran's building regulations on junctions, coupled with the proportions of the plot, imposed a weird triangular footprint on the project. This confining rule turns out to be the beginning point of the design process. First, the two edges of the triangle that form the façade, were unfolded and the whole façade was designed as one single face. After specifying the spaces and designing the openings, the façade was folded back again, but this time none of the folding lines at each level were the same.

Iranian Artists' Forum, main entrance

Chizari Apartment , street view

Rendering of Valiasr Mosque

Valiasr Mosque
Masjed-e Valiasr
مسجد ولیعصر

331 G

Khiyaban-e Valiasr, Tehran
35.70008, 51.40562
Fluid Motion Architects
AD: from 2008 / AH: from 1428 /
Yaz: from 1377

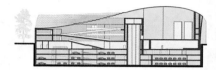

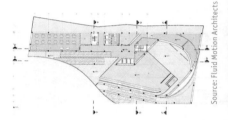

Floor plan and section

In the late Pahlavi time, a shopping centre was planned at this location but rejected by the people. After the Islamic revolution, the plan for a mosque with cultural centre was tackled. The original design was similar to a traditional mosque with a dome of 52 m and two minarets. By 2008, the mosque's basement was built, causing cracks and damages to the adjacent Shahr Theatre. The project was suspended when artists of the Shahr staged protests. In 2008 the city of Tehran called on two young architects, Reza Daneshmir and Catherine Spiridonoff – known for their successful cineplex project – to continue with the planning. They proposed to develop the mosque as part of the urban landscape, connecting on one side to Daneshjoo Park and the Shahr theatre situated there, and on the other hand retaining the urban structure of Enghelab Street. In addition, the design should incorporate contemporary ideas of mosque architecture, so that the building is "relevant for the present but rests with one foot in history". After consultation with Dr. Mehdi Hojjat, professor at the university of Tehran, the project came a step closer to approval. His analysis was that it should be a horizontal mosque rising up from earth to heaven. Therefore, the entrance hall is inspired by the spiral access of the Sheikh Lotf Allah mosque without copying it. Also, the design shows neither dome nor minarets, which was criticised by the Imam of Masjed Asr. However, the architects were able to create their vision of the urban landscape; the mosque is built at the same height as the adjacent buildings so that a balance between low and high buildings could be maintained. The realisation and development of the future roofscape is to be in harmony with the meticulous mosaic façade of the Shahr Theatre opposite.

Park façade under construction

Absar Waterpark
Majmueh-ye Absar
مجموعه آبسار

Sepahan Shahr, Isfahan
32.55503, 51.67317
Polsheer Consultants
AD: 2009/AH: 1430/Yaz:1378

The Absar Waterpark was planned by Polsheer Consultants, Mohammad Reza Ghaneei, from 2003 to 2009. The water-park is a unique complex of recreational and sporting activities with a special and somewhat different architecture for Iran.

Reza Ghaneei decided to design a build-ing that relates to scenography as an art of staging. Therefore the term *atmos-phere* plays an important role. Based on images of Iran's bathing culture, Reza Ghaneei developed the idea of a cav-ern, which appears as a porous, hollowed stone. The use of the bath is separate for men and women – women on even days, men on odd days. On Fridays women can use the water park from 10.00 to 15.30 h, while men can use it from 16.30 to 24.00 h. The building was given an award by *Memar* Magazine in 2010.

M Coffee
Cafe M
کافه M

Velenjak Shopping Centre,
Khiyaban-e Velenjak, Tehran
35.80722, 51.39333
Hooman Balazadeh
AD: 2009/AH: 1430/Yaz: 1378

Coffee shops are extremely popular places among young Iranians. M Coffee, with its modest dimensions, is located on the second floor of a shopping centre. The objective of the project was to cre-ate a single space with different spatial qualities in a limited area. The project is functionally divided into two main areas, the kitchen and the lounge. In the main hall, walls and ceiling as well as lighting elements are merged into a single unit, resulting in a number of different per-spective views. In the main hall a white casing continuously covers walls and ceil-ing, whilst the rear section is restricted to a dark wooden colour and heavy furni-ture in dark brown leather.

Source: Behdari, Yousef/ Bavani, Pardis Khabaz (CAOI)

Axonomeric projection of the indoor swimming pool

Indoor swimming pool

Source: Behdari, Yousef/ Bavani, Pardis Khabaz (CAOI)

M Coffee interior

Source: Nextoffice

Bamboo structure of 70 bamboo trunks

Entrance

Bamboo Structure
Kolbeh Bambu
کلبه بامبو

334 A

Katalom, Iran
36.86744, 50.72944
Pouya Khazaeli Parsa
AD: 2009 / AH: 1430 / Yaz: 1378

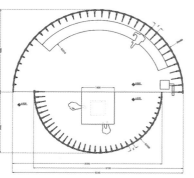

Floor plan and section

When Pouya Khazaeli Parsa was approached by Manouchehr Mirdamad to design a modest resort town near the forests of Katalom in northern Iran, he decided to use bamboo as building material, because it is locally-available, cheap and easy to obtain. He used seventy bamboo poles with two bamboo poles forming a curve from one side of the structure to the other side. The bamboo was cut two days prior to use. This ensured that it was still soft and flexible during construction and would become rigid once built. Gas pipes from the local market made the base for the bamboo, but were not fixed to the ground, providing for the possibility of moving the structure by simply taking out the bamboo poles from the plugs and installing them again in another location. In completing the membrane, bunches of straw from one of the many post-harvest rice fields in the area were collected. Each bunch was bundled at the top and the structure was covered by overlapping these "straw-bricks" around it. A major benefit of using rice straws for this purpose is that when they become wet in rainy weather, they expand to the extent that they do not allow rain to pass through the membrane. On the other hand, in sunny and warm weather, they become dry and allow wind to pass through lots of small holes, providing natural cool ventilation. Local material can be utilized in every part of the world, changing the appearance of the structure to reflect its setting, whilst ensuring that costs are kept low.

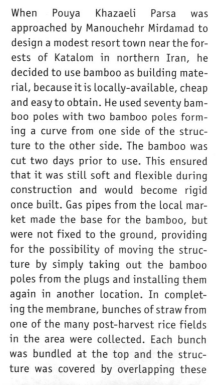

Model picture

Low angle view of the roof

Interior view

Checker Box Office Building
Mojtame-ye Edari-ye Khorsand
مجتمع اداری خرسند

Khiyaban-e Khorsand 16,
Khiyaban-e Valiasr, Tehran
35.78406, 51.41528
Arsh Design Studio
AD: 2009/AH: 1430/Yaz: 1378

According to the Arsh Design Studio, the city of Tehran is an absurdly constructed landscape, where the conventional typology for achieving high density through the use of towers is replaced by a completely different spatial strategy where density is achieved through massive deployment of a mid-rise building type, namely the four to five-storey apartment buildings.The dominance of this type has yielded a somewhat absurd urban morphology whereas the exterior manifestation of the apartment buildings from a street point of view is limited to a single two-dimensional façade. Furthermore, due to the particular dynamics of the real estate market, where the price of land in Tehran has reached unbelievable heights, investors demand architects to design spatial scenarios where the maximum allowed envelope is built to maximize the profit. This intensifies the importance of the façade design in the overall process of design,

development and construction of buildings, since investment in this single façade is the way to make the building stand out as unique in its context and therefore architecturally attractive. Under such circumstances, the architect does not have much room to manoeuvre in volumetric composition. What is left for him is basically the design of the main façade of the building with a maximum depth of 20 to 40 cm. With the above mentioned goals in mind, the design strategies which were incorporated in the conception and development of the "Checker Box" created a building with the maximum-allowed building envelope into saleable inhabitable space. It provided a design based on variations that allow the building to stand out as a unique piece of engineering and artistic intervention in its spatial context, ensuring that the adopted design strategies in spatial composition, proposed construction techniques and technologies and choice of materials do not compromisethe financial feasibility of the investment.

Main façade when closed

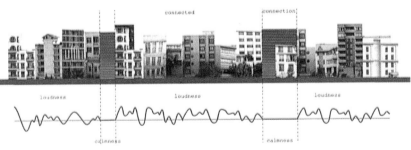

Façade development at Khiyaban-e Khorsand

Courtyard of Valiasr Office Building

Façade detail of the office building

Source: RYRA Studio

Valiasr Office Building
Sakhteman Edari-ye Tejari-ye Valiasr
ولیعصر تجاری ساختمان اداری

Khiyaban-e Valiasr, Tehran
35.71861, 51.40778
RYRA Studio
AD: 2009/AH: 1430/Yaz: 1378

The Valiasr Commercial Office Building is located on a rectangular site which has approximately 15 m of frontage along the west side of Vali Asr Avenue. Due to municipal building regulations, only a two-storey structure could be built, so there was no possibility to create a balance in elevation with adjoining buildings. The design of the commercial office building intents to shape the façade as a skin, bringing motion and dynamism of the location into the skin, as if

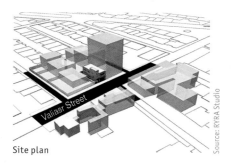

Site plan

Source: RYRA Studio

it were influenced by movement of people. Moreover, the main objective was that the façade should form a continuous skin which is not disturbed by different materials. The diagram finally chosen shows how different spaces transfigure and connect into each other to create overall integrity. This unity can be experienced by walking through the main passages between the spaces.

Holy Defense Museum
Muzeh-ye Defa-ye Moqadas
موزه دفاع مقدس

Abbasabad, Tehran
35.75200, 51.42603
Jilia Norouzi
AD: 2010/AH: 1431/Yaz: 379

The Iranian Holy Defense Museum dedicated to the history of the Iran–Iraq-war was designed by Jila Norouzi between 2006 and 2010. It is a big, shiny, 100 m long decorated shelter. The visitor is guided through the eight-year war by a kind of reality show with panoramas, computer animations, movies, weapons and a variety of other technologies including a misty waterfall, on which a film is projected, and an interesting interior design. The Iran–Iraq war lasted

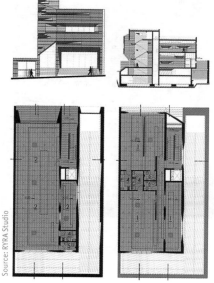

Floor plans of Valiasr Office Building

Source: RYRA Studio

from 22 September 1980 to 20 August 1988. There was no victor; it ended in a truce and with high human and material losses on both sides. No peace treaty exists to this day. The Iran–Iraq war is a national trauma; the betrayal of Iran by the UN is still an open wound which is so painful that even this exhibition is unable to give an objective view on the conflict. There are also depictions of the 1979 Islamic revolution as well as libraries and a café-restaurant. The museum provides a good insight into the Iranian understanding of politics. The museum succeeds in meeting the visitor's need of a landmark, a low-lying building that merges into the surrounding landscape with a gently sloping folded roof influenced by the topography of the hills. The design is also influenced by the view to the green valley, Persian garden and the lake. The building becomes a folded entity of large metallic forms, a dramatic contrast between the green hills and the metallic building, which takes its form from a camouflage net.

Holy Defense Museum, site plan

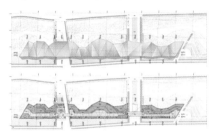

Floor plan of the Holy Defense Museum

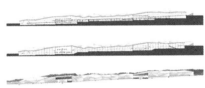

Longitudinal section of the museum

Cross sections of the museum

Source: Behdari, Yousef / Bavani, Pardis Khabaz (CAOI)

Aerial view of the museum complex

Source: Mohsen Jazayery (Pouya Khazaeli Parsa)

Pending building mass

Villa in Darvishabad
Villa dar Darvishabad
ویلا در درویش آباد

Darvishabad
36.66775, 52.42450
Pouya Khazaeli Parsa
AD: 2010/AH: 1431/Yaz: 1379

The Villa in Darvishabad is hermetic. Despite its proximity to the Caspian Sea it appears as an independent, other-worldly object that barely allows onlookers a glimpse into its interior. This is an object-house that respects the rules of international minimalist architecture, but also establishes a subtle connection with the local architectural tradition and the traditional Iranian house. Pouya Khazaeli Parsa designed this house for his wife, the artist Nastaran Shahbazi.

The floating building touches the ground on all sides, with only a slender pillar in the centre of the façade, making the corners appear to be floating in space. The sensitivity to the architecture of the region is also evident in the fact that the building is raised above ground on four columns to prevent absorption of moisture from the soil. In this case, the architect, with the simple act of placing the columns of a house along the orthogonal axes of the square plan, avoids a banal reproduction of the native hut with corner columns. The Shahbazi residence consists of three vertically stacked areas – garden, house and roof terrace. On the ground floor, a path winds towards a steep staircase rising without railing or parapet through a narrow gap in the façade. The straight and narrow staircase

Source: Mohsen Jazayery (Pouya Khazaeli Parsa)

Roof terrace

Source: Mohsen Jazayery (Pouya Khazaeli Parsa)

Interior view

emphasises the open space of the house, divided mainly by movable partitions. Thus the space maintains the flexibility typical of traditional houses in which the main functions, sleeping, eating and spending time together, can take place in different spaces depending on the season or time of day. The high entrance hall – a modern piano nobile – has white double doors, white walls and white radiators. It is organised around a void represented by a glass funnel-like element that captures sunlight and brings it to the centre of the house. Khazaeli Parsa argues that this is inspired by Iran's traditional architecture, where most spaces are organised around a central courtyard or patio. From there the path continues to the roof terrace where a *chambre à ciel ouverte* is found behind high walls, similar to the famous design by Le Corbusier. The roof is another reference to the Persian homes. This kind of courtyard is not open to the surrounding area but is enclosed by a high wall leaving only a view of the sky. In this way, the family's privacy is protected from prying eyes and the terrace space simulates the intimacy of the central courtyards of traditional houses. Of course the nine-square plan has precedents in many architectural cultures and the arrangement can be compared to western modernity or

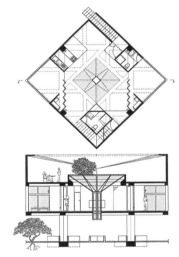

Source: Pouya Khazaeli Parsa

Upper floor plan and section

Middle Eastern traditional private rooms. However, there is a surprise: A light shaft opens from the roof terrace downwards and appears inside as a central glazed column, a lantern by day and night, which is also used for ventilation and rainwater drainage. It appears as a metaphorical tree, which, in contrast to the basic structure, is transparent: a void at the core of this fascinating house. Khazaeli Parsa's creation is representative of the route taken by many young Iranian architects in search of their indigenous and, at the same time, international identity.

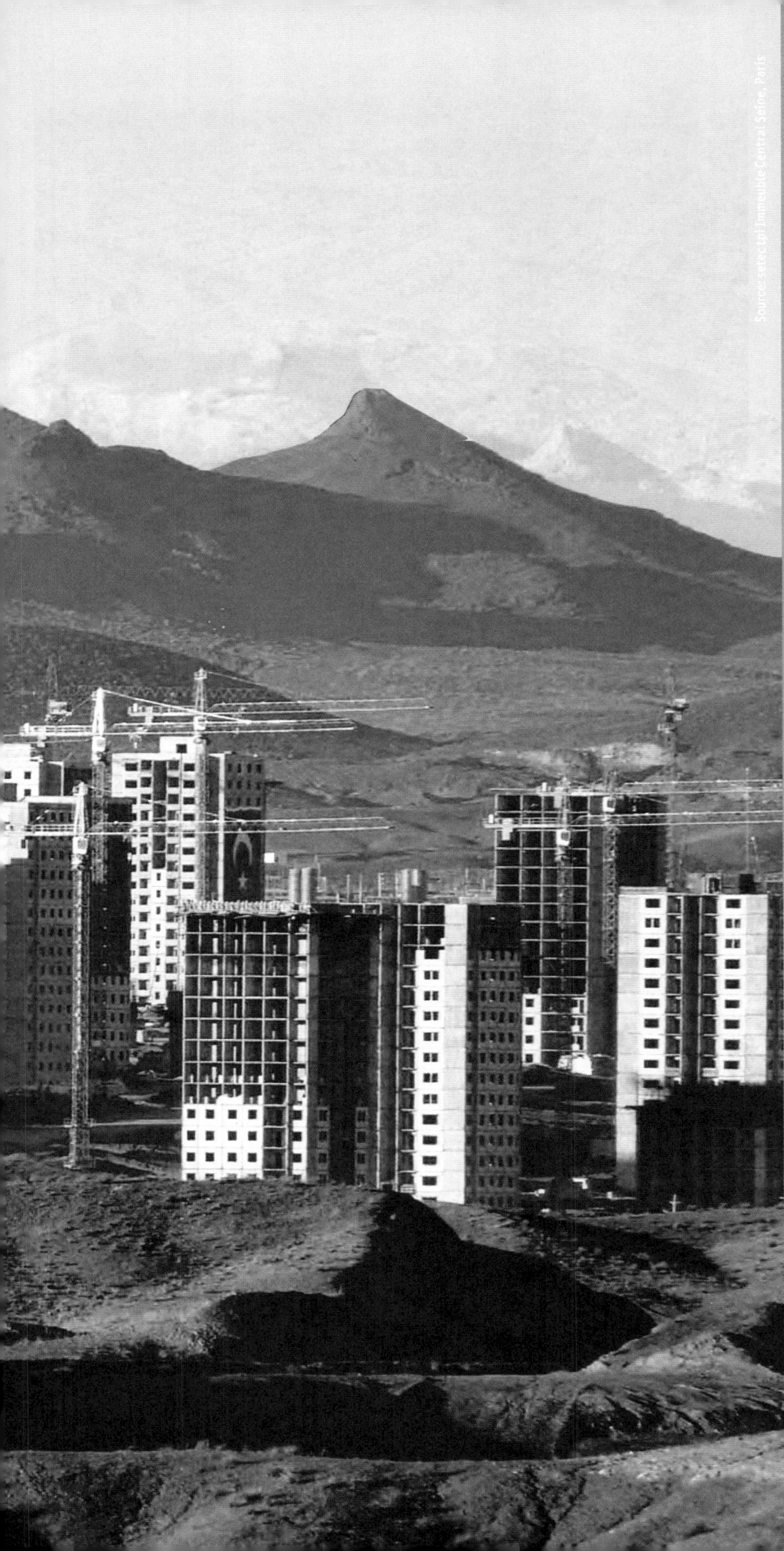

Source: setec cpl Immeuble Central Seine, Paris

Aerial view of the New Town Parand

New Town Parand
Shahr-e Jadid-e Parand
شهر جدید پرند

Parand, ca. 50 km southwest of
Tehran
35.46660, 50.98300
Kayson Company
AD: ca. 2011/AH: ca. 1432/Yaz: ca. 1380

The New Town Parand is located about
50 km southwest of Tehran en route to
Imam Khomeini International Airport.
It was planned for 80,000 inhabitants
on the discharge of Tehran and offers
an alternative to the informal settlements. Originally designed for an average density, the New Town got a new master plan, which now relies on high density in the form of high-rise buildings. In
1960, only one third of the Iranian population lived in urban areas, whereas today
there are already 70 per cent. In addition
to the dynamics, the nature of urbaniza-
tion has changed. Today megacities ar no
longer the fastest growing places, but
rather the suburbs. In objectives and spatial shaping the New Town Parand orients
itself to the European welfare state New
Towns after 1945. Thereby urban planning
and urban design are primarily regarded
as technically-oriented fields of action
enabling construction of the most possible living space in the shortest time.
Row of houses and over-sized outdoor
areas are divided by huge transport axis.
The interfaces of the mono-functional

urban spaces are not worked out, a total
identity cannot be read. Alongside
the largely deficient completed buildings, it paints a rather sad picture.

Apartment No. 1
Aparteman-e Maskuni Shomareh yek
آپارتمان مسکونی شماره یک

Mahallat
33.91111, 50.45306
Architecture by Collective Terrain
AD: 2011/AH: 1432/Yaz:1380

In the small town of Mahallat, the majority
of the workforce is engaged in the energy-
intensive business of cutting and treating
stone, which is highly dependent on fossil
fuels and produces an enormous amount
of waste due to an inefficient stone-cut-
ting technique. The Apartment No.1 project by the architectural office AbCT
of, Seoul, South Korea, turns the inef-
ficiency to economic and environmental advantage by reusing leftover stones

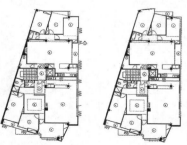

Floor plans of Apartment No. 1

for both exterior and some interior walls, which led to the increasing adoption of stone recycling by local builders. Thus, the project is able to connect the building with the unique context of the city and also proves that a creative architectonical solution can help to preserve valuable natural resources and reduce costs. The five-storey structure comprises two ground-level retail spaces and eight, three-bedroom apartments above. Small windows are shielded by triangular stone protrusions, and larger ones have wooden shutters which allow residents to regulate light and temperature levels. The austere, prismatic form of the building is balanced by the warmth of the natural materials.

Borj-e Melal Beinol Tehran, in the urban context with the Alborz mountains in the background

Tehran International Tower
Borj-e Beinol Melal Tehran
برج بین المللی تهران

341

Eslamshahr, Tehran
35.74268, 51.39914
François Dubuisson
AD: 2011 / AH: 1432 / Yaz: 1380

Tehran International Tower, the tallest residential building in Iran, is located north of Youssef Abad, near the Kordestan and Resalat expressways, with excellent transport links to major highways. The tower is divided into three wings, each offset by 120°, granting a sweeping panoramic view of Tehran's skyline. It has 572 units, with apartments ranging in size from 42 to 500 m² on fifty-six floors, accessed by fifteen public elevators.

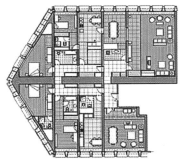

Floor plan of an apartment in Borj-e Beinol Melal

The tower is made of reinforced concrete walls and ceilings with high stiffness arranged star-shaped for earthquake protection. Tehran International Tower is one of the most expensive residential buildings in Tehran.

Apartment No. 1 from recycled Stones

Street elevation

Detail of façade

Source: www.designboom.com

Brick façade

Source: www.designboom.com

Construction phase

Brick Pattern House
Khaneh Ajor Baft
خانه آجر بافت

Jeyhoon, Tehran
35.69669, 51.36431
Alireza Mashhadmirza
AD: 2011 / AH: 1432 / Yaz: 1380

Architecture in many countries is reality, but in Iran it is a luxurious fantasy. The Brick Pattern House is located in one of Tehran's poorest districts, in Jeyhoon, where one is hard pressed to find a building that complies with minimum standard requirements. Owners cannot afford the costs of a contractor and instead build their houses themselves. Alireza Mashhadmirza has always looked at the social role of architecture. This project was a challenge to show that architecture has a place even in such economically and culturally challenged areas.

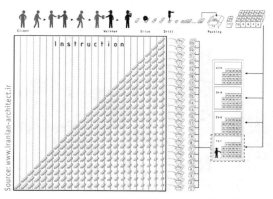

Source: www.iranian-architect.ir

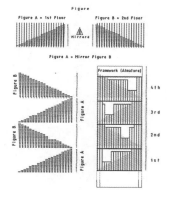

Instruction for the construction of the Brick Pattern House

Nevertheless, the Brick Pattern House is not a village cottage but a city building with an earthquake-resistant structure, energy-saving walls, acceptable acoustic properties, fire safety and functional technical services. The space requirements are similar to any small scale modern apartment building. The cost of labour in Iran is proportionally low and it is therefore easier to create special designs on smaller scales than in developed countries. Alireza Mashhadmirza went back to traditional architecture by using brick as the main building material, and he made a kind of contemporary mashrabiya to cover the whole façade to mitigate the glaring sunlight of Tehran. In view of the low budget, the architect created a method which does not need many drawings and does not require a great amount of time for supervision. He invented a new and extremely easy means of communication based on a table which listed all information necessary to build a façade. This is something similar to the instructions traditionally given in carpet workshops to coordinate the activities of several weavers working on the same carpet. This project has been shortlisted for the housing category for the 2012 world architecture festival and received an award from *Memar* magazine for one of the best architectural achievements of the year.

Father's Inn
Mehmansaray-e Pader
مهمانسرای پدر

Khansar, Isfahan
33.21906, 50.31597
ZAV Consulting Engineers
AD: 2011/AH: 1432/Yaz: 1380

In order to respect the scale of the city, the building volume is divided into three blocks, reflecting the dimensions of the neighbouring buildings with their openings. In addition, the height of the volumes was staggered so that they can only be partially seen. The architects reinterpreted the local building tradition and detailing. They applied the typical Khansar pattern of "place and path" inside the building as well, thus linking the house to the city. "Indoor life" was another pattern picked up by these architects, resulting in an enhancement of the courtyard instead of the street. In the local dialect khane, which means house in Farsi, translates rather to room, perhaps because all activities in a house take place in rooms. The rooms of the houses in Khansar usually open to the courtyard to which they are connected by a semi-open space and doors. All these features were implemented in the new construction. In 2012, Father's Inn was awarded the *Memar* Prize and published in *Memar* Magazine No. 70.

Source: Contemporary Architecture of Iran (CAOI)

Interior view

Staggered structure of Father's Inn

Ski Resort Barin
Barin Eski Tochal
.برین اسکی توچال

Shemshak, Tehran
36.01134, 51.48808
RYRA Studio – Ashkan Bagheri
Aghdam, Navid Nasrollahzadeh
AD: 2011/AH: 1432/Yaz:1380

Barin Ski Resort with Alborz mountains in the background

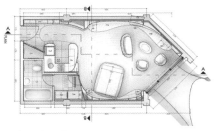

Floor plan of an apartment

This ten-storey resort is located near the Shemshak ski resort, the second largest skiing area in Iran and only half an hour's drive from the capital. In 2008, the clients requested architects to redesign a ski resort as a cozy and snug place for young people to relax in after skiing in extremely cold weather. The location is defined by snow-covered landscapes. The Barin Ski resort picks up on the philosophy of designing buildings so that the form emulates the immediate environment in a fluid way. Barin ski resort looks as one with the snow-covered mountains, almost as if windswept onto the mountain side like an iced rock formation. The individual rooms, sixty-seven in total, each of a different size, from 45 m² studio flats to 270 m² penthouses, seem carved into a mountainous ice block like natural caves. Each dome-shaped unit enhances the feeling of a warm, homey cave to relax in after skiing in the cold. This design approach continues inside the rooms and passages, which are also organically formed, as well as the pebble-shaped windows that offer stunning views of the surrounding mountain range. Taken together, all of these factors make the Barin Ski Resort a holistic building that complements its incredible natural habitat.

Façade detail

Interior view of an apartment

Source: RYRA Studio, Persia Photography Centre

Ghaneei House
Khaneh-ye Ghaneei
خانه ی قانعی

Mir St., Isfahan
32.63502, 51.67495
*Polsheer Consultant, Mohammad
Reza Ghaneei, Ashkan Ghaneei*
AD: 2012/AH: 1433/Yaz:1381

Khaneh-ye Ghaneei is an old house located on the south side of the home of the architect's father. As the children grew up, more space was needed, so two other rooms were added on the top floor on the north side of the existing building. Similar to ancient Persian buildings such as Chehel Sotun palace, a porch was built on top of these new rooms, to accommodate the whole family. Thereafter a driveway was built on the east side of the house, connecting the house to the entrance in the back alley. Finally, a staircase with three stairs was built to connect the east to the west parts. The aluminum covering of the main structure resembles a contemporary form of ancient Persian houses, orosi, which allows full control and view to the outside but no view from outside as coloured window glass was installed. The circulation system is an up-to-date form of the circulation system present in old Persian houses, providing horizontal transition into three vertical levels.

The orosi window, which allows full control and view to the outside but no view from outside

Floor plan

Plants play an important role. The old mulberry tree in the yard attracts every viewer's attention, followed by the image of the cedar tree at the end of the stairs, and this beautiful green picture will end with the image of the old pine tree which is located in the father's house.

View into living room

View into courtyard

484

Entrance area of Niavaran Apartment Complex

Apartment complex from the entrance

Source: Behdari, Yousef/Bavani, Pardis Khabaz (CAOI)

Niavaran Apartment Complex 346
Majmueh-ye Niavaran
مجتمع مسکونی نیاوران
Shemiran, Tehran
35.81222, 51.47047
Mohammad Reza Nikbakht
AD: 2012/AH: 1433/Yaz: 1381

Mohammad Reza Nikbakht's Niavaran residential complex is located in the Shemiran area at the foot of the Alborz mountains. It was used as a summer resort until 40 years ago and was known for its numerous gardens and trees, of which only a few exist today due to massive urbanisation. The parcel allocated to this project also boasts a number of old trees and their preservation was considered as the first priority in designing the complex. The preliminary design concept is based on the inclusion

of the existing old trees on the building site and considering the main axis of the trees, the building mass was divided into two main sections. The preservation of the green area alongside this axis also affected the arrangement of the sides and the overall shape of the building.

Danial Apartment 347
Aparteman-e Maskuni Danial
آپارتمان مسکونی دانیال
Khyiaban-e Pasdaran,Tehran
35.79678, 51.47536
Reza Sayadian, Sara Kalantary
AD: 2012/AH: 1433/Yaz: 1381

In 2010, Reza Sayadian and Sara Kalantary were commissioned to build a seven-storey residential building in which the creation of a dynamic façade was all-important. The whole exterior façade consists

Ground floor plan of the apartment complex

Upper floor plan

Source: Behdari, Yousef/Bavani, Pardis Khabaz (CAOI)

Courtyard within Niavaran Apartment Complex

Façade with sliding tree-panels

Floor plan of Danial Apartment

of tree-like panels that can be moved manually, providing infinite choices to the residents who can control the panels from inside. The variety of shapes of the façade, added by the angle of sunlight, has a unique effect on the interior since different light and dancing shadows are created by every movement. The different depths convey a feeling of unlimited space.

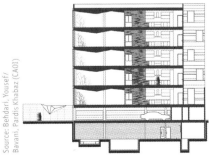

Section of Danial Apartment

Interior of Danial Apartment

Aerial view of Stone Carpet Pit Garden in Tabriz

Stone Carpet Tabriz
Tabriz Sangh Farsh
سنگ فرش

Shahid Beheshti Square, Tabriz
38.07121, 46.30467
Sharestan Consultants
AD: 2012/AH: 1434/Yaz:1381

The Stone Carpet functions as a land-mark within the city. The project is actually a pit garden, equivalent in size to the Maidan-e Naqsh-e Jehan in Isfahan and serves as an urban hub connecting the surrounding buildings and the urban context below ground level. The carpet's pattern is inspired by the oldest Tabriz carpet kept in the city's museum.

Both the design and the supervision of the construction was done by Sharestan Consultants. This huge creation is made from 500,000 pieces of coloured tile stones. It will be part of the new Ipak Trading Centre.

Detail of Stone Carpet Pit Garden in Tabriz

Stone Carpet Pit Garden in Tabriz

Padideh Kish
Padideh Kish
پدیده کیش

Insel Kish
26.49897, 53.98969
Shirdel and Associates Architects
AD: 2013/AH: 1434/Yaz: 1382

In 2013, Shirdel Associates won first prize in the competition hosted by Padideh Kish, a hotel complex on the holiday island of Kish, the most important tourism hub in Iran and the fourth-largest in the Middle East. The magnitude of the project and the diversity of structures to be designed demanded an approach similar to the planning of a city. The master plan is a result of juxtaposition, the interaction and development of concepts where each one is dependent on "the architectural achievements and architectural history of Iran with the aim to provide a range of fantastic and exciting scenarios for leisure and sport". Bahram Shridel, who returned to Iran in 1994, exerts a lasting influence on Iranian architects. Shirdel was director of the graduate design program at the Architectural Association School of Architecture in London and taught design theory at Harvard and various other universities in the US. His work was exhibited at the 1984 Venice Architecture Biennale and in 1992 in the Museum of Modern Art in New York. In 1996, Bahram Shridel and Seyed Hadi Mirmiran, two of the most important Iranian architects, worked together on various projects and developed a perfect synthesis of their two very-different approaches.

Bird's-eye view of the hotel complex

Rendering of the huge complex on Kish Island

Source: Nextoffice

Main façade in open state

Sharifi-ha house
Khaneh-ye Sharifi-ha
خانه شریفی‌ها

Khiyaban-e Sharifi, Khiyaban-e
Saleh Hossein, Darrous, Tehran
35.77389, 51.45656
Nextoffice
AD: 2013 / AH: 1434 / Yaz: 1382

350

The seven-storey Sharifi-ha House is located north of Tehran, where summers are hot and winters are cold. Alireza Taghaboni found an unconventional answer to this. On three floors of the building he developed revolvable wooden boxes which can be moved out in summer, offering a projecting volume with wide, large terraces, and closed down on the terrace during snowy winter months, providing minimal openings and a total absence of those wide summer terraces. Taghaboni draws on traditional Iranian houses, which dynamically serve as seasonal modes of habitation by offering their residents both a Zemestan-Neshin, or winter living room, and Taabestan-Neshin, or summer living room. The three turning boxes contain the breakfast room on the first floor, a guest room on the second floor and a home office on the third. Each box has a side door, giving access to the terrace when it is open, and to the inside of the house when closed. In order to adapt the change in the façade, the terraces are furnished with tiltable balustrades. A central courtyard allows daylight to enter even when the façade is closed.

Source: Nextoffice

Main façade in closed state

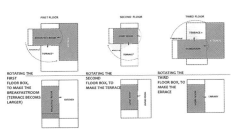

Scheme of Rotation Process

Suspension bridges connect the two fixed volumes on both sides of the seven-storey courtyard. The sensational, spatial qualities of the interiors, as well as the formal configuration of its exterior, directly respond to the displacement of turning boxes that cause the building's volume to become open or closed, introverted or extroverted.

Source: Nextoffice

View into the covered courtyard

Villa Kouhsar
Villa-ye Kouhsar
ویلای کوهسار

Kurdan, Tehran
35.92092, 50.83381
Nextoffice
AD: 2013/AH: 1434/Yaz: 1382

The Kouhsar Villa rests in a wide landscape, capturing the delightful vistas of the Alborz mountains in the background. It forms a cube with an elastic façade that receives tension from a dynamic vacuum on the southern face. Stretching the façade towards the void and columns did not merely meet the structural necessities but also provided spatial qualities for both the interior and exterior. The building was named Kouhsar, Mountain, to recall the old name for the location of the house. The front façade is equipped with a generous ayvan, formed by columnar walls, showing references to the Persian ingenuity of developing floor plans of traditional buildings. Particularly interesting is the view from the central interior space which spatially recalls the Forty Columns Palace. The portal is wide open towards the outdoor space where the "free" exterior and the "enclosed" interior are brought in such close relation that it is difficult to say where the one begins and the other ends, an effect that is enhanced by the pool placed in front of it. Upstairs the construction is intersected by galleries and rooms, each of which has its own shape. The ayvan open towards the garden connects garden and villa.

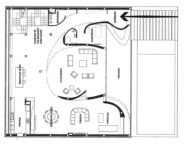

Floor plan and section

Interior of the Villa with views into the surrounding environment

Source: Behdari, Yousef/Bavani, Pardis Khabaz (CAOI)

Shams Pavilion
Kushk-e Shams
کوشک شمس

Saveh, Markazi
35.03978, 50.31994
Karand Group
AD: 2013 / AH: 1434 / Yaz: 1382

Shams Pavilion is situated in a village near Saveh, 70 km west of Tehran. The client is a journalist who requested a recreational house close to the family farm corresponding to the Iranian mentality. Pursuing the client's needs and considering the warm and dry climate of the site, the Koushk, a Persian traditional summer house, was redefined. Koushk, or pavilion, is a kind of extroverted architecture which is commonly located in a garden with semi-open balconies. Irrigation on site was used to create a pool surrounding the building footprint. The water reflects the building as well as the daylight into the house. The building envelope forms a cube in which the interior spaces are arranged as closed or semi-open rooms and recessed to protect them from direct sunlight. Generous porches were built on the north, south and west sides, supported by a pair of large, thin columns. The natural vistas on the other hand led to the creation of an L-shaped terrace on the second floor, expanding from south to north and connecting with the shell to form a continuous surface.

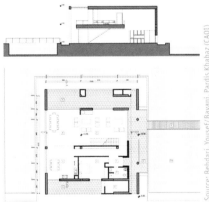

Source: Behdari, Yousef/Bavani, Pardis Khabaz (CAOI)

Ground floor plan and section

Source: Kaveh Seyed Ahmadian (Contemporary Architecture of Iran)

Open-plan interior of the pavilion

Niayesh Office Building, view from Farhanb Boulevard

Niayesh Office Building, detail of street façade

Niayesh Office Building
Sajteman Idar-e Niayesh
ساختمان اداری نیایش
Saadat abad, Tehran
35.77726, 51.38830
Behzad Atabaki Studio,
Behzad Atabaki
AD: 2013/AH: 1434/Yaz:1382

The Niayesh office building overlooks a busy expressway and is set on a disproportionate semi-triangular site. The main objective in the design was to create a form that would not reflect this disproportion. The central concept was to set the layers free from a monotonous repetition or other structural confinements. The floor layers, whilst not exactly similar, were built up in a free style and have a light, single-material stone cladding to create a harmonious and homogeneous quality for the building. The building's identity also takes its cue from the high level of kinetic energy surrounding the site in that it resembles a photographic image of a fast moving object that is seen in stretched, sometimes wave-like lines. The interior moves along the same concept of spatial smoothness and flow. Large windows have been installed to benefit from the daylight and the fascinating views of city, mountains, and sky.

House of 40 knots
Khaneh-ye Chehel Girih
خانه چهل گره
Kahrizak, Tehran
35.52100, 51.35965
Habibeh Madjdabadi and
Alireza Mashhadimirza
AD: 2014/AH: 1435/Yaz:1383

Persian carpets are world-famous, and bricks have a strong relationship with Iranian historical architecture. Here they are fused into a contemporary façade which appears as a collection of intricately interwoven components. Creating a small and low budget apartment building in Tehran does not leave much room for creativity, yet an architect can try to do something with the material, textures, outer envelope and light. In light of that, a modern interpretation of the ancient mashrabiyya was conceived by using bricks available on the local market. In order to reduce costs in the construction of this five-storey building, unskilled workers, unable to read technical drawings, were employed instead of master craftsmen. All the construction data was transformed into simple instructions to be recited by the supervisor during every step, resulting in a protruding irregular geometry, designed

East view

brick by brick, a system devised by watching carpet weavers in traditional workshops. The building is entirely covered with a mesh of bricks impaled on rod bars as contiguous pearl necklaces. The distances between the bricks were adjusted to create an opaque effect, through which light does not pass, but when there is a window behind the mesh, it becomes a transparent grid.

Detail of façade

Source: Muze-ye Honarha-ye Ziba

Tabiat Bridge
Pol-e Tabiat
پل طبیعت

between Taleghani-Park und
Abo-Atash-Park, Tehran
35.75411, 51.42024
Leila Araghian
AD: 2014/AH: 1435/Yaz: 1383

Tabiat Bridge is the largest pedestrian bridge ever built in Iran. It is 270 m long and connects two public parks, the Taleghani and Abo Atash Park, over Shahid Modarres highway in northern Tehran. Although bridges are usually considered as structural projects, the approach here is more architectural. The "nature" bridge is the first project of the Iranian architect Leila Araghian,

who won the competition whilst studying at Shahid Beheshti university and then founded Diba Tensile Architecture together with Alireza Behzadi. "I did not want to create just a bridge connecting a park to another" says the now 31-year old architect, "I wanted to create a place where people dwell, enjoy and think". The result is a three-dimensional truss with two continuous levels on three tree-shaped columns. All the levels are connected to each other by stairs and ramps, providing multiple paths throughout the bridge to get from one level to another. The curved pier, with variable widths and turnarounds, seating areas, green areas and restaurants, decelerates and creates a mysterious world of its own. The bridge was opened by Tehran's mayor Mohammad Bagher Ghalibaf in October 2014, after a construction period of just two years. It is considered the third landmark of Tehran and before long became a popular meeting place. The bridge is reminiscent of famous predecessors in Isfahan, the Siosepol and Pol-e Khaju bridges. They were also places for public events, poetry readings and offered space for traditional teahouses. The bridge received several awards, among others the 2015 Architizer A+ Award.

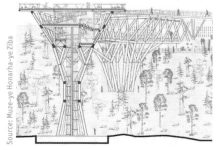

Source: Muze-ye Honarha-ye Ziba

Section

Source: Fluid Motion Architects

Jaam Tower
Burj-e Jaam
برج جام

Khiyaban-e Shariati, Tehran
35.74934, 51.45013
Fluid Motion Architects
AD: 2015/AH: 1436/Yaz: 1384

356 F

Dynamic and fluid structures form an important guiding principle in the work of Fluid Motion Architects. Commissioned by Mellat Bank, the tower comprises a stack of rectangular volumes, all of which follow a slightly upward curve. A balance has been created by the slight shifting of the glass blocks in relation to each other, giving the office building a rather striking appearance. Jaam Tower is adjacent to Shariati Avenue, one of two central and historic arteries in Tehran running along a north-south axis. Jaam

Tower is composed of two volumes: a horizontal commercial platform with a footprint coverage of 80 per cent on two levels, and a vertical office tower with a footprint coverage of ca. 25 per cent on twenty five floors. The simple cubic form of the modern office tower was broken down into repeatable modules designed with 7.6 m spans, ideal for different office and commercial spaces as well as parking areas. The modules are stacked in a way to allow for views of the park on lower levels, and to avoid blocking sunlight and airflow on the north side. With an unusual transformation, the horizontal platform allows direct access from the park and adjacent sidewalks to the roof garden of the commercial volume, and visually merges the green space of the park with the project, creating a connection between workspace and landscape. In addition to providing suitable solutions to urban and climatic issues, and seamlessly combining horizontal and vertical volumes, the project sets aside the cliché of modern cuboid towers, replacing it with a penetrating, floating structure. Tehran's natural slope from north to south makes this project a distinctive landmark that is visible from many different parts of the city.

Source: Fluid Motion Architects

Reza Daneshmir, design sketches of Jaam Tower

Street artist at work

Residential Villa
Villa-ye Maskuni
ویلای مسکونی

Labbaf St., Tehran
35.71326, 51.41345
ARSH 4D studio, Alireza Sherafati,
Pantea Eslami
AD: 2015 / AH: 1436 / Yaz: 1384

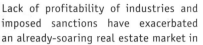

357 G

Lack of profitability of industries and imposed sanctions have exacerbated an already-soaring real estate market in

View into the courtyard

Courtyard elevation

Interior view

Tehran. As a result, the city is now faced with a growing number of infill projects whose aesthetic challenges are generally reduced to envelope design. In the Residential Villa project, the site is located at the end of a dead-end alley. It does not have a view of the street and it is not seen by passersby. To address the unique design challenges of this project, the architects suggested the creation of a view for a project with no view. Inspired by the popular children's story, *The Last Leaf*, and utilizing the talent of a street artist, they decided to paint a landscape on the 18 m high cement wall to create a view for the inhabitants. They reused the bricks from an old building which existed on this site. When the demolition was complete, the bricks were sorted and used in the façade and other parts of the building. Considering that the observable façade from the alley is about 3 m wide, the design progress of the mass is intended to invite passers-by to come into the building.

ARG Shopping Mall
Arg Tajrish
ارگ تجاری

Maidan-e Tajrish, Tehran
35.807899, 51.426249
ARSH 4D studio, Alireza Sherafati, Pantea Eslami
AD: 2015/AH: 1436/Yaz: 1384

In 2012, Alireza Sherafati and Pantea Eslami won the competition to design a new façade, landscape, roofscape, and interior for the ARG Shopping Mall, which was already designed and under construction. Re-composing the façade, they decided to simplify the massing and create a smooth and neutral surface to counteract the chaos of the neighbourhood. Glass is used to reflect the old trees of the surrounding area and highlight the mountains to the north. Elevation differences of the site are solved by landscape – steps turning into long benches provide connections from the sidewalk and create a public outdoor auditorium.

Source: Parham Taghioff

View from Tajrish Square

Kahrizak Residential Project 359

Project Maskuuni-ye Kahrizak

پروژه مسکونی کهریزک

Kahrizak, Tehran

35.51915, 51.36021

CAAT Studio, Mahdi Kamboozia

AD: 2015 / AH: 1436 / Yaz: 1384

Kahrizak is an underprivileged urban district located southwest of Tehran. Due to its proximity to Tehran, the population in this region is steadily growing. As a result, the region is changing rapidly and many poor-quality residential dwellings are being built. The choice of material was a significant parameter in this project mainly because it had to be something affordable and easy to supply to the site. As a result, CAAT Studio considered clay blocks produced in a factory nearby, benefiting not only the project but also local businesses. The bricks to create the modules of the residences are placed within a concrete frame, resulting in a grid façade that allows for the views and climatic conditions. The selection of concrete and brick for this project reduces its cost to the minimum whilst at the same time creating high quality living spaces. Each module is designed in relation to the function of the space behind it. Despite the variety of the brick modules, they are coherent and homophonic. This is how it resulted in a smooth façade to represent both Iranian brick architecture and the essence of residential dwelling.

In addition, this geometry is practical for local workmen and thus facilitates the construction process. The geometry is also present in traditional residential architecture of desert areas of Iran. CAAT Studio was not only responsible for designing the residential project but also assisted the local workmen by training them how to handle this unique arrangement of the brick modules. There is a basic principle in Iranian architecture, namely the richness in details in coexistence with the depiction of simplicity in overall scale, which finally merges with the context and matches its functions. The Kahrizak residential project respects these typologies; it is shaped around them and the history of the place.

Source: Parham Taghioff

General view of the project

Source: Ashkan Radnia

Detail of front elevation

Hashtgerd Planned City
Shahr-e Jadid-e Hashtgerd
شهر جدید هشتگرد

Hashtgerd New Town,
Tehran-Karaj
35.98250, 50.73528
Technische Universität Berlin
AD: 2016 / AH: 1437 / Yaz: 1385

Site plan of the Young Cities Project

The planned city Hashtgerd was founded by the Iranian urban development authority in 1993. The town had 40,000 inhabitants in the year 2000, which will have increased to 500,000 inhabitants by 2016. It is located at the western end of the almost completely developed Greater Tehran-Karaj. It is the largest new town in the country and planned for about half a million inhabitants. The experimental Young Cities Project is located at the present outskirts of the town where, on a 35 ha site, a residential area for about 8,000 residents was established in 2013. Invited by the local developer, Technische Universität Berlin developed a design proposal which aims to establish an urban identity. The pilot project acknowledges the need for privacy in Islamic society, with a spatial hierarchy of district over neighbourhoods right down to individual units, which does justice to the Islamic understanding of public and private spheres. The urban design is characterised by the topography at the foot of the Alborz mountains. Compact, south-oriented housing clusters on ridges form spatially combined neighbourhoods, each for 250 to 300 inhabitants. In the centre of each neighbourhood, small commercial units are arranged around a courtyard-like space. The open spaces are not considered isolated but are creatively and spatially integrated into the neighbourhood. The central park is linked to the community centre, and the gardens are allocated to the private living quarters. The historic Islamic town offers numerous possibilities for contemporary climate-friendly architecture, like the compact design and introverted house typology. Through these, a reduction of enveloping surfaces and self-regulation of microclimate via shading and thermal cooling can be achieved. Both affect the energy demand. The housing for the aggregated housing clusters follows this approach with a modular courtyard house typology.

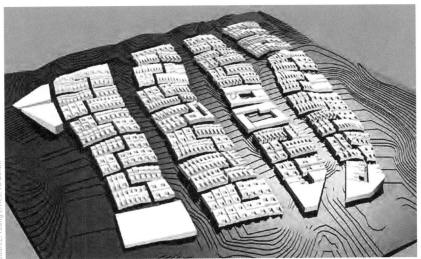

Model of the Young Cities Project

Index

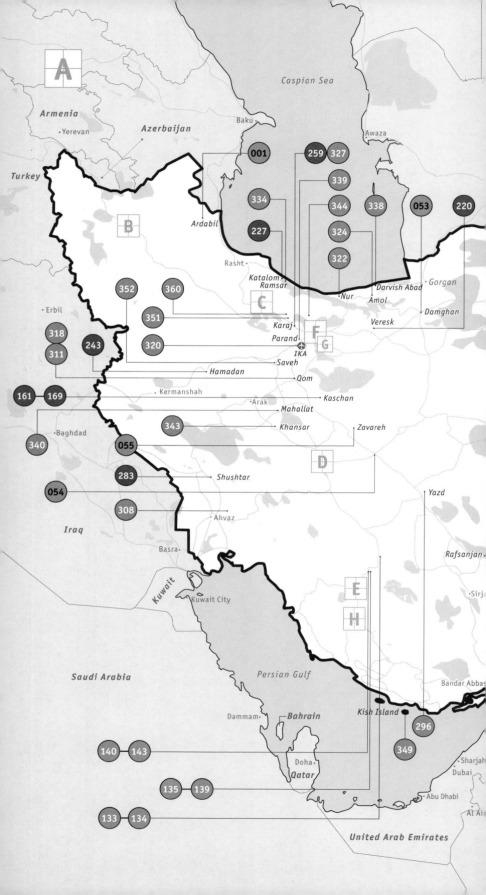

Uzbekistan

Khiva

Bukhara

Turkmenistan

244

210

Ashgabat

Bojnurd

Tus

Mashhad

Sabzevar   Neyshabur

Herat

Birjand

Afghanistan

Zabol

Kerman

Zahedan

Islamic Republic of Iran

Pakistan

305

Chabahar

Masqat

Arabian Sea

Oman

0   200 km

https://goo.gl/BQN1nu

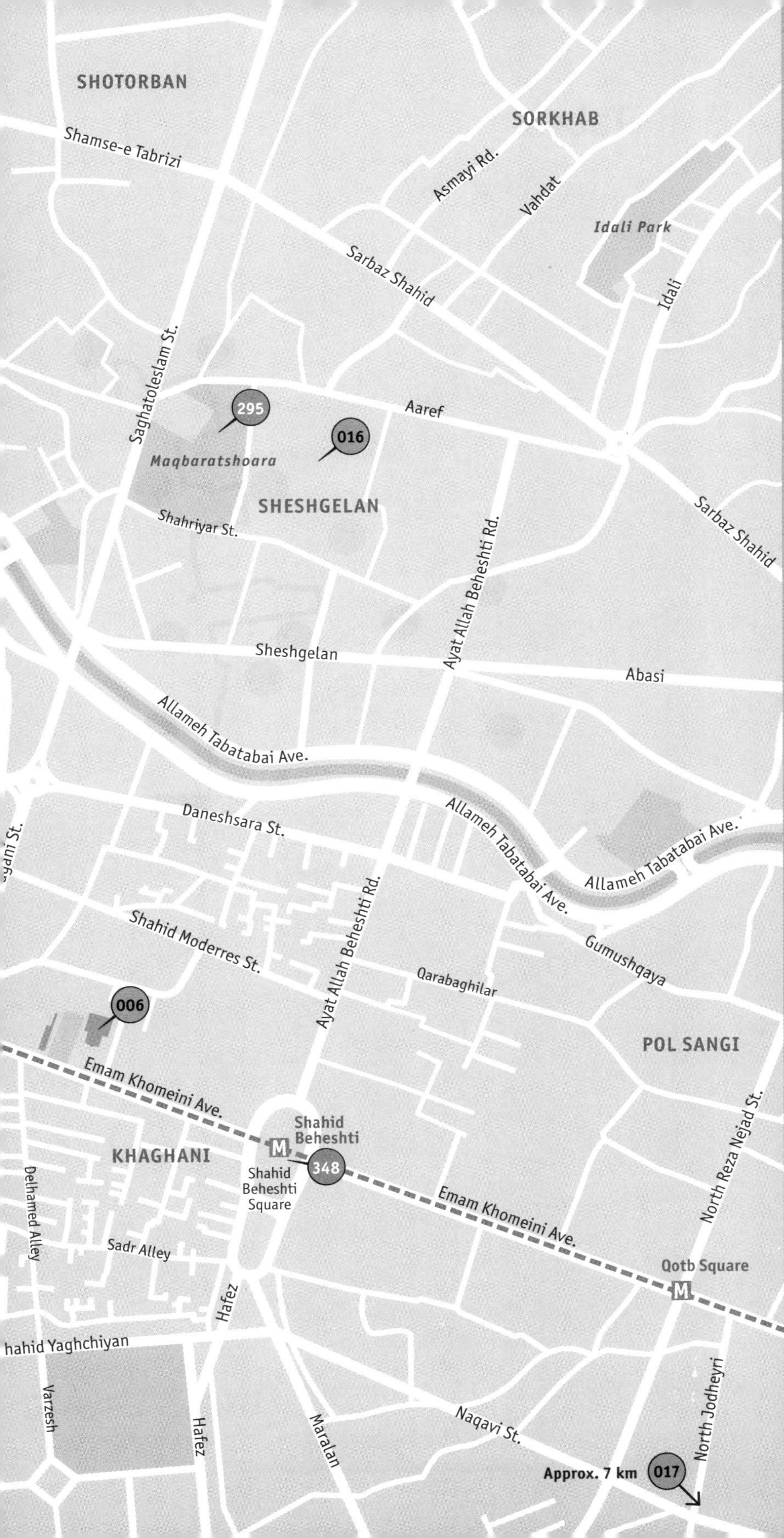

SHOTORBAN

SORKHAB

Shamse-e Tabrizi

Asmayi Rd.

Vahdat

Idali Park

Idali

Sarbaz Shahid

Saghatoleslam St.

Aaref

295

016

Maqbaratshoara

SHESHGELAN

Shahriyar St.

Ayat Allah Beheshti Rd.

Sarbaz Shahid

Sheshgelan

Abasi

Allameh Tabatabai Ave.

Allameh Tabatabai Ave.

Allameh Tabatabai Ave.

Daneshsara St.

Gumushqaya

Shahid Moderres St.

Ayat Allah Beheshti Rd.

Qarabaghilar

006

POL SANGI

Emam Khomeini Ave.

Shahid Beheshti

KHAGHANI

M

348

Shahid Beheshti Square

Emam Khomeini Ave.

North Reza Nejad St.

Delhamed Alley

Sadr Alley

Qotb Square

M

hahid Yaghchiyan

Varzesh

Hafez

Hafez

Maralan

Naqavi St.

North Jodheyri

Approx. 7 km

017

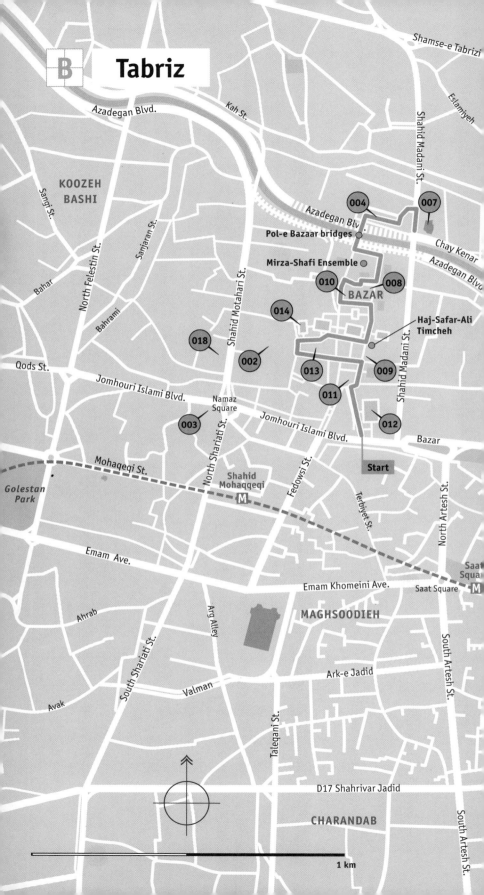

SHOTORBAN

SORKHAB

Shamse-e Tabrizi

Asmayi Rd.

Vahdat

Idali Park

Sarbaz Shahid

Idali

Saghatoleslam St.

Aaref

Sarbaz Shahid

Maqbaratshoara

SHESHGELAN

Shahriyar St.

Ayat Allah Beheshti Rd.

Sheshgelan

Abasi

Allameh Tabatabai Ave.

Daneshsara St.

...ghani St.

Shahid Moderres St.

Ayat Allah Beheshti Rd.

006

Emam Khomeini Ave.

Shahid
Beheshti

KHAGHANI

Shahid
Beheshti
Square

Delhamed Alley

Sadr Alley

Hafez

Shahid Yaghchiyan

Varzesh

Hafez

Maralan

City Walk 1
Tabriz – First Safavid Capital
Begin your walk through the Tabriz at the **Amir Ensemble (012)**, and continue through the **Haji-Sheikh-Kazem Timcheh (011)**, turn 45° with respect to the bazaar and head through **Haji-Mohammad-Qoli Timcheh and Sara (009)** and **Mozaffaryeh Timcheh (013)**, one of the most beautiful buildings in the bazaar. Go to the historically-important **Jameh Mosque (002)**, where Shah Ismail I introduced Shia as the Iranian state religion. Continue through **Mir-Abol-Hasan Sara (014)** and Haj-Safar-Ali Timcheh to **Malek Timcheh (010)**, a handsome Qadjar-period bazaar building. Make a detour to the elaborated Mirza-Shafi Ensemble and continue to the historical Pol-e Bazaar bridges with shops connecting the two parts of the bazaar on either side of Quri river. Go through the former **Bagh-e Sahib-abad (004)** and finish your tour in the **Shah Tahmasp Mosque (007)**, built by the son and successor of Shah Ismail I.

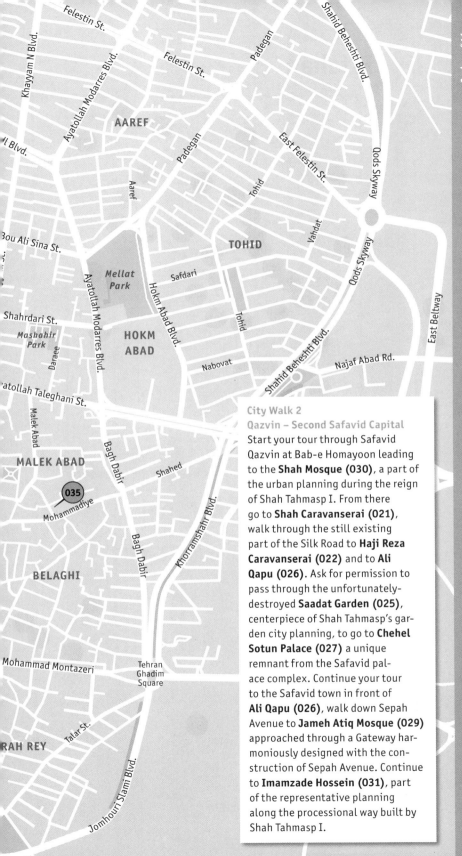

City Walk 2
Qazvin – Second Safavid Capital
Start your tour through Safavid Qazvin at Bab-e Homayoon leading to the **Shah Mosque (030)**, a part of the urban planning during the reign of Shah Tahmasp I. From there go to **Shah Caravanserai (021)**, walk through the still existing part of the Silk Road to **Haji Reza Caravanserai (022)** and to **Ali Qapu (026)**. Ask for permission to pass through the unfortunately-destroyed **Saadat Garden (025)**, centerpiece of Shah Tahmasp's garden city planning, to go to **Chehel Sotun Palace (027)** a unique remnant from the Safavid palace complex. Continue your tour to the Safavid town in front of **Ali Qapu (026)**, walk down Sepah Avenue to **Jameh Atiq Mosque (029)** approached through a Gateway harmoniously designed with the construction of Sepah Avenue. Continue to **Imamzade Hossein (031)**, part of the representative planning along the processional way built by Shah Tahmasp I.

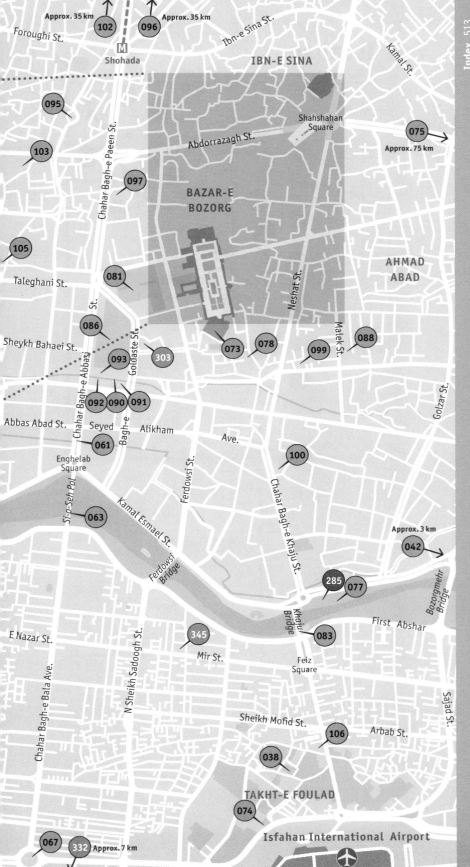

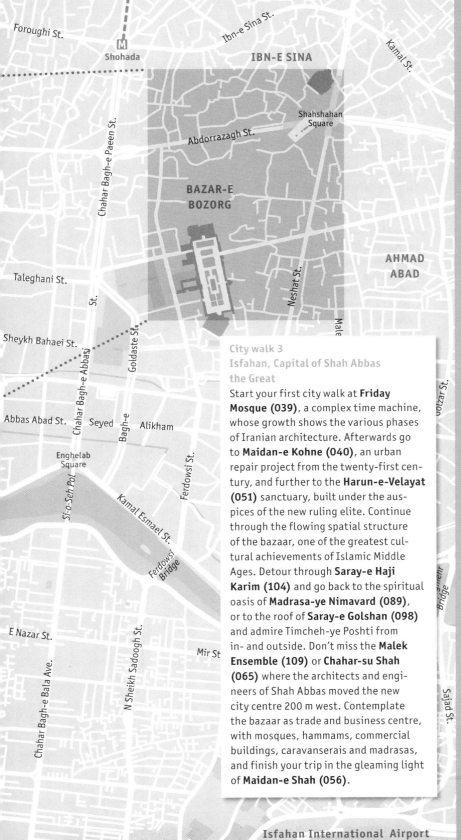

Foroughi St.

Shohada

IBN-E SINA

Ibn-e Sina St.

Kamal St.

Shahshahan
Square

Abdorrazagh St.

Chahar Bagh-e Paeen St.

BAZAR-E
BOZORG

AHMAD
ABAD

Taleghani St.

Neshat St.

Male

Sheykh Bahaei St.

Goldaste St.

St.

Chahar Bagh-e Abbasi

Abbas Abad St.

Seyed

Bagh-e

Alikham

Enghelab
Square

Ferdowsi St.

olzar St.

Si-o-Seh Pol

Kamal Esmael St.

Ferdowsi
Bridge

nehr

Bridge

E Nazar St.

N Sheikh Sadoogh St.

Mir St

Chahar Bagh-e Bala Ave.

Sajad St.

City walk 3
Isfahan, Capital of Shah Abbas
the Great
Start your first city walk at **Friday
Mosque (039)**, a complex time machine,
whose growth shows the various phases
of Iranian architecture. Afterwards go
to **Maidan-e Kohne (040)**, an urban
repair project from the twenty-first century, and further to the **Harun-e-Velayat
(051)** sanctuary, built under the auspices of the new ruling elite. Continue
through the flowing spatial structure
of the bazaar, one of the greatest cultural achievements of Islamic Middle
Ages. Detour through **Saray-e Haji
Karim (104)** and go back to the spiritual
oasis of **Madrasa-ye Nimavard (089)**,
or to the roof of **Saray-e Golshan (098)**
and admire Timcheh-ye Poshti from
in- and outside. Don't miss the **Malek
Ensemble (109)** or **Chahar-su Shah
(065)** where the architects and engineers of Shah Abbas moved the new
city centre 200 m west. Contemplate
the bazaar as trade and business centre,
with mosques, hammams, commercial
buildings, caravanserais and madrasas,
and finish your trip in the gleaming light
of **Maidan-e Shah (056)**.

Isfahan International Airport

D | Isfahan

City walk 4
Capital of Shah Abbas the Great
Continue your walk through
the Safavid town following the pro-
longation of the bazaar a few meters
to the south until the beginning
of the pre-Safavid Hassan Abbad
Bazaar, which follows the course
of the original Silk Road. Pass by
Imamzadeh-ye Ahmad and visit **Saru
Taqi Mosque (078)**. Stray through
Naqshe Jahan Quarter behind
Shah Mosque or visit the old typical **Arastoie House (099)** of the
Isfahan Calligrapher's Association
or **Khaneh-ye Mosafer al-Molk
(088)**, a large house with decorative
wood carvings. Continue your way
to Chahar-su Naghashi, proof that
even the south part of the bazaar was
completely roofed. Visit the remarkable **Madrasa-ye Sadr-e Khaju (100)**
and make a detour at Manouchehri
street along the Jubes, the traditional fresh water supply of the town.
Have a look at the Mausoleum of
Arthur Upham Pope and Phyllis
Ackerman, a mirror to their philosophy, before you end your trip at
Khaju Bridge (083).

Kharrazi Expy.

Kashani St.

Masjed-e Se

Mirdamad

Saheb Rowzat Ave.

Jahad St.

Shahpoor St.

LONBAN

Motahari St.
Koudak
Park

BISHE
HABIB

Felezi Bridge

Mellat

Zayandeh Rud

Marnan Bridge

Saedi St.

Vahid Bridge

W Nazar St.

Tohid St.

Mirza Kuchak Khan Expy.

Bagh-e Daryacheh

Khaghani St.

Hakim Nezami St.

Sohrevardi

Rudaki St.

Tohid St.

Daqiqi St.

Shariati St.

HOSEIN

1 km

Artesh

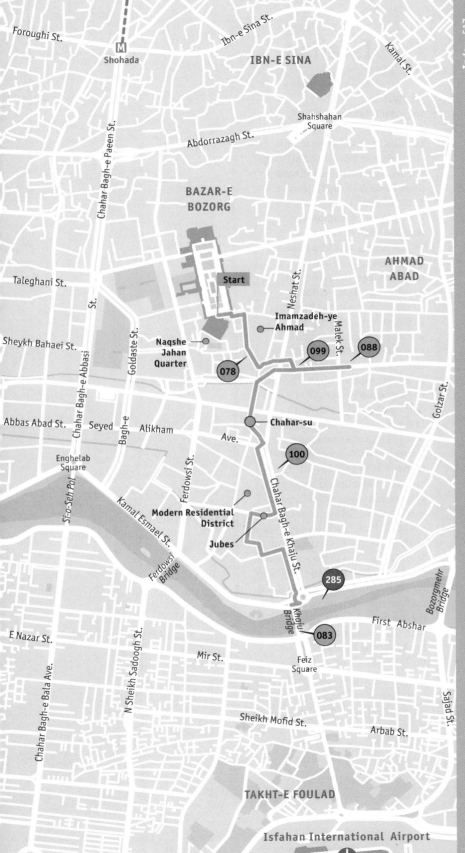

Foroughi St.

Ibn-e Sina St.

Kamal St.

Shohada

IBN-E SINA

Shahshahan
Square

Abdorrazagh St.

Chahar Bagh-e Paeen St.

**BAZAR-E
BOZORG**

**AHMAD
ABAD**

Taleghani St.

Start

Neshat St.

Malek St.

Sheykh Bahaei St.

**Imamzadeh-ye
Ahmad**

**Naqshe
Jahan
Quarter**

099

088

Goldaste St.

078

Abbas Abad St.

St.

Chahar Bagh-e Abbasi

Seyed

Bagh-e

Alikham

Ave.

Chahar-su

Golzar St.

Enghelab
Square

Ferdowsi St.

Chahar Bagh-e Khaiu St.

100

Si-o-Seh Pol

Kamal Esmael St.

**Modern Residential
District**

Jubes

Ferdowsi Bridge

285

Bozorgmehr Bridge

Khaiu
Bridge

First Abshar

E Nazar St.

N Sheikh Sadoogh St.

Mir St.

Feiz
Square

083

Sajad St.

Chahar Bagh-e Bala Ave.

Sheikh Mofid St.

Arbab St.

TAKHT-E FOULAD

Isfahan International Airport

D   Isfahan

City Walk 5
Imperial Isfahan

Dedicate a whole day to Imperial Isfahan. Start in the morning in the middle of **Sio-o-Seh Pol bridge (063)**, and walk through **Chahar Bagh Boulevard (061)**, the model of the Champs-Elysées. If it is a Friday, visit **Madrasa-ye Madar-e Shah (092)** and go to the Caravanserai, today **Abbasi Hotel (091)**, where you can sip tea in the legendary teahouse. Pass through **Bazar-e Honar (093)** and go to **Hasht Behesht (086)**, the only surviving palace along the Chahar Bagh. Take a look at **Tohid Khaneh (094)**, one of the few preserved structures of the Royal Palace. Then go to **Chehel Sotun Palace (081)** a highlight of every visit to Isfahan. In the afternoon, take your time for the buildings that have made Isfahan world-famous: **Maidan-e Naqsh-e Jehan (056)** with its juxtaposition of religion, economy, politics and legitimation. Start with **Ali Qapu (058)**, the access to the Royal Palace, and visit **Masjed-e Shah (073)**, the Royal Mosque of Shah Abbas – one of the most beautiful in the world. Head to the colourful **Sheikh Lotfollah Mosque (069)**, built to demonstrate the piety of the Safavid court. Finish your walk with the visit to the **Qeysaryeh Bazaar Portal (060)** and enjoy the hustle and bustle of the bazaar.

Kharrazi Expy.

Masjed-e Sey

Kashani St.

Mirdamad

Saheb Rowzat Ave.

Jahad St.

Shahpoor St.

LONBAN

Motahari St.

BISHE HABIB

Koudak Park

Felezi Bridge

Azar Bridge

Mellat

Marnan Bridge

Zayandeh Rud

Tohid St.

Saedi St.

W Nazar St.

Sohrevardi

Rudaki St.

Khaghani St.

Hakim Nezami St.

Tohid St.

Daqiqi St.

Shariati St.

HOSEIN

1 km

Artesh

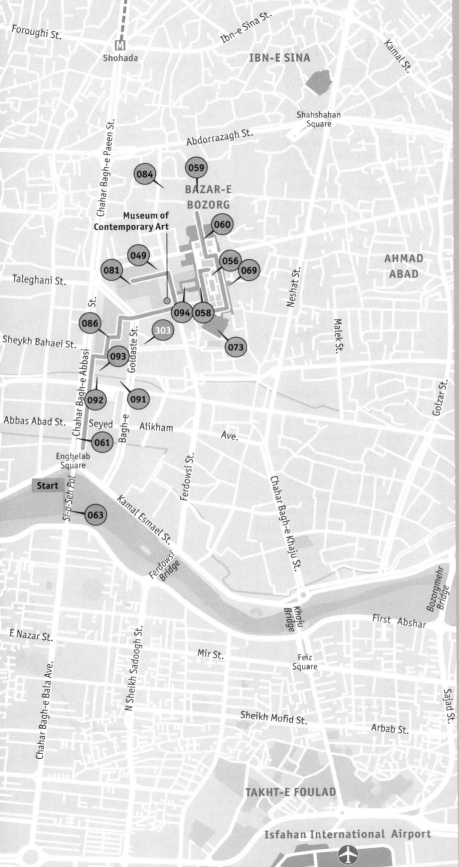

Foroughi St.

Ibn-e Sina St.

Kamal St.

M
Shohada

IBN-E SINA

Shahshahan
Square

Abdorrazagh St.

084

059

**BAZAR-E
BOZORG**

060

**Museum of
Contemporary Art**

049

056
069

081

Taleghani St.

Neshat St.

**AHMAD
ABAD**

Chahar Bagh-e Paeen St.

Malek St.

086

Sheykh Bahaei St.

094 058

303

073

Goldaste St.

093

Chahar Bagh-e Abbasi St.

092

091

Abbas Abad St.

Seyed

Alikham

Bagh-e

Ave.

Golzar St.

061

Enghelab
Square

Start

Ferdowsi St.

Chahar Bagh-e Khaju St.

063

Kamal Esmael St.

Si-o-Seh Pol

Ferdowsi Bridge

Bozorgmehr
Bridge

Khaju
Bridge

First Abshar

E Nazar St.

Chahar Bagh-e Bala Ave.

N Sheikh Sadoogh St.

Mir St.

Feiz
Square

Sajad St.

Sheikh Mofid St.

Arbab St.

TAKHT-E FOULAD

Isfahan International Airport

D Isfahan

City Walk 6
Suburbs of Isfahan
Start your journey in the middle of **Sio-o-Seh Pol bridge (063)** and walk through Chahar Bagh E Bala Avenue, recently redesigned by Naqsh-e Jahan Pars architects. Walk through the Sichan neighbourhood and learn about the principles of today's Zoroastrianism in the modern Zoroastrian Fire Temple. Walk to **St. Mary's Church (064)**, whose interior combines frescoes, stucco reliefs and tiles with oil paintings imported from Venice. Then go over the animated Julfa Square to the Armenian-Apostolic **Kelisa-ye Vank (062)**, which reflects the glorious history of the Armenian community in architecture and style. Continue your walk through the European-esque Julfa to **Zovelian House (066)**, the headquarters of an Armenian merchant family, now housing Polsheer, a contemporary Iranian architectural office. And finish your walk in the precious **House of David-Isfahan** from the Safavid period located in the Tabrizi section of the Julfa neighbourhood, the present-day home of the faculty of conservation of the Art University of Isfahan.

Kharrazi Expy.

Masjed-e Sey

Kashani St.

Mirdamad S

Saheb Rowzat Ave.

Jahad St.

Shahpoor St.

LONBAN

Motahari St.
Koudak
Park

BISHE
HABIB

Felezi Bridge

Azar Bridge

Marman Bridge

Zayandeh Rud

Mellat

Saedi St.

068

Tohid St.

070

W Nazar St.

Meydan-e Julfa

Mirza Kuchak Khan Expy.

062   064

Bagh-e Daryacheh

Khaghani St.

Armenian suburb

H. Nezami St.

Sohrevardi

066

Rudaki St.   House of David-Isfahan

Tohid St.

Daqiqi St.

Shariati St.

HOSEIN

1 km   Artesh

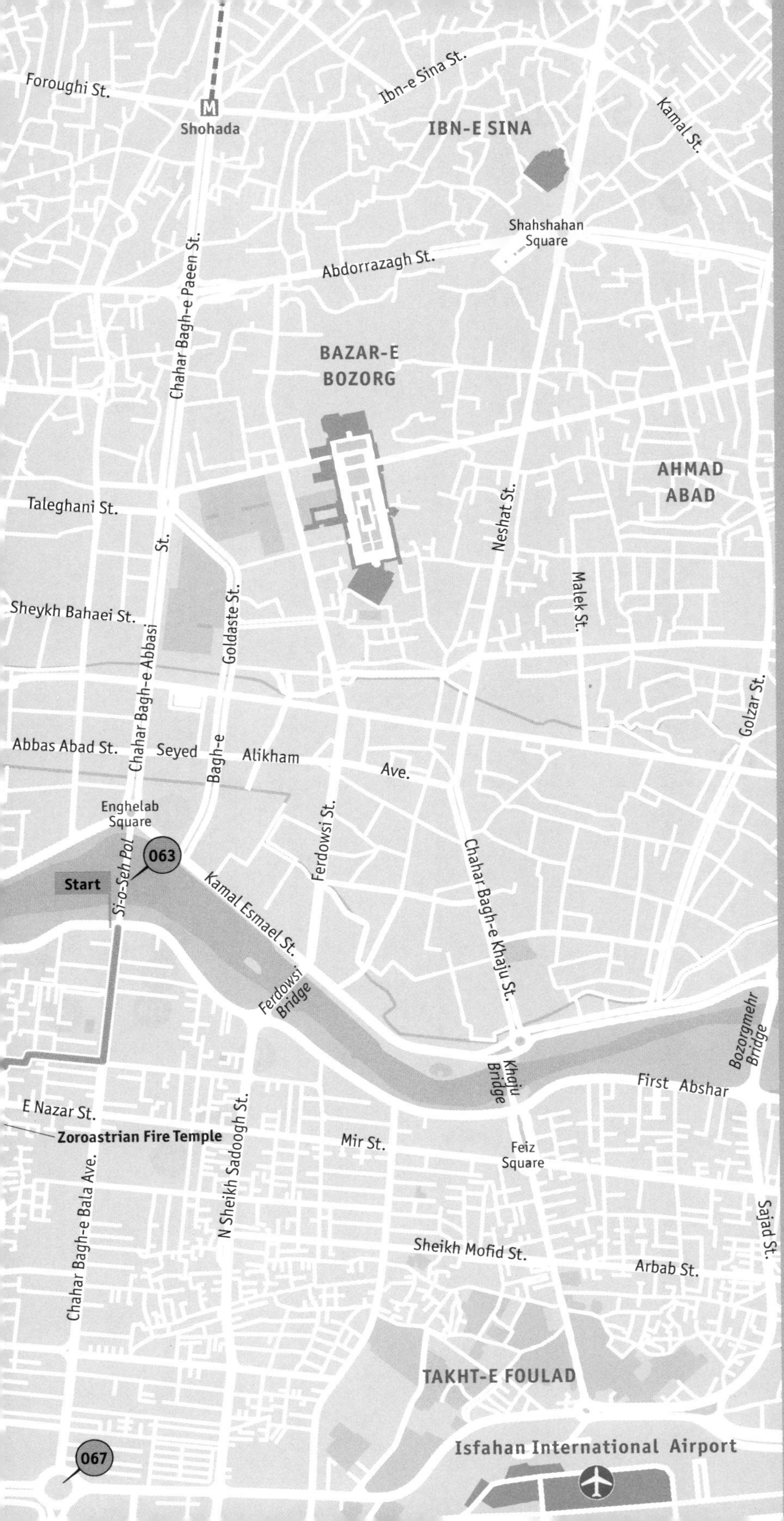

Foroughi St.

Ibn-e Sina St.

Kamal St.

Shohada

IBN-E SINA

Shahshahan Square

Abdorrazagh St.

BAZAR-E BOZORG

Chahar Bagh-e Paeen St.

Neshat St.

AHMAD ABAD

Taleghani St.

Malek St.

Goldaste St.

St.

Sheykh Bahaei St.

Chahar Bagh-e Abbasi

Golzar St.

Abbas Abad St.

Seyed

Bagh-e

Alikham

Ave.

Ferdowsi St.

Enghelab Square

063

Chahar Bagh-e Khaju St.

Start

Si-o-Seh Pol

Kamal Esmael St.

Ferdowsi Bridge

Khaju Bridge

Bozorgmehr Bridge

First Abshar

E Nazar St.

Zoroastrian Fire Temple

N Sheikh Sadoogh St.

Mir St.

Feiz Square

Sajad St.

Chahar Bagh-e Bala Ave.

Sheikh Mofid St.

Arbab St.

TAKHT-E FOULAD

Isfahan International Airport

067

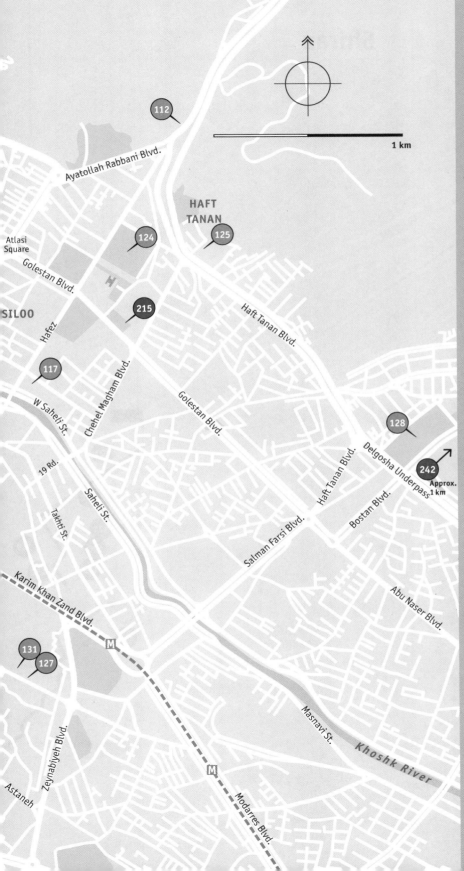

1 km

112

Ayatollah Rabbani Blvd.

HAFT
TANAN

124

125

Atlasi
Square

Golestan Blvd.

SILOO

215

Haft Tanan Blvd.

Hafez

117

W Saheli St.

Chehet Magham Blvd.

Golestan Blvd.

128

Delgosha Underpass

242

Approx.
1 km

19 Rd.

Saheli St.

Takhti St.

Haft Tanan Blvd.

Bostan Blvd.

Abu Naser Blvd.

Karim Khan Zand Blvd.

M

Salman Farsi Blvd.

131
127

Zeynabiyeh Blvd.

M

Masnavi St.

Khoshk River

Astaneh

Modarres Blvd.

City Walk 1
Residential Town of Zand Dynasty

Start your first tour in Shiraz at Shohada Square and visit **Arg-e Karim Khan Zand (123)** a purely residential building with a palatial central complex, walk to **Bagh-e Nazar (122)**, today Pars Museum, which served for the reception of royal guests and foreign ambassadors. Continue to **Bazar-e Vakil (119)**, considered the finest example of a cross-bazaar with several large, simultaneously-built khans. Visit **Vakil Mosque (120)**, one of the most important artistic buildings remaining from the Zand period, **Hammam-e Vakil (121)** adjacent to the mosque, and the **Cistern at the Moshir (132)** or Golshan complex, one of the most sophisticated buildings in the bazaar. Try to climb the roof, where you have a good overview of the bazaar structure, before you go to the **Madrasa-ye Khan (118)**, one of the most beautiful Koranic schools of Iran. Begin the afternoon with the biruni of **Bagh-e Narenjestan (127)**, and visit then the corresponding andaruni, **Khaneh-ye Zinat (131)**, opposite the small alley. Go from there to Masjed-e Jameh Atiq, the most interesting building in the old town and enter the Shrine of **Seyyed Mir-Ahmad (116)**, King of Light, the third most important pilgrimage destinaton in Iran.

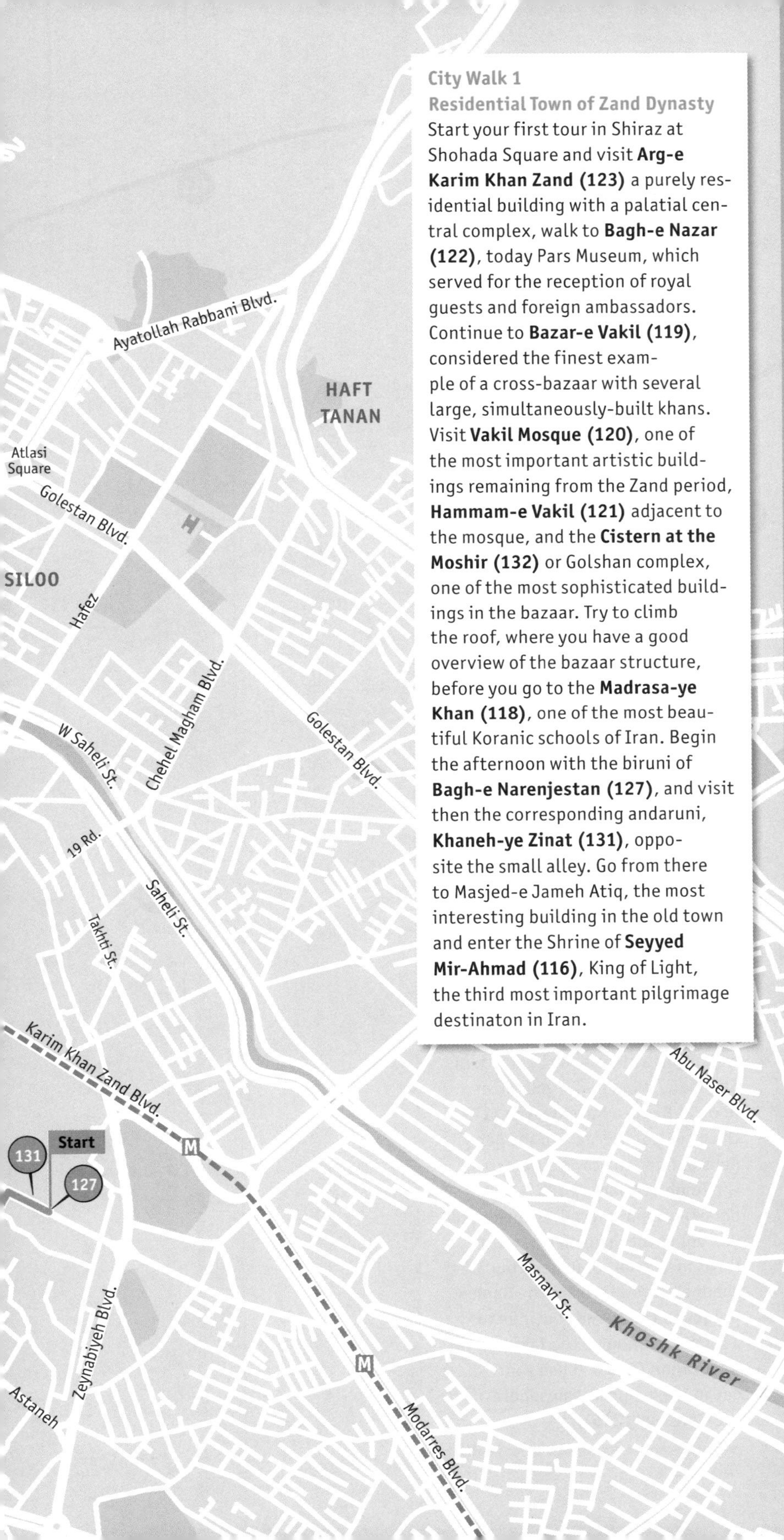

Ayatollah Rabbani Blvd.

HAFT TANAN

Atlasi Square

Golestan Blvd.

SILOO

Hafez

Chehel Maghari Blvd.

Golestan Blvd.

W Saheli St.

19 Rd.

Saheli St.

Takhti St.

Karim Khan Zand Blvd.

Abu Naser Blvd.

Start

131

127

M

Zeynabiyeh Blvd.

Astaneh

Masnavi St.

Khoshk River

M

Modarres Blvd.

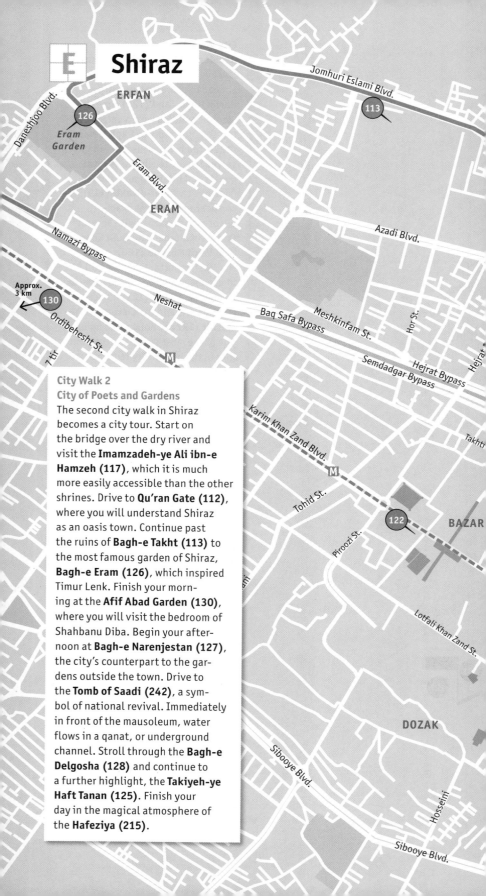

E Shiraz

City Walk 2
City of Poets and Gardens
The second city walk in Shiraz becomes a city tour. Start on the bridge over the dry river and visit the **Imamzadeh-ye Ali ibn-e Hamzeh (117)**, which it is much more easily accessible than the other shrines. Drive to **Qu'ran Gate (112)**, where you will understand Shiraz as an oasis town. Continue past the ruins of **Bagh-e Takht (113)** to the most famous garden of Shiraz, **Bagh-e Eram (126)**, which inspired Timur Lenk. Finish your morning at the **Afif Abad Garden (130)**, where you will visit the bedroom of Shahbanu Diba. Begin your afternoon at **Bagh-e Narenjestan (127)**, the city's counterpart to the gardens outside the town. Drive to the **Tomb of Saadi (242)**, a symbol of national revival. Immediately in front of the mausoleum, water flows in a qanat, or underground channel. Stroll through the **Bagh-e Delgosha (128)** and continue to a further highlight, the **Takiyeh-ye Haft Tanan (125)**. Finish your day in the magical atmosphere of the **Hafeziya (215)**.

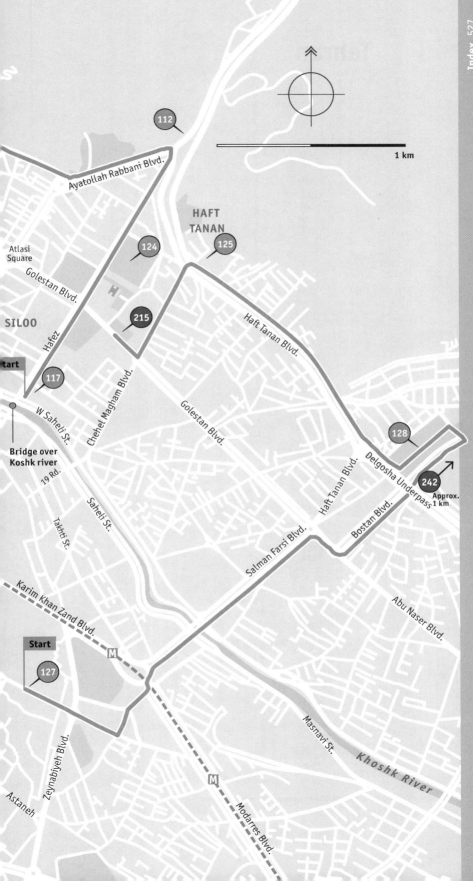

1 km

112

HAFT
TANAN

Ayatollah Rabbani Blvd.

Atlasi
Square

124

125

Golestan Blvd.

SILOO

215

Haft Tanan Blvd.

Hafez

start

117

W Saheli St.

Bridge over
Koshk river

19 Rd.

Chehel Magham Blvd.

Golestan Blvd.

128

Delgosha Underpass

242

Approx.
1 km

Haft Tanan Blvd.

Saheli St.

Takhti St.

Salman Farsi Blvd.

Bostan Blvd.

Abu Naser Blvd.

Karim Khan Zand Blvd.

Start

127

M

Zeynabiyeh Blvd.

Astaneh

Masnavi St.

M

Modarres Blvd.

Khoshk River

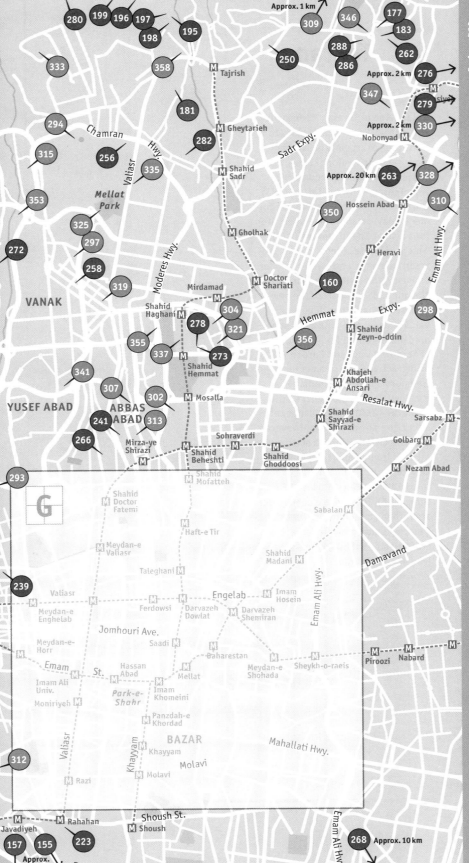

F Tehran

City Walk 1

Golden Age of Iranian Modernism
This city walk necessarily leads to
a bus tour. Start early on a Friday
morning to drive along some of
the jewels of Iranian modernism
from **Tehran Railway Station (223)**
through the 20-km long Vali Asr, former Pahlavi street to the north, stop
for a visit at **Shahr Theatre (274)**,
which integrates Greek, Roman and
traditional Persian as well as modern
elements and visit the nearby **Valiasr
Mosque (331)**, as part of the new
urban landscape. Continue along
Vali Asr street and walk a few hundred meters uphill for a coffee break
at **Ferdowsi Villa and Garden (181)**,
an attractive Qajar summer residence
transformed into the Iranian Film
Museum. Pass by **Gio Ponti's Villa
Nemazee (250)**, now in danger of
being torn down, and visit **Niaveran
Cultural Centre (286)**, a masterpiece of Iranian modern garden
architecture by Kamran Diba. Walk to
the gate of the **Secretariat of Farah
Diba (288)**, located in a demarcated
area. Then go for lunch to Darband,
a quite popular and busy area, the
starting point of hiking trails that
lead all over Tehran.

Yadegar-e Emam Hwy.

Niayesh Exp.

Hemmat Expy.

*Pardisan
Forest Park*

Ashraf Esfahan Expy.

Yadegar-e Emam Hwy.

**AMIR
ABAD**

Tehran
(Sadeghiyeh)

M Tarasht

TARASHT

M Sharif Univ.

Shademan   To

Meydan-e
Azadi

Ostad
Moein

Doctor
Habib-o-llah

Shahid
Navab
Safavi

Mehrabad International Airport

JEY

JAVADIYE

5 km

Azadegan Expy.

Saidi Expy.

Ghaleh
Morghi M

280 199 196 197 198 195

Darband

250 288 286 262

Tajrish

181

Gheytarieh

Chamran

256

Hwy.

Sadr Expy.

Nobonyad

Aghdasiyeh

Shahid Sadr

Mellat Park

Hossein Abad

Valiasr

258

Gholhak

Heravi

Mirdamad

Doctor Shariati

Emam Ali Hwy.

VANAK

Moderes Hwy.

Shahid Haghani

Hemmat

Expy.

Shahid Zeyn-o-ddin

YUSEF ABAD

Shahid Hemmat

Mosalla

Khajeh Abdollah-e Ansari

Resalat Hwy.

Shahid Sayyad-e Shirazi

Sarsabz

241

Mirza-ye Shirazi

Sohraverdi

Shahid Beheshti

Shahid Ghoddoosi

Golbarg

266

Nezam Abad

Shahid Mofatteh

Shahid Doctor Fatemi

Sabalan

Haft-e Tir

Meydan-e Valiasr

Shahid Madani

Damavand

Taleghani

Valiasr

331

Ferdowsi

Engelab

Imam Hosein

Emam Ali Hwy.

Meydan-e Enghelab

274

Darvazeh Dowlat

Darvazeh Shemiran

Jomhouri Ave.

Meydan-e Horr

Saadi

Baharestan

Meydan-e Shohada

Sheykh-o-raeis

Piroozi

Nabard

Emam St.

Hassan Abad

Mellat

Imam Ali Univ.

Park-e Shahr

Imam Khomeini

Moniriyeh

Panzdah-e Khordad

Valiasr

BAZAR

Mahallati Hwy.

Khayyam

Khayyam

Molavi

City Walk 4–6

Start

Razi

Molavi

Javadiyeh

Rahahan

Shoush St.

Shoush

223

Besat Expy.

Tehran

City Walk 2
Golden Age of Iranian Modernism
After lunch and the breathtaking view from **Valenjak** over the city of eight million, visit the **Centre for Management Studies (272)**, today Sadegh University, of Louis Kahn's pupil Nader Ardalan and pass through the imposing **Shahrak-e Gharb (287)** skyscrapers and the **Pardisan Ecology Park (290)** to Shahrak-e Ekbatan **(281)**, the then-largest residential development in the Middle East. Continue to **Shahyad Aryamehr (271)**, an interesting monument that represents modern Iran before and after the revolution. End your tour before the **Senate Building (248)** a testament to the inspiring era of modern thinking in Iranian art and architecture.

Yadegar-e Emam Hwy.

Niayesh Exp.

Hemmat Expy.

287

290

Pardisan Forest Park

Hakim Hwy.

Bakeri Hwy.

Sattari Hwy.

Ashraf Esfahan Expy.

Yadegar-e Emam Hwy.

AMIR ABAD

Eram Park

Ekbatan (Eram-e Sabz)

Tehran (Sadeghiyeh)

Tarasht

Azadi Stadium

TARASHT

281

Sharak-e Ekbatan

Sharif Univ.

Shademan   To

Bimeh

Meydan-e Azadi

271

Ostad Moein

Doctor Habib-o-llah

Shahid Navab Safavi

Mehrabad International Airport

JEY

5 km

JAVADIYE

Azadegan Expy.

Saidi Expy.

Ghaleh Morghi

View from Valenjak

195

M Tajrish

M Gheytarieh

Aghdasiyeh M

Chamran Hwy.

Sadr Expy.

Nobonyad M

Valiasr

Mellat Park

M Shahid Sadr

Hossein Abad M

Start

272

Moderes Hwy.

M Gholhak

Heravi M

Emam Ali Hwy.

VANAK

Mirdamad M

Shahid Haghani M

M Doctor Shariati

Hemmat

Expy.

M Shahid Zeyn-o-ddin

YUSEF ABAD

ABBAS ABAD

M Shahid Hemmat

M Mosalla

Khajeh Abdollah-e Ansari M

Resalat Hwy.

M Shahid Sayyad-e Shirazi

Sarsabz M

Mirza-ye Shirazi M

M Sohraverdi

M Shahid Beheshti

M Shahid Ghoddoosi

Golbarg M

M Nezam Abad

M Shahd Mofatteh

M Shahid Doctor Fatemi

Sabalan M

M Haft-e Tir

M Meydan-e Valiasr

Shahid Madani M

Damavand

M Taleghani

Engelab

Emam Ali Hwy.

M Valiasr

M

M Ferdowsi

M Darvazeh Dowlat

M Darvazeh Shemiran

M Imam Hosein

Meydan-e Enghelab

Jomhouri Ave.

Piroozi M

Nabard M

Meydan-e Horr M

248

M Saadi

M Baharestan

Meydan-e Shohada M

Sheykh-o-raeis

Emam St.

Hassan Abad

M Mellat

Imam Ali Univ.

Park-e Shahr

Imam Khomeini M

Moniriyeh M

Panzdah-e Khordad M

Valiasr

Khayyam

BAZAR

Khayyam

Molavi

Mahallati Hwy.

M Razi

M Molavi

City Walk 4–6

M Rahahan

Shoush St.

Javadiyeh M

M Shoush

Besat Expy.

Emam Ali Hwy.

F Tehran

City Walk 3
Architecture of the Iranian Revolution

Start your morning early at Navab Expressway, a 6 km highway with many new buildings on either side commissioned in 1999. Then drive to visit the Mosque of **Sharif University (300)**, an example of early Islamic post-revolutionary architecture. Drive to **Borj-e Milad (326)** and get the panoramic view from the new post-revolutionary landmark of Tehran. Pass by **Borj-e Beinol melal Tehran (341)**, the **Lawyers' Chamber (307)**, **Armita office tower (313)** to the **Mosalla-ye Imam Khomeini (302)**, a gigantic complex for religious events and symbol of the new Islamic Republic of Iran. Drive for lunch to **Tabiat Bridge (355)**, a three-dimensional, curved pier, with turnarounds, seating areas, green areas and restaurants. Walk over the bridge in the afternoon and visit the **Holy Defense Museum (337)**, dedicated to the history of the Iran–Iraq-war. Pass by the **New National Library (321)** and complete your walk in the small but architecturally-important **Masjed-e Al-Ghadir (298)**, whose interior exemplifies the post-revolutionary tension between continuity and transformation.

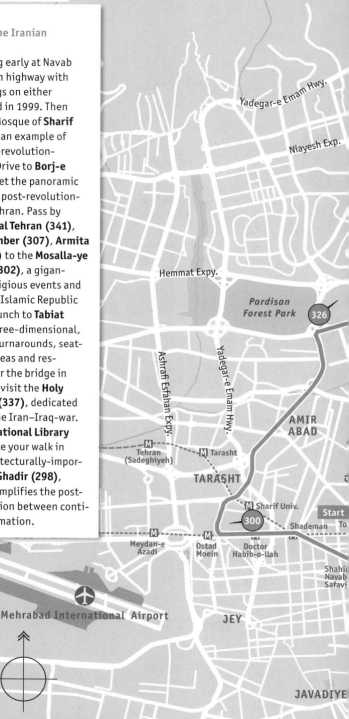

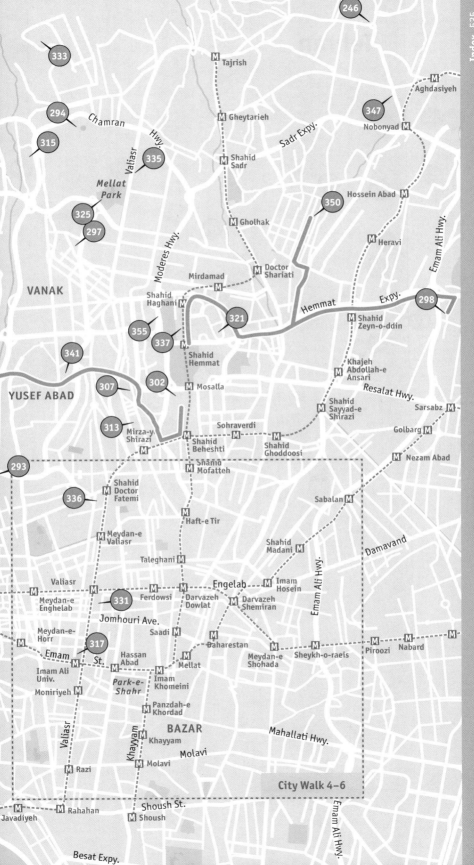

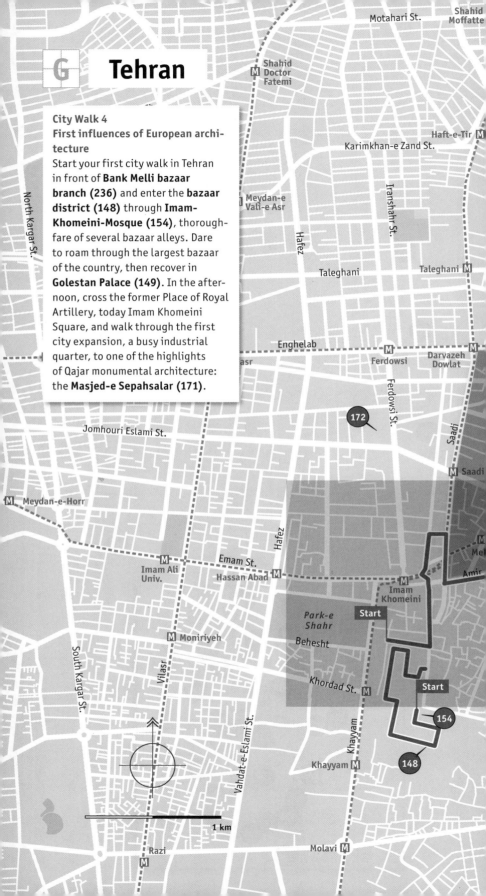

G Tehran

City Walk 4
First influences of European architecture
Start your first city walk in Tehran in front of **Bank Melli bazaar branch (236)** and enter the **bazaar district (148)** through **Imam-Khomeini-Mosque (154)**, thoroughfare of several bazaar alleys. Dare to roam through the largest bazaar of the country, then recover in **Golestan Palace (149)**. In the afternoon, cross the former Place of Royal Artillery, today Imam Khomeini Square, and walk through the first city expansion, a busy industrial quarter, to one of the highlights of Qajar monumental architecture: the **Masjed-e Sepahsalar (171)**.

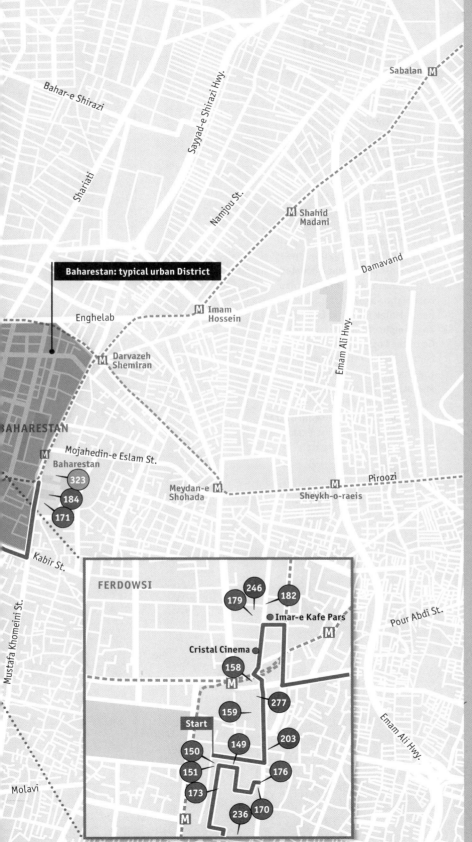

Sabalan Ⓜ

Bahar-e Shirazi

Sayyad-e Shirazi Hwy.

Shariati

Namjou St.

Shahid
Madani Ⓜ

Damavand

Baharestan: typical urban District

Enghelab

Ⓜ Imam
Hossein

Emam Ali Hwy.

Ⓜ Darvazeh
Shemiran

BAHARESTAN

Ⓜ Mojahedin-e Eslam St.
Baharestan
323
184
171

Meydan-e
Shohada Ⓜ

Piroozi
Ⓜ
Sheykh-o-raeis

Kabir St.

Mustafa Khomeini St.

FERDOWSI

246
179
182

● Imar-e Kafe Pars
Ⓜ

Pour Abdi St.

Cristal Cinema ●
158
Ⓜ

277

159

Start

149

203

150

151

176

173

Emam Ali Hwy.

236 170
Ⓜ

Molavi

G Tehran

City Walk 5
Discovery of the National Identity
Take the metro to Imam Khomeini Metro Station and visit **Imam Khomeini Square (158)** with **Shahi Bank (178)**, the first bank of Iran, and continue to **Bagh-e Melli (190)** the first construction of the Pahlavi dynasty. Pay a brief visit to the courtyard of the **General Post Office (209)**, then compare the **Police Building (204)**, one of the most prominent examples in the development of an Iranian national style, with the contemporaneous **Malek National Library (224)**, an example of Iranian Islamic style. Go to the **Cossack Garrison (000)**, constructed for the bodyguards of the Shah, then go to the art deco **Ministry of Foreign Affairs (208)** by Gabriel Guévrékian.Finish your day in the **National Museum of Iran (230)**,a most convincing examples of this recourse to the past.

Motahari St.

Shahid Moffatte

Ⓜ Shahid Doctor Fatemi

Haft-e-Tir Ⓜ

Karimkhan-e Zand St.

Iranshahr St.

Ⓜ Meydan-e Vali-e Asr

Hafez

Taleghani

Taleghani Ⓜ

192

Enghelab

Ⓜ Ferdowsi

Darvazeh Dowlat

asr

Ferdowsi St.

Saadi

Atashkadeh ●

193

Ⓜ Saadi

Ⓜ Meydan-e-Horr

Start

Ⓜ

Me

Hafez

200

Emam St.

Amir

Ⓜ Imam Ali Univ.

Hassan Abad Ⓜ

Ⓜ Imam Khomeini

Park-e Shahr

Ⓜ Moniriyeh

Behesht

South Kargar St.

Vilasr

Khordad St. Ⓜ

Khayyam

Vahdat-e-Eslami St.

Khayyam Ⓜ

North Kargar St.

1 km

Razi Ⓜ

Molavi Ⓜ

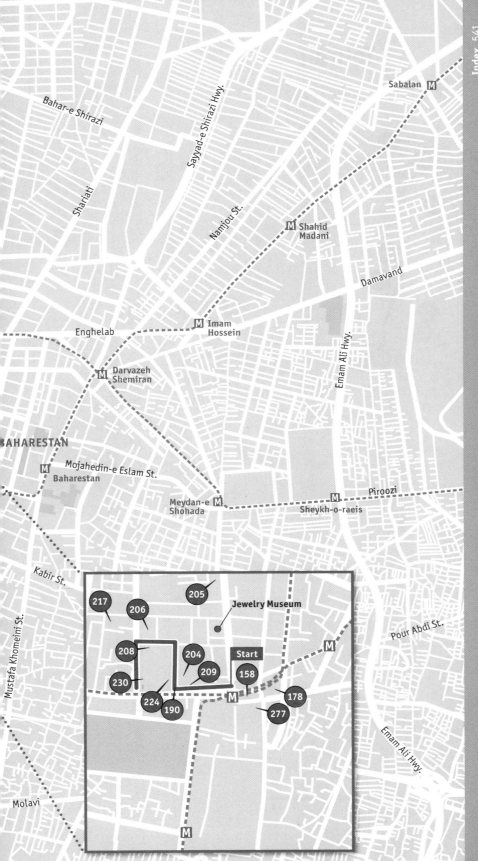

City Walk 6
Arrival of Modernism in Iranian Architecture
Start your walk in front of **Alburz High School (192)**, one of the architectural gems of Tehran, and walk through Shah Reza Avenue, today Khiaban Enqelab Islami. The avenue runs where, until 1932, the quayar wall bounded the city, to **Vahdat Hall (265)**. Go through Daneshjoo Park to **Shahr Theatre (274)**, modelled on the classic Greek and Roman as well as Iranian theatres and visit the nearby **Valiasr Mosque (331)**, developed as part of the urban landscape. The development on the Khiaban Enqelab Islami dates back to the 1930s and is thus a fairly uniform example of Iranian premodern and early modernism. Visit Jørn Utzon's Enqelab branch of **Melli Bank (255)**, inspired by Isfahan's bazaar. Cross the street and enter the **University of Tehran (252)** pass by the **University Club (213)** and **University of Fine Arts (231)**, milestones of modernity in Iran, go along the **Faculty of Law and Political Science (222)** and finish your trip at the **Medical Faculty (212)**, the university's main building, designed by Mohsen Foroughi.

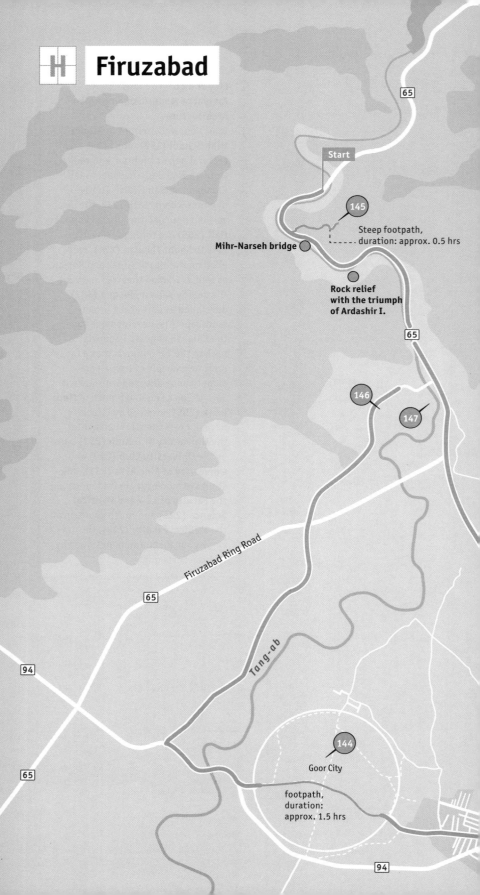

Firuzabad

Start

145

Steep footpath,
duration: approx. 0.5 hrs

Mihr-Narseh bridge

**Rock relief
with the triumph
of Ardashir I.**

65

146

147

Firuzabad Ring Road

65

94

Tang-ab

65

144

Goor City

footpath,
duration:
approx. 1.5 hrs

94

Excursion:
Origin of Ayvan

After an early morning departure to Firuzabad, walk to **Qaleh Dokhtar (145)**, an early Sassanid fortress, described by Robert Byron as a milestone in architectural development. Then drive to the remains of the Mihr-Narseh bridge and the two **rock reliefs (146)**. After lunch, walk to the circular centre of the residence town, **Ardashir Khureh (144)**, then continue to **Ardashir I Palace (147)**, a well-preserved Sassanid period building with a central ayvan, around a former garden.

2 km

Kavar–Firuzabad Road

RUZABAD

94

Valiasr Park

94

94

Glossary

Abbasid Caliphate third Caliph dynasty (749-1258), abolished the Umayyads

Achaemenid Empire first Persian empire, from 700-330 BC

AD Anno Domini; Gregorian calendar, starting from the year of Christ's birth. The Christian chronology does not know a year zero

AH Anno Hegirae; Islamic calendar, based on a moon calendar and the day of Hijra, July 16, 622 (see also Yaz)

Amir title of nobility, sovereign, prince, governor

Andaruni private area of a residence

Arabesque intertwined lines of stylized plants

Arg citadel

Atashgah Fire temple, Zoroastrian place of worship

Ayn well, spring

Ayvan Farsi, also Ivan or Liwan, a room, open to the courtyard, surrounded by a three-sided, arched hall

Ayvanaches vaulted arcades enclosed on three sides, open to a courtyard

Ayyubid Dynasty Sunni dynasty, founded by Salah ad-Din in 1174

Badgir literally "wind catcher", a traditional Persian architectural element used for ventilation of buildings

Bagh garden (see also Chahar Bagh)

Balakhaneh loggia above the entrance to the garden, gateway

Bazaar Farsi (Arabic suq), place of shopping in the Middle Eastern-Islamic cultural area

Bey Turkish ruling title, similar to Amir

Behesht Farsi, paradise

Biruni public area of a residence

Buyid Dynasty major Shiite dynasty (930-1062)

Borj tower

Bustan garden, orchard, planting

Buyutat commercial building of a residence

Chahar Bagh literally "four gardens" a garden divided into four parts

Chahar-su covered crossroads with four entrances or streets

Chal-e Hose swimming pool

Caravanserai courtyard building as station in long distance trade

Caravan travel companies

Dar house, flat

Darvazeh entrance, door

Daryacheh literally "small sea", pond

Dasht-e Lut literally "sandy desert", largest desert in the Iranian highlands. Measurements from 2003 to 2010 testify that this is the hottest point on Earth with surface temperatures of up to 70.7 °C

Dasht-e Kavir literally "salt desert", lies in the high basin between the Zagros mountains in the southwest and the Alborz mountains. Because of the sterile and hostile conditions caused by the salt zones, the Kavir is uninhabited

Dowlatkhaneh complex of royal residence, royal palace

Dervish description of a Sufi, a member of a religious order, generally known for his modesty and discipline

Divankhaneh audience hall

Driba tight area, home access

Farsakh Persian measure of length, approximately 6 km

Farman Farsi, also ferman, firman, meaning "decree" or "order" in Islamic countries

Favvare water-jet, fountain

Firdaws paradise

Garmkhaneh warm part in a hammam

Girih tiles set of five tiles, designed to be infinitely arrayed

Gholam military slave, mostly of Turkish or Caucasian origin, mercenaries, some of whom belonged to the elite of the Safavid court

Golestan rose garden, also a landmark of Persian literature by Saadi

Hajj Islamic pilgrimage to Mecca, one of the five pillars of Islam

Haft rangi Farsi, literally "Seven Colours", technology for processing tiles with up to seven colours

Hammam Public bathing, usually consists of different rooms for the bathing procedure

Harem Private dwelling area

Hasht Behesht literally "eight paradises", pavilion, whose base is divided into nine rectangles

Hasht-o Nim Hasht regular octagon, with four sides smaller than the other four

Howz basin, cistern

Howzkhaneh room with a basin

Hojreh storage space for commercial buildings, storage boxes

Imam in Shia, an Imam is not only presented as the man of God but as participating fully in the names, attributes, and acts that theology usually reserves for God alone. Twelver and Ismaili Shia believe that these imams are chosen by God to be perfect examples for the faithful and to lead all humanity in all aspects of life. These leaders must be followed since they are appointed by God

Imarat building, palace, dwelling house

Islamic revolution also Iranian revolution or 1979 revolution, refers to events involving the overthrow of the Pahlavi dynasty and its replacement with an Islamic Republic under the Grand Ayatollah Ruhollah Khomeini

Jannat garden, paradise

Juy water channel

Kaaba central sanctuary of Islam, cuboid cube in the courtyard of the mosque in Mecca, destination of the great pilgrimage (Hajj)

Khaneh house

Khanqah a building designed specifically for a Sufi brotherhood, a place for spiritual retreat

Khiyaban avenue, street

Qu'ran/ Qur'an holy book of Islam, according to Islamic faith, the literal revelation of God by the angel Gabriel to the Prophet

Kufi one of the oldest calligraphic forms of Arabic writing

Mahdi also Imam Mahdi, according to traditional Shiite beliefs, the descendant of the Prophet, who appears at the end time and abolishes injustice in the world

Masjid smaller mosque, mostly in the district area

Masjid-e Jam'a Friday mosque, mosque in which the Friday prayer takes place

Madrasa higher theological training centre with boarding school

Maidan square, place

Minaret elevated stand or tower for the prayer caller (muezzin)

Muqarnas stalactic vault, an important decorative style element of Islamic architecture

Mehrab prayer niche of the mosque, which displays the prayer direction (qibla)

Mezzanin intermediate storey

Muhandisin builder, architect, engineer

Namaz Khaneh open air prayer room

Namakdan salt cellar

Naqqara Khaneh literally "house of drummers", building of the court orchestra, vestibule of the palace

Glossary

Narenjestan orange grove

Ottoman Empire also Turkish Empire or Turkey, for several centuries the decisive power in Asia Minor, the Middle East, the Balkans, North Africa and the Crimea

Pahlavi Dynasty last ruling dynasty of Persian Shahs. The Pahlavi came to power in 1925 as successor to the Qadjars. On 12 December 12 1925, Parliament decided to take Reza Khan as a Shah. He reigned until 1941, surrendering to his son Mohammad Reza Pahlavi, who was the last Shah of Persia and Iran, and ruled until 1979

Pishtaq rectangle framing a pointed arch or ayvan

Qadjar Dynasty Persian dynasty founded by Agha Mohammed, who united Persia and made Tehran his capital. After 1896 the dynasty decayed; the last ruler, Shah Ahmed was deposed in 1925 by Reza Shah

Qibla prayer direction of the Muslims to Mecca

Qishlaq winter pasture, winter quarters, winter camps of semi-nomadic Turkic people

Qizilbash also Kizilbash, fanatical followers of the Shiite Sufi Order (Safaviyya) named "red heads" because of their red head covering

Ribat fortified monastery

Riwaq arcade or portico of a courtyard mosque

Safavid Dynasty Persian dynasty, originally from the Sufi Ordermaster Safi od–Din from Ardebil. The dynasty founder of Turkish descent from Azerbaijan, Shah Ismail I (1501-24), united the Iranian highlands, introduced the Twelve Shia and established a theocratic regime. Ismail's son and successor Tahmasp I (1524-1576) moved the residence from Tabriz to Qazvin in 1529. Abbas I (1588-1629), under whom the dynasty reached the summit of its power, made Isfahan the capital of the Safavid Empire in1598. Among the successors of Abbas I there was a decline of power (1638, loss of Baghdad). The Afghans finally ended the Safavid dynasty (1722); Nader Shah was crowned in 1736.

Sahn Arabic, courtyard of a mosque

Salad ritual prayer, one of the five pillars of Islam

Salsabil water stone, cascade

Sara inner courtyard of a building for trade, commerce and accommodation

Sarbineh dressing room in a hammam

Salsabil water stone, cascade

Sassanid Empire second Persian empire, who co-ordinated the destinies alongside China and Rome

Shabestan literally "land of the night", a cool, shaded, often subterranean summer place, usually found in traditional mosques

Shah literally "king", the highest Persian ruler title

Shahanshah literally "king of kings," an absolute ruler, comparable to a great kingship or emperor

Shahbanu literally "queen"; Farah Diba Pahlavi was the first, crowned Shahbanu of modern Iran

Shah Neshin literally "seat of the king"

Shahada Islamic creed, one of the five pillars of Islam

Sheikh Arabic, honorary title for men of rank and name

Silk Road network of caravan routes whose main route connected the Mediterranean by land via Central Asia to East Asia

Chronology

1501–1525 …… Shah Ismail I

1501 …………………… Conquest of Tabriz by the Qizilbash, Tabriz becomes the capital of the new dominion

1501 …………………… July, Ismail takes the title of Shah-hanshah, orders the Friday prayer to be performed on behalf of the twelve Imams, curses the first three caliphs and introduces Shia as "state religion"

1501–1512 ……… Shah Ismail I expels the Turkmen from Iran and establishes the rule of the Safavids

1504–1530 ……… Foundation of Mughal Empire by Babur

1510 …………………… Battle of Marv ends with a decisive victory for the Safavids over the Uzbek

1510 …………………… Habsburg–Persian alliance between Habsburg and Safavid Empire in their common conflict against the Ottoman Empire

1512 …………………… Construction of Harun-Velayat Mausoleum in Isfahan

1514 …………………… Battle of Chaldiran, Sultan Selim I defeats Ismail I, who loses his supernatural air and aura of invincibility

1515 …………………… Subjugation of Hormuz Island by the Portuguese

1515 …………………… Construction of Mashhad-e Fatima in Qum

1524 …………………… Ismail I dies at the age of thirty-six, succeeded by his son Tahmasp I

1524–1576 …… Shah Tahmasp I

1526 …………………… Civil war among the differing factions

1529 …………………… First Siege of Vienna by the Ottoman Empire, led by Suleiman the Magnificent

1532–1555 ……… Ottoman–Safavid War, one of the many military conflicts fought between the two archrivals, where thousands of Christian Armenians were captured and deported

1541 …………………… Publication of *Divan* manuscript by Shah Ismail I, written under the pen name Hatayi

1544–1555 ……… Mughal emperor Humayun gets asylum at Tahmasp's court

1548 …………………… Dislocation of the capital to Qazvin under Shah Tahmasp I

1548–1598 ……… Qazvin, second Safavid capital

1555 …………………… Peace of Amasya frees Iran from Ottoman attacks for three decades

1571 …………………… Birth of Prince Abbas, later Shah Abbas I the Great in Herat

1576 …………………… Tahmasp I dies of poison, unclear whether by accident or on purpose

1576–1577 …… Shah Ismail II

1576 …………………… Coronation of Shah Ismail II, son of Shah Tahmasp I

1576 …………………… November, Ismail II dies after consuming poisoned opium

1578–1587 …… Shah Mohammad Khodabanda

1578–1590 ……… Ottoman–Safavid War, Sultan Murad III begins war with Safavid Iran

1581 …………………… Khorasan becomes autonomous

1585 …………………… Prince Abbas comes under guardianship of Qizilbash leader Murshid Qoli Khan

1585 …………………… Conquest of Tabriz by Ottoman army, the city remains in Ottoman hands for 20 years

1587 …………………… Mohammad accepts his dethronement and is banished to Alamut prison

Chronology

1647	Publication of Adam Olearius' book about his visit to Persia
1647	Reconstruction of the Forty Columns Palace in Isfahan
1648	Safavid empire expands to Afghanistan
1650	Construction of Khaju Bridge
1651–1653	Russo-Persian War
1654–1715	Reign of Louis XIV in France
1656–1663	Construction of Hakim Mosque in Isfahan
1666	Shah Abbas II dies without revealing who should be his successor
1666–1694	**Shah Safi II/Shah Suleiman**
1666	Sam Mirza, son of Shah Abbas II, crowned as Shah Safi II
1666	Jean Chardin appointed Court Jeweler by Shah Safi II
1667	Construction of Champs-Élysées by André Le Nôtre in Paris
1667	Earthquake in Shamakhi, estimated 80,000 people die
1667	Second coronation of Sam Mirza as Shah Suleiman I
1669	Construction of the garden palace Hasht Behesht in Isfahan
1673–1677	Jean Chardin's second stay in Isfahan
1683	Battle of Vienna, fought by allied forces of Holy Roman Empire of German Nations and Polish–Lithuanian Commonwealth against Ottoman Empire
1686	Publication of Jean Chardin's *Voyages en Perse and aux Indes orientales*
1694	Suleiman dies on 29 July, at Isfahan, as a result of heavy drinking.
1694–1722	**Sultan Husayn**
1694	Coronation of Sultan Husayn, nicknamed Yakhshidir, "Very well"
1695	Shifting of power to leading clerics, measures against Sufi order as well as prohibiting consumption of alcohol and opium and restrictions on the behaviour of women
1706	Construction of the Caravanserai and Madrasa Madar-e Shah and Bazar-e Honar
1709	Ghilzai Afghans rebel and break away from Safavid rule
1710	Revival of Shia Islam leads to increased intolerance towards Sunni Muslims, Jews, Zoroastrians and Christians
1715	Persian embassy to the court of Louis XIV causes a dramatic flurry
1715	Establishment of a permanent Persian consulate in Marseille, main French Mediterranean port for trade with East
1716	Safavid expeditions to bring Afghans under control end in failure
1717–1720	Revolt of Sunnis in Kurdistan and Shirvan calling Ottoman Turks for support
1721	Sack of the Shamakhi, massacre of Shia population and raid of property of Christian and foreign nationals
1722–1723	Russo-Persian War, Tsar Peter the Great declares war in an attempt to expand Russian influence in the Caspian and Caucasus regions
1722	Ghilzai Afghans sweep westward, aiming at Shah's capital Isfahan
1722	Battle of Gulnabad between military forces from Hotak and the army of Safavid Empire
1722	Siege of Isfahan, starvation and disease force Isfahan into submission, estimated 80,000 inhabitants die. Devastation of Isfahan
1722	Sultan Husayn abdicates and acknowledges Mahmud Hotak as new Shah of Persia

1722 to 1729   Afghan Rebellion

1722–1725 ...... Shah Mahmud Hotak
1722 .... Shah Mahmud Hotak acknowledged Shah of Persia
1722 .... Prince Tahmasp establishes his government in Tabriz and declares himself Shah of Persia
1723 .... Treaty of Saint Petersburg, Russian victory ratified for Safavid Irans'
cession of their territories in Transcaucasia and Northern Iran
1725 .... Publication of Montesquieu's *Lettres persanes*, a satiric critique of
French society
1725 .... Palace revolution by Afghan officers which places Ashraf Hotak on
the throne

1725–1729 ...... Shah Ashraf Hotak
1725 .... Ashraf Hotak succeeds as Shah of Persia
1727 .... Battle near Kermanshah between Ottoman Empire, who want to rees-
tablish Safavid Shah Tahmasp II, and Shah Ashraf Hotak's army
1729 .... Battle of Damghan, the royal Persian army under the leadership of
Nader Khan drives the Afghans back to what is today Afghanistan

1729–1736   Safavid restoration

1729–1732 ...... Shah Tahmasp II
1729 .... Shah Tahmasp II returns to Isfahan and the Safavids have the empire
under control again
1729 .... Shah Tahmasp II crowned as penultimate ruler of Safavid dynasty
1730–1735 ...... Ottoman – Persian War between Safavid and Ottoman Empire
1730 .... Nader Khan, a talented young general, attacks the Ottomans and
regains most of the territory lost during the collapse of the Safavid
Empire
1732 .... Nader Khan forces Shah Tahmasp II to abdicate in favour of his baby
son, Abbas III, to whom Nader becomes regent

1732–1736 ...... Abbas III
1732 .... Infant Abbas appointed nominal ruler of Iran. Nader Khan assumes
the positions of deputy of state and viceroy
1734 .... Battle of Yeghevard, where the Ottoman army is utterly destroyed by
Nader's army
1736 .... Abbas III deposed, when Nader Khan has himself crowned as Nader
Shah Afshar. This marks the official end of the Safavid dynasty

1736–1796   Afsharid dynasty

1736–1747 ...... Nader Shah Afshar
1736 .... Nader Khan crowned Shah of Persia in attendance of an "exceptionally
large assembly" composed of military, religious and nobility, as well as
the Ottoman ambassador
1736–1747 ...... Dislocation of the capital to Mashhad
1738–1740 ...... Campaign against Indian Mughal Empire, Afsharids annex all lands west
of the Indus and establish hegemony over the region
1738 .... Nader Shah conquers Kandahar, the last outpost of the Hotak dynasty

Chronology

1739	Battle of Karnal, Nader Shah crushes the Mughal army and enters Delhi, ordering his troops to plunder and sack the city and capture Peacock Throne and Kohinoor Diamond
1740	Tahmasp II and his son Abbas III executed by Nader Shah
1743	Nader Shah builds a Persian navy, recapture Bahrain and conquer Oman
1743–1746	Ottoman–Persian War between Ottoman Empire and Afsharid dynasty
1743	Ottomans capture Kirkuk, Arbil and Mosul, forcing Nader Shah to retreat
1743–1744	Revolts break out because of taxes for the military campaigns, and are crushed ruthlessly by Nader Shah, who builds towers from his victims' skulls in imitation of his hero Timur
1745	Battle of Kars results in complete destruction of Ottoman army
1746	Treaty of Kerden signed between Ottoman Empire and Afsharid Iran; the boundary line between the two countries is restored as a century ago
1747	Nader Shah assassinated at a complot, succeeded by his nephew Ali Qoli, who is probably involved in the assassination

1747–1748 Adil Shah Afshar

1747	Nader Shah's officers offer the crown to Ali Qoli Khan, declared Shah under the name of Adil Shah, the "righteous"
1747	Adil Shah defeats his Kurdish allies and had several of his supporters put to death on suspicion of conspiracy
1748	In a futile attempt to bend the Qajar tribe into submission, Adil Shah has the Qajar chieftain killed and his four-year-old son, the future Agha Mohammad Khan, castrated
1748	During this struggle all provincial governors declare independence, establish their own states, and the entire Empire falls into anarchy

1748–1748 Ebrahim Shah Afshar

1748	Ebrahim Mirza topples his brother. Two months later, his own troops rebel against him
1748	Ebrahim succeeded by Nader's grandson, Shahrukh

1748–1796 Shahrukh Shah Afshar

1748	Shahrukh Shah Afshar elected by the nobles, makes Mashhad his capital
1758	Agha Mohammed Khan, later the first Qajar Shah, becomes chieftain of Qavanlu tribe
1760	When Karim Khan takes control of Persia, the realm of Shahrukh is reduced to the province of Khorasan
1796	Agha Mohammad Khan conquers Khorasan and has Shahrukh tortured to death

1750–1794 Zand dynasty

1751–1779 Mohammad Karim Khan Zand

1750	Karim Khan and other Bakhtiari chieftains divide the country and raise the Safavid sprout Ismail III to Shah to legitimize their power as Vakil, "servant" of the king and soothe the people

1789 to 1924   Qajar dynasty

Chronology

1797 .... Agha Mohammad Khan falls victim to the assassination of two servants in his tent near Shusha. His successor is his nephew Baba Khan, crowned as Fat'h-Ali Shah Qajar

1779–1834 .... **Fat'h-Ali Shah Qajar**
1797 .... Fat'h Ali ascends the throne and uses the name of Fat'h-Ali Shah Qajar
1804–1813 .... Russo–Persian War between the new Qajar king Fat'h-Ali Shah and the also-new Tsar Alexander I of Russia
1804 .... Fat'h-Ali Shah orders the invasion of Georgia under pressure from the Shia clergy
1807 .... Treaty of Finckenstein between Napoleon and a Persian delegation establishing the Franko-Persian Alliance, directed against Russia and United Kingdom
1809 .... Napoleon makes peace with Russia, which enables the Russians to increase their war efforts in the Caucasus
1813 .... Russian troops successfully storm Lankaran, invade Tabriz and force Persia to sign the Treaty of Gulistan with Russia, ending the Russo–Persian war
1813 .... Construction of Imaret-e Badgir in the Golestan Palace
1818 .... Battle of Kafir Qala between Qajar dynasty and the victorious forces of Durrani Empire of Afghanistan
1822 .... Amir Kabir appointed to the post of military registrar for the army of Azerbaijan
1826–1828 .... Russo-Persian War between the Russian Empire and Qajar dynasty
1826 .... Fat'h-Ali Shah decides to occupy the lost territories, invades very successfully, and manages to regain most of their lost territories
1827 .... October, General Eristov captures Tabriz
1828 .... Treaty of Turkmenchay, Iran loses all of its Caucasian territories to Imperial Russia
1830–1895 .... Beginning of the Great Game, a political and diplomatic confrontation between Britain and Russia over Afghanistan and neighbouring territories in Central and Southern Asia
1831 .... Fat'h-Ali Shah has himself and other Qajar princes engraved in the rock
1834 .... Fat'h-Ali Shah dies on 23 October

1834–1848 .... **Mohammad Shah Qajar**
1834 .... Mohammad Shah Qajar mounts the throne
1834 .... Beginning of modernisation and the industrialisation of Persia with the help of European consultants
1835 .... Mohammad Shah, wearied of the discussions with his Prime Minister, lets him suffocate rolled into a carpet
1837–1838 .... Siege of Herat, an unsuccessful attack on the Afghan city during the time of the Great Game
1847 .... Amir Kabir appointed chief tutor to the crown prince Naser al-Din
1848 .... Mohammad Shah issues a farman banning the maritime trade of slaves
1848 .... Mohammad Shah dies of gout, his eldest son Naser al-Din becomes the new Shah

1848–1896 .... **Naser al-Din Shah**
1848 .... Naser al-Din Shah assumes the throne. Amir Kabir makes the necessary arrangements

Chronology

1891	Tobacco Protest climaxes in an edict against tobacco use by the most important religious authority in Iran
1892	Naser al-Din Shah cancels the tobacco concession. The protest is one of the issues leading to the Persian Constitutional Revolution
1894	Reza Khan, later Reza Shah Pahlavi, joins the Persian Cossack Brigade
1896	Naser al-Din assassinated whilst praying in the shrine of Shah-Abdol-Azim in Ray

1896–1907   Mozaffar ad-Din Shah Qajar

1896	Mozaffar ad-Din Shah ascends the throne, unprepared for the burdens of office
1900	Construction of Pavilion Ahmad Shahi, summer residence of the Shah in the Niaveran Garden
1901	D'Arcy Concession signed by Mozaffar ad-Din Shah and William Knox D'Arcy which gives D'Arcy the exclusive rights to prospect for oil in Persia
1896–1905	Mozaffar ad-Din Shah visits Europe three times, borrowing money from Nicholas II of Russia for his traveling expenses
1905–1911	Persian Constitutional Revolution leads to the establishment of a parliament in Iran
1905	Protests over the increase of taxes to pay back the Russian loan for Mozaffar ad-Din Shah's royal tour to Europe
1906	Mozaffar ad-Din Shah capitulates, agreeing to surrender power to a new "house of justice"
1906	First Iranian legislative election held after Iranian Constitutional Revolution, Persia becomes constitutional monarchy
1906	First meeting of the majles, who immediately give themselves the right to make a constitution
1906	Mozaffar ad-Din Shah signs the constitution, from there on the Shah is "under the rule of law, and the crown became a divine gift given to the Shah by the people."
1906	Mozaffar ad-Din Shah dies of a heart attack 40 days after granting this constitution

1907–1909   Mohammad Ali Shah Qajar

1907	Mohammad Ali Shah Qajar crowned as Shah of Persia
1907	Anglo-Russian Entente delineating the spheres of interest between British India and Russian Central Asia in the borderland areas of Persia, Afghanistan and Tibet
1908	William Knox D'Arcy and his team find large quantities of oil in Maidan-e Naftun
1908	Mohammad Ali Shah has the Majlis bombed with military and political support of Russia and Britain, arrests many of the deputies and closes down the assembly
1909	Pro-Constitution forces march to Tehran, depose the Shah, and re-establish the constitution
1909	The parliament votes to place Mohammad Ali Shah's son, Ahmad Shah, on the throne. Mohammad Ali Shah abdicates following the new Constitutional Revolution
1909	Mohammad Ali Shah flees to Odessa, Russia

Chronology

1935 .... Inauguration of the main campus of the University of Tehran, an example of first Pahlavi era Modernism
1936–1941 .... Women's Awakening movement and elimination of chador from Iranian society led to opposition from the Mullahs and the religious establishment
1937 .... Commissioning of Tehran Central Station influenced by contemporary German and Italian architecture
1939 .... Handover of Trans-Iranian Railway from the Persian Gulf to to the Caspian Sea
1939 .... World War II breaks out in Europe, Iran declares neutrality
1941 .... Great Britain and the Soviet Union become allies. Division of Iran by the Soviet Union and the British into three zones
1941 .... Great Britain and the Soviet Union force Reza Shah to abdicate. His son Mohammad Reza Shah is sworn in as a second Shah of the Pahlavi dynasty
1941 .... Great Britain and USSR invade Iran, arrest the monarch and send him into exile to South Africa

1941–1979 ...... **Mohammad Reza Pahlavi**
1941 .... British and Soviet troops march into Tehran and take control of the Iranian government
1942 .... United States, ally of Britain and USSR, sends a military force to operate the "Persian Corridor" by which supplies are transferred to the Soviet Union
1943 .... In September, Shah Mohammad Reza Pahlavi declares war on Germany
1943 .... Shah Mohammad Reza hosts Tehran Conference between Churchill, Roosevelt, and Stalin
1944 .... Mohammad Mosaddegh, the "first and last father of Persian democracy" elected to parliament
1945 .... End of World War II in Europe
1945–1946 .... Iran crisis, British and US begin to withdraw their troops as agreed, the Soviets remain and thus trigger the first postwar international crisis, seen as one of the early conflicts in the growing Cold War
1949 .... Assassination attempt on Mohammad Reza Shah
1950 .... Point IV program, a bilateral agreement between the US and Iran for reconstruction
1951 .... Nationalization of the Iranian oil industry by Prime Minister Mohammad Mosaddegh, cancelling the oil concession of Anglo-Iranian Oil Company
1953 .... Operation Ajax orchestrated by United Kingdom and US CIA to overthrow of Prime Minister Mohammad Mosaddegh, who is placed under house arrest
1954 .... Anglo-Iranian Oil Company (AIOC) becomes British Petroleum Company (BP)
1954–1959 .... Construction of a new Senate building, testimony of modern thinking in Iranian art and architecture
1955 .... Opening of Mehrabad airport for national and international flights
1961–1970 .... First Kurdish–Iraqi War, an attempt to establish an independent Kurdish state
1963 .... Mohammad Reza Shah launches the White Revolution, a series of far-reaching reforms

Chronology

Chronology

Index of architects

Sorted by page numbers

Index of architects

Sorted by page numbers

Index of places

Sorted by page numbers

Index of places

Sorted by page numbers

Author

Thomas Meyer-Wieser
Thomas Meyer-Wieser is an architect
and urban planner. He is a graduate of
the Swiss Federal Institute of Technology
in Zurich and has had a keen interest in the architecture and town planning of the Islamic world since his university days. He did practical training with Modam Consulting Architects
in Tehran, and in 1979 he worked on
a UNESCO project for the consolidation and restoration of the Sassanid
Palace Ghala Dokhtar in Firuzabad, Iran.
Between 1995 and 2002, he was Lecturer
in the Landscape Architecture Division
of the Technical University Rapperswil.
Thomas Meyer-Wieser is the author of
the *Architectural Guide Cairo*, published
in 2014 by DOM Publishers.

The Deutsche Nationalbibliothek
list this publication in the Deutsche
Nationalbibliografie; detailed bib-
liographic data are available on
the Internet at http://dnb.d-nb.de.

ISBN 978-3-86922-570-8

Translation
Monika Golightly

Proofreading
Molly O'Laughlin

Design
Masako Tomokiyo

Maps
Katrin Soschinski

QR-Codes
Christoph Gößmann

Print
Tiger Printing (Hong Kong) Co., Ltd.
www.tigerprinting.hk

**DOM
publishers**